DATE DUE

~~AG 7 02~~			

DEMCO 38-296

The American West

The American West

A NEW INTERPRETIVE HISTORY

Robert V. Hine & John Mack Faragher

YALE UNIVERSITY PRESS   New Haven & London

Published with assistance from the foundation
established in memory of Philip Hamilton
McMillan of the Class of 1894, Yale College.

Set in Minion and Egiziano types by
The Composing Room of Michigan, Inc.
Printed in the United States of America.

Library of Congress
Cataloging-in-Publication Data
Hine, Robert V., 1921–
The American West : a new interpretive
history / Robert V. Hine & John Mack Faragher.
        p.   cm.
Includes bibliographical references and index.
ISBN 0-300-07833-1 (cloth : alk. paper). —
ISBN 0-300-07835-8 (pbk. : alk. paper)
1. West (U.S.)—History.   2. Frontier and
pioneer life—West (U.S.)   I. Faragher, John
Mack, 1945–   .   II. Title.
F591.H662   2000
978–dc21   99-43653
                                                CIP

A catalogue record for this book is available
from the British Library.

The paper in this book meets the guidelines for
permanence and durability of the Committee
on Production Guidelines for Book Longevity
of the Council on Library Resources.

10   9   8   7   6   5   4   3   2   1

FOR SHIRLEY

"Under the wide and starry sky . . . "

—RLS

Contents

Preface

In alighting out for the West (that's the way Huck Finn put it) we intend to interpret the story of the American frontier with little pretense of being comprehensive or completely objective. Instead we face with wonder the deep contradictions in our history and try to make sense of them. The explosion of new and provocative scholarship since the last revision of this book has given us much to consider and much to incorporate. Long ago the two of us discovered our congruous mindsets, so readers will find no dramatic interpretive departures from previous editions. But there is substantial new material with a steadier emphasis on Native Americans, the role of ethnicity, environmental issues, and the participation of women in the events of western history. There are many more voices, speaking directly from their own experience. There are new illustrations and maps. There are notes to guide readers to the sources of quoted material, and lists of suggested readings at the end of each chapter. The task of revision has fallen mainly on the shoulders of John Mack Faragher, who used the old edition as the anvil on which to hammer out a new work from beginning to end.

This book is illustrated with twenty-three maps and 233 historic illustrations, all of them contemporaneous with the period under discussion. Many of the images come from the Collection of Western Americana, Beinecke Rare Book and Manuscript Library of Yale University, which for brevity is simply listed in the captions as "Beinecke."

Many friends and colleagues contributed ideas and support. At the Riverside and Irvine campuses of the University of California: Carlos E. Cortes, Edwin Scott Gaustad, Irving G. Hendrick, Spencer C. Olin, and Henry C. Meyer. At Mount Holyoke College: Daniel Czitrom and Joseph J. Ellis. At Yale University: Nancy Cott, Robert Johnston, Howard R. Lamar, Steven B. Stoll, and Robin Winks. In the wider historical world we are indebted to: Kathryn Abbott, Robert Berkhofer, Edwin R. Bingham, Alan Bogue, Elizabeth Fenn, Greg Hise, Paul W. Hirt, Wilbur Jacobs, Elizabeth Jameson, Earl Pomeroy, Rodman Paul, Ruth Sutter, and Elliott West. Over the years the essays and theses of our undergraduate students inspired us and supplied important historical details.

Three generations of students helped with the research for this book. We applaud the good work of Laurel Angell, James T. Brown, Robert Campbell, Jack Goldwasser, Jeff Hardwick, Allison Hine-Estes, Jennifer Howe, Benjamin H. Johnson, Jammes Kessenides, J. C. Mutchler, Christina Nunez, Elizabeth Pauley, Robert Perkinson, and Nora Sulzmanm. For this edition Andrew Lewis greatly assisted in the search for historical images. The transformation of manuscript into book was the responsibility of the skilled staff of Yale University Press. We especially want to thank Kathryn Levesque and Ki Joo Choi, as well as our splendid editors, Laura Jones Dooley and Charles Grench.

Introduction: Dreams and Homelands

"The West has been the great word of our history. The Westerner has been the type and master of our American life." When the future president Woodrow Wilson wrote these words in 1895 he was neither the first nor the last to so grandly interpret the American West. That "great word" was never pure fact but was always tinged deeply with myth, and though interpretations of the facts change, the myth survives. The history of the West has been consistently revised in accord with the dream.[1]

Centuries before they first sailed to the Americas, Europeans were dreaming of unknown lands to the West, places inhabited perhaps by "the fabulous races of mankind," men and women unlike any seen in the known world. The people might be frightening, but their world would surely be a paradise, a golden land somewhere beyond the setting sun.

> See, see before us the distant glow,
> Through the thin dawn-mists of the West,
> Rich sunlit plains and hilltops gemmed with snow,
> The Islands of the Blest!

Glossing these lines of Horace, the Roman poet Plutarch imagined that "rain falls there seldom, and in moderate showers, but for the most part they have gentle breezes, bringing along with them soft dews, which render the soil not only rich for ploughing and planting, but so abundantly fruitful that it produces spontaneously an abundance of delicate fruits, sufficient to feed the inhabitants, who may here enjoy all things without trouble or labour." Written nearly two thousand years ago, these are words worthy of a nineteenth-century western real estate promoter.[2]

Such visions inspired the great explorations of the early modern world. According to his son, Christopher Columbus longed to see the mythical western isles "of which so many marvels are told." Sailing west across the Atlantic to reach the wonders of the Indies, the admiral conflated an exotic East with rumors of an imagined West. On his third voyage in 1498, as his ship coasted the shores of Trinidad, Columbus convinced himself he was skirting the Garden of Eden, "because all men say that

Anticipating contact with unknown peoples: the "Fabulous Races of Mankind." From Liber Chronicarum (Nuremberg Chronicle) *(Nuremberg, 1493). National Gallery of Art, Washington. Gift of Paul Mellon, in Honor of the 50th Anniversary of the National Gallery of Art.*

it's at the end of the Orient, and that's where we are." He was the first but certainly not the last European to seek paradise on Caribbean beaches. Similar dreams sent others in quest of the Fountain of Youth, the golden Cities of Cíbola, and the mystical isle of California, populated by beautiful but fierce Amazons. Centuries of "California Dreaming" inspired the conquest and colonization of the West.[3]

During the epoch of European colonialism, with nation-states in competition for the resources of the Americas, the dream took an imperial cast. "Westward the course of empire takes its way," Bishop George Berkeley of England famously declared in the mid-eighteenth century, and the first generation of American nationalists adopted his rhetoric as their own. "True religion, and in her train, dominion, riches, literature, and art have taken their course in a slow and gradual manner from East to West," the Reverend John Witherspoon preached at Princeton in 1775, and "from thence forebode the future glory of America." Even as he spoke, pioneers were planting the first American settlements west of the Appalachians. Westward Ho! In the nineteenth century American expansionists coupled the imagined West to the idea of American greatness and called the process Manifest Destiny.[4]

But beyond the misty horizon of dreams was a real world, throbbing with human possibility. Though European explorers believed they had discovered "Mundus Novus"—a New World—for thousands of years the Western Hemisphere had been home to peoples with histories and dreams of their own. Native Americans lived in more than two thousand distinct cultures, spoke hundreds of different languages, and made their livings in scores of dissimilar environments. Columbus called the people of the Caribbean *los Indios,* mistakenly thinking he had arrived in the East Indies. Within a half-century "Indian" had passed into English, used to refer to all Native Americans, ridiculously lumping together Aztec militarists, Hopi communalists, and Pequot horticulturists. Just as the term *European* includes dozens of nationalities, so the term *Indian* encompasses an enormous diversity among the native peoples of the Americas.

The Indians were descendants of ancient hunters who migrated from Asia to America across the Bering land bridge some thirty to forty thousand years ago, about the time migrants elsewhere were settling the British Isles. Huge continental glaciers blocked movement south for most of the last Ice Age, but archaeologists believe that during several periods a narrow corridor through the ice may have opened, leading along the eastern base of the Rocky Mountains. After many generations of small movements these first American settlers emerged onto the northern Great Plains, a hunter's paradise teeming with animals of great variety. Even at the slow rates of population growth that characterize foraging peoples, it would have taken only a few thousand years to settle the whole hemisphere. Remarkably, the oral traditions of

The creation of man and woman. Painted pot, Mimbres River culture of southwestern New Mexico, c. 1000. National Museum of the American Indian.

many Indian people depict a long journey from a distant place of origin to a new homeland. The Pima people of the Southwest sing an "Emergence Song":

> This is the White Land; we arrive singing,
> Head dresses waving in the breeze.
> We have come! We have come!
> The land trembles with our dancing and singing.

Ancient migrants were first to meet the many challenges of the American land. They developed a unique tradition of stone tool-making that archaeologists have named Clovis, after the New Mexico site where these distinctive artifacts were discovered in 1932. Scientists have since unearthed Clovis points and choppers at diggings from Montana to Mexico, Nova Scotia to Arizona.[5]

But about ten thousand years ago the global warming that ended the Ice Age radically altered the North American climate. The glaciers retreated northward and ice melt raised the level of the surrounding seas, flooding the Bering Strait and creating a new continental system of lakes and rivers. These monumental transformations resulted in new patterns of wind, rainfall, and temperature, reshaping the ecology of the continent and producing the distinct North American regions of today. The Clovis tradition fragmented, and the Indian peoples of North America embarked on their long journey toward the development of regionally distinct cultures.

Much of the continent—from the arid heartland of the Great Plains to the forests and muskeg stretching from Alaska to the northern Atlantic coast—was colonized by small bands of foragers whose way of life was based on the harvest of wild plant foods and the pursuit of game. Peoples like the Utes of the Great Basin or the Micmacs of northern Nova Scotia had migratory lives, moving with the game and the shifting resources of the seasons. Ethics of mutual sharing in combination with their nomadic way of life prevented the accumulation of goods and reinforced values of

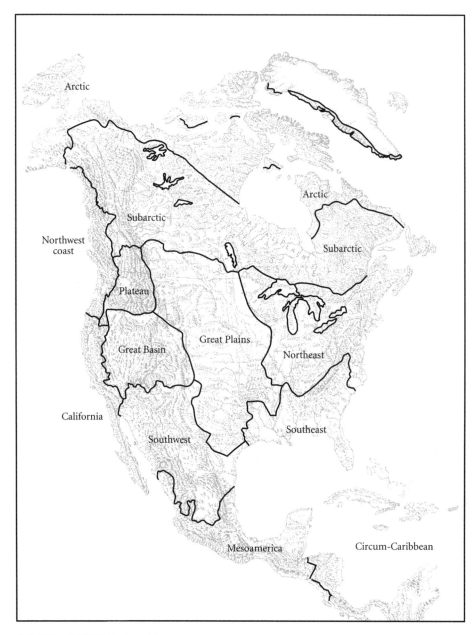

Arctic

Arctic

Subarctic

Subarctic

Northwest
coast

Plateau

Great Plains

Northeast

Great Basin

California

Southwest

Southeast

Mesoamerica

Circum-Caribbean

NATIVE CULTURE AREAS

social equality among them. Decisions were made by consensus among adults, and leadership tended to be informal, based on proven achievement and reputation. Intermarriage created a sense of common ethnic identity among scattered bands sharing cultural and linguistic traditions.

These peoples struck Europeans as materially impoverished. Nineteenth-century American pioneers disdainfully labeled the Utes, Shoshones, and other desert

An Aztec farmer cultivates his corn. Aztec drawing, from Codice Florentino *(ca. 1550). Department of Library Services, American Museum of Natural History.*

peoples "Diggers" because they foraged for edible roots. But forager diets were considerably more varied and higher in protein than those of farmers, whose foodways concentrated on corn or grains. Why sweat all day in the fields, desert peoples wondered, when in an hour or two one could gather sweet prickly pear or pine nuts sufficient to last a week? Colonizers may have thought of them as inferior, but foragers considered their way of life superior to any other. "There is no Indian who does not consider himself infinitely more happy and more powerful than the French," a Micmac chief once told a Jesuit missionary.[6]

In the myth of western conquest, all Indians were nomadic, but foragers were actually far outnumbered by native peoples with other strategies for procuring a living. An early French visitor to the Florida coast was amazed at the abundant harvests Timucua fishermen took from the sea. They used elaborate weirs, he wrote, "made in the water with great reeds so well and cunningly set together, after the fashion of a labyrinth or maze, with so many turns or crooks, as it is impossible to do with more cunning or industry." Across the continent, the peoples of the Northwest Pacific coast were among the most densely settled of all North Americans. Their staff of life was the salmon, which spawned in numbers so great that they sometimes filled the rivers to overflowing. The catch allowed the Tlingits, Haidas, Kwakiutls, and other coastal peoples the abundance to develop a rich and refined material culture, including grand clan houses with distinctive carved and painted wood, fantastic totem poles, and magnificent blankets woven of wild goat's wool. Theirs was a world of powerful clans, ruling families, and fierce warriors in formidable war canoes.[7]

Even more numerous than the fishing peoples were the farmers living in the arid Southwest or in the fertile river system of the Mississippi. North America was one of four world sites where late stone-age people invented the practice of growing their own food. The uniquely American crop complex of corn, beans, and squash—known by the Iroquois as "the three sisters"—originated in the Mexican highlands some five to ten thousand years ago and gradually spread northward. Farming made possible a more elaborate social and cultural life for Indians, but it also enabled the settlement of North America by Europeans. Without corn and potatoes—and such other New World crops as tobacco, rubber, and short-staple cotton, each of which became the basis for important modern industries and markets—it is fair to say that the history of the modern world would have been far different.

For hundreds of years farming undergirded Indian societies wherever the climate was temperate and water adequate. Agricultural civilizations rose and fell. By the time Europeans arrived in their lands, the apartment-dwelling Anasazis and the mound-building Mississippians were gone, leaving only ruins and artifacts to echo their greatness. But their descendants—the Pimas and the Pueblos in the Southwest, the Cherokees and the Iroquois in the East—inherited the farming tradition and built civilizations of their own.

Farming demands a sedentary way of life as well as elaborate customs and institutions to manage planting, harvest, and storage. Like fishing peoples, native farmers devised complicated systems of kinship to perform these tasks. Families aligned in clans with different social, political, or ritual responsibilities, and clans with common ethnic, linguistic, and territorial identity banded into tribes. In contrast to foragers with their shifting leadership, tribal government was formalized, with chiefs and councils of elders. Much more frequently than foragers, farming tribes were warring tribes, sometimes fighting one another over territory. To Europeans, Indian tribes seemed like little states, and colonial officials often designated them "Indian nations." But with the exception of the Aztecs, these tribes had no standing armies and no bureaucracies.

———

This was but one of several important differences between Indians and Europeans. Europeans also had great difficulty understanding the authority of tribal chiefs. One of a chief's primary responsibilities was the supervision of the farming economy. Yet the community judged his performance not by how much wealth and power he accumulated but rather by how well he disbursed resources to clans and families. A good chief was often an impoverished chief. From the European perspective this made little sense, but Indians found Old World traditions equally puzzling. In the early seventeenth century a young Huron visited France, and upon his return he reported his shock at the conditions he had found there. "Among the French," he told his tribesmen, "men were whipped, hanged and put to death without distinction of innocence or guilt." He had seen a "great number of needy and beg-

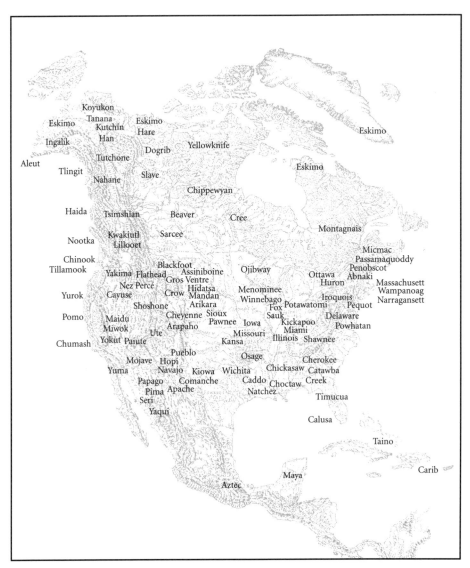

TRIBAL LOCATIONS

gars," and could not understand why the French people tolerated such conditions, "saying that if [they] had some intelligence [they] would set some order in the matter, the remedies being simple."[8]

Although distinctions of wealth sometimes arose within Indian farming communities, cultural traditions of sharing prevented the development of great inequalities. Nowhere in North America did native cultures employ the concept of individual ownership of land. Productive resources were invariably considered the common property of kinship groups, clans, or the whole tribe. This pattern contrasted dramatically with the European tradition of private property, and colonists doubted that there could be individual responsibility without individual ownership. Sometimes colonial officials used these differences in cultural values to justify the dispossession of native communities, denying that Indians had any rights to the land at all.

Probably the most fundamental distinction between invading Europeans and indigenous Indian cultures came down to religion. There were, of course, religious differences among native cultures. But in the religion of most North Americans human beings were thought to share a kinship with all other living things and a pantheon of supernatural forces linked together all of nature. If that chain was broken, the great cycles were damaged, and illness and disorder ensued. Native religion connected Indian people intimately with nature and encouraged a strong sense of belonging to their own places, their homelands. As the Navajos sing in their Blessingway ceremony:

> Before me it is blessed, behind me it is blessed,
> Below me it is blessed, above me it is blessed,
> Around me it is blessed, my speech is blessed,
> All my surroundings are blessed as I found it, I found it.

Europeans, by contrast, were less concerned with sacred places than with sacred time, the movement toward a second coming or a new millennium, a way of thinking that encouraged people to believe in progress, to believe that by picking up and moving to a new land they might better their future. Christians were monotheists, attracted to the simplicity of grand designs and single causes, believing in a hierarchical reality. The Bible taught them that they were separate and distinct from the rest of nature, granted dominion over "every living thing that moveth upon the earth." The Christian God revealed himself as a man, not as a coyote or a raven.[9]

The European invasion of North America created a frontier between natives and newcomers. The American frontier, declared Frederick Jackson Turner at the end of the nineteenth century, was "the meeting point between civilization and savagery." His phrase rang with the arrogance of the victors in the centuries-long campaign of colonial conquest. Frontiers were indeed the site of violent confrontations, as colonizers sought to conquer territory and Indians struggled to defend native homelands. But, at the beginning of a new millennium many Americans are less sure than Turner who exactly was the savage and who the civilized.[10]

The history of the frontiers of North America, moreover, is not simply the story of warfare. To paraphrase historian Sarah Deutsch, frontiers are "what happens when cultures meet." The colonization of the North American continent created a multidimensional world inhabited by peoples of diverse backgrounds, including

"*The Arrival of the Englishmen in Virginia.*" *Engraving by Theodore de Bry, based on a watercolor by John White, from Thomas Harriot,* A Briefe and True Report of the New Found Land of Virginia *(Frankfurt, 1590). Beinecke.*

many of mixed ethnic ancestry, the offspring of a process of interaction that spanned many generations. Frontier history tells the story of the creation and defense of communities, the use of the land, the development of markets, and the formation of states. It is filled with unexpected twists and turns. It is a tale of conquest, but also one of survival, persistence, and the merging of peoples and cultures that gave birth and continuing life to America.[11]

Frontier and *West* are key words in the American lexicon, and they share an intimate historical relation. From the perspective of the Atlantic coast, the frontier *was* the West. "At different periods in our history," an Indiana newspaperman reflected in 1837, "the 'Far West' has been differently located. At one time Indiana was the far west; at another . . . the Mississippi. But now, it has been determined that no point short of half a mile this side of sundown deserves the appellation." *West* might remain as a regional nominative artifact—the Western Reserve, the Old Northwest, the Middle West—but *the* West moved on with the frontier. Where then is the West? The question has puzzled generations of Americans, for its location has changed with the times. "Phantom-like it flies before us as we travel," wrote frontier artist George Catlin in the mid-nineteenth century. Even today there is little consensus on its location. A recent survey of western historians, writers, and editors found that about half believe that the West begins at the Mississippi or the Missouri River, while others propose the eastern edge of the Great Plains or the front range of the Rockies. Most consider the Pacific to be its western boundary, but a sizable minority insist that the states of the "left coast" are not part of the West at all. "I wouldn't let California into the West with a search warrant," the late western historian Robert Athearn cracked. His view has been around for quite a spell. "When I am in California," insisted President Theodore Roosevelt, "I am not in the West. I am west of the West." Roosevelt's little joke is a reminder that *West* is a relative term. Adopting the perspective of Latino settlers moving from Mexico, the frontier was the *North;* for the Canadian *métis* moving onto the northern plains of the Dakotas or Montana it was the *South;* for Asian migrants headed for California it was the *East.*[12]

Whatever its boundaries, in American history the West is not only a modern region somewhere beyond the Mississippi but also the process of getting there. That may make the western story more complicated, but it also makes it more interesting and more relevant. The history of the frontier is a unifying American theme, for every part of the country was once a frontier, every region was once a West.

1

A New World Begins

The Indians who first met Columbus were the Tainos. On their island homes in the Bahamas they cultivated corn and yams, made brown pottery and cotton thread, and fashioned deadly little darts from fish teeth and wood, which they used to protect themselves from their aggressive neighbors, the Caribs (for whom the Caribbean Sea is named). But Columbus thought the Tainos had no weapons, a conclusion he based on a curious test. Handing them swords he observed that they grasped the blades and cut their fingers. Steel had come to a people who previously had worked only with bone and stone. It was a typical surmise for Columbus, who assumed the superiority of his own culture in all things. "They are all naked, men and women, as their mothers bore them," he condescended in his report to the Spanish monarchs. Columbus made his landfall in October 1492, when the prevailing Caribbean temperatures were balmy, and the natives he saw were attired in much the same costume as bikini-clad vacationers who flock to those same beaches today. Although he could not understand the Tainos' language, Columbus believed he could read their minds. When the natives lifted their hands to the sky, it was an indication they considered the Spaniards to be gods. It was only one of several possible explanations. Perhaps the Tainos were exclaiming, "Great God, what now!"[1]

We are more sure of what was on the minds of the Spaniards. After noting the Indians' loving, cooperative, and peaceful reception, Columbus concluded that "all the inhabitants could be made slaves," for "they have no arms and are all naked and without any knowledge of war. They are fitted to be ruled and to be set to work, to cultivate the land and to do all else that may be necessary, and you may build towns and teach them to go clothed and adopt our customs." His impression of natives as a people vulnerable to conquest is clear in the image produced to accompany the published version of the Columbus report. Before he sailed home Columbus kidnapped

King Ferdinand directs Columbus to the New World. From Giuliano Dati, Isole trovate nuovamente per el re di Spagna *(Florence, 1495). Beinecke.*

a number of native men and women to display for the monarchs at the Spanish court.[2]

"There are many spices and great mines of gold and of other metals," Columbus reported. In fact, none of the Asian spices familiar to Europeans grew in the Caribbean, and there were only small quantities of precious metals in the river beds of the islands. But noticing the little gold ornaments the Tainos wore, Columbus contracted a bad case of gold fever. More than anything else, it was the possibility of setting the natives to work mining gold that convinced the monarchs to finance a large return expedition. "The best thing in the world is gold," Columbus once wrote in his diary, "it can even send souls to heaven." As Hernán Cortés, the conqueror of Mexico, once put it: "We Spaniards suffer from a disease of the heart, the specific remedy for which is gold."[3]

For the native inhabitants, the Spaniards' lust for gold and hostages were ominous signs. The invasion of America would be marked by scenes of frightful violence. In the wake of Columbus, conquering armies marched across the Caribbean islands, plundering villages, slaughtering men, capturing and raping women. The conquistadors who followed Columbus were equally sure of their culture, their God, their church, and their superiority. They were also skilled in the arts of conquest because of their long experience fighting "infidels" in Iberia. Moslems from Africa had flooded western Europe to a high-water mark in the eighth century and thereafter the Christians slowly pushed back. The wars of the "Reconquest" absorbed the energies and directed the crusading propensities of many generations of young Spaniards. In 1492—that most extraordinary year—Granada, the last Moorish stronghold in Iberia, fell to the Christian warriors led by Isabella and Ferdinand of Castile and Aragon. The royal couple thereupon united their kingdoms to form the new Christian state of Spain and followed up their victory by expelling thousands of Jews. Now their Catholic majesties turned their attention westward, across the ocean sea.

In the New World, Columbus and his successors established a feudal institution known as the *encomienda,* which placed Indian workers at the disposal of Spanish lords, who set them to work dredging the streams for alluvial gold, working the fields, and building new colonial towns. Rather than work as slaves, many Indians took poison, hanged themselves, and killed their children. Whole villages were rumored to have committed suicide rather than submit to Spanish conquest.

Although they proved a poor match for mounted warriors with steel swords and vicious bloodhounds, native people resisted the conquest. The Caribs—from the more southeasterly islands of the West Indies—successfully defended their homeland until the end of the sixteenth century, ruthlessly wiping out all Spanish attempts to colonize or missionize. One chronicler of the conquest told of a particularly ironic torture some Indians invented for captured Spaniards with a hunger for gold. Heating the metal to its melting point, they would pour the molten stuff down the throats of their prisoners.

Soon the alluvial gold on Hispaniola had been depleted, leading to the invasion of Puerto Rico and Jamaica in 1508, then Cuba and Central America in 1511. Over the next few years the Spaniards undertook several expeditions along the mainland Caribbean coast as far north as Yucatán. The people they encountered lived in far more complex societies than those of the Caribbean Tainos, with splendid towns and even libraries of handwritten, illustrated books. One Central American native reacted with surprise when he saw a Spaniard reading a European book. "You also have books?" he exclaimed. "You also understand the signs by which you talk to the absent?" In 1517 a small party of Spaniards became the first Europeans to enter one of the Mayan towns along the coast of Yucatán. The residents offered them many trea-

Indians pour molten gold down the throats of conquistadors. From Girolamo Benzoni,
La historia del mondo nuovo *(Venice, 1565). Beinecke.*

sures, wrote the chronicler of this expedition, "and begged us kindly to accept all this,
since they had no more gold to give us." But pointing westward, "in the direction of
the sunset," the Indians insisted that the Spaniards would find plenty. "They kept on
repeating: 'Mexico, Mexico, Mexico,'" reads the account, "but we did not know what
Mexico meant."[4]

Rumors of the land called Mexico created a sensation among officials of Cuba, the
center of the growing Spanish empire in the Caribbean. In a search for more sources
of treasure, in 1519 a fleet of eleven ships with 530 Spanish soldiers, several hundred
Cuban Indian porters, and a number of Africans set out for the unknown lands of
the West. There were sixteen horses—"the nerves of the wars against the natives" one
Spanish chronicler called them—and numerous fighting dogs. Mexico, they
thought, might be some powerful principality of the Great Khan of Cathay
(China)—for the Spaniards still believed that the islands of the Caribbean lay directly off the Asian mainland. Nearby must be fabled California, which was said to
be located "on the right hand of the Indies . . . , very close to the region of the terrestrial paradise."[5]

The Spaniards land in Mexico. Aztec drawing, from Codice Florentino, *c. 1550. Department of Library Services, American Museum of Natural History.*

Leading this expedition was the man who would become known as the archetypal conquistador, Hernán Cortés. An officer in Cortés's army of conquest, Bernal Díaz, described his commander as sexually attractive and physically strong, with broad chest and shoulders, slow to anger but sometimes roused to speechless fury, the veins swelling in his neck and forehead. He demanded absolute obedience from his men. He also read Latin, wrote poetry, and wore around his neck a golden chain bearing "the image of Our Lady the Virgin Saint Mary with her precious son in her arms." Diaz described Cortés as fond of gambling at cards and dice. Now he gambled for the highest stakes in the New World. The expedition would "bring us both honor and profit," Cortés told his men, "things which very rarely can be found in the same bag." Shortly after his arrival on the Mexican coast, near present day Veracruz, he ordered the ships dismantled. The game was winner take all, and the Virgin Mary was on his side.[6]

All the while Cortés and his men were being observed by spies of Montezuma II, the emperor of the Aztecs, a powerful empire in the central valley of Mexico. They recorded the strangers' movements in a set of detailed drawings. "Their flesh is very light, lighter than ours," the spies reported, "they all have long beards, and their hair comes to their ears." We know these details because of the extraordinary efforts of a Spanish friar, Bernardino de Sahagún, who after the conquest learned the Nahuatl language and, with the help of native informants, recorded the Aztec view of events.[7]

The people of Mexico differed vastly from the Tainos who had greeted Columbus. They lived in several dozen city-states, most under the domination of the Aztecs, the inhabitants of Tenochtitlán in the central highlands. Built on an island in the midst of a large lake, the Aztec capital was resplendent with stepped pyramids, stone temples, golden vessels, and causeways with cleverly engineered dams and irrigation canals, built and maintained with the tribute the Aztecs demanded from the conquered peoples whom they governed. The Aztecs were as certain of themselves as were the Spaniards. "Are we not the masters of the world?" Montezuma remarked to his council when he first heard of the landing of the Spaniards, and an Aztec poem asked rhetorically:

> Who could conquer Tenochtitlán
> Who could shake the foundation of heaven?[8]

Yet Montezuma seems to have sensed that two worlds were on a collision course. The Aztecs had myths of their own. For several years there had been evil omens—strange comets, heavenly lights, monstrous two-headed births, foaming lake waters, an insane woman wailing through the night, "My children, where shall I take you?" Very much like Europe's kings, Montezuma held his office in trust for the gods, and as he and his high priests worried over these signs there came the news of the strange appearance of the invaders from over the waters. Didn't they ride on weird creatures, larger than deer, from whom flecks of foam fell like soapsuds? Were not the bodies and heads of the men covered with iron, and did they not use strange rods that spit fire and killed? Moreover, the year of 1519 was 1-Reed in the Aztec calendar, an ominous year. In the words of one of their old books:

> They knew that, according to the signs,
> If he comes on 1-Crocodile, he strikes the old men, the old women;
> If on 1-Jaguar, 1-Deer, 1-Flower, he strikes at children;
> If on 1-Reed, he strikes at kings.

Perhaps Cortés had come to fulfill the prophecy, to strike at the king, Montezuma.[9]

The Aztecs might easily have crushed the several hundred Spaniards at this point, as they struggled to survive amid the sand dunes and mosquitoes of the Gulf coast. But Montezuma was undecided about the right course to pursue. "If you do not admit the embassy of a great lord such as the King of Spain appears to be," a member of

Montezuma and the evil omen. Aztec drawing, from Diego Durán, Historia de las Indias de Nueva España e islas de Tierra Firme *(c. 1580; Mexico City, 1867–80). Beinecke.*

his council advised him, "it is a low thing." But another lord warned him "not to allow into your house someone who will put you out of it." Yet confident of the enormous power of his empire and his army, Montezuma indulged his desire to see these strangers from another world. "Come forward, my Jaguar Knights," the emperor called to his generals, "come forward. It is said that our lord has returned to this land. Go to meet him. Go to hear him. Listen well to what he tells you; listen and remember."[10]

He sent the Spaniards "divine adornments" and his messengers kissed the earth before Cortés. In the words of the Aztec account: "They gave them emblems of gold, banners of quetzal plumes, and golden necklaces. And when they gave them these, the Spaniards' faces grinned: they were delighted, they were overjoyed. They snatched up the gold like monkeys. They were swollen with greed; they were ravenous; they hungered for that gold like wild pigs. They seized the golden standards, they swung them from side to side, they examined them from top to bottom. They babbled in a barbarous language; everything they said was in a savage tongue." This remarkable description recaptures the native perspective of the dramatic encounter between civilizations. To the Aztecs the Spaniards were outsiders, barbarians, perhaps barely human.[11]

How Cortés conquered an empire that could at any time raise thousands of well-trained fighting men remains mysterious. Certainly there was more to it than the

Malínche translates for the Spaniards. Aztec drawing, from Codice Florentino, *c. 1550. Department of Library Services, American Museum of Natural History.*

Aztec preoccupation with signs and omens. Cortés proved masterful at the art of diplomacy, but he was ignorant of the language and the subtleties of Aztec history and could not have directed these efforts without native help. His first assistance came in the form of one of the cleverest women of history, a girl by the name of Malíntzin, whom the friars baptized Doña Marina but who is best known by the Hispanicized verson of her native name, La Malínche. Malínche was born in a Nahuatl-speaking community but was sold into slavery as a child. Cortés received her from a local Mexican chief who was attempting to curry favor. Malínche made the decision to align herself with the Spaniards. Possessing an enormous talent for languages—perhaps the heritage of a childhood among strangers—she quickly mastered Spanish and made herself into Cortés's indispensable interpreter. But not only did she translate, she also proved a master interpreter of Aztec intentions. In the words of Bernal Díaz, Malínche was "the great beginning of our conquests." In the Aztec images of the conquest Malínche is nearly always shown by Cortés's side.[12]

Malínche was a powerfully complex character, and the Mexican people have never ceased arguing over her meaning. Her name symbolizes the betrayal of native culture, synonymous with the worst traitor. Malínche became Cortés's mistress, and she bore him a son before eventually marrying another conquistador. Other Mexicans, however, see Malínche as the mother of *la rasa*, the new people that arose out of the blending of Indian and Spanish, native and European, ancient gods with new. Thus she symbolizes not only betrayal but also the mixing of cultures and peoples that is the essence of modern Mexico. Malínche stands for much of what is distinctive about the frontier cultures of the Americas.

Lusting for the treasures of Tenochtitlán, Cortés and his men pushed into the Mexican interior, invading Tlaxcala, a small republic that lived under the heavy heel of Aztec domination. The Tlaxcalans fought fiercely, and the Spaniards lost dozens of men and horses to the Indians' obsidian-tipped wooden broadswords that cut like razors. This was the fiercest fighting the Spaniards had yet encountered in the Americas. The Spaniards knew that the Tlaxcalans had been defeated by the Aztecs, and the soldiers began to mutter that if they had to fight so hard here, what would it be like when they confronted the great Aztec army? But then the Tlaxcalans made an offer of peace. "The Tlaxcalans prefer slavery amongst us to subjection to the Mexica," Cortés remarked cynically. Thousands of Indian warriors now joined the Spaniards on their march over the mountains to the great city of Tenochtitlán. The conquest of Mexico would largely be the work of Indians fighting Indians—this was the most powerful lesson Europeans would draw from Cortés's victory.[13]

One after another of Montezuma's allies fell before Cortés, yet the emperor vacillated and agonized: "My heart burns and suffers, as if it were drowned in spices!" When the Spaniards and their Tlaxcalan allies arrived at the outskirts of Tenochtitlán, the emperor was present to officially welcome them. He led Cortés and his men down a great causeway leading to the island capital. Bernal Díaz described the scene: "The pyramids and buildings rising from the water, all made of stone, seemed like an enchanted vision. Indeed, some of our soldiers asked whether it was not all a dream. . . . I stood looking at it, and thought that no land like it would ever be discovered in the whole world." Indeed, Tenochtitlán was one of the sixteenth-century world's greatest cities. It seemed as if the age-old dream of a western paradise finally had become real. Writing in the 1570s, fifty years after the conquest, Díaz ended his description of the city on a note of great regret: "Today all that I then saw is overthrown and destroyed; nothing is left standing."[14]

Montezuma gave the Spaniards the use of large quarters near his palace, and across the cultural divide the emperor and Cortés entered into a dialogue, conversations recorded in both the Aztec and the Spanish sources. "I do not understand," Cortés declared, pointing to the Aztec religious shrine in his quarters, "how such a great lord and wise man as you are has not realized that these idols are not gods, but bad things, called devils." He knocked down the objects and set up a little Catholic altar in its place. Montezuma was shocked by such a brazen act. He had been trained as a priest. Aztec priests practiced rituals of human sacrifice, inflicting terrible death on captives by cutting open their chests and tearing the pulsing hearts from their living bodies. But the priests also subjected themselves to terrible self-torture, spending their days and nights praying, slashing their own bodies with obsidian blades, and piercing their tongues and penises with cactus thorns to draw the blood that was the ultimate sacrifice to the gods. The Aztecs were, in short, as thoroughly committed to their religious beliefs and practices as were the Spaniards. And so Montezuma replied to Cortés: "We have worshipped our own gods here from the beginning and know them to be good. No doubt yours are good for you also. But please do not trouble to tell us any more about them."[15]

Cortés now conceived the impossibly bold plan of seizing Montezuma and making him a prisoner in his own palace, thinking that perhaps with a single blow he could behead the Aztec kingdom and place himself on its throne. Incredibly, Montezuma allowed himself to be taken. To his council the emperor explained that he had prayed about it, "but the gods no longer replied as of old," and he took this as a sign that he must acquiesce. Constantly praying and sacrificing captives to the gods, Montezuma and the Aztec priests desperately looked for a sign for what they should do.[16]

The Aztecs finally were forced to act when the Spaniards attacked an assembly of the nobility, gathered for a religious festival. In the words of the Aztec account, at the very moment of the festival "when the dance was loveliest and when song was linked to song, the Spaniards were seized with an urge to kill the celebrants." Brandishing their swords they ran headlong into the dancers. "They attacked the man who was drumming and cut off his arms. They cut off his head, and it rolled across the floor. They attacked all the celebrants, stabbing them, spearing them, striking them with their swords. They attacked some of them from behind, and these fell instantly to the ground. . . . They struck others in the shoulders, and their arms were torn from their bodies. They wounded some in the thigh and some in the calf. They slashed others in the abdomen, and their entrails all spilled to the ground. Some attempted to run away, but their intestines dragged as they ran; they seemed to tangle their feet in their own entrails. No matter how they tried to save themselves, they could find no escape." The massacre destroyed the flower of the Aztec ruling class, but it also precipitated a revolt within Tenochtitlán. The army rallied and besieged the Spaniards within the emperor's palace. "Mexicanos, come running!" the surviving leaders cried to the people. "Bring your spears and shields! The strangers have murdered our warriors."[17]

Cortés marched the prisoner Montezuma to a balcony overlooking the public square and told him to call off the Aztec forces. "We must not fight them," the emperor shouted to the people, according to the Aztec account. "We are not their equals in battle. Put down your shields and arrows. . . . Stop fighting, and return to your homes." But the people cursed him, crying out, "Who is Montezuma to give us orders? We are no longer his slaves," and then "it seemed as if the sky was raining stones, arrows, darts, and sticks." Montezuma was hit three times. According to legend, the stone that killed him was thrown by his cousin Cauauhtémoc, who would lead the Aztec defense against the invaders.[18]

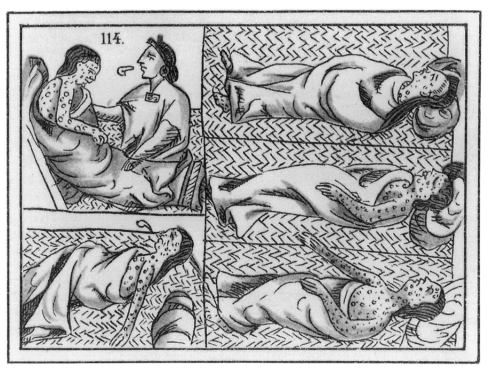

Aztecs suffer with the smallpox. Aztec drawing, from Codice Florentino, *c. 1550. Department of Library Services, American Museum of Natural History.*

After a siege of seven days, the Spaniards made a bold attempt to flee the city by night. An Aztec woman, drawing water at the edge of a canal, spied them and cried out, "Mexicanos, come running! They are crossing the canal! Our enemies are escaping." Two-thirds of the Spanish troops died that night. Dressed in heavy armor, loaded with gold and precious stones looted from Montezuma's treasure house, many drowned in the canals, poetic justice for those afflicted with gold lust. So clogged did the channel become with their bodies, it was said, that those who managed to escape did so by running across the backs of the dead. After the battle the Aztecs dredged the canal and brought up the bodies in order to retrieve the treasure—but left the carcasses to rot in rows along the roadway, a warning if the Spaniards thought to return.[19]

But return they did, reinforced by troops from Cuba as well as thousands of Indian allies who now grabbed the opportunity to overthrow their Aztec overlords. During the intervening year Tenochtitlán was struck by an epidemic plague of smallpox spread to them by the invaders. "They died in heaps, like bedbugs," one Spaniard wrote unsympathetically. Compare the Aztec account: "There came amongst us a great sickness, a general plague. It raged amongst us, killing vast numbers of people. It covered many all over with sores: on the face, on the head, on the chest, everywhere. It was devastating. Nobody could move himself, nor turn his head, nor flex any part of his body. The sores were so terrible that the victims could not lie face down, nor on their backs, nor move from one side to the other. And when they tried to move even a little, they cried out in agony. . . . The worst phase of this pestilence lasted 60 days, 60 days of horror." This epidemic killed thousands; some contemporaries estimated that it reduced the population by half. Cortés attacked the city at the conclusion of the plague. After terrible fighting, the invaders fought their way to the central pyramid, where the final battle took place. After it was all over, wrote Díaz, "we could not walk without treading on the bodies of dead Indians. . . . The dry land and the stockades were piled with corpses. Indeed, the stench was so bad that no one could endure it." Modern estimates are that as many as a hundred thousand Aztecs died in the fighting. The Aztec leaders were captured and tortured to reveal the location of the state treasure house.[20]

The Spaniards imposed the encomienda system on the Mexicans, forcing them to build the new capital of Mexico City on the ruins of Tenochtitlán and to labor in the fields or in the fabulous gold and silver mines the Spaniards opened in northern Mexico. Unlike the peoples of the Caribbean, the peoples of Mexico were familiar with a system of tribute and taxation, and they were better at adapting to their new rulers. Catholic missionaries also began a wholesale assault on Aztec religion. A few years ago, in the Vatican archives, researchers discovered an eloquent Aztec plea for the survival of their traditions: "Do not force something on your people that will bring them misfortune, that will bring them catastrophe. . . . Is it not enough that we have already lost? That our way of living has been lost, has been annihilated?"[21]

There were Spaniards who protested the horrors of the conquest and worked to obtain justice for the Indians. Principal among them was Bartolomé de Las Casas, a priest who had participated in the plunder of Cuba in 1511 but afterward suffered a crisis of conscience and began to denounce the conquest. The Christian mission in the New World was to convert the Indians, he argued, and "the means to effect this end are not to rob, to scandalize, to capture or destroy them, or to lay waste their lands." Centuries before the world recognized the concept of universal human rights, Las Casas proclaimed that "the entire human race is one." His brave stand earned him a place as one of the towering moral figures in the history of the Americas.[22]

The controversy over the treatment of the Indians was waged at the highest levels of the Spanish state. In 1512 the crown responded to criticisms of its Indian policy by issuing stricter protections, but abuses continued. Las Casas became a troublesome critic, and his moral critique persuaded many members of the royal court. Finally in the 1540s he was permitted to organize an official debate over the treatment of the Indians. Those seeking to justify the conquest argued that the Indians were savages who practiced horrible vices, for which they deserved to be punished. It was

Bartolomé de las Casas. From Oeuvres de don Barthélemi de las Casas . . . , *2 vols. (Paris, 1822). Yale University.*

widely reported, for example, that the Indians were drug users. One of the first published accounts, written by a man who accompanied Columbus, described how the Indians of Hispaniola used a little straw to sniff a powder up their noses. "This produces such intoxication," he wrote, "that they do not know what they are doing, and they say many senseless things." The Spanish also noted the wide use of coca leaves in South America and peyote in Central and North America.[23]

Another charge was that the natives were sexual libertines and homosexuals. "The Indians are sodomites," declared one conquistador. "Very common is the nefarious sin against nature. The Indians who are headmen have youths with whom they use this accursed sin, and those consenting youths, as soon as they fall into this guilt, wear skirts like women." The Indians "did not keep faith or order," wrote a Franciscan priest, "husbands were not loyal to their wives nor wives to their husbands." But the most common complaint was that the Indians were cannibals. Images depicting the Caribs (from which was derived not only the word *Caribbean* but also the word *cannibal*) devouring the flesh of captured Spaniards were used to justify the conquest. In Mexico, Cortés argued that the ultimate goal of the conquest was to stamp out the horrible rituals of human sacrifice.[24]

These charges were a slander against the native peoples of the Americas, Las Casas replied. "The Spaniards have defamed the Indians with the greatest crimes," making them seem "ugly and evil." The charge of sodomy he dismissed as "a falsehood," and he compared the native use of drugs to the communion of the Catholic church, pointing out that it was part of a ceremony of divination in order to "learn what good, adversity, or evil were to come." He even made a remarkable effort to explain Aztec human sacrifice in its own terms. "It is not surprising that when unbelievers who have neither grace nor instruction consider how much men owe to God," he explained to the court, "they devise the most difficult type of repayment, that is, human sacrifice in God's honor." To think this way was an error, Las Casas admitted, but the Church should aim to correct such practices through enlightenment, not punishment.[25]

Las Casas carried the day in this official debate, and the Spanish monarchy concluded by declaring the Indians fully human and demanding that they be treated fairly. Las Casas was appointed a bishop in Chiapas, Mexico, where he experimented with colonies that excluded soldiers and firearms. But his was a voice in the wilderness, and in time these ideals gave way to more typical patterns of colonization. As Cortés once said, "I came to get gold, not to till the soil like a peasant." Dreams of riches easily corroded ideals.[26]

Perhaps Las Casas's most enduring contribution was his brilliant history of the conquest, *The Destruction of the Indies,* published in Spain in 1552. In this book, one of the most influential in the history of the early modern world, Las Casas blamed Spaniards for the deaths of millions of Indians and indicted them for what today we would call genocide. His arguments were later used by other European powers to condemn Spain while covering up their own dismal records of colonial conquest. Subsequent scholars, doubting Las Casas's estimates of huge population losses, criticized his work as part of a "Black Legend" of the Spanish conquest. Even the good bishop himself anticipated such doubts. "Who of those born in future centuries will believe this," he wrote. "I myself, who am writing this and saw it, and know most about it, can hardly believe that such was possible."[27]

Las Casas's claims continue to arouse a great deal of controversy among historians, although many find his numbers more believable. Lacking good statistics, all population figures for this period are educated guesses. Estimates of the indigenous population of Hispaniola, for example, range from several hundred thousand to several million. But the indisputable fact is that by 1517, as one Spanish official observed, the Indians had diminished to "as few as grapes after a harvest," and fifty years after Columbus's landing the native population of the island numbered but a few hundred. The Tainos eventually disappeared completely from the face of the earth. Faced with severe shortages of Indian labor, the Spaniards began importing slaves from Africa, and by 1560 Africans had become the majority population on Hispaniola. By the end of the sixteenth century African slaves vastly outnumbered both the native and European populations in the Caribbean colonies.[28]

Estimates of the size of the native Mexican population on the eve of conquest range from eight to twenty-five million. A century later it stood at little more than a million. For the rest of the continent, north of Mexico, historians argue over estimates that vary from four million to eighteen million native inhabitants at the be-

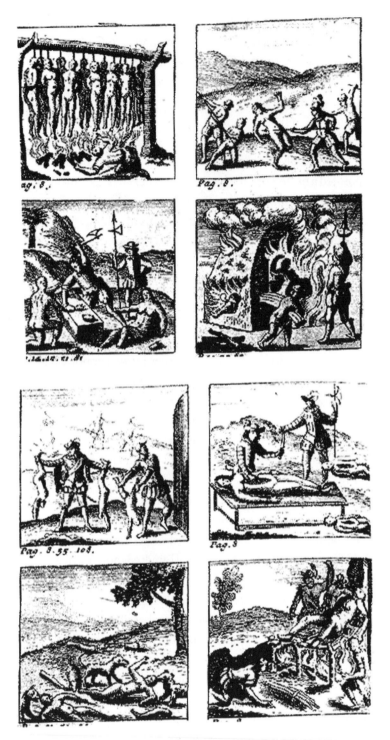

"The Cruelties us[e]d by the Spaniards on the Indians." From Bartolomé de las Casas, The Spanish Colonie . . . (London, 1583). Mount Holyoke College.

ginning of the sixteenth century. But there is no disputing the fact that over the next four hundred years the native population dropped to about 250,000. Despite disagreement over the number of Indians in the Americas before European conquest, most scholars now acknowledge that the collapse of native populations was the greatest demographic calamity in human history.

Las Casas attributed the destruction of the Indians to warfare and overwork. But by far the greatest loss of life resulted from the introduction of Old World diseases. Pre-Columbian America seems to have had no contagious epidemic diseases, and because of this, Indian peoples lacked the antibodies necessary to protect them from European germs and viruses. A shipload of colonists from Spain carried smallpox to Hispaniola in 1516, and the expedition of Cortés brought it to Mexico, where it devastated the Aztecs. Infected Indians unintentionally spread the disease along the trading network linking distant communities. Thus disease frequently preceded conquest. Peru was devastated by smallpox in 1524, strategically weakening the Inca empire eight years before it was attacked by conquistador Francisco Pizarro. Spanish chroniclers wrote that this initial pandemic of smallpox killed up to half the Native Americans it touched.

Disease was the secret weapon of the European invaders of the New World, and it helps explain their almost unbelievable success at conquest. The outstanding difference between the European colonial experience in the Americas and elsewhere—Africa and Asia, for example—was this extraordinary reduction in the Indian population. After the conquest, the Indians of Mexico sang of earlier times:

> There was then no sickness.
> They had then no aching bones.
> They had then no high fever.
> They had then no smallpox.
> They had then no burning chest.
> They had then no abdominal pains.
> They had then no consumption.
> They had then no headache.
> At that time the course of humanity was orderly.
> The foreigners made it otherwise when they arrived here.[29]

Yet, because the rate of Spanish immigration was relatively low, Indians continued in the majority, and by the end of the sixteenth century native populations in Mexico had begun to rebound from their disastrous collapse. The cities and towns were predominantly Spanish, while the countryside remained predominantly Indian. "This state of New Spain," observed a convention of missionaries meeting in

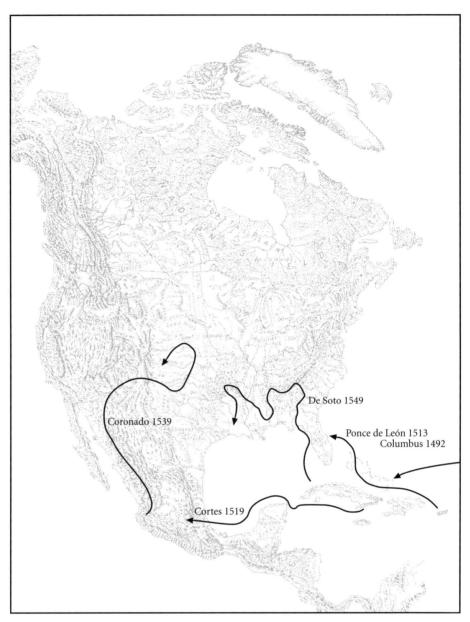

Coronado 1539

De Soto 1549

Ponce de León 1513
Columbus 1492

Cortes 1519

THE SPANISH INVASIONS

Mexico City in 1594, "is made up of two nations, Spaniards and Indians." But a third group was becoming increasingly important. Because the great majority of the Spanish immigrants to the New World were young, single men, there quickly developed a pattern of cohabitation between colonists and native women, and soon there arose a large population of mixed ancestry, the *mestizos*. By the eighteenth century mestizos constituted nearly a quarter of the whole population of New Spain, and by the nineteenth century they had become the majority. *Mestizaje*, or ethnic intermixing, was one of the most important phenomenons of post-conquest societies in the New World.[30]

The Spanish New World empire was divided into two parts: New Castile in South America, and New Spain, stretching from the Isthmus of Panama to Mexico, from the Caribbean islands west across the Pacific to the Philippines. At the heart of New Spain was Mexico City, an imperial seat with shady parks, well-dressed people parading in coaches, splendid churches towering over the sites of Montezuma's temples, a university (founded in 1553), a government mint, hospitals, monasteries, and wealthy homes. Commanding this colonial empire was the viceroy—the new Montezuma—regent of the Spanish king, and in the New World a man as powerful as the king himself. There were sixty-one viceroys during the nearly three hundred years before Mexico gained its independence from Spain in 1821. Beneath them, bureaucratic control reached down through provinces and finally to the local magistrate—the alcalde—who administered justice, executed imperial policies, and collected taxes in more than two hundred cities and towns. The empire ran on the suffering labor of millions of peons and slaves, Indians and Africans.

Fanlike, Spanish conquistadors and colonists spread northward, creating the northern borderlands of New Spain, the southern region of what is now the United States. The first North American Indian people forced to the defense of their homeland were the Timucuas of Florida, attacked in 1513 by Juan Ponce de León, governor of Puerto Rico. Ponce may have been interested in rumors of a limestone spring, supposedly the Fountain of Youth, an old European legend, but there is no doubt that he was also hunting for slaves for his colony. He landed on the southern Atlantic coast, which he named in honor of the Easter season—*pascua florida*—making Florida the oldest European place-name in the United States. Native warriors beat back this invasion and several more that Ponce led before the Timucuas killed him in battle in 1521.

In 1528 an expedition to settle Florida was dispatched from Spain under the leadership of Pánfilo de Narváez, but storms wrecked the ships on the Florida coast, and within a year only a handful of men were left. Over the subsequent seven years they lived and wandered among the Indian peoples of the Gulf coast and the Southwest

Timucua chief and French Hugenot in Florida. Watercolor by Jacques le Moyne, 1564. New York Public Library.

and thus became the first Europeans to make the overland western trek. In 1536 the last two survivors chanced upon a Spanish expedition seeking Indian slaves in the far northern Mexican province of Sonora. One of them, Alvar Núñez Cabeza de Vaca, wrote an account of his adventures in which he told of a North American empire known as Cíbola, with cities larger than the city of Mexico, where the king took his siesta under a tree of golden bells. These heady myths were based on nothing firmer than the adobe pueblos of New Mexico, but the report inspired two Spanish attempts to penetrate the mystery of North America.

The first was an invasion of Florida led by Hernán de Soto, a veteran of the conquest of Peru who, in the words of one Spaniard who knew him, was "much given to the sport of hunting Indians on horseback." Landing at Tampa Bay in 1539 with a Cuban army of over seven hundred men and thousands of hogs and cattle, he pushed hundreds of miles through the heavily populated Southeast. A member of the expedition recorded the reaction of one chief to de Soto's arrival at his village. "The sight of you and your people . . . astride the fierce brutes, your horses, entering with such speed and fury into my country, . . . strike[s] awe and terror into our hearts." I hope, he continued, "that you will tell me who you are, whence you come, wither you go, and what it is you seek." Like the other conquistadors de Soto sought a golden city, but he failed to locate another Aztec empire. In present-day Alabama, thousands of Tuscaloosa warriors besieged his army, and a few months later ancestors of the modern Chickasaws chewed the Spaniards apart. De Soto died on the banks of the Mississippi, and some 300 survivors eventually reached Mexico on rafts in 1543. The native peoples of the South had turned back Spanish invasion, and they would remain in control of their country for another 250 years.[31]

In the 1560s a group of French Protestants from Normandy, led by Jean Ribault, established a small colony on Florida's Atlantic coast. At their first location, on Parris Island along the South Carolina coast, the colonists nearly starved, but they saved themselves by relocating to a location south of present-day Jacksonville, near a cluster of Timucua villages. The Timucuas were hospitable, welcoming the French into their homes with food and drink, likely seeing them as potential allies against the slave-raiding Spaniards.

But the Spaniards would not tolerate the existence of a French colony along the southern coast—especially one inhabited by infidel Protestants. "We are compelled to pass in front of their port," wrote one Cuban official, "and with the greatest ease they can sally out with their armadas to seek us." In 1565 the Spanish crown sent Don Pedro Menéndez de Avilés, captain-general of the Indies, to crush the Huguenots. He established the fort of Saint Augustine south of the French, then marched overland through the swamps to surprise them with an attack from the rear. "I put Jean Ribault and all the rest of them to the knife," Menéndez wrote triumphantly to the king, "judging it to be necessary to the service of the Lord Our God and of Your Majesty." Menéndez left more than five hundred French colonists lying dead on the white sandy beach, ending the French attempt to colonize the temperate latitudes of North America. The Spanish triumph was an even greater disaster for the Timucuas, who suffered enslavement and depopulation and over the next two centuries completely disappeared as a distinct people.[32]

The second Spanish *entrada de conquista* into North America was aimed at the north of Mexico, what today is called the Southwest. Francisco Vásquez de Coronado led three hundred Spaniards, both mounted troops and infantry, as well as eight hundred Tlaxcalan warriors north along a well-marked Indian trading path that connected central Mexico to the northern region known as Aztlan—the legendary homeland of the Aztecs. Like de Soto, Coronado was looking for Cabeza de Vaca's golden cities of Cíbola.

The expedition passed through the settlements of the Pimas near the present border of the United States and Mexico, and finally reached the village of the Zunis, the southernmost town of the Pueblo peoples. The Zunis resisted, but the invaders quickly smashed them. Coronado moved on to the communities along the Rio Grande, where after some persuasive violence, the Indians allowed him to establish a base camp. These towns "of stone and mud, rudely fashioned," as one of Coron-

The Spaniards arrive in the Southwest. Navajo pictogram, Canyon del Muerto, Arizona, c. eighteenth century. Photograph by Helga Teiwes, Arizona State Museum, University of Arizona.

ado's companions described them, were deeply disappointing to the Spaniards. "I have not seen any principal houses," wrote this chronicler, "by which any superiority over others could be shown." There were, in other words, no signs that these villages were part of an empire. Still hopeful, however, Coronado sent expeditions out in all directions. They brought back word of the Colorado River and the Grand Canyon, but nothing to match the rumors of golden Cíbola. Coronado himself took his army as far north as the Great Plains, and they were the first Europeans to see great herds of buffalo—Coronado called them "shaggy cows"—and made contact with nomadic hunting peoples, but they returned without gold. After a winter in the Southwest, the discouraged army dragged back to Mexico. For the next half-century Spain had no interest in the Southwest.[33]

When the Spaniards finally returned it was as Catholic missionaries. The dense, settled farming communities of the Pueblos may not have had any wealth to plunder, but they did offer a harvest of souls. Franciscan missionaries came up the trading road and began to proselytize among the Pueblos during the 1580s. Soon rumors were drifting south of rich silver mines along the Rio Grande. Gold and silver mining had become major industries in New Spain, and men were anxious to make new

Zuni Pueblo, New Mexico. Photograph by Timothy O'Sullivan, c. 1872. Beinecke.

strikes. It would not be the last time that rumors of gold would spark new colonization of the West.

In 1598 an expedition left New Spain led and financed by Juan de Oñate, member of a wealthy mining family of northern New Spain and married to a woman descended from both the emperor Montezuma and the conquistador Cortés. Oñate's party consisted of 130 predominantly mestizo and Tlaxcalan soldiers and their families, along with some twenty Franciscans. The name that Spanish officials bestowed on the region at this time—Nuevo Mexico—registered their hopes that Oñate would discover a new Aztec empire in the north.

Reaching the valley of the Rio Grande, Oñate advanced from town to town, announcing the establishment of Spanish authority. The reaction of the Pueblos ranged from skepticism to hostility. Encountering the most resistance at the town of Acoma, "the sky city" built high atop a commanding mesa, Oñate lay siege. Indian warriors killed dozens of invaders with their arrows, while native women bombarded the attackers with a hail of stones. The Spaniards finally succeeded in climbing the rock walls, killing eight hundred men, women, and children in the battle, and laying waste to the town. Each surviving warrior had one of his feet severed, and more than five hundred people were carried off into slavery. Why had they resisted, Oñate asked one of the Acoma chiefs. "Some Indians wanted to make peace," he replied, "but others did not. And because they could not agree, they would not sub-mit."[34]

The Spanish conquest of the Pueblos was marked by many such scenes of vio-lence. But it was Oñate's failure to locate the storied mines, not the violence, that caused consternation in Mexico City, and after several years he was recalled. The of-ficials of New Spain were about to abandon the colony when at the last minute it was saved by the Spanish monarch, who decided to subsidize New Mexico as a special missionary project. In 1609 a new governor founded the capital of La Villa Real de la Santa Fe de San Francisco—"the royal town of the holy faith of Saint Francis"—and from this base at Santa Fe the Franciscans penetrated all the surrounding Indian vil-lages.

The real conquest of the Pueblos—the Franciscan effort to convert them to Chris-tianity—was a cultural struggle. The missionaries entered an Indian world they found difficult to understand. Pueblo society was sharply divided into separate do-mains for men and women, and contrary to Spanish norms the Pueblos reckoned descent through the mother's line, with women exercising nearly complete control over their households. "The woman always commands and is the mistress of the house," wrote one Franciscan, "not the husband." Men and women, wrote another, "make agreements among themselves and live together as long as they want to, and when the woman takes a notion, she looks for another husband and the man for an-other wife." Men formed into religious societies, and their proper sphere was what we might call "external" affairs—hunting, trading, warfare, and ceremonial reli-gion.[35]

Accustomed to the norm of the patriarchal family, the Spanish friars found this system incomprehensible. There was, for example, a great deal of private and public competition between the sexes. One missionary reported that when Pueblo women bore a girl-baby they placed a seed-filled gourd over her vulva and prayed that she would grow up to be fertile; but they sprinkled a boy-baby's penis with water and prayed it would remain small. Not surprisingly, this angered Pueblo men, and in some of their public ceremonies they put on giant phalluses as an assertion of their fertility and sang scornfully to the women that this was "the thing that made the women happy." The Pueblos and the Spaniards had very different understandings of sexuality. Sexual intercourse was to the Pueblos a symbol of the powerful force bring-ing the separate worlds of men and women together and was thus their symbol for community.[36]

The Franciscans presented a striking contrast. Their sexual celibacy not only as-tounded the Indians, it horrified them, for it marked the priests as only half-persons. When the Franciscans indulged in their practice of self-flagellation and encouraged their converts to do the same, the Pueblos looked on this much as a Freudian might—as an aspect of the priests' repressed sexuality. "You Christians are crazy," one Pueblo religious chief told a Franciscan. "You go through the streets in groups, flagellating yourselves, and it is not well that the people of this pueblo should be encouraged to commit such madness." Indeed, the Franciscans seem at least as preoccupied with sex as the Pueblos. At Taos Pueblo a priest humiliated men by grabbing their testicles and twisting until the victims collapsed in pain. One Taos man complained in court that a priest had "twisted his penis so much that it broke in half." Priests punished other young men by forcing them onto all fours and "buggering" them with sticks.[37]

The difference in the Pueblo and Franciscan points of view is well illustrated by an incident that occurred while one of the missionaries was conducting an outdoor ceremony. Preaching in favor of monogamy, he was challenged by a woman who argued vigorously against it. Suddenly, according to the Catholic account, "a bolt of lightning flashed from a clear untroubled sky, killing that infernal agent of the demon." To the priest, God had struck her dead. But the Pueblos interpreted the event differently. For them, persons struck by lightning immediately became cloud spirits, and thus the woman's death confirmed that what she had said was morally true.[38]

The missionaries had their greatest success among Pueblo youth, many of whom were taken from their families and raised by the priests. The religious leaders of the Pueblos scornfully called these converts "wet-heads," because of the Christian practice of baptism. The Indians of the outlying towns—the Acomas, the Zunis, and the isolated Hopis—were the most successful at resisting Christian conversion and retained their old customs, including the system of matrilineal kinship. But the Pueblos of the Rio Grande valley were dramatically affected by Spanish and Christian customs, and over time the power of women and of the mothers' lineages faded, providing one of the earliest examples in the history of the frontier of what is called *acculturation*. As one Pueblo tale put it, "When Padre Jesus came, the Corn Mothers went away."[39]

The colonial economy of New Mexico was based on small-scale agriculture and the raising of sheep and cattle introduced by the Spaniards. Livestock were transported to Mexico from the Caribbean almost before Cortés had conquered the Aztec capital. "The hardy and tough-sinewed Spanish cattle," writes Tom Lea, "tinged with the savage blood of the fighting bulls of the plazas, seemed exactly fitted to thrive in the new continent's wilderness." The colonists exploited the labor of the Indians, creating the conditions for lordship and leisure. As one Spanish official put it, "No one comes to the Indies to plow and to sow, but only to eat and loaf."[40]

Most of the soldiers who came with Oñate were themselves Mexican Indians, mestizos or mulattoes, but their service to the crown earned them the aristocratic title of *hidalgo*, and descendants in their lineage inherited all the rights and privileges of that class. Thus did men of mixed ancestry proudly claim the status of *españoles* in New Mexico and received titles as *encomenderos* with the right to command Indian labor. In the northern Spanish colonies, writes historian Quintard Taylor, "color presented no insurmountable barrier to fame, wealth, or new ethnoracial status." Moreover, after the initial conquest, few new colonists came up the dusty road from Mexico, and the growth of population was almost entirely the result of mixing between local Indian women and settler men.[41]

By the late seventeenth century this northernmost outpost of the far-flung Spanish-American empire was populated by about three thousand mostly mestizo settlers clustered in a few settlements along the Rio Grande. Surrounding them were an estimated fifty thousand Pueblos in some fifty villages. In spite of this imbalance between colonists and Indians, the native population was in the midst of a precipitous decline—largely because of the introduction of European epidemic diseases. As the number of Indians fell, the exploitation of labor by encomenderos became less profitable, and colonists began instead to extend their land holdings, their agriculture, and particularly their stockraising activities. The result was increasing conflict with Pueblo people, who considered these lands their own. A severe drought that caused widespread hunger in the 1670s seems to have been the last straw. Some twenty thousand Pueblos had converted to Catholicism over the previous few decades, but now there was a resurgence of traditional Pueblo religion.

In response the Spaniards attempted to outlaw and stamp out native ceremonies. With the support of soldiers the Franciscan missionaries invaded the underground kivas and destroyed sacred artifacts. They publicly humiliated holy men and compelled whole villages to perform penance by working in irrigation ditches and fields. The governor of New Mexico had three Pueblo holy men executed and dozens more whipped for practicing their religion.

One of those humiliated priests, Popé of San Juan Pueblo, became the leader of a movement dedicated to overthrowing the colonial regime. In August 1680, executing a secret plan with superb timing, the Pueblos rose in revolt. The Indians killed four hundred colonists, including several dozen priests, whose mutilated bodies they left strewn upon the altars. Then they ransacked the churches, desecrating the holy furnishings. Two thousand Spanish survivors fled to the security of the Palace of Governors in Santa Fe, where they were besieged by three thousand angry warriors. After a siege lasting five days the Spanish counterattacked and fled south, in the words of one account, with "the poor women and children on foot and unshod, of such a hue that they looked like dead people."[42]

The victorious Pueblos now transformed the governor's chapel into a traditional kiva, his palace into a communal dwelling. On the elegant inlaid stone floors where

Palace of the Governors, Santa Fe, New Mexico. Photograph by Ben Wittick, c. 1881.
Museum of New Mexico.

the governor had once held court, Pueblo women now ground their corn. The corn mothers had returned. Santa Fe became the capital of a Pueblo confederacy with Popé in the position of leadership. He forced Christian Indians to the river to scrub away the taint of baptism. He also ordered the destruction of everything Spanish, but this most Pueblos found they could not do. The colonists had introduced horses and sheep, fruit trees and wheat, new tools and new crafts that the Indians found useful. Although they looked forward to a world without Jesus, they could not imagine a world without iron or sheep or peaches. The Spaniards, moreover, had provided support in the struggle against the Pueblos' traditional enemies, the nomadic Navajos and Apaches. With stolen horses and weapons, these nomads now became considerably more dangerous, their raids on the Pueblo villages much more destructive. With chaos mounting, the Pueblos deposed Popé in 1690.

The Spaniards returned in 1692, beginning a violent reconquest that in six years of fighting reestablished colonial authority. But both sides had learned a lesson, and over the next generation the colonists and the Pueblos reached an implicit understanding. Pueblos observed Catholicism in the missionary chapels, while missionaries tolerated the practice of traditional religion in the Indians' underground kivas. Royal officials guaranteed the inviolability of Indian lands, and Pueblos pledged loyalty to the Spanish crown. Pueblos voluntarily turned out for service on colonial lands, and colonists abandoned the system of forced labor. Together the Spaniards and the Pueblos held off the nomadic tribes for the next 150 years. Colonist and Indian communities remained autonomous, but they learned to live with one another.

In New Mexico and elsewhere in their New World colonial empire, the Spanish established a "frontier of inclusion." Their colonial communities were characterized by *mestizaje,* including a great deal of intermarriage between male colonists and native women. Thousands of Indians died of warfare and disease, but thousands more passed their genes on to successive generations of mestizo peoples. The children of Old World fathers and New World mothers became the majority population of New Spain. Thus although the coming of the Spaniards to the Americas was characterized by the destruction of peoples, it also resulted in the birth of new ones.

FURTHER READING

Alfred W. Crosby, Jr., *The Columbian Exchange: Biological and Cultural Consequences of 1492* (1972)

Ramón Gutiérrez, *When Jesus Came, the Corn Mothers Went Away: Marriage, Sexuality, and Power in New Mexico, 1500–1816* (1991)

Lewis Hanke, *The Spanish Struggle for Justice in the Conquest of America* (1949)

Miguel Leon-Portilla, ed., *The Broken Spears: The Aztec Account of the Conquest of Mexico* (1962)

Samuel Eliot Morison, *The European Discovery of America: The Southern Voyages, A.D. 1492– 1616* (1974)

Kirkpatrick Sale, *The Conquest of Paradise: Christopher Columbus and the Columbian Legacy* (1990)

Edward H. Spicer, *Cycles of Conquest: The Impact of Spain, Mexico, and the United States on the Indians of the Southwest, 1533–1960* (1962)

David E. Stannard, *American Holocaust: Columbus and the Conquest of the New World* (1992)

Quintard Taylor, *In Search of the Racial Frontier: African Americans in the American West, 1528–1990* (1998)

Hugh Thomas, *Conquest: Montezuma, Cortés, and the Fall of Old Mexico* (1993)

David J. Weber, *The Spanish Frontier in North America* (1992)

Ronald Wright, *Stolen Continents: The Americas Through Indian Eyes Since 1492* (1992)

2

Contest of Cultures

The woodland Indians on the shores of the Atlantic first discovered Europeans on some unknown day in the late fifteenth century, as they watched ships from beyond the sunrise manned by a people who fished the salt sea. The Micmacs of Nova Scotia later told of seeing the approach of "a singular little island, as they supposed, which had drifted near to the land and become stationary there. There were trees on it, and branches to the trees, on which a number of bears, as they supposed, were crawling about. . . . What was their surprise to find that these supposed bears were men, and that some of them were lowering down into the water a very singularly constructed canoe, into which several of them jumped and paddled ashore." Ships from ports in England, France, Spain, and Portugal probably were plying the waters of the great fishing grounds of the North Atlantic years before Columbus made his first voyage to the Caribbean. Certainly by 1500 dozens of European ships and hundreds of sailors were regularly fishing in coastal waters, many making landfall to take on water and fuel and to dry their catch.[1]

The first European to record making contact with the native people of eastern North America was Giovanni da Verrazano, a gentleman from Florence sailing for the French, who in 1524 reconnoitered the Atlantic coast from Florida in the south to Cape Breton Island in the north. Reaching a fine harbor at 30° of latitude he was greeted by dozens of natives who came paddling out to greet his ship, the *Dauphine*. They were a people known as the Narragansetts, and this great bay would later take their name. "These are the most handsome people," Verrazano recorded, "of bronze color, some inclining to white, others to tawny color; the profile sharp, the hair long and black and they give great attention to its care; the eyes are black and alert, and their bearing is sweet and gentle, much in the manner of olden days." Verrazano, too, was a believer in edenic myths. But further north along the coast of Maine he en-

Canadian Indian. Drawing by Louis Nicolas, from Codex Canadiensis, *c. 1700. The Thomas Gilcrease Institute of American History and Art, Tulsa.*

countered a more troublesome people, *mala gente* he called them, who kept the Frenchmen at a distance and shot arrows at a shoreside exploring party. But they made it clear they wanted to trade for knives, fishhooks, or edged metal. The Narragansetts apparently had had no previous contact with Europeans, but these Indians were experienced enough to be wary of ships and their crews while also understanding the value of their technology.[2]

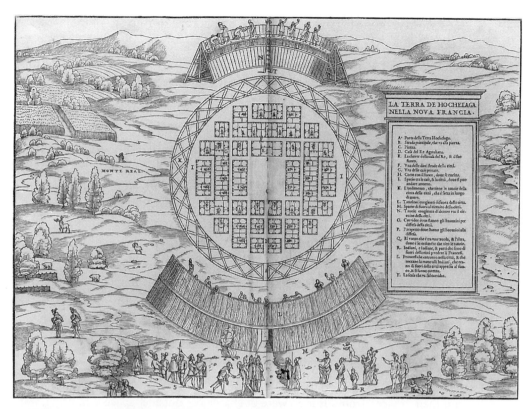

Hochelaga as described by Jacques Cartier. From Giovanni Battista Ramusio, Terzo volume delle nauigationi et viaggi . . . *(Venice, 1556). Beinecke.*

Ten years later—while Cabeza de Vaca was wandering among the tribes of the Gulf coast—the Indians of the Saint Lawrence valley marveled at two ships that came sailing up their river. The vessels were mastered by Jacques Cartier, whose king, Francis I of France, was ready to compete with imperial Spain. Cartier had come to seek the Northwest Passage to India and to establish French claims to lands "where it is said that he should find great quantities of gold." But Spanish vessels had already been in this vicinity. When Cartier met natives along the Newfoundland coast they greeted him with the only European words they knew—*acá nada,* "nothing is here" in Spanish. And thinking this was the name of the place, Cartier called it "Canada."[3]

At another landing up the Saint Lawrence, Cartier was welcomed by at least a thousand Indians who escorted the Frenchmen down a well-worn road to the village of Hochelaga, through what Cartier described as "land cultivated and beautiful, large fields full of the corn of the country." The town was "circular and enclosed by timbers," Cartier wrote, with "galleries with ladders to mount to them, where stones are kept for protection and defense."[4]

Warfare was a prominent fact of life among the Iroquois and Algonquian peoples of the northeast, and violence would permeate the frontier era as well. Scalping seems to have been a part of the warfare complex of the Northeast. For Indians it was a practice filled with religious significance, for the special way in which a man chose to wear his hair was a token of his spirit, and a warrior sought to gain that spiritual power by taking his enemy's scalp lock. The invasion of North America by Europeans would raise the level of woodland violence and do much to spread the practice. Imperial conflict in the northeastern woodlands would scar the continent until its resounding climax in the eighteenth century.

Hochelaga was composed of "some fifty houses," Cartier observed, each "fifty or more paces long and twelve to fifteen wide, made of timbers and covered, roof and sides, by large pieces of bark and rind of trees." These were the famous "longhouses" of the Iroquois peoples. "Inside," he continued, "are a number of rooms and chambers and in the center of the house is a large room or space upon the ground, where they make their fire and live together, the men thereafter retiring with wives and children to their private rooms." Like the Pueblos, they were matrilineal people, and each longhouse was a communal clan dwelling, headed by a clan mother. When they married, men left the longhouses of their mothers to reside in the longhouses of their wives.[5]

Women controlled domestic and village space. The women "are much respected," a French priest wrote some years later. "The Elders decide no important affair without their advice." Iroquois men were in charge of "outside" space—hunting, warfare, diplomacy. Men brought meat back for their sisters and mothers, not their wives, and the most important male figures in the lives of Iroquois children were maternal uncles, not fathers. Most chiefs were men, but their succession, wrote another missionary, "is continued through the women, so that at the death of a chief, it is not his own, but his sister's son who succeeds him, or, in default of which, his nearest relation in the female line."[6]

Cartier also provided a detailed description of the Indian enthusiasm for trading. "The savages showed marvelous great pleasure in possessing and obtaining iron wares and other commodities," he noted. Like the Indians Verrazano met, they appreciated the usefulness of European technology. Cartier, meanwhile, noticed the beautiful fur coats of his hosts. "They make their clothes of the pelts of otter, beaver, marten, fox, lynx, deer, stag, and others." In Europe only nobles and priests had the right to wear ermine, sable, and other luxurious furs, but there was a demand for pelts of all kinds for winter wear. The growing population had depleted the wild game of Europe, and even supplies of furs from Russia and Scandinavia were seriously declining.[7]

So here was the potential for rich profit. "They do not value worldly goods," wrote Cartier, "being unacquainted with such." In exchange for cheap goods and trinkets, the Indians were willing to give over valuable furs. Europeans most prized beaver, for it could be processed into a waterproof material for coats and hats. To do so, however, required the removal of the long outer hairs, and it turned out that the very best pelts were those that Indians had already used for a season, wearing them down. What a bargain, the Indians must have thought. These fools are willing to trade scarce metal, glass, and woven goods for our greasy old coats! The Europeans "have no sense," declared a Montagnais of eastern Canada, "they give us twenty knives like this for one Beaver skin." A mutual misunderstanding thus lay at the heart of the fur trade—the belief on the part of both sides that each was getting the better of the other.[8]

It requires imagination to recapture the context of this early frontier on the Atlantic coast. Indians were in the commanding position, vastly outnumbering Europeans, who had boldly ventured into a land they scarcely understood. Because of heavy competition among traders, Indians frequently could extract very good exchange rates. They had a sharp eye for quality, and insisted on superior goods of their own specification—large bolts of heavy woolen cloth to take the place of leather or hide clothing, for example, in the Indians' favorite colors of deep blue, dark red, and steel gray. Think of the Hudson Bay trade blankets, still renowned as the highest quality in the world: they were designed to Indian specifications. Many decades would pass before Indians would fit the description of simply the victims of European traders.

Cartier and his crew spent the winter of 1535 at the village of Stadacona. The residents were remarkably cooperative and helpful. They suggested, for example, a potion of boiled bark that cured almost magically an epidemic of scurvy threatening to wipe out the company. The bitter cold, however, was beyond relief. Mountainous snowdrifts lay against the ships in the harbor, their bulwarks encased in ice four inches thick. By May 1536 the French were on their way home. Although Cartier made further attempts at colonization, not until the dawn of the seventeenth century did the French permanently settle the Northeast.

But in the meantime trade continued and grew increasingly important, especially at the annual summer trade fair at the village of Tadoussac near the mouth of the Saint Lawrence River. The early connections between Europeans and Indians in the Northeast were thus quite different from those that characterized the Spanish-Indian frontiers of northern New Spain, for in the north they were based on commerce rather than conquest. These, too, were colonial relationships, of course, and there would be negative consequences for Indian people. Epidemic European diseases soon began to ravage their communities, and as the value of furs increased, intense and deadly rivalry broke out among tribes over access to hunting territory. In the resulting warfare the communities of Stadacona, Hochelaga, and numerous smaller villages disappeared, and the Saint Lawrence became a no-man's-land for Indians, opening the way for European settlement. Moreover, as manufactured goods became essential to their way of life, Indians gradually grew dependent upon European supplies. Europeans might acquire elsewhere goods offered by Indians, but Indians found it difficult or impossible to produce the goods they wanted from Europeans. Trade was stacked in favor of Europeans.

The French were the most numerous traders at work in the Northeast, and at the turn of the seventeenth century they devised a strategy to capture a monopoly of the trade. Samuel de Champlain, as a result of his travels to the West Indies and to Mexico City between 1599 and 1601, envied Spanish success in the New World. Backed both by his king and by merchants, he commanded a colonizing expedition that arrived on the north Atlantic coast and established the outpost of Port Royal on the Bay of Fundy in 1605. Within three years he had planted the first permanent French settlement in the New World, a place he called Québec, located at the site of the former Indian town of Stadacona, on the bluffs above the river where he could intercept the flow of furs to the Atlantic.

As a vigorous governor for twenty-five years, until he died on Christmas Day in 1635, Champlain always sensed the importance of good relations with the Indian tribes, and he relied on the tradition of commercial relations that had developed between natives and Europeans during the sixteenth century. As his first task he forged an alliance with the Huron confederacy living to the north of Lake Ontario, in what is today the fruitful agricultural heartland of the Canadian province of Ontario, where they controlled access to the rich hunting territory of the northern lakes. But good relations with some Indians meant war with others. The Hurons were traditional enemies of the Five Nation League of the Iroquois (the Mohawk, Oneida, Onondaga, Cayuga, and Seneca tribes). According to Iroquois oral history, the league was formed in the fifteenth century by the great orator Hiawatha and Chief Deganawida, the lawgiver. This alliance suppressed violence among its members but did not hesitate to encourage war against outside groups such as the neighboring Hurons. Now Champlain sealed his alliance by joining the Hurons in making war on the Five Nations. Like the Spanish with the Tlaxcalans, the French initiated their American empire by allying themselves with a powerful Indian force, demonstrating once again the importance of native people in the making of continental history.

As an industry the fur trade of New France rivaled cattle raising and mining in New Spain. And just as the ranches and mines of Mexico depended on native labor, so the trapping of beaver and otter in New France relied on the work of the Indians. Champlain understood this simple necessity and therefore sent his agents and traders in canoes to negotiate with Indians and to live in their villages, learning their languages and customs, in order to direct the flow of furs to Quebec and to Montreal, built upriver at the site of Hochelaga in 1642.

Champlain joins the Hurons in battle against the Mohawks, 1609. From Samuel de Champlain,
Les voyages de la Novvelle France Occidentale . . . *(Paris, 1632). Beinecke.*

Meanwhile, along the Saint Lawrence, the French installed their own version of
European feudal society. Cardinal Richelieu, prime minister of Louis XIII, devised a
scheme that the king proclaimed in 1628, granting a "Company of One Hundred Associates"—young nobles, army officers, and merchants—immense privileges in exchange for supervision of the religious and economic development of the area. The
company had to transport to the New World at least four thousand settlers and an
appropriate number of priests, all of whom they had to support. The company held
a monopoly over the fur trade and all commercial activities, except fishing and mining. It could grant land, which it did in large swaths along the waters of the Saint
Lawrence. Because rivers were everywhere in New France, and such easy highways,
the lord, or *seigneur,* of each manor divided his land in ribbons from river frontages.
Usually fewer than eight hundred feet wide, these properties would run back ten
times that length. The riverbank farmers, the *habitants,* owed the seigneur homage
and dues.

These obligations, though pittances, were seldom paid, for the growing season
was short and productivity low. The company had trouble attracting its quota of
colonists and eventually surrendered its charter, leaving care of New France to the
crown. A spurt of activity came in the 1660s under the leadership of Governor Jean
Talon. He injected new prosperity into agriculture as well as the fishing and trapping
industries. Under Talon the French population doubled. But by 1700 New France had
only fifteen thousand colonists. Quebec City, the administrative capital, was small

by Spanish colonial standards, and Montreal remained little more than a frontier outpost.

———

Because of the importance of the fur trade, the communities of the Saint Lawrence looked west toward the continental interior rather than east across the Atlantic. It was typical for the sons of habitants to take to the woods in their youth, working as agents for fur companies or as independent traders. Most returned to take up farming, but others remained in Indian villages, where they married Indian women and raised families. The contact between French traders—the *coureurs de bois* or "runners of the woods"—and Indian peoples resulted in much cultural exchange: Indians adopted many aspects of European material culture, and Europeans adopted many of the Indians' lifeways. Like the Spanish-Indian frontier, the French in the Northeast also established a "frontier of inclusion," but it developed a unique character.

There was a great deal of sexual mixing. Among most of the native groups with whom the French had contact, young women were free to make their own decisions about their associations. "A young woman is allowed to do what she pleases," one Frenchman wrote, "let her conduct be what it will, neither father nor mother, brother nor sister, can pretend to control her. A young woman, say they, is master of her own body, and by her natural right to liberty is free to do what she pleases."[9]

For many Europeans, the encounter with these women fulfilled an erotic fantasy often associated with colonialism. As one experienced trader wrote in his journal, "Our young Canadians who come here are seen everywhere running at full speed like escaped horses into Venus's country." A western chief asked one of the traders, "I was wondering whether you white people have any women amongst you?" The way the men act, he exclaimed, "one might suppose they had never seen any before." The European colonial record is filled with glowing comments on the beauty of young Indian women. "As for the Indian women," one English trader wrote, "when young and at maturity, they are as fine-shaped Creatures as any in the Universe. They are of a tawny Complexion, their Eyes very brisk and amorous, their Smiles afford the finest Composure a Face can possess, their hands are of the finest make, with small, long fingers, and as soft as cheeks, and their whole Bodies of a smooth Nature."[10]

To be sure, exploitation was often a component in these relationships. Prostitution, unknown among the Indians before the colonial era, soon became a prominent institution at every fur trade post and fort. Many colonists who came into fur trade country took Indian women as lovers, then abandoned them without a word or a sign of the least consideration for the children they left behind. But there was opportunity for exploitation on both sides. Indian women established liaisons with traders to bring valuable trade connections to their families, their clans, or themselves. Most of these peoples were matrilineal, and women expected rather weak marital connections. Moreover, polygamy and divorce were common.

So for the most part, these marriages seem to have been mutually advantageous. "When a Frenchman trades with them," wrote one observer, "he takes into his services one of their Daughters, the one, presumably, who is most his taste; he asks the Father for her, & under certain conditions, it is arranged; he promises to give the Father some blankets, a few shirts, a Musket, Powder & Shot, Tobacco & Tools; they come to an agreement at last, & the exchange is made. The Girl, who is familiar with the country, undertakes, on her part, to serve the Frenchman in every way, to dress his pelts, to sell his Merchandise for a specified length of time; the bargain is faithfully carried out on both sides." Note the practical considerations here. The Indian wife of a trader or trapper prepared the furs and skins for market, did the cooking, helped to carry the packs. "One woman can carry, or haul, as much as two men can do," a Chipewyan chief told a trader. "They also pitch our tents, make and mend our clothing, keep us warm at night; and in fact there is no such thing as traveling any considerable distance, or for any length of time, in this country without their assistance." Most of the connections made between traders and Indian women seem to have been stable, permanent, and constant, lasting for years, with a great deal of commitment on the part of the men to their children. Many traders remained in Indian country and raised mixed families.[11]

The French-Indian frontier was the site of cultural learning on both sides. Consider language. Young men who entered the trade were advised on how best to get along. If you want to do well in Indian country, they were told, sleep with a dictionary. Thus the fur trade spawned a special language—linguists call these "pidgin" languages—that combined both French and native tongues. "There is a certain jargon between the French and Savages," wrote a priest, "which is neither French nor Savage; and yet, when the French use it, they think they are using the Savage tongue, and the Savages in using it, think they are using good French." This was another of the "fictions" that kept the system of cultural relations running smoothly.[12]

Out of this process of intermixing, which the French called *métissage,* there developed not only a new language but a new people, the *métis.* In the Great Lakes region and to the west many of these people of mixed ancestry gradually formed a separate grouping, a "people in between." Often bilingual, sometimes trilingual—speaking their mother's, their father's, and sometimes their own métis language as well—with highly developed skills of moving across the cultural boundaries, these people became guides, interpreters, and often traders in their own right.

Some of the métis were the coureurs de bois who were living among the Indians of the Great Lakes as early as the 1620s. Fifty years later they were on the reaches of the upper Mississippi River. Governor Louis de Frontenac, Talon's successor, added

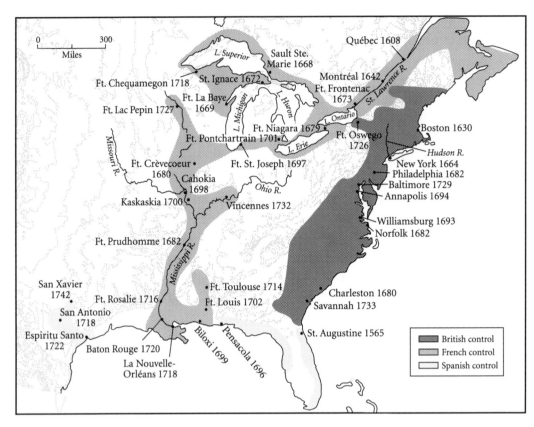

THREE NORTH AMERICAN EMPIRES IN THE EIGHTEENTH CENTURY

official sanction to this French Canadian impulse to plunge deeper into the continent. More than a century after Coronado marched northward into the Mississippi basin, Frontenac authorized tests of the Spanish imperial drive in roughly the same region. In 1673 Jacques Marquette, a Jesuit priest, and Louis Joliet traveled two-thirds of the way down the Mississippi to the Arkansas River. Then in 1682 Robert Cavelier de La Salle, leading a bickering but courageous expedition, traveled all the way to the river's mouth on the Gulf of Mexico. There in the swampy delta he planted a cross, turned a spade of earth, and claimed all land drained by those waters for King Louis XIV.

The Spanish empire had fleshed out its basic form in the seventeenth century, the French in the early eighteenth. New France became a giant crescent—the interior heartland of North America embracing the two immense river systems of the Saint Lawrence and the Mississippi joined by the five Great Lakes. Its dimensions were nearly as breathtaking as the sweep of New Spain, whose northeastern borders it touched. The boundaries of the two empires, vague as they were, actually overlapped. The French, too, founded settlements along the Gulf coast—at Biloxi (in 1699, seventeen years after La Salle stood at the mouth of the Mississippi) and at New

Orleans (1718). Except for these ports, however, the French turned inward to the land they named for King Louis XIV, Louisiana.

———————

Economics motivated the French, but like the Spanish they also had religious aspirations: they wished to see the Indians converted to the Catholic faith. In 1611, three years after Champlain founded Quebec, the first Jesuit missionaries arrived in New France, bearing from the king an exclusive jurisdiction to convert the Indians. The Jesuits often accompanied traders into Indian country, and sometimes they led the way. At first Indians looked upon these "Black Robes" as culturally inferior. They wore inefficient and sexually ambiguous clothing, they hid their faces behind deforming beards, and they were uninterested in women, which Indian men found incomprehensible, especially in the context of the heightened sexual contacts with other Europeans. And the Jesuits lacked the most basic survival skills. During the seventeenth century quite a number of Jesuits died martyrs' deaths in pursuit of their missionary goals.

They faced overwhelming cultural differences. Jesuits often unknowingly broke important taboos, like speaking the names of the dead, something Indians never did. It was a horrible insult, for example, to repeat the phrase "Our Father who art in Heaven," or to quote the injunction to "Honor thy father and mother" to men and women whose parents were dead. The Indians had difficulty understanding the concept of celibacy or other sexual mores of the missionaries. One Jesuit, preaching on the Sixth Commandment, which forbade adultery, was interrupted by laughter from the assembled Indians. "It must be impossible to keep that one," one of them explained. To a missionary preaching against the sin of divorce, a Huron man expressed a point of view with which most modern Americans would agree. "You make no sense. My wife does not agree with me, and I cannot agree with her. She will be better suited with another [man] who does not get on with his present wife. Do you wish us four to be unhappy the rest of our days?"[13]

Such articulate and reasoned responses expose the lie in the stereotype of the silent, stoic Indian, with his grunts and "ughs." Another Jesuit recorded a wonderful exchange with a Micmac chief of present-day Nova Scotia. "Thou sayest of us that we are the most miserable and most unhappy of all men," he told the missionary, "living without religion, without any rules, like the beasts in our woods and our forests, lacking bread, wine, and a thousand other comforts." Strange to say, he went on, "we are very content with the little that we have." Then he concluded with unimpeachable logic, "Thou deceivest thyself greatly if thou thinkest to persuade us that thy country is better than ours. For if France, as thou sayest, is a little terrestrial paradise, art thou sensible to leave it?"[14]

Only when the Jesuits began to allow Indians to build bridges between their own

Huron Catholic converts. Detail from Novae Franciae accurata delineatio, *engraved map by G. F. Pesca, 1657. Yale University.*

customs and Christianity did they succeed in their mission. "One must be very careful before condemning a thousand things among their customs, which greatly offend minds brought up and nourished in another world," a Jesuit wrote in 1647. "It is easy to call irreligion what is merely stupidity, and to take for diabolical working something that is nothing more than human; and then, one thinks he is obliged to forbid as impious certain things that are done in all innocence, or, at most, are still not criminal customs. I have no hesitation saying that we have been too severe in this point." Unlike the Spanish Franciscans, who linked conversion to the acceptance of European cultural norms, the Jesuits succeeded because they introduced Christianity as a supplement to the Indian way of life.[15]

Among the Indians of the Northeast, several factors led to the acceptance of the missionaries and their message. Many came to respect the bravery of the priests and their apparent ability to command powers of healing and communion with the spirit world, like shamans. Most important, however, was the enormous social and cultural dislocation that began soon after European contact, caused mainly by disease. During the 1630s the Hurons, for example, were struck by a horrible smallpox epidemic. In a few years as many as half of the Hurons perished, their population falling from thirty thousand to less than fifteen thousand.

Many Hurons blamed the Jesuits for these plagues. To them, the missionaries were sorcerers who sapped the spiritual power of communities and introduced disease by practicing their strange rites. Priests went about baptizing dying people, establishing in the minds of many Indians a connection between this ritual and death. For other Hurons, however, the plagues were the occasion for the loss of faith in their religious beliefs. Traditional healers were unable to handle these massive outbreaks of deadly disease. Traditional practices like communal steam treatments or sitting with the sick only spread the highly infectious disease. In the aftermath of the smallpox epidemic, Jesuit conversions picked up dramatically.

The missionaries seemed particularly successful among Huron women. Just as these women were free to choose European lovers and husbands, so also they could choose to follow Jesuit priests. The Jesuits consciously appealed to women through the cult of the Virgin, the veneration of female saints, and the sisterhood of nuns. They were especially critical of the abuse of women—whether by Indian or European men—organized special women's groups and encouraged adolescent girls to commit themselves to lives of virginity. It was largely through the special appeal to women that the Jesuits became so successful among the Hurons. By the 1640s they had succeeded in converting about 40 percent of the Huron nation.

As a rule the French Jesuits lived and worked with the natives on their own ground, whereas the Spanish Franciscans attempted to concentrate them at their missions. Both exploited Indians for commercial profit, but both also considered them human beings with souls worth saving. By no means would all subsequent inheritors of the North American continent agree.

The English first turned toward the New World in the mid-sixteenth century, during the reign of Queen Elizabeth I. The "sea dogs," among them such privateers as Francis Drake, ventured into Spanish waters to raid the galleons carrying Indian treasure home across the seas. From one such voyage Drake was said to have returned with booty valued in the millions, greatly enriching those who had invested in the enterprise, including Queen Elizabeth herself. The English thus began their American adventure by looting the Spaniards who had in turn looted the Indian empires of the New World.

A consensus soon developed among Elizabeth's closest advisers that the time had come for entering the competition for America. In a remarkable state paper, "A Discourse of Western Planting," written in 1584, the Queen's adviser Richard Hakluyt laid out the advantages that would come from colonies: bases from which the privateers might raid the Spanish Caribbean empire, posts where English traders could tap the Indian market, plantations for growing tropical products that might free the nation from a reliance on the long-distance trade with Asia. These colonies could be populated by the "multitudes of loyterers and idle vagabonds" who populated English cities and the countryside. Hakluyt urged Elizabeth to establish colonies "upon the mouths of the great navigable Rivers" from Florida to the Saint Lawrence. The queen would not commit to Hakluyt's plan, but she did authorize and invest in several private attempts at exploration and colonization. Martin Frobisher conducted three voyages of exploration to the North Atlantic in the late 1570s, on one voyage kidnapping and bringing back to England an Eskimo man, woman, and child as well as samples of worthless ores.[16]

Another attempt at colonization came in 1585 when Sir Walter Raleigh, a favorite of the queen, sponsored the establishment of a base of English soldiers and mercenaries on the Outer Banks of North Carolina from which they might better raid the Spanish to the south. At an island that the local Algonquian Indians called Roanoke, an advance party treated with the local chief, Wingina, who seems to have viewed his visitors as potential allies in the struggle to extend his authority. When the English returned to make preparations for the colonizing expedition, Wingina sent two of his men back with them to keep watch on their plans.

Manteo and Wanchese, the Indian emissaries, were extremely helpful in preparing the scientific component of the mission, under the direction of the Oxford scholar Thomas Harriot and the artist John White. These four men worked at learning one another's languages and developed a good deal of mutual respect. It showed in Harriot's published report of the expedition, a sensitive depiction of Indian culture that provided a detailed description of a Native American people on the eve of colonization. White's watercolors were the most accurate images of Indians made before the nineteenth century.

But the colony itself, which Raleigh christened Virginia in honor of the Virgin Queen, was a dismal failure. The men—there were no women or families—proved incapable of supporting themselves, preferring to hunt for precious metals or raid nearby villages for treasure, visions of Cortés before their eyes. At first Wingina fed them, but when his stores grew short the colonists mounted a surprise attack, killing several of the leading men and beheading the chief. Soon thereafter they returned to England, leaving a legacy of violence and hatred in their wake. In 1587 Raleigh arranged for White to return as governor of a new colony, this one composed of sixty-five single men and twenty families, including White's daughter Elenor and her husband, Ananias Dare. White had put forth a plan for a colony of farmers who would live in association with the native people of the country. "There is good hope," wrote Thomas Harriot, that "through discreet dealing" the Indians may "honor, obey, fear and love us." Harriot and White clearly believed that English culture was superior to that of the Indians, but their vision nevertheless differed greatly from that of the plunderers.[17]

The Algonquians, however, had learned from the first attempt at English colonization. Wanchese told his fellow villagers about the savage inequalities he had seen

The Algonquian town of Secota. Engraving by Theodore de Bry, based on a watercolor by John White, from Thomas Harriot, A Briefe and True Report of the New Found Land of Virginia *... (Frankfurt, 1590). Beinecke.*

in England and warned them not to let the colonists get a foothold in their land. Within the first month of White's return one of the Englishmen had been killed, his body shot full of arrows as he fished for crabs. Knowing that the project hung in the balance, White sailed home in the one small seaworthy ship the colonists possessed to press Raleigh for reinforcements. War with Spain broke out during his absence, and it was three long years before he could return. He found the colony in ruins and the colonists gone without a trace, except for the word *Croatan* carved in a tree. Roanoke became known as the "Lost Colony," the ultimate fate of the colonists one of the great enduring mysteries of the English colonial frontier.

Many historians today believe that the Indians probably incorporated those English men and women into their villages as adoptees. Unlike Wanchese, Manteo had remained a friend of the English and had argued that their goods and technology would be powerful additions to Algonquian life. His home village was called "Croatan," and that is probably where the colonists went for safety. If that was the case, the children of the Roanoke colonists would have married into Indian families when they reached adulthood. The marriage of John White's granddaughter Virginia Dare to an Algonquian warrior would have been an ironic fulfillment of White's vision of a colonial community of English and Indians living side by side.

———

The war between England and Spain suspended further efforts at English colonization in the Americas, but at its conclusion in 1604 King James I issued a number of royal charters for the colonization of the mid-Atlantic region to a number of joint-stock companies. The joint-stock company was basic to English colonization. It sold shares of stock in various quantities, and the money raised in this manner met initial costs without financial assistance from the monarch. The stockholder was liable only for the amount he invested, and if the venture failed he could not be sued for his remaining resources. Raleigh had discovered how much failure could cost a single investor when he lost forty thousand pounds in the Roanoke disaster. A company would have distributed the loss among many small investors.

In 1607 a group of one hundred colonists in the employ of the Virginia Company built a fort on the Chesapeake Bay, named Jamestown in honor of the king. It was to become the first permanent English settlement in North America. The Chesapeake was already home to an estimated twenty thousand Algonquian villagers, most of them united in a powerful chiefdom. Their leader was a man named Powhatan who had already had a bad experience with the Spanish. When Powhatan was a boy, his brother had been kidnapped by Spaniards, taken to Mexico City, and given the name Luis de Velasco. Several years later Velasco returned as an interpreter with a party of Jesuits intent on establishing a mission on the Chesapeake. Velasco escaped to his people, then led a group of warriors who attacked and killed the Catholics. He took a new name, Opechancanough, "he whose soul is white," and became an implacable foe of the Europeans. Powhatan, however, saw positive possibilities in the arrival of the English. Like Wingina, he viewed them as protection against the Spanish and as potential allies in the struggle to extend his confederacy over outlying tribes. Moreover, he looked forward to a valuable trade. As was the case among the Tlaxcalans in Mexico and the Hurons of Canada, the Algonquians of the Chesapeake used Europeans to pursue ends of their own.[18]

For their part, the Jamestown settlers, like the colonists of Roanoke, saw themselves as latter-day conquistadors. Abhorring the idea of physical labor, they survived the first year only with Powhatan's assistance. "In our extremity the Indians brought us Corne," wrote the colony's military leader, Captain John Smith, "when we rather expected they would destroy us." When the English demanded more than Powhatan thought prudent to supply, events took a familiar turn. Smith inaugurated an armed campaign to plunder food from surrounding villages, and Powhatan retaliated by attempting to starve the colonists out. He now realized, he declared to Smith, that "your coming is not for trade, but to invade my people and possess my country." The English came, in other words, not in the mode of the French but in the pattern of the Spanish. During the terrible winter of 1609–10 scores of English colonists starved and a number resorted to cannibalism. By the spring only sixty persons remained of the more than five hundred sent by the Virginia Company.[19]

The company was determined to prevail. It sent out a large additional force of men, women, and livestock, committing themselves to a protracted war against the Indians. By 1613 the colonists had established firm control over the territory between the James and York rivers. Worn down by warfare and disease, Chief Powhatan accepted a treaty of peace in 1614. "I am old and erelong must die," he declared. "I knowe it is better to eat good meat, lie well, and sleep with my women and children, laugh and be merrie than to be forced to flie and be hunted." Powhatan abdicated in favor of his brother, Opechancanough.[20]

Powhatan sent his daughter Pocahontas, who had become fluent in English, to be his ambassador at Jamestown. As in Mexico, the role of mediator would once again be played by an Indian woman. John Rolfe, a leading Jamestown settler, was smitten by her. "My heart and best thoughts are and have been a long time so entangled and enthralled in so intricate a laborynth" when thinking of her, he wrote, "that I was even awearied to unwind my selfe." But alas, they could not marry, for she was "an unbelieving creature." Pocahontas removed that last obstacle by converting to Christianity, taking the name Rebecca, and they were married. Theirs was the best known of many intimate connections between Indians and English during those early years. Similar to the Spanish and French, early English colonization included a good deal of mixing among Europeans and Indians. There was even hope that the couple would beget a Christian line of succession for the Chesapeake chiefdom of Pow-

VIRGINIA. MATOAKA ALS REBECCA FILIA POTENTISS PRINC: POWHATANI IMP: VIRGINIÆ.

Ætatis suæ 21. A.
1616.

Matoaks als Rebecka daughter to the mighty Prince
Powhatan Emperour of Attanougskomouck als virginia
converted and baptized in the Christian faith, and
wife to the worℓℓ Mr Joh Rolff.

Si: Paß: sculp: Compton Holland excud:

Pocahontas in England. Engraving by Simon van de Passe, from Baziliologia: A Book of Kings
(London, 1618). National Portrait Gallery, Smithsonian Institution.

hatan. But the plan was aborted when Pocahontas fell ill and died while visiting England in 1617. Her only child remained there, never to return to Virginia.[21]

History took a different turn. Yet John Rolfe himself provided the key to Virginia's future by developing a hybrid of hearty North American and mild West Indian tobacco, and by 1615 the Jamestown colony was shipping cured tobacco to England. Tobacco first had been introduced to English consumers by Francis Drake in the 1580s, and even though King James described the habit as "loathsome to the eye, hateful to the nose, harmful to the brain, dangerous to the lungs," by the 1610s a craze for smoking created strong consumer demand. Tobacco made the Virginia colony a success. Soon the company began to send over large numbers of indentured servants—Hakylut's "loyterers and idle vagabonds"—to work the tobacco fields. Gradually a society of English families began to take shape in Virginia. There now was no need to incorporate Indians into the population as workers. In contrast to the Spanish and French, who built societies based on the inclusion of Indian people, the English established a "frontier of exclusion," pushing Indians to the periphery rather than incorporating them within colonial society.[22]

The English pressed the Indians for further concessions of land on which to plant their profitable crop, and Opechancanough prepared his people for what he hoped would be an assault that would throw them back into the sea. He was joined by an Algonquian shaman named Nemattanew, who instructed the villagers to reject the English and their ways. This would be the first of many movements of Indian resistance to colonial expansion led by the partnership of a military chief and a religious prophet. Opechancanough's uprising began on Good Friday, March 22, 1622, completely surprising the English. Nearly 350 people, a quarter of the colonists, died before Jamestown mobilized its defenses. Yet the colony managed to hang on, and the attack stretched into a ten-year war of attrition.

The war bankrupted the Virginia Company and in 1624 the king converted Virginia into a royal colony. But the tobacco economy boomed, leading to a doubling of the English colonial population every five years from 1625 to 1640, by which time it numbered approximately ten thousand. Native population, in the meantime, was decimated by warfare and disease, and thus numerical strength shifted in favor of the English. In 1644 Opechancanough, now almost a hundred years old, organized a final desperate assault in which more than five hundred colonists died, but within two years the Virginians had crushed the Algonquians. Opechancanough—"he whose soul is white"—was taken prisoner, then shot in the back and killed by a Jamestown settler.

The state of war continued to exist between tough frontier tobacco farmers and native peoples west of the Chesapeake. Aware that they were losing ground, Indians regarded the establishment of all new settlements as a provocation. In the 1670s the Susquehannocks of the upper Potomac River came into conflict with expanding colonists. In 1675 the wealthy backcountry planter Nathaniel Bacon and his neighbors took the law into their own hands and launched a series of violent raids against Indian communities that included a good deal of indiscriminate murder, although Bacon termed it "a mighty conquest." The effort of Virginia governor William Berkeley to suppress these unauthorized military expeditions so infuriated Bacon and his followers that in the spring of 1676 six hundred of them turned their fury against the colonial capital of Jamestown. Berkeley fled across the Chesapeake while Bacon pillaged and burned the capital. Soon thereafter, however, Bacon died of dysentery, a common fate of the day, and his rebellion collapsed.

Bacon's Rebellion of 1676 was the first expression of frontier agrarian dissent in American history. During his reign as "General of Virginia," Bacon had issued a manifesto demanding the death or removal of all Indians from the colony as well as an end to the rule of aristocratic "grandees" and "parasites." Western farmers were testing the limits of Indian endurance and the strength of eastern seaboard controls. In 1677, in a replay of Virginia events known as Culpepper's Rebellion, backcountry men in the newly settled region of North Carolina overthrew the government and established one of their own before English authorities finally suppressed them. But as a result both Virginia and North Carolina shifted their policy in favor of armed expansion into Indian territory, thereby hoping to gain the support of the backcountry by enlarging the stock of available colonial land. The issues raised in these rebellions would become increasingly important in the years ahead.

Many Indians fled westward. Colonial authorities required those who remained to sign formal treaties granting them small reserved territories. By the 1680s, when the English population of the Virginia region numbered more than fifty thousand, only a dozen tribes with about two thousand residents remained. Over the next three centuries, however, these Indian communities struggled to remain on the land, and today some fifteen hundred people claiming descent from the original tribes continue to live in the Chesapeake area. With their own churches and schools, they work at fishing and farming or commute to work in metropolitan Richmond or Washington, D.C.

In their northern colonies the English carried out a similar policy of exclusion, although in almost every other way the history of their northern frontier colonies was quite different. Coastal New England seemed an unlikely spot for the English, for at the beginning of the seventeenth century the region was dominated by Dutch traders on the Delaware, Hudson, and Connecticut rivers, and the French controlled the Indian trade as far south as Cape Cod.

But a twist of fate provided the English with an opening. From 1616 to 1618 a widespread epidemic of some unknown infectious disease ravaged the native peoples of the northern coast. Whole villages disappeared, and the trade system of the French and the Dutch collapsed. Indians perished so quickly and in such numbers that few remained to bury the dead. The scattered "bones and skulls made such a spectacle," wrote an Englishman, "it seemed to me a new found Golgotha." A surviving Indian reported that "the population had been melted down by this disease, whereof nine-tenths of them have died." The native population of New England as a whole dropped from an estimated 120,000 to less than 70,000, and so crippled were the surviving coastal societies that they were unable to provide effective resistance to the planting of English colonies.[23]

When in 1620 a group of English religious dissenters landed at the site of the Algonquian village of Patuxet, they found it abandoned, with the bones of the unburied dead scattered before them. They fell on their knees to thank God for "sweeping away great multitudes of natives" to "make room for us." But the Pilgrims, as later generations of Americans would know these colonists, had themselves arrived stricken with scurvy and weakened by malnutrition, and over the first New England winter nearly half perished. Like the settlers of Jamestown, the Pilgrims were rescued by Indians. Massasoit, the sachem or leader of the Wampanoags, offered food and advice to them in the early months of 1621, anxious to establish an alliance with the newcomers as protection against the Narragansetts, the powerful neighboring tribe who had been spared the ravages of the plague.[24]

The translator in these negotiations was an Indian named Squanto. A former resident of Patuxet, he had been kidnapped in 1614 by the crew of an English ship and, after a series of adventures that took him to the Caribbean, Spain, and England, had returned five years later, hitching a ride on another English ship by working as a guide and translator. Squanto spoke beautiful English. But on his return he made the horrifying discovery that plague had wiped out his entire village. Knowledgeable in the ways of the Europeans, Squanto became an invaluable adviser to Chief Massasoit. When the Pilgrims arrived, Squanto resumed his former residence, but now working as an interpreter for the English in the village they called Plymouth. He secured seed corn for the colonists and instructed them on its cultivation.

The Algonquians of southern New England found these Europeans considerably different from the French and Dutch traders who had preceded them. Their principal concern was not commerce but the acquisition of land for their growing settlements. Like Indian leaders elsewhere, Massasoit attempted to use the colonists to his own advantage, but the English used warfare against his enemies as the pretext for their own expansion. In 1623, on Massasoit's urging, the Pilgrim military commander Miles Standish attacked a group of Massachusetts Indians north of Plymouth. Yet Standish brought back the chief's severed head and placed it on a pike outside

Plymouth's gates as a "warning and terror" to the Wampanoags. The meaning of the gesture was not lost on them. If we are allies, one of them demanded, "how cometh it to pass that when we come to Patuxet [note the use of the Wampanoag rather than the English name for the village] you stand upon your guard, with the mouths of your pieces [guns] presented to us?" Soon the Wampanoags were calling their English allies by the name used by Algonquians all along the coast: *wotowequenage*, "cut-throats."[25]

The Puritans of Massachusetts Bay, a much larger group than the Pilgrims, believed they had the God-given right to take "unused" lands—those not being used for farming—and the depopulated village sites of the Massachusetts Indians became prime targets. Although the official seal of the Bay Colony featured the figure of a native asking the English to "Come Over and Help Us," the Puritans were actually more interested in helping themselves. "The country lay open," wrote Puritan leader John Winthrop, "to any that could and would improve it." Potential conflicts among settlers over title, however, made it necessary to obtain legal deeds from Indians, and the English used a variety of pressure tactics to push them into signing quitclaims. The Puritans allowed their livestock to graze native fields, making them useless for cultivation; they fined Indians for violations of English law, such as working on the Sabbath, then demanded land as payment; and they made deals with fraudulent chiefs. Disorganized and demoralized, many of the coastal Algonquians soon placed themselves under the protection of the English; it was one of the few survival strategies open to them.[26]

The English and Narragansetts destroy the Pequot village at Mystic, Connecticut. From John Underhill, Newes from America *(London, 1638). The Library Company of Philadelphia.*

Indian peoples to the westward, however, remained a formidable presence. They blocked Puritan expansion until they were hit in 1633–34 by an epidemic of smallpox that spread with devastating consequences from the Saint Lawrence River south to Long Island Sound. The epidemic occurred at the same moment that hundreds of new English migrants were crowding into coastal towns. "Without this remarkable and terrible stroke of God upon the natives," recorded the minutes of one Puritan town meeting, "we would with much more difficulty have found room, and at far greater charge have obtained and purchased land." In the aftermath of the epidemic, colonists established a number of new inland towns along the lower Connecticut River.[27]

English expansion was contested, however, by the powerful Pequot tribe, the principal trading partner of the Dutch, who lived near the mouth of the Connecticut River. The Puritans offered an alliance, but they demanded concessions of tribute and an acknowledgment of English sovereignty, something the proud Pequots were unwilling to do. So in 1637 the Puritans joined with the Pequots' traditional enemies, the Narragansetts, who lived to the east along the shores of Narragansett Bay, and went to war. On a foray led by Captains John Mason and John Underhill, English soldiers and Narragansett warriors wiped out the main Pequot village on Connecticut's Mystic River, killing most of its slumbering residents, including women and children. Unaccustomed to warfare of such brutality, the shocked Narragansetts cried out to the English: "It is too furious, it slays too many men." Alfred Cave, author of the definitive history of the conflict, concludes that the Puritan destruction of Mystic was nothing short of "an act of terrorism," intended to send a message to the other Indian tribes of the region. Pequot territory was quickly absorbed by colonial expansion.[28]

During the nearly forty years of relative peace that followed the Pequot War of 1637, English colonists and the remaining Algonquian Indians of New England lived in close, if tense, contact. A number of Puritan ministers conducted a series of brief experiments in Indian conversion. Roger Williams, who had broken with the Puritans and established a colony for dissidents in Rhode Island, had a special relationship with the Narragansetts. Overflowing with zeal to bring Christ to the Indians, he occasionally went to live with them in their "filthy, smoky holes," struggling to learn their language. The Narragansetts trusted him because he maintained that Europeans had no right to land except with prior Indian agreement. As Edmund S. Morgan has summarized, "He despised their religion and found many of their customs barbarous, but he was ready to live with them and deal with them on equal terms." Efforts to convert the Indians were institutionalized in New England as early as 1643 by the establishment of the Society for the Propagation of the Gospel. Working for the society in Massachusetts, clergyman John Eliot learned Indian languages, translated the Bible into Algonquian, evangelized among the tribes on the fringe of the English settlements, and brought together fourteen villages of "praying Indians." These self-governing communities were the closest the English came to the Spanish missions.[29]

But all the while the gradual but inexorable expansion of the Puritan population continued. Although immigration from England fell off, the fertility of colonial English women was extraordinarily high. As the New Englander Philip Vincent argued, he and his fellow colonists enjoyed a biological edge over native peoples through their capacity "to beget and bring forth more children than any other nation in the world." Population growth in turn produced a hunger for new land, creating pressures for expansion into Indian territory.[30]

A number of independent Indian tribes remained, including the Wampanoags, the Narragansetts, and the Abenakis of northern New England. Although the Wampanoags were still formally allied with the English of Plymouth, they had been forced to concede authority over an ever increasing proportion of their tribal lands.

These humiliations convinced their chief Metacomet, the English-educated son of Massasoit, that his people had no alternative but armed resistance. The English, meanwhile, prepared themselves for a final war of conquest in southern New England.

The conflict boiled over in early 1675 when a Christian Indian working as a spy for Plymouth was found murdered. English authorities arrested three of Metacomet's men, tried, and executed them. Within days Wampanoags attacked a colonial town and killed several colonists. Metacomet appealed to the neighboring Narragansetts for a defensive alliance, but before the Narragansetts had a chance to reply, the English—claiming conspiracy—invaded Narragansett country, attacking and burning villages. Metacomet, who had been given the name King Philip by his English teachers, escaped into the New England interior with a guerrilla army. What became known as King Philip's War was actually a general Indian uprising. Warriors from many tribes attacked and torched dozens of towns throughout New England. As they left the smoking ruin of the town of Medfield, the fighters tacked a message to a tree. "Thou English man hath provoked us to anger & wrath," it read. "We have nothing but our lives to loose but thou hast many fair houses, cattell & much good things."[31]

Things at first went well for the Indians. But by the beginning of 1676, their struggle was in collapse. While his warriors suffered through a miserable winter in western Massachusetts, Metacomet appealed to the Mohawks along the Hudson River for supplies and support. But the Mohawks attacked and dispersed his forces. Metacomet retreated to his Rhode Island homeland, where an English colonial army, significantly aided by Christian Indians and other natives with grudges against the Wampanoags, attacked and burned villages, killing hundreds of men, women, and children. Finally, in a battle known as the Great Swamp Fight, the rebels were defeated and Metacomet was killed. The colonists mutilated his body and triumphantly marched his head on a pike through their towns, then sold his wife and son, among hundreds of other captives, into West Indian slavery.

At the conclusion of the war some four thousand Algonquians and two thousand English colonists were dead. Dozens of English and Indian towns lay in ruins. Measured in relation to the size of the population, it was one of the most destructive wars in all American history. Fearing attack from Indians close at hand, in the last stages of the war the Puritan colonists rounded up hundreds of praying Indians and concentrated them on desolate islands in Boston harbor. Eliot worked hard to protect his converts, but to little avail. Although a few Christian communities remained after the war—in isolated locations on Cape Cod or Martha's Vineyard—most of the Christian Algonquians who survived the war fled west. Even Roger Williams, lame and in his seventies, after finding his own house burned along with most of the others in Providence, led Rhode Island troops against his former friends, the Narra-

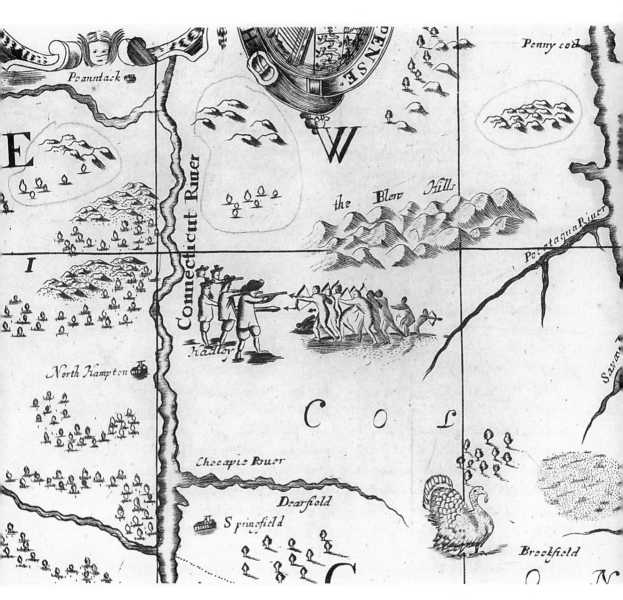

Indians and New Englanders skirmish during King Philip's War. Detail from A Mapp of New England, 1675, *by John Seller. John Carter Brown Library, Brown University.*

gansetts. With few exceptions, the English seemed to see only two alternatives for dealing with the Indians—removal or extermination.

The war marked the end of organized Indian resistance in southern New England. The population of Indians in the region had slipped far below that of the English, from ten to twenty thousand natives compared with fifty to seventy-five thousand colonists. Yet small communities of Narragansetts, Pequots, and other tribal groups survived into the twentieth century, as anyone who has gone to the Pequot casino of Foxwoods in Connecticut knows. These several thousand native residents have an alternative perspective on the history of New England. In the homeland of Metacomet, his descendants claim that because he was denied a proper burial, his ghost still rises and walks among the Indian spirits at night.

———

The wars between the natives and the Puritans deeply influenced the way Americans would think about the frontier. Puritans interpreted their victories as part of God's plan. "Let the whole Earth be filled with his Glory!" wrote John Mason after he had torched the Pequots. "Thus the Lord was pleased to smite our Enemies in the hinder Parts, and give us their land for an Inheritance." Increase Mather, the influential Puritan divine, wrote that the Indian defeat "must be ascribed to the wonderful Providence of God." Here are the origins of what a later generation would call "Manifest Destiny."[32]

Out of the wars also came two frontier literary classics, the first in 1682, when Mary Rowlandson published an account of her captivity among the Indians during King Philip's War. Torn from her community, with many of her family murdered, Rowlandson wrote of being taken deeper and deeper into the wilderness, where she witnessed the wild bacchanal of the Indians. "Oh the roaring, and singing, and dancing, and yelling of those black creatures in the night, which made the place a lively resemblance of hell." But she came to accept her torment as a reminder of *The Sovereignty and Goodness of God*, the title she gave to her narrative. "It is good for me that I have been afflicted," she wrote, for "I have learned to look beyond present and smaller troubles, and to be quieted under them." Rowlandson's narrative was an immediate best-seller and was reissued in at least fifteen editions before the Revolution. It stimulated the publication of dozens, perhaps hundreds of other stories of captivity, most with far less religion and a great deal more gore.[33]

American readers clearly found something significant in these accounts. For one thing, many colonists endured similar captivity experiences, and that may explain some of the popularity of the form. But the captivity narrative was also an "archetype of the American experience," writes Richard Slotkin. "The situation of the captive presented an exaggerated and emotionally heightened illustration of the moral and psychological situation of the community. The New Englanders had left their homes voluntarily, albeit under compulsion of conscience, and come to dwell close to the Indians. Their ties with their families, with civilization itself, had been forsaken for the sake of their God's will." Even in New England, where settlement followed a compact pattern, authorities could not restrain colonists from migrating west and north into Indian country, breaking virgin land with their plows, building homes, and establishing new communities. "They that profess themselves Christians have forsaken Churches, and Ordanances, and all for land and elbow-room," railed Increase Mather, and his son, Cotton Mather, condemned the continual process of

A
NARRATIVE

OF THE

CAPTIVITY, SUFFERINGS AND REMOVES

OF

Mrs. *Mary Rowlandfon,*

Who was taken Prifoner by the INDIANS with feveral others,
and treated in the moft barbarous and cruel Manner by thofe
vile Savages : With many other remarkable Events during her
TRAVELS.

Written by her own Hand, for her private Ufe, and now made
public at the earneft Defire of fome Friends, and for the Benefit of the afflicted.

B O S T O N :

Printed and Sold at JOHN BOYLE's Printing-Office, next Door
to the *Three Doves* in Marlborough-Street. 1773

1773

Title page of the 1773 edition of Mary Rowlandson's captivity narrative. American Antiquarian Society.

"swarming into New Settlements." Captivity narratives provided a way of addressing the fear and guilt that accompanied the emerging American pattern of profound mobility.[34]

The second classic to emerge from the Puritan-Indian wars was the memoir of Benjamin Church, the officer who led the settlers against Metacomet at the Great Swamp Fight. Church was American-born—one of those seekers after "elbowroom" the Mathers so deplored—and in his account he presented himself as the wilderness expert without whom the war could not have been won. Ridiculing other officers who attempted to use "regular" tactics, Church argued that to fight Indians successfully the colonists had to learn the Indian way of war. In the course of his narrative, Church becomes more and more like an Indian himself, actively seeking the amalgamation of European and Indian characteristics. After the final battle he sits up all night with Philip's lieutenant, Annawon, swapping tales of their adventures, and Church implies that a bond of mutual respect and even affection developed between them. Later he is horrified to find Annawon's head on a pike at Plymouth. His anger at this dishonorable treatment of a fellow warrior, wrote Church's son, led to "the loss of the good will and respects of some before were his good friends." In Richard Slotkin's phrase, Church is "the man who knows Indians" yet remains loyal to his own people. The first of a long line of similar characters, the perspective of men like Church added a degree of ambivalence and ambiguity to the flourishing confidence of English settlers that they were on God's side.[35]

When the Mohawks attacked Metacomet instead of supporting him, they were motivated by self-interest. Casting themselves in the role of powerful intermediaries between neighboring Indians and the English colonies, the Mohawks and the other tribes of the Five Nation League of the Iroquois sought to place themselves in a dominant position.

European trade goods first began to reach the peoples of the Five Nations through indirect means as early as the mid-fifteenth century. In many Iroquois graves dating to that period archaeologists find brass, iron, and glass items. Their first direct access to these valuable goods came when Dutch traders established posts along the Hudson River in the 1610s. But the Iroquois had a problem. The best source of beaver pelts came from colder climes to the north. To supply themselves with the means to trade, the Mohawks, Cayugas, Onondagas, Oneidas, and Senecas thus began to raid their northern neighbors, plundering their stores of furs and bringing the pelts south to trade with the Dutch. These raids began a long series of seventeenth-century conflicts known as the Beaver Wars in which warriors of the Five Nations attacked other Indian peoples as far west as the Illinois country, making themselves into the most powerful Indian confederacy on the North American continent.

Seneca warriors return from war with scalps and a captive. French drawing, c. 1666, from Edmund B. O'Callaghan, ed., Documents Relative to the Colonial History of the State of New York, *15 vols. (Albany, 1853–87). Yale University.*

But the Beaver Wars were spurred by another factor besides economics. Imported European diseases had hit the Iroquois hard. By the 1640s the population of the Five Nations had been cut nearly in half. Warfare against their neighbors not only gave the Iroquois access to the great fur grounds of the northern Great Lakes but offered the opportunity to take captives.

The Iroquois directed their most furious attacks against the Hurons, allies of the French. "So far as I can divine," one Jesuit missionary wrote, "it is the design of the Iroquois to capture all the Hurons, if it is possible; to put the chiefs and great part of the nation to death, and with the rest to form one nation and one country." In 1647 and 1648 the Mohawks and Senecas massed a brutal attack against the Hurons, destroying both Indian towns and Jesuit missionary stations. The Iroquois suffered enormous losses, but they inflicted even greater ones on the Hurons, and they so demoralized their enemies that those who were not killed or captured dispersed and fled westward. Hundreds of Hurons were marched south to the Seneca and Mohawk towns and were adopted into the villages.[36]

Many of these Hurons were Christians, and they were the first to introduce European religion among the Five Nations. So dependent were the Iroquois on keeping their adoptees happy that eventually they were forced to invite Jesuits into their homeland to minister to these Christian Hurons, thus giving the missionaries an opportunity to work among the Five Nations. Experiencing the same disruption and cultural trauma that had made the Hurons vulnerable to the Jesuit appeal, many Iroquois converted to Catholicism. Rates of conversion were especially high among the

Mohawks—the people most directly affected by their contact with European traders on the Hudson River. By the 1660s there were strong factions of pro-French Christians in all the Iroquois towns of the Five Nations.

Christianity introduced a serious conflict into Iroquois society. Many Christians rejected participation in traditional ceremonies, asserting that they no longer believed in them. "The black gowns had turned his head," the traditionalists said about a converted Onondaga leader named Garakontie. "He had abandoned the customs of the country, [and] had also ceased to have any affection for it." As the level of domestic conflict rose, many of the Christian Iroquois moved north, settling nearer the French, where the Jesuits created special villages for them. One of those emigrants was Kateri Tekakwitha, a Mohawk convert who fled her village and settled in the Christian Iroquois town of Kahnawake, near Montreal. Practicing the most extreme forms of fasting and self-punishment, Tekakwitha died at the young age of twenty-four. The Jesuits made her into a martyr of the cause of conversion—and she is now well on her way to sainthood in the Catholic church.[37]

The Iroquois responded to this cultural crisis by strengthening the Five Nation League that bound them together. In the 1660s New Netherlands became New York when the English took Manhattan without firing a shot. The new English authorities were anxious to strike an alliance with the Iroquois, using them to exercise control over the other Indian peoples on the frontier. Traditionalists among the Iroquois hoped that an alliance with the English might help counter the growing power of the French to the north, as well as the rising influence of Catholics within their own communities. For them, the lack of English missionary activity was a point in their favor. When they smashed Metacomet, the Iroquois were proving their worth to the English authorities.

In a series of negotiations conducted at Albany in 1677, the Five Nation League and the colony of New York created an alliance known as the "Covenant Chain." The Iroquois carefully walked a path between the competing French and English, but they were always clear in asserting their autonomy. The Onondaga leader Otreouti ("Big Mouth") put it well in a speech to the English in 1683: "You say we are Subjects to the King of England and Duke of York, but we say, we are Brethren. We must take care of ourselves." Understanding the history of colonialism in the Northeast requires appreciating the role of the Iroquois—for they were as much a great power as the English or the French.[38]

The Iroquois had a perspective of their own on the history of colonialism. "You think that the Axe-Makers are the eldest in the country and the greatest in possession," declared the Onondaga orator Sadekanaktie in the 1690s. "Yes, all the Axe-Makers think the same. But no! Oh no! We Iroquois are the first, and we are the eldest and the greatest. These parts and countries were inhabited and trod upon by the Iroquois before there were any Axe-Makers."[39]

James Axtell, *The European and the Indian: Essays in the Ethnohistory of Colonial North America* (1981)

———, *The Invasion Within: The Contest of Cultures in Colonial North America* (1985)

Alfred A. Cave, *The Pequot War* (1996)

William Cronon, *Changes in the Land: Indians, Colonists, and the Ecology of New England* (1983)

W. J. Eccles, *The Canadian Frontier, 1534–1760*, rev. ed. (1986)

Francis Jennings, *The Invasion of America: Indians, Colonialism, and the Cant of Conquest* (1975)

Jill Lapore, *The Name of War: King Philip's War and the Origins of American Identity* (1998)

Samuel Eliot Morison, *The European Discovery of America: The Northern Voyages, A.D. 500–600* (1971)

Daniel K. Richter, *The Ordeal of the Longhouse: The Peoples of the Iroquois League in the Era of European Colonization* (1992)

Neal Salisbury, *Manitou and Providence: Indians, Europeans, and the Making of New England, 1500–1643* (1982)

Richard Slotkin, *Regeneration Through Violence: The Mythology of the American Frontier, 1600–1860* (1973)

Robert S. Tilton, *Pocahontas: The Evolution of an American Narrative* (1994)

Peter H. Wood et al., *Powhatan's Mantle: Indians in the Colonial Southeast* (1989)

3

The Struggle of Empires

The Algonquian peoples of Virginia and southern New England were crushed by the English colonists. But between those two regions, along the mid-Atlantic coast, relations between Indians and Europeans took a more positive turn. Perhaps it was because both the native and colonizing peoples of the seventeenth-century Delaware valley were loosely organized and somewhat autonomous. The indigenous residents of the central Atlantic coast were village peoples. Many places in the area still echo their traditional names: the Tappans, the Raritans, the Nyacks, the Hackensacks. The English called these people the Delawares, a nomenclature borrowed from the river named for the first governor of Virginia colony, Lord De La Warr. But although these villagers sometimes joined together for large hunting drives or mutual defense, unlike the Iroquois Five Nations or Powhatan's Algonquians of the Chesapeake, the Delawares were not a single tribe with centralized leadership. Colonists also lived under frail central authority. The first Europeans in the region were Scandinavians—Finns, Swedes, and Danes—who came to the short-lived colony known as New Sweden, founded in 1638. Attacked and taken by the Dutch in 1655, then by the English in 1664, the colony remained weak well into the eighteenth century.

Loose organization and local autonomy fostered a cultural fusion between native and settler cultures that proved one of the most notable—and least understood—developments of early American history. The natives were both farmers and hunters; Indian women raised gardens of corn, beans, and squash, while Indian men hunted for furs, hides, and meat. Such a sexual division of labor was much like the one practiced by Swedish and Finnish settlers. In the hardscrabble environment of northern Europe Scandinavian women had been accustomed to practicing forms of shifting cultivation, and they immediately understood Indian horticulture. Colonial women of the Delaware valley quickly adopted the crops of Indian women, while Indian

71

Dutch colonists and Algonquian Indians in New Sweden. From Thomas Campanius Holm,
Kort beskrifning om provincien Nya Swerige uti America . . . *(Stockholm, 1702). Beinecke.*

women welcomed European metal hoes, as well as pigs and chickens. Just as quickly,
Scandinavian men took to hunting. In France and England hunting had long been
reserved as a sport for the nobility, and few French or English settlers had much experience in handling firearms or understanding the patterns of game animals. But
Scandinavian men were receptive to learning the calls, disguises, and decoys, the sur-
rounds and fire hunting methods of the local Algonquians. In turn Indians readily
incorporated into their hunting routines European steel knives, firearms, and linen
hunting shirts, which were much more comfortable in wet weather than buckskin.

The most ubiquitous symbol of pioneer America, the log cabin, emerged in the

An early depiction of a log cabin. From Georges-Henri-Victor Collot, A Journey in North America . . . *(Paris, 1826). Beinecke.*

Delaware valley, and ought to serve as a symbol of this composite culture. Log construction with axes was a tradition brought to North America by the pioneers of New Sweden, particularly the Finns. It was quickly picked up by other settlers, for with the resources of the American woods, a few tools, and a little training, several men could erect a rough shelter in a day, a solid house in a week. What is truly fascinating is that Indians quickly learned these construction techniques and probably did as much as colonists to spread the practice of building in wood across the frontiers of North America. Descriptions of the Indian towns of Pennsylvania and later Ohio frequently remark on their resemblance to American pioneer settlements—with the difference being that Indians tended to cluster their cabins rather than spreading them across the face of the country, and they often built a large, impressive log council house in the center of their towns.

The Delaware valley was what geographers call a "cultural hearth," an originating place, for a unique woodland material way of life that combined traits from both the Indian and European worlds. Indians and colonists even created a lingua franca—

a frontier pidgin language based in Algonquian but combined with elements of Swedish and eventually English—allowing them to communicate. In many details, the lifeways of Indians and colonists came to greatly resemble one another. Indeed, visitors from Europe or more refined areas of the colonies sometimes described backcountry pioneers as "white people who live like savages."[1]

No account of frontier history should omit William Penn, who flourished a generation after John Eliot and Roger Williams but towers above them as a symbol of generous understanding with native people. To a degree not previously known in the colonization of North America he attempted to deal fairly with the Indians, not permitting colonization to begin until he negotiated the right to settle and purchased the land. Indeed, the composite woodland culture of the Delaware valley flowered precisely because of the relative peace that Penn and his Quaker followers brought to this distinctive mid-Atlantic frontier.

In 1682, during his first few months in America, Penn met with the leaders of the local Algonquians at the village of Shackamaxon near his colonial capital of Philadelphia. He negotiated with a council he described as being made up of "all the Old and Wise men of the Nation, which perhaps is two hundred People." On the sidelines were all the warriors of the assembled villagers, to whom the leaders turned for consensus in a form of direct democracy. The treaty that Penn and the chiefs signed was commemorated in a Great Treaty Wampum Belt, which the Delawares presented to Penn, an artifact that symbolizes the best hopes of the American frontier experience. In it a figure of a Quaker in distinctive hat—Penn himself, perhaps—clasps in friendship the hand of an Algonquian said to be Chief Tammany, a leader renowned for his benevolence and independence. In subsequent years the mythical figure of Tammany appeared in many popular stories and myths among both Indians and colonists, and by the time of the Revolution his name had become emblematic of the American spirit of independence. Tammany Hall, the Democratic political society of New York City, was named in his honor.[2]

Benjamin West's painting of Penn under a spreading elm shows him presenting the Indians with the English version of the treaty. Surely this image has done much to color our opinion, but there can be no doubt that Penn treated the natives as human beings with rights and feelings. He did his best to protect the Indians from the liquor traffic and from unscrupulous traders. There was no frontier warfare in Pennsylvania while Penn lived. Indeed, during his lifetime a number of Indian groups resettled in his Quaker colony. Relations would sour after Penn's death—mostly because of his descendants' shift to a policy of more aggressive treatment and shady dealings. But the toleration and accommodation of early Pennsylvania created the

Penn's Treaty with the Indians. *Painting by Benjamin West, c. 1771. The Pennsylvania Academy of the Fine Arts, Philadelphia. Gift of Mrs. Sarah Harrison (The Joseph Harrison, Jr. Collection).*

conditions for the development of a distinctive American backcountry culture, a tradition that affected and changed Indians as much as it did colonists.

By the first decades of the eighteenth century the English colonies were expanding rapidly. "Our People must at least be doubled every 20 Years," Benjamin Franklin concluded after studying the phenomenon in 1751. He was only slightly off in his calculation, the doubling occurring every quarter-century. The 250,000 colonists of 1700 would explode to more than 1.3 million fifty years later. The British colonial population of North America experienced what the English economist Thomas Malthus described as "a rapidity of increase probably without parallel in history."[3]

Several factors were at work, extremely high levels of fertility prominent among them. English colonial women commonly bore seven or more children, and birth rates in the backcountry were pushed to the maximum. Rebecca Bryan Boone, wife of frontier hero Daniel Boone, for example, bore ten children, and the couple was surrounded by sixty-eight grandchildren in their old age! Such high fertility was combined with relatively low mortality. Blessed with fertile lands and the produc-

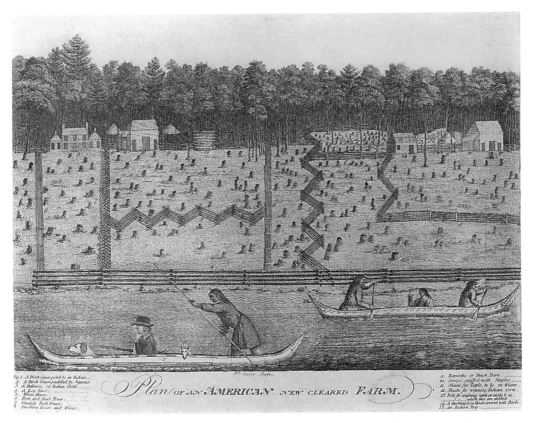

American farm on the Pennsylvania frontier. From Patrick Campbell, Travels in the Interior Inhabited Parts of North America. In the Years 1791 and 1792 . . . *(Edinburgh, 1793). Beinecke.*

tivity of Indian agricultural techniques, famines simply did not occur in North America. It is true that colonial cities were notoriously unhealthy places, and that some rural areas—notably the lowland South—were plagued by malaria and other tropical diseases. But for most colonists, living in the open air of the countryside, North America was a remarkably healthy environment. Death rates were 15 or 20 percent lower than in Europe. Most important for the growth of population were the relatively low level of infant mortality and the extraordinary number of people who survived to reproductive age.

There was also immigration. Large movements of Germans and Scots-Irish to the fringes of English settlement had an immense impact on the American frontier. William Penn began recruiting European settlers for his colony as early as the 1680s. By the second decade of the eighteenth century Germans by the thousands were streaming out of the Rhineland as the result of depressed farm conditions, wars in which they did not believe, and New World advertisements. They were Pietists, pacifists, and good farmers. They sought fertile land in the interior, first along the Mohawk valley in New York, where they had trouble with speculators, then in Pennsylvania, where they flourished. Some of the Germans, such as the Mennonites and Amish, came to be known as the Pennsylvania Dutch ("Deutsch"). Wherever they went they were found to be a people willing to endure hardships if the future promised harvests and well-filled barns.

The Scots-Irish, who began pouring into western areas about the same time, colored the frontier even more. They had been transplanted from Scotland to northern Ireland around Ulster, and their struggles with local Catholics encouraged aggressive qualities. They also learned to hate and fight Englishmen, and it is not surprising that in America they immediately got as far away from the seaboard colonists as possible. The Scots-Irish were fighters, hunters, marksmen, and they bred leaders like Andrew Jackson, John C. Calhoun, and Sam Houston.

By the 1720s, squeezed by population growth in coastal regions, and now benefiting from the adaptive advantage of the composite Indian-European frontier culture of the Delaware valley, these peoples began to push into the backcountry, down the great Shenandoah valley, running southwest along the eastern flank of the Appalachians. This was the first of the great pioneer treks that took Americans into the continental interior, and the Shenandoah became the site of British America's first "west." Within a generation settlers could be found all along the front range of the Appalachians, from Pennsylvania south to the Carolina backcountry. Many, perhaps most, of these pioneers held no legal title to the lands they occupied but simply hacked out and defended their squatters' rights.

They laid claim to the lands of Indian peoples who found themselves literally pressed to the mountain wall. While English colonial society underwent rapid expansion, these coastal Indian societies continued to undergo traumatic population decline, mostly as a result of the terrific beating inflicted by European epidemic disease. During the eighteenth century the European colonial population overtook the native population of the continent. But population loss did not affect all Indians equally. Although the number of coastal natives declined precipitously, the population of interior peoples such as the Creeks and Cherokees actually stabilized and grew in the mid-eighteenth century. The invasion of backcountry pioneers, however, presented a new and deadly threat to their homelands. Rising fears and resentments over this expanding population would be the cause of much eighteenth-century warfare.

The colonies of New France also experienced growth. But France was dedicated to keeping its colony exclusively Catholic and refused to admit the thousands of French Protestants who sought immigration to Canada, preventing the colony from achieving the impressive growth of the English colonies. Although Canadian population climbed from fifteen thousand in 1700 to more than seventy thousand by mid-

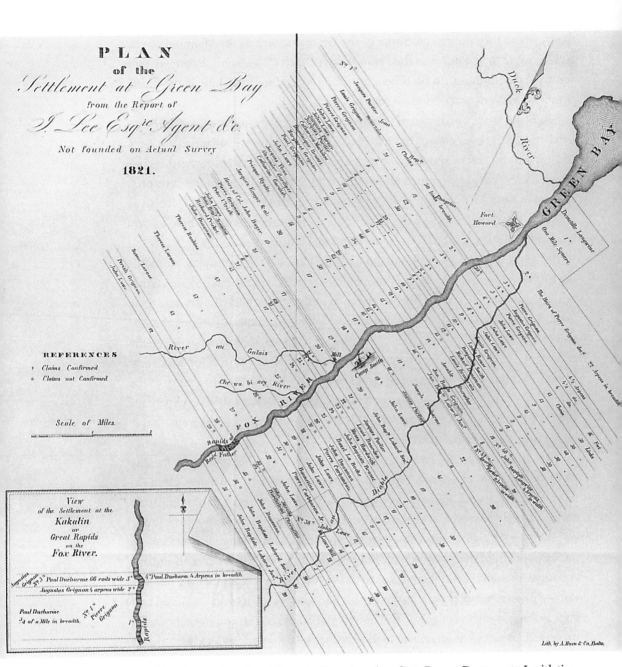

French long lots at Green Bay, Wisconsin. From American State Papers: Documents, Legislative and Executive *(Washington, D.C., 1832–61). Yale University.*

century, it was relatively puny beside the English colonial behemoth of more than a million.

In the absence of large numbers, French colonial policy in North America aimed at blocking British expansion by a system of trade networks and alliances with Indian peoples. The French worked to strengthen their great crescent of military posts and isolated settlements extending from the mouth of the Saint Lawrence down the river to the Great Lakes, then down the length of the Mississippi River to the Gulf of Mexico. The scattered French settlements in the western country anchored this colonial crescent at strategic locations. At each site—from the sugar plantations of the lower Mississippi to the farms of the Illinois country and the fur posts at Prairie du Chien—the French recreated the "long lot" pattern of the Saint Lawrence; it was the distinctive Franco-American stamp on the landscape. The persistence of these forms on the land is revealed by aerial photographs. There were also French settlements at each of the strategic passages of the Great Lakes: Mackinaw, Sault Sainte Marie, and Detroit, this last by midcentury a community of a hundred métis farm families who worked their land close to the villages of Ottawas, Potawatomies, and Hurons.

These French frontier communities combined both European and Indian elements. Detroit looked like "an old French village," one observer testified, until one got closer and noticed that its houses were "mostly covered with bark," Indian style. "It is not uncommon to see a Frenchman with Indian shoes and stockings, without breeches, wearing a strip of woolen cloth to cover what decency requires him to conceal," wrote another visitor; "yet at the same time he wears a fine ruffled shirt and a laced waistcoat, with a fine handkerchief on his head." Family and kinship also took on local Indian patterns. There was a good deal of intermarriage between colonial men and native women, and soon there were groups of métis in every French settlement. Households were frequently composed of several related families, and in the Indian fashion most women limited their fertility, bearing an average of only two or three children. There was arranged marriage and occasional polygamy, but wives had easy access to divorce and enjoyed full rights to property. Yet unlike their Indian kin, these people focused their activities on commerce and overwhelmingly identified themselves as Catholics. Choosing a path of mutual accommodation, the French and Indians established some of the most interesting and distinct communities in all of North America.[4]

Although in general the French had better relations with native peoples than the English, they sometimes came into conflict with Indians as they pursued their expansionist plans. When the Foxes of the upper Mississippi attempted to block French access to the interior, interposing themselves in the fur trade, the French did not hesitate to wage bloody war upon them, eventually forcing them to sign a treaty in 1738. On the lower Mississippi, the French fought the Natchez, who opposed their arrival, a war that concluded with a horrible decimation and dispersion of the entire Natchez tribe in 1731. Whether by friendship or by force, the French thus laid a thin colonial veneer over a vast territory, creating the basis for what they hoped would be the future development of a great continental empire. Though it was true that British colonists far outnumbered the French, observed a military officer of New France, numbers were not of first importance, for "the Canadians are brave, much inured to war, and untiring in travel. Two thousand of them will at all times and in all places thrash the people of New England."[5]

The colonial period of North American history was marked by a series of bloody wars involving French, Spanish, and English colonists, punctuated by periods of armed and uneasy peace. Indians played a role in all these conflicts, national rivalries fanning ancient tribal hostilities. Such wars decimated many Indian peoples but strengthened others. By the late seventeenth century, for example, the Five Nation League of the Iroquois was one of the most important empires in North America. In the Southeast, many Indian communities joined to form strong confederacies: the Cherokees, Creeks, Chickasaws, and Choctaws in what would later become the states of Georgia, Alabama, Tennessee, and Mississippi. The Choctaws were allied to the French, the others to the English. Neither Indians nor Europeans understood the colonial wars as racial conflicts of red against white but rather as a kind of free-for-all, with every group fighting for itself, allied as circumstance and interest demanded. Indian fought Indian and colonist fought colonist at least as much as Indian fought colonist.

Many of the North American wars had European origins, but they also had colonial aims. What English colonists called King William's War began in 1689 when King Louis XIV of France declared war rather than accept the ascension of William of Orange to the English throne. But in America the war was fought over access to the rich fur grounds of the north and west. In 1670 the English chartered the Hudson's Bay Company to counter French trade dominance in the far north, while on the southern flank of New France the English sought to extend their control of the Indian trade through their "covenant chain" allies, the Five Nations. The hostilities opened with an English-supported Iroquois massacre of French settlers at the village of Lachine, near Montreal. The next year the French and their Indian allies counterattacked, burning frontier settlements in New York, New Hampshire, and Maine, and pressing an attack on the Iroquois towns. The same year a Massachusetts fleet briefly captured and held the strategic French harbor at Port Royal in Acadia, but a combined English colonial force failed in an attempt to conquer the French settlements along the Saint Lawrence. The inconclusive war ended with a European treaty of 1697 that established an equally inconclusive peace.

In 1702, only five years later, the dynastic fighting officially resumed in Europe when the grandson of Louis XIV was crowned king of Spain, arousing English fears of a powerful French-Spanish combination. But in North America during Queen Anne's War, as English colonists called this conflict, frontier antagonisms once again provided a focus for the fighting. The English attacked French settlements in the maritime region, while the French and their Indian allies raided English settlements

Iroquois warrior. French watercolor, c. 1780.
Library of Congress.

like the frontier village of Deerfield, Massachusetts, dragging more than a hundred prisoners into captivity in 1704. In the South, South Carolina troops invaded Spanish Florida in 1702, burning and plundering Saint Augustine, and four years later a combined French and Spanish fleet took revenge by bombarding Charleston. Indian allies played an important part in the fighting on both sides. This war officially ended in 1713, but English slave traders encouraged their Indian allies to continue the attack against natives allied with Spanish Floridians and French Louisianans. Over the next quarter-century these raids and attacks destroyed the last of the Spanish mission stations of Florida. Thousands of mission Indians were captured and sold into slavery in the Caribbean, and thousands more were killed or dispersed.

The Creeks would resettle Florida. They joined with fugitive African-American slaves from South Carolina—encouraged by Spanish authorities who were anxious to weaken the rival British colony—and formed a new mixed group known as the Seminoles. The word "Seminole" itself is an interesting linguistic example of cultural interchange. It originated in the Spanish *cimmaron,* meaning "wild" or "untamed," which colonists in Florida used to refer to fugitive slaves living side by side with the Creek settlers. The Muskogee language of the Creeks has no "r" sound, so when the Indians used the word they pronounced it "cimaloe," which eventually became "Seminole."

Another of the Indian victims of this fighting were the Iroquoian-speaking Tuscororas of North Carolina. Badly defeated in 1713, the survivors moved north to join their New York cousins. In 1722 the Iroquois Confederacy admitted the Tuscororas as full partners; thereafter it was known as the *Six* Nations. Not only did the Iroquois incorporate tribes within their confederacy, but by means of war and diplomacy they asserted their dominance over others, like the Delawares. Iroquois diplomats became experts at playing the French off against the British. Badly shaken by Canadian attacks on their towns during King William's War, in 1701 the Iroquois negotiated a treaty of neutrality with New France while maintaining their alliance with the English, attempting to maintain a neutral position between the rival colonial powers. "To preserve the Ballance between us and the French," wrote one New York official, "is the great ruling Principle of the Modern Indian Politics." Iroquois neutrality was not passive, however, for factions within the Confederacy were free to ally themselves with either the British or the French. In a similar way the southern confederacies attempted to carve out space for themselves between the British colonies and those of the French in Louisiana and the Spanish in Florida. The Indian position was well expressed by the Onondaga chief Otreouti. "We are born Freemen," he declared, "we have a power to go where we please, conduct who we will to the places we resort to, and to buy and sell where we think fit."[6]

After several decades of armed and uneasy peace between England and France, new struggles over royal succession resulted in renewed warfare in the 1740s. In North America the outcome of what would be called King George's War depended in great part on whether the French or the English could count on the Six Nations. At a conference held with the Indians at Lancaster, Pennsylvania, in 1744, the English appealed for support. But the Iroquois were unhappy. Like other native peoples, they felt under siege. A chief named Canasatego gave a long speech in which he looked back to a time before the European invasion: "We then had room enough, and plenty of deer, which was easily caught; and though we had not knives, hatchets, or guns, such as we have now, yet we had knives of stone, and hatchets of stone, and bows and arrows, and those served our uses as well then as the English ones do now." But times had changed: "We are now straitened, and sometimes in want of deer, and liable to many other inconveniences since the English came among us, and particularly from that *pen-and-ink work* that is going on at the table." Here Canasatego pointed to the scribe that was taking down his speech.[7]

At Lancaster the Six Nations agreed to support the British—in exchange for payments of gold and promises of fair dealing in the future—and with the Iroquois protecting their northern borders, the English colonists felt safe enough on that frontier to devote most of their manpower to the capture of the strategic French fortress of Louisbourg, at the entrance to the Gulf of Saint Lawrence. But "pen-and-ink" frauds remained much on the Indians' minds. Most alarming were a series of seizures

Delaware chief Tishcohan. Painting by
Gustavus Hesselius, 1732. Historical Society
of Pennsylvania.

of Delaware lands by the colony of Pennsylvania, notably the "Walking Purchase" of
1737. Under terms negotiated by William Penn a half-century before, the Delawares
agreed to cede lands vaguely bounded by the distance a man could travel in a day and
a half. The Indian understanding was that this was to be a walk taken at the "common" pace, pausing at noon for a midday meal and a pipe. But Pennsylvania authorities prepared a cleared path for a group of specially trained "walkers" who ran
and covered more than sixty miles in the specified time. The runners succeeding in
turning this vague provision into a huge tract encompassing the entire upper
Delaware and Lehigh valleys and dispossessing a large number of Indian communities. It was a clear violation of the spirit of the earlier agreement and displayed an obvious contempt for the Indians. Overturning Pennsylvania's history of fair dealing,
the Walking Purchase was yet another disturbing sign of things to come.

Another was the Indians' growing dependence on European traders and their
goods. The Indians were "straitened," as Chief Canasatego put it. Being able to purchase manufactured goods at the trading post was "a vast advantage to the Six
Nations," another Iroquois spokesman declared. "But we think, Brother, that your
people who trade there have the most advantage by it, and that it is as good for them
as a Silver mine." He understood that the profits flowed in one direction only, away
from the Six Nations.[8]

Moreover, by the eighteenth century, with the easy availability of European goods,
native manufacture in the Northeast had practically disappeared. A list of items sent
to the Iroquois about this time suggests how essential trade had become. It included
weapons and ammunition, knives, hatchets, needles, scissors, and flint strikers for
starting fires, steel and brass wire, glass bottles, heavy blankets and other textiles,

ready-made shirts and dresses, paint for body decoration, glass beads and wampum, tobacco and pipes, and liquor, much liquor.

Alcohol abuse among the Indians was one of the signs of the disorientation that colonialism introduced. Liquor was illegally manufactured in New England distilleries from contraband sugar smuggled in from the Spanish or French West Indies. In the eighteenth and nineteenth centuries, the alcohol trade to the Indians was much like the modern cocaine business, with the traders acting like drug lords. Indian communities became the setting for communal drinking bouts with violent results. "Strong liquor is the root of all evil," a chief of the Senecas declared, but the chiefs found themselves unable to stop the flow of the drug. One missionary was witness to a drunken brawl among the Senecas in 1750. "The yelling and shrieking continued frightfully in the whole village. It is impossible to describe the confusion to any one who has not witnessed it."[9]

By the mid-eighteenth century such violent scenes had become commonplace features of Indian life in eastern North America. To find refuge, many Indian families moved westward, settling in ethnically mixed Indian towns; others remained in their traditional homelands but dispersed themselves over the face of the country, trying to put distance between themselves and their neighbors, much as backcountry colonists did. Gradually the traditional communal longhouse gave way to single-family log cabins.

———

The struggle between Britain and France for control of North America reached its climax in what a later generation of Americans would call the French and Indian War. The Ohio country—the great trans-Appalachian watershed of the Ohio River—became the primary focus of British and French attention. British traders began to challenge the French with goods of superior quality and more competitive prices. The rich land of the interior was also a prime target of frontier land speculators and backcountry settlers. The French worried that their traders would be crushed by British commercial competition and their settlements overrun by an expanding British population. The loss of the Ohio, they feared, would threaten their North American trading empire. To reinforce their claims, in 1749 they sent a heavily armed force of Canadians and Indians down the Ohio to warn off the British, and they violently expelled British traders from the region. As a barrier to any British return to the west, in 1753 they began constructing a series of forts that extended south from Lake Erie to the forks of the Ohio River, the junction of the Allegheny and Monongahela rivers. Deciding to challenge the French directly, the British strengthened existing forts and constructed new ones along the frontiers, and the king conferred an enormous grant of land on the Ohio Company, organized by Virginia and

London capitalists. The company made plans to build a fort of its own at the forks of the Ohio.

The coming conflict did not merely involve competing colonial powers, however, for the Indian peoples of the interior had other interests. In addition to its native inhabitants, the Ohio Country became a refuge for Indian peoples who fled the Northeast—Iroquois, Hurons, Delawares, and Shawnees among them. Most of the Ohio Indians opposed the British and were anxious to preserve the Appalachians as a barrier to westward expansion. They were also disturbed by the French moves into their country, but unlike the British, French outposts did not become centers of expanding agricultural settlements. Indian diplomats understood that it was in their interest to perpetuate the existing colonial stalemate. Their position would be greatly undermined in the event of an overwhelming victory for either side.

In 1754 the governor of Virginia sent Colonel George Washington, a young militia officer, to expel the French from the region granted to the Ohio Company. But when Washington was confronted by a superior force of Canadians and Indians, he was forced to surrender his troops, and the French, from their base at Fort Duquesne, which they built at the forks of the Ohio and named for the governor of Canada, now commanded the interior country. The next year General Edward Braddock, a Scottish Coldstream Guard, led more than two thousand English troops and fifty Indian scouts from Virginia toward the fort. Among them was Washington, who knew that wilderness reasonably well. The French and their Indian allies ambushed the army, and in Britain's worst defeat during the eighteenth century, Braddock lost his life. His body was buried in the trail, and the entire English detachment was marched over it to destroy the traces.

Braddock's defeat was the first of a long series of setbacks for the British. Canadians captured their forts in northern New York, and Indians pounded backcountry settlements, killed thousands of settlers, and raided deep into the coastal colonies, throwing British colonists into panic. Prime Minister William Pitt, an enthusiastic advocate of colonial expansion, committed the British to the conquest of Canada and the elimination of all French competition in North America. To win the support of colonists, he promised that the war would be fought "at His Majesty's expense." To win the support of the natives, British officials promised the Six Nations and the Ohio Indians that the crown would "agree upon clear and fixed Boundaries between our Settlements and their Hunting Grounds, so that each Party may know their own and be a mutual Protection to each other of their respective Possessions." Pitt dispatched more than twenty thousand regular British troops across the Atlantic, and in combination with colonial forces he massed over fifty thousand men against French Canada.[10]

These measures reversed the course of the war. A string of British victories cul-

The Death of General Wolfe. *Engraving by William Woolett, based on a painting by Benjamin West, 1776. Yale Center for British Art, Paul Mellon Collection.*

minated in the taking of Fort Duquesne in 1758, which was renamed Fort Pitt and later Pittsburgh. The last of the French western forts fell the next year. In the South, the Cherokees attempted to maintain the critical balance between the colonial powers by entering the war against the British, but regular and provincial British troops invaded their homeland and crushed them.

The decisive British victory came in 1759. British forces converged on Quebec, the heart of French Canada. Approaching up the Saint Lawrence, General James Wolfe, redheaded and romantic (he once said he would rather have written Thomas Gray's "Elegy" than take Quebec), ordered his troops to "burn and lay waste the country," and they plundered the farms of habitants and shelled the city. Seeking a final showdown with the French, commanded by the Marquis de Montcalm, Wolfe and his men twice made frontal assaults on Quebec from the river, failing both times. He then devised a scheme worthy of a wilderness scout—a night maneuver up a cleft in the bluffs two miles behind the city. At dawn on September 13, 1759, the French on the Plains of Abraham behind Quebec faced a British force of forty-five hundred men, as large as their own. In a day's hard fight, Montcalm was killed and Wolfe was shot three times. Before Wolfe died, he knew the battle was won. In effect, at that moment England supplanted France in North America.[11]

In the final two years of the war the British swept French ships from the seas, and because Spain was an ally of France, invaded and captured several Spanish colonies in the Caribbean, as well as the Spanish Philippines in the Pacific. At approximately the same time England also conquered India, thus becoming the greatest imperial power the world had yet known.

The bells were loud in London and silent in Paris. New France was no more. In *Candide,* Voltaire could describe Canada as a few acres of worthless snow, but England could afford to smile as its firms took over the lucrative fur trade. In the Treaty of Paris, signed in 1763, France gave up all its North American possessions, ceding its claims east of the Mississippi to Great Britain, with the exception of New Orleans, which along with its other trans-Mississippi claims it passed to the control of Spain. In exchange for the return of its Caribbean and Pacific colonies, Spain ceded Florida to Britain. The imperial rivalry in eastern North America that began in the sixteenth century now came to an end with what appeared to be the final victory of the British empire. All territory east of the Mississippi was now claimed by the English—a thousand green valleys and fair forests for those who bore the long rifles and carried the maps.

When the Ohio Indians heard of the French cession of the western country to Britain they were shocked. "Having never been conquered, either by the English or French," British Indian agent William Johnson wrote, the Indians "consider themselves as a free people." A new set of British policies soon shocked the Indians all the more. Both the French and British in America had long used gift-giving as part of the diplomatic protocol with the Indians. The Spanish officials who replaced the French in Louisiana made an effort to continue the old policy, but the British military governor of the western region, General Jeffrey Amherst, in one of his first official actions, banned presents to Indian chiefs and tribes, demanding that they learn to live without "charity." Not only were Indians angered by Amherst's reversal of custom, they were also frustrated by his refusal to supply them with the ammunition they required for hunting. Because Indians were completely dependent upon the British for their supplies, many were left in a starving condition.[12]

In this climate, hundreds of Ohio Indians became disciples of an Indian visionary named Neolin ("The Enlightened One" in Algonquian), known to the English as the Delaware Prophet. The core of Neolin's teaching was that Indians had been corrupted by European ways, that they needed to purify themselves by returning to their traditions and prepare themselves for a holy war against the colonists. "If you suffer the English among you, you are dead men. Sickness, smallpox, and their poison will destroy you entirely," he declared, and urged his followers to "drive them out!" The prophet's ideas prepared the way for the rising influence of chiefs who laid plans for a coordinated attack against the British in the spring of 1763. The principal figure among them was a proud Ottawa named Pontiac, a renowned orator and political leader who was thoroughly incensed by Amherst's policies. The combination of inspirational religious and political leadership had fired the Algonquian resistance on the Chesapeake early in the seventeenth century, and it would recur numerous times in the long history of Indian resistance to colonial expansion in North America.[13]

In May 1763 the Indians simultaneously attacked all the British forts in the west. At Mackinaw, located at the narrows between Lakes Michigan and Huron, Indians overran the fort by scrambling through the gates in pursuit of a ball during a lacrosse game, cheered on by the unsuspecting soldiers. In raids throughout the backcountry, Indians killed more than two thousand settlers. At Fort Pitt, General Amherst proposed that his officers "Send the *Small Pox* among those Disaffected Tribes of Indians" by distributing infected blankets from the fort's hospital. Germ warfare spread this epidemic from the Delawares and Shawnees to the southern Creeks, Choctaws, and Chickasaws, killing hundreds. The Indians sacked and burned eight British posts but failed to take the key forts at Niagara, Detroit, and the forks of the Ohio. Although Pontiac fought on for another year, most of the Indians sued for peace, fearing the destruction of their villages; the British came to terms because they knew they could not overwhelm the Indians.[14]

Yet the British made a significant concession to the Indian nations. Even before the uprising began, British authorities were at work on a policy they hoped would resolve frontier tensions. In accordance with wartime agreements with their Indian allies, the king assumed jurisdiction over Indian lands and issued the famous Royal Proclamation of 1763, which set the terms for continuing colonial policy toward Indian peoples. Some areas would be opened for settlement, but these would be at the geographical extremes of North America—Quebec in the north and Florida in the south. The proclamation set aside the trans-Appalachian region as "Indian country" and required the specific authorization of the crown before the purchase of these protected Indian lands. British authorities promised to maintain commercial posts in the interior for Indian commerce and to fortify the border to keep out land-hungry settlers. Indians were pleased with the proclamation, but land speculators and backcountry British Americans were outraged.

Backcountry colonists expected that with the removal of the French threat, they could move unencumbered into the West, regardless of the wishes of the Indian inhabitants. They could not understand why the British would reward territory to Indian enemies who slaughtered more than four thousand settlers during the previous war. In fact, the British proved unable and ultimately unwilling to prevent the

B.West inv.   *Grignion sculp.*

The Indians giving a Talk to Colonel Bouquet in a Conference at a Council Fire, near his Camp on the Banks of Muskingum in North America, in Oct.ʳ 1764.

Ohio Indians meet with the British in 1764. Engraving by Benjamin West, from William Smith,
An Historical Account of the Expedition Against the Ohio Indians . . . *(London, 1766).*

westward migration that was a dynamic part of the colonization of British North America. Within a few years of the war, New Englanders by the thousands were moving into the northern Green Mountain district, known by the corrupted French name of "Vermont." In the middle colonies, New York settlers pushed ever closer to the homeland of the Iroquois, while others located within the protective radius of Fort Pitt in western Pennsylvania. Hunters, stock herders, and farmers crossed over the first range of the Appalachians in Virginia and North Carolina, planting pioneer communities in what are now West Virginia and eastern Tennessee.

The press of population growth and economic development turned the attention of investors and land speculators to the area west of the Appalachians. Fresh from his service in the war, investing heavily in western lands, George Washington believed the proclamation line to be merely "a temporary expedient." In 1768 the Ohio Company sent surveyors to mark out its grant in the upper Ohio. In response to settlers and speculators, British authorities were soon pressing the Iroquois and Cherokees for cessions of land in Indian country. No longer able to play the balancing game between rival colonial powers, Indians found themselves reduced to a choice between compliance and resistance, and weakened by the recent war, they chose to sign away their rights to land. In 1768 the Cherokees ceded a vast tract on the waters of the upper Tennessee River—where British settlers had already planted communities—and the Iroquois gave up their claim of possession to the Ohio valley, hoping to deflect English settlement away from their homeland.[15]

———

Backcountry pioneers wanted to do as they pleased, assuming that they knew the best way to get ahead—cutting timber, trapping furs, speculating in land, planting farms on the rich soil. They supported whoever stood to help them. They fought against restrictions such as the Proclamation Line, but not because they wanted the government to get out. They petitioned strenuously for government assistance against the Indians; if the colonial governments refused it, they became furious, as Nathaniel Bacon in Virginia had, and took the law into their own hands. Pioneers were conservative, Tory, Whig, liberal, democrat, republican, radical, rebel—whatever they had to be to protect their own interests.

Far on the western fringes of Pennsylvania, in a log-cabin cluster called Paxton on the smooth waters of the Susquehanna, the frontier farmers viewed the government in Philadelphia as if through the wrong end of a telescope and felt themselves only weakly represented there. The Paxton community, largely Presbyterian, looked askance at the Quakers who controlled Pennsylvania. How could those sons of William Penn, effete Philadelphia pacifists and notorious coddlers of savages, know the needs of westerners? Thirty miles from Paxton lay a village of Conestoga Indians—poor, peaceful descendants of a tribe that had long lived in submission. There

The Paxton Boys murder Conestoga Indians, 1764. Library of Congress.

were rumors, though, that the Conestogas were spying on Paxton, and in those troubled days that was enough to raise a lynch mob.

In December 1763 a small band of men calling themselves the Paxton Boys massacred twenty Conestoga men, women, and children. Other Indians became frightened enough to seek protection, and more than a hundred fled to Philadelphia. The Paxton Boys were so incensed that they marched on the capital. Philadelphia officials, genuinely alarmed, sent out the militia, including a troop of artillerymen, and dispatched negotiators led by Benjamin Franklin. Franklin had already written an essay expressing his sympathy with the Indians and calling the Paxton Boys "Christian white savages." But he satisfied the frontiersmen that their cause would be heard by the colonial assembly and the governor; so, leaving a long written remonstrance, the farmers marched home to Paxton.[16]

In the petition the Paxton Boys admitted that their conduct bore "an appearance of flying in the face of Authority" (a lovely euphemism for an armed rebellion). But, they argued, their grievances were great, chiefly because the government showed a "manifest Partiality for Indians." The Conestogas had been "cherished and caressed as dearest friends" by the politicians. The public had thereby been made "tributaries to savages," and the poor frontier farmers were forced to fend for themselves. As the remonstrance continued, deeper frictions surfaced. The frontiersmen wanted more effective political representation and the abolition of property qualifications for voting. Further in the background lay the economic indebtedness of western farmers to eastern financiers. Altogether the uprising in Pennsylvania was an agrarian revolt not unlike that of Nathaniel Bacon, and it had mounted to the point of threatening the colonial establishment.[17]

In 1767 in the backwoods of South Carolina murders, thefts, and anarchy reached a peak. Even members of a new religious sect, the Weberites, turned homicidal and murdered their "holy ghost" (an African American) and their "holy son" (a white man). Miscreants were often captured and, when tried in Charleston, almost as often pardoned. The established law thus seemed to be in the wrong place producing the wrong results. And so men on the frontier began to take the law into their own hands. When they were able to identify an outlaw group, farmers would band together to descend on the hideout and scatter the outlaws. The governor was upset and called the farmers licentious spirits, but the settlers banded together and called themselves Regulators. One thousand of them signed an agreement to protect one another until the crime wave was stopped. Occasionally designated Rangers, especially when mounted, they roamed the backcountry, pursuing suspected criminals as far as necessary, whipping some, hanging others, but usually bringing them in to be tried in the proper manner.

Their violent and bloody methods were often as notorious as those of their quarry. Richard Maxwell Brown asserts that "the cruelty of outlaws who burned and tortured their victims was matched by the sadism of honest and respectable Regulators who shredded the flesh of miscreants at orgiastic flogging sessions while fiddles played." The dubious morality on both sides was undoubtedly the consequence of barbarities still fresh in these men's minds from the recent Cherokee War. Like the Paxton Boys, the backcountry Regulators clothed their criminal savagery in the cloak of political legitimacy. They wanted better representation in the colonial legislature, better courts in the frontier areas, more schools and jails, increased regulation of taverns and public houses, more restrictions on hunters and lawyers (both of whom were offensive), and even distribution of Bibles at public expense. A remonstrance covering most of these points was signed by four thousand men. Nevertheless, by March 1768 sentiment was rising against the Regulators' illegal actions. They themselves could argue, however, that their work was done, the crime wave was over, and their remonstrances were made.[18]

The South Carolina Regulator movement is sometimes paired with the actions of the Paxton Boys as an example of a frontier rebellion. In some ways they were radically different. The Pennsylvanians challenged the authority of the government. The Regulators were concerned more with ridding their local areas of crime, and although they acted unlawfully, like the Paxton Boys, their goals were different. Both groups were agrarian dissenters. The men from Paxton, however, functioned like a lynch mob, attacking a minority and then using the occasion to carry their grievances further. The Regulators were vigilantes, allegedly responsible members of society trying to clean up local corruption. Both lynch mobs and vigilantes would appear and reappear in only slightly varied guises on every American frontier. The terms *regulator* and *regulation* were first used in the backcountry of South Carolina but soon became standard until events in San Francisco in 1851 shifted popular usage to *vigilante* and *vigilance committee*.

Thousands of miles from the violence tearing through the eastern woodlands, on the fog-bound coasts of the northern Pacific, New World natives and Old World colonists were locked in yet another bloody confrontation. Driven by the search for valuable furs, Russians conquered Siberia and eventually moved across the icy sea to the Aleutian archipelago, homeland of the Aleuts, hunters of sea mammals and perhaps the most amphibious people on the face of the earth. We know this region by the name *Alaska,* derived from an Aleutian word meaning "great land," but it was rarely used to describe this country until the American purchase in 1867, when Senator Charles Sumner suggested it to Secretary of State William Seward. With the arrogance of colonizers, the Russian invaders called it Russian America.

Tsar Peter the Great commissioned the Danish-born naval officer Vitus Bering to lead an exploring expedition across the Pacific, and in 1741, after several preliminary voyages, Bering sailed east across the sea that now bears his name and discovered the Aleutian Islands. Although he died on the return voyage, his associates brought back a cargo of sea otter furs valued at the fabulous sum of ninety thousand rubles, beginning a rush of Russian independent fur trappers and traders called *promyshleniki.* By 1763 hundreds of promyshleniki had followed the Aleutian chain to the mainland and were sending home a steady supply of furs, valued in the millions of rubles, that were traded into China in exchange for the tea to which the Russians were addicted.

The Russian expansionists of the eighteenth century employed methods as brutal as any colonial power involved in North America. As they had done with native communities in Siberia, promyshleniki held Aleut villages hostage, forcing the men to trap and the women to perform sexual service. In 1748 the Russian state declared the Aleuts a conquered people and saddled them with the duty of paying *yasak,* or tribute, to the tsar, effectively legalizing their exploitation. Native resistance was sporadic and local at first, but it soon broadened into a large-scale revolt. The Aleuts had no military tradition, yet in 1762 the natives of a number of villages effectively coordinated an uprising that destroyed a fleet of Russian ships. They prevented the promyshleniki from returning for three years, but in 1766 a force of Russians crushed the rebel Aleuts, destroying dozens of native villages and carrying out deliberate "reductions" of the native population. When word of the revolt reached Moscow, Tsarina Catherine ordered the promyshleniki to be more cautious in the treatment of the natives: "Impress upon the hunters the necessity of treating their new brethren

Колумбы Росскіе презрѣвъ угрюмый рокъ
Межъ льдами новый путь отворятъ на Востокъ,
И наша досягнетъ въ Америку, Держава,
И по во всѣ концы, досигнетъ Россовъ слава.

Russians trade with the Aleuts. From Greigorii Ivanovich Shelikhov, Puteshestvie G. Shelekhova . . . *(Saint Petersburg, 1812). Beinecke.*

and countrymen, the inhabitants of our newly acquired islands with greatest kind-ness." But as the promyshleniki put it: "God is in his heaven, and the tsar is far away." Tsarina Catherine abolished yasak, but otherwise very little changed.[19]

In 1799 the tsar approved the charter of the Russian-American Company, which took charge of operations. The company ameliorated the harshest practices of the promyshleniki, but by the end of the century the Aleut population had fallen from a high of twenty-five thousand to perhaps six thousand. The causes were familiar: war-fare, alcoholism, disease. But sexual relations and intermarriage between promysh-leniki and Aleut women created a substantial group of mixed-ancestry people the Russians called *Creoles*—the equivalent of the French métis and the Spanish mesti-zos—who assumed an increasingly prominent position in the northern Pacific fur trade as navigators, explorers, clerks, and traders.

The Spanish responded fearfully to the activity of Russians, French, and English in North America. In the early eighteenth century, concerned over French designs in the lower Mississippi River valley, officials of New Spain began the construction of a string of Franciscan missions among the Indian peoples of Texas. By the time the French ceded their trans-Mississippi claims to the Spanish in 1763, the main Texas settlement at San Antonio de Béxar, including the mission that would later become known as the Alamo, was the center of a developing frontier province. With the elim-ination of the French threat, the Spanish began to focus on the vague reports of Rus-sian movements along the northern Pacific coast. In 1769 officials in Mexico ordered Gaspar de Portolá, governor of Baja California, to begin planting missions along the Alta California coast. The next year Portolá established his headquarters at the fine bay of Monterey to defend the empire against the Russian attack he believed was imminent. He was a little premature in his expectations, for the Russians had yet to establish a single permanent base on the American mainland. But such fears drove the Spanish to push the boundaries of their American empire northward.

In both Texas and California, the mission was a most important frontier institu-tion. The old missions, with their quaint adobe walls and cracked tiles, fascinate tourists today. But these visitors seldom perceive the reality of the mission institu-tion: a tough, pioneering agency that served as church, home, fortress, town, farm, and imperial consulate. This corporate body made it possible for two missionaries with three or four soldiers to create an orderly town out of several thousand Indi-ans, often from diverse and mutually hostile clans. Indeed, the hostility of the natives in the north made difficult the expansion of the encomienda, thriving as it did on the docility of native labor.

The primary aim of the mission was to Christianize people who had not yet heard the true word of God. But the mission also shared the aims of the encomienda—eco-

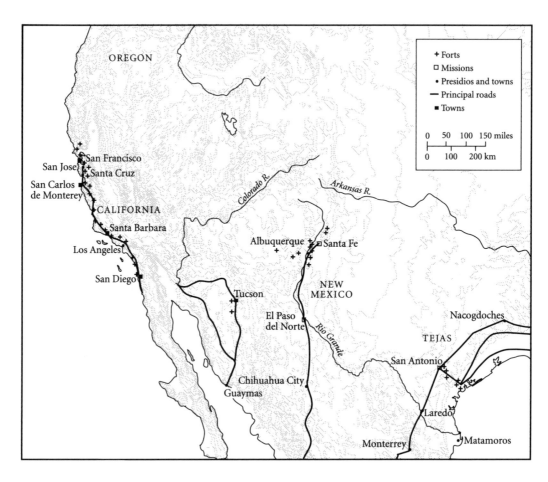

THE SPANISH NORTH IN THE EIGHTEENTH CENTURY

nomic development and social discipline. The mission, an arm of the state, also worked as a defensive fortress before the presidios were manned. Priests sent reports and observations to Mexico City to be studied by generals and civil administrators. In some years the funds for missions and war were kept in the same account. Such a practice was sensible because, where few Spaniards were available, Indians conceivably could be transformed into citizens. These Indian colonials would be unified through education and language. The Indians learned Spanish readily, and unification through a common tongue was not a far-fetched idea; a century or so later it worked well enough for the British in India. The mission introduced breeds of cattle and such agricultural products as grapes and citrus, laying economic foundations that are still apparent. In an unexpected way, the padres promoted their provinces in letters and reports, extolling the beauties and values of their new homes, rather like modern-day chambers of commerce. It is not surprising that colonial ad-

Spanish lancers bring captured California Indians to a mission. From Louis Choris,
Voyage pittoresque autour du monde . . . *(Paris, 1822). Beinecke.*

ministrators were willing to support the missions from their royal treasuries, though in fulfilling their principal purpose, the conversion and reeducation of Indians, the missions were only marginally successful.

In Alta California the mission system was directed by the Franciscan Junípero Serra, and from San Diego to Sonoma he and his fellow Franciscans founded twenty-one missions. Secular officials, meanwhile, established a half-dozen garrisoned presidios and pueblos, including San Francisco, founded in 1776, and Los Angeles, settled by a group of mestizo and mulatto colonists from Sinaloa in 1781. But the colonial population of California never exceeded thirty-five hundred. It was Indian labor, both at the missions and in the towns, that herded the cattle, sheep, and horses, irrigated the fields, and produced a flourishing California economy. One of the most prosperous missions was San Juan Bautista, inland from Monterey Bay, with thousands of sheep, cattle, and horses, fertile fields of wheat, and a treasury loaded with gold. The great cathedral with thick adobe walls was built on Spanish and Moorish patterns, with interior paintings of saints in European style and decorative abstract designs in the native manner.

At the end of the eighteenth century the missions of Alta California housed more than twenty thousand "neophytes" (as the padres called them), but their mortality rate was high, and historians estimate that their numbers had already fallen by about a third. The Indians suffered from changes in diet and confinement in close quarters, and they died of dysentery, fevers, and venereal disease. Father Felipe Arroyo de

California mission Indians gambling. From Louis Choris, Voyage pittoresque autour
du monde . . . *(Paris, 1822). Beinecke.*

la Cuesta, of Mission San Juan Bautista, wrote that "the number of deaths here ex-
ceeds that of births," and the mission's funeral records during a terrible smallpox epidemic in 1838 noted that "the old graveyard close to the church is filled up with bodies to such an extent as to saturate the Mission with their smell." We cannot tell how
much death resulted from the harsh discipline of the padres—shackles, solitary confinement, and whipping posts. "The Indians at the mission were very severely treated
by the padres," remembered Lorenzo Asisaro, who was raised at Mission Santa Cruz.
If there was any disobedience or infraction of the rules "then came the lash without
mercy, the women the same as the men." There were occasional acts of Indian resistance, such as the murder at Santa Cruz of a priest who thrashed the Indians too often for his own good. In fact, there was native rebellion from the beginning. In 1775
the villagers around San Diego rose up and killed several priests, and the history of
many missions is punctuated by revolts, although the arms and organization of
Spanish soldiers were usually sufficient to suppress uprisings. One form of protest
was flight, and sometimes whole villages fled to the inaccessible mountains.[20]

Observers often noted the despondence of the neophytes. "I have never seen any
of them laugh," one European visitor wrote, "I have never seen a single one look anyone in the face. They have the air of taking no interest in anything." Visitors such as
Frenchman Jean François de Lapérouse charged that the Indians were being transformed not into new men but into slaves. Lapérouse compared the missions to plan-

tations in the Caribbean. He wrote that the missionaries were convinced "either by prejudice or by their own experience that reason is almost never developed in these people, which to them is sufficient motive for treating them as children."[21]

But other missionaries left evidence of considerably more self-determination on the part of the Indians. "Even today they show more respect and submission to their chiefs than to the alcaldes who have been placed over them for their advancement as citizens," one padre wrote. Father Gerónimo Boscana told of witnessing a dying man refuse confession and the sacraments. "If I have been deceived whilst living," he declared with his last breath, "I do not wish to die in the delusion!" According to Boscana, defiance of this kind was commonplace.[22]

Looking backward from the twentieth century, some historians have called the missions charnel houses and have compared them with Nazi concentration camps. But this analogy is almost as misleading as that picture of Indians as silly sheep and the padres as gentle but effective shepherds. Perhaps the modern anthropologist Alfred L. Kroeber came closest to proper balance when he wrote, "It must have caused many of the fathers a severe pang to realize, as they could not but do daily, that they were saving souls only at the inevitable cost of lives."[23]

FURTHER READING

Richard Maxwell Brown, *South Carolina Regulators* (1963)

Hector Chevigny, *Russian America: The Great Alaskan Venture, 1741–1867* (1965)

Gregory Dowd, *A Spirited Resistance: The North American Indian Struggle for Unity, 1745–1815* (1992)

Francis Jennings, *The Ambiguous Iroquois Empire: The Covenant Chain Confederation of Indian Tribes with English Colonies from Its Beginnings to the Lancaster Treaty of 1744* (1984)

———, *Empire of Fortune: Crowns, Colonies, and Tribes in the Seven Years War in America* (1988)

Terry G. Jordan and Matti Kaups, *The American Backwoods Frontier: An Ethnic and Ecological Interpretation* (1989)

James H. Merrell, *Into the American Woods: Negotiators on the Pennsylvania Frontier* (1999)

Martin J. Morgado, *Junípero Serra's Legacy* (1987)

Francis Parkman, *Montcalm and Wolfe* (1884)

Jack M. Sosin, *The Revolutionary Frontier, 1763–1783* (1967)

Ian K. Steele, *Warpaths: Invasions of North America* (1994)

Richard White, *The Middle Ground: Indians, Empires, and Republics in the Great Lakes Region, 1650–1815* (1991)

J. Leitch Wright, Jr., *Creeks and Seminoles: The Destruction and Regeneration of the Muscogulge People* (1986)

4

The Land and Its Markers

There was no unified support for the American Revolution in the backcountry. How could the Carolina Regulators, for example, rally behind the leaders of a provincial government they had so recently defied? Fleeing the violence that ripped through their backcountry communities, during the Revolution hundreds of settlers crossed the Appalachians, plenty of Loyalists among them. The Patriot Committee of Safety at the new settlement of Harrodsburg petitioned the Continental Congress in 1776 for help to prevent Kentucky from becoming "an asylum to those whose principles are inimical to American liberty."[1]

The frontier provided no asylum from the fighting, however. The Revolution continued the conflict between settlers and Indians for control of the West that began with the French and Indian War and would not reach a conclusion until the Battle of Fallen Timbers in 1794. At least two thousand Americans, and Indians in countless thousands, lost their lives in this, the bloodiest phase of the three-century campaign for the conquest of North America. Relative to population, the West during the Revolution suffered greater losses than any other section of the country. There were about ten war-related deaths for every one thousand persons in the thirteen coastal colonies, but better than seventy per thousand in Kentucky. Though not unified on the politics of revolution, backcountry Americans could agree on the Indian menace.

The British held an essential advantage because they kept the tribal allies they had won in their long fight against the French. In 1775 British agents began to press the Iroquois Six Nations, long one of the most significant political forces in colonial North America, to ally with them against the Patriot cause. "We are unwilling to join on either side of such a contest, for we bear an equal affection to both Old and New England," one Oneida chief responded. "Let us Indians be all of one mind, and live

Indians at Independence Hall, Philadelphia. From William Birch, The City of Philadelphia . . . *(Philadelphia, 1800). The Winterthur Library: Printed Book and Periodical Collection.*

with one another; and you white people settle your own disputes between your-selves." Disease, alcohol abuse, and economic dependency had terribly weakened the once powerful Six Nations, and the French departure from North America made it difficult to play the traditional balancing game. Many Iroquois chiefs saw neutrality as their only course.[2]

But the British had powerful supporters among the Six Nations chiefs, principally the Mohawk leader Thayendanegea, whose English name was Joseph Brant. De-scended from a powerful family, Brant was the brother-in-law of British Indian agent Sir William Johnson, who sent him to Anglican mission school and then to an Indian academy (later known as Dartmouth College), where Brant proved himself a brilliant scholar. As the fighting broke out at Lexington and Concord, Brant went to London at the request of British authorities to negotiate an anti-Patriot alliance between the Six Nations and the British. He toured the capital in the company of no less a Londoner than James Boswell and sat for his portrait in oils by no less a painter than George Romney. (He would later also be painted by Gilbert Stuarto)

Mohawk support, Brant told the British, would be conditional on questions of land and sovereignty being "settled to our satisfaction whenever the troubles in America were ended." Receiving British assurances that the Six Nations could write their own terms at the conclusion of the conflict, Brant returned to his homeland to lobby for the British within the Six Nations council.[3]

Mohawk leader Joseph Brant. Painting by Gilbert Stuart, 1786. Copyright New York State Historical Association, Cooperstown, New York.

When he was unable to get a hearing at the council fire, however, Brant called his own meeting of sympathetic chiefs at the British trading town of Oswego. Representatives of four nations—Mohawks, Cayugas, Onondagas, and Senecas—agreed to fight for the English king, and Brant himself assumed command. But Oneida and Tuscorora chiefs decided to side with the Patriots, and thus, for the first time since the founding of the confederacy in the fifteenth century, warriors of the Iroquois nations would face each other in battle. Over the next several years the Iroquois not

George Rogers Clark. *Painting by John Wesley Jarvis, c. 1820. The Filson Club Historical Society, Louisville, Kentucky.*

only suffered from the devastating raids of Americans but were torn by fratricidal civil war. For some Iroquois, Joseph Brant was remembered as a hero, but others condemned him as a traitor to the cause of Iroquois unity.

Brant led Indian victories along the Mohawk River at Oriskany in 1777 and Cherry Valley in 1778, and his name came to summon more fear to western hearts than any Indian since Pontiac. Despite devastating Patriot invasions, the Iroquois threw the Americans out of their homeland and pushed the frontline of battle back almost to Albany. "We are now deprived of a great portion of our most valuable and well inhabited territory," declared Governor George Clinton of New York. Meanwhile the Shawnees, Delawares, Miamis, Mingos, and other Indian peoples of the Ohio valley formed an effective defensive confederacy centered at Detroit, where they were supplied by the British. In 1777 and 1778 they sent warriors south against pioneer communities in Kentucky and western Virginia that had been founded in defiance of the Royal Proclamation of 1763. The Americans barely held out.[4]

The only western officer who could match the leadership skills of Brant was George Rogers Clark, who for a time managed to turn the war in the West in favor of the Americans. Clark, a six-foot, redheaded Virginian who knew well the lands along the Ohio River in Kentucky, held as a truism that if land was worth claiming (something he had already done), it was worth protecting (something he was about to do). His first victory against the British, at the French town of Kaskaskia in 1778, was followed by successes at Cahokia and at Vincennes, where he captured the British commander. Clark's successes were supplemented by the campaign against the British waged by the Spanish, who refused to establish a formal alliance with the Americans but regarded the Revolution as an opportunity to regain Florida. They threw the

British out of the Mississippi River towns of Natchez and Baton Rouge in 1779, the Gulf ports of Mobile and Pensacola in 1780 and 1781. But the Americans were unable to follow up on these victories. Clark lacked the strength to mount an attack on the strategic garrison at Detroit, and though they frequently raided the Indian towns north of the Ohio, the Americans were unable to do much more than defend their forts in Kentucky and their newly conquered territory in Illinois.

General Charles Cornwallis surrendered for the British at Yorktown in 1781, and the fighting in the East came to an end. But the conflict accelerated in the West as Brant mounted a new set of offensives that cast a shadow over Clark's successes. American militiamen from western Pennsylvania invaded the Ohio valley but, failing to engage the enemy, turned instead to a brutal massacre of unresisting Christian Delawares at the mission village of Gnadenhutten, hacking the bodies of ninety-six men, women, and children and bringing home scalps to nail over the doors of their cabins. In retaliation outraged Indian warriors invaded Kentucky and at the Battle of the Blue Licks in August 1782 ambushed an army of militiamen, leaving the mutilated bodies of 146 Kentuckians on the battleground.

By 1783, therefore, the western Indians had every reason to think they were winning the war. They were thunderstruck when word came of peace between the Americans and the British. They were even more shocked when the details of the treaty became known: the Americans had won the right to the entire trans-Appalachian country, from the Great Lakes to the Mississippi River to Florida, a region the British had reserved for the Indians since the Royal Proclamation of twenty years before. Why had the British abandoned their Indian allies? Cynical realpolitik. The English minister, Lord Shelburne, shrewdly understood the difficulties of limiting backcountry Americans behind a political boundary at the Appalachians. By returning Florida to the Spanish and strengthening their fortifications in Canada, the British sought to ensure that the new republic would be flanked north, south, and west by jealous European powers. Although the treaty specified that the British would evacuate their forts in ceded territory "with all convenient speed," London instructed Canadian authorities to "allow the posts in the upper country to remain as they are for some time." The British assured the Indians that they still considered them the rightful owners of the western country and that they could rely on British power against the Americans.[5]

When the thirteen colonies achieved their independence, they took from under the British crown three million white people and uncounted Indians living on 541 million acres, an area roughly seventeen times the size of England. The trans-Appalachian lands, those beyond the generally accepted boundaries of the new states, covered about 230 million acres, nearly half of the new country. There were serious questions about this western territory: Did it belong to the Indians, to the respective states, or to the general government (embodied in the national Confederation Congress)? In what manner should the lands be distributed? How were they to be governed? These may seem abstract questions, but they were wrung from human dreams—the dream of homelands, the hope of owning land and prospering from laboring upon it, the promise of liberty and independence. In a predominantly rural society such dreams were important enough to cause the rise and fall of political systems.

The Indian residents of the West naturally assumed that they held the equivalent of title to their traditional lands. But although neither the Iroquois, the Cherokees, nor the western tribes considered themselves defeated, the United States assumed that victory over the British meant victory over their Indian allies as well. The national government claimed the *right of conquest*—the seizure of the lands and property of all who had fought against the Revolution. Indians must suffer the same fate as the Tories. "When you Americans and the King made peace," declared the Seneca leader Red Jacket, "he did not mention us, and showed us no compassion, notwithstanding all he said to us, and all we had suffered." The Americans paid no attention to such complaints. Seizing hostages and forcing compliance, commissioners of the Confederation Congress forced the Six Nations in 1784 to sign a new Treaty of Fort Stanwix ceding a large portion of their homeland. Joseph Brant and his Iroquois followers fled north to Canada, creating de facto separate Iroquois confederacies on either side of the international boundary. The next year the commissioners forced the same terms on the Ohio Indians, eliminating aboriginal title to the lands in the southeastern portion of what would become the state of Ohio. Even Indian nations that had fought with the Patriots, tribes such as the Oneidas and the Tuscoraras of the Six Nations, suffered similar losses to the Americans. The Penobscots and Passamaquoddys of northern New England had fought with Massachusetts during the Revolution in exchange for a promise that the state would protect their lands. After the war, however, they too were compelled to make large cessions. The arrogant way in which the Americans treated the Indians guaranteed a continuation of bloody warfare in the West.[6]

The king, through his charters, had given the land to the colonies, so it might have followed that the states, counterparts of the colonies, would take possession of it. Understandably inclined to this position were the seven states with colonial charters granting them boundaries running westward beyond the Appalachians (in some cases all the way to the "South Sea"). But the six landlocked states without such charters demanded that Congress assume authority over the western lands for "the good of the whole." This dispute lasted for four years, delaying ratification of the Articles of Confederation until 1780, when Congress finally passed a resolution promising that any ceded western territory would "be disposed of for the common benefit of

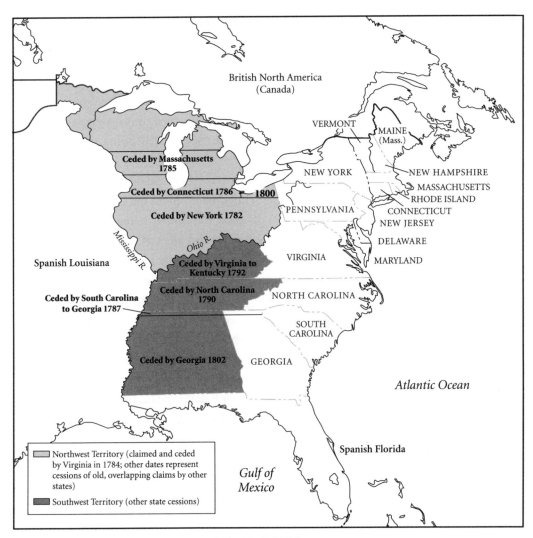

British North America
(Canada)

VERMONT

MAINE
(Mass.)

Ceded by Massachusetts
1785

NEW YORK

NEW HAMPSHIRE

MASSACHUSETTS
RHODE ISLAND

Ceded by Connecticut 1786   1800

CONNECTICUT
NEW JERSEY

PENNSYLVANIA

Ceded by New York 1782

DELAWARE

Mississippi R.

Ohio R.

VIRGINIA

MARYLAND

Spanish Louisiana

Ceded by Virginia to
Kentucky 1792

Ceded by North Carolina
1790

NORTH CAROLINA

Ceded by South Carolina
to Georgia 1787

SOUTH
CAROLINA

Ceded by Georgia 1802

GEORGIA

Atlantic Ocean

Northwest Territory (claimed and ceded
by Virginia in 1784; other dates represent
cessions of old, overlapping claims by other
states)

Southwest Territory (other state cessions)

Spanish Florida

*Gulf of
Mexico*

WESTERN LAND CLAIMS OF THE STATES

the United States, and be settled and formed into distinct republican States, which
shall become members of the Federal Union, and have the same rights of sovereignty,
freedom and independence as the other States." New York was the first state to give
up its western claims, followed by an indication from Virginia that it would go along.
By 1790 all the states but Georgia had given up their pretentions to western territory,
thus creating a vast public domain under the control of the Confederation Congress.[7]

Now there was the problem of what to do with the land. On this question the Confederation Congress did not start from scratch. The colonies used systems of land
distribution that intriguingly wove together both geographical and sociological factors. In the flinty hills of New England, for example, colonial governments granted

land not to individuals but to congregations and community groups, and they discouraged migrants from moving too far from existing communities, preferring to keep settlement compact and contiguous. Before moving, an advance party of settlers surveyed their grant, designating the appropriate place for the town center, with its church, roads, pasturage, and most fertile farming fields. Each family in the group received a lot in the center, as well as farm, pasture, and timber lots on the outskirts. As the Puritan church lost its dominant social position in the eighteenth century this system fell into disuse, but Yankee pioneers continued to practice prior survey and compact settlement. A different settlement system developed in the South, where land and climate made possible single-crop plantation agriculture (tobacco, rice, later cotton) and larger farms than in the North. The pioneer planter typically sought out a large tract that he found appealing, even if it was relatively far from the nearest settlement, and requested a grant from the colonial government. Unlike the communal tradition of the Yankees, the southern pioneer assumed the obligation for independent development. The law that Congress wrote, the Land Ordinance of 1785, pragmatically drew from both traditions. From New England it borrowed the idea of prior survey and orderly contiguous development, from the South the practice of allocating land directly to individuals.

Yet what was most notable about the Land Ordinance was not its incorporation of tradition but its invention of a new and revolutionary system of measuring and bounding the land. Surveyors traditionally employed a technique known as "metes and bounds," in which each parcel was described by the distinctive lay of the countryside and the successive property lines of previously surveyed lots. This time-tested method worked well on a case-by-case basis, but it could produce big problems when used to survey vast new territories. The haphazard and hurried survey of Kentucky, for example, which took place amid the chaos and turmoil of the Revolution, resulted in considerable conflict, even violence, over confusing boundaries and titles, and it was with the cautionary tale of Kentucky in mind that the Congress broke with tradition.

All the land in the western territory, the Land Ordinance declared, would be divided "into townships of six miles square, by lines running due north and south, and others crossing these at right angles." A great grid of "Principal Meridians" and "Base Lines" would divide the whole American West into numbered ranges of townships, with each township divided into thirty-six square-mile sections, each section further divisible into half-sections, quarter-sections, and quarter-quarter-section parcels of forty acres. Every farmer's field would be instantly identifiable by its range, township, and section numbers. As Elliott West writes, the "surveyor's stake was a kind of polestar of national development, the anchored point of reckoning for more than a billion acres. Nowhere else in the world would an area of such size be laid out in a uniform land system." The system, which owed much to Enlightenment ratio-

An Ordinance for ascertaining the mode of disposing of Lands in the Western Territory.

Be it ordained by the United States in Congress assembled, that the Territory ceded by individual States to the United States which has been purchased of the Indian inhabitants shall be disposed of in the following manner.———

A Surveyor from each State shall be appointed by Congress, or a Committee of the States, who shall take an Oath for the faithful discharge of his duty, before the Geographer of the United States, who is hereby empowered and directed to administer the same; and the like Oath shall be administered to each Chain carrier by the Surveyor under whom he acts.———

The Geographer, under whose direction the Surveyors shall act, shall occasionally form such regulations for their conduct, as he shall deem necessary; and shall have authority to suspend them for misconduct in Office, and shall make report of the same to Congress, or to the Committee of the States, and he shall make report in case of sickness death or resignation of any Surveyor.———

The Land Ordinance of 1785. National Archives.

nalism, had all the advantages and disadvantages, clarity and distortion, of any rational approach to human affairs. The national survey would assure clear boundaries and firm titles, highly important in wild new lands. But it would press upon the land a uniformity that took no account of different valleys, climates, or men who might wish for other arrangements.[8]

The Land Ordinance also created the system for converting western lands to private ownership. Thomas Jefferson had argued for giving western land away "in small quantities" to actual settlers. "I am against selling the lands at all," he declared. The people on the frontier were poor and "by selling the lands to them, you will disgust them, and cause an avulsion of them from the common union." They would simply ignore the law and "settle the lands in spite of everybody." Jefferson clearly understood the mentality of western settlers (and his thinking anticipated the Homestead Act of 1862), but in 1785 he was out of step with most other American leaders. Instead of giving the land away, as Jefferson advised, Congress decided to auction it off in chunks no smaller than 640 acres, and at a price no less than one dollar per acre. This was well beyond the means of most farmers, but Congress was interested in providing a revenue base for the national government, not equality of opportunity for western settlers. The Land Ordinance did reserve the revenue of one section in each township for the maintenance of public schools. Narrowly defeated was an attempt to set aside another section for the support of religion.[9]

Although Jefferson's plan was rejected, there were great hopes for the role the West would play in the development of the new nation. In what was perhaps the best-selling American book of the decade, *Letters from an American Farmer* (1782), the French immigrant J. Hector St. John de Crèvecoeur announced that America would find its destiny in the West. "Scattered over an immense territory" and "animated with the spirit of an industry which is unfettered and unrestrained," Americans were building "the most perfect society now existing in the world." The limitless West was the best guarantee that the American people would maintain their economic independence, the foundation of republican government. Jefferson echoed these sentiments, writing in 1787 that Americans would remain virtuous as long as they maintained their roots in the agricultural soil. But he recognized a darker side to Crèvecoeur's vision. Once the western lands were exhausted, he wrote, Americans would "get piled upon one another in large cities, as in Europe, and go to eating one another as they do there."[10]

The surveyors headed west in late 1785 as soon as the Iroquois and the Ohio Indians ceded lands there, but running the lines and marking the township boundaries proved to be slow and torturous work. Impatient to begin the flow of badly needed revenue, in 1787 Congress ordered a public auction of the first surveyed ranges in New

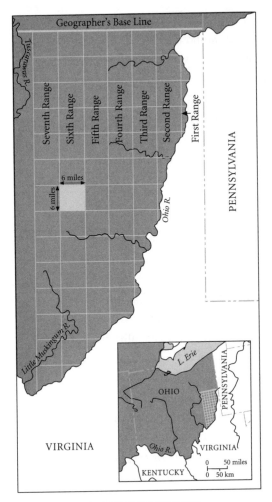

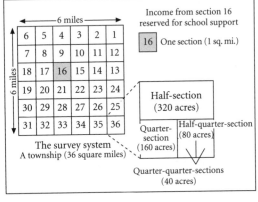

THE SURVEY SYSTEM

York City, hoping to attract the interest of land speculators. The results were extremely disappointing, producing nothing like the windfall that was expected. While skeptical eastern capitalists sat on their hands, however, western settlers were proving Jefferson right by simply moving onto tracts of their choice north of the Ohio River and claiming ownership by the right of occupancy. Congress was forced to call out troops to sweep areas clean of squatters. "There is scarcely one bottom on the river but has one or more families living thereon," Ensign John Armstrong reported to his superiors, and he predicted that if Congress did not "fall on some speedy method to prevent people from settling," the country would soon be populated by "a banditti whose actions are a disgrace to human nature." Armstrong's unhappiness with frontierspeople was widely shared among middle- and upper-class easterners. Fresh in their memories was the protest of Daniel Shays, a poor farmer and Revolutionary

Daniel Shays (left) and Job Shattuck. From Bickerstaff's Boston Almanack *for 1787, 3d ed. (Boston, 1787). National Portrait Gallery, Smithsonian Institution.*

War hero from western Massachusetts, who in the tradition of the Regulators led a protest against monetary policies and farm foreclosures. In 1786 Shays and hundreds of local farmers prevented the local county courts from sitting, and state authorities called out troops to quell the rebellion.[11]

Faced with frontier squatting, the disappointing initial sale of western lands, and the crying need for revenue, Congress now charted a different course that seemed to contradict its own land law. In 1787 a Massachusetts lobbyist named Manasseh Cutler approached a number of congressmen with a proposal for a huge western land grant to a group of wealthy New England capitalists known as the Ohio Company of Associates (not to be confused with the Virginians' Ohio Company of the pre-Revolutionary era). Cutler was a restless Yale divine with a parish in Massachusetts and an eye that often roved from heaven to a quick business dollar, one of those unquenchable spirits who combined a multitude of lives into one. He studied and practiced law, then turned to the church. Thereafter, through a great variety of activities, he always led his parish, but in addition he studied medicine, astronomy, botany, and electricity. In his household he taught as many as twenty boys at once. Somewhere in his full life, he also found time to pursue one of the largest business deals of his day.

The Ohio Company wanted a grant of one and a half million acres of lush green Ohio hills and valleys. The associates were unwilling to pay the dollar-an-acre price mandated by the Land Ordinance, but Cutler proposed a convenient dodge for the conscience of the Congress. Let them pay in depreciated revolutionary currency, worth only eight or nine cents on the dollar. The Land Ordinance expressly prohibited such a practice, and a number of congressmen balked. They were brought around, however, by the threat that if Congress refused to sell, the Ohio Company would buy from individual states, presumably those yet to cede their western lands, thus costing the national government a tidy sum of which it was desperately in need. As a final coup Cutler agreed to yet another scheme, the Scioto Company, in which recalcitrant congressmen could themselves profit from a grant of five million acres along the Ohio River. The Ohio Associates had wrested from the government a principality in exchange for a pittance.

A considerably more outrageous western land scam took place in Georgia, the only state continuing to claim trans-Appalachian lands. In 1795 land speculators bribed members of the state legislature into granting them an enormous tract of land in what would later become the states of Alabama and Mississippi. Georgia's authority over that territory was dubious at best; indeed, the Spanish still claimed much of it. The lack of secure title, however, did not bother the speculators, who quickly sold their "rights" to land jobbers, who resold them to thousands of gullible investors, anxious to participate in what was expected to be an enormous profit as the lands came on the market. After the sale was declared a fraud by no less an authority than President Washington, the Georgia legislature repealed the Yazoo Act, so-named for a meandering river in the region. The repeal caused even more controversy, as thousands of naive speculators throughout the country faced the loss of their investment. A congressional commission took years to investigate the various claims, and in an attempt to limit its liability Georgia finally ceded its western claims to the federal government in 1802. The matter came before the Supreme Court in the case of *Fletcher v. Peck* in 1810. In his justly famous decision, Chief Justice John Marshall ruled that the constitutional guarantee of the sanctity of contracts meant that Georgia could not revoke its actions, however corrupt. Congress finally voted to award the speculators more than four million dollars (fifty million dollars in today's values). The Ohio Company and Yazoo affairs testified to the victory of speculators over actual settlers in the land policy of the early republic.

Still unsettled was the question of the political relationship of the new western settlements to the established states. Many Americans assumed that the western lands would move quickly toward full, independent statehood within the union. Again Thomas Jefferson played the most important role in attempting to create a democratic colonial policy. His plan would have divided the western public domain into distinct territories, each granted immediate self-government and republican institutions. Once the population of a territory reached twenty thousand, the residents could call a convention and establish a constitution and government of their choosing. Admission to statehood would be automatic as soon as the population grew to equal the smallest of the original thirteen states.

But the continuing Indian warfare, the squatter problem, and a general sense about the unruliness of western society convinced Congress to reject Jefferson's territorial plan. It was necessary, explained Richard Henry Lee of Virginia, "for the security of property among uninformed and perhaps licentious people, as the greater part of those who go there are, that a strong toned government should exist." In the Northwest Ordinance of 1787, Congress divided the territory "northwest of the river Ohio" into a number of separate districts. A governor, secretary, and three judges would be appointed to govern each district until its male population reached five thousand, at which time they could elect an assembly. But the assembly was empowered to do little more than nominate a list of men from whom Congress would select a legislative council, which functioned as an upper house. The governor enjoyed absolute veto power and could select from the laws of the thirteen states those he wished to incorporate into the code of his district. These provisions were more strict and authoritarian than the colonial governments overthrown by the Revolution. When any district grew to include sixty thousand residents, it could be admitted to the Union on equal terms with the existing states.

An ORDINANCE for the GOVERNMENT of the TERRITORY of the UNITED STATES, North-West of the RIVER OHIO.

BE IT ORDAINED by the United States in Congress assembled, That the said territory, for the purposes of temporary government, be one district; subject, however, to be divided into two districts, as future circumstances may, in the opinion of Congress, make it expedient.

Be it ordained by the authority aforesaid, That the estates both of resident and non-resident proprietors in the said territory, dying intestate, shall descend to, and be distributed among their children, and the descendants of a deceased child in equal parts; the descendants of a deceased child or grand-child, to take the share of their deceased parent in equal parts among them: And where there shall be no children or descendants, then in equal parts to the next of kin, in equal degree; and among collaterals, the children of a deceased brother or sister of the intestate, shall have in equal parts among them their deceased parents share; and there shall in no case be a distinction between kindred of the whole and half blood; saving in all cases to the widow of the intestate, her third part of the real estate for life, and one third part of the personal estate; and this law relative to descents and dower, shall remain in full force until altered by the legislature of the district. ———— And until the governor and judges shall adopt laws as herein after mentioned, estates in the said territory may be devised or bequeathed by wills in writing, signed and sealed by him or her, in whom the estate may be, (being of full age) and attested by three witnesses; — and real estates may be conveyed by lease and release, or bargain and sale, signed, sealed, and delivered by the person being of full age, in whom the estate may be, and attested by two witnesses, provided such wills be duly proved, and such conveyances be acknowledged, or the execution thereof duly proved, and be recorded within one year after proper magistrates, courts, and registers shall be appointed for that purpose; and personal property may be transferred by delivery, saving, however, to the French and Canadian inhabitants, and other settlers of the Kaskaskies, Saint Vincent's, and the neighbouring villages, who have heretofore professed themselves citizens of Virginia, their laws and customs now in force among them, relative to the descent and conveyance of property.

Be it ordained by the authority aforesaid, That there shall be appointed from time to time, by Congress, a governor, whose commission shall continue in force for the term of three years, unless sooner revoked by Congress; he shall reside in the district, and have a freehold estate therein, in one thousand acres of land, while in the exercise of his office.

There shall be appointed from time to time, by Congress, a secretary, whose commission shall continue in force for four years, unless sooner revoked, he shall reside in the district, and have a freehold estate therein, in five hundred acres of land, while in the exercise of his office; it shall be his duty to keep and preserve the acts and laws passed by the legislature, and the public records of the district, and the proceedings of the governor in his executive department; and transmit authentic copies of such acts and proceedings, every six months, to the secretary of Congress: There shall also be appointed a court to consist of three judges, any two of whom to form a court, who shall have a common law jurisdiction, and reside in the district, and have each therein a freehold estate in five hundred acres of land, while in the exercise of their offices; and their commissions shall continue in force during good behaviour.

The governor and judges, or a majority of them, shall adopt and publish in the district, such laws of the original states, criminal and civil, as may be necessary, and best suited to the circumstances of the district, and report them to Congress, from time to time, which laws shall be in force in the district until the organization of the general assembly therein, unless disapproved of by Congress; but afterwards the legislature shall have authority to alter them as they shall think fit.

The governor for the time being, shall be commander in chief of the militia, appoint and commission all officers in the same, below the rank of general officers; all general officers shall be appointed and commissioned by Congress.

Previous to the organization of the general assembly, the governor shall appoint such magistrates and other civil officers, in each county or township, as he shall find necessary for the preservation of the peace and good order in the same: After the general assembly shall be organized, the powers and duties of magistrates and other civil officers shall be regulated and defined by the said assembly; but all magistrates and other civil officers, not herein otherwise directed, shall, during the continuance of this temporary government, be appointed by the governor.

For the prevention of crimes and injuries, the laws to be adopted or made shall have force in all parts of the district, and for the execution of process, criminal and civil, the governor shall make proper divisions thereof——and he shall proceed from time to time, as circumstances may require, to lay out the parts of the district in which the Indian titles shall have been extinguished, into counties and townships, subject, however, to such alterations as may thereafter be made by the legislature.

So soon as there shall be five thousand free male inhabitants, of full age, in the district, upon giving proof thereof to the governor, they shall receive authority, with time and place, to elect representatives from their counties or townships, to represent them in the general assembly; provided that for every five hundred free male inhabitants there shall be one representative, and so on progressively with the number of free male inhabitants, shall the right of representation increase, until the number of representatives shall amount to twenty-five, after which the number and proportion of representatives shall be regulated by the legislature; provided that no person be eligible or qualified to act as a representative, unless he shall have been a citizen of one of the United States three years and be a resident in the district, or unless he shall have resided in the district three years, and in either case shall likewise hold in his own right, in fee simple, two hundred acres of land within the same:——Provided also, that a freehold in fifty acres of land in the district, having been a citizen of one of the states, and being resident in the district; or the like freehold and two years residence in the district shall be necessary to qualify a man as an elector of a representative.

The representatives thus elected, shall serve for the term of two years, and in case of the death of a representative, or removal from office, the governor shall issue a writ to the county or township for which he was a member, to elect another in his stead, to serve for the residue of the term.

The general assembly, or legislature, shall consist of the governor, legislative council, and a house of representatives. The legislative council shall consist of five members, to continue in office five years, unless sooner removed by Congress, any three of whom to be a quorum, and the members of the council shall be nominated and appointed in the following manner, to wit: As soon as representatives shall be elected, the governor shall appoint a time and place for them to meet together, and, when met, they shall nominate ten persons, residents in the district, and each possessed of a freehold in five hundred acres of land, and return their names to Congress; five of whom Congress shall appoint and commission to serve as aforesaid; and whenever a vacancy shall happen in the council, by death or removal from office, the house of representatives shall nominate two persons, qualified as aforesaid, for each vacancy, and return their names to Congress; one of whom Congress shall appoint and commission for the residue of the term; and every five years, four months at least before the expiration of the time of service of the members of council, the said house shall nominate ten persons, qualified as aforesaid, and return their names to Congress, five of whom Congress shall appoint and commission to serve as members of the council five years, unless sooner removed. And the governor, legislative council, and house of re-

The Northwest Ordinance of 1787. National Archives.

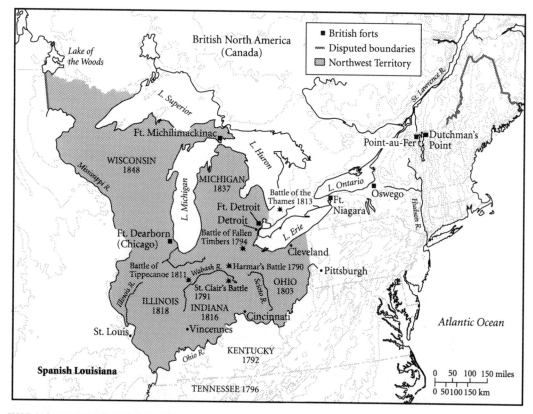

THE NORTHWEST TERRITORY

The Northwest Ordinance has been called, rather extravagantly, one of America's greatest contributions to political theory. Attention is often called to the fact that it outlawed involuntary servitude north of the Ohio River, but actually this was merely a recognition of the fact that the northern states were already in the process of abolishing slavery. It might be noted that Jefferson's original territorial plan called for keeping slavery out of the *entire* trans-Appalachian West, but Congress rejected that radical notion out of hand. Southern politicians insisted that the nation do nothing to impede the expansion of slavery into the country west of the Appalachians and south of the Ohio River. Indeed, when North and South Carolina ceded their western claims in the late 1780s, it was with the understanding that the slave prohibition in the Northwest Ordinance would not apply, and Congress included no antislavery provision when it created the Southwest Territory in 1789.

Praise for the Northwest Ordinance may be justifiably aimed, however, at the final stage of the plan, namely, the complete equality of the admitted states. With the exception of Texas and California (and Nevada, for which the minimum population regulation was overlooked), all the western states were admitted to the Union in accordance with this ordinance. The policy succeeded because it provided for an orderly abolition of the territorial or colonial status. Yet the Northwest Ordinance represented no triumph of democracy or self-government. The negative attitude of the East toward the West—first apparent in the undermining of the Land Ordinance through company grants—was evident in the congressional distrust of western self-government. In fact, in an early instance of government in the hands of developers, Congress chose Arthur St. Clair, a prominent leader of the Ohio Company of Associates, to be the first governor of the Northwest Territory. The East seemed to demand that the West mature, throw off its frontier ways, and become heavily populated with easterners before being accepted as a full-fledged member of the national society. In the territorial phase the plan finally adopted was autocratic, reflecting eastern fears of violent mobs and frontier roughnecks that had been aroused by the Regulators, the Paxton Boys, and Daniel Shays.

Easterners never fully understood westerners and always held ambiguous attitudes toward them. "Heathen" Indians or Mexican "greasers," were beyond the pale, of course. But the antipathy often extended to American backwoodsmen, too. To some the man of the frontier was a magnificent, self-reliant hunter roaming the untrod forest wilderness, but to others he was lowdown, shiftless, lazy riffraff. Some of these ambiguities are apparent in the life and legend of Daniel Boone.

Boone was born on the Pennsylvania frontier in 1734, and when he was fifteen he migrated with his parents to the North Carolina backcountry. There he married a hearty pioneer woman named Rebecca Bryan. By all accounts she was a strong and commanding woman who in midlife stood nearly as tall and as broad as her husband and could handle an ax or a gun as well as most men. In the typical frontier division of labor, not only did she manage the household and raise their family of ten children, but she and the kids did practically all the farming, while Boone devoted himself to his occupation as a professional hunter and woodland guide, a pursuit that took him ever westward in search of game. As a teamster with General Braddock's army during the French and Indian War Boone heard tales of the beautiful bluegrass valleys of Kentucky, and by the late 1760s he found his way there and fell in love with the western country. In 1773 he tried to move his family across the mountains, but at the Cumberland Gap Indians attacked, killing his oldest son and turning the party back. Two years later he led another attempt, this one part of the grand colonization scheme of the North Carolina land speculator Richard Henderson. Boone helped build Boonesborough and brought his family and others to settle the bluegrass, but Henderson's company failed and Boone lost the lands promised him. During the colonies' struggle for independence he was captured and held hostage by the Shawnee allies of the British, and in 1778 he proved his frontier skills by escaping from

Daniel Boone kills a bear and escapes from the Indians. From Timothy Flint, The First White Man of the West; or, The Life and Exploits of Col. Dan'l Boone . . . *(Cincinnati, 1854). Yale University.*

the Indians and leading the defense of besieged Boonesborough, earning a reputation as one of the frontier heroes of the Revolution.

After the war Kentucky became the new "land of promise, flowing with milk and honey," where "you shall eat bread without scarceness and not lack any thing," in the words of schoolmaster John Filson, whose promotional tract of 1784 convinced thousands of settlers to head west over the Cumberland Gap in the Appalachians. The stories told about Kentucky had been told before about Pennsylvania, Virginia, and North Carolina, and they would be told again about later Wests. There was the tale about the productivity of the soil—corn would yield twenty bushels to the acre if it was planted and cultivated carefully, ten bushels if it was planted and neglected, and seven bushels if it wasn't planted at all. "What a Buzzel is amongst People about Kentuck," wrote a Virginia minister. "To hear people speak of it one Would think it was a new found Paradise." Like hundreds of others, Daniel Boone staked claims to thousands of acres of bluegrass. Such desires to engross land were typical. The frontiersman Simon Kenton, one of Boone's contemporaries in Kentucky, wounded nearly to death from Indian torture, returned almost immediately to begin plans for claiming new lands. But the claims of Boone—and Kenton, and many others—

proved defective, and Boone grew unhappy with Kentucky. He and his large extended family crossed the Mississippi and settled in Spanish Missouri in 1799. He lived the rest of his life near Saint Charles on the Missouri River, working as a hunter until he died in 1820.[12]

Americans would have remembered none of this if John Filson hadn't included a stirring account of Boone's adventures in his book on Kentucky, presenting him as a pathfinder, "an instrument ordained to settle the wilderness." Others saw him differently, however. A missionary in North Carolina complained that Boone did "little of the work" around his farm but left it to his wife and children. "There are many hunters here who work little," he wrote, and "live like the Indians." Boone and pioneers like him were refugees, "placing themselves at a distance from the deceit and turbulence of the world," as literary romantic Henry Marie Brackenridge wrote in 1814. Still others argued that Boone was a misanthrope, a man who, as one critic put it, wanted "to live as remote as possible from every white inhabitant." Thus Boone could be different things to different people. Was Boone a lazy drifter or a truly free man?[13]

—————

During the 1780s and early 1790s there was no respite from the fighting along the Ohio River, and the continuing violence claimed the lives of thousands of Indians and pioneers. The cause of the fighting was no mystery. From just a few hundred American settlers at the beginning of the Revolution, by 1785 the population of Kentucky stood at thirty thousand; it had grown to nearly ninety thousand by the time it was admitted as a state in 1792. Without waiting for the official opening of lands of the Northwest Territory, and making no distinction between the public domain and Indian homelands, pioneers began to press north across the Ohio, squatting and settling illegally. This incursion, combined with the arrogance of the new nation's "conquest" theory—that natives possessed no rights to land because they were a conquered people—sent the Indians of the Ohio valley a clear message: the Americans were about to dispossess them of their lands.

The Ohio Indians included native inhabitants who had lived there for centuries, like the Miamis and the Potawatomies, as well as Delawares, Shawnees, and Mingos, newcomers from Pennsylvania and New York who moved west to escape violent conflicts with Americans. They built communities of log cabins in the woods, cleared forests for their fields of corn and beans, grazed their herds of horses and cattle in the meadows, and hunted in the woods, very much like the American settlers in Tennessee and Kentucky. In the late 1780s native and newcomer Indians formed a defensive confederacy with a council fire at Detroit, where they were encouraged and supplied by the British. Joseph Brant and other Canadian Iroquois—the bitter lessons of the Revolution still fresh—became the principal spokesmen for pan-

Indian unity at Detroit. The Indians east of the Appalachians had lost their lands, one Iroquois chief declared, because they had fought one another instead of uniting against the Europeans. The Americans, by contrast, had succeeded because of "the unanimity they were prudent enough to preserve, and consequently none of the divided efforts of our ancestors to oppose them had any effect."[14]

There was considerable irony here, for advocates of union among the colonies, and later the states, frequently cited the Iroquois as their model of unity. "It would be a strange thing," declared Benjamin Franklin, "if Six Nations of Ignorant savages should be capable of forming such a union and be able to execute it in such a manner that it has subsisted for ages, and appears indissoluble, and yet a like union should be impracticable for ten or a dozen English colonies." During the Revolution an American delegation to the Iroquois thanked them for their example: "The Six Nations are a wise people. Let us hearken to them and take their counsel, and teach our children to follow it. . . . Divided, a single man may destroy you; united, you are a match for the whole world."[15]

Now, speaking to the Ohio Indians, the Iroquois chiefs urged the emulation of American political models. Let us profit by their example, the Iroquois spokesman continued, "and be unanimous, let us have a just sense of our own value. And, if after that, the Great Spirit wills that other colors should subdue us—let it be—we then cannot reproach ourselves for misconduct." All the Indians of the Ohio country must "eat out of one bowl with one spoon," Joseph Brant told them. "Whilst we remain disunited, every inconvenience attends us. The Interest of any one Nation should be Interests of us all, the welfare of the one should be the welfare of all the others." Thus as Americans were uniting under a new constitution, the Ohio confederacy was agreeing to the principle that all Indians, whatever their tribe, held their lands in common and that unanimous consent of all would be necessary to cede any part of it. They demanded that the United States accept the Ohio River as the boundary between the Indians and the Americans.[16]

When George Washington assumed office as the first president of the new federal government, the troubled West was the most pressing problem facing him. The western Indian confederacy seemed unified and determined. Great Britain continued to maintain a force of at least a thousand troops at northwestern posts like Detroit, from where they managed the fur trade and supplied the Indians with guns and ammunition. Spain also encouraged and supplied native resistance to the expansion of American settlements in the South, refusing to accept the territorial settlement of the Treaty of Paris and claiming that the northern boundary of Florida extended all the way to the Ohio River. The Spanish secretly employed a number of prominent westerners, including George Rogers Clark and General James Wilkinson, as informants and spies.

Washington and his secretary of war Henry Knox knew that the attempt to en-

Facsimile of federal peace medallion presented to Seneca chief Red Jacket in 1792. From Red Jacket *(Buffalo, 1885). Beinecke.*

GEORGE WASHINGTON
PRESIDENT.
1792.

force an American "right of conquest" had failed, and in desperation they put to-gether a new approach that would set the terms and tone of American Indian policy during the first half-century of the young republic. Actually the language of the Northwest Ordinance of 1787 had first signaled this departure. "The utmost good faith shall always be observed towards the Indians," it read; "their lands and property shall never be taken from them without their consent; and in their property, rights, and liberty, they shall never be invaded or disturbed, unless in just and lawful wars authorized by Congress." This amounted to a rejection of the conquest theory of In-dian relations and a recognition of the independent character of Indian tribes.[17]

These sentiments became law in the Indian Intercourse Act of 1790, the basic law regulating "trade and intercourse with the Indian tribes." The act created a legal dis-tinction between the territorial jurisdiction of the states and that region known as Indian country, a concept taken directly from the Royal Proclamation of 1763. Indians residing within the territory of the United States were not citizens of the Re-public but rather subjects of their own nations, nations enjoying jurisdiction over their own homelands, with their own government and laws. Indian nations, in other words, retained much of their original sovereignty, with the exception that they were not permitted to engage in "state-to-state" relations, neither with the individual states nor with foreign governments—the British in Canada or the Spanish in Florida and Louisiana. Establishing and maintaining relations between the United States and the Indian nations would be achieved through treaty-making. The power to make treaties was detailed in the Constitution—the president was vested with the authority to negotiate them, while the Senate was given the power to approve or reject them. [18]

Typical was the first Indian treaty negotiated by the Washington administration, with "the Creek Nation of Indians" in 1790. In exchange for Creek cessions of land and an acknowledgment that they were "to be under the protection of the United States of America, and of no other sovereign whosoever," the federal government pledged itself to protect the boundaries of the Creek Nation and acknowledged the Indians' right to punish "as they please" Americans who invaded their boundaries or violated their laws.[19]

The Indian Intercourse Act of 1790 also declared that it was official federal policy "to promote civilization among the friendly Indian tribes." The president was authorized to furnish them "with useful domestic animals, and implements of husbandry" in order to encourage their transformation into farmers. Henry Knox believed that only when Indians acquired "love for exclusive property" could they become good citizens of the Republic. Moreover, to eliminate unscrupulous abuses, the federal government created a licensing system for traders and authorized the creation of subsidized federal trading posts (called "factories") in Indian country, where Indians could obtain goods at fair and reasonable prices. The Congress also soon began an attempt to curtail the destructive flow of alcohol to the Indians. Unfortunately, because these programs were never adequately funded with many tribes, they never really started.[20]

To be sure, there were enormous contradictions in America's Indian policy. On one hand was the pledge to protect Indian homelands. On the other was the program to survey, sell, and create new political institutions in those very same lands. As Elliott West writes, "A policy that could make such promises, all within the same pair of documents, had moved beyond contradiction to schizophrenia." Yet the legal principles were more than simply hypocritical fictions. In the twentieth century many Indian tribes successfully appealed for the return of lands taken by states or private individuals in violation of the provisions of the Indian Intercourse Act. In the 1970s, for example, nearly two centuries after the fact, federal courts declared illegal the seizure of Penobscot and Passamaquoddy lands by the state of Massachusetts and awarded the native peoples of Maine a settlement of hundreds of thousands of acres of land and millions of dollars.[21]

Yet violent conflict, not "utmost good faith," characterized Indian-American relations in the Ohio country, where the growing population of settlers pressed ruthlessly against the rich farming lands held by Indian villagers. "Though we hear much of the Injuries and depredations that are committed by the Indians upon the

Little Turtle, Miami chief and war leader of the Ohio confederacy. Copy of a lost portrait by Gilbert Stuart, c. 1796. Indiana Historical Society Library.

Whites," wrote Governor St. Clair of Northwest Territory, "there is too much reason to believe that at least equal if not greater Injuries are done to the Indians by the frontier settlers of which we hear very little." According to one American officer, there was not a jury in the West who would punish a white man for these crimes. With provocations like these, the Ohio confederacy proved unable to restrain and coordinate the passions of its many members. Chiefs could not control their warriors as Indians struck back at Americans with equally indiscriminate violence.[22]

One of the most important leaders of the Ohio confederacy was Little Turtle, a brilliant war chief of the Miamis. In the fall of 1790, an American expeditionary force led by General Josiah Harmar invaded the Ohio country, but Little Turtle trapped the army and badly defeated him. The British, encouraged by this victory, began the construction of Fort Miami in the Maumee valley west of Lake Erie, well within the region ceded to the United States at the end of the Revolution. Meanwhile the Spanish closed the port of New Orleans to American commerce, threatening to choke off economic development. For the infant federal government, the future of the nation was at stake.

In November 1791 the Americans once again invaded the Ohio country, this time with a large but poorly trained army under the command of the governor of the Northwest Territory, Arthur St. Clair. Little Turtle's Indian forces subjected them to a terrible and humiliating defeat. With a loss of more than nine hundred American dead and wounded, this would go down as the single worst defeat of an American army by Indian warriors, a far more serious loss than the famous defeat of General George Armstrong Custer at the Little Bighorn in 1876.

Knowing that he required a dramatic victory in the West, Washington now committed over 80 percent of the federal government's operating budget to a massive campaign against the western Indians and appointed General Anthony Wayne to lead a greatly strengthened American force to subdue the Ohio confederacy and secure the Northwest. On August 20, 1794, at the Maumee villages, three thousand troops under "Mad Anthony" (as Wayne was known to his men, who suffered under his fierce discipline) engaged the Indian forces under Little Turtle. The Indians drove back the first wave of Americans, inflicting heavy casualties. But as the warriors advanced to take advantage, Wayne brought up his reserves, overwhelming and outflanking them. Indian warriors scrambled for the protection of Fort Miami, but the British officers, thinking better of an engagement with a superior American force, closed and barred the gates, and Wayne directed his men to pick off the fleeing warriors. The Battle of Fallen Timbers was a decisive defeat for the Ohio confederacy and an important victory for the United States. Realizing that they could no longer count on British support, the confederacy fell apart. Hundreds of Indians joined kinsmen and women who had already left the Ohio and emigrated west across the Mississippi. Many of those who planned to remain now prepared to come to terms with the Americans.

The representatives of twelve Indian nations, led by Little Turtle, ceded a huge territory encompassing most of present-day Ohio, much of Indiana, and other enclaves in the Northwest, including the town of Detroit and the tiny village of Chicago. The strengthened American position in the West—as well as the rising threat of revolutionary France—encouraged the British to settle their differences with the Americans and withdraw from American soil. The next year the United States settled its boundary dispute with Spain, which agreed to grant Americans free navigation of the Mississippi River with the right to deposit goods at the port of New Orleans.

Defeated in wars of conquest, and suffering from the effects of colonization, the Indians of the trans-Appalachian West now had to learn to live under the dominating authority of the United States. Different peoples chose different paths, but many included forms of spiritual revitalization. When cultures seem overwhelmed, a prophet often emerges, offering a message of cultural salvation. In the late eighteenth century it happened first among the Iroquois.

Their frustration stemmed from their reduced homelands, mere fractions of the land they once held, and the previous half-century's awful toll on their people. Before the Revolution the British estimated Iroquois strength at about ten thousand, but by 1800, after the bloody warfare of those intervening years, their numbers had fallen to four thousand. Anthony Wallace has described the Iroquois communities of that era as "slums in the wilderness." Alcoholism and drunkenness were major

RED JACKET.
Seneca War Chief.

Philadelphia Published by E. C. Biddle

Red Jacket wears the Washington peace medal. Engraving based on a painting by Charles Bird King, from Thomas L. McKenney and James Hall, History of the Indian Tribes of North America . . . , 3 vols. *(Philadelphia, 1836–44). Beinecke.*

problems and there was economic despair as their hunting territory was severely constricted. "It appears to me," one Iroquois testified with tears rolling down his cheeks, "that the great Spirit is determined on our destruction."[23]

It was about this time that a group of enthusiastic Quakers appeared among the Iroquois. Preaching a message of Christian love, they set up schools and offered employment, and many Indians came under their influence. Iroquois leaders had different opinions on their presence. The Seneca chief Cornplanter came to believe in accommodation. "We are determined to try to learn your ways," he declared to one Quaker missionary. But Cornplanter was opposed by Red Jacket, leader of the Senecas' traditionalists. "You say that you are sent to instruct us how to worship the Great Spirit," he told a missionary, but "we also have a religion, which was given to our forefathers, and has been handed down to us, their children. We worship in that way. It teaches us to be thankful for all the favors we receive; to love each other, and to be united." The conflict between "progressives" and "traditionalists" that tore the Iroquois apart in the 1790s continues in many Indian communities today.[24]

It fell to a new leader to find a middle way. Handsome Lake had been a distinguished war leader of the Six Nations during the Revolution. But in the aftermath of defeat, like many other warriors he despaired and became an alcoholic. After a long bout of drinking in 1799 he fell into a coma, and his family thought him dead. But he finally awakened and began to preach a glorious message of renewal. His words were taken up by hundreds of followers, and within a generation the teachings of Handsome Lake had become a major force of reform within the Six Nations. Urging a return to the ancient rites and rituals of the people, Handsome Lake seemed to be a traditionalist. But he also advocated that Iroquois men forsake hunting and take up farming and that women give up their traditional power within Iroquois society.

Handsome Lake's followers thus tried to emulate their American neighbors in many things, but they gathered in traditional longhouses for their services. The "Longhouse Religion," as it came to be called, combined Iroquois spirituality with the values of Quaker Christianity: temperance, nonviolence, frugality, an emphasis on personal good and evil. The Bible found a place within the longhouse alongside more traditional Iroquois oral texts and teachings. Although the Longhouse Religion did not solve the Iroquois problem of living as a colonized people, it restored their self-respect and gave them the means to revitalize their culture.

The Indians who remained in the Ohio country after the American conquest were besieged by many of the same problems as the Iroquois. There, too, an Indian prophet arose to point the way to a revitalized future. He was a Shawnee and, like Handsome Lake, a dissolute alcoholic; in a drunken stupor he had once poked out his own eye. One day in 1805 he collapsed into a trance so deep that his family feared

Tenskwatawa, the Shawnee Prophet. From James Otto Lewis, The Aboriginal Port-Folio . . . *(Philadelphia, 1835–36). Beinecke.*

he had died. But he awoke and told them that the Master of Life had sent him back from the dead to lead the Indians to redemption. He took the name Tenskwatawa, meaning "The Open Door." Among Americans he became known as the Shawnee Prophet.

Tenskwatawa's teaching focused on the decline of traditional values and mores. He condemned alcohol as "the white man's poison." He told his followers that they must abandon white ways—including clothing, tools, and weapons—and return to the traditions of the people, demonstrating a keen understanding of the dangers of economic dependency. His emphasis on the rejection of colonial ways marked an important difference with the Longhouse Religion, yet the new rituals of the Shawnee Prophet also showed the influence of Christianity. In a brilliant adaptation of Christian imagery he preached that all the Indians who followed him would be wonderfully rewarded in the afterlife but that all the bad Indians would join the Americans in a hell of fire and brimstone—an image surely borrowed from frontier preachers of the day. Here was a shrewd man. Once, in an attempt to undercut the growth of the revitalization movement, Governor William Henry Harrison of the Northwest Territory urged the Ohio Indians to insist on a demonstration of Tenskwatawa's power. "If he is really a prophet, ask of him to cause the sun to stand still," Harrison dared; if he accomplished such a feat "you may then believe he has been sent from God." Taking up Harrison's challenge, on June 16, 1806, Tenskwatawa assembled his followers and declared that he would darken the sun. In a delicious reversal of the classic explorer's trick, he exploited his knowledge of the total eclipse predicted for that day, and meeting Harrison's standard he instantly converted hundreds. By 1809 Tenskwatawa's large following was living in a new multitribal Indian community called Prophetstown at a place called Tippecanoe near the Wabash River.[25]

Tenskwatawa's opponents within the Indian world of the Ohio were progressives like Little Turtle, the Miami chief who had led the fight against the Americans but now argued for accommodation. American officials supported the progressives but responded as well to the demands of white settlers and pressed for more cessions of the diminishing Indian homelands. William Henry Harrison, the new governor of the Northwest Territory, forced accommodationist chiefs like Little Turtle to sign away more than three million acres. Thus the federal government undercut the progressives and increased the appeal of Tenskwatawa's traditionalist message.

Joining the prophet at Tippecanoe was his brother Tecumseh, a traditionalist Shawnee chief who adopted his brother's religious vision and used it to fight the progressives. Tecumseh was a remarkable man, a brilliant orator with a powerful understanding of the Indians' tragic history. "Where today are the Pequot?" he asked his followers. "Where are the Narragansett, the Mohican, the Pokanoket, and many other once powerful tribes of our people? They have vanished before the avarice and oppression of the white man, as snow before a summer sun." Tecumseh worked to rebuild the Ohio confederation, in ruins after the Battle of Fallen Timbers, and he even traveled among the tribes of the South with his message of united opposition to American expansion. "Let the white race perish!" he thundered before an assembly of Creeks. "They seize your land; they corrupt your women; they trample on the bones of your dead! Back whence they came, upon a trail of blood, they must be driven! Back—aye, back to the great water whose accursed waves brought them to our shores! Burn their dwellings—destroy their stock—slay their wives and children, that the very breed may perish. War now! War always! War on the living! War on the dead!"[26]

In 1810 Tecumseh and a delegation of chiefs and warriors from Prophetstown came to Harrison's headquarters at Vincennes to proclaim their intention of keeping federal surveyors off the lands recently ceded by treaty. The Great Spirit, he told Harrison, intended the land to be "the common property of all the tribes"; it could not be sold "without the consent of all." Traditionalist Indians by the hundreds were drawn to the banner of the two brothers—the classic combination of religious prophet and political leader—and Harrison feared their growing power. In the fall of 1811, while Tecumseh was organizing in the South, Harrison attacked Prophetstown. The Battle of Tippecanoe did not defeat the traditionalists, but it began the war in earnest. "What other course is left for us to pursue," wrote Harrison, "but to make a war of extirpation upon them."[27]

As the United States and Great Britain moved closer to war over maritime problems in the Atlantic, the British again adopted the policy of using the western Indians to destabilize the young republic. They supplied Tecumseh and his followers, and

Tecumseh confronts Gov. William Henry Harrison of Northwest Territory, 1810. Engraving by W. Ridgeway, c. 1850. Cincinnati Museum Center.

encouraged them to think that the British supported the creation of an Indian republic in the Great Lakes region. In 1812 the United States once again went to war against the British. Ostensibly the objective was to maintain American maritime rights. But the congressional "War Hawks" were mostly interested in expanding into British territory under the cover of the conflict. The Canadian campaign, however, was a fiasco, resulting in the surrender of Detroit to the British in 1812 and the sack and burning of Buffalo, New York, by the Canadians the next year. By 1814 the British were in complete control of the Atlantic coast. In retaliation for the American burning of the Canadian city of York (modern Toronto), British troops invaded Washington, D.C., and burned nearly all the public buildings, including the Capitol and the president's house (which became known as the White House when it was rebuilt and freshly painted after the war). Preoccupied with the struggle against Napoleonic France, however, Great Britain agreed to settle the conflict without consolidating its gains.

If the war's outcome was a wash for the United States and Great Britain, it was a disaster for the Indians of the Northwest. The hopes of the traditionalist followers of Tecumseh turned to ashes in 1813, early in the conflict, when they were defeated at the Battle of the Thames, northeast of Detroit. Compounding the damage, Tecumseh himself was killed. Tenskwatawa lived until the 1820s, but he had lost his power as a prophet.

_____

The Cherokees provide a final example of the revitalization movements that swept through the Indian nations of the trans-Appalachian West during the first decades of the nineteenth century. After the Revolution the Cherokees were devastated. Like that of the Iroquois the conflict had taken on aspects of civil war, with the people divided and fighting one another. Patriots had invaded the Cherokee towns and burned them to the ground. Hundreds were killed.

In the aftermath, men of mixed ancestry such as Major Ridge and John Ross, the sons of native mothers and American traders, claimed leadership of the nation. These leaders were enthusiastic supporters of the federal Indian "civilization" program established by the Washington administration. They owned land and slaves and sought to transform their tribe into a modern nation along the lines of the American states. But these new ways ran afoul of traditional Cherokee values. It was impossible to run a store or a plantation, as many of these leaders did, without violating traditional ethics of sharing. Chiefs had always distributed their possessions freely, a system historian William McLoughlin called "upside down capitalism." But the new leadership practiced real capitalism.[28]

In the years surrounding the War of 1812 traditionalists among the Cherokees and other Indian nations in the Southeast rallied to the cause of Tecumseh. Prophets arose who echoed the language of Tenskwatawa. Among the Cherokees there was a visionary named Tsali, who preached to the people to "get the white men out of the country and go back to your former ways." He was upset by the new values of the mixed-blood leadership. "Kill the cattle, destroy the spinning wheels and looms, throw away your plows, and everything used by the Americans," he thundered.[29]

The conflict between progressives and traditionalists was swept into the turmoil of the War of 1812. A large faction of Tecumseh supporters among the Creek Nation, known as the Red Sticks, went to war against American settlers, attacking and killing most of the five hundred men, women, and children held up in Fort Mims on the Tombigbee River. In retaliation, Andrew Jackson, commander of the Tennessee militia, led an army of two thousand against the Creek militants. He was joined by the progressive Cherokee leaders and their followers, which turned the campaign into something of a civil war among Indians. In March 1814, at the Battle of Horseshoe Bend, Jackson's combined force defeated the Red Sticks, killing more than eight hundred. Jackson went on to repulse a British invasion at New Orleans, the only major American victory of the war.

The slaughter at Horseshoe Bend so disgusted traditionalist Cherokees that many of them left the traditional Cherokee homeland in the southern Appalachians, moving westward across the Mississippi and settling on the Arkansas River. But rather than take this as rejection, the progressive leadership exploited the exodus to proclaim themselves the true defenders of Cherokee nationalism. "I scorn this movement of a few men to unsettle the nation, and trifle with our attachment to the land of our forefathers," declared head chief Major Ridge to a large assembly of his people. In the battle for the hearts and minds of the Cherokees, Ridge and the progressives were ultimately the more successful. Underlying this success was the fact that during the preceding two decades a substantial minority, if not a majority, of the Cherokees had taken up farming and slave ownership like the progressives, were selling their goods in the market, and had begun to accumulate homes and possessions.[30]

Led by Ridge, the Cherokee Nation emerged from the War of 1812 in a strengthened condition. To a greater extent than any other Indian nation or tribe in North America, the Cherokees took the early Indian policy of the United States at its word and fulfilled its most extravagant expectations. With the assurance of federal protection of their homeland and their sovereignty, the Cherokees listened to their agents and missionaries, took up the Americans' economic system, and modeled their government on the institutions of the United States. The nation built a new capital at Echota, elected a representative assembly, and codified their laws. Missionaries introduced education and the leading men of the nation became literate in English.

Perhaps the best symbol of this Cherokee renaissance was the invention by a man named Sequoyah (his English name was George Guess) of a written phonetic system for spoken Cherokee—the first writing system to be invented by a North American Indian. Sequoyah was a traditionalist who had removed to the Arkansas River, and he was seeking a way to communicate with kith and kin back home in the Cherokee Nation. His syllabary proved very easy for Cherokees to learn, and it immediately caught on. Within a few years of its invention, a majority of Cherokees both in the West and in the nation had learned to read and write using Sequoyah's system. Literacy rates among the Cherokees were higher than among their American neighbors. "Guess's alphabet is spreading through the nation like wildfire," wrote an admiring missionary. The nation set up its own newspaper, the *Cherokee Phoenix,* published in both English and Sequoyan.[31]

In a remarkable talk given before a white audience, Elias Boudinot, the Cherokee editor of the *Cherokee Phoenix,* addressed himself to the revitalization and renaissance of his people. "There is, in Indian history, something very melancholy," he told them. "We have seen everywhere the poor aborigines melt away before the approach of the white population." But the Cherokees intended to write a new chapter. "I can view my native country, rising from the ashes of her degradation, wearing her puri-

Sequoyah and his Cherokee syllabary. Engraving by A. T. Bewens, 1836. National Anthropological Archives, Smithsonian Institution.

fied and beautiful garments, and taking her seat with the nations of the earth." How would the United States answer? "I ask you," he concluded, "shall red men live, or shall they be swept from the earth? Must they perish? Let humanity answer."[32]

FURTHER READING

Stephen Aron, *How the West Was Lost: The Transformation of Kentucky from Daniel Boone to Henry Clay* (1996)

Colin G. Calloway, *The American Revolution in Indian Country: Crisis and Diversity in Native American Communities* (1995)

Andrew Cayton, *The Frontier Republic: Ideology and Politics in the Ohio Country, 1780–1825* (1986)

R. David Edmunds, *The Shawnee Prophet* (1983), and *Tecumseh and the Quest for Indian Leadership* (1984)

John Mack Faragher, *Daniel Boone: The Life and Legend of an American Pioneer* (1992)

Isabel Thompson Kelsay, *Joseph Brant, 1743–1807: Man of Two Worlds* (1984)

William G. McLoughlin, *Cherokee Renascence in the New Republic* (1986)

Peter S. Onuf, *Statehood and Union: A History of the Northwest Ordinance* (1987)

Francis Paul Prucha, *The Great Father: The United States Government and the American Indians* (1984)

Roy M. Robbins, *Our Landed Heritage: The Public Domain, 1776–1936*, rev. ed. (1976)

Malcolm J. Rohrbough, *The Trans-Appalachian Frontier: People, Societies, and Institutions, 1775–1850* (1978)

John Sugden, *Tecumseh: A Life* (1997)

David Szatmary, *Shays' Rebellion: The Making of an Agrarian Insurrection* (1980)

Anthony F. C. Wallace, *The Death and Rebirth of the Seneca* (1969)

5

The Fur Trade

Nothing proved more important to the American nation than the frequent addition of large tracts of the North American continent: the gain of trans-Appalachia in the peace settlement at the close of the Revolution, the purchase of Louisiana, the seizure of Florida, the annexation of Texas and the Oregon country, the conquest of northern Mexico. This history of expansion was unparalleled in the modern world.

James Madison, "the father of the Constitution," placed expansion at the heart of the American political system. "Extend the sphere," he argued, "and you make it less probable that a majority of the whole will have a common motive to invade the rights of other citizens." American republican government was thus tied to an ever-expanding system, to what Madison called "one great, respectable, and flourishing empire." George Washington also envisioned the United States as a "rising empire," a growing, expanding sovereign state. The American people, he asserted, were "placed in the most enviable condition as the sole Lords and Proprietors of a vast Tract of Continent, comprehending all the various soils and climates of the World. They are, from this period, to be considered as the Actors on a most conspicuous Theatre." Many Americans entertained similar continental ambitions. "The Mississippi was never designed as the western boundary of the American empire," declared Jedediah Morse in *American Geography*, the popular textbook he published in 1789, the year the Constitution was ratified. "It is well known that empire has been traveling from east to west. Probably her last and broadest seat will be America, . . . the largest empire that ever existed. . . . We cannot but anticipate the period, as not far distant, when the AMERICAN EMPIRE will comprehend millions of souls west of the Mississippi."[1]

American expansion moved from pipe dream to policy with President Thomas Jefferson's purchase of Louisiana from France, which historian Bernard De Voto called "one of the most important events in world history." Louisiana irrevocably turned the nation's eyes westward, brought it incalculable natural wealth, and insured the emergence of the United States as a world power. This acquisition was the beginning of the American continental empire. At first Jefferson did not appear to envision the importance of the great West to the nation. In his first inaugural address in 1801 he expressed the opinion that the nation already possessed "a chosen country, with room enough for our descendants to the thousandth and thousandth generation." Yet his interest in the West was deep and long-standing. "For Jefferson, more than any other major figure in the revolutionary generation, the West was America's future," writes biographer Joseph Ellis, "America's fountain of youth." In 1793 Jefferson had contributed funds to the Frenchman André Michaux, who planned a western botanical expedition. He listened sympathetically to a young dreamer by the name of John Ledyard, who proposed an expedition to the West. Then, one month before his inauguration, Jefferson asked Meriwether Lewis to prepare for a major western exploration.[2]

This expedition would travel through territory claimed by European empires. In 1762, before the treaty with Great Britain that concluded the French and Indian War, France had transferred its claim on Louisiana to Spain. The boundaries of this huge cession were vague, but they were generally understood to begin at the Mississippi on the east (but including the city of New Orleans on the east bank of the delta), following the northern border of Spanish Texas on the south, extending to the sources of the Mississippi on the north, and reaching the crest of the Rocky Mountains on the west. During the years they controlled New Orleans, the Spanish periodically made clear their hostility to the new American republic by closing the port to American shipping on the Mississippi. Westerners were certain that the economic development of the West depended on continued access to the Gulf via the Mississippi, and after long negotiations Spain agreed in 1795 to reopen the port to the United States.

But soon American concerns shifted to France. Napoléon Bonaparte, the new French leader, had New World imperial dreams of his own, envisioning a revived empire that would unify France's Caribbean colonies with the mainland colony of Louisiana. In 1800 Napoléon invaded and defeated Spain and dictated a peace treaty transferring Louisiana back to French control. At first the treaty of cession was kept secret, and Americans heard of it only by rumor, but a few months into his presidency Jefferson became fully aware of the terms. Justly concerned about continued American access to New Orleans, he sent an American delegation to France to negotiate for the purchase of the port. In the knowledge that French intelligence was monitoring his diplomatic correspondence, the president dropped broad threats of the consequences of renewed French imperialism in North America. "The day that

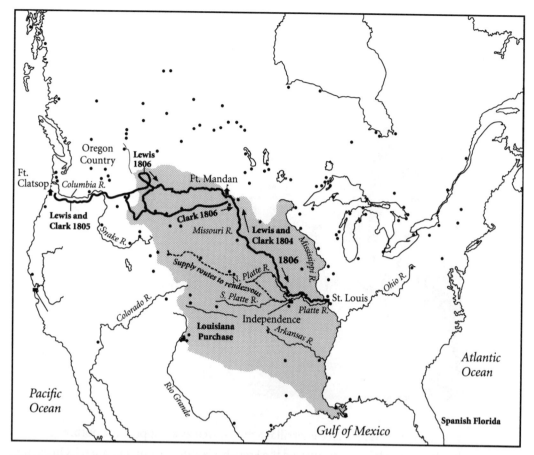

THE LOUSIANA PURCHASE AND THE FUR TRADE

France takes possession of New Orleans," he wrote, "we must marry ourselves to the British fleet and nation."[3]

Napoléon did not abandon his imperial plans because of this hollow threat but rather because of the revolt of the Haitians, led by the revolutionary François-Dominique Toussaint, one of the era's great generals. Born a plantation slave, Toussaint acquired enough education to read the writings of revolutionary Frenchmen as well as Julius Caesar's account of his conquests. When Haiti's slaves rebelled against their French masters in 1790, he rose to leadership, taking the name L'Ouverture, "The Opener." By 1798 the Haitians had thrown out their former French masters and installed L'Ouverture as governor for life. There was quiet panic throughout the slaveholding world. Napoleon sent twenty thousand troops to oppose L'Ouverture's eight-thousand-man army. Unwilling to support L'Ouverture publicly for fear of inspiring the hopes among slaves in their own South (and on their own plantations!), Jefferson and his Secretary of State James Madison nevertheless attempted to frustrate the French by encouraging a secret flow of supplies to the

Captain Meriwether Lewis. *Watercolor by Charles B. J. F. Saint Memin, c. 1807.* © *Collection of The New-York Historical Society.*

Haitian rebels. With fierce guerrilla tactics as well as an opportune outbreak of yellow fever, the Haitians decimated the French. Captured by his enemies, L'Ouverture died in a miserable dungeon, but his followers fought on. By early 1803 it had become clear that the Haitians had successfully defended their independence, and Napoléon decided to cut his losses. His attention had begun to center on Europe, and even for a man as ambitious as Napoléon one continent at a time was enough.

In April 1803 the American negotiators in Paris were shocked when French foreign minister Talleyrand suddenly asked, "What will you give for the whole?" The Americans cautiously asked what the boundaries of "the whole" might be. "Whatever it was we took from Spain," the minister answered with a shrug. The Americans offered fifteen million dollars (perhaps the equivalent of two hundred million dollars today), an incredible deal, only slightly more than they had been prepared to offer for New Orleans alone. "You have made a noble bargain for yourselves," Talleyrand declared at the conclusion of the negotiations. "And I suppose you will make the most of it."[4]

Jefferson intended to do just that. His interest in far western exploration now assumed new meaning, even urgency. The expedition, commanded jointly by Meriwether Lewis and William Clark, became the most illustrious exploring party in American history. Much has been made of Jefferson's scientific intentions—the investigation of the botany, zoology, and geology of the unknown regions of the West—and they were clearly important to both the president and to Lewis. But most important were the expedition's economic objectives, for the incorporation of this vast tract of continent into the nation hinged on finding a way to exploit it. Jefferson hoped that his explorers would open an easy route across the continent by waterway, even though some of it would cross foreign soil. Such a route could redirect the lucrative fur trade of western Canada into American channels. Corollary gains included more effective ways to exploit the sea otter trade of the northern Pacific coast and through that means establish commercial connections with China. The friendship of the native nations was essential to these goals, and thus Indian diplomacy was also high on the explorers' agenda.

In the spring of 1804 the company pushed off from its base camp on the Illinois side of the Mississippi, across from the mouth of the Missouri. The forty men made up a motley crew: backwoodsmen of British or Irish descent, métis of mixed ancestry, and Lewis's black slave York. As they rowed up the Missouri they passed communities more motley still: towns of French-speaking Creoles and métis who had lived here since the mid-eighteenth century, villages of emigrant Indians more recently displaced from the Ohio valley, and clusters of recent arrivals from the American backwoods, like old Daniel Boone himself, who lived surrounded by his kith and kin on the north side of the Missouri about fifty miles west of Saint Louis.

It took all summer to ascend the Missouri to the earth lodge villages of the Mandan and Minnetaree Indians in what is now central North Dakota. These Indians were farming people whose towns were trading centers for the northern Great Plains. The Americans found French traders living among them with Indian wives and métis children. Frenchmen had been visiting the Mandans since 1738, when the party of fur trader Pierre de La Vérendrye arrived, part of a wave of French traders pushing westward from the Great Lakes. Lewis warned them off, announcing, "This is now American territory." But a number of the resident traders hired on to the expedition as interpreters, and one, Toussaint Charbonneau, offered the interpretive skills of one of his wives, a fifteen-year-old Shoshone captive named Sacajawea. She became the only woman to accompany the expedition over the mountains to the Pacific. "The sight of this Indian woman," wrote Clark, convinced the Indians "of our friendly intentions, as no woman ever accompanies a war party of Indians in this quarter."[5]

The winter the Americans spent with the Mandans and Minnetarees introduced them to the complicated world of the Great Plains, a region that had been transformed over the preceding century. Soon after the Pueblo Revolt in 1680, horses stolen from the Spanish settlements had found their way through the Indian trad-

The Mandan village on the Missouri River. From George Catlin, Catalogue of Catlin's Indian Gallery of Portraits . . . *(New York, 1837). Beinecke.*

ing network to the tribes living on the southern fringe of the plains. Horses, which Indians were soon breeding in great numbers, enabled hunters to exploit the huge buffalo herds of the plains much more efficiently, making possible a whole new way of life, an elaborate and distinctive nomadic culture. In the centuries preceding the European invasion of the Americas a prolonged drought had depopulated the plains, but the horse allowed Indian peoples to reclaim the arid North American heartland. Here is another of those fascinating ironies of frontier history. The first settlers of the Great Plains during the colonial era were not Europeans but Indians. And the mounted warrior of the plains—the ubiquitous and romantic symbol of native America—was in fact not an aboriginal character at all but one born from the colonial collision of cultures.

Although there were important differences among the nomadic peoples who settled the plains, they had much in common. They shared a material culture, all of them dependent upon the horse and the buffalo, all of them using the tepee, a snug and portable house that could be rolled up and easily transported. They also shared a way of looking at the world, a symbolic religious system derived from the ancient North American hunting tradition but focusing on the buffalo rather than the bear as the master of animals. Success in hunting and warfare they believed was an indication of great spiritual power. Many of them practiced the Sun Dance, in which young warriors tested themselves in rituals of self-torture. And in what had formerly been egalitarian societies, men who were particularly successful at the hunt began to accumulate large herds of horses. In classic plains Indian culture there were wealthy men with many horses and poor men with few. Here is yet another wonderful irony, for theirs was a world in which male talent was rewarded with material plenty and great status, the very values that such eighteenth-century Americans as Benjamin Franklin were declaring sacred.

The great social and cultural revolution introduced by the horse was of dubious value to native women on the plains. The new nomadic way of life was hardest on them, for aside from hunting and making war, they were required to do practically everything else. The rise of the trade in buffalo hides and robes meant an enormous increase in women's workload. It took about three days of constant labor to cure a single hide; and a great hunter might bring in a dozen hides from a successful hunt. Successful hunters not only acquired many horses but began to take many wives, for women were the primary producers of hides, and a hunter could trade only as many as his women could manufacture.

The basic social unit of these nomadic peoples of the plains was the hunting band. As bands moved, their allegiance and loyalty often shifted, and tribal identities emerged only gradually. The great tribes of western fame did not actually consolidate until their nineteenth-century confrontations with the expanding United States. But on the eighteenth-century Great Plains it was the Indians who were doing the expanding. Mounted peoples converged on the interior of the continent from all directions. The Comanches, for example, originated as a Shoshone people of the Great Basin. After adopting the horse, they migrated onto the plains, and over several generations they gradually moved southeastward toward present-day Oklahoma and Texas. The Comanches illustrate the enormous distance mounted nomads could travel, circulating within territories from five to seven hundred miles in diameter. Their numbers were never large, but because of their range and their ferocity they became legendary as the rulers of the southern plains, raiding Indian and Mexican villages from the Mississippi all the way west to the Rio Grande.

In the northern plains a number of nomadic groups contested one another for hunting space. The Crows first broke away from their mother group of farming peoples on the Missouri River around 1700. A little later the Cheyennes left their farming homeland in present-day Minnesota and also moved west. In the vicinity of the Black Hills these two groups met in violent clashes. Long before Europeans or Americans reached the plains the Crows and the Cheyennes had engaged in several generations of warfare. The migration of the Cheyennes was propelled by the competition of an even stronger and more populous people, the Lakotas. Before the era of the horse they, too, practiced hunting, gathering, and a little farming on the northern fringe of the plains, but as French traders pushed beyond the Great Lakes, their

Plains Indian pictogram on a buffalo robe. Watercolor copy by Samuel Seymour, c. 1819. Beinecke.

Algonquian allies, the Ojibwas and Crees, went to war with the Lakotas, driving them west. Indeed, the name by which we generally know the Lakotas—the Sioux—is a French transliteration of an Algonquian word meaning "enemy." On the plains the Sioux pressed the attack against both Cheyennes and Crows in a decades-long struggle for control of the territory surrounding the Black Hills. By the late eighteenth century they were the most powerful mounted group on the northern plains.

Nomads such as the Sioux existed in an uneasy but necessary relationship with the Mandans, the Minnetarees, and other village peoples of the river valleys like the Pawnees and the Wichitas. These villagers also adopted the horse and took up buffalo hunting, but they also continued to farm. Soon their earth lodge villages became the shopping centers of the eighteenth-century plains. Nomads with their buffalo robes came to bargain not only for food but for the European goods that found their way to the villages in the packs of French traders or via the convoluted but effective Indian trading network. Villagers also became a target for periodic nomadic raiding, although the mounted warriors were careful not to destroy what they could not live without. The Lewis and Clark expedition tensely encountered a band of Sioux just before reaching the Mandan towns, and when the Mandans requested American help in defending against Sioux raids the Americans were sympathetic. "We were ready to protect them," wrote Clark, "and kill those who would not listen to our Good talk." Thus from the first moment the expanding Americans entered into the world of the plains, they willingly counterpoised themselves against the most powerful of the nomadic peoples.[6]

The company constructed "Fort Mandan" and spent the winter among the villagers, becoming part of its social life. There were dances and joint hunting parties, frequent visits to the earth lodges, long talks around the fire, and, for many of the men, pleasant nights spent in the arms of Mandan women. When the party departed in the spring Clark wrote (with his usual atrocious spelling) that the members of the company were "generally helthy except for Venerials Complaints which is verry Common amongst the natives and the men Catch it from them."[7]

Following charts and maps drawn with the help of their Mandan friends, the company followed the Missouri and Jefferson rivers to the continental watershed ("the distant fountain of the waters"). Obtaining crucial horses from Sacajawea's Shoshone relatives, they reached the westward-flowing Snake River and followed it to its junction with the Columbia. Finally, in the rainy November of 1805 they stood on the shores of the Pacific in present-day Oregon. After a difficult and depressing winter, they largely retraced their route, and in September 1806 the hardened band returned, twenty-eight months after it had left.

Lewis and Clark left a great drama in the eight volumes of their journals. They brought back an incredible amount of scientific information, including descriptions of hundreds of species of fish, reptiles, mammals, birds, plants, and trees (as well as the preserved skins, bones, and horns of dozens of animals, and even live birds and prairie dogs). The journals featured Lewis's long-winded philosophizing on the future route of empire and the record of his diplomacy with the Indians, who on several occasions might have wiped the expedition from the record. Clark left a record of frontier know-how, something he shared with his brother, George Rogers Clark of Revolutionary fame. The journals detail the endurance of Sacajawea, who bore a baby along the way, a boy Clark loved and subsequently adopted. They document snow blindness and snakebite, and the one death that occurred from a burst appendix, a malady that would have been fatal anywhere. The journals were published in an unauthorized version in 1809, and an official edition followed five years later. They have inspired generations of Americans ever since.

Given the drama, was the trip worthwhile? The captains made contact with dozens of Indian tribes and distributed more than a hundred impressive silver peace medals and dozens of American flags. Despite the troubles with the Sioux, they

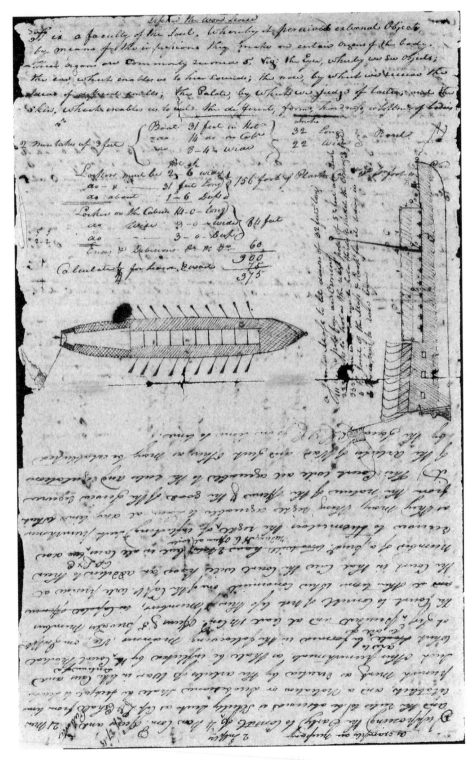

Page from William Clark's field notes of the Lewis and Clark expedition, January 18, 1804. Beinecke.

found most Indians anxious for allies against their expansionist neighbors as well as for better trading connections. But at best the commercial objectives of the expedition were only partly realized. They failed to find what Jefferson had declared the most important object of the exploration, a commercial route linking the waters of the Atlantic and the Pacific. The route that Lewis and Clark charted over the Rockies was impossibly hard going and practically useless.

In the long view the most important accomplishment was locking Louisiana territory securely into the minds and plans of the nation and associating the distant Oregon country so closely with it that Americans thereafter assumed it was their own preserve. Although another generation passed before American settlement poured into that part of the continent, the expedition aroused popular interest in the Far West. No other exploration was so influential, wrote Bernard De Voto. "It satisfied desire and it created desire: the desire of a westering nation."[8]

The Lewis and Clark expedition also set a pattern, establishing a precedent for a strong government role in the development of the American West. Theirs was the first American exploration mounted and pursued with government encouragement and financing. Historians have tended to overlook the basic preparations for westward expansion undertaken by the government—surveying the land, marking the routes, building the wagon roads, clearing the rivers for navigation, dredging the harbors along the coasts, planning and digging canals, subsidizing railroads, suppressing the protests of Indians, and in general standing close beside the pioneers as they elbowed their way to the Pacific.

———

After three centuries of operation, the fur trade continued to be one of the largest and most important commercial enterprises in North America. When Meriwether Lewis, upon his return in 1806, described the region of the upper Missouri River as "richer in beaver and otter than any country on earth," it seemed to suggest that trapping and trading might offer the greatest promise for the commercial exploitation of the huge new western territory of the nation.[9]

The fur trade depended on Indian labor—the work of male hunters and trappers and of Indian women who made jerky and pemmican (buffalo fat mixed with dried berries) and prepared hides and pelts. But the western fur trade of the day was controlled by two large combinations whose directors sat in London and Montreal. The Hudson's Bay Company, which the British monarchy chartered in 1670, held the exclusive right to the Indian trade over the whole watershed of Hudson's Bay. It coordinated a far-flung network of field directors and workers (*engagés*), supplying them with traps, horses, boats, food, whiskey, and trade goods for Indians, indicating the best routes for the largest returns, and preparing, collecting, warehousing, and distributing the pelts. The company was an example of centrally directed enterprise, even in the field, where the business operated out of forts or "factories," with Indians assigned to trapping and bringing the furs into the forts, where the engagés readied them for shipment. So great was the power and prestige of the company, it was said, that the initials "HBC" stamped on shipping boxes, invoices, and packs of furs stood for "Here Before Christ."

The HBC was locked in brutal competition with a newcomer, the North West Company, a Montreal partnership including French Canadian and Highland Scots traders that the British government chartered in 1784. Unlike the Hudson's Bay Company, the strategy of the North West Company was based on going where the furs were. The Nor'Westers, as these company men were called, built sustained ties with natives. They had a special spirit and manner about them, less bound by protocol and formula than Hudson's Bay men, more willing to risk all and venture far in pursuit of furs. In 1793, more than ten years before Lewis and Clark, Nor'Wester Alexander Mackenzie became the first European to reach the Pacific by way of the continental interior when Indians guided him down the maze of western Canadian rivers to the coast, where on a rock he inscribed: "Alexander Mackenzie, from Canada, by land, the twenty-second of July, one thousand seven hundred and ninety-three." Reading Mackenzie's published account of his journey was one of the factors that pushed Jefferson to send Lewis and Clark on their way.[10]

With all its color and flair, the North West Company was as natural a magnet for restless energies as the life of a cowboy would later be. One young spirit, John McLoughlin, as a boy in Quebec watched Nor'Westers swagger through the streets. His uncles, Alexander and Simon Fraser, were partners of the company. Sent to Scotland to become a medical doctor, McLoughlin dutifully finished his training, but returning to Canada in 1804, barely out of his teens, he became an apprentice Nor'Wester. He entered a world of relentless and rampant competition between the two rival companies. The lure of high profit was coupled with few controls, and relations with the Indians were subverted with empty promises and cheap whiskey. Finally, to curb the excesses of cutthroat competition, the British government forced the two companies to combine, and in 1821 the Nor'Westers were absorbed into the HBC. McLoughlin weathered the transition and became a partner. Convinced of McLoughlin's good judgment and devotion, the company named him in 1824 to the general superintendency of the far western Columbia River District.

Whether McLoughlin's flowing mane of prematurely white hair, a distinguishing characteristic, resulted from the stress of ambition no one can say; but his dignified appearance certainly did not hurt his rise to executive status. Ensconced in the Oregon country, he came to symbolize probity. Like most of his fur trade contemporaries, McLoughlin found intimate company among Indian women. In 1811 he

Dr. John McLoughlin, c. 1850. Oregon Historical Society.

married Marguerite Wadin, the métis widow of another trader. It was a lifelong relationship, and together they had four children. McLoughlin was representative of those traders who never wavered in their commitment to their native wives, and his children were proud of their métis heritage. The Indians respected him and it is said gave him the title White-Headed Eagle. Whether they used that term or not, McLoughlin was as proud and regal as the cloud-crested bird, and for more than twenty years he majestically dominated the region from his post at Fort Vancouver on the Columbia River.

The mouth of the Columbia had been the great western target of the only American who in the first decade of the nineteenth century rivaled the prosperity and power of the Canadian traders. John Jacob Astor was a stout, arrogant man who never lost the accent of his native Germany. As a young man he left his homeland and joined his brother in a small musical instrument shop in London. After the American Revolution Astor took all his worldly capital—seven flutes—and emigrated across the Atlantic. On the advice of a fellow traveler, he transferred his interests from flutes to furs and made his fortune organizing and exploiting the trade of the Northwest Territory after the British evacuation in 1795. He eventually became the richest man in America, with assets at the time of his death in 1848 of some twenty million dollars (the equivalent, perhaps, of four hundred million dollars today). Astor's was the first of the great American fortunes, and it was built on furs.

Astor was quick to exploit the Louisiana Purchase by forming the American Fur Company. He dreamed of a western empire controlled from a post on the Columbia, where pelts from the interior could be shipped to the Orient, exploiting the commercial link forged by Russian traders along the northern Pacific coast. In 1811 he sent a ship, the *Tonquin,* mounted with twelve guns and manned by thirty-three young Scots and Canadian voyageurs. To back them up Astor organized an overland expedition of fifty men. The two companies were to meet at the mouth of the Columbia and construct the fortified post of "Astoria." Astor invested nearly two hundred thousand dollars in the scheme, an amount he considered not excessive if it came to fruition. Influential Americans were ebullient about his plans. "I view it as the germ of a great, free, and independent empire on that side of our continent," Jefferson gushed in a letter to Astor, "liberty and self-government, spreading from that as well as this side, will insure their complete establishment over the whole."[11]

Astoria was, indeed, little more than a germ planted along a coast that was fiercely contested among the Spanish, British, and Russians. In 1774 Juan Pérez explored the coast as far north as latitude 55°, establishing the Spanish claim. Four years later Captain James Cook of the Royal Navy ventured up the coast. The publication in 1784 of Cook's account of his Pacific voyage set off an international rush to those shores. The impressive and wealthy Indian societies along the coast were testimony to the potential riches Europeans envisioned; there were sea otter along the coast and beaver in the streams, whales and limitless supplies of salmon, great stands of spruce and fir, as well as thousands of Indian consumers who promised a brisk commerce in trade goods. But the viceroy of New Spain considered this an invasion of his extended coastline, and he sent a warship north to warn off the intruders. At Nootka Sound, located at latitude 50°, the Spanish seized two British trading vessels and their crews and arrested a British captain. The Spanish monarchy proved unwilling to pursue the conflict begun by their viceroy, however, and in the Nootka Convention of 1790 Spain agreed to return prisoners and property and to share the coastline with the British. Two years later George Vancouver of the Royal Navy surveyed and mapped the coastline, and in 1793 the Nor'Wester Alexander Mackenzie journeyed down the interior rivers to the coast.

Over the next ten years trading vessels from all over the world plied these waters, exchanging goods for furs with the native chiefdoms along the coast, some even attempting to hunt sea otter like the Russians. This aggression, of course, was worrisome for the Russian-American Company, which controlled the coastline to the north. With their trained force of Aleut hunters, the Russians were making fabulous profits from the trade in sea otters, tea, and silk between Alaska and China; but they were in danger of hunting the animals to extinction in the waters off Alaska. The new competition from British, French, and American traders forced them to push south to establish a claim to the coast. In 1802, Aleksandr Baranov, the director of operations for the Russian-American Company, established a new American headquarters on Sitka Sound at latitude 57°. This was the homeland of the Tlingits, a wealthy society of clan matrons and fierce warriors. The Tlingits had already established connections with American traders whom the Indians called "Bostons." Arming themselves with American guns, the Tlingits attacked Baranov's fort, leaving the heads of dozens of Aleuts and Russians impaled on stakes before the smoking ruins. Baranov threw his forces against the local Tlingits and rebuilt the headquarters. Relations remained tense, but eventually the Indians came to accept the Russian presence. By 1811, when the Astorians arrived, the Russians controlled the northern coast.

Astor thus confronted opponents on all sides. His dream quickly turned into a nightmare. Captain Jonathan Thorn, in command of the *Tonquin*, turned out to be murderous, if not mad. He was on leave from the navy, a veteran of the war with the Tripolitanian pirates, and a kind of Captain Bligh, quick-tempered, haughty, and cruel. Hating the sound of both a Scottish burr and a French accent, he was hardly the man to be involved with a trade so heavily loaded with Scotsmen and Frenchmen. The voyage was colored from the start with quarrels, suspicions of mutiny, and harsh disciplinary acts. There were also serious accidents, such as the loss of eight men who drowned searching for the channel at the mouth of the Columbia. Once the ship reached shore, the back-breaking work of construction got under way. The *Tonquin* sailed north to Vancouver Island for some trading. In the haggling, Captain Thorn, true to his character, provoked the Indians, whom he also hated, into a surprise attack on the ship. In the resulting melee the captain and so many of the crew were killed that the ship became helpless. In a vicious final bloody scene, a single re-

ASTORIA, AS IT WAS IN 1813.

Astoria in 1813. From Gabriel Franchère, Narrative of a Voyage to the Northwest Coast of America . . . *(New York, 1854). Beinecke.*

maining white man waited until the largest possible number of Indians were aboard or nearby and then blew up the ship, killing himself and at least a hundred natives.

Meanwhile, Wilson Price Hunt, in charge of the overland expedition, had encountered mountainous difficulties crossing the continent. His party left the Missouri settlements in April 1811 and through summer, fall, and early winter carried Astor's hopes into the face of almost every obstacle the wilderness could raise. Voyageurs plotted and deserted, Indians grew hostile, horses ran off, men were lost, boats that were built for river transport were wrecked and discarded. At times hunger, thirst, cold, sickness, and death rode with the men; toward the end they splintered into isolated, struggling groups. Hunt himself reached Astoria in the cold February of 1812, ten months after leaving the Missouri settlements.

But it was the War of 1812 that delivered the coup de grâce to Astoria. When a British warship challenged Astoria in October 1813, several former Nor'Westers in Astor's employ simply signed over the deed to the North West Company for fifty-eight thousand dollars. The British jubilantly raised their flag, broke open a bottle of wine, and renamed the post Fort George, while the local Indians looked on in bewilderment, expecting the Americans to become slaves. Even under the new name the settlement was abandoned shortly thereafter for a better location up river known as Fort Vancouver. It would be thirty years before another generation of Americans would lay a new claim to the Oregon country, one based not upon furs but on farms.

The first Americans to challenge the Canadians successfully and exploit the great fur-bearing regions of the West came not from the east, as did Astor, but from Saint Louis, a small western town near the convergence of the Missouri and Mississippi rivers. When Saint Louis became part of United States territory, with the acquisition of Louisiana, the most important traders there were the Chouteaus, a family prominent among the town's founders in 1764. Led by the widowed matriarch Marie-Thérèse, the Chouteaus made a fortune in the Missouri valley Indian trade during the period of Spanish sovereignty. With the coming of the Americans in 1804, Marie's sons, René-Auguste and Jean-Pierre Chouteau, quickly established important connections with the new regime, securing positions as agents and officers of the territory. Jefferson even appointed Auguste-Pierre Chouteau, one of Marie's grandsons, to West Point. The Chouteaus provided the link between the French and American Wests, and over the next half-century they would raise much of the capital for the expanding western fur trade as well.

But the first of the Saint Louisans to exploit the rich beaver grounds of the upper Missouri was one of the Chouteaus' local rivals, Manuel Lisa. Half French, half Spanish, and half grinning alligator, Lisa had moved up the river from New Orleans as a boy of eighteen looking for his big chance. When Lewis and Clark returned, he immediately set into motion plans to organize and exploit the newly discovered lands. Lisa persuaded John Colter, who had scouted for Lewis and Clark, to guide his traders into the mountains. On this expedition Colter became the first American to explore the Yellowstone River country. In 1808, in partnership with other Saint Louis traders, including the Chouteaus, Lisa organized the Missouri Fur Company. It proved a very profitable operation. One happy season Lisa made thirty-five thousand dollars, this in an age when a successful merchant might clear a thousand dollars a year.

The market for furs had its ups and downs, however. During the War of 1812 In-

Manuel Lisa, c. 1820.
Missouri Historical Society.

dians of the northern plains, allied with the Canadian traders, drove the Americans back down the Missouri, ending their dream as effectively as the British had Astor's. There followed a decade of serious depression in the fur business. Demand for beaver did not rebound until the early 1820s, when the day's fashion called for broad-brimmed, stovepipe beaver hats. With style dictating, the fur trade boomed once again.

One of the men who chose this time to invest was William H. Ashley, a respected Saint Louis gentleman, brigadier general in the militia, and lieutenant governor of the new state of Missouri. In the Saint Louis *Missouri Republican* for March 22, 1822, he advertised his intention to bankroll an expedition of one hundred "enterprizing young men" to the sources of the Missouri River. The project was an enormous success, and the fabulous cache of beaver brought back the first year made Ashley a rich man.

The alumni of Ashley's first brigade included some of the most notable characters in the history of the West. Mike Fink, the "ring-tailed roarer" of Mississippi flatboatmen, certainly could not have qualified as "young," for he had been born near Pittsburgh in 1770 and had worked keelboats up and down the river for nearly forty years. Now with the coming of the steamboat he and others of his type were being pushed off the river, and Ashley must have been glad to have a man of Fink's experience to guide his big boats up the Missouri. In American legend, Fink was the original frontier braggart. "I'm a land-screamer—I'm a water-dog—I'm a snapping turtle," he shouts in a typical tale. "I can out-run, out-dance, out-jump, out-dive, out-holler, and out-lick any white thing in the shape o' human that's ever put foot within two thousand miles o' the big Massassip." Once in beaver country Fink quarreled with one of his two companions. After ostensibly making up, they agreed to play a friendly game—shooting cups of whiskey off each other's heads from a distance of sixty yards. With his first shot, Fink drilled his companion between the eyes. Realizing, with Fink being the marksman he was, that this could hardly be an accident, the third man shot Fink dead. Among a collection of scoundrels, Fink might have been the worst, a man Don Berry described as "a lying, sadistic, foul-mouthed braggart, a treacherous and murderous psychopath." But along with Daniel Boone and Davy Crockett, Mike Fink quickly found a place in the Valhalla of frontier heroes.[12]

Ashley's group also included old Hugh Glass, another veteran of the frontier. No one seems to have known how old he really was, but it was said that early in the century he had served under the command of Jean Laffite, the privateer. Glass's character may not have been strikingly better than that of Fink, but he illustrates the courage and stamina of the mountain men. While out trapping he was attacked by a mother grizzly protecting her cubs; she tore open his throat and left his body covered with bleeding lacerations. Abandoned for dead by his two companions, Glass pulled himself to a spring, sustained himself on berries and the carcasses left by wolves, and dragged himself across nearly a hundred miles of present-day South Dakota until he was rescued by friendly Indians. For a year he searched for his faithless companions like an avenging angel. One put himself out of reach by joining the army. The other Glass found but spared because he was only a boy of seventeen.

The boy's name was Jim Bridger. He would became one of the best known of the mountain men, working for all the important outfits, organizing companies himself, building posts and forts, scouting for explorers and generals. He came to know the northern Rockies better than any man alive, his mind a veritable atlas of peaks, passes, and meadows. Bridger was a friend to the native people of the Rockies, living among them and romancing their women. In 1835 he fell in love with a Flathead girl named Cora, the daughter of a chief, and before her untimely death they had three children together. In 1848 he married a Ute woman whose name went unrecorded; she died giving birth to their daughter the next year. In 1850 Bridger married a Shoshone named Mary, bought a house in Westport, Missouri, and settled his wife and children there. "Old Gabe," as he was known to intimates, returned to the mountains to trade and trap each season, but he arranged to have all his children educated in missionary schools and convents.

Perhaps the most remarkable of Ashley's remarkably "enterprizing men" was a clean-cut, serious, blue-eyed boy who neither swore nor smoked. Jedediah Strong Smith spent only a decade in the West, but he firmly left his stamp upon it. In 1824 Indians guided him to the great South Pass across the Rockies, and Smith's discovery allowed American trappers to exploit the far side of the Continental Divide. Two years later he traveled over the great southwestern desert to California and became the first American to cross the Sierra Nevada west to east. He explored the Great Basin

Jim Bridger, c. 1850. Beinecke.

and dipped his toes in the Great Salt Lake. Smith's physical endurance allowed him to cover the West like a real Paul Bunyan, with steps too large to be believed. His accomplishments were not fully appreciated until historians compiled the complete record of his many explorations.

But what really set Smith apart was his moral code, his religious dedication. His conscience seemed to bear a heavy weight. "O, the perverseness of my wicked heart," he once wrote. "I entangle myself altogether too much in the things of time." Instead of tramping the wilderness, he felt he should be helping the poor, "those who stand in need," wherever they were. But the wilderness, giving him few such opportunities, instead turned him in on himself, intensifying his guilt. Coupled with his vague search for personal fulfillment, this sentiment made for an interesting phenomenon, and it may have appeared often enough on the frontier to explain some of the restlessness. Smith probably never resolved his frustrations. He died alone on the southern plains in 1831, his mouth undoubtedly still unprofaned but his body punctured with Comanche lances.[13]

Ashley's second trapping expedition in 1823 was attacked by the Arikara Indians, a group living along the Missouri who resented this intrusion of their homeland and sensed how profoundly it would alter their world. The Arikaras killed fifteen men

Fur Trade Rendezvous near Green River. Painting by Alfred Jacob Miller, c. 1840. American Heritage Center, University of Wyoming.

and, despite a punitive military campaign later that year, succeeded in keeping the river route closed for a few years. This disaster led Ashley to experiment with a set of innovations that restructured the American fur trade of the Rockies. Avoiding the Missouri altogether, he sent his men directly overland to the mountains, pioneering a path across the plains that would later become the Overland Trail. His mounted brigades wintered in their own mountain camps, doing their own trapping. Rather than investing in fixed posts in the style of the Hudson's Bay Company, Ashley used the same overland route to supply his men by pack and wagon train, meeting them at a predetermined summer "rendezvous." Ashley opened his rendezvous to any and all trappers in the mountains. With these innovations the era of the engagé gave way to the day of the "free trapper."

There was an annual rendezvous each summer for the next fifteen years, the flush times of the Rocky Mountain fur trade. No other assemblies in American history—excepting the Mardi Gras of New Orleans—matched the color and excitement of the rendezvous. Fur trading companies would agree on a location a year in advance, any one of a thousand green meadows with streams and timber: in the Wind River Mountains, along the banks of the Bear or the Green River, in Jackson's or Pierre's Hole. There for a week in July or August, the poorest season for trapping, the mountain trappers would straggle in, their mules top-heavy with the season's harvest of skins, converging with the merchant caravans from the east, drawn like bears to the honey of profit, which was often several hundred percent. Indians would come, sometimes whole tribes, to barter furs or just to watch. And there was plenty to see.

As if they were sailors home from a long voyage, the trappers were ready for a wild debauch. They drank Saint Louis whiskey and Taos lightning (*aguardiente*—brandy flavored with red peppers). They bargained with Indian women, compliant in the soft grasses. There were fights among drunken men, duels among the sober, and gambling everywhere—on horse and footraces, at cards and dice. The lilt of a French-Canadian song ("A la claire fontaine") might melt into a Highland fling or a Mexican fandango. A big rendezvous could attract more than a thousand trappers and traders. Imagine such a setting—sundown behind the Teton ridges, hundreds of tepees and tents, the smoke of wood fires rising above the cedars, the sounds and smells!

In the flush years of the late 1820s, traders, if not trappers, took in handsome returns at the rendezvous. In 1825 Ashley brought home furs worth nearly fifty thousand dollars, and in 1826 he made enough to retire with a fortune. The Rocky Mountain Fur Company, as new owners renamed his enterprise, took back 168 packs of beaver pelts worth eighty-five thousand dollars in 1832. That is the equivalent of more than a million dollars in today's values, a reminder that the fur trade was indeed a business and that many of the mountain men were "expectant capitalists," as historian William Goetzmann puts it. Examining the lives of a large number of Rocky Mountain trappers, he found that a third of them left the mountains to pursue other careers. Many became businessmen, investing their savings in stores or saloons.[14]

Two of the more enterprising men were the brothers Charles and William Bent, who in 1832 brought back to Saint Louis 131 packs of beaver pelts. They succeeded spectacularly in diverting the flow of furs from the southern Rocky Mountain region away from New Mexico. Operating out of their trading post on the upper Arkansas, the Bents collected furs from trappers operating in the southern region. Furs had long been important to the northern Spanish colony. "Without this trade," the Spanish governor wrote in 1754, the New Mexicans "could not provide for themselves, for they have no other commerce than that of these skins." Throughout the eighteenth century, furs constituted New Mexico's chief export. Like the French in the north, Spanish traders from New Mexico beat Americans into the Rockies by at least fifty years. But by the late eighteenth century Americans were invading their grounds. "Although American colonists live a great distance from that frontier," a Spanish official wrote of New Mexico in 1795, "it is not impossible that they plan to go there." Indeed, Manuel Lisa had trappers working the streams of the southern Rockies by the time of Lewis and Clark's expedition, and during the 1820s the Spanish had their hands full trying to round up the American frontiersmen working rivers from the

Arkansas south to the Gila. Among them was young Christopher "Kit" Carson, who moved from Missouri to Taos to trap beaver and for a time worked as a hunter at Bent's Fort on the Arkansas. Because of the Bents, furs now moved northeast to Saint Louis rather than south to Chihuahua.[15]

The free trapper was the backbone of the American trade. A wonderful example is William Sherley Williams, known to his trapping contemporaries as "Old Bill"— "old" being more a title of honor than a description of age. Bill was more religious in early life than was Jedediah Smith. He was only sixteen when in 1803 he got the call and became a hell-storming Baptist preacher in Missouri. That was the year of the Louisiana Purchase, and soon Bill's eyes turned west. Within a few years he was taking the Word to the Osage Indians, and conversion quickly followed: the Osages converted Bill.

He settled down with them, married an Osage woman, and had two daughters. He later told his family that he liked the Indian way of life better than the white, and indeed his Indian religious beliefs seemed to deepen as he aged. He embraced the transmigration of souls, for example, and through revelations projected his own reincarnation as a distinctively marked elk. After his death, he warned his friends, if they saw his antlered head raised in the meadows, don't shoot—it would just be Old Bill still roaming the wilderness. Yet Williams stood between two cultures, an intimate of neither. When his Osage wife died, he guided a party southwest to New Mexico. He married a well-off New Mexican widow, Antonia Baca, and tried to settle down running a little store in Taos, but sitting behind the counter so irked him that he threw the bolts of cloth down the streets like rolls of confetti, laughed as the señoritas fought over the pieces, and took off for his only true home, the mountains. He grew close to the Ute Indians who, like the Osages, adopted him, and he took a Ute woman for his wife.

Even in his own day Williams was the subject of tall tales. Over six feet tall, red-headed, his pants shiny with grease, he was sometimes called Old Solitaire. He remained a loner, keeping his favorite trapping grounds secret and never working with more than a few others at a time. He was the patriarch of the mountains yet ruled over none but his lone, free self. If freedom is defined as the absence of external restraint, then old Bill Williams was a supreme example of a free man, and in American thought and legend he has often been so considered. But if freedom is a state of mind, it is arguable that a man like Williams was maladjusted and that his aversion to society was based on a restless pursuit of something he could neither find nor define. Jedediah Smith, once hallucinating from thirst and hunger, said he dreamed not of gold nor honor but of family, friends, and home. A quest for freedom that becomes a relentless prod to move on is shallow at best.

Yet there was another side to the experience of the mountain men, a side of deepening connections to the human world. Bernard De Voto imagined that the trapper serenely pulled the wilderness round him "like a robe." If so, that robe was of Indian design. This "white Indian" worked and lived intimately with real Indians. He traded with them and picked their brains; he fought with and against them and appreciated their courage. He recognized their cruelty and he often shared in it. To the mountain man the Indian warrior could be both friend and enemy. At times he esteemed him less than he did the beaver, at times more highly than he did the wind spirits on the peaks. The Indian woman he knew as both temporary whore and tender wife. He understood how vital the woman was to the Indian economy and that her role as camp-keeper and hide-tanner was no less important to him. He knew that she could increase his opportunities through kin and tribe. In short, the mountain man knew Indians too well to generalize. Like anyone else, they were a mixed lot. Indeed, a life in the fur trade was all about mixing.[16]

The trappers did their job so well that there was some danger that the beaver, like the sea otter, would become extinct. Intense competition threatened to kill the golden goose. In the late 1820s the hundreds of free trappers in the mountains were joined by trappers employed by Astor's American Fur Company, which had moved into the vacuum on the Missouri River, establishing a series of fixed fur posts along the river in Hudson's Bay Company style. Along the Columbia River, John McLoughlin sent out brigades with instructions to trap beaver out along the western slope of the northern Rockies in an attempt to discourage the American trappers from penetrating the Oregon country. The resulting oversupply of beaver on the international market precipitated a steep fall in prices and profits.

In 1830 William Clark, who was western superintendent of Indian affairs at Saint Louis, wrote of "a very perceptible decrease of the furred animals." A quarter-century earlier he and Lewis had heard the constant slapping of beaver tails on western streams. The trappers had intervened. American trapper James Ohio Pattie once witnessed the destructive tactics firsthand as he followed another party down the Gila River. The group in the lead had so scoured the valley that Pattie could locate not a single animal, but ranging ahead of the others he took thirty-seven beaver on his first night. Such intensive trapping, with no thought for the following season, was typical. In 1834 the men of the Rocky Mountain Fur Company, experts all, sold out to others. Their chief reason for quitting? The supply of beaver had simply slipped too low.[17]

We can only guess at the number of beaver killed. In 1800 more than 245,000 beaver skins were exported from eastern ports alone. A little later one English ship carried more than 21,000 pelts to Canton. Extrapolating from such shreds of evi-

*Indians and trader examine furs, late nineteenth century. Keystone-Mast Collection, UCR/
California Museum of Photography, University of California, Riverside.*

dence, and assuming a continuous rate of destruction, we must conclude that the beaver might not have held out. What saved it was a decline in the market for its pelt. Fashions changed. "I very much fear beaver will not sell well," Astor wrote from Paris in 1832; "it appears that they make hats of silk in place of beaver." With his acute nose for business, two years later Astor sold his western operations to the Chouteaus, shifting his investments into the booming New York real estate market. It was a sign of the times. The last real rendezvous took place in 1840; in the following year only a few wagons met a handful of dispirited trappers. The trade continued, focusing on other kinds of fur, with less frantic activity and greater control by large companies. By the 1850s, large numbers of beaver tails once more slapped the waters of the upper Missouri country, but few free trappers heard them.[18]

FURTHER READING

Stephen E. Ambrose, *Undaunted Courage: Meriwether Lewis, Thomas Jefferson, and the Opening of the American West* (1996)

Don Berry, *A Majority of Scoundrels: An Informal History of the Rocky Mountain Fur Company* (1961)

Bernard De Voto, *Across the Wide Missouri* (1947)

Joseph J. Ellis, *American Sphinx: The Character of Thomas Jefferson* (1996)

John C. Ewers, *Plains Indian History and Culture: Essays on Continuity and Change* (1997)

LeRoy R. Hafen, ed., *The Mountain Men and the Fur Trade of the Far West*, 10 vols. (1965–72)

Ted C. Hinckley, *The Canoe Rocks: Alaska's Tlingit and the Euramerican Frontier, 1800–1912* (1996)

Richard E. Oglesby, *Manuel Lisa and the Opening of the Missouri Fur Trade* (1963)

Lewis Saum, *The Fur Trader and the Indian* (1965)

Richard W. Van Alstyne, *The Rising American Empire* (1960)

Sylvia van Kirk, *"Many Tender Ties": Women in Fur-Trade Society in Western Canada, 1670–1870* (1980)

David J. Weber, *The Taos Trappers: The Fur Trade in the Far Southwest, 1540–1846* (1971)

David J. Wishart, *The Fur Trade of the American West, 1807–40: A Geographical Synthesis* (1979)

6

From Texas to Oregon

Settlement was the key to America's conquest of the continent. Common folks—un-moneyed farmers, artisans, and their families—craved a piece of land. A Connecticut Yankee named Moses Austin joined crowds of them pushing across the Appalachians to Kentucky in 1797. "Ask these Pilgrims what they expect when they git to Kentuckey," Austin noted in his diary, "the answer is Land. Have you any? No, but I expect I can git it. Have you any thing to pay for land? No. Did you ever see the country? No, but Every Body says its good land." Such great expectations were far more powerful than soldiers in establishing the sovereignty of the United States over the West.[1]

Propelling this surge was the enormous growth in American population, which through the Republic's first seventy-five years nearly doubled every twenty years, just as Benjamin Franklin had predicted in the mid-eighteenth century. Neither Mexico nor Canada experienced explosions of such proportions. Mexican authorities prod-ded their people to move to the northern borderlands, but with only modest results. The Hudson's Bay Company succeeded in establishing fur posts flung like distant stars across the map of the Far West, but there was no great movement into western Canada before the late nineteenth century. All the while Americans were pushing their wagons and cattle westward. By 1840 eight new states had formed in trans-Appalachia (Kentucky, 1792; Tennessee, 1796; Ohio, 1803; Indiana, 1816; Mississippi, 1817; Illinois, 1818; Alabama, 1819; Michigan, 1837) with three more carved from the Louisiana Purchase (Louisiana, 1812; Missouri, 1821; Arkansas, 1836). The first federal census in 1790 counted fewer than one hundred thousand Americans west of the Ap-palachians. Fifty years later there were more than seven million, better than 40 per-cent of the nation's population.

Pioneers did not go unaided, of course. One of the principal contributions of the federal government was to explore the land of the trans-Mississippi West and assess its potential for settlement. In 1806, even before the return of Lewis and Clark, President Jefferson dispatched a second major expedition, this one under the command of Lieutenant Zebulon Pike, to reconnoiter the southern reaches of the Louisiana Purchase territory. On a previous mission Pike had failed to find the sources of the Mississippi; on this new one he was equally unsuccessful in locating the headwaters of the Arkansas in the southern Rockies. He marveled at the grand summit later named Pike's Peak in his honor—although he did not manage to scale it. He turned south in search of the Red River, by which he was instructed to return, but instead blundered across the Sangre de Cristo range into New Mexico, where Spanish dragoons arrested him. "What, is not this the Red River?" Pike asked his captors incredulously. "No, Sir!" came the reply, "The Rio del Norte." Obviously Pike's importance to history should not be sought in his skill as a navigator.[2]

The Spanish forced Pike and his men to return with them to the New Mexican capital at Santa Fe, then escorted them south to the provincial capital of Chihuahua, where officials questioned Pike closely before finally conducting him back home through the provinces of Coahuila and Texas to the American post at the old French town of Nachitoches in Louisiana. Pike's expedition had done little to clarify the boundary line, but he was the first American to provide detailed intelligence on the northern provinces of New Spain. The region impressed him, but unfavorably. "These vast plains," he wrote, "may become in time equally celebrated as the sandy deserts of Africa; for I saw in my route, in various places, tracts of many leagues, where the wind had thrown up the sand, in all the fanciful forms of the ocean's rolling wave, and on which not a speck of vegetable matter existed." Deserts were places "deserted" of people; true, Indians might hunt and live in such regions, but they could be dismissed as wild nomads. The only advantage Pike could imagine arising from the "immense prairies" lying in the center of the continent was that "our citizens being so prone to rambling and extending themselves on the frontiers will, through necessity, be constrained to limit their extent on the west to the borders of the Missouri and Mississippi, while they leave the prairies incapable of cultivation to the wandering and uncivilized aborigines of the country."[3]

Pike's opinion soon would be seconded by another American explorer of the West, Stephen H. Long, a Phi Beta Kappa graduate of Dartmouth who joined the Army Corps of Topographical Engineers after teaching mathematics at West Point. During his trip across the plains to the Rocky Mountains in 1820, Long visited with the Indians and surveyed the country. The account of this expedition concluded that the region was "almost wholly unfit for cultivation, and of course uninhabitable by a people depending upon agriculture for their subsistence," and included a map on which the present states of Oklahoma, Kansas, and Nebraska were labeled the "Great American Desert." That phrase, used in most of the atlases and grammar-school geographies published in America before the Civil War became the commonsense way

Pawnees in council with the Stephen Long expedition. Watercolor by Samuel Seymour, 1819. Beinecke.

of referring to the Great Plains. "When I was a schoolboy," wrote explorer and army officer Colonel Richard Irving Dodge later in the century, "my map of the United States showed between the Missouri River and the Rocky Mountains a long and broad white blotch, upon which was printed in small capitals 'THE GREAT AMERICAN DESERT—UNEXPLORED.'"[4]

Pike was more favorably impressed with Mexico's northern province of Tejas (which Americans knew as "Texas"). He wrote of the fertility of the soil, the luxuriance of the grasslands, and the "general urbanity and suavity of manners" among the Tejanos, the native-born Mexicans. In Pike's conversations with the leading men he found them interested in but three topics—money, horses, and women, in ascending order of importance. They spoke earnestly to him about their interest in opening trade with the United States. Most were *rancheros* who raised longhorn cattle and were, Pike observed, "always ready to mount their horses" on which they "spent nearly half the day." Cattle ranching, introduced into Mexico by the first Spanish colonists, provided the foundation of the Texas economy, and Tejano leaders had hopes of supplying the market for beef in places like New Orleans. As to the last topic, Pike had to agree that the Tejanas were most agreeable. They enchanted him with their short skirts

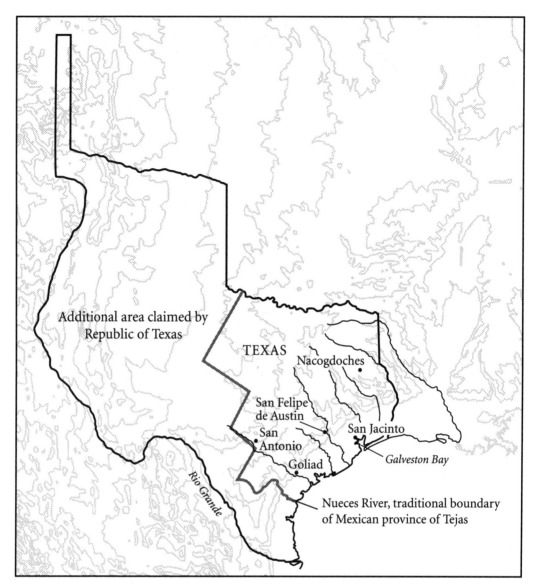

TEXAS

and their high-heeled shoes, silk shawls drawn coquettishly around their faces, "but from under which you frequently see peeping large, sparkling black eyes."[5]

A few years after Pike's departure, the Texas he admired lay in ruins. During the turmoil of Mexico's independence rebellion against Spain in the 1810s, the province became a target for American adventurers known as *filibusters*—a word derived from "freebooter"—but these were pirates who operated on land. In 1813 a filibuster army took San Antonio by storm, then was routed by a royalist army whose commander executed three hundred Tejanos for collaboration, leaving San Antonio in ruins. In 1819 an expedition of American mercenaries took over the east Texas town of Nacog-

Stephen F. Austin, c. 1825. Beinecke.

doches and held it for several months before being chased out by Spanish forces. As a result of the fighting, by 1820 the population of Texas had been reduced by half.

Unless the province was strengthened, Spanish authorities knew that it was only a matter of time before it would fall victim to American aggression. Unable to attract migration from central Mexico, they proved receptive to an idea proposed by entrepreneur Moses Austin, who had prospered as the owner of lead mines in Missouri. After a visit to Texas in 1820 Austin made application for a large grant of land on which he would settle three hundred American families. Clearly inviting Americans in was taking a risk, but Austin promised to settle a different kind of American, and the Spanish reasoned that unless the province was developed it would inevitably fall to the United States. In 1821 they approved Austin's plan, granting him two hundred thousand acres of rich Texas soil.

On his trip home Austin was fatally stricken with pneumonia, but his son received the father's dying injunction to carry on with the Texas enterprise. Stephen F. Austin had been sent to school at a private academy in Connecticut, with instructions from his father that the teachers teach him to think clearly and to write effective English. The elder Austin must have been dismayed when the young man returned to Missouri with a decided bent for music and dancing. By the time of his father's sudden death, however, Stephen's best dancing days were over. At the age of only twenty-seven he had already made a dignified mark on his community as a representative to the Missouri territorial legislature and a circuit judge. He would remain a bachelor, later claiming that Texas was his bride. What William Penn had been to Pennsylvania and Brigham Young would later be to Utah, Austin was to Anglo Texas.

The new Mexican government confirmed the generous grant to the younger Austin. His lands stretched along the rich bottoms of the Colorado and Brazos rivers, rolling gently down to the Gulf coast. These were among the richest alluvial lands in all the

West. Settlers were given the choice of claiming 177 acres of farmland or 4,428 acres for grazing—not surprisingly, most of Austin's colonists declared in favor of ranching. The herds of cattle that fattened on these ranges and the cotton that flourished in these soils were soon major exports, almost all of which went to the United States.

The Mexican government made three more grants to Austin, allowing him to colonize an additional nine hundred American families. He was one of a number of *empresarios*, land speculators given the authority to settle families in exchange for awards of thousands of acres to themselves. But unlike other Texas empresarios, Austin adopted the perspective of a patriarch. "I feel almost the same interest for their prosperity that I do for my own family," he wrote of his colonists. "In fact I look upon them as one great family under my care." Other speculators were less careful. Many Americans simply drifted into Texas and squatted on the best land they could find. Unpredictable as the flooded delta channels of the Mississippi and as irksome as its bars and snags, these squatters were the frontier types that Austin carefully excluded from his own "family." By 1823 the fifteen hundred settlers in the Austin colony had been supplemented by at least three thousand squatters in the east Texas region bordering Louisiana. The Texians, as the Americans called themselves, were rapidly outnumbering the Tejanos, concentrated in the southern half of the province.[6]

───────

One of the fundamental principles of the Mexican independence movement was the abolition of slavery and the equality of all citizens regardless of color. Attracted by these ideals, a small number of free African Americans emigrated from the United States to Texas during the 1820s. Samuel H. Hardin and his wife came, he wrote, because Mexico's laws "invited their emigration," and Virginian John Bird moved because he believed he and his sons "would be received as citizens and entitled as such to land." Several free black heads of household were granted land by the Mexican government, and there were at least two African-American settlers in the Austin colony.[7]

But the number of free blacks was insignificant compared to the thousands of slaves who came with the white settlers. Slavery was a founding institution of the region that early nineteenth-century Americans called the Southwest—the states of Tennessee, Alabama, Mississippi, and Louisiana and the territory of Arkansas. Black labor cleared the pine forests and drained the swamps, opening plantations and making cotton production the engine of the region's economy. Many slaves arrived with their masters, but most were brought in by traders. "We require more slaves," settler William Dunbar wrote from the Mississippi frontier in 1799; "ordinary men are worth $500 cash, women $400 and upwards. There is no country where they are better treated." What nonsense! Planters on this frontier were infamous for driving their slaves beyond the point of endurance, and slaves in the upper South trembled at the thought of being "sold down the river," a threat frequently employed by masters to keep their hands in line.[8]

Slaves being driven to the Mississippi frontier. From Wilson S. Armistead, A Tribute for the
Negro *(New York, 1848). Yale University.*

It was a common fate. For slave children throughout the southern states, writes historian Michael Tadman, "the cumulative chance of being 'sold South' by 1860 might have been something like 30 percent." Carol Anna Randall, who lived a life as a Virginia slave, described the sale and forced migration of her sister as "de saddes' thing dat ever happen to me." Ex-slave Laura Clark remembered being loaded into a wagon with other black children and given a piece of candy to keep her quiet. Delighted with her prize, she could not understand why her mother, standing nearby, wept so miserably. "I knows now," she reflected, "and I never seed her no mo' in dis life." Travelers in the Old Southwest often encountered slave traders with their human livestock. Edwin L. Godkin overtook a group struggling through a Mississippi swamp. "The hardships the negroes go through who are attached to one of these emigrant parties baffle description," he wrote. "Thousands of miles are traversed by these weary wayfarers without their knowing or caring why, urged on by the whip and in the full assurance that no change of place can bring any change to them. Hard work, coarse food, merciless floggings, are all that await them, and all that they can look to." Westering without hope—this version of American pioneering has not received sufficient attention, but it, too, is an essential part of the nation's frontier history.[9]

Slavery lent its full measure to the violent character of frontier life. Samuel Townes was one of many southwestern masters who drove his slaves hard. Impatient that his black women were picking less than half the cotton of the men, he insisted that his overseer "make those bitches go to at least 100 [pounds a day] or whip them like the devil." The lashings, he later noted with satisfaction, had measurably improved their productivity. Combining the everyday violence of slavery with the unsettled social conditions of the frontier—large numbers of unattached men, excessive drinking, and endemic Indian-hating—produced a lethal brew. Visitors were horrified by the dueling, fistfighting, and brutal practical joking. Historian Joan Cashin, after studying the personal papers of several dozen pioneer southwestern planters, argues that as a group they were obsessed with independence and adopted a particularly aggressive posture, both in society and at home. Don't "hang around Mother and drivel away your life," Townes wrote to his younger brother in South Carolina. Come West, where "you can live like a fighting cock with us." The fighting cocks would rule the old Southwest.[10]

It was the dawning "age of the common man"—for white men, anyway. The political rhetoric of the day, which pitted ordinary men against the privileged, was especially strong in the Southwest, where a new set of rough-and-tumble characters were emerging as new political heroes. David Crockett of Tennessee provided a prototype. Working his way up the local political ladder in the 1820s, Crockett cultivated the persona of a backwoods bumpkin who consistently bested his highborn opponents by using native wit and wisdom. During his successful run for Congress, Crockett and his opponent appeared together at a boisterous rally of settlers. After Crockett had felt the sting of criticism from his competitor he stepped up and blasted the man with a number of serious charges. When his opponent rose to complain, Crockett had to admit that he had been lying. "They told stories on me," he explained to the voters, "and I wanted to show them, it if came to that, that I could tell a bigger lie than they could. Yes, fellow citizens, I can run faster, walk longer, leap higher, speak better, and tell more and bigger lies than my competitor, and all his friends, any day of his life." The crowd roared its approval, and Crockett's astounded opponent soon dropped out of the race. "If a man can get five hundred votes for telling a lie, and one thousand for acknowledging the fact," he complained, "an honest man may well be off!"[11]

Crockett and others might speak the boisterous language of frontier democracy, and even win election to high office, but the Southwest was quickly becoming a society of great inequality, a land of "nabobs and nobodies," in the words of historians Thomas D. Clark and John D. W. Guice. By the 1820s the "nabobs"—the elite class of planters—included some of the wealthiest Americans of the day. More millionaires lived in the Natchez district of Mississippi, it was said, than anywhere else in the country, even New York City. But the vast majority of whites were "nobodies"—small aspiring planters with a handful of slaves, or hardscrabble farmers subsisting on the thin soils of the pine barrens or grazing cattle on the prairie grasses.

As the nabobs grew richer they gobbled up the farms of the nobodies. "Our wealthier planters," wrote an Alabamian, "are buying out their poorer neighbors, extending their plantations, and adding to their slave force. The wealthy few . . . are thus pushing off the many." Thus the need for new frontiers, where opportunity still beckoned for the little man. And thus did an army of nobodies push off for Texas.[12]

The arrival of Americans—many of them with slaves—caused great concern in Mexico. In 1824 political leaders in Mexico City adopted a new national constitution that reaffirmed the abolition of slavery throughout the country. Southwestern slaveholders worried that Texas would become a haven for fugitive slaves much as Spanish Florida had been. In Texas there was momentary panic, but with the support of leading Tejanos, local authorities created a paper fiction called "contract labor," allowing planters to hold their slaves in bondage for ninety-nine years. It was an uneasy solution to a sensitive problem.

The 1820s also brought change to the Mexican province of New Mexico, a liberalization of formerly restrictive commercial policies. In early 1822 Missouri Indian trader William Becknell returned home from a trading expedition on the southern plains with a smile on his face and Mexican silver jingling in his pockets. He had met up with a company of soldiers from New Mexico, but rather than arresting him they escorted him to Santa Fe to do business. Not only did he make a handsome profit on the sale of his goods, but the New Mexican governor "expressed a desire that the Americans would keep up an intercourse with that country." The next summer Becknell blazed a wagon route from Missouri to New Mexico, across the southern plains and over Glorieta Pass in the Sangre de Cristo Mountains. By mid-decade hundreds of wagons were heading down the Santa Fe Trail each spring, and soon the value of American imports into New Mexico averaged $145,000 annually (the equivalent of $2.4 million today). Traders from the United States hauled tools and household utensils, bolts of fabric and the latest fashions, wallpaper and window glass, ending two centuries of isolation for Santa Fe. The markup was fabulous. By the 1830s New Mexican merchants were participating in this traffic and were playing a major role in the transnational trade by the eve of the Mexican War. "Of about 200 wagon loads which I have escorted this year," trader Josiah Gregg wrote in 1843, "I do not believe 10 have belonged to Americans."[13]

Wagon freighting on the Santa Fe Trail continued to be important until the establishment of rail connections with the Southwest in the 1880s. Mexican money and Mexican mules did much to transform frontier Missouri. The silver peso was, for several decades, the principal medium of exchange in the West, much preferred to the highly unstable and inflated paper currency issued by state banks. More than half the goods freighted down the trail from the United States were destined for the

"The Arrival of the Caravan at Santa Fe." From Josiah Gregg, Commerce of the Prairies . . .
(New York, 1845). Beinecke.

northern Mexican cities of Chihuahua, Durango, and Zacatecas, mining towns
where a great deal of silver was in circulation. And the stubborn but nearly inde-
structible Mexican mules that came back with the traders soon became the most important work animal of the nineteenth-century West. Before long Missourians were
importing jackasses of their own to use as breeding stock.

The Santa Fe trade was a demonstration of the mutual benefits of strengthened
connections between the United States and Mexico. It was little cause for concern
among Mexican officials. But Texas was more worrisome. The persistent attempts of
Presidents James Monroe and John Quincy Adams to negotiate a purchase of the
border province added to deepening feelings in Mexico City that the presence of
Americans there would be used as an excuse for annexation. As the Texians called for
increased local independence, the Tejanos found themselves torn between their
hopes of economic development and their loyalty to the new Mexican nation.

In an attempt to protect their border province, in 1830 the Mexican congress
passed a Colonization Law, canceling all pending empresario contracts, banning further immigration from the United States, and authorizing the occupation of the
province by the Mexican army. It was one thing to send troops, raising panic and fear
among Texians, but quite another to close the border to Americans determined to
cross it. By the early 1830s the Southwest was experiencing an epidemic of "Texas
Fever." Mary Austin Holley, acting as press agent for her cousin, penned a promotional account that intensified the outbreak. Texas, she wrote, has "a soil that yields
the fruit of nearly all latitudes, almost spontaneously, with a climate of perpetual

summer." The cattle were fatter, the sugar cane was taller, and the cotton was finer than any other country in America. In short, Texas "is adapted, beyond most lands, both to *delight* the senses and *enrich* the pockets." Hundreds of cabins in Alabama, Mississippi, and Louisiana soon stood deserted, signs pinned to their doors printed with the initials *GTT*—"Gone to Texas." Over the next five years the Texian population rose from seven thousand to nearly thirty thousand, and by 1835 Tejanos were outnumbered seven to one.[14]

Texians were divided into two political factions. Austin's group, known as the Peace Party, argued for Texas continuing in the Mexican union with more autonomy, the complete legalization of slavery, and the elimination of all barriers to free trade with the United States. Leading Tejanos shared many of these sentiments. Indeed, marriage frequently sealed the alliance of Texians and Tejanos. Erastus "Deaf" Smith, one of the first Anglos to settle in San Antonio, married into the prominent Duran family, and James Bowie, a Louisianan best known for the shape and effectiveness of his trademark knife, courted and married the daughter of the vice governor of the province, bringing him into close association with the most prominent Tejano families. At Austin's request the *ayuntamiento* (town council) of San Antonio issued a statement supporting much of his political program. "North Americans reclaimed a considerable part of these lands from the desert," the council declared. "They planted cotton and sugar cane, introduced the cotton gin, and imported machinery for the cultivation of sugar and sawmills to cut wood economically. We owe these advances to the efforts of these hard-working colonists." But fearing that the Anglo majority would reduce them to political impotence, the Tejanos of San Antonio refused to endorse Texas statehood. As historian David J. Weber writes, "They sought reform in a way that would protect their own interests."[15]

Austin's moderates were opposed by the Texian War Party, which demanded the secession of Texas from the Mexican federation and its annexation by the United States. William Barret Travis, a volatile and ambitious young lawyer from Mississippi, became the rallying point for this group. Like many other settlers, Travis had come to Texas to escape creditors and a failed marriage, leaving his wife behind to nurse his infant son and fend off the bill collectors. He was motivated by a combination of patriotism and profit-seeking. "If the country should be saved, I may make him a splendid fortune," he wrote to his son's guardian back in Mississippi. "But if the country should be lost and I should perish, he will have nothing but the proud recollection that he is the son of a man who died for his country." In 1835 Travis and a group of hot-headed followers forced the surrender of a Mexican garrison supervising the collection of import duties at Galveston Bay. The actions of the War Party were condemned by the moderates, who placed their faith in Austin, in Mexico City making their case.[16]

Austin, however, fell under the growing Mexican suspicion of all Americans, was

thrown into jail, and was kept for eighteen months in a small windowless cell. When finally released, he was a convert to independence. But Austin's day had passed. A more volatile breed of Texian was now in the saddle. There was David Crockett, who had recently lost his congressional seat. "I told the people of my district that if they saw fit to reelect me, I would serve them faithfully as I had done," he told a crowd. "But if not, they might go to hell, and I would go to Texas. I was beaten, gentlemen, and here I am." Then there was Samuel Houston, a giant of a man whose girth was matched by his enormous charisma. He had served two congressional terms in Tennessee and began a promising term as governor. But when his young wife abandoned him, he resigned and escaped to the life of an Indian trader. His travels brought him to Texas in the early 1830s, and by 1835 he had relocated there. Houston and Crockett hoped to make a new start on this new frontier. They arrived just in time for a revolution.[17]

The attack on the garrison at Galveston Bay convinced conservatives in Mexico City that the Texians were in revolt. Rebellion against central authority was simmering in other provinces as well, and in October Mexican president Antonio López de Santa Anna issued a decree abolishing all state legislatures and placing the central government directly in charge of local affairs, essentially transforming himself into a dictator. With an army of four thousand, Santa Anna marched north, crushing all opponents in his path. In Texas there was panic. The Mexican army was advancing, wrote a committee of Texians in Matagorda, "to give liberty to our slaves and to make slaves of ourselves."[18]

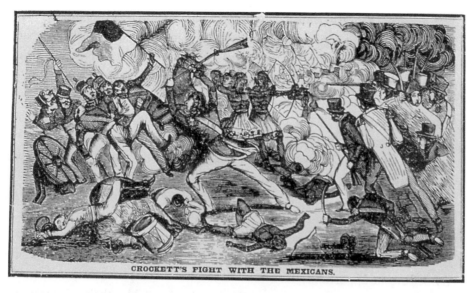

"Crockett's Fight with the Mexicans." From Ben Hardin's Crockett Almanac, 1842 *(Boston, 1841). Yale University.*

Texians now took up arms, joined by a number of leading Tejanos. They besieged San Antonio and at the cost of much destruction forced the withdrawal of the Mexican troops stationed there. "Our army owes many thanks to the brave inhabitants," one Texian veteran wrote a number of years later, for they "ranked themselves on the side of liberty, and fought bravely with the Texan forces. Were all the Mexicans such ardent lovers of liberty." But Tejano supporters of the rebellion were on dangerous ground. Condemned as traitors by Mexican authorities, they also came under suspicion of disloyalty by many Texians. "Two different tribes on the same hunting ground will never get along together," declared Houston, who had been named commander in chief of the motley independence army. Considering San Antonio and the southern half of the province indefensible because of its Tejano majority, he ordered his troops north, leaving only a small detachment under the command of William Travis to hold San Antonio. At the approach of Santa Anna's army most Tejanos fled the city and the Texians—including James Bowie and David Crockett—fortified themselves in the ancient mission ruin of the Alamo. "The citizens of this municipality are all our enemies," Travis raged. "Those who have not joined us in this extremity should be declared public enemies."[19]

In fact there were Tejanos with the Texians in the Alamo—a group of armed horsemen under the command of Captain Juan Seguín, son of a prominent provincial leader. Travis might have led a retreat—there was no strategic significance to holding the Alamo when Santa Anna could simply have swept north, leaving a regiment to keep the Texians boxed up. But instead he dispatched Seguín and his men with an urgent appeal to Houston for support and issued a "liberty or death" proclamation swearing not to give an inch. Probably thinking to terrorize the Texians, Santa Anna decided he would destroy the Alamo and all its defenders. His siege ended in a five-hour assault on March 6, 1836, that cost the lives of some 600 Mexican soldiers and 187 Texians. Santa Anna had their bodies burned so that there would be no memorial. Yet the slogan "Remember the Alamo" became the emotional fulcrum that helped keep doubters in the camp of independence and potential deserters in the ranks. At the little village of Washington-on-the-Brazos an emotional meeting of delegates declared Texas an independent republic.

Santa Anna moved on to the town of Goliad, where he captured and executed 371 Anglo prisoners, whom he castigated as "pirates" (filibusters), then pushed north as the Texian army fell back in panic. But then the Mexican general made a disastrous error, dividing his army to terrorize the people by burning and plundering the country. Seizing the opportunity, Houston and 900 Texians surprised Santa Anna and a rump force of 1,200 at the San Jacinto River on April 21. Taking their revenge for the Alamo and Goliad, the Texians slaughtered more than 600 of the disorganized Mexicans. Santa Anna was captured and, under duress, signed a treaty granting Texas independence.

The Texian-Tejano alliance survived the revolution, but just barely. Houston was elected president of the Texas republic with Mexican empresario Lorenzo de Zavala as his vice president. Juan Seguín, who led a troop of Tejano cavalry at the Battle of San Jacinto, became the mayor of San Antonio. But bitter anti-Tejano sentiment flourished among Texians in the aftermath of the war. Seguín did his best to protect the Tejano community, but it was a losing battle. "At every hour of the day and night, my countrymen ran to me for protection against the assaults or exactions of these adventurers," he later recalled. "Could I leave them defenseless, exposed to the assaults of foreigners, who, on the pretext that they were Mexican, treated them worse than brutes?" Finally, under threat of murder, Seguín was forced to flee with his family to Mexico. His personal story told of the Tejano tragedy. "White folks and Mexicans were never made to live together, anyhow," an American woman declared shortly after the war. "The Mexicans had no business here." Over the next two decades entire Tejano communities were uprooted and expelled. By the 1850s San Antonio had been "half-deserted" by its Spanish-speaking population. As Juan Seguín wrote, he had become "a foreigner in my native land."[20]

The United States recognized the independent Republic of Texas on March 3, 1837. The new Texas constitution legalized slavery and barred the residence of all free persons of color. "I love the country, but now look at my situation," free black rancher Greenbury Logan, who owned a spread in the Austin colony, wrote in a petition to Texas authorities requesting permission to remain in the country. "Every privilege dear to a free man is taken away." His request was denied. Logan's story, like Seguín's,

Juan Seguin. *Painting by Jefferson Wright, 1838. Texas State Library and Archives Commission.*

stood for something larger. The problem of slavery and race was immediately thrust into the national and congressional debate over the admission of Texas to the union of states. Texas would remain on the back burner until American expansionists could find a way to subsume this controversy within a general enthusiasm for "continentalism."[21]

A quarter-century or more before the first great movement of Americans across the Mississippi, communities of Shawnees, Delawares, Cherokees, and other eastern Indians migrated across the river in an attempt to avoid the bloody warfare of the late eighteenth century. These Indian migrations often were defensive, but they were also voluntary. In 1804 Congress authorized the president to assist those tribes who sought to avoid the encroachments of American settlers by removing west of the Mississippi, and during the next two decades a number of Indian communities from the South established emigrant colonies in the West.

But as cotton production expanded, and the price of land skyrocketed, many white southerners demanded the final liquidation of all Indian title within their borders. Georgia presented the most difficult case. In 1802 the state finally agreed to relinquish its lingering claim to lands in the Old Southwest in exchange for a federal promise to extinguish all remaining Indian title within its boundaries. Over the next quarter-century, however, the Cherokees resisted all federal attempts to broker an exchange of their homeland in the northern highlands of Georgia for lands west of the Mississippi. By 1825 the "Cherokee problem" had become the driving issue in Georgia politics. In the words of a popular tune of the day:

> All I want in God's creation
> Is a pretty little wife and a big plantation
> Away up yonder in the Cherokee Nation.[22]

It was not "virgin land" the Georgians wanted. The Cherokee Nation had prospered. Cherokee farmers had improved their holdings and participated in the booming cotton economy. Cherokee leaders had centralized their tribal government and replaced the old law of blood with a formal legal code. In 1827 they adopted a republican constitution and declared themselves an independent nation, with complete jurisdiction over their own territory and affairs. The governor of Georgia railed against what he called "this presumptuous document," contending that the state would never consent to *imperium in imperio*. Along with the other tribes of the South—the Creeks, Choctaws, Chickasaws, and Seminoles—the Cherokees were the great success story of American Indian policy, commonly referred to as "The Five Civilized Tribes." That very success, however, exposed the unresolved contradiction at the heart of that policy. Few political leaders of the United States were prepared to

Andrew Jackson. *Painting by Ralph Eleaser Whiteside Earl, c. 1835. Yale University Art Gallery, Mabel Brady Garvan Collection.*

accept an outcome in which Indians adopted many customs of the dominant society but retained independent cultures and polities.[23]

The crisis came soon after the Cherokee declaration of independence. For many years rumors had persisted of gold in the streams of the Cherokee Nation. Indeed, many Cherokees knew this to be true; a young Indian boy found a large gold nugget in a stream near his home in 1815, but his family kept the discovery quiet. In July 1829, however, American prospectors found gold in quantity in the northern Georgia hills, precipitating a frantic rush that by year's end had some ten thousand miners scouring the watercourses of the Cherokee homeland. Cherokee people call this event the "Great Intrusion."

Andrew Jackson had just become the first westerner to be elected president. Jackson took the position that it was farcical for the federal government to treat Indian nations as if they were sovereign and independent states. Thus assured of presidential sympathy, the Georgia legislature extended the state's jurisdiction over Cherokee territory and sent the Georgia Guard to protect American miners and squatters and intimidate Cherokee families. Almost simultaneously Jackson presented Congress with his Indian Removal Act, a comprehensive plan for the relocation west of the Mississippi of all eastern Indians. Removal was to be voluntary, the president insisted, but in the context of the times everyone understood that Jackson's policy was tantamount to eliminating federal protection and exposing Indians to the aggression of the individual states. The passage of the Removal Act in 1830, despite significant opposition, made it clear that the federal government would ignore the actual accomplishments of nations such as the Cherokees in order to respond to the demands of land speculators, miners, and white settlers.

Federal commissioners soon pressured the Choctaws, Chickasaws, and Creeks into signing treaties of removal. The Cherokees, however, remained adamant in their opposition to removal. With the assistance of missionary and lawyer friends they brought suit in federal court against Georgia's infringement of their sovereignty. Heading their legal team was William Wirt, formerly attorney general in the administration of John Quincy Adams. In Washington to help prepare the case, John Ross, the elected paramount chief of the Cherokee Nation, spoke to a delegation of Iroquois who came to offer support. "Our position may be compared to a solitary tree in an open space," he told them, "where all the forest trees around have been prostrated by a furious tornado."[24]

Chief Justice John Marshall wrote the majority opinion in *Cherokee Nation v. Georgia* (1831). There could be no doubt, Marshall declared, that the Cherokee Nation was "a distinct political society, separated from others, [and] capable of managing its own affairs and governing itself." But, he continued, "it may well be doubted whether those tribes which reside within the United States can, with strict accuracy, be denominated foreign nations. They may, more correctly, perhaps, be denominated *domestic dependent nations.*" Because only foreign nations could bring suit against one of the states, Marshall threw out the Cherokee case against Georgia. President Jackson took this as a vindication, but Marshall's opinion seemed to suggest that Indian communities might claim a place within the federal system of countervailing checks and balances. Within months the Georgia legislature created an opportunity to test that implication when it passed an act regulating the presence of white men in Cherokee territory. When two missionaries to the Cherokees defied the state's authority over their movements, they were imprisoned, and one of them, Samuel Worcester, brought a federal suit against Georgia. The case quickly found its way to the Supreme Court as *Worcester v. Georgia* (1832). Writing for the majority, Chief Justice Marshall concluded that the Cherokees constituted "a distinct community, occupying its own territory, with boundaries accurately described, in which the laws of Georgia can have no force, and which the citizens of Georgia have no right to enter, but with the assent of the Cherokees themselves, or in conformity with treaties, and with the acts of Congress."[25]

"Glorious news!" the Cherokee leader Elias Boudinot wrote home. Jackson had a different reaction. "The decision of the Supreme Court has fell still born," he wrote, and predicted that the court "would find that they cannot coerce Georgia to yield to its mandate." Indeed, encouraged by Jackson, Georgia ignored the Court's ruling. The president was perfectly willing to violate the Constitution to get rid of the Indians.[26]

The Cherokees now faced an impossible choice. If they remained in Georgia they would surely lose their lands as well as their political identity. If they agreed to removal they might maintain that identity, but at the cost of surrendering the homeland they had fought for two centuries to hold. One faction among the leadership—including Major Ridge, his son John Ridge, and Elias Boudinot—came around to the view that further resistance was useless. "We all know," John Ridge wrote to Chief John Ross, "that we can't be a Nation here. I hope we shall attempt to establish it somewhere else!" But Ross rejected the views of the so-called Treaty Party, which represented a minority of the Cherokees.[27]

In 1835 Georgia authorities arrested Ross and his supporters among the Cherokee leadership, and while they languished in prison federal commissioners negotiated an agreement with leaders of the Treaty Party. They agreed to relinquish the Cherokee homeland for five million dollars (nearly one hundred million dollars in today's values) and the promise of permanent lands on the Arkansas River, west of the Mississippi. "An intelligent minority has a moral right, indeed a moral duty, to save a blind and ignorant majority from inevitable ruin and destruction," Elias Boudinot offered in justification. "I have signed my death warrant," John Ridge pronounced as he put down his pen. "We can die," replied Boudinot, "but the great Cherokee Nation will be saved." From prison, Ross denounced this "fraud upon the Cherokee people." Fifteen thousand Cherokees—nearly the entire population—signed a petition to the Senate opposing the treaty, and there was a public outcry among supporters of the Cherokees throughout the country. In the end the Senate approved the treaty by only one vote. The Treaty of New Echota, declared former president John Quincy Adams, would endure as "an eternal disgrace upon the country."[28]

A small group of Treaty Party supporters left for the West, but most Cherokees refused to leave. Finally in the spring of 1838 seven thousand army troops under the command of General Winfield Scott began systematically rounding them up. An eyewitness testified to the horror:

> Squads of troops were sent to search out with rifle and bayonet every small cabin hidden away in the coves or by the sides of mountain streams, to seize and bring in as prisoners all the occupants. Families at dinner were startled by the sudden gleam of bayonets in the doorway and rose to be driven with blows and oaths along the weary miles of trail that led to the stockade. Men were seized in their fields, or going along the road, women were taken from their spinning wheels and children from their play. In many cases, on turning for one last look as they crossed the ridge, they saw their homes in flames, fired by the lawless rabble that followed on the heels of the soldiers to loot and pillage.

Eighteen thousand Cherokees were herded into concentration camps. There were inadequate supplies and many people suffered from malnutrition and dysentery. Hundreds, perhaps thousands, died of epidemic disease. Despite his bitter opposi-

Major Ridge, Cherokee chief. From Thomas L. McKenney and James Hall, History of the Indian Tribes of North America . . . , *3 vols. (Philadelphia, 1836–44). Beinecke.*

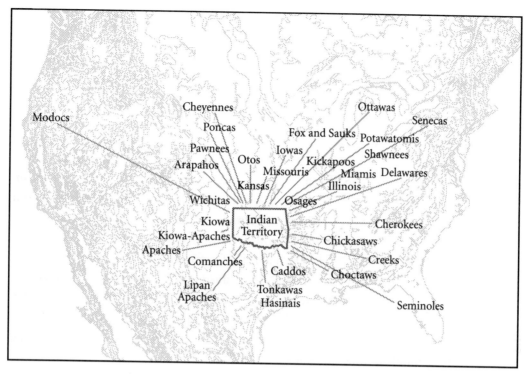

INDIAN REMOVAL

tion to removal, Chief Ross felt compelled to take charge of the exodus. Nearly every family lost a loved one during the forced march westward of more than a thousand miles. Quatie Ross, the chief's wife, died during the trip, which the Cherokees call the "Trail on Which We Cried."

In 1839, citing a Cherokee law that proscribed death for any leader selling tribal land without the council's permission, a group of Ross supporters ambushed and killed Major Ridge, John Ridge, and Elias Boudinot. Terrorism would become a staple of Cherokee politics, and the bitter factional fighting continued for many years. "Murders have become so frequent," one Cherokee wrote several years later, that "the people care as little about hearing these things as they would hear the death of a common dog. I think now there is to be no end to bloodshed."[29]

There were other violent episodes of Indian removal. The most infamous was the campaign to remove the Seminole people of Florida. The problem here was the presence in the Seminole Nation of many African Americans, including runaway slaves—some integrated and intermixed in Indian communities, others living in separate but affiliated villages. Southerners were not so much interested in Seminole lands—mostly the swamps of central Florida—but they were dedicated to reclaiming fugitive slaves and enslaving the other African Americans who lived among the Indians.

A few Seminole chiefs signed a removal treaty in 1832, but the majority refused to abide by it. When the army moved into central Florida to enforce the removal order in 1836, the war chief Osceola struck back and inflicted a humiliating defeat. The war dragged on for years, with the United States unable to root out the Seminoles from the swamps. "We have committed the error of attempting to remove them when their lands were not required for agricultural purposes," wrote General Thomas S. Jesup, commander of the operation, "when the greater portion of their country was an unexplored wilderness, the interior of which we were as ignorant of as of the interior of China." Acknowledging defeat, the army offered Osceola safe conduct to a peace negotiation, then treacherously captured him and threw him into prison, where he languished and died. By 1842 the majority of Seminoles had been harried into moving west, and even though hundreds remained in the Everglades, the federal government finally called off the operation, which had become extremely unpopular. What did this war accomplish? The removal of some three thousand Seminoles to Indian Territory, but at the cost of twenty million dollars and the lives of more than fifteen hundred American soldiers.[30]

Under the terms of Jackson's removal policy thousands of Indians from the states of the Old Northwest were also forcibly removed to the trans-Mississippi West. Many of them had been extremely successful in the ways of the whites, becoming landowners, farmers, stockraisers, even businessmen, while still maintaining their distinct cultural identity. Now Americans began to also press them to cede their lands in exchange for territory in the West. For the most part there was little violence, although Indians resisted removal for as long as they were able. Many, like the Winnebagos of Wisconsin, eventually drifted back to their former homes, unable to adjust to the arid western environment and longing to return to the graves of their ancestors.

In the case of the Sauk and Fox people of Illinois, pressures for removal resulted in a brief but brutal war. Several chiefs signed a treaty ceding their lands east of the Mississippi and settled on a reservation across the river. But a dissident leader by the name of Black Hawk protested. "My reason teaches me that land cannot be sold," he declared. "The Great Spirit gave it to his children to live upon, and cultivate, as far as is necessary for their subsistence. Nothing can be sold but such things as can be carried away." In 1832 Black Hawk led two thousand followers back across the Mississippi into Illinois, precipitating a general panic among settlers. Soon the state militia confronted the Indians. Black Hawk sent a delegation to negotiate under a flag of truce, but when the excited volunteers fired on them, the chief unloosed his five hundred experienced warriors, who routed the Illinoisans. Black Hawk and his people then fled into Wisconsin, where they were finally cornered by the outraged militia.

Black Hawk and his lieutenants in chains. From George Catlin, Catalogue of Catlin's Indian Gallery of Portraits . . . *(New York, 1837). Beinecke.*

At the Massacre of Bad Ax River, dozens of Indians were slaughtered, including many women and children.[31]

Emigrant Indians found the arid western plains far different from their eastern homelands. Most had left their goods behind, and many lacked even basic equipment. Native peoples of the plains resented these incursions into their territory, and the emigrants were frequently required to defend themselves against fierce attack. But Indian settlers successfully transplanted their communities to the river valleys of the trans-Mississippi West, and gradually their settlements expanded as they opened new farms and plantations. Within a few years the Five Civilized Tribes were shipping cotton, grain, and livestock to markets in neighboring states. Each of the southern nations reestablished their governments, built towns, and opened schools. Emigrant Indians "were carriers of Western civilization, of Anglo-American culture, onto the plains," historian Arrell Gibson concludes. They "introduced schools, churches, constitutional government, commercial agriculture and stock raising, and slaveholding into the western wilderness fifty years before the process of cultural transformation was taken up by Anglo-American and European immigrant settlers."[32]

While Indians were settling the eastern fringe of the Great Plains, many Americans were focusing on the far-western region of Oregon. The story began in New England, where Yankees in the 1790s had become aware of the commercial potential of the Pacific Northwest. Great sailing ships returned to Boston harbor smelling of tea and spice, their holds spilling out rich profit from a trade that began with barter among the coastal Indians for sea otter furs, which were carried to China, where they were traded for prized Oriental goods. John Quincy Adams, delegate at the negotiations concluding the War of 1812, knowing how lucrative this Pacific trade could be, pressed for fixing the boundary between the United States and British North America at the forty-ninth parallel. If extended to the Pacific, this would have given his country sole possession of present-day Oregon and Washington. The British refused. Since the Nootka Convention of 1790 they had considered themselves sovereign along the coast between California and Russian America. The problem of the boundary was relegated to an international commission.

The claims of the United States to the Pacific Northwest were weak by comparison with the British, or even the Russians, both of whom had established substantial outposts along the coast at Fort Vancouver and New Archangel, respectively. The Americans pointed out that in 1792 the American captain Robert Gray had been first to pilot a vessel into the mouth of the region's great river, leaving his ship's name, the *Columbia,* upon its waters; that in 1804 Lewis and Clark had traversed and mapped the Columbia; and that in 1811 the American trading post of Astoria had been the first imperial settlement on its banks. Yet these claims meant little against the effective occupancy of the Pacific coast by other powers. No matter. Adams, an avid expansionist when he became secretary of state in the cabinet of President James Monroe in 1817, was determined to extend American sovereignty to the Pacific. "Our proper dominion," he confided in his diary, is "the continent of North America. . . . The United States and North America are identical."[33]

Adams pursued his goal through the use of effective diplomacy—so effective, in fact, that among diplomatic historians he has the reputation of being the greatest of all American secretaries of state. Adams had served a long stint as American ambassador to Russia, and parlaying his connections there he threatened the British with a Russian-American alliance and was able to win acceptance of a northern boundary at the forty-ninth parallel, extending from the Great Lakes to the Rockies. Although the British refused to concede the Columbia River—most of which runs south of 49°—they agreed that the Pacific Northwest country would remain "free and open" to the subjects of both countries for ten years. It was essentially the same formulation that the British had wrung from the Spanish during the Nootka controversy.

Meanwhile, Adams opened negotiations with the Spanish, who were preoccupied with their crumbling Latin American empire. In the midst of discussions over border disputes with ambassador Luis de Onís, word reached the negotiating table that General Andrew Jackson, hero of the War of 1812, had invaded Florida. To Spanish

Tlingit village of Howkan, Alaska. Photograph by John G. Brady, c. 1890. Beinecke.

protests Adams replied that Florida had for too long been a refuge for hostile Indians, runaway slaves, and bandits and that unless Spain established order on the border, the United States would have no choice but to seize the province in self-defense.
In the comprehensive Adams-Onís Treaty of 1819 beleaguered Spain agreed to cede
Florida to the United States, to draw a definitive boundary between Texas and
Louisiana, and to withdraw all claims in the West north of the forty-second parallel,
the northern border of present-day California, Nevada, and Utah.

Finally the secretary of state turned his attention to Russia. In an attempt to protect the domain of the Russian-American Company, in 1821 the czar declared the
northern coast off limits to all but his people. Adams's response—"The American
continents are no longer subjects of any new European colonial establishments"—
was the first articulation of the principle he later embodied in the famous Monroe
Doctrine, which the president announced in 1823. Countering public bluster with
private negotiation, however, in 1824 Adams agreed to regulate more closely the activity of American traders (who continued to stir up trouble for the Russians, selling arms and liquor to coastal Indian peoples), in exchange for a voluntary Russian

limitation of their claims to latitudes north of 54° 40′, today's southern boundary of Alaska. When Great Britain and the United States renewed their "joint occupancy" agreement in 1827, they remained as the last of the imperial competitors for the Oregon country. It was evident that both nations were buying time, and time for the Americans meant settlement. [34]

The two men who first brought Oregon to public attention represented rampant idealism and speculative capitalism. Hall Jackson Kelley was an eccentric Boston schoolteacher whose interest in the region was aroused by the reports of Lewis and Clark. In a flood of letters, speeches, and pamphlets during the 1820s, Kelley vividly brought Oregon—"the most valuable of all the unoccupied parts of the earth"—to public attention. He talked of a new Massachusetts Bay Colony in the Far West, another "city on a hill" throwing light into the wilderness. Only "the active sons of American freedom," Kelley argued, could save Oregon from "the disastrous consequences of a foreign and corrupt population." In 1832 he organized the "Oregon Colonization Society," but the group never got beyond the discussion stage. Kelley's efforts, however, inspired Nathaniel Wyeth, a Cambridge entrepreneur in the ice business, who had more concrete ventures in mind. From 1832 to 1836 Wyeth sought to lock up the trade in furs and fish along the Columbia River, twice journeying overland to the Oregon Country. But the supply ships he sent around the Horn failed to reach him in time, and Wyeth's company collapsed. Although their schemes failed, Kelley's propaganda and Wyeth's enterprise helped to make Oregon a household word.[35]

The first actual American settlement had religious motivations. In 1834, in response to what was thought to be a call for missionaries by the native people of the region, the Methodists sent a small company led by the Reverend Jason Lee overland to Oregon with Wyeth's expedition. Once located in Oregon's Willamette Valley, however, Lee seemed quickly to forget about the Indians, ministering instead to a community of retired trappers and their native wives. Lee was the first of numerous Protestant missionaries in Oregon who served the settlers better than they did the natives. Not to be outdone, the Congregationalists and Presbyterians made plans to send their own missionaries to Oregon. They selected Marcus Whitman, a young medical doctor from western New York, who yearned to combine his new medical skills with his religious zeal. The board frowned on bachelor missionaries—worried, perhaps, that they would succumb to the charms of native women—and so when an associate told Whitman of a young woman in a nearby town whose application for missionary work had been denied because she was unmarried, Whitman hurried there. In a quick weekend courtship Whitman and Narcissa Prentiss agreed to enter missionary work together. "There was no pretense about romantic love," writes Narcissa's biographer, Julie Roy Jeffrey. "Both saw the marriage as the means of fulfilling cherished dreams." In 1836 the newlyweds joined Henry and Eliza Spalding, another missionary couple, in the first overland migration of American families to Oregon.[36]

The wives quarreled and the men disagreed, and when they reached Oregon they established mission stations a hundred or so miles apart—the Whitmans at Wai-ilatpu near the future Walla Walla, Washington, and the Spaldings at Lapwai, near modern-day Lewiston, Idaho. The strong faith of the group persisted, but all were severely challenged by what Narcissa called "the thick darkness of heathenism." During their whole time in Oregon country no more than twenty Indians were baptized. A lack of sympathy separated the Protestants from their potential flock. The local Cayuse people staunchly defended their customs, and the Whitmans saw them as "insolent, proud, domineering, arrogant, and ferocious," in Narcissa's words. "The Dr. and his wife were very severe and hard," the Indians told an interpreter, "which occasioned frequent quarrels." Meanwhile Catholic missionaries in the region, led by the Jesuit Pierre De Smet, were enjoying a good deal of success, precisely because of their skill at crossing cultural boundaries.[37]

Gradually the Whitmans turned their attention to groups of American settlers who began to appear in the area. "It does not concern me so much what is to become of any particular set of Indians," Whitman wrote candidly to Narcissa's parents. "I have no doubt our greatest work is to be to aid the white settlement of this country." He went east and promoted Oregon as a promised land for settlers. In 1843 he returned triumphantly with the "Great Migration" of 1843, more than a thousand emigrants bound for Oregon.[38]

The Oregon settlement that Whitman helped to prime would indirectly bring a grim conclusion to his life's work. The colonists who marched down the Blue Mountains through the Grand Ronde and the stark hills of the upper Columbia carried diseases such as measles, deadly to native people without immunity. The Cayuse were one of the tribes nearly decimated by an epidemic in 1847, and survivors turned their grief to lashing hatred. On a cold November morning in 1847, with the ghosts of their dead children behind them, Cayuse men broke into the Whitman mission and murdered Marcus, Narcissa, and ten others.

How do historians explain the overland migration to the Pacific, one of the most remarkable of the many remarkable incidents in the epic of the American West? It resulted from a convergence of circumstances. During the mid-1830s a mania for land speculation caused the disappearance of the last of the public domain in the trans-Appalachian West. Soon thereafter the Panic of 1837 inaugurated a prolonged depression. The wholesale price index of farm products fell to the lowest level in American history. Many westerners set to wondering if they might not better their

Cayuse Indians attack the Whitman mission, 1847. Yale University.

circumstances elsewhere. A hatred of slavery kept many from considering Texas, while others believed that the West beyond the Missouri was a desert, fit only for nomads, buffalo hunters, and the emigrant Indians forced to abandon their eastern homelands. Perhaps Pike and Long had been right, perhaps westering would end here.

This was the moment when the missionary effort in the Far West came to wide public attention. People heard speeches by Jason Lee and Marcus Whitman or read about them in their local newspapers. Others learned from the propaganda of Hall Kelley. In 1841 and 1842 small parties of adventuresome emigrants headed west via the Platte River trail pioneered by the fur companies. Suddenly hundreds of people throughout the West came down with a previously undiagnosed illness. "The Oregon fever has broke out," wrote an observer in early 1843, "and is now raging like any other contagion." Oregon fever was little different from the popular hope that motivated the settlement of Texas. One emigrant from Missouri later recalled hearing the recruiting speech of Peter H. Burnett, an organizer of the "Great Migration" of 1843. He stood on a box and gave a regular stump speech. Oregon was a land with soil so rich, a farmer could raise huge crops of wheat with little effort; with a climate so mild, livestock could forage for themselves all winter. "And they do say, gentlemen, they do say," Burnett concluded with a wink, "that out in Oregon the pigs are running about under the great acorn trees, round and fat, and already cooked, with knives and forks sticking in them so that you can cut off a slice whenever you are hungry." Pioneers had told the same tall tale about Kentucky, about Missouri, about Texas.[39]

But Oregon was farther—much farther. Emigrants counted off the two thousand

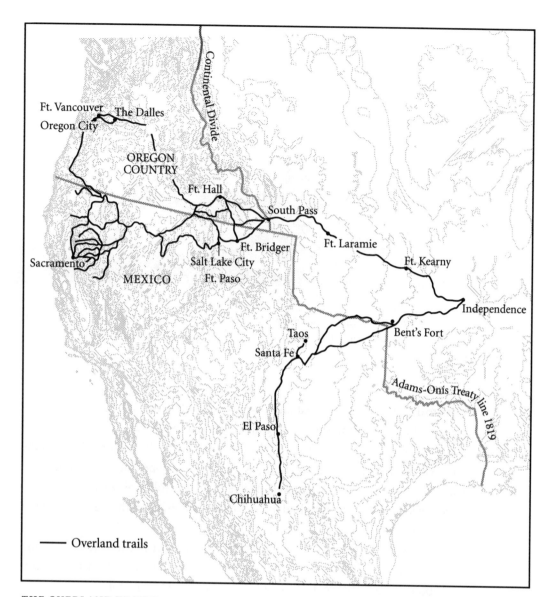

THE OVERLAND TRAILS

miles of the Oregon Trail at the rate of just twelve to fifteen miles per day, the speed of oxen and wagons. They departed in the spring, as soon as the grass was high enough for the stock to graze, and prayed they would make it over the Far Western mountains before the first winter storms. They spent May and June crossing the Great Plains, following the Platte River to Fort Laramie, a lingering landmark of the fur trade. Heading up the Sweetwater River they traveled over the broad saddle in the Rockies known as South Pass, then followed timber and water over rough terrain to Fort Hall, which they reached in early August. At that point they had traveled two-thirds the distance, but their journey was only about half completed. It was here they

VIEW DECENDING THE GRAND ROUND FOOT OF THE BLUE MOUNTAIN.

Emigrant wagons in the Blue Mountains of Oregon. From Major Osborne Cross, A Report . . . of
the March of the Regiment of Mounted Riflemen to Oregon . . . *(Washington, D.C., 1850).*
Beinecke.

began to discover the heart-breaking thing about the Oregon Trail: the closer the destination, the tougher and slower the going. The next few weeks they spent clinging to the torturous cliff ledges of the Snake River leading to the dreaded Blue Mountains, which they could surmount only with the aid of ropes, pulleys, and quickly made winches. Finally, if all went well, they reached the Columbia River in early October and ferried the final hundred miles downriver to the mouth of the Willamette River, their destination.

"How do the old woman and the girls like the idea of such a long journey?" one farmer asked a neighbor who had decided to remove to Oregon. "They feel mighty peert about it," came the reply, "and Suke says she shan't be easy till we start." Other women were not so "peert"—a frontier colloquialism meaning "perky." "Oh let us not go," Mary Jones cried when her husband, John, told her of his decision. But "it made no difference," she lamented. Lucy Deady, daughter of an emigrant family, wrote that her despairing mother knew "nothing of this move until father had decided to go." One study of women's overland trail diaries found not a single wife who initiated the idea of moving, while nearly a third actively objected. One emigrant wife told a hired hand that "the journey for which she was bending all her energies in preparation was not in her judgment a wise business movement. But 'Wilson wished to go,' and that settled the question with her."[40]

There is no way of knowing how many women successfully kept their husbands at home sweating out the fever, but it is worth noting that only a small minority

Wagon train passing through Castle Creek Valley. Photograph by W. H. Killingworth, date unknown. Beinecke.

risked the overland trek to Oregon. From the 1840s until the completion of the transcontinental railroad in 1869, perhaps fifty thousand emigrants traveled to Oregon, and the American population there grew from a few hundred to somewhat more than one hundred thousand. That is substantial growth, but it needs to be kept in perspective. During the same period Iowa's population rose to 1.2 million, better than ten times that of the Pacific Northwest. Americans were still ramblers, but most rambled to the next county or the next state, not all the way to Oregon.

———

During this period the federal government became increasingly involved in the emergent West. One sign was the growing autonomy of the Corps of Topographical Engineers, which by act of Congress in 1838 took its assignments directly from the president and the secretary of war. The scientific orientation of the corps was clear; its officers frequently represented the scientific community in such organizations as the American Philosophical Society, where Thomas Jefferson and Meriwether Lewis had made their plans. The fraternization of science and government was further encouraged by the founding of the Smithsonian Institution in Washington, D.C., in 1846. The Topographical Engineers cooperated closely with these and other eastern scientific groups to plan observations and collections in the West. Printed reports of the corp's expeditions typically included expensive illustrations and appendixes detailing the botany, zoology, geology, meteorology, ethnology, and cartography of the new land. But the agenda of the corps was also practical, for its pursuit of knowledge was in the service of expansion across the continent.

John C. Frémont. Engraving by J. C. Buttre, c. 1856. Beinecke.

No one better embodied this combination than John Charles Frémont, the best known and most controversial officer of the Topographical Engineers. An illegitimate child, Frémont had an eye for opportunity that may have been related to the insecurity of his birth. He took advantage of one friendship to get a naval appointment, which enabled him to master mathematics and engineering. With these scientific tools at his command, he caught his next golden ring in the courtship and marriage of Jessie Benton, daughter of Thomas Hart Benton, senator from Missouri and a powerful western voice in Washington. Benton's contacts were strung along all the lines of command, and he cried out for attention to the needs of the West— greater support for explorations and surveys, land developers, and railroads. Jessie inherited her father's outlook, energy, and iron will. She defied him and eloped when he opposed her marriage to the young, little-known Frémont. Reconciliation came quickly, and Benton became Frémont's powerful patron.

Frémont's first assignments for the corps—which Benton secured—made him into one of the great celebrities of his day. From 1843 to 1844 he surveyed the Oregon Trail with a company made up mostly of metís voyageurs, following a route carefully planned by Benton and President John Tyler himself. They wanted the expedition to appear strictly scientific, and science did provide an important motivation. Frémont and his party brought the best European equipment—barometers, field telescopes, chronometers, and all the rest—taking special pains that they not be jostled or cracked. They calculated innumerable latitudes, longitudes, and elevations and observed such phenomena as the emergence of the first satellite of Jupiter. They collected fossils from the rocks, new plants (such as *Fremontia*), and hundreds of birds, fish, and mammals.

But Frémont's report—skillfully ghostwritten by Jessie Frémont—was more

Jessie Benton Frémont. Photograph by Carleton Watkins, c. 1850. Beinecke.

than a scientific treatise. Attention to availability of water and fuel, grass for pasturage, and the ease of the grade all spoke directly to the needs of overland emigrants. He noted the passage of westering emigrants and even reported spotting domesticated cows, refugees from the wagon trains, grazing among the herds of buffalo. These passages were calculated to communicate the fact that an American move to Oregon was in full swing and that the government was behind it 100 percent. Senator Benton arranged for the printing and distribution, at government expense, of ten thousand copies of the report, including an excellent map of the trail produced by the expedition's cartographer, Charles Preuss. Overnight Frémont became known as the "Great Pathfinder." In reality Frémont was guided by others. His expeditions included a number of Indian scouts and mountain men, including Kit Carson, whose intimate knowledge of the West was a product of nearly twenty years spent as a fur trapper in the southern Rockies. Jessie's narrative neglected the Indians, but was careful to give Carson his due, and he soon became equally famous, the mid-nineteenth-century inheritor of Daniel Boone's mantle (Carson had, in fact, been raised in the home of a Boone descendant). It was a vivid demonstration of the combination of science, practicality, and popular culture that characterized the Topographical Engineers.

Frémont's report became a bestseller among easterners as well as emigrants, exciting talk in New York drawing rooms and Missouri barns. Western writer Joaquin Miller later recalled reading the report as a boy. "I fancied I could see Frémont's men, flags in the air, Frémont at the head, waving his sword, his horse neighing wildly in the mountain wind, with unknown and unnamed empires on every hand." Thousands of pioneers carried Frémont with them as they set out for the empire of the far West.[41]

The most impressive western migration of the era was undertaken by the Mormons, a uniquely American religious sect. In 1847, in one of the greatest treks in all of American history, thousands of members of the Church of Jesus Christ of Latter-day Saints left the Mississippi valley headed for the isolated desert country of the Great Basin, between the Rockies and the Sierra Nevadas.

The founder of the Mormons was Joseph Smith, a visionary who claimed to have discovered, near his home in upstate New York, a set of hammered golden plates covered with strange hieroglyphs. With divine assistance, Smith translated the plates into the *Book of Mormon*, which he published in 1830. It told a tale of one of the lost tribes of Israel that had wandered to the shores of the New World. Eventually the migrants were blessed by the arrival of Jesus, who after his crucifixion in Jerusalem had come to found his true church in America. But in the fullness of time, decadence overwhelmed the tribe and it fell into warring factions, finally self-destructing in a climactic battle reminiscent of Armageddon. The few survivors, the Lamanites, were the ancestors of the American Indians. The *Book of Mormon*, with its references to America as the "land of promise," the "choice above all other lands," offered what historian Jan Shipps calls a "powerful and provocative synthesis of biblical experience and the American dream."[42]

The upper Hudson valley was, in those days, a boiling cauldron of religious enthusiasm, and in that context Smith was able to build a following of several hundred converts within a few years. One of the things that most attracted them was the communitarian emphasis of the Latter-day Saints. The "Saints" lived in exclusively Mormon communities, either at the headquarters Smith founded in Kirtland, Ohio, or a satellite settlement in western Missouri where Smith hoped to build a new "Kingdom of God." Pooling their labor and resources, and distributing goods according to the needs of the people, the Mormons hammered out doctrines that placed the survival of the group above that of the individual. They drew on the same longing for community and order that motivated other utopian experiments of the day, such as those at the communities of Brook Farm in Massachusetts, Oneida in New York, or New Harmony in Indiana. But there was another side to all this. The community was ruled theocratically by Smith and his inner circle. And viewing themselves as the "chosen people," the Mormons kept their distance from their neighbors. In Missouri, surrounding farmers felt threatened by the Mormons' combination of economic collectivism and political authoritarianism, especially when it was practiced by anti-slavery Yankees, and soon the Mormons found themselves under attack by hostile vigilantes. Smith responded by organizing his men into military companies that only inflamed the conflict. Finally in 1838 there was an explosion of violence, encouraged by Missouri's governor, that drove Smith and his followers from the state.

The Mormons reassembled on the banks of the Mississippi in Illinois. With renewed vigor they set to building once again, and the new community—which Smith christened Nauvoo—soon grew into the state's largest town, with more than fifteen thousand residents. Smith began to think big. He built an enormous temple and organized a large military force known as the Nauvoo Legion to protect the Saints. He announced his intention to run for president of the United States and with his closest advisers sketched out a plan for a fabulous Mormon empire in the American West. But soon the Mormons had become involved in the same hostile relations with their neighbors.

Perhaps most fateful was the development of the practice of "plural marriage" among the Saints. For years there had been rumors of sexual improprieties among the Mormon elite, and evidence suggests that Smith and his inner circle had begun practicing polygamy by the early 1840s. It was an age of dramatic change, as expanding commerce and industry transformed the ways ordinary people lived. Utopian reformers began to experiment with different ways of organizing social life, and especially the relationships between men and women. The Shakers advocated celibacy, the Oneidans "free love," the Mormons "plural marriage." But not surprisingly many Mormons found the new custom difficult to accept. When a group of disaffected members published a broadside condemning plural marriage and other secret practices of the Mormon elite, Smith had their press destroyed by the Nauvoo Legion. The dissidents pressed charges, and state authorities arrested Smith and his brother, Hyrum, for destruction of private property. In June 1844, as they awaited trial, an enraged anti-Mormon mob broke into their cell and murdered both men.

The next two years were a time of terrible struggle for the Mormons, as competing factions jostled for control of the sect. Eventually the leadership was seized by Brigham Young, one of the most talented of Smith's loyal elite. A supporter of the Mormon vision of a western empire, Young laid plans for an exodus that would finally remove the Mormons from harm's way. The great migration began in early 1846. As they evacuated Nauvoo, anti-Mormon mobs were bombarding the town with cannon, destroying the great temple, the proudest of Smith's achievements. The Saints first moved to temporary winter quarters near Omaha, Nebraska. Then, in the spring of 1847, several thousand set out on the Overland Trail, keeping to the north side of the Platte to avoid conflict with other migrating Americans. Crossing the plains and the mountains, they finally arrived that fall at the Great Salt Lake, where Young determined to build a permanent refuge. By 1852 more than ten thousand people were residing in the new Mormon utopia of Salt Lake City, irrigating the desert and making it bloom.

Brigham Young. Engraving by Frederick H. Piercy, 1855. Beinecke.

In addition to Oregon and the Great Salt Lake the other important far western destination of the mid-1840s was the Mexican province of California, where the governor had made it clear that American settlers were welcome. Independence from Spain precipitated great changes in California, most importantly the "secularization" of the mission system. The missions had always legally held title to their lands in the name of the Indians, to be divided among them once they had become good citizens. But Mexican liberals, anxious to curtail the power of the conservative Catholic church, pointed out that the mission padres were unlikely to initiate such a process, for it would lead to a loss of power. So in 1833 Mexico finally ordered the Franciscans to relinquish control over the neophytes. Mission resources were placed in the hands of civil administrators who were charged with distributing them to the Indians. These men, however, made sure that most of the lands and herds stayed in their own hands or passed into the possession of friends and associates. Years later Julio César, a Christian Indian raised at Mission San Luis Rey, remembered the way the administrators "left the mission stripped bare, making an end of everything, even to the plates and cups. . . . [They left] scarcely any furniture in the house and . . . in the storehouse there was nothing at all." The rancho system, and the emerging class of rancheros, built itself up by plundering the missions. In 1820 there were only twenty ranchos in California; by 1840 there were more than six hundred, most carved from the mission estates.[43]

Most former mission Indians set up their own little *ranchería* communities and found work on the ranchos as field hands, or *vaqueros*. According to Salvador Vallejo, a prominent ranchero, "Indians tilled our soil, pastured our cattle, sheared our sheep, cut our lumber, built our houses, paddled our boats, made tiles for our homes, ground our grain, slaughtered our cattle, dressed their hides for market, and made our unburnt bricks; while the Indian women made excellent servants, took care of our children, made every one of our meals." Although they gained a degree of cultural independence in this transition, many Indians were bitter over what amounted to a second round of dispossessions.[44]

The rancheros were soon enmeshed in the international Pacific market, with Americans as their principal trading partners. At first American merchant seamen traded along the California coast for sea otter pelts that they transported to China as part of the great trans-Pacific trading circuit. By the 1820s, however, the sea otter population was in serious decline after years of exploitation, and Americans began bartering manufactured goods and Asian luxuries for the hides and tallow of the vast cattle herds of the ranchos; these raw materials were soon supplying the shoe and soap industries of New England while Californians became dependent upon American products. To increase their production, the rancheros began to mount expeditions into the great central valleys of the province in search of Indian captives to enslave, for more workers meant more cattle.

But the independent Indians of the interior had different ideas. Like the peoples of the plains a century before, they became mounted warriors, supporting themselves by raiding the herds of the rancheros. When Frémont led his expedition through California in 1844 he encountered these fierce people who, he wrote, made "frequent descents upon the settlements west of the Coast Range, which they keep constantly swept of horses; among them are many refugees from the Spanish missions." The Miwoks of the San Joaquin valley were especially successful at raiding; in the south, a number of former neophytes became vaquero chieftains of large warrior bands of Cupeños and Cahuillas. The Indians sold horses to American mountain traders, who herded them to eastern markets across the mountains and deserts.[45]

By encouraging foreigners to settle the interior valleys, California officials hoped to gain control over these tribes. The most prominent settler was John A. Sutter, a Swiss emigrant, who in 1839 obtained a large tract on the interior Sacramento River, where he built a large trading post. Sutter had spent several years in western Missouri, had worked as a trader on the Santa Fe Trail, and had traveled overland to Oregon. He came to California via Fort Vancouver, Honolulu, and the Russian headquarters at New Archangel. As historian Howard Lamar points out, Sutter had seen for himself how "the most successful trading posts in the entire West worked." He brought with him ten Hawaiian workers, who lived in Polynesian grass shacks until Sutter made arrangements for local Indians to construct his headquarters. Like the rancheros, Sutter was utterly dependent upon Indians for labor; they harvested his

John A. Sutter. Photograph by Pach, 1877. Beinecke.

wheat, herded his cattle and horses, and provided the warriors for a ragged but effective militia. Sutter's Fort on the Sacramento became a lodestone for American settlers headed for California.[46]

The first framework for government in Oregon was drawn by the Americans in May 1843. To social-compact theorists, the process would have been more interesting had these settlers worked with a tabula rasa, but in fact they cribbed what they could from *The Organic Laws of the State of Iowa,* the only volume of statute law they had available. Like the Articles of Confederation of the United States after 1783, the new constitution of Oregon provided for an executive committee of three men rather than a governor, and it stipulated voluntary instead of compulsory taxation. The next summer, after the arrival of a new wave of settlers, the constitution was revised. The committee became a single executive, and taxes were made compulsory. Alcoholic drink was prohibited, and African Americans were forbidden from settling and were to be whipped at intervals of six months until they left, a law little enforced but on the books in Oregon until the 1920s.

By 1845 there were already five thousand Americans in the Willamette valley, and their numbers were growing with each annual migration. John McLoughlin, at the Hudson's Bay Company post of Fort Vancouver, graciously took an oath of allegiance to the Oregon provisional government, but he remained responsible for the 750 British subjects scattered north of the Columbia, many of whom expressed alarm at the growing number of Americans with bowie knives and long rifles south along the Willamette. The fur trade of the area was dwindling, and that summer the London directors of the HBC decided to move their post north to a site on Vancouver Island, which has since grown into the city of Victoria, British Columbia. McLoughlin, who wanted to stay where he was, quarreled with the company and resigned. He built a fine home in Oregon City and invested in a millsite, which he later lost because he was not a naturalized citizen. He and his métis wife eked out a modest existence until their deaths in the 1870s.

Once the HBC had literally given ground, the time seemed right for a settlement of the boundary controversy between Great Britain and the United States. President James K. Polk, the Democrat who had beaten the Whigs in a campaign of spread-eagle expansionism, privately asked the British ambassador for acceptance of the forty-ninth parallel, the boundary first proposed by John Quincy Adams after the War of 1812 and supported by every subsequent American president. When the ambassador refused, an angry Polk publicly declared that he would accept nothing less than the whole of the disputed territory from the northern border of California to the southern boundary of Alaska at latitude 54°40'. A stump speech conveys the spirit of the times: "Whar, I say *whar* is the individual who would give the first foot, the first outside shadow of a foot of the great Oregon? There aint no such individual. Talk about treaty obligations to a country over which the great American eagle has flown! Some people talk as though they were affeerd of England. Hav'nt we licked her twice, and can't we lick her again? Lick her! Yes, jes as easy as a bar can slip down a fresh peeled saplin." *Fifty-four forty or fight!* That was the slogan of the hour. There was bluster on both sides of the Atlantic, newspapers printed ominous reports of preparations for war. But there were also voices of reason. A war over Oregon, declared the editor of a prominent Whig paper, would be one of "the most reckless and insane exhibitions that the civilized world has ever witnessed." Such a war soon would come, but it would not be fought over Oregon.[47]

FURTHER READING

Susan Calafate Boyle, *Los Capitalistas: Hispano Merchants and the Santa Fe Trade* (1997)
Thomas D. Clark and John D. W. Guice, *The Old Southwest, 1795–1830: Frontiers in Conflict* (1996)
William C. Davis, *Three Roads to the Alamo: The Lives and Fortunes of David Crockett, James Bowie, and William Barret Travis* (1998)
John Mack Faragher, *Women and Men on the Overland Trail* (1979)
William H. Goetzmann, *Exploration and Empire: The Explorer and the Scientist in the Winning of the American West* (1966)

Julie Roy Jeffrey, *Converting the West: A Biography of Narcissa Whitman* (1991)

Paul D. Lack, *The Texas Revolutionary Experience: A Political and Social History, 1835–1836* (1992)

David Montejano, *Anglos and Mexicans in the Making of Texas, 1836–1986* (1987)

Kenneth N. Owens, ed., *John Sutter and a Wider West* (1994)

Andrew Rolle, *John Charles Frémont: Character as Destiny* (1991)

William W. Slaughter and Michael Landon, *Trail of Hope: The Story of the Mormon Trail* (1997)

John D. Unruh, *The Plains Across: The Overland Emigrants and the Trans-Mississippi West, 1840–60* (1979)

Anthony F. C. Wallace, *The Long Bitter Trail: Andrew Jackson and the Indians* (1993)

David J. Weber, ed., *The Mexican Frontier, 1821–1846: The American Southwest Under Mexico* (1982)

7

War and Destiny

If he could have his way, young Stephen A. Douglas of Illinois declared on the floor of Congress in 1845, he "would blot out the lines on the map which now marked our national boundaries . . . and make the area of liberty as broad as the continent itself." An empire for liberty! This oxymoron was an old American ideal, but never before had Americans asserted it so boldly or with such aggressive intent. "Acquisitions of territory in America, even if accomplished by force of arms, are not to be viewed in the same light as the invasions and conquests of the States of the old world," asserted the editor of the *New York Morning News* in 1845. "Our way lies, not over trampled nations, but through desert wastes." How would Tejano patriot Juan Seguín or Chief John Ross of the Cherokees have replied to such nonsense?[1]

The *Morning News* was one of the dozens of cheap newspapers—the "penny press"—that revolutionized the dissemination of information in the 1830s and 1840s. Its editor, John L. O'Sullivan, was not only a journalist but a scholar, a lawyer, a bon vivant, "one of the most charming companions in the world," a friend later recalled. He was also a propagandist for the Democratic Party, an important member of the group of intellectuals and politicians who concocted a new ideology of American expansion in the 1840s. O'Sullivan coined one of the most famous phrases in American history when he insisted on "our manifest destiny to overspread the continent."[2]

Over the years many Americans had called attention to the demographic realities that underlay expansion. "Go to the West and see a young man with his mate of eighteen, and [after] a lapse of thirty years, visit him again, and instead of two, you will find twenty-two," asserted representative Andrew Kennedy of Indiana during the congressional debate on the Oregon question. "That is what I call the American multiplication table. . . . How long, under this process of multiplication, will it take to cover the continent with our posterity, from the Isthmus of Darien to Behring's straits?" Combining this idea with the old Puritan certainty that they were fighting on God's side, O'Sullivan argued that American fecundity amounted to nothing less than a revelation of "the manifest design of Providence." What his pronouncement ignored, of course, was the purposeful federal policy and the ruthless military power that were necessary prerequisites to the conquest of the continent. The United States did not gain an empire simply by doing what came naturally. But the idea of "manifest destiny" deliberately avoided such hard realities, focusing instead on natural, immutable, and "providential" forces. This is a classic instance of ideological thinking—propaganda formulated for public consumption rationalizing, naturalizing, or otherwise masking the true state of things in the interests of established power.[3]

"Manifest destiny" was not, as historians so often imply, a deeply held American folk belief. Rather, it was the self-conscious creation of political propagandists like O'Sullivan, determined to uncouple the politics of expansion from the growing sectional controversy over slavery. That conflict first threatened to divide the country in 1820, when Missouri applied for admission as a slave state. "This momentous question, like a fire bell in the night, awakened and filled me with terror," wrote the elderly former president Thomas Jefferson. "I considered it at once as the knell of the Union." But Congress was able to fabricate a compromise, balancing Missouri's admission with Maine's and agreeing that henceforth slavery would be "forever prohibited" in the territory of the Louisiana Purchase north of 36°30′. The controversy next resurfaced over the question of admitting Texas to the Union in 1837. With abolitionists organizing to prevent the creation of another slave state, Presidents Andrew Jackson and Martin Van Buren decided to steer clear of annexation, believing that the preservation of the Democratic sectional coalition required keeping mum on slavery. The issue came up again during the term of President John Tyler, who assumed office after the sudden death of William Henry Harrison just a month into his term in 1841. Tyler negotiated a treaty of annexation with the Texans but failed to win the necessary two-thirds majority in the Senate.[4]

By the presidential campaign year of 1844 expansionists had become desperate to break the logjam. James K. Polk of Tennessee, candidate of the Democrats, ran on an explicitly expansionist platform calling for the "reoccupation of Oregon and the reannexation of Texas at the earliest practicable period." Here was another cynical contribution to the propaganda war. Linking Texas with Oregon, the phrase attempted to shift the focus from the expansion of slavery to expansion per se; employing the prefix ("reoccupation . . . reannexation"), it implied that these territories had always been part of America's "providential" domain; yet by remaining vague about timing ("the earliest practicable period"), it seemed to strike a moderate tone. The Whigs were skeptical about expansion. Polk "did not believe in enlarging our field," the

young Illinois Whig Abraham Lincoln declared, "but in keeping our fences where they are and cultivating our present possession, making it a garden, improving the morals and education of the people." What the country needed, argued the Whigs, was *improvement,* vigorous federal support for economic development. No, countered the Democrats, what the country needed was *expansion,* vigorous federal action to acquire more land, and with it more opportunity for the ordinary man and his rapidly multiplying offspring.[5]

But if the election was touted as a referendum on expansion, its outcome suggested a nation of closely divided opinions. With just 49.6 percent of the national vote, Polk became only the second president to win election without a popular majority, although he carried fifteen of twenty-six states. Had Henry Clay attracted but five thousand additional ballots in the state of New York—where a third party drained support—he would have won in the electoral college. The Democrats nevertheless insisted they had won a mandate for a program of national expansion. Presidential elections, of course, are not about gauging public opinion but about capturing political power and putting it to use. A mandate is what you make of it, and the Democrats were about to make a western empire with theirs.

After the election, lame-duck Tyler, with his eye on history, pressed Congress to admit Texas through the device of a joint resolution, which required only a simple majority. The Democrats pushed the measure through, presenting Polk with an accomplished fact when he assumed office in March 1845. The president promptly notified the Texans of the offer of admission, and by the end of the year the Lone Star had become one of twenty-eight on the flag of union.

Flushed with success, the Democrats moved on to the Oregon question. In his first annual message to congress, Polk had announced his intention of seizing the Pacific Northwest from the British. What did it matter that the United States could offer no valid precedent for a claim to the northern land of 54°40′? "Away, away with all these cobweb tissues of rights of discovery, exploration, settlement, contiguity, etc.," John O'Sullivan asserted with typical bombast. "The American claim is by the right of our manifest destiny to overspread and to possess the whole of the continent which Providence has given us for the development of the great experiment of liberty and federative self-government entrusted to us." Polk similarly blustered in public, but in private he arranged an amicable treaty with the British, dividing Oregon at the forty-ninth parallel. The president wanted to concentrate on the greater prize he could obtain by confronting Mexico and did not feel that he could risk armed confrontations on both the southern *and* northern borders. The Senate ratified the international agreement with Great Britain in June 1846. By that time Polk desperately needed it, for he had already provoked a full-scale war with Mexico.[6]

For decades American filibusters had sought to subvert the northern provinces of Mexico, while American presidents simultaneously sought to purchase them. As far as the Mexicans were concerned, it amounted to gringo imperialism either way. After the Texas Revolution relations between the North American neighbors grew steadily worse. In 1843 Mexico's president, Antonio López de Santa Anna, formally

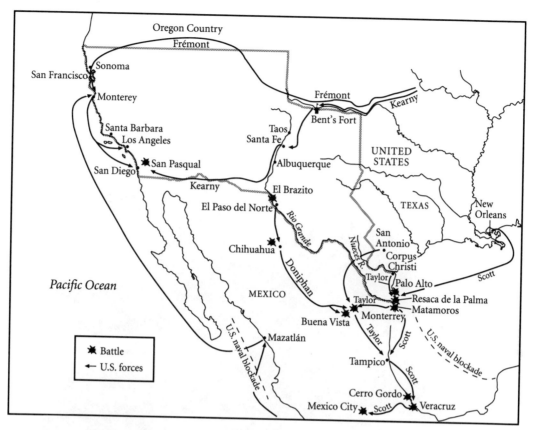

THE U.S.-MEXICAN WAR

notified the American government that the annexation of Texas would be "equivalent to a declaration of war."[7]

As soon as the Mexicans heard of the congressional vote for annexation they severed diplomatic relations, and soon both nations had moved troops to the contested border region. Secretly Polk sent Democrat partisan John Slidell of Louisiana to Mexico City to negotiate a settlement. He found that although the Mexicans officially disclaimed the legitimacy of Texas independence, in private they were willing to accept annexation if the United States would agree to the traditional provincial boundary at the Nueces River. The Mexican public was deeply hostile to the United States, which gave Mexican officials little room to maneuver. But, following Polk's instructions, Slidell insisted on a boundary along the more southerly Rio Grande. The region in dispute—often called the Nueces Strip—was a hundred-mile swath along the left bank of the Rio Grande, extending from the Gulf to the headwaters in the southern part of present-day Colorado, populated almost entirely by Tejanos. Slidell also pressed the Mexicans to sell the provinces of New Mexico and California. Knowing that such an agreement would be the equivalent of signing their own death warrants, Mexican leaders had no choice but to terminate the negotiations, and

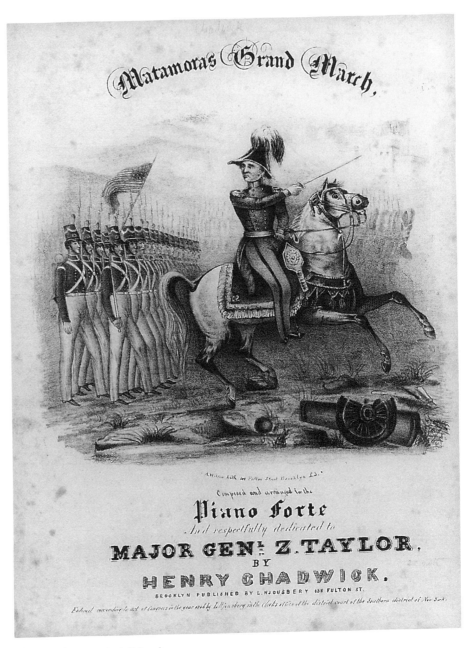

Sheet music cover, 1846. Beinecke.

Slidell returned to Washington empty-handed. "We can never get along well with them until we have given them a good drubbing," he told the president.[8]

The Mexicans were angry, but they were not about to invade the United States to reclaim a province they had lost ten years before. Polk, however, was spoiling for a fight. He announced to his cabinet that the acquisition of California—with the fine Pacific ports of San Diego and San Francisco—was the prime goal of his presidency. To force the issue, in March 1846 he ordered General Zachary Taylor, veteran of campaigns against Tecumseh, Black Hawk, and the Seminoles, to march his "Army of Observation" into the Nueces Strip. The Mexicans warned Taylor to retire, but he refused, and on April 24 they crossed the Rio Grande, attacked a party of United States dragoons, and killed eleven Americans. Polk had his rationale for war. "Mexico has passed the boundary of the United States," he announced in his war message to Congress, "has invaded our territory and shed American blood on the American soil." In the lexicon of manifest destiny, desire took the form of declaration. Congress voted for war on May 13.[9]

"I wish now that you would judge these events with a Mexican heart," the distinguished Mexican journalist Carlos María de Bustamante appealed to the American people soon after the war began. "Ask yourself: which has been the aggressor country? What would your government have done in the controversy with England over the Maine border if that nation had brought in troops, large or small in number? Without any doubt your government would have declared war and would not have entertained any propositions put forth until the armed force had evacuated the territory." There were many Americans who agreed with him. "That region belonged to Mexico. *Certainly* it did not belong to the United States," argued Whig senator Charles Sumner of Massachusetts. "Here was an act of aggression." The war was "one of the most unjust ever waged by a stronger nation against a weaker nation," Ulysses S. Grant wrote years later. "It was an instance of a republic following the bad example of European monarchies, in not considering justice in their desire to acquire additional territory."[10]

But most Americans overwhelmingly supported the war. Volunteers from Illinois, Missouri, Texas, and the states of the Old Southwest marched off singing new verses to the tune of "Old Dan Tucker":

> We're on our way to Rio Grandey
> On our way to Rio Grandey
> On our way to Rio Grandey
> And with arms they'll find us handy.
>
> We're on our way to Matamoros
> On our way to Matamoros
> On our way to Matamoros
> And we'll conquer all before us![11]

The Mexican War ostensibly began as a limited war for limited objectives. It was, in fact, a war of conquest and proved far easier to start than to finish. The Mexican army performed badly, but the Mexican people excelled at guerrilla fighting, which took a bloody toll. In the final tally it would cost the United States Treasury nearly

General John E. Wool and his staff entering Saltillo, Mexico, 1847. Beinecke.

one hundred million dollars to win California and the new Southwest. By official and conservative government reckoning, it was also the most destructive war in which the United States had yet engaged, claiming the lives of nearly thirteen thousand Americans and at least twenty thousand Mexicans.

Polk planned a campaign with three principal theaters of operations. In the first, an American army under General Taylor invaded northern Mexico, sweeping south and in January 1847 destroying the numerically superior Mexican army of General Santa Anna at the Battle of Buena Vista, near Saltillo, the provincial capital of Coahuila. From Buena Vista, Taylor's road to the presidency in 1849 would be direct and short. But it took him only a third of the distance to Mexico City, and Santa Anna refused to negotiate peace while the American army remained on Mexican soil.

The conquest of New Mexico, the second theater, was directed by General Stephen Watts Kearny. Like Taylor, Kearny had served on the frontier continuously since the War of 1812. His sixteen hundred men entered Santa Fe in August 1846 without firing a shot. There were rumors that New Mexico's governor, Manuel Armijo, capitulated so readily because of the bribe of a satchel of gold coins. Kearny appointed the American trader Charles Bent to be the first American governor of the province. Re-

Lowering the bear flag and raising the American flag at Sonoma, California, 1846. Sonoma Valley Historical Society.

lated by marriage to a prominent Hispano family and a close associate of former governor Armijo, Bent seemed the perfect accommodationist choice. But he had his enemies and became the focus of a good deal of postconquest bitterness. In 1847 Taos Indians and New Mexicans rose in a brief rebellion that, though quickly suppressed, claimed the lives of several Americans, including Bent.

California, Polk's principal objective, was the third front. After mopping up in New Mexico, Kearny set out for the Pacific coast. On the way he learned that California had already fallen to an American force. On an early morning in June 1846 a small irregular force of American settlers had ridden into the village of Sonoma in the northern part of the province, invaded the home of General Mariano Vallejo, and proclaimed the independence of the "California Republic." They were supported by Captain John Charles Frémont of the Topographical Engineers. Frémont and his forty men were on another scientific expedition into the Far West. Although Polk and his advisers were careful not to leave any traces in the public record, Frémont later reported that the president had instructed him that in the case of war with Mexico he was to act decisively to secure California for the United States. If this local uprising was not the war Frémont had expected, so what?

Appointing Frémont their leader and spokesman, the American rebels raised a flag with a lone star and a crude drawing of a brown bear. The star signaled the intention of the Americans to "play the Texas game," while the bear indicated their intention to secure "rough justice." But to the Mexican Californians (or Californios) cattle-thieving bears, *los osos,* were symbols of piracy, and these "Yankee Osos" were "savage hordes." The Americans played the part expected of them. In the name of an empire of liberty they imprisoned and insulted Vallejo and other important Californios, they plundered homes, they killed civilians. "We must be conquerors," declared Benjamin Ide, one of Los Osos, or else "we are robbers." Mexican Commandante José Castro called on the Californios "to rise en masse, irresistible and just."[12]

The Bear Flag Republic, however, lasted only one month. In July, Commodore John Sloat of the United States Navy sailed into San Francisco Bay with the news that the United States and Mexico were at war. Promising guarantees of Californio lives and property, Sloat put a stop to Frémont's terror. This could have been the end of it. A good number of Californios, including General Vallejo himself, agreed that the province should break with Mexico. But Sloat, who was ailing, was soon relieved by Commodore Robert Stockton, a bellicose old salt whose attitude toward Mexicans and Catholics is best indicated by the fact that ten years later he stood for the presidential nomination of the anti-immigrant, anti-Catholic American Party, better and more appropriately known as the "Know Nothings." Sloat commissioned Frémont as commander of a new fighting unit, the California Battalion of Volunteers, composed of scientific sharpshooters, Bear Flaggers, and Indian mercenaries hired at Sutter's Fort. Frémont's marauders so outraged the Californios that he managed to stimulate the growth of an effective guerrilla resistance that ousted the American force in Los Angeles.[13]

Unaware that the Californios had retaken most of southern California, Kearny had sent most of his force back to New Mexico and arrived with only 125 men. At the small village of San Pasqual, in the hills west of San Diego, General Andrés Pico and a force of mounted defenders inflicted heavy casualties on Kearny's unsuspecting troop, even wounding the general himself. Only Stockton's rush of emergency forces saved them from complete destruction. The next month Kearny and Stockton finally recaptured Los Angeles. But in spite of the presence of a general and a commodore, it was Captain Frémont who loftily accepted the surrender of the city, foreshadowing conflicts among the three men in the military governance of the conquered province. With egotistical bravado, Captain Frémont refused orders from General Kearny, his superior, and reported instead to Commodore Stockton. It led to his court-martial on charges of mutiny and his resignation from the army.

By early 1847, then, the Americans were in control of all northern Mexico. But there was little evidence that the Mexican government was about to give up. The United States might simply retain what it had conquered, of course, but the idea of seizing territory without the benefit of legal cover did not sit well, even with an expansionist like Polk. A treaty duly ratified by both governments would be preferable.

BATTLE OF CERRO GORDO.
APRIL 18th 1847.

Mexican War lithograph, 1847. Beinecke.

Surely the Mexicans would negotiate if the United States seized their capital. In March, General-in-Chief of the Army Winfield Scott, directing the first large-scale amphibious operation in United States military history, landed ten thousand troops at Vera Cruz, more than five hundred miles down the Mexican Gulf coast from the mouth of the Rio Grande. Securing his position, he marched his troops over the mountains Cortés had traversed more than two centuries before. As they marched to the halls of Montezuma, American soldiers passed around copies of William H. Prescott's best-selling *Conquest of Mexico* (1843), imagining themselves modern-day conquistadors.

Through the spring and summer Scott engaged the Mexican army in a long series of engagements, including the crucial Battle of Cerro Gordo. Mexican losses were followed by rear-guard guerrilla actions, harassing supply lines and slowing progress. Americans retaliated with outrages against civilians. A Mexican editor described the invaders as a "horde of banditti, of drunkards, of fornicators, . . . vandals vomited from hell, monsters who bid defiance to the laws of nature, . . . shameless, daring ignorant, ragged, bad-smelling, long-bearded men with hats turned up at the brim, thirsty with the desire to appropriate our riches and our beautiful damsels."

This was to be expected. But American officers, too, were critical of the operation. Lieutenant Ulysses Grant wrote home that "some of the volunteers and about all the Texans seem to think it perfectly right to impose on the people of a conquered city to any extent, and even to murder them where the act can be covered by dark. And how much they seem to enjoy acts of violence too!" Even General Scott admitted that his troops had "committed atrocities to make Heaven weep and every American of Christian morals blush for his country," including "murder, robbery and rape of mothers and daughters in the presence of tied-up males of the families." The Americans reached Mexico City in September, storming Chapultepec, the palace of the viceroys in the suburbs, then swiftly moving to seize the center of the capital itself. On September 14, 1847, Mexicans sullenly watched the supreme ignominy of United States Marines raising the American flag above the National Palace. More than a century and a half later it is a memory that still stings.[14]

───────

This was the first American war to be covered by Samuel F. B. Morse's telegraph system, which began operations in 1844. President Polk learned of the fall of Veracruz by reading about it in the *Baltimore Sun*. The Democrats anticipated that a patriotic war for territorial expansion would unify the country, but the detailed press coverage seemed only to inflame the opposition. As the war dragged into its second year American public opinion polarized. The majority continued to believe Polk's rhetoric about the duty of the nation to protect the cause of liberty. The president affirmed early in the war that the United States would never fight for conquest and that forced annexation was unthinkable, but he soon began to hedge under the guise of seeking repayment for the escalating costs of the war. California, Polk's prime objective from the beginning, seemed a logical reparation, and geopolitical logic demanded that the territory between Texas and California be included in the package. The region was worthless to Mexico, so the argument ran, but was strategically essential to the United States, especially for a transcontinental railroad skirting the Rocky Mountains.

But grander dreams were abroad. Extreme expansionists argued that the Mexicans were backward economically, their political institutions were chaotic, and consequently they deserved to lose jurisdiction over regions that Americans could develop so much more efficiently. Out of these arguments grew a movement for the complete annexation of Mexico. While Polk was talking of honor and duty, Treasury Secretary Robert J. Walker commissioned a study of the fiscal implications of total annexation, and Secretary of State James Buchanan reported to the cabinet that Mexicans dreaded the day when American troops would withdraw, so great were the benefits of American occupation. "More! More! More!" shouted O'Sullivan from the pages of the *New York Morning News*. "Why not take all of Mexico?"[15]

The attack on the all-Mexico position came from southerners who trembled at the thought that American institutions would be contaminated by "the colored and mixed-breed" population of Mexico. Senator John C. Calhoun of South Carolina led the opposition. "We make a great mistake, sir," he argued on the floor of the Senate, "when we suppose that all people are capable of self-government." More than half of Mexico's residents were Indians, and the rest were "impure races, not as good as the Cherokees or Choctaws." The Spanish made the "fatal error of placing these colored races on an equality with the white race," Calhoun lectured his colleagues, and "destroyed the social arrangement which formed the basis of society." Race mixture was the inevitable result. Were Mexico annexed and made a territory of the United States, those mongrel peoples would be placed on a equal level with the racially pure Americans. "I protest utterly against such a project," Calhoun thundered.[16]

A third body of opinion considered the war immoral and unworthy of the nation. Abolitionists charged that the South had incited the war as a way of extending slavery into Mexican territory. The war made him "sick at heart," declared the abolitionist leader Frederick Douglass, himself an escaped slave. "The spirit of slavery reigns triumphant throughout all the land. Every step in the onward march of political events is marked with blood—innocent blood; shed, too, in the cause of slavery." Henry David Thoreau, believing that the war was fought to extend slavery, refused to pay his taxes and went to jail for a night before his friends bailed him out. The experience became the basis for his famous essay on civil disobedience. There was also a republican argument against the war, made most effectively by eighty-seven-year-old Albert Gallatin, whose service as adviser to Presidents Jefferson and Madison permitted him to speak with the authority of the founders. "Your mission is to improve the state of the world, to be the 'Model Republic,' to show that men are capable of governing themselves," he lectured his fellow citizens in a widely reprinted pamphlet. But this was a war of "unjust aggrandizement by brutal force." Transcendentalist writer Margaret Fuller took up the same theme, lamenting that the nation's gaze was "fixed not on the stars, but on the possessions of other men," and concluding that "the spirit of our fathers flames no more, but lies hid beneath the ashes."[17]

Yet even in the writings of these opponents there is little concern for the struggles and the bravery of the Mexicans. Antiwar activists tended to adopt the same demeaning and racist rhetoric as the war's supporters. Who credited the band of Californios, armed only with lances and muskets, who nearly turned back the Americans at San Pasqual? Who applauded the guerrillas defending their homeland along the road to Mexico City or celebrated the quiet devotion of a Catholic people in the face of Protestant bombast and egotism? Few Americans of the day paid attention to the Mexican side of the war. Few do today.

President Polk sent a peace emissary, Nicholas Trist, to march with Scott and seek negotiations at the first opportunity. Trist was instructed to win Mexican acceptance of Texas annexation and acquire California and New Mexico. Mexican officials were deeply divided about what to do, and negotiations went slowly. Trist reported that "the condition of the inhabitants of the ceded or transferred is the topic upon which most time is expended." Receiving this news, and yielding to the demands of the all-Mexico extremists in his party, the president recalled his negotiator to issue new, presumably more extensive demands for territory. But in Mexico City, Trist sensed that keeping up the pressure would result in Mexican concessions. He stubbornly ignored Polk's message, kept negotiating, and in January 1848 won a treaty based on the earlier American aims. When news of his accomplished fact arrived in Washington, it undercut the extremists. Polk felt he had no choice but to submit the treaty to Congress, which ratified the agreement in March. The Treaty of Guadalupe Hidalgo confirmed the annexation of Texas and set the Rio Grande as the international boundary. As reparations for the cost of the war, Mexico ceded California and the province of New Mexico (the present-day states of New Mexico, Arizona, Utah, Nevada, and southern Colorado). The United States paid Mexico $15 million and reimbursed American citizens for claims they held against Mexico amounting to $3.75 million. In today's dollars the total price, including the cost of the war itself, would be in the range of $2.3 billion—real money, but still a bargain.[18]

A joint United States–Mexico commission was established with the power to draw an exact boundary from Texas westward to the Pacific. The American half of the commission had the impossible task of separating a surveying problem from sectional politics. When a New Englander, John Russell Bartlett, allowed the boundary to be the most northerly line of several possibilities, southerners howled. To make up for his gaff, in the Gadsden Purchase of 1853 (named for American negotiator James Gadsden) the United States acquired for $10 million the land south of the Gila River in present-day New Mexico and Arizona. The total loss to Mexico, including Texas, came to 602 million acres, a third of its national domain.

The Treaty of Guadalupe Hidalgo stipulated that "male citizens of Mexico" in the transferred territory could choose either to retain their Mexican citizenship or become citizens of the United States and be "maintained and protected in the free enjoyment of their liberty and property, and secured in the free exercise of religion without restriction." In the war's aftermath, however, Mexicans found their civil rights slipping away, their property in jeopardy, and their Catholic religion under assault. The 1850s were notable for the rise of intense nativism and anti-Catholicism in the United States, and Anglo newcomers treated the native population as "Mexicans" regardless of their formal American citizenship. Anglo Americans expected either conformity or exclusion, and the tenacity with which Mexican Americans attempted to hold on to their traditions gave Anglos a justification for relegating them to menial economic and social status. For their part, most Mexican Americans thought of Anglos as marauding and materialistic.[19]

The Spanish-speaking people of the conquered Southwest had long been tied to the land. But Mexican holdings were treated as fair game by the American settlers pouring into the new territories, and courts were faced with complicated inconsistencies between Mexican and United States law. Many Mexican landowners lost their titles or were forced to sell to cover legal costs, and the poor people who worked for them were also thrown off the land. Nineteenth-century historian and philosopher Josiah Royce commented ironically on how all this appeared to many Anglo Americans. "Providence and manifest destiny were understood in those days to be on our side and absolutely opposed to the base Mexican," he wrote. "And so the worthlessness of Mexican land-titles was evident."[20]

One consequence was the rise of social banditry, the frequent response of persecuted peoples in times of social disruption. Robbing the rich to provide for the poor, the bandit was a criminal in the eyes of the state but a hero in the eyes of the people from whom he sprang. There were numerous Mexican social bandits in the years following the conquest, but the most famous was Joaquín Murrieta, a semifictional hero who combined the exploits of at least five men. Facts were less important than the legend, distilled in an important book written in 1854 by John Rollin Ridge, a descendant of chief John Ridge of the Cherokees, a beautiful example of a representative of one persecuted people finding meaning in the story of another. According to Ridge, the Murrieta family had been attacked on their land by a group of Yankees who tied up Joaquín, flogged him, and forced him to watch while they raped his wife. Murrieta's vow of revenge echoed the frustration of California's oppressed Mexicans.

Murrieta and his outlaw band so terrorized the Anglo community that the California governor placed a thousand-dollar bounty on his head. One day, according to Ridge, as a group of Anglos stood reading the wanted poster, a Mexican rode up and dismounted. Pulling out a pencil, he wrote across the poster, "I will give $10,000 myself—Joaquín Murrieta," and then with a spring he mounted his horse and swiftly rode away. The authorities called in Harry Love, an experienced bounty hunter. In pursuit of the Murrieta gang, Love and his posse came upon a small group of Mexicans sitting around a campfire. A gunfight ensued, and Love brought back the head of the gang's apparent leader, which was pickled in whiskey and displayed to thousands of curious Californians. But Mexican Californians claimed that their hero had escaped, a belief reinforced by a letter, supposedly from Murrieta, printed in the *San Francisco Herald.* "My alleged capture seems to be the topic of the day," the letter read, but "I inform the readers of your worthy newspaper that I retain my head." For the next half-century Murrieta's accomplishments were celebrated in the ballad "El corrido de Joaquín Murrieta," sung throughout communities on both sides of the bor-

JOAQUIN, THE MOUNTAIN ROBBER.

Joaquín Murrieta. From the Sacramento Steamer Union, *April 22, 1853. California State Library.*

Juan Cortina, c. 1870. Texas State Library and Archives Commission.

der. In a sense, Murrieta never died. "To the Mexicans he was a great liberator, come out of Mexico to take California back from the hands of the gringos," his cousin later wrote. "They did not call his 'looting' and 'killing' banditry. They called it war."[21]

In the valley of the Rio Grande in Texas, where Tejanos long remained a majority, discontent indeed moved beyond social banditry to guerrilla warfare. Law in south Texas was administered through the guns of the Texas Rangers, an irregular force originating during the Texas rebellion. The Rangers considered Mexicans their natural enemies. "I can maintain a better stomach at the killing of a Mexican than at the crushing of a body louse," one Ranger boasted in the 1850s. The Rangers' kind of arrogant bullying was deeply resented by Tejanos, including Juan Nepomuceno Cortina, son of a respected ranchero family and a veteran of Mexican defeats during the Mexican War. One day in 1859, while Cortina was conducting business in the predominantly Anglo town of Brownsville, he witnessed the marshal pistol-whipping an old vaquero who worked for his family. Jumping on his horse and charging forward, Cortina fired a shot and wounded the marshal; then, swinging the old man up behind him, he galloped out of town to the cheers of Tejanos on the street. When the authorities filed charges of attempted murder, Cortina and seventy-five supporters returned to free all the prisoners in the jail, in the process killing four of the town's residents, two of them Anglos with notorious reputations for abusing Mexicans.[22]

Proclaiming the "sacred right of self preservation," Cortina issued a broadside to Tejanos. "You have been robbed of your property, incarcerated, chased, murdered, and hunted like wild beasts," he declared, and "to me is entrusted the work of breaking the chains of your slavery." During the subsequent "Cortina War," several hundred Mexican rebels destroyed the property of dozens of Anglos. Cortina was finally chased into Mexico by federal troops under the command of Colonel Robert E. Lee, but for the next two decades he continued to operate as a Tejano Robin Hood. He was long celebrated in the *corridos,* the folk ballads of the border region.

> The famed General Cortina
> Is quite sovereign and free,
> The honor due him is greater,
> For he saved a Mexican's life.

Violence along the Rio Grande persisted well into the twentieth century, creating a harsh climate of ethnic relations. The Texas Rangers often took it upon themselves to "keep the Mexicans in their place."[23]

There were also decades of skirmishing between the native residents of northern New Mexico (known as Hispanos) and newcomer Americans. Clustered in little village communities, the Hispanos depended on communal rights to grass, timber, and water. But these resources—redefined as federal "public domain" lands after the conquest—were frequently claimed by Anglo squatters. By the end of the century the Hispanos had lost more than 90 percent of their communal lands. Night-riding Hispano vigilantes—groups with romantic-sounding names like Las Manos Negras (The Black Hands) or Las Gorras Blancas (The White Caps)—cut the fences erected by Anglo ranchers and sometimes burned their barns. "Our purpose," read one of the manifestos left nailed to a barn door, "is to protect the rights of the people."[24]

With the acquisition of Oregon, Texas, California, and the new Southwest, the United States became a transcontinental nation. The unorganized territory of the trans-Mississippi West constituted 49 percent of the country's land. In this vast region, the federal government would assume unprecedented authority over the next forty years. The native peoples of the West would be conquered by federal armies, the land surveyed by federal engineers, and the territories administered by federal bureaucrats. As historian Richard White argues, by exercising its power in the West, the federal government greatly expanded its own authority. In the American federal system, states and localities exercised countervailing power with the national government. But the Indian and Mexican communities of the West were targets of federal conquest and colonization—disempowerment. Thus "the West provided an arena for the expansion of federal powers that was initially available nowhere else in the country," says White. "The West itself served as the kindergarten of the American state."[25]

One of the first steps in this process was the creation by Congress, in 1849, of the

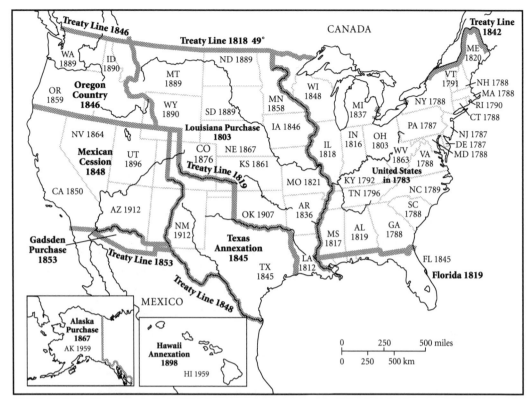

TERRITORIAL ACQUISITIONS AND STATEHOOD

Department of the Interior, consolidating in one government agency the Bureau of Indian Affairs and the General Land Office, and soon adding the Geological Survey and the Territorial Office. The federal department charged with protecting the Indians' rights to their lands thus also became responsible for assessing the value of and dividing up the national domain, distributing it to settlers, and creating new territories and states. That this did not strike Americans as an absurd contradiction speaks volumes about the attitude of the government on the eve of the violent period of disempowerment that was beginning.

The designation of the Great Plains as Indian country in perpetuity had been essential to the logic of "Indian Removal." Both native peoples and emigrant Indians were signatories to federal treaties promising to protect their homelands "for as long as the grass grows and the waters run." But the new geopolitical reality of continentalism invalidated this premise. Already officials were seriously discussing possible routes for a transcontinental railroad, and thousands of Americans were traveling across the plains on the overland trails to the Pacific. Although few Americans were as yet settling the plains themselves, emigrants were consuming the timber of the river bottoms for their campfires, grazing their livestock on the crops of native farmers, and hunting buffalo and antelope by the thousands. Frequently they blundered into conflicts with Indian hunting parties or sometimes with war parties battling with other native warriors for access to hunting territories. "How are we to develop, cherish, and protect our immense interests and possessions on the Pacific, with a vast wilderness fifteen hundred miles in breadth, filled with hostile savages, and cutting off all direct communication?" asked Senator Stephen Douglas of Illinois. "The Indian barrier must be removed."[26]

In treaties negotiated with plains peoples in the 1850s, the United States began the construction of a new order in Indian country. In 1851 federal officials called on the tribes of the northern plains to send delegates to a conference at Fort Laramie on the North Platte River. More than twelve thousand Indians stood witness as the leaders of the Sioux, Northern Cheyennes, Arapahos, Crows, Assiniboines, Mandans, and Arikaras negotiated with the Americans. In exchange for annuities compensating them for the loss of game, the Indians agreed to grant the United States the right to establish posts and roads across the plains. In 1853 the tribes of the southern plains—including the Southern Cheyennes, Comanches, and Kiowas—agreed to similar provisions in the Treaty of Fort Atkinson, which secured safe passage for Americans on the Santa Fe Trail. These agreements presaged the end of permanent Indian country.

The Americans also pressed the plains nomads to agree to territorial boundaries, hinting at the reservation system that would become the hallmark of federal Indian policy in coming years. But the lines on a map were practically meaningless for nomadic peoples whose way of life required them to circulate within huge territories in pursuit of buffalo, and Indians chafed at the idea of territorial restriction. "You have split my land I don't like it," declared Black Hawk, a spokesman for the Oglala Sioux, at the Fort Laramie conference in 1851. "Those lands once belonged to the Crows, but we whipped those nations out of them. And in this we did what the white men do when they want the lands of the Indians." The American negotiators were forced to concede his point and acknowledge the Sioux's right to hunt south of the Platte. It was a recognition that the Sioux had become the dominant Indian power on the plains.[27]

It was among peoples like the Crows and the Pawnees—who had suffered substantial losses to the expanding Sioux and the Comanches—that Americans would find their most important allies during the coming wars for the plains. To those peoples, the Sioux represented a far greater danger than the Americans. It is important not to think of the Indian allies of the Americans as collaborators against their own people, however, for the strongest loyalty Indians felt was to their band, their community, or their linguistic group. Pan-Indian identity would not begin to develop until after the completion of the American conquest.

White Horse, Pawnee scout. Photograph by W. H. Jackson, c. 1869. National Anthropological Archives, Smithsonian Institution.

If the outcome of the Mexican War exposed the sham of "permanent" Indian country, it also killed the hope that sectional differences over slavery might be subsumed in the national enthusiasm for expansion. "Our system may be safely extended to the utmost bounds of our territorial limits," Polk had declared in his inaugural address; "the bonds of our Union, so far from being weakened, will become stronger." In the tradition of Founding Father James Madison, who had argued that Americans could defeat factionalism and division if they would "extend the sphere," the Democrats had anticipated that a patriotic war for territorial expansion would unify the country. It did not work that way. Instead, the Mexican War opened a divisive and violent new conflict on the question of slavery's extension that led directly to the Civil War.[28]

That controversy began during the first months of the war when Congressman David Wilmot of Pennsylvania introduced an amendment to an appropriations bill that applied the precise restriction of the Northwest Ordinance to land acquired from Mexico: "neither slavery nor involuntary servitude shall ever exist in any part of said territory." Wilmot was no antiwar Whig but a Democrat who feared that his party had been captured by southern interests. Neither was he an abolitionist. Believing that "the negro race already occupy enough of this fair continent," he wanted to preserve the West for "the sons of toil of my own race and own color."[29]

The debate over the Wilmot Proviso shattered the expansionist coalition. The legal stipulations over slavery in the new lands now had to be determined by a sectionally divided Congress. The House passed the proviso, but southerners in the Senate blocked it; having furnished a majority of the soldiers for the victory, the slave states refused to be shut out of the spoils. Should the magic Missouri Compromise line be extended indefinitely westward? To do so would be to legalize slavery in the new Southwest and in the southern part of California. While Congress stewed, California waited for two years under military government. Finally another "grand compromise" was patched together in a series of bills passed in 1850. California, which rejected slavery in its own state constitution in 1849, would be admitted as a free state, skipping the territorial interlude altogether. New Mexico and Utah territories would be organized without restrictions on slavery, the residents of each territory left to decide the question themselves in good time, a solution the Democrats called "popular sovereignty."

But the peace of 1850 was shortlived, broken just four years later when Senator Stephen Douglas offered a bill to organize the old Louisiana Purchase territory beyond the Missouri River into the territories of Kansas and Nebraska. Douglas was eager to promote a transcontinental railroad that would begin in his home state of Illinois and head west across Kansas, but such a project required the formation of a territorial government. Not daring to alienate the southerners in the Democratic Party, he proposed to abandon the old Missouri Compromise line—which would have barred slavery in Kansas—invoking instead the principle of popular sovereignty.

Over the next four years the Kansas prairie became a killing field where men took sides and fought for their uncompromising beliefs. Proslavery militias organized by Senator David Atchison of Missouri crossed the border to battle heavily armed abolitionist settlers from New England. "The game must be played boldly," Atchison asserted, for "if we win we carry slavery to the Pacific Ocean, if we fail we lose Missouri, Arkansas, Texas, and all the territories," and he incited his followers "to kill every God-damned abolitionist in the Territory." In the spring of 1856 a "posse" of eight hundred proslavery men from Missouri invaded the antislavery town of Lawrence, Kansas, demolishing the two newspaper offices, plundering shops and homes, and killing one man. Senator Charles Sumner of Massachusetts condemned this "Crime against Kansas" as the work of "murderous robbers from Missouri, hirelings picked from the drunken spew and vomit of an uneasy civilization." Several days later, on the floor of the Senate, Sumner was beaten senseless by an outraged proslavery congressman from South Carolina. When the abolitionist settler John Brown of Kansas learned of the beating, he vowed to "fight fire with fire." In an act designed to "strike terror in the hearts of the proslavery people," he and four of his sons—all dedicated to freedom and righteousness—seized five peaceful proslavery settlers on Pottawatomie Creek and laid open their skulls with broadswords. Brown was enacting the traditional role of the western vigilante. But never

Antislavery militia in Kansas, c. 1856. Kansas State Historical Society, Topeka.

before had white American settlers used such violence against each other. It was a dark omen of things to come.[30]

The old politics finally expired on the plains of Kansas, and a new politics arose to take its place. In order to win a national election the Republicans, an antislavery party of northern interests, needed western support. In 1856 they played the western card by running peripatetic John C. Frémont under the banner "Free Soil, Free Men, Frémont." Frémont lost, but not by much. Indeed, the Republicans came very close to uniting the North and West against the South. The Jacksonian coalition had depended on the political alliance of the Old Northwest and the Old Southwest, the linking of farmers and planters via the commerce of the Mississippi. But the construction of the Erie Canal, one of the greatest engineering feats of the nineteenth century, the development of steam transportation on the Great Lakes, and finally the construction of railroad lines redirected the commercial connections of the Old Northwest from New Orleans to New York. These prospering economic connections generated support for the program of the new Republican Party: protective tariffs for northern industry, internal improvements and cheap public land for westerners. That sectional political bargain was finally sealed in 1860 when the Old Northwest voted as a block for Abraham Lincoln and the Republicans. When the South refused to accept the outcome of the election and seceded, the other two sections joined forces to preserve the Union. The payoff came when Congress, purged of southern representation, enacted two of the West's most cherished political goals—a Homestead Act providing free land for settlers and a Pacific Railroad to sew together the distant allies with steel.

The most important controversy leading to the Civil War was the question of the territories. "The territorial question sectionalized American politics and resulted in the election of a sectional president," writes historian Michael A. Morrison, and "the election of a sectional president produced disunion." Donald Frasier goes a step further, persuasively arguing that the creation of a Confederate slave empire in the West "was a basic goal of Southern independence." Confederate president Jefferson Davis took a strong interest in the territory acquired from Mexico. While serving as secretary of war during the 1850s, he noted with interest the long tradition of irrigated cotton cultivation by Indian and Mexican farmers. It was also Davis who secured the Gadsden Purchase from Mexico to provide the route for a southern transcontinental railroad. It was thus logical that one of the first strategic military moves of the Confederacy was an attempt to grab New Mexico Territory. In the first weeks of the war an army of thirty-five hundred Texans pushed up the Rio Grande from El Paso and forced the retreat of Union forces. This victory gave the proslavery minority in the area the opportunity to proclaim the Confederate Territory of Arizona.[31]

During the following winter of 1861–62 the Texans extended their control by capturing Albuquerque and Santa Fe. Gold had been discovered in the front range of the Rockies in 1859, and with the aim of seizing these valuable Colorado mines the troops advanced on Fort Union, east of Santa Fe, the largest federal facility in the Southwest. But at Glorieta Pass in the Sangre de Cristo Mountains they were turned back by Colorado volunteers. Leading the charge with "a pistol in each hand and one or two under his arms" was Major John M. Chivington, a Methodist minister known to his men as the "fighting parson." Chivington's maneuver broke the Texan lines and forced a Confederate retreat from New Mexico.[32]

An even more important Confederate goal in the West was control of the state of Missouri, which would put them in command of the entire west bank of the Mississippi River. As part of this strategy, the Confederate government sent agents to court the leaders of the Five Civilized Tribes in Indian Territory, directly south of strongly Unionist Kansas. The Choctaws and Chickasaws quickly signed Confederate treaties without much dissent in 1861, but among the Creeks, Seminoles, and especially the Cherokees, there were strong pro-Union factions. These new divisions reopened old wounds. Chief John Ross of the Cherokees, for example, found his principal support among those who had opposed removal from Georgia to the bitter end, including most of the full bloods and traditionalists. The pro-Confederate faction, by contrast, was led by Stand Watie, brother of Elias Boudinot, the lone survivor of the group of leaders who had signed the removal treaty. Watie's supporters also included most of the Cherokee slaveowners. Ross tried to maintain Cherokee neutrality but was seriously undercut when federal troops withdrew from Indian Territory in April 1861. By then Watie was already organizing fighters from the "United Nations of Indians" for the Confederacy.

In Missouri, meanwhile, ad hoc Unionist forces blocked the attempt of the governor to take his state into the Confederacy. When a rebel army composed of troops from Indian Territory and the state of Arkansas undertook an invasion of the state in March 1862, they were defeated by federal forces at Pea Ridge in the Ozarks, a battle that saved Missouri for the Union. But the violence metastasized throughout the region in the form of vicious guerrilla fighting. Armed bands of abolitionist "Jayhawkers" crossed the Kansas border into Missouri, burning and looting. Confederate "bushwackers" like William Quantrill and "Bloody Bill" Anderson answered in kind. Ordering his men to "kill every male and burn every house," Quantrill stormed the abolitionist town of Lawrence in 1863, leaving 182 men and boys slaughtered and 185 buildings destroyed, one of the most heinous acts of the war. "More than any other state, Missouri suffered the horrors of internecine warfare," writes Civil War historian James McPherson, and "produced a form of terrorism that exceeded anything else in the war."[33]

This judgment applies equally well to Indian Territory, where factional guerrilla fighting nearly destroyed the Indian nations. "From being the once proud, intelligent, and wealthy tribe of Indians," wrote a federal official, "the Cherokees are now stripped of nearly all." Fleeing the devastation, ten thousand Indian refugees flooded north into Kansas, where they mingled with thousands of proslavery refugees who had been evicted from their western Missouri homes. Both western Missouri and Indian Territory would remain wastelands for years. The victorious federal government later made the Five Civilized Tribes pay dearly for their Confederate alliance, forcing them to relinquish half of their lands.[34]

The tribes also had to make room for the emigrant Indians being evicted from Kansas to accommodate American settlers. In 1860 there were already 136,000 Americans living along the west bank of the Missouri River in eastern Kansas and Nebraska, and when the price of wheat shot up during the war it greatly accelerated the pace of settlement. Emigrants traveling across the plains on the Overland Trail in the mid-1860s passed fenced fields and plowed land, and by 1870 the combined population of the plains states of Kansas and Nebraska—admitted in 1861 and 1867, respectively—had reached nearly half a million.

During the war the Republican Congress carved the rest of the trans-Mississippi West into territories in preparation for their settlement. It was one thing, however, to organize a territory in Washington, D.C., and quite another to establish it on the ground. The incorporation of the trans-Mississippi West into the political structure

Innovations in handguns (from top to bottom): Colt 1851 Navy Revolver; Colt 1860 Army Revolver; Colt 1873 Peacemaker Single-Action Army Revolver. Buffalo Bill Historical Center, Cody, Wyoming. Gift of Olin Corporation, Winchester Arms Collection.

of the nation required a generation of offensive warfare. For the several hundred thousand Indian people who called the West home, it meant thirty years of desperate resistance.

Suffering and slaughter became commonplace and changed the expectations and behavior of thousands of western Americans. New means of violence facilitated these new habits. In 1836 Samuel Colt patented the first modern revolver, an inexpensive weapon that had no utility as a hunting piece but was designed solely for violent human confrontations. Colt advertised his guns with heroic scenes—a man protecting his wife and child from Indians armed only with a Colt revolver. Sales were brisk. The weapon soon found its way into the hands of the Texas Rangers, whose example made it the weapon of choice for irregular forces. By the 1850s the Colt factory in Hartford, Connecticut, was turning out a variety of new handguns—the .36-caliber "Navy" model was a favorite among border guerrillas—while the Sharps and Winchester companies perfected the manufacture of new breech-loading and repeating rifles. During the Civil War hundreds of thousands of these weapons were issued to troops, and the West was soon flooded with firearms of every type and description, from tiny pocket derringers to .50-caliber buffalo guns. In a recent study of nineteenth-century gun ownership, historian Michael Belleîles found that the proportion of Americans with firearms doubled during the quarter-century leading up to the Civil War, increasing from about one in six households to nearly one in three, with rates highest in the rural South and West. The Civil War, he writes, "brought guns into the home, making them part of the domestic environment and an unquestioned member of the American family."[35]

The arming of western America was accompanied by a hardening and coarsening of attitudes toward the Indians. "The instinct of antipathy against an Indian grows in the backwoodsman with the sense of good and bad, right and wrong," wrote novelist Herman Melville in 1854. "In one breath he learns that a brother is to be loved, and an Indian to be hated." Adults instructed children with "histories of Indian lying, Indian theft, Indian double-dealing, Indian fraud and perfidy, Indian want of conscience, Indian blood-thirstiness, Indian diabolism—histories which, though of wild woods, are almost as full of things unangelic as the Newgate Calendar or the Annals of Europe." With such irony Melville tried to communicate the absurdities of racism, but his was a lonely voice. Indeed, new "scientific" theories of race were providing authoritative support for long-assumed beliefs in Indian inferiority. "The aboriginal barbarous tribes cannot be forced to change their habits," ethnologists Joshia C. Nott and George R. Gliddon wrote in the 1850s. "It is as clear as the sun at noon-day, that in a few generations more the last of these Red men will be numbered with the dead." They offered these words as prediction, but they could as easily be read as a death warrant.[36]

A new rhetoric of violence also appeared in the official government discourse regarding the Indians. Officials of the Indian Bureau did not shirk from the draconian design of their new reservation policy. "It is indispensably necessary that [Indians] be placed in positions where they can be controlled and finally compelled by sheer necessity to resort to agricultural labor or starve," one bureaucrat wrote of the plains Indians. "A stern necessity is impending over them," another official warned. "They cannot pursue their former mode of life, but must entirely change their habits, and, in fixed localities, look to the cultivation of the soil and the raising of stock for their future support. There is no alternative to providing for them in this manner but to exterminate them, which the dictates of justice and humanity alike forbid." Get out of the way or be damned! Such was the thinking of Commissioner of Indian Affairs Alfred B. Greenwood expressed in the annual report of the Bureau of Indian Affairs for 1859.[37]

The West harvested the first bitter fruits of these trends among the Eastern Sioux of Minnesota in 1862. In treaties of 1851 and 1858 the United States forced these communities to relinquish title to twenty-eight million acres in exchange for annuities and a crowded reservation on the Minnesota River. Their agent described the regimen on the reservation as designed "to break up the community system among the Sioux; weaken and destroy their tribal relations; individualize them by giving each a separate home and having them subsist by industry—the sweat of their brows; till the soil; make labor honorable and idleness dishonorable; or, as it was expressed in short, '*make white men of them.*'" It is hardly surprising that the Sioux resisted. "If the Indians had tried to make the whites live like them," said Big Eagle, one of the Sioux chiefs, "the whites would have resisted, and it was the same with many Indians."[38]

By the summer of 1862 a combination of crop failure and diminished supplies of game had reduced the Eastern Sioux to practical starvation, yet their authoritarian agent refused to depart from standard procedures and issue emergency stores from the abundant supplies in the agency warehouse. Chief Little Crow, a man inclined to accommodation, approached one of the reservation traders with a group of Sioux men. "We have no food, but here are these stores," he said through a translator. "When men are hungry they help themselves." Furious at what he considered this veiled threat, the trader's response lit the fuse on this powder keg: "So far as I am concerned, if they are hungry let them eat grass or their own dung." When his reply was translated the Sioux were thunderstruck, and they stormed off, filling the air with their war whoops. Two days later the reservation exploded. In an orgy of violence directed against surrounding farms, towns, and forts, the Sioux killed some five hundred settlers before the state militia crushed the rebellion. The body of the offending trader was later found, his mouth stuffed with grass. After the state militia suppressed the uprising, thirty-eight Sioux, convicted of rape and murder, were executed before

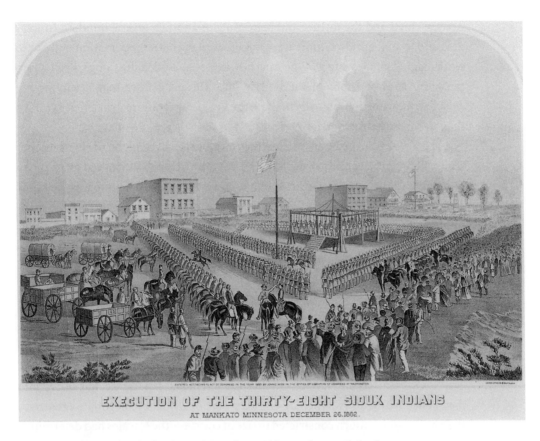

EXECUTION OF THE THIRTY-EIGHT SIOUX INDIANS
AT MANKATO MINNESOTA DECEMBER 26.1862.

Minnesota Sioux executed after the uprising of 1862. Lithograph, 1883. Beinecke.

a cheering crowd of settlers; several hundred more were imprisoned, and the remaining Eastern Sioux were forcibly removed to a reservation in Dakota Territory.[39]

The Southwest became the focus for the next round of violence between the federal government and the Indians. In the spring of 1862 Colonel James H. Carleton promised the Hispanic and Pueblo residents of the Rio Grande valley to eliminate the raids of the Navajos and the Apaches that had been a fact of life for at least three centuries. But the raids not only continued, they accelerated, for now the nomads were attracted by the goods and the horses of the Americans as well.

Carleton commissioned the former mountain man Kit Carson—made famous by Frémont's reports—to lead a campaign to eradicate the raiders. "There is to be no council held with the Indians nor any talks," Carleton ordered. "The men are to be slain whenever and wherever they can be found. The women and children may be taken as prisoners." At a desolate spot in arid east-central New Mexico called Bosque Redondo, Carleton established a reservation on which he intended to exile the subdued Indians. In a brutal campaign that included the murder of two surrendering

Apache chiefs and the torture and beheading of another, several hundred Indians died and several hundred more were forced onto the barren reservation and put to work digging ditches. Most of the Apaches, however, eluded the troops, fleeing into the mountains or south of the border into Mexico. Rather than pacifying the Apaches, the campaign actually marked the beginning of more than twenty years of their fierce resistance to the Americans.[40]

Carleton next turned Carson onto the Navajos who lived in the northern border region between New Mexico and Arizona. A group of chiefs attempted to arrange a peace with Carleton, but he insisted that removal to Bosque Redondo was their only option. Like the Apaches, the Navajos had long raided Hispano and Pueblo communities, but unlike their cousins they were a farming and pastoral people, with gardens, orchards, and large flocks of sheep and goats. Consequently Carson ordered a scorched-earth policy for the Navajo homeland, destroying hogans and crops, burning orchards, killing livestock. By the late winter of 1864 the Navajos were desperate. "Owing to the operations of my command," Carson reported, "they are in a complete state of starvation, and many of their women and children have already died from this cause." By winter's end some eight thousand Indians had surrendered and been forced to march four hundred miles through the desert to Bosque Redondo. The "Long Walk," as the Navajos call this brutal removal experience, was seared into their collective memory. When in 1868 they were finally able to negotiate a return to their homeland—much constricted in size of course—the Navajos had determined to give up raiding and never again to go to war against the Americans.[41]

From Minnesota to New Mexico the Americans proved themselves ruthless and effective conquerors. But in the annals of Civil War Indian fighting, few events could match the infamy of what happened in Colorado. In 1861, anxious to clear the title to land in the newly created Colorado Territory, the Indian Bureau arranged a treaty with some of the Arapahos and Southern Cheyennes of the region, assigning them to a barren reservation along the Arkansas River. It was country in which they found it nearly impossible to support themselves, and they fumed as they watched American ranches and taverns spring up at every one of their traditional watering holes. Finally in the summer of 1864 the militant Dog Soldier society of the Cheyennes struck the Platte River road connecting Denver with the east, burning stage stops, driving off livestock, and taking captives. John Evans, the territorial governor, raised a regiment of volunteers and issued a proclamation "authorizing all citizens of Colorado . . . to go in pursuit of all hostile Indians on the plains."[42]

That fall, however, a group of conciliatory chiefs visited the governor and his staff in Denver. "We want to take good tidings home to our people, that they may sleep in peace," Black Kettle, a Cheyenne chief, told Evans. "I have not come with a little wolf's

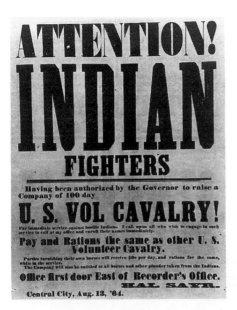

Colorado recruitment poster, 1864. Colorado Historical Society.

bark, but have come to talk plain with you. We must live near the buffalo or starve." Evans offered nothing but threats in return, for he was hoping that war would give him an excuse to clear all the Indians from the territory. ("What shall I do with the Third Colorado Regiment if I make peace," he wondered aloud to an associate, "they have been raised to kill Indians, and they must kill Indians.") As the meeting was about to conclude, Colonel John Chivington, the hero of Glorieta Pass and now military commander of the territorial militia, told Black Kettle that only one course was open. "My rule of fighting white men or Indians is to fight them until they lay down their arms and submit to military authority."[43]

Black Kettle and the other chiefs were puzzled by what Chivington said, but to avoid any possibility of conflict, the chief returned to his Cheyenne band and brought them into Fort Lyon in southeastern Colorado, asking to be placed under the protection of the soldiers. Following the instructions of the fort commander, Black Kettle led his people forty miles to the northeast and set up camp on Sand Creek. The encampment was a fair representation of the inclusive world of the upper Arkansas valley frontier; counted among the hundred or more lodges of the Cheyennes and Arapahos were a few white men married to Indian women and a liberal number of métis. Three of the four children of trader William Bent and his two Cheyenne wives were there. "All the Indians had the idea firmly fixed in their minds that they were here under protection and that peace was soon to be concluded," wrote George Bent.[44]

But Chivington was acting under instructions received from the militia commander of the region: "I want no peace till the Indians suffer more." Chivington was

George Bent and his Cheyenne wife, Magpie, niece of Black Kettle, c. 1867.
Colorado Historical Society.

the man for the job. Soon he was leading the seven hundred men of the Third Colorado Regiment toward Sand Creek. The colonel made his position very clear to his men. "I have come to kill Indians," he told them, "and believe it is right and honorable to use any means under God's heaven to kill Indians."[45]

The Colorado volunteers surprised the Cheyenne camp at sunrise on November 29, 1864, while most of the young warriors were away hunting. No Cheyenne ever forgot that day. George Bent awoke to the sound of excited people rushing by his lodge. "From down the creek a large body of troops was advancing at a rapid trot," he later wrote. "All was confusion and noise, men, women, and children rushing out of the lodges partly dressed; women and children screaming at sight of the troops; men running back into the lodges for their arms, other men, already armed, or with lassos and bridles in their hand, running for the herds. . . . Black Kettle had a large American flag tied to the end of a long lodgepole and was standing in front of his lodge, holding the pole, with the flag fluttering in the gray light of the winter dawn. I heard him call to the people not to be afraid, that the soldiers would not hurt them; then the troops opened fire." It was a slaughter.[46]

White Antelope, a chief who had long promoted peace with the Americans, stood before his lodge singing his death song: "Nothing lives long / Only the earth and the mountains." Mounted soldiers shot him dead. Many Indians ran for the high bank of the creek, where they desperately attempted to bury themselves in the sand. The Coloradans followed, firing round after round. Some women desperately exposed their bodies so that they would not be mistaken for warriors, but this only inflamed the ruthless fury of the troops. As George Bent ran down the creek he could see "men, women, and children lying thickly scattered in the sand, some dead and the rest too badly wounded to move." In the end the bodies of some two hundred Cheyennes and Arapahos littered the cold ground, three-quarters of them women and children. Chivington, reflecting his disposition, boasted that his men killed nearly five hundred.[47]

"Colorado soldiers have again covered themselves with glory," the *Rocky Mountain News* gloated. But there was public outrage in the East. A congressional committee investigated and issued a published report. "From the sucking babe to the old warrior," it read, "all who were overtaken were deliberately murdered. Not content with killing women and children, who were incapable of offering any resistance, the soldiers indulged in acts of barbarity of the most revolting character; such, it is to be hoped, as never before disgraced the acts of men claiming to be civilized." The summary report spared the details, but witnesses testified that the troops had carved the genitals from women's bodies, stretching them over their saddle horns or pinning them to their hats. "No attempt was made by the officers to restrain the savage cruelty of the men under their command," the report concluded; "they stood by and witnessed these acts without one word of reproof, if they did not incite their commission." Governor Evans was forced to resign, but Chivington had already left the state militia and was beyond the reach of military law. He became a sheriff of Denver and later served as county coroner. Indian-hating was respectable in the West. In 1868 western commander General Philip S. Sheridan put the public sentiment into a memorable phrase: "The only good Indians I ever saw were dead."[48]

In the aftermath of the Sand Creek Massacre, the entire central plains exploded into war. Previously the Cheyennes had been divided on the issue of war or peace, but the Colorado brutality settled the matter. In early 1865 Sioux, Cheyenne, and

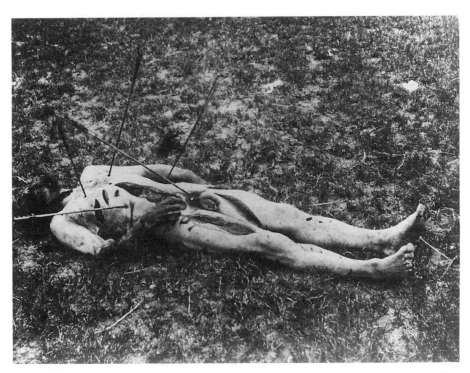

Corpse of Sgt. Frederick Williams on the plains of western Kansas. Photograph by William Bell, 1867. Smithsonian Institution.

Arapaho bands retaliated for Chivington's attack by burning virtually all the ranches and stage stations along the South Platte, killing scores of American men, women, and children. Efforts to subdue the warriors were ineffective. "At night the whole valley was lighted up with the flames of burning ranches and stage stations," said George Bent. Among the attackers was his métis brother, Charles, who became known as the fiercest of the Dog Soldiers. Renounced by his father, Charles swore vengeance on all white people, including his kin.[49]

Now, as the struggle for the Union concluded in the East and war-weary soldiers clamored to be sent home to their families, it became difficult for the U.S. Army to find volunteers for the renewed Indian fighting in the West. In response to this crisis, Congress sanctioned the recruitment of soldiers from the ranks of Confederate prisoners-of-war and authorized the formation of the African-American Twenty-fourth and Twenty-fifth Infantry and the Ninth and Tenth Cavalry, the famous "Buffalo Soldiers"—as they were christened by the Indians, in reference to the texture of the soldiers' hair. The black troops were segregated and paid significantly less than white soldiers, but they compiled an extraordinary record for discipline, courage, and high morale; over the next quarter-century fourteen troopers won the Congressional Medal of Honor. Thus, in 1865, regiments of Yank veterans, "White-washed Rebs," and former slaves joined in the fight against the western Indians.

Donald S. Frazier, *Blood and Treasure: Confederate Empire in the Southwest* (1995)

Norman A. Graebner, *Empire on the Pacific: A Study in American Continental Expansion* (1955; reprint, 1983)

Robert V. Hine, *Bartlett's West: Drawing the Mexican Boundary* (1968)

Robert W. Johannsen, *To the Halls of the Montezumas: The Mexican War in the American Imagination* (1985)

Alvin M. Josephy, Jr., *The Civil War in the American West* (1991)

Frederick Merk, *Manifest Destiny and Mission in American History: A Reinterpretation* (1963; reprint, 1995)

Michael A. Morrison, *Slavery and the American West: The Eclipse of Manifest Destiny and the Coming of the Civil War* (1997)

Leonard Pitt, *The Decline of the Californios: A Social History of the Spanish-Speaking Californians, 1846–1890* (1966)

Cecil Robinson, ed., *The View from Chapultepec: Mexican Writers on the Mexican-American War* (1989)

David Svaldi, *Sand Creek and the Rhetoric of Extermination: A Case Study in Indian-White Relations* (1989)

Robert M. Utley, *The Indian Frontier of the American West, 1846–1890* (1984)

Albert K. Weinberg, *Manifest Destiny: A Study of Nationalist Expansionism in American History* (1935; reprint, 1979)

8

Mining Frontiers

"Boys, by God I believe I have found a gold mine!" James Marshall, in charge of constructing a sawmill for John Sutter, shouted those words to his workers on January 24, 1848, beginning the California gold rush. Some Americans argued that this discovery, coming just ten days before the official announcement of the treaty ending the Mexican War, was a kind of divine reparation. "God kept that coast for a people of the Pilgrim blood," preached a New England minister. "He would not permit any other to be fully developed there. The Spaniard came thither a hundred years before our fathers landed at Plymouth; but though he came for treasure, his eyes were holden that he should not find it."[1]

It was true that Spanish colonists had always been preoccupied with precious metals. Their quest, in fact, had launched the European age of colonization. Columbus was obsessed with gold, mentioning it sixty-five times in the journal of his first voyage. Cortés crossed the mountains to the valley of Mexico in pursuit of golden dreams, and after the conquest of the Aztecs he had what was left of Tenochtitlán torn apart, stone by stone, in search of Montezuma's golden treasury. By the middle of the sixteenth century the Spanish had Indian slaves working the silver mines of northern Mexico, and several decades later Juan de Oñate, son of a mining baron from the province of Zacatecas, led an army to the valley of the upper Rio Grande, chasing rumors of the golden Cities of Cíbola. The lust for precious metals, in short, was a basic, underlying cause of the conquest of the Americas. "Let us be strictly truthful," the sixteenth-century English humanist Peter Martyr candidly remarked to the pope in a conversation concerning the American Indians. "The craze for gold was the cause of their destruction. For these people were in the past accustomed, as soon as they had sown the fields, to play, dance, sing, and chase rabbits. But now they have been set to work mercilessly, extracting and sifting gold."[2]

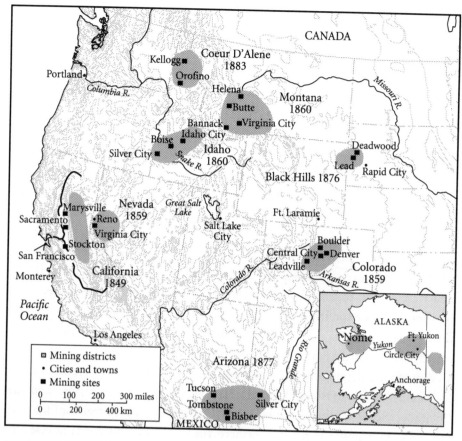

WESTERN MINING

The Spanish economy in California, however, did not create conditions conducive to the discovery of gold. Settlements there clustered around the harbors, and missions spread over the coastal valleys. Stock raising does not involve disturbing the earth, so minerals were unlikely to be revealed, even accidentally. Adobe construction of the missions required digging, but for clay rather than gold-bearing quartz rock. (The mission fathers, in fact, noted a few insignificant finds of gold in their region but kept them quiet, knowing, as Peter Martyr did, how gold rushes could ruin their evangelical work by destroying native peoples.) Newly arrived Anglo-American farmers in the Sacramento valley, however, wanted wooden houses, and men such as Sutter built sawmills among the large pines in the foothills to meet the demand. Sawmills require waterpower, the diversion of water from stream to spillway, and it was at such a site that Marshall found those first several bits of glittering gold. Americans discovered gold in California because of their demand for lumber, not the workings of Providence.[3]

California is counted as the first of the great mining rushes of the nineteenth century, but the little-known Georgia gold rush of 1829 actually prefigured it. Thousands of miners clamored into the foothills of the southern Appalachians, extracting as much as ten million dollars in gold and pushing the Cherokees off their homeland. Shockingly disorderly mining towns appeared overnight. One miner wrote home of "gambling houses, dancing houses, drinking saloons, houses of ill fame, billiard saloons, and tenpin alleys that were open day and night." Yet within a couple of years, mining companies had consolidated most individual claims, and the men who remained working in the diggings were toiling for wages. What happened in Georgia was a preview in miniature of what would happen in the Golden State, as well as dozens of other mining strikes throughout the West.[4]

The California experience, however, provided the lodestone for the exploitation of the Far West in the second half of the nineteenth century. Up to the 1840s the United States absorbed and incorporated new territory contiguously, but the gold rush caused the sudden movement of tens of thousands across the continent to the Pacific Coast. The census of 1850 revealed a new pattern that would characterize this new West: clusters of settlement separated by hundreds of miles. The further development of mining confirmed it. From California, prospectors spread out across the mountains and deserts, making a series of strikes that spawned a seemingly endless round of rushes: to the Fraser River in British Columbia in 1858; the Colorado Rockies west of the emerging city of Denver and the Washoe country of Nevada in 1859; Idaho and Montana in 1860 and 1862; the Black Hills of the Dakotas in 1876; Leadville, Colorado, and Tombstone, Arizona, in 1877; the Coeur d'Alene region of Idaho in 1883; and, closing out the era, the northern Yukon country of Canada in 1896–97, which quickly spread to Nome and Fairbanks, Alaska. Each rush created new isolated centers of population.

Practically every rush also presented the familiar kaleidoscope of lonely prospectors with their mules and pans, crowds of jostling men of every conceivable nationality, jerry-built stores along muddy streets, mirrored saloons, prostitutes and dance hall girls, outlaws, claim jumpers, and vigilance committees—all soon supplanted by smelters and mills, slag heaps and underground burrows, company towns, and labor unions, leading finally to strikes with the fist instead of the shovel. Mining added a significant dimension to the social, economic, and imaginative development of the West.

——————

John Sutter tried to keep the discovery of gold at his millrace quiet. "I had a talk with my employed people all at the Sawmill," he later remembered, and asked "that they would do me the great favor and keep it a secret." A vain hope. Yet Sutter succeeded in slowing the spread of the news. Reports did not reach San Francisco until May. The *California Star* denounced them as "a sham, a superb take-in as was ever got up to guzzle the gullible," but within days the town was emptied of able-bodied

California placer mining, 1848. Beinecke.

men. The cry of gold quickly spread throughout the territory. One man described the effect of the news: "A frenzy seized my soul. Piles of gold rose up before me at every step; castles of marble, dazzling the eye with their rich appliances; thousands of slaves, bowing to my beck and call; myriads of fair virgins contending with each other for my love, were among the fancies of my fevered imagination. The Rothschilds, Girards, and Astors appeared to me but poor people. In short, I had a very violent attack of Gold Fever." Editors suspended publication of their newspapers and city councils adjourned for months. Americans, Mexicans, and Indians alike poured into the foothills with picks, shovels, and pans.[5]

Fanning outward, they learned that the mother lode lay some five hundred miles along the Sierra Nevada. The icy streams of the higher range cut and eroded the rock, washing out the gold-bearing ores and depositing them in the alluvial sands of the rivers. A man needed little knowledge and minimal skill to swish the sand in a flat pan with enough water to wash away the lightest ores, leaving the heavier gold grains in the bottom. But the work was backbreaking and the icy waters could quickly bring on a case of rheumatism. "A person thinking of coming to California ought to consider whether he can stand to work all day, under a hot sun, up to the knees in water and mud," wrote John Eagle. "You will have to work in water & mud Morning until night," concurred F. T. Sherman in a letter to his parents, "it is no boys play." This was placer mining, and during the summer of 1848 many men struck a bonanza. These were Spanish words—*placera* meaning alluvial sand, *bonanza* rich ore—and the fact that both were incorporated into the American argot at this moment suggests the important role of Mexican miners in educating the first rushers, the "forty-eighters." In 1848 plenty of streams held an abundance of sand for all who came, and the lore was rich in tales of men panning gold worth thousands of dollars in a week. A territorial report estimated that ten million dollars was taken out of Sierra streams that first year.[6]

Fragmentary news of what was happening on the Pacific coast reached the eastern United States in the fall of 1848 but raised little interest until President Polk confirmed the rumors in his State of the Union address in early December, supplying tangible evidence by displaying nearly four thousand dollars of California gold at the offices of the War Department. It was the spark that ignited the frenzy of 1849. The news spread via telegraph. Apocryphal stories from California were printed in first one local newspaper, then wired to another and reprinted, a process repeated dozens of times with all the exaggeration and distortion one expects in a game of "telephone"—tales of the $10 in dust found in the bottom of the washtub after washing curtains soiled in a dust storm, of the man who washed $16 in gold dust from his beard, of the sick miner who sweated out gold worth $49.50 in a Turkish bath. (Multiply these figures by twenty to convert to today's values.) This "news" hit while the country was still awash with thousands of dislocated and unsettled veterans of the Mexican War, not only in the United States but in Mexico as well. In Europe residents of the capital cities were recovering from the revolutions of 1848, which had pushed a fearful establishment into severely repressive measures. In Ireland rural people were in flight from a long famine resulting from a blight on potatoes. By slim clippers around Cape Horn, by square-rigged ships from Hawaii, Australia, and China, over the Isthmus of Panama and across the plains and mountains, Sweet Betsy from Pike and more than eighty thousand Ikes jostled into California.

But almost immediately the easily obtained surface supply of ore ran thin, and the miner's take was drastically reduced. The supply of placer gold was running out before the first of the forty-niners arrived in California. The big moneymakers of the gold rush were the men who realized the fortunes to be made selling supplies. Levi Strauss, a young Jewish dry goods merchant from New York, made his by manufacturing the durable canvas and denim pants that became the standard in western ware. "I find that all shrewd calculating men," miner Henry Kent noted soon after arriving in California, "get into other business besides mining." Prices skyrocketed, and men found that most of what they made quickly ended up in the pockets of merchants. Procuring supplies for the mines—pan and pick, tent and blanket, food and incidentals—easily cost a miner more than a hundred dollars. "Between the ten of us, we didn't have the money necessary to outfit completely a single one of us!" wrote

Hydraulic mining in California. Photograph by Lawrence and Houseworth, c. 1860. Beinecke.

the Belgian miner Jean-Nicholas Perlot, who had come with a group of compatriots.[7]

Placer mining gave way to quartz mining, which required the application of industrial processes to extract the gold from the surrounding rock. In 1852, only four years after the first discovery, there were already 108 crushing mills pounding out the ores that time and the river had not yet reached. If machinery could crush, it could also erode, and as early as 1853 men were employing high-pressured jets of water to flush mountains of alluvial deposits into the rivers. "The effect of this continuous stream of water coming with such force must be seen to be appreciated," wrote a horrified observer, for "wherever it struck it tore away earth, gravel and boulders. . . . It is impossible to conceive of anything more desolate, more utterly forbidding, than a region which has been subjected to this hydraulic mining treatment." These hydraulic operations required large capital investment as well as a substantial labor force, so the disillusioned Ikes who had rushed across the continent to get rich quick were forced to go to work for wages. Mining ceased being an individual pursuit and instead became a corporate enterprise. "I think all of the old mining ground that is now called worked out will yet pay millions of dollars by working them Systematically," wrote miner Seldon Goff in 1850. "Capitalists will take hold of it and make money out of it."[8]

The amount of gold and silver dug out of California and the rest of the West over the next several decades dwarfed all previous mining, not only in the United States but worldwide. In 1848 and 1849 the federal government reported the mining of seventy-six tons of gold, more than twice the total recorded since bookkeeping had begun in 1792. The production of silver, previously calculated in thousands of ounces, surged to millions with the discovery in 1859 of the Comstock Lode in Nevada. Almost all this precious metal came from far western mines. As a result the world production of gold and silver more than doubled in the second half of the century. Output remained high as the cycle of strike, rush, and corporatization brought new operations on line.

Historians debate the economic effects. Most experts believe that during the mid-1840s the manufacturing Northeast had moved into a phase of self-sustained industrial growth, replacing the cotton South as the most dynamic sector of the nation's economy, but that view requires the perspective of hindsight. For most ordinary Americans of the day, the country still seemed mired in the economic hard times that began with the Panic of 1837. For them, the California gold rush marked the passage to a new economic era, the midcentury economic boom that would continue until the Panic of 1873. The impact of the gold rush was not all psychological, however. From 1848 to 1851 the nation's gold coinage increased twentyfold, creating a unique opportunity for the expansion of the money supply with only a mild rate of inflation (the Civil War years excepted). Not only did the new supply of specie provide a medium for the greatly increased pace of investment during this critical half-century of industrialization, but much of that investment was financed by western gold and silver. Precious metal made possible the importation of capital goods, particularly railroad iron.

California gold created the first of the great extractive industries that dominated the economic history of the American West for a full century. Mining, lumbering, ranching, and commercial farming were all enterprises in which western workers produced raw materials and sent them to distant markets. Each was highly susceptible to wild economic swings of boom and bust. Each was financed in large part by eastern capitalists with little regard for the balanced economic development of the West. According to American mythology, of course, a gold rush was supposed to be a golden opportunity for the little man, and more than enough success stories lent credibility to that legend. But the idea of frontier social mobility best applied to earlier Wests, not to the industrial Far West born during the California gold rush. In the words of historian Richard Hofstadter, "The westward movement involved the conquest of resources and their incorporation into the machinery of American capitalism." The California experience pointed the way to a new kind of economic colonialism.[9]

The gold rush jump-started the California economy. Within months of Marshall's discovery, the state had become the center of a booming Pacific market that made everything that had come before seem mere prelude. The "creation of large new markets out of nothing," Friedrich Engels wrote with some shock to his collaborator Karl Marx in 1852, was something they had "not provided for in the *Communist Manifesto*." Western mining booms were a vivid demonstration of the growing interdependence of the world's economies. Into the port of San Francisco in 1849 came dozens of foreign ships loaded with Chilean wheat, Mexican coffee and cocoa, Australian potatoes, Chinese sugar and rice, Alaskan coal, fish, and even ice. As soon as they docked their ships and unloaded their cargoes, the foreign crews jumped ship and rushed for the diggings. San Francisco's waterfront soon was clogged with rotting hulks from all over the world.[10]

Gold rush society was composed of the most polyglot collection of nationalities since Babel. Mrs. Louisa Amelia Knapp Clappe, who wrote literate and observant letters to eastern newspapers under the pseudonym "Dame Shirley," walked through a mining camp called Indian Bar in the Sierras and overheard conversations in English, French, Spanish, German, Italian, and Kanakan (Hawaiian), as well as various American Indian languages. The camp was "a perambulating picture gallery, illustrative of national variety," she wrote in her colorful prose. In the middle of the nineteenth century, gold rush California was perhaps the most multicultural spot on the globe.[11]

But for the lapse of a few years, of course, American citizens would have been the foreigners. In the California mining regions, however, there had been no previously settled Californio population, and with the flood of forty-niners Americans instantly formed the majority. But some fifteen or twenty thousand Latino miners were not far behind—Californios and Mexicans, as well as Peruvians and Chileans. Many were experienced placer miners, in great demand as technical advisers. It was one of several glimmers of interethnic cooperation. The California constitutional convention of 1849 included eight Californios among the forty-eight elected delegates, and thousands of former Mexican citizens participated in the balloting when the document was submitted to the voters for ratification. Travel writer Bayard Taylor witnessed the scene as registrars circulated among the Californio miners of one camp determining whether they wished to declare American citizenship. "Como

*Deserted ships in San Francisco Bay, c. 1850. The Bancroft Library,
University of California, Berkeley.*

no?" one man shrugged, "Soy Americano ahora" ("Why not? I'm an American
now"). Taylor thought that "by pursuing a similar course, the future government of
the State will soon obliterate the differences of race and condition, and all will then
be equally Californian and American citizens."[12]

If Taylor had read the proceedings of the convention he might have been less sanguine. During a contentious debate over granting the franchise to former "male citizens of Mexico"—a provision of the Treaty of Guadalupe Hidalgo—one delegate proposed amending the phrase with the adjective "white." Noriega de la Guerra of Santa Barbara rose in protest. "Many citizens of California have received from nature a very dark skin," he told the convention, and "it would be very unjust to deprive them of the privilege of citizens merely because nature had not made them white." Nevertheless, with all Californio delegates casting votes in the negative, the amendment was approved, along with another provision barring Indians and Negroes from testifying against whites in court. Several years later another of the Californio delegates, Manuel Dominguez of Los Angeles, a wealthy landowner and elected county supervisor, was prohibited from testifying in a civil suit because the court declared that "Indian blood" ran in his veins.[13]

As it became evident that not everyone was going to get rich in the goldfields, the tight jaw of prejudice set in. "Mexicans have no business in this country," a veteran of the late war wrote to the *Stockton Times*. "The men were made to be shot at, and the women were made for *our* purposes. I'm a white man—I am! A Mexican is pretty near black. I hate all Mexicans." Yet there is good reason to suspect that much of the hostility toward Mexicans had less to do with their race than with their skill and success as miners. "The reason for most of the antipathy against the Spanish race was that the majority of them were Sonorans who were men used to gold mining and consequently more quickly attained better results," believed Californio Antonio Franco Coronel. The American miner may have learned to pan gold from his Mexican neighbors, wrote English observer William Kelly, but "as soon as [he] got an inkling of the system, with peculiar bad taste and ingenious feeling he organized a crusade against these obliging strangers."[14]

Like most crusades, however, this one had official sponsorship. In January 1849 the military governor of California issued an order warning foreigners that they were mining "in direct violation of the laws." There were, in fact, no such laws. Indeed, until the federal government formally opened the public domain to private mining in 1866, practically every miner in the West was an illegal trespasser. But the order provided official cover for groups of miners calling for the expulsion of foreigners from the diggings. The mass expulsions of Mexicans awaited the enactment of a Foreign Miners' Tax by the California legislature in the spring of 1850, a prohibitive monthly levy of twenty dollars on all "aliens." Over the next several months mobs of American miners accompanied county tax assessors on their rounds, collecting the tax from Mexican miners who could pay and driving the rest from the mines. Ramon Jil Navarro, a Chilean forty-niner working a valuable claim near the Mokelumne River with a group of his countrymen, awoke one morning to find notices tacked on the pines and oaks notifying all "foreigners" to abandon the country. A few days later a mob of Americans descended on his camp. They "despoiled every man of everything

Chinese and American miners work the head of Auburn Ravine, 1852. California State Library.

of value he had on his person," Navarro wrote, "then they demolished each house, not leaving a single wall standing, but taking care to steal the canvas that covered the roofs." Although Navarro's comrades were Chileans, most of the expelled miners probably would have qualified as citizens under the terms of the Treaty of Guadalupe Hidalgo. There is no evidence, however, that any assessor bothered to distinguish Mexican-American citizens from Mexican aliens, nor that foreigners from Europe were required to pay a penny.[15]

Some Californians protested this latest version of removal. At the height of the expulsions a miners' meeting at Roger's Bar resolved "that the citizens of this Bar will discountenance any act of violence committed against peaceable persons of any race, living or traveling in this community." The *Daily Alta California* of San Francisco declared that "we are sorry to observe that some of our contemporaries in the most savage and unseemly manner have attempted to fling obloquy and disgrace upon so-called 'greasers.' Shame! Shame! To spit on a man because he was born under a warmer sun than shone upon our birth." Unfortunately, it would not be the last time when humane and cosmopolitan voices found themselves drowned out by the vulgar chorus of political pandering and popular prejudice.[16]

The place of thousands of departing Sonorans, Chileans, and Peruvians was soon taken by another group of immigrant miners. Several hundred Chinese arrived in California in 1849, and within a year they were passing through the Golden Gate by the thousands. Historians of immigration often speak in terms of "push and pull" factors. These men were pushed out of their homeland by peasant rebellions and the British Opium Wars, pulled by the lure of Gam Saan, "Gold Mountain." "Americans are very rich people," read one Chinese circular promoting migration to California. "They want the Chinaman to come and make him very welcome. There you will have great pay, large houses, and food and clothing of the finest description. . . . Money is in great plenty and to spare in America." By 1859 an estimated thirty-five thousand Chinese were working the California diggings, and they joined in the rush to each subsequent strike in the West. Dressed in their distinctive blue cotton shirts, baggy pants, and broad-brimmed hats, with a single long braid, or queue, hanging down their backs, the Chinese proved diligent and enterprising workers, often forming companies to work over the deposits rejected by American miners and making them pay.[17]

The Chinese came as temporary sojourners, intending to return as soon as their savings warranted, and indeed, every year thousands took passage home with their hard-won savings. Most were married, but almost none brought their wives to Gold Mountain. Respectable Chinese women were expected to remain at home, and families believed that keeping them there was the best insurance of a husband's returning. The California census of 1852 listed only seven Chinese women in the state, and over the next three decades most of the women who immigrated from China were prostitutes, many of them slaves. The trade in enslaved Chinese women, writes historian Annette White-Parks, "was the most widely known secret in the American West in the mid-nineteenth century."[18]

In the cities, towns, and mining camps of the West lonely Chinese men clustered in their own little "Chinatowns" that included social clubs, temples, opium dens, and brothels, most under the control of Chinese companies and tongs (fraternal societies). In the eyes of many white Americans, this huddling made the Chinese even more suspect than the Mexicans. A California newspaper described groups of twenty or thirty Chinese "inhabiting close cabins, so small that one . . . would not be of sufficient size to allow a couple of Americans to breathe in it." The "clannishness" Americans loved to hate, however, was largely the result of discrimination and prejudice. In 1852 the California legislature passed a new Foreign Miners' Tax targeting the Chinese. Before the tax was voided by the Civil Rights Act of 1870, Chinese miners had contributed more than five million dollars to the state's coffers, a quarter of the state's revenue for those years.[19]

Paying more than their fair share, however, did not insure the Chinese the equal protection of the laws. In the case of *People v. Hall* (1854) the California Supreme Court stripped the Chinese of the most basic legal protection. On the basis of Chinese eyewitness testimony, George Hall and two white companions had been convicted and sentenced to hang for the murder of a Chinese man. Hall's attorneys appealed on the ground that Chinese testimony should be excluded, since California statute excluded the evidence of African Americans, Indians, and other peoples of color. Exchanging their judicial robes for the scholarly gowns of ethnologists, the judges declared that because "this continent was first peopled by Asiatics, who crossed Behring's Straits," the Chinese should be considered Indians and thus prohibited from testifying against white Americans. They were "a race of people whom nature has marked as inferior and who are incapable of progress or intellectual development beyond a certain point." Hall's conviction was overturned and the murderer set free.[20]

Historian Liping Zhu argues that Idaho proved an exception to the pattern of discrimination the Chinese suffered throughout most of the West. Prospectors discovered gold on the feeder streams of the Boise River in 1862, and Chinese miners were among the first to rush into the district. As the placers ran thin most white miners left but many Chinese remained, working abandoned claims for the last traces of gold. By 1870 the Chinese made up nearly 50 percent of the miners in the Boise district and were an overwhelming majority in many camps. Their confidence rose with their numbers. With Bowie knives and Colt revolvers tucked in their belts, they refused to play the expected part of victim. "A Chinaman is slow to deeds of desperation," wrote the editor of the *Idaho World,* "but when he starts in he generally means business."[21]

In 1864 the Idaho territorial legislature passed its own version of the Foreign Miners' Tax, known locally as the "China Tax," but the Boise Chinese decided to challenge the law. "Taxee man no good, Chinaman no likee," declared one excited miner at one Chinese rally, according, at least, to a reporter for the *Idaho World* who transcribed his words. First, Chinese leaders succeeded in getting local courts to break with the California precedent and allow the testimony of their countrymen. Indeed, it became common practice for Chinese witnesses to be sworn in according to their own custom—an oath written on a piece of paper, dipped in the blood of a freshly

Two Chinese toughs, Blackfoot, Idaho, c. 1870. Idaho State Historical Society.

killed chicken, then burned. "What does it mean," a perplexed but interested judge asked a Chinese interpreter, who explained that blood signified solemnity and the smoke alerted the heavens to the proceedings. If the witness lied, God would kill him, like a chicken. Then, using their access to the courts, the Chinese challenged the constitutionality of the China Tax. Although they lost that suit, most refused to pay the tax, and there is no record of Chinese prosecutions for tax evasion. The Chinese miners continued to use the courts to settle claims among themselves and with Americans. "Although hardly perfect," Zhu concludes, Idaho "offered Chinese immigrants opportunities far beyond the proverbial 'Chinaman's chance.'" Size matters, at least when it comes to the assertiveness of an ethnic community.[22]

In spite of prejudice, discrimination, and attempts at removal, the Chinese, the Mexicans, and immigrants from dozens of European countries were in the West to stay. Whether narrow-minded Americans liked it or not, a multicultural West was aborning.

———

Once the Indians who worked at his fort learned about gold and its value, they were "impatient to run to the mines," wrote John Sutter. "Nothing as the Dollars could bring them to work," he lamented in his typically broken English, and because Sutter was willing to pay only a pittance, the gold rush ruined his ten-year-old enterprise on the Sacramento. Sutter's Indian workers were joined by hundreds of other Native Americans in the rush to the mines. When California's territorial governor toured the diggings in the summer of 1848 he found four thousand miners at work, "of whom more than half were Indians." Many labored for Anglo and Mexican contractors. "A few men who are working 30 to 40 Indians are laying up to $1000 to $2000 a week," American consul Thomas O. Larkin wrote in July. Other Indians mined for themselves or for their communities. A Chilean miner came across a group of Miwoks collectively working a stream in the Sierras. "The men dug and gave the mud to the children, who then carried it in baskets to the women." Panning with "grass baskets of the most perfect construction," the women carefully separated the gold, then tied up small portions in bits of rag. These they used "to trade with, just as if they were money."[23]

Indian mining came to an abrupt end with the arrival of the forty-niners. Suddenly Indian homelands were overrun by tens of thousands of Americans. Violence broke out immediately. In one typical incident in early 1849, a group of Oregon prospectors on the American River shot up a Maidu village, raping women and killing several men. The outraged Indians retaliated by ambushing and killing five of the miners, and in return the Oregonians attacked a completely unconnected village, murdering twelve people, taking others captive, then executing them. There were dozens of similar incidents. The Indians "could not understand why they should be murdered, robbed, and hunted down in this way, without any other pretense of provocation than the color of their skin," traveler J. Ross Browne wrote sympathetically. It "never occurred to them that they were suffering for the great cause of civilization, which, in the natural course of things, must exterminate Indians."[24]

Miners drove the natives into the barren high Sierras, depriving them of their food supplies and forcing them to raid the livestock of valley ranchers to survive. Ranchers retaliated with attacks on Indian retreats in the mountains. Americans, wrote one federal official, "value the life of an Indian just as they do that of a *cayota* or a wolf, and embrace every occasion to shoot [them] down." Federal Indian agents charged with protecting the Indians found themselves powerless to stop the carnage. When one conscientious agent attempted to file charges against a group of murdering miners, the United States attorney in San Francisco refused to act, saying that "he was not aware of the existence of any law which would apply" and suggesting that the matter be referred to local authorities. But, wrote the agent, "the gentleman who commanded the party in this unfortunate affair was soon after elected county judge," and he "did not think it worth while to prosecute him in his own county."[25]

As this story suggests, much of the violence was condoned, even sponsored by government officials. In 1851 federal commissioners negotiated a set of treaties with the California tribes, creating a series of reservations scattered throughout the state, but the governor and legislature opposed the treaties, claiming that they set aside too much land, and instead argued for the removal of all Indians from the state. The Indians would never stand for that, the commissioners responded. "You have but one choice," they wrote, "kill, murder, exterminate, or domesticate and improve them." The treaties were forwarded to the United States Senate, which followed the lead of California's congressional delegation and rejected them in 1853, in effect withdrawing the federal government from its constitutional responsibility to oversee Indian affairs in California. In the breech the state assumed unprecedented authority. In a special message to the legislature, Governor Peter Burnett made it clear that he was choosing the first of the commissioners' options. "A war of extermination will continue to be waged between the races," he declared, "until the Indian race becomes extinct." Over the next few years, with the encouragement and sponsorship of the state, thousands of Indians were murdered by miners, ranchers, and militia. It was the clearest case of genocide in the history of the American frontier.[26]

Adding greatly to native suffering was the "Act for the Government and Protection of Indians," passed by the legislature in 1850, which, as historian Albert Hurtado puts it, "protected them very little and governed them quite a lot." The pretense was that the law provided a way of disciplining dangerous Indian vagrants and caring for dependent Indian orphans, but in fact, under its cover of legality, thousands of Indian men, women, and children were kidnapped and sold to Anglo and Mexican employers. One federal agent apprehended three kidnappers with a group of nine Indian children ranging from three to ten years of age. The men defended themselves by claiming that the seizure of the children had been "an act of charity" because their parents had been killed. How do you know that? asked the agent. Because, one of the kidnappers replied, "I killed some of them myself." Spanish and Mexican California had been built by forced Indian labor, and until this pernicious 1850 law was repealed in 1863 (as a direct result of President Lincoln's Emancipation Proclamation), Anglo Californians contributed their own dark pages to that history. Perhaps most shocking was the public support for the measure. "This law works beautifully," wrote an enthusiastic editor of the *Humboldt Times*. "What a pity the provisions of this law are not extended to greasers, Kanakas, and Asiatics. It would be so convenient, you know, to carry on a farm or mine when all the hard and dirty work is performed by apprentices." The conclusion of anthropologists Robert Heizer and Alan Almquist is admirably candid: "This was a legalized form of slavery of California Indians. No other possible construction can be made of the facts."[27]

As a result of the genocidal violence, the forced labor, and the inevitable epidemics of disease, the Indian population of California, estimated at 150,000 in 1848, had

Mining operation near Helena, Montana, c. 1880. Beinecke.

fallen to only 30,000 by 1860: 120,000 lives lost in just twelve years, a record of brutality without parallel in the history of the United States. A minority of the remaining natives lived in isolated rancheritas, but most clustered in dingy shanties on the outskirts of towns like San Jose or Los Angeles, eking out a livelihood as cheap day laborers. It wasn't until the mid-twentieth century that California Indians used the courts to obtain compensation for the lands stolen from them during the gold rush, but the final awards totaled less than a thousand dollars per person. This settlement brings to mind the comment of Bartolomé de Las Casas when he learned of the official Spanish policy of offering Indians conversion before attacking their villages: one doesn't know whether to laugh or to weep.

────────

All the mining strikes in the West were an unmitigated disaster for Indians. The Georgia and California experiences were repeated in the Colorado rush of 1859, which led directly to the massacre of Black Kettle's band of Cheyennes at Sand Creek. Thus when gold was discovered in the Yellowstone country of Montana, and miners blazed the Bozeman Trail northwest from Fort Laramie across prime buffalo range in 1864, the Sioux, longtime allies of the Cheyennes, took it as an ominous sign. As the army worked to construct forts along the road to protect traveling miners, Oglala chief Red Cloud prepared to evict them. "The white men have crowded the Indians back year by year," he declared in a meeting at Fort Laramie. "And now our last hunting ground, the home of the people, is to be taken from us. Our women and children will starve, but for my part I prefer to die fighting rather than by starvation." With these words he strode across the parade ground and out the gates to the Oglala camp, his warriors following him.[28]

In the three years of fighting that followed, the Sioux and Cheyennes defeated most of the American forces sent against them. "The Great Father sent his soldiers out here to spill blood," Red Cloud told a peace delegation. "The Great Spirit raised me in this land, and has raised you in another land. What I have said I mean. I mean to keep this land." The federal government concluded that it would have to abandon the forts along the Bozeman Trail, settling for an Indian agreement guaranteeing the security of the main east-west overland routes through the central plains, critical for the construction of the transcontinental railroad. In the Treaty of Fort Laramie of 1868 federal commissioners "set apart for the absolute and undisturbed use and occupation of the Indians" the "Great Sioux Reservation," which stretched from the Missouri River westward through the Black Hills. Sioux rights to the adjacent Powder River country of Montana were left deliberately vague.[29]

In spite of his victories, however, Red Cloud sensed that the days of Indian armed resistance were over. A tour of the eastern United States in 1870 confirmed him in the belief that his people must attempt to reconcile themselves to the inevitable. In the hope of saving the Sioux from destruction, he and other accommodationist chiefs led the majority of their people onto the reservation. But militants like Red Cloud's fellow Oglala Crazy Horse, and Sitting Bull of the Hunkpapa, opposed this strategy; drawing followers from each of the tribes, they totaled perhaps a third of the western Sioux. Refusing to participate in what he called the "piecemeal penning" of his people, Crazy Horse continued to follow the buffalo, as his fathers had done, and to smell the sweet grass of the plains as he willed. Sitting Bull, a holy man as well as a

Sioux Indians at Fort Laramie for the treaty conference, 1868. National Anthropological Archives, Smithsonian Institution.

war chief, argued that compromise would get the Sioux nowhere. "The whites may get me at last, as you say," he told a group of reservation Indians, "but I will have good times till then. You are fools to make yourselves slaves to a piece of fat bacon, some hard-tack, and a little sugar and coffee." In hostility and intensity the factional conflict among Indians rivaled the fighting with the Americans.[30]

It was in this volatile context that rumors began to circulate of yet another gold strike, this time in the Black Hills on the Sioux reservation. A rush into the area was assured after Colonel George Armstrong Custer led an army expedition into the area and trumpeted the news that "from the grass roots down it was 'pay dirt.'" Within two years the town of Deadwood was swarming with ten thousand miners and the nearby Homestake Mine was exploiting the richest lode of ore in American history. The Sioux treaty of 1868 required the army to keep miners and settlers off the reservation, but officers deliberately looked the other way, hoping that miners on the ground would force the Sioux into agreeing to sell the Black Hills. A federal commission attempted to negotiate a purchase, and although Red Cloud and most of the reservation chiefs were willing to sell, they set a price the government was unwilling to pay. But Sitting Bull was contemptuous. "I want you to go and tell the Great Father that I do not want to sell any land to the government," he declared. And bending down he picked up a pinch of dust: "Not even as much as this." With gold beckoning, the federal government was in no mood to wait on stubborn Indians.

Sitting Bull. Photograph by Bailey, Dix, and Meade, 1882. Beinecke.

Reasoning that if they smashed the rejectionist Sioux they would have an easier time negotiating a bargain price with more cooperative chiefs like Red Cloud, officials began to plan for a campaign of total war.[31]

Knowing what was coming, free bands of Sioux, Cheyennes, and Arapahos joined together for the summer buffalo hunt of 1876. In June, with leaves full in groves along the Powder River and the nearby Rosebud and Little Bighorn, more than four thousand men, women, and children assembled in what was the largest encampment any of the chiefs could remember. At a summer solstice Sun Dance ceremony, Sitting Bull experienced a vision in which he saw many dead American soldiers "falling right into our camp." His dream reflected the Indians' confidence and their determination to defend themselves against the two army regiments of some thousand troops sent out against them. In the first major encounter along the Rosebud, Crazy Horse and General George Crook fought with roughly equal numbers, and though Crook claimed victory he was immobilized for nearly a month.

On June 25 Custer, leading six hundred troops of the Seventh Cavalry on a reconnoiter, came upon the combined Indian camp. Custer was a cavalry hero of the Civil War who had become a leader in the army's struggle against the plains Indians. In 1868 at the Washita River in Indian Territory he had led a victorious charge through a sleeping village of Southern Cheyennes that left 103 Indians dead, including Chief Black Kettle, sad survivor of the Sand Creek Massacre. Now Custer would attempt to repeat the same maneuver at the Little Bighorn. "Hurrah, boys, we've got them," he called out to his men as they prepared to begin the engagement. All the players were in place for the most famous moment in the war for the plains.[32]

Wooden Leg, an eighteen-year-old Cheyenne warrior, awoke from an afternoon nap in the Indian camp to the sounds of great commotion. He roused his sleeping brother. "We heard shooting. We hurried out from the trees so we might see as well as hear. Women were screaming and men were letting out war cries. Through it all we could hear old men calling: 'Soldiers are here! Young men, go out and fight them.' We ran to our camp and to our home lodge. Everybody there was excited. . . . Children were hunting for their mothers. Mothers were anxiously trying to find their children. I got my lariat and my six-shooter." The first concern of the warriors was the protection of their families.[33]

Foolishly refusing to wait for reinforcements, Custer made a fatal decision to divide his forces; he flanked the encampment to the north with about two hundred men while Major Marcus Reno attacked the southern end. Wooden Leg jumped on his horse and joined the skirmishing on the south. "Many hundreds of Indians on horseback were dashing to and from in front of a body of soldiers. The soldiers were on the level valley ground and were shooting with rifles. Not many bullets were being sent back at them, but thousands of arrows were falling among them." Suddenly the American soldiers panicked, mounted, and raced for the river. "We gained rapidly on them. I fired four shots with my six-shooter. I do not know whether or not any of my bullets did harm. I saw a Sioux put an arrow into the back of a soldier's head. Another arrow went into his shoulder. He tumbled from his horse to the ground. Others fell dead either from arrows or from stabbing or jabbings or from blows by the stone war clubs of the Sioux. Horses limped or staggered or sprawled out dead or dying. Our war cries and war songs were mingled with many jeering calls, such as: 'You are only boys. You ought not to be fighting. You should have brought more Crows or Shoshones with you to do your fighting.'" The warriors inflicted heavy casualties on Reno's troops, but the Americans were able to regroup and hold out in an entrenched position until the Indians withdrew the next evening.[34]

The troops under Custer's command were not so lucky. None of them would see the sun go down that day. Custer seems to have directed them in an attack on the northern fringe of the large camp. "I saw flags come up over the hill," recalled the Cheyenne chief Two Moons, "then the soldiers rose all at once." He and hundreds of other warriors raced across the river on horseback and met the charge head-on. Custer's troops were quickly overwhelmed and surrounded. "The shooting was quick, quick," said Two Moons. "Pop–pop–pop, very fast. Some of the soldiers were down on their knees, some standing. Officers all in front. The smoke was like a great cloud, and everywhere the Sioux went the dust rose like smoke. We circled all round them—swirling like water round a stone. We shoot, we ride fast, we shoot again. Soldiers drop, and horses fall on them." The battle lasted only minutes though it seemed like hours. Afterward, Sitting Bull's nephew White Bull was walking among the dead with another Hunkpapa who had known some of the soldiers. He pointed out a naked corpse and identified it as Custer's. "He thought he was the greatest man in the world, and there he is."[35]

Custer sought personal acclaim, the kind bestowed by the nation on those who hunted down Indians and took care of them permanently. But indirectly he was also the instrument of many western interests—the men of the gold rush to the Black Hills, a rush he helped create; railroad investors who saw their tracks rusting because the Sioux would not lay down their arms; cattlemen who saw the plains ready for expanded herds from Kansas and Texas; settlers bearing seeds of wheat and hollyhocks and dreams of neat furrows across the earth. Compared with the seriousness of Sitting Bull, who believed that his people must have the buffalo country or perish, Custer with his flowing hair, his red-top boots, and his grandiose ambition may seem faintly ridiculous. But he represented historical forces of immense magnitude, and in his death he achieved an apotheosis that outranks almost any other American hero.

The last stand for the Seventh Cavalry turned into the last major stand of the Sioux. The American army pursued the free bands relentlessly, keeping them from hunting or gathering food. No rations were distributed on the reservation. When the war ended that winter, it was not because the Americans had beaten the Indians in battle but because they had starved them into submission. By the end of the year the reservation chiefs agreed to cede the Black Hills. Not until the following spring, however, did Crazy Horse surrender at the Red Cloud Agency in Nebraska. Rumors understandably flew that he would not remain on the reservation. When the army tried

A Sioux version of the Battle of Little Bighorn. From Hartley Burr Alexander, Sioux Indian Painting, *2 vols. (Nice, France, 1938). Beinecke.*

to arrest him in September, he offered just enough show of resistance to give the soldiers a pretext for bayoneting him. Crazy Horse died within hours.

Sitting Bull meanwhile had escaped with his followers across the border into Canada, where he petitioned the authorities for food and land. But Canadian officials were worried about their own Indian problems and the precedent such an action might set, and they refused. Sitting Bull was eventually forced to return to the United States, where federal authorities made him a prisoner. Yet to his people he remained a beloved spiritual leader to whom they listened: "We have now to deal with another race—small and feeble when our fathers first met them but now great and overbearing. These people have made many rules that the rich may break but the poor may not. . . . They claim this mother of ours, the earth, for their own and fence their neighbors away; they deface her with their buildings." Sitting Bull summed up his feelings about the Americans in a phrase that still stings more than a century later: "Possession is a disease with them."[36]

In 1867 the United States purchased Russian America for the bargain-basement price of $7.2 million (the rough equivalent of $85 million in today's dollars). Although some Americans ridiculed the region as an icebox, others saw it as a storehouse. To Senator Charles Sumner (who came up with the name "Alaska," an Aleut

An American version of the Battle of Little Bighorn. Engraving by A. R. Waud, from Frederick Whittaker, A Popular Life of Gen. George A. Custer ... *(New York, 1876). Beinecke.*

word meaning "the big land"), the region was the sum of its resources: "forests of pine and fir waiting for the ax; mineral products among which are coal and copper, if not iron, silver, lead and gold; ... furs, including precious skins of the black fox and sea-otter; and lastly the fisheries, which in waters superabundant with animal life beyond any of the globe, seem to promise a new commerce." For most Americans, however, Alaska did not register on their mental maps until the discovery of gold. A few months after the purchase, a San Francisco newspaper reported that near Sitka, the administrative capital of the Russian-American Company, "the Indian women wear necklaces of gold and nuggets picked up from the surface." Suddenly there was a good deal of talk about the north country.[37]

Neither the Russians nor the local Indians had been interested in gold. The principal concern of the Russian-American Company was furs, although before the American purchase they had exploited Alaskan timber, coal, and even ice (making a fine profit on the shipment of clear glacial crystal to the purveyors of San Francisco's deluxe hotels). The Tlingit Indians of the northern Pacific coast grew prosperous not only by supplying the Russians with foodstuffs but, more important, by the old strategy of controlling much of the trade between the Russians and interior tribes. By the time of the American purchase the orientation of the Tlingit economy had shifted from subsistence to commerce, but this development only strengthened their traditional social organization and culture. Indeed, this was the golden age of Tlingit art: beautiful Chilkat blankets woven from the rare wool of mountain goats, wooden screens fabulously painted in the classic form-line pattern of the Northwest coast,

Interior of Tlingit chief's house, Chilkat, Alaska. Photograph by Winter and Pond, c. 1890. Beinecke.

totem poles carved from monumental Sitka spruce. The Tlingits offer an instructive contrast to the general devastation of Indian peoples by colonialism. "They were a confident group," write anthropologists Douglas Cole and David Darling, "astute in their business dealings and more exploiting than exploited."[38]

The departure of the Russians and the arrival of the Americans marked a dramatic shift in Tlingit fortunes. Their initial confidence was clear in their welcome to the Americans. "True, we allowed the Russians to possess this island," a chief told the delegation who had come to Sitka to accept the Russian cession and raise the Stars and Stripes, "but we did not intend to give it to any and every fellow that comes along." The Americans were little interested in continuing the operations of the Russian-American Company, and consequently the Tlingits lost their valuable intermediary role. In 1877, with Indian warfare raging on the Great Plains and in the Rockies, the War Department ordered the transfer of troops from Sitka to the West, and before their steamer had cleared the harbor, the Tlingits were tearing down the stockade and taking over government buildings. The Americans were soon back, punishing the proud Tlingits by bombarding their coastal villages. The decline of Tlingit power and prosperity dates not from the first contact with Europeans but from the beginning of the American period.[39]

Indians found few roles to play in the mining economy that the Americans wished to establish, although some found work as guides. Prospectors arrived in the 1870s to explore the coastal ranges. The first important discovery took place in 1880, when a Tlingit chief led the French Canadian Joe Juneau and his partner Richard Harris to a site near a village of the Chilkat band where the miners found gold. Within a year the number of white men at the Juneau mines was greater than the population of the

Packing up Chilkoot Pass to the Yukon gold fields, 1899. Yukon Archives, MacBride Museum, Whitehorse, Canada.

rest of Alaska combined. Working hundreds of stamping mills that pulverized tons of quartz rock and extracted traces of gold, the Juneau miners produced more than $170 million over the next sixty years. Tlingits worked alongside East European immigrants in the mills and mines but were prevented from sharing in the prosperity. Federal authorities removed the Chilkat band and refused to compensate them for the loss of their lands. A number of Indians attempted to file mining claims, but because they were not citizens, the federal government rejected their applications.

Soon Tlingit guides were leading prospectors over the coastal mountains to explore the rivers of the interior. In 1886 gold was discovered on a feeder stream of the Yukon River, and within a few years as many as a thousand Americans, Canadians, and Indians were working the interior valley. Yields were low, but that changed in 1896 when George Carmack and his Indian partners Dawson Charley and Skookum Jim scooped up a single pan of gravel containing four dollars' worth of gold and realized they had struck a bonanza. The word spread quickly, and by the next year a full-scale rush to the Yukon was on. Over the next several years some one hundred thousand miners steamed north from Seattle through the Inside Passage, landing at the boomtown of Skagway and making their way over the treacherous Chilkoot and White passes. This stampede remade the world of the interior Athabascan people overnight. Dawson Charley, Skookum Jim, and a few other Indians made fortunes, but for most natives the effects of the gold rush were disastrous. The miners dis-rupted the pattern of native hunting and fishing, and in order to support themselves Indians were forced to find employment as laborers and packers. In a familiar story many communities were devastated by disease and alcoholism. Although there was little interethnic violence during the high tide of placer mining in the Yukon—nor much violence when operations shifted to the Alaskan coast of Nome, then the Tanana valley (where the town of Fairbanks developed) a few years later—gold again proved to be a plague for Indians. Perhaps the Indian perspective was best captured in the declaration of an Athabascan chief to a delegation of Americans near the site of Fairbanks in 1915. "We want to be left alone," he told them. "God made Alaska for the Indian people, and all we hope is to be able to live here all the time."[40]

———

Luckily for the Athabascans, most of the miners soon moved on, and by the 1920s the Indians got their wish to be left alone. Western miners had the highest rates of mobility of any group in American history. In his careful study of two California mining communities, for example, Ralph Mann finds that of every hundred persons there in 1850, only five remained in 1856. When rumors swept through the California camps in 1858 of rich pay dirt in British Columbia, some thirty thousand men left the California mines for the Fraser River. The following year there was a similar rush to Colorado, but after it became clear that the initial take suffered by comparison with California's, an estimated 60 percent of the miners left. Many hurried on to the great Comstock Lode in Nevada, where a series of independent finds had been made by such prospectors as James "Old Virginny" Fenimore and Henry "Old Pancake" Comstock. In its heyday more than three hundred million dollars was taken from those mines, but it would feed the fortunes of a small group of "Silver Kings." Henry Comstock sold one of his claims for eleven thousand dollars, the other for two mules, and rambled on to Oregon, Idaho, and Montana.

Comstock's mobility was typical. According to Granville Stuart, a Montanan of the 1860s, late one wintry evening the rumor of a new strike made the rounds: thirty miles away, it was said, the gravels were so rich you could shovel out pans of gold worth one hundred dollars each. Within hours the town was deserted as men streaked off without provisions despite the January weather. The ore turned out to be fool's gold, but the miners' frame of mind remained unchanged. Some miners spent their lives chasing rumors. "I've dug in Alaska and made a bit," says Howard, the old prospector in B. Traven's classic novel of gold fever, *The Treasure of the Sierra Madre*. "I've been in the crowd in British Columbia and made there at least my fair wages. I was down in Australia, where I made my fare back home, with a few hundred left over to cure me of the stomach trouble I caught down there. I've dug in Montana and in Colorado and I don't know where else." Something extraordinary was going on here. Gold rushers, writes the historian Douglas Fetherling, "were very much like Crusaders. It was the journey and the process, not the destination or the fact, that lent mystery and substance." Bayard Taylor caught something of this in his description of men on their way to California by ship, "clustered on the bow, sitting with their feet hanging over the guards, and talking of Ponce de Leon, De Soto, and the early Spanish adventurers." The men agreed "that the present days were as wonderful as those, and each individual emigrant entitled to equal credit for daring and enterprise." Rushing among dozens of gold, silver, and hard-rock mining regions for seventy years after the California furor instilled the West with obsessive restlessness. The itinerant western army of miners was the origin of what historian Carlos Schwantes calls "the wageworkers' frontier."[41]

Gold rushing was a kind of nineteenth-century rite of passage for American men, an opportunity, as contemporaries put it, "to see the elephant." This phrase entered the American glossary in the mid-1830s but became particularly associated with the California gold rush. It originated with the tale of the western farmer who hitches his team and drives to town to see the circus and on the way encounters the parade of exotic animals led by the elephant. The farmer's terrified horses buck, pitch, and overturn the wagon. How was the show? asks the man's wife on his return. "Didn't get to the circus," he replies with a crooked smile, "but I've seen the elephant!" The analogy is revealing: the gold might be elusive—but oh, the thrill of the rush![42]

William Swain's letters home from California in the 1850s offer vivid testimony on the restlessness of the mining frontier. When Swain arrived he declared himself "proud of the miners, both for their honesty and their sobriety," but soon he was lamenting "the rapidity with which they have retrograded. . . . Drinking has become very prevalent, swearing a habitual custom, and gambling has no equal in the annals of history." Part of the problem, he wrote to his brother, was that the miners considered California "but a temporary stopping place," a place to make money. "Perhaps one-half of those who try the mines do not remain a month," he wrote. Consequently, there was "an almost total lack of social organization." But soon even the money-making stopped. "The fact is, we are too late in this country to make a fortune," Swain complained to his mother, "and every season makes the matter worse." Nine-tenths of his fellow miners, he believed, were "sick at heart! Aye!! Downhearted and discouraged!!! And many of them have great reason to be disheartened. Thousands who one month ago felt certain that their chances were sure for a fortune are at this time without money or any chance of any and hundreds of dollars in debt. Certainly such a turn of fortune is enough to sicken the heart of any man." Desperate hope kept the men digging. "It is hard for a man to leave here with nothing where there is so much money made," another miner wrote to his sister. "Still clinging to the hope that he will strike it soon, he hangs on until he spends what little he has and is then forced to stop. . . . I have no pile yet but you can bet your life I will never come home until I have something more than when I started." Many a lonely and heart-sick miner delayed his return in the hope that he would finally make enough to return home with his self-respect.[43]

Swain recognized that California contrasted with other frontiers. "The emigration to this country has been marked with a different stamp and character from any other," he wrote. "It has generally been the emigration of individuals, not of families." And those individuals were nearly all male. The pattern among the Chinese was duplicated among the Americans. The census of 1850 reported that women made up less than 8 percent of the state's population, and in the diggings their numbers were even lower. In El Dorado County, the most densely populated of the mining counties, the census enumerator counted 19,062 men and only 459 women. "Women to society is like a cement to the building of stone," opined the *Daily Alta California*. California "has no such cement, its elements float to and fro upon the excited, turbulent, hurried life." As William Swain put it, to men without families "vice seems more alluring" and comes "to be a substitute for common amusement."[44]

"My old man has left me & has gon to Califorma and took my wagon and left me and my Children in a bad situation." So Elizabeth Cress of Illinois wrote to her parents in North Carolina, appealing for a loan to see her through the winter of 1851. Consider the number of "gold rush widows" left behind, tending the children, running the farm or the business, waiting for the mail, worrying through the days and nights. Women responded in a variety of ways. Abby Jenkins urged her husband, Harry, to return and "lift the burden off [my] shoulders and take the lead." Ridiculing "the fuss that is made about the rights of Woman," she insisted that all she wanted was the "right to my own husband." But some women took their husband's absence as the opportunity to claim new rights. From the Colorado mines James Fergus wrote his wife, Pamelia, a patronizing letter suggesting that his sojourn away from home would "be a great benefit to you, by throwing you on your own resources and learning you to do business for yourself." He got more than he bargained for. When they finally reunited, after four years of he mining and she doing for herself, Pamelia was no longer the acquiescent wife. They disagreed, sometimes in public, and frequently quarreled. "The great trouble is that you pay no attention to the wishes of your husband," the flabbergasted James wrote in a chastising letter. But eventually the couple adjusted, and many years later, after his dear wife had died, James confessed to his daughter that he and Pamelia had never really understood each other "until she had her own way."[45]

Some wives simply forbade their husbands going. "The Rolling Stone," a song popular throughout the Midwest during the 1850s, recounted such a struggle:

Since times are so hard, I'll tell you, my wife
I've a mind for to shake off this trouble and strife,
And to California my journey pursue
To double my fortunes as other men do.
For here we may labor each day in the field
And the winters consume all that summers doth yield.
Dear husband, remember your land is to clear,
It will cost you the labor of many a year.
Your horses, sheep and cattle will all be to buy,
And before you have got them you are ready to die.
So stick to your farming; you'll suffer no loss,
For the stone that keeps rolling can gather no moss.

The wife of the song, like thousands of uncounted women, succeeded in keeping her feverish husband at home. Other women took a different approach. When Gay Hayden came down with gold fever in early 1850, he announced to his wife, Mary Jane, that he was leaving her behind. "I was nearly heart-broken at the thought of the separation," she remembered, but she wisely adopted an aggressive defense: "I said 'we were married to live together' (he saying 'yes'), 'and I am willing to go with you to any part of *God's foot stool* where you think you can do best, and under these circumstances you have no right to go where I cannot, and if you do you need never return for I shall look upon you as dead.' So it was settled that *we* should go the next year."[46]

Like Mary Jane Hayden, a number of wives accompanied their husbands to the camps, and many immediately found themselves in demand. Upon her arrival at the diggings near Nevada City, California, Luzena Wilson was interrupted at her campfire by a miner gazing longingly at her simple cooking. "I'll give you five dollars, ma'am, for them biscuit," he drawled. She was startled. "It seemed like a fortune to me," she remembered, "and as I hesitated at such, to me, a very remarkable proposition, he repeated his offer to purchase, and said he would give ten dollars for bread made by a woman, and laid a shiney gold piece in my hand." Knowing a good thing when she saw it, Wilson determined to set up her own makeshift boardinghouse. "With my own hands I chopped stakes, drove them into the ground, and set up my table. I bought provisions at a neighboring store, and when my husband came back at night he found, mid the weird light of the pine torches, twenty miners eating at my table. Each man as he rose put a dollar in my hand and said I might count him as a permanent customer. I called my hotel 'El Dorado.'" Mrs. Wilson's boarding produced far more income than Mr. Wilson's mining. The census of 1850 recorded only twenty-three women in Nevada City, but fifteen of them were running boardinghouses or taverns. "A smart woman can do very well in this country," a young woman

*Female prospectors on their way to the Yukon.
Photograph by B. W. Kilburn, 1899. Beinecke.*

wrote home. "True there are not many comforts and one must work all the time and work hard but [there] is plenty to do and good pay. . . . It is the only country that I ever was in where a woman received anything like a just compensation for work."[47]

Throughout the mining West women played important roles as laundresses and cooks or proprietors of restaurants and boardinghouses. Indeed, at the end of the century a number of single women joined the rush to Alaska precisely to take advantage of these entrepreneurial opportunities. "Yes, there are women going into the mines alone," returned Klondiker Ethel Bush Berry declared in 1898, "widows and lone women to do whatever they could for the miners, with the hope of getting big pay." Belinda Mulrooney was a single woman in Juneau in the summer of 1896 when she heard of the Klondike strike. Recognizing her chance to make good, she set out on her own. By the time she was twenty-six she had become one of the wealthiest residents of the Klondike, holding a number of claims and managing several businesses.[48]

Women in the camps found themselves the object of a good deal of attention. C. C. Mobley wrote in his diary how his heart "leaped with joy" when he heard one evening "the voice of a pretty girl raised in song—a thing I have not heard before for months." The sound of a woman's voice drew men like the siren's song. When the Alverson girls performed a piano concert in Stockton, California, in 1892, there were "scores of men in the street as far as the eye could see, and some were sobbing." "I tell you the women are in great demand in this country no matter whether they are married or not," Abby Mansur wrote her sister from the camp of Horseshoe Bar in the Sierras in 1852. "You need not think strange if you see me coming home with some good looking man some of these times with a pocket full of rocks. You may rest assured that I shall not take up with no common stalk. It is all the go here for Ladys to leave there Husbands. Two out of three do it." But sometimes there was the devil to

*Prostitutes in Dawson City, Yukon Territory.
Photograph by B. W. Kilburn, 1899. Beinecke.*

pay. A young girl at a mining camp called Shaws Flat watched a developing flirtation between her neighbor Mrs. Smith and a gambler. But catching wind of the affair, "Mr. Smith met him and beat his face nearly off; he broke his nose, and knocked out several teeth, and told him to leave the Flat. He certainly left."[49]

It was inevitable, given their overwhelming male character, that the camps attracted prostitutes by the dozens, many from outside the states. As the miners of Butte sang: "First came the miners to work in the mine. / Then came the ladies to live on the line." Crowded into one small house in the mining camp of Coloma the census enumerator found six prostitutes ranging in age from seventeen to thirty and hailing from Canada, Ireland, Chile, Mexico, and New York. From Boise, Idaho, in 1863 Louisa Cook wrote her mother that "I have but two or three Lady acquaintances in this country. *Ladies* are not plenty. There are a great many in all the mining towns who wear the form of a woman, but oh so fallen and vile, a living, burning shame to the sex they have so disgraced. As soon as the miners began to flock to this country these women began to come out." Whoring could be a profitable business, according to historian Paula Petrik. A "fancy lady" in late nineteenth-century Helena, Montana, could expect a monthly income of $233, compared to less than $100 a month for a miner. A small group of "dowager queens of the *demimonde*" became prominent landladies in Helena's tenderloin. But as Anne Butler demonstrates in her careful study of western prostitutes, most came from the poorest and most exploited groups on the frontier and were often the victims of violence, disease, drug abuse, and suicide. Half the prostitutes in Helena were Chinese, and Petrik acknowledges that there is no record of any of them owning property.[50]

For lonely miners, however, "the whore with the heart of gold" was more than simply a myth. Alf Doten, a journalist working in Virginia City in the 1860s, kept a candid diary of his many encounters with prostitutes, but in reading the entries one senses a longing not only for sex but for tender loving care. "I went with Sam Glasser down to Chinatown—drank at Tom Poos'—went to Mary's house—we were in her room with her—she gave us each a cake left from the holiday of yesterday—filled with nuts & sweetmeats—we laid on a bed with her & smoked opium with her—a little boy some 2 years old sleeping there, belonging to one of her women—long and interesting chat with her."[51]

When Francis Parkman left the Missouri settlements in 1846, he bid "a long adieu to bed and board and the principles of Blackstone's Commentaries." It was a feeling widely shared. It was not merely the common law that the miners reconstructed with difficulty; they also had to create a corpus of mining law, for which they brought almost no usable precedent. Practical questions arose immediately. Who owned what? How could a man stake out land on which to dig or pan for gold? How much could he claim—a mountain ridge or a whole valley? Where would the deed be recorded? Could a man own land and leave it to be worked later? Who would protect the weak from the strong, the unarmed from the armed?[52]

In California, in a process that happened hundreds of times, a group of miners came together in a kind of mass meeting, elected officers, and drafted a few rules. No one has estimated how often it occurred throughout the West. Similarities emerged, partly because the problems were predictable and partly because of the movement of men from one place to another. Models worked out in California were often adopted elsewhere. In general the laws allowed a man to stake out any "reasonable" amount of land, by which was meant an amount he could work in a season. He had to mark it clearly and file a claim with the local recorder. Most important, he had to work the land. If he left it, he lost it. There would be no absentee owners in the mines. The Spanish-Mexican influence was evident in the attachment of water rights to all land. Thus, even if a man claimed a parcel far back from the banks of a stream, he still had the right to divert a reasonable amount of water to wash his dry gravels. Conflicting claims were arbitrated by committees, panels, juries, or sometimes by entire town meetings. In some respects these miners' codes appear highly idealistic, weighted in favor of the small miner. Large mining companies amassing extensive holdings found them quaint and irrelevant. They needed more uniformity between various districts. As individualism in the mines gave way to corporatism, local codes gave way to state law. By then the first comers, like Henry Comstock, were long gone.

Yet many westerners looked back fondly on the days of the miners' meetings. They admired the idea of a group of men sitting together, applying common sense to their immediate problems, and they praised the miners' directness and the lack of humbug or legal complexity in their proceedings. For Charles Howard Shinn—whose *Mining Camps: A Study in Frontier Government* (1884) has become a classic—it was a demonstration of the "Saxon love of fair play." But when life and civil liberties are

TREMENDOUS EXCITEMENT !

Samuel Whittaker and Robert Mc Kenzie rescued from the authorities, an. hung by the Vigilance Committee, on Sunday August 24ᵗʰ at 3 o'clock P.M. in the presence of Fifteen thousand People.

Lith. & Publ. by Justh. Quirot &Cᵒ Calif corner Mong. 4ᵗ S.F.

A lynching conducted by the San Francisco Vigilance Committee, 1851. Beinecke.

challenged, the lack of humbug and the disregard for due process appear far less attractive, for legal complexity is what protects people from harm until they are proven guilty. The miners' meetings were a principal agency of violence against Indians, Latinos, and Chinese, and miners were quick to resort to lynchings and vigilante action, with or without the approval of courts and legal systems. The spirit of the Regulators and the Paxton Boys was alive and well in the Far West. Though he praised the miners' "instinctive cleverness" at self-government, philosopher Josiah Royce condemned the "popular passion" of their extralegal justice and argued that "you cannot build up a prosperous and peaceful community so long as you pass laws to oppress and torment a large resident class of the community."[53]

Royce made his point most effectively by pointing to the operation of lynch law in San Francisco. After a series of violent crimes in early 1851, a group of businessmen took command of a hysterical mob and constituted themselves as the city's "Committee of Vigilance." Over a period of several months, the committee arrested, tried, and convicted several dozen men, hanging five and banishing twenty-eight. In September they smugly declared San Francisco clean and adjourned, receiving plaudits from all over the state. The episode was an example of what Richard Maxwell Brown calls "socially constructive" vigilantism. The committee reappeared in 1856, claiming once again that criminals had swept away order. More than six thousand citizens, mostly businessmen, volunteered to enforce vigilante order. But this time there was much dispute over the alleged crime wave. A smaller group of citizens protested against the need for extralegal justice, but they were ignored. Through the summer the committee arrested suspects and held trials. Legally constituted courts issued writs of habeas corpus, demanding the release of those jailed, but the vigilantes refused to honor them on the grounds of popular sovereignty. Eventually California's governor declared the city in a state of insurrection, but William Tecumseh Sherman, major general of the California militia, declined to move against the vigilantes. Many suspected that his reluctance stemmed from close connections with the business community. Sherman resigned and shortly after, in a letter to his brother, wrote that "being in a business where large interests are at stake, I cannot act with that decision that would otherwise suit me." How many others acquiesced in the work of the committee for the same reason?[54]

In August the committee held a jubilant parade and disbanded. They had executed five men and deported thirty. Hundreds of others had fled the city in fear. San Francisco had been saved. But saved from what? Practically every person deported was Irish. In retrospect the movement turned out to be less about suppressing crime than seizing political control of the city from Irish Democrats. The Committee of Vigilance organized its own People's Party, which proceeded to sweep the city elections and place in office a government that drastically reduced taxes on businessmen. The budget was cut so badly that some schools were forced to close. This was vigilantism of a different kind; it was a "Business Man's Revolution," as Royce put it, a group of entrepreneurs engineering a panic over crime to further their own economic interests. Vigilante actions serving such narrow interests infected every region of the West. While sometimes vigilantes acted in accord with wider civic interest, more frequently they were characterized by class interest and appeared as part of the everlasting tension between the rich and the poor, the white and the colored, the elite and the outcast, the established and the disinherited.

Though eighty million dollars in gold was taken out of California in 1852, it ceased enriching the independent prospector. The social ramifications of gold rushes spread widely. Storekeepers had to be supplied with goods, of course. Urban centers, freighting, shipbuilding, and the merchant marine felt the boom. The most dramatic effect was seen in the form of the clipper ship, designed to bring cargoes as quickly as possible from the East to San Francisco. In their high noon during the 1850s, the ships placed America in the forefront of the world's maritime powers. In California fortunes were made by men who could corner markets in crucial items. Collis P. Huntington would row out in a dinghy to meet incoming ships with so many gold bags around his belt that capsizing would have sent him straight to the bottom. With gold on the barrel head he would buy every shovel on board.

Booms in food supplies were to be expected. Here the results were not simply in trading and transportation but in local farming as well. The cattle ranches of southern California supplied meat for the northern mines, and Yankees like the elder James Irvine acquired the vast acreage that would later become the Irvine Ranch (and still later the planned city of Irvine) in order to participate in the boom. "Cattle on a thousand hills" is the phrase Robert Glass Cleland used to describe southern California at this time. In the San Joaquin valley the increase in wheat farming was even more dramatic. According to John W. Caughey, annual production there in the decade after 1850 bulged from seventeen thousand bushels to nearly six million. This initial expansion was underwritten by eastern capital.[55]

By the 1870s the mining industry throughout the Far West was concentrated in the hands of a wealthy elite. Some of these "bonanza kings" had clawed their way up from the diggings. George Hearst, father of the newspaper baron William Randolph Hearst, crossed the plains on foot in 1850 and within a few years had made a pile in placer and quartz mining. In 1859 he invested in the Comstock Lode and laid the foundation for a great fortune. "If you're ever inclined to think that there's no such thing as luck," Hearst once remarked, "just think of me." In 1877 Hearst and his partners purchased the Homestake Mine in the Black Hills and, by gradually buying up the claims of competing and adjoining miners, turned their property into the most fabulous of all western gold mines. More frequently capital came from investors who had never lifted a spade. Eastern and British capitalists loaned huge sums to western bankers who in turn invested in western mining. William Ralston of the Bank of California financed the integration of mines, mills, smelters, railroads, and lumber companies on the Comstock Lode. It was a classic story of American capitalism.[56]

Although individual prospecting and mining continued, by the 1860s the majority of western miners were laboring for corporations. "The situation is much different from what we in Denmark imagine," a journalist reported home to a newspaper in Copenhagen. "When we speak of a goldminer, we mean a kind of King Midas who simply has to thrust his spade into the ground to find a nugget. But that is not how it is. A goldminer is a common mine worker who labors for a company." Within a few decades the most fabulous profits were in the mining of base metals rather than precious ones. After a brief moment as a gold and silver mining center, the Montana town of Butte became the mother of all western copper mining—"The Richest Hill on Earth," in the phrase of local promoters. At the turn of the century there were copper strikes at such places as Globe and Bisbee in southern Arizona and at the Bingham open-pit mine near Salt Lake City—which jokesters lampooned as "The Rich-

Homestake Mine, Lead City, Dakota Territory. Photograph by J. C. H. Grabill, 1888. Beinecke.

est Hole on Earth." These operations were in the hands of large mining corporations with names like Kennecott, Phelps-Dodge, and Anaconda. By the eve of World War I the West was producing 90 percent of the nation's copper as well as most of its lead and other heavy metals. Work in these hard-rock mines was extremely dangerous. One investigation of Butte's deepest shaft measured the air temperature at 107°F, the water temperature at 113°F, the rock temperature at 113°F, and the relative humidity at 100 percent. The heat and humidity magnified the overwhelming odor of human excrement, sweat, blasting powder, rotting food, and tobacco. Men sometimes dropped dead from such conditions. The accident rate was incredibly high. Western mining had become the most hazardous industry in the country.[57]

One of the biggest challenges confronting union organizers was the ethnic diversity among western miners. Mining towns tended to divide into ethnic enclaves, and ethnic identity frequently compromised working-class solidarity. The Americans fought the Irish, the Irish fought the English, the English fought the Germans, and all in turn fought the Mexicans and especially the Chinese. As early as the 1860s, however, miners began to organize unions that brought groups of Americans and Europeans together, although for the most part they continued to exclude African Americans, Latinos, and Asians. The first successful labor organizing began on the Comstock Lode of Nevada, where miners struck successfully to maintain the four-dollar daily wage in 1864. The defensive struggle to maintain wage rates became the hallmark of western miners' unionism. During the 1860s competition among mine owners kept rates high, but when the national economy soured after the Panic of 1873, there was constant pressure to lower wages. In 1878 when the copper miners of Butte came up from their shifts to receive their monthly paychecks they discovered that the company had cut wages by a quarter, to three dollars. Parading through the streets they called a mass meeting at which they organized the Butte Workingmen's Union. Solidarity eventually made the union strong enough to force the mine owners not only to bring wages back up but to accept the union demand for a closed shop. Miners' unions were equally committed to mutual aid. In response to the dangers that beset miners on the job, unions created trust funds that paid benefits to sick and injured workers and provided assistance to miners' widows and orphans. This dual strategy characterized all the miners' unions of the West.

A second problem for organizers was the miners' continuous movement from rush to rush in an attempt to find diggings where a man could still work his own claim. When hundreds of men left the Comstock Lode for rumors of gold in Idaho, the local newspaper noted that they were leaving a region "where the mines are worked only by companies, for a country where every man can work for himself." The Butte union was a leader in the effort to build a regional miners' organization, affiliating in the 1880s with several dozen other locals to form the Silver Bow Trades and Labor Assembly, which claimed several thousand members by 1891.[58]

Miners remained relatively moderate in their demands until the strike for union recognition at the mines in the Coeur d'Alene region of Idaho in 1892. In a confrontation between strikers and troops seven miners were killed. The next year, at a meeting in Butte, organizers formed the Western Federation of Miners (WFM). One of their planks called for a prohibition of the use of armed force against workers, a direct reference to the wounds of Coeur d'Alene. From the start the WFM took a radical position, arguing for fundamental change in the economic and social system of the country. Soon there were organizers for the union in nearly every mining town and camp in the West. As a young miner in Silver City, Idaho, Bill Haywood was approached by an organizer. "I had never heard of the need of workingmen organizing for mutual protection," Haywood later wrote in his colorful autobiography, but the older man "told me about the unions he had belonged to, the miners' union in Bodie, California, and the Virginia City Miners' Union in Nevada." Converted to the cause, like thousands of others, Haywood soon joined the WFM leadership. Within

Miners, Central City, Colorado. Photograph by Donald Kemp, c. 1890. Denver Public Library, Western History Department.

a few years the union enrolled more than fifty thousand members and became the strongest workers' organization in the American West.[59]

The Western Federation of Miners was one of the unions that helped found the Industrial Workers of the World (IWW) in 1905. Not only miners but all kinds of migratory workers of the western "wageworkers' frontier" were attracted in large numbers to the IWW. Unlike craft unions affiliated with the American Federation of Labor, the IWW made it easy for itinerant workers to transfer from one local to another as they moved from place to place, and it specialized in organizing among the unskilled, including African Americans, Mexicans, and Chinese. One story attributes the groups' nickname, the Wobblies, to the mispronunciation of Chinese recruits: "i-wobbly-wobbly." The Wobbly leaders, Haywood included, were implacable foes of industrial capitalism, and over the next ten years they battled the captains of the West's great extractive industries in the name of revolution. In 1917, after the United States had entered World War I, they led strikes in the great copper mines of Montana and Arizona; the strike ended in Butte when the National Guard occupied the town, in Bisbee when local vigilantes and sheriffs deported more than twelve hundred strikers, threatening violence to any who returned. Soon thereafter President Woodrow Wilson's Justice Department raided IWW offices throughout the West, arresting leaders on charges of obstructing the war effort. Local, state, and federal authorities combined to crush the movement.

But the IWW success in organizing among miners, lumberjacks, longshoremen, and migrant harvest workers was an indication of how the West had changed from the early days of the California rush. "Working men who travel westward are for the most part imbued with the restless spirit of enterprise, born of the desire for improved conditions," wrote one IWW organizer. "But unlike the old pioneer seeking a homestead and finding it, the modern wage worker who 'goes West' finds no alternative except to hunt for a master." The Industrial Workers of the World were an ironic outcome, perhaps, of the great rush for gold and riches in the West. But they succeeded because they understood something essential about the restless way of life on the wageworkers' frontier.[60]

FURTHER READING

Louise Barnett, *Touched by Fire: The Life, Death, and Mythic Afterlife of George Armstrong Custer* (1996)

Anne M. Butler, *Daughters of Joy, Sisters of Mercy: Prostitutes in the American West, 1865–90* (1985)

Douglas Fetherling, *The Gold Crusades: A Social History of Gold Rushes, 1849–1929* (1988)

Marion S. Goldman, *Gold Diggers and Silver Miners: Prostitution and Social Life on the Comstock Lode* (1981)

Robert F. Heizer and Alan F. Almquist, *The Other Californians: Prejudice and Discrimination under Spain, Mexico, and the United States to 1920* (1971)

Albert L. Hurtado, *Indian Survival on the California Frontier* (1988)

JoAnn Levy, *They Saw the Elephant: Women in the California Gold Rush* (1990)

Paula Mitchell Marks, *Precious Dust: The American Gold Rush Era, 1848–1900* (1994)

Mary Murphy, *Mining Cultures: Men, Women, and Leisure in Butte, 1914–41* (1997)

Rodman Wilson Paul, *Mining Frontiers of the Far West, 1848–1880* (1963; reprint, 1974)

Malcolm J. Rohrbough, *Days of Gold: The California Gold Rush and the American Nation* (1997)

Robert M. Utley, *The Lance and the Shield: The Life and Times of Sitting Bull* (1993)

David Williams, *The Georgia Gold Rush: Twenty-Niners, Cherokees, and Gold Fever* (1993)

Mark Wyman, *Hard Rock Epic: Western Miners and the Industrial Revolution, 1860–1910* (1979)

9

The Power of the Road

Bret Harte, western writer and editor of the *Overland Monthly,* was among the crowd at Promontory, Utah, in 1869, that witnessed the driving of the golden spike to join the tracks of the first transcontinental railroad. He watched as the steam engines, with overblown smokestacks and ox-sized cowcatchers, faced off for one of the most iconic photographs in American history. Harte wondered:

> What was it the Engines said,
> Pilots touching—head to head,
> Facing on the single track,
> Half a world behind each back?

No one could doubt the power of the railroad to transform. Over the previous quarter-century it had reshaped the landscape of the eastern half of the continent, propelled the country into sustained industrial growth, and made possible the victory of the Union over the Confederacy. "Railroads are talismanic wands," one promoter wrote during the Civil War. "They do wonders—they work miracles." What miracles would they work for the West?[1]

Certainly hopes were high. "The iron key has been found to unlock our golden treasures," gushed the editor of the *Helena Independent.* "With railroads come population, industry, and capital, and with them come the elements of prosperity and greatness to Montana." Once it was in place, the national railroad system would undergird a fabulously valuable exchange of people and products between East and West. Thousands of settlers would steam onto the plains and over the mountains to the Pacific coast, settling on farms, ranches, and in dozens of rapidly growing cities and towns, scattered like oases across the western countryside. The late nineteenth-century West was inconceivable without the railroad. "The West is purely a railroad

274

East and West shake hands at the laying of the last rail. Photograph by A. J. Russell, 1869. Beinecke.

enterprise," declared an executive of one of the transcontinental lines and then added, with a wink, "We started it in our publicity department." Backcountry folks may have been isolated in an earlier era, but the railroad would provide the people of the West with easy access to eastern goods. In turn, the West would become a vast resource windfall for industrial America, supplying bread and meat, lumber and minerals. Wealth and power would ride the rails, but they would be ticketed east-bound, always moving from the West toward the metropolitan centers of the Atlantic coast and Europe. Consider what the railroad would bring to Montana: the copper boom at Butte, which attracted thousands of people, made enormous fortunes, and turned that town into what historian Richard O'Connor describes as "possibly the most miserable city in the Western world." The railroads would bring the best and the worst of Gilded Age America. "What was it the engines said?" Too often they spoke with forked tongue.[2]

Red River carts and Indians. Photograph by Stanley Morrow, c. 1870. Beinecke.

The golden spike made earlier methods of transportation seem antiquated and primitive. But before 1869 people, mail, and freight had moved rather efficiently through the West by horse and mule transport. During the Civil War farm wagons continued to roll along the Overland Trail through the Platte River valley as hundreds of families fled the violence. Among them were bands of men "armed with rifles & revolvers," according to one Union soldier, "all of the Southern sympathizing class." After the war there was another of those periodic surges of westward migration. Major General John Pope saw "great throngs" of former Confederates and displaced Southern families heading west. Overland wagon travel would decline after the completion of the first transcontinental line, but poor folks would continue moving west by wagon until well into the twentieth century.[3]

On the northern plains the characteristic vehicle was the two-wheeled, ox-drawn cart, or *charette,* of the métis communities that lived along the Missouri River and on the banks of the Red and Assiniboine rivers north of the forty-ninth parallel. Agriculture was marginal in this northern country, and after planting their crops in the spring, families would pack their belongings into their charettes and set out by the hundreds to follow the buffalo herds, making meat, pemmican, and robes, which they sold to traders on their return in the winter. During a tour of the northern plains in 1854, Governor Isaac Stevens of Washington Territory overtook a caravan of thirteen hundred métis men, women, and children in 824 carts. So linked were these people to their distinctive Red River carts, that in the sign language of the plains the word *métis* was indicated by circling the hands about each other, then drawing a finger down the center: half wagon, half man.

Much to the chagrin of the Hudson's Bay Company, which tried to maintain a monopoly within its realm, during the 1840s the métis had begun to trade with the Americans moving into the newly opened territory of Minnesota. After a protracted struggle, in 1849 the HBC finally loosened its restrictions, opening two decades of prosperous trading between the Red River communities and the Saint Paul merchants. Down a series of rough paths and roads known as the Red River Trail, métis traders drove their carts to American markets. The screech of the ungreased wooden axles, according to one observer, sounded like "the scraping of a thousand finger nails on a thousand panes of glass." The métis might appear exotic, with their "swarthy complexions, straight long black hair, and wild, devil-may-care look," wrote one Saint Paul editor, but he urged his readers to think of them as "our fellow citizens." Uppermost in his mind was the value of the métis trade. In 1865, when the Red River Trail was experiencing peak traffic, the métis generated more than $250,000 of business for Saint Paul traders. This probably exceeded the annual value of the Santa Fe trade of the 1840s, but somehow the charettes of the northern plains failed to find a place in the lore of western America, perhaps because they chronicle a Canadian rather than an American story.[4]

On the Santa Fe Trail itself, freight was hauled by big, heavy Conestoga wagons, drawn by large teams of mules. In the years following the Mexican War the military became the biggest customer on the plains, and after several years of unsatisfactory ad hoc arrangements, the army in 1854 awarded a huge contract for supplying all its western posts to the company of Russell, Majors and Waddell, organized by several experienced Santa Fe traders. This government business—worth more than six million dollars annually by the time of the Civil War—turned Russell, Majors and Waddell into the largest freighting business in the country. By 1865 western freighting companies were hauling an estimated 125 million pounds of merchandise from the Mississippi valley to army posts and towns in the West; without this service, mining and military operations could not have succeeded.

Federal subsidies were also critical to the development of western stage lines. After the Mexican War, at an annual cost of more than seven hundred thousand dollars, Congress established a maritime mail service between New York and San Francisco. But impatient with the months required for ocean delivery, in 1856 some seventy-five thousand Californians laid a petition before Congress urging the establishment of an overland mail route. Washington responded quickly, and the next year the first large-scale federal contract for overland mail service went to John Butterfield of New York. A self-made capitalist who had achieved wealth and fame in the eastern freight and stage business, in 1850 Butterfield merged his interests with those of Henry Wells and William Fargo—operators of a system of California stage lines—

Stagecoach at Elko, Nevada. Photograph by A. J. Russell, c. 1869. Beinecke.

to form the American Express Company. The government provided grading, bridges, and 141 station stops along the "Ox Bow Route"—so called because it avoided the Rockies in a great festooned loop through the Southwest—2,795 miles from Saint Louis to Fort Yuma to Los Angeles, then up the inland valleys of California to San Francisco. These improvements, in addition to the annual federal subsidy of six hundred thousand dollars, allowed Butterfield and his partners to build the Overland Mail into a stagecoaching business of imperial design, employing eight hundred men to operate 250 leather-braced Concord coaches. With luck, passengers embarking in Saint Louis on the twice-weekly "jackass mail" could arrive in San Francisco twenty-five days later.

The Civil War forced Butterfield to abandon the Ox Bow Route, and for a brief period the focus shifted to the Pony Express, a mail service between Missouri and California organized by Russell, Majors and Waddell. The Pony Express was speed incarnate. The jockey-sized riders covered 1,966 miles in an average of ten days, less than half the time of the Overland Mail. One hundred fifteen stations were provided for change of horses, and 120 men mounted the relays. In an effort to conserve weight, the horseman carried no guns; speed was his only protection. The mail pouches were kept slim by the prohibitive cost of the letters—$10 an ounce, the equivalent of $180 in today's dollars! The Pony Express lasted for less than two years, but Americans have always loved its memory—so efficient, so organized, so dependent on the physical stamina of a rider alone against the elements. It was, in fact, a quixotic operation. Even as the first riders galloped over their route they saw workers stringing telegraph wires westward from Kansas City and eastward from Sacramento. The lines were

Pony Express rider, c. 1861. Beinecke.

joined on October 24, 1861, killing the Pony Express. Russell, Majors and Waddell went bankrupt the next year.

The firm was taken over by Ben Holladay, a boisterous westerner who worked as saloonkeeper, postmaster, and Indian trader before making his fortune freighting for the army. He won a series of federal western mail and freighting contracts during the Civil War that netted nearly two million dollars, and with twenty thousand wagons and coaches and more than 150,000 animals on the trails became known as the "Stagecoach King." Holladay decked himself out royally, with an emerald stickpin, an enormous gold watch hanging from a heavy chain, and a money belt stuffed with thousands in cash. It was a Holladay coach that Mark Twain rode when he went "roughing it" to Nevada during the Civil War. Twain delighted in the story of a boy who belittled Moses for the forty years he took to get the children of Israel across the desert: "Ben Holladay would have fetched them through in thirty-six hours."[5]

The finale in this series of mergers and takeovers occurred in 1866, when the American Express Company bought out Holladay, consolidated his lines with Butterfield's, and turned the entire operation over to the Wells Fargo division. Concord coaches would continue to link small western communities and isolated mining camps to the railroad towns for another forty years, but the days of the Overland Mail were numbered. States barely east of the Mississippi were already laced with rails. The Illinois Central was thriving, even advertising in Europe for settlers and allowing farmers to pay off mortgages with produce. The stagecoach age had created comfortable fortunes, but these would be small potatoes compared to the fortunes ahead for the builders of the Pacific railroads. After leaving the stagecoach business Ben Holladay invested his capital in Pacific railroad stock.

————

The first serious proposal for a transcontinental railroad came from Asa Whitney, a New York dry goods merchant who made a fortune in the China trade and became convinced that America's future prosperity depended on an overland rail connection to the Pacific. In 1844 he opened a campaign to convince Congress to authorize a western railroad, funding it with a vast subsidy of fertile land along the route. In 1849 Senator Thomas Hart Benton of Missouri, father-in-law of John Charles Frémont, put forward an alternate plan for a Pacific railway funded by the proceeds from the sale of public lands. Such a project, he argued, would complete civilization's "circumambulation of the globe." Benton was a believer in what historian Jan Willem Schulte Nordholt calls "the heliotropic myth." From its origins in Asia, empire had been moving successively westward; first to Mediterranean Greece and Rome, then to France and England, finally crossing the Atlantic to America with the Revolution. When the United States succeeded in constructing a new civilization in the Far West, when at last the pioneers could rest on the shores of the Pacific and gaze over the waters to the ancient place of their Asian origin, human destiny would be fulfilled. It would "realize the grand idea of Columbus," Benton declared. "The rich commerce of Asia will flow through our centre. And where has that commerce ever flowed without carrying wealth and dominion with it?" For too long the East had controlled and limited the West, and the railroad would be the instrument for liberating the region and fulfilling its promise.[6]

Benton's high hopes for western economic development were countered by a sober rejoinder from Princeton geographer Arnold Guyot. A western railroad would indeed be a good thing for the country, Guyot agreed, but "brilliant as may be the prospects the West may aspire to, life and action will always point toward the [East] coast, which can only derive fresh accessions of prosperity from the prosperity of the interior." His reminder that eastern capital would largely control western development contained the "hard core of truth," wrote Henry Nash Smith. "The East would long be able to maintain its economic control over the West."[7]

By the 1850s there was no doubt that the transcontinental railroad would be built. The only questions were where, when, and how. Everyone agreed that the nation could initially afford only a single main line, so the issue quickly became enmeshed in sectional antagonism. New Orleans, Saint Louis, and Chicago were all competing for the privilege of becoming the eastern terminus of the transcontinental trunk line. In 1853, hoping that scientists and engineers might cut this political knot, Congress passed the Pacific Railroad Survey Act, appropriating four hundred thousand dollars to ascertain the "most practical and economical route for a railroad from the

Mississippi River to the Pacific Ocean." Four western expeditions surveyed potential routes along the forty-seventh, thirty-ninth, thirty-fifth, and thirty-second parallels, their work supervised by the newly organized Smithsonian Institution, which supplied apparatus and instruments, issued instructions for collectors and observers, and cataloged the specimens sent back to Washington, D.C. Artists and daguerrotypists kept a detailed pictorial record. The results were published by the federal government in fourteen magnificent volumes, "a priceless compendium," writes Dee Brown, "of the virgin West immediately before its despoliation by the Iron Horse." But the survey teams concluded that there were good routes to the Pacific at each of the four parallels, thus failing to transcend sectional politics.[8]

The where, when, and how were settled only after the South seceded from the Union in 1861, leaving Washington to Lincoln and the Republicans. Indeed, as historian James McPherson writes, the Civil War Congress "did more than any other in history to change the course of national life," restructuring the tariff, the tax and banking system, and the manner and method of financing government. It was what Charles and Mary Beard, in their classic history of the United States, called the "Second American Revolution," a power shift from agrarian to industrial and financial interests. "Human ingenuity would have had difficulty contriving a more perfect engine for class and sectional exploitation," financial historian Robert Sharkey asserts in regard to the Republican program, "creditors finally obtaining the upper hand as opposed to debtors, and the developed East holding the whip over the undeveloped West and South." There would be plenty of complaints about "colonialism" from westerners in the future. But in 1862 their attention was transfixed by congressional action on two programs uppermost on the wish list of the West—free land for settlers in the Homestead Act and a transcontinental line in the Pacific Railroad Bill.[9]

The railroad legislation empowered two corporations, the Union Pacific and the Central Pacific, to construct (westward and eastward, respectively) "a continuous railroad" along the forty-second parallel, the Platte River route of the Overland Trail. The companies secured a four-hundred-foot right-of-way and were granted alternate sections of the public domain within ten miles of each side of the line, amounting to ten sections (ten square miles) for each linear mile of track. To prime the pump of private capital the legislation authorized the federal government to loan the companies construction money in amounts ranging from sixteen thousand dollars per mile of level ground to forty-eight thousand dollars per mountainous mile, all in the form of thirty-year bonds at 6 percent interest.

Congress assumed that private enterprise would not build the transcontinental line unaided. Over most of the route between Missouri and California, population and markets were as sparse as trees on the Nevada desert. If society at large wished to bind together the coasts, society would have to pay a good deal of the cost. Some politicians—old Thomas Hart Benton among them—argued that the government should build the road itself and rent the line to private carriers, but such notions ran against the scruples of constitutional strict constructionists and capitalists alike. Much better, from a business point of view, were government guarantees that removed much of the risk but allowed ample room for profit making. The trinitarian formula of right-of-way, land grant, and loan, however, proved insufficient to produce the additional private investment required to get the corporations moving. "I do not believe that there is one man in five hundred who will invest his money and engage in the building of this road as the law now stands," declared Senator Hiram Price of Iowa. By holding out for two years, the companies got the federal government to up the ante by a factor of two. In 1864 Congress passed a new bill, increasing the land grants to twenty sections per mile instead of ten and reconfiguring the bonds as a second mortgage, allowing the companies themselves to issue bonds and reducing their risk to nil.[10]

These lavish federal subsidies were controversial at the time and remain controversial today among historians. "The federal government seems in these matters to have assumed the major portion of the risk," historian Stuart Daggett concludes, while the railroads "derived the profits." There has been little argument over the bond issue, which cost the taxpayers nothing—here the federal government was advancing credit, not cash, and the bonds were eventually repaid in full with interest, although not before both the corporate descendants of the Union Pacific and Central Pacific attempted to renege on their obligations. The controversy has always focused on the grant of public lands. To be sure, this was a time-honored American method of financing "internal improvements." The original Land Ordinance of 1785 had provided grants of land to the states for public education, and in the early nineteenth century both the state and federal government used land grants to encourage the construction of roads and canals. The first grant for a railroad came in 1850 when Congress voted a generous donation to the Illinois Central. Over the next quarter-century the federal government gave away more than 131 million acres to support the construction of transcontinental trunk routes and numerous feeder lines.[11]

Federal beneficences turned the railroad companies into "empire builders," landlords on a par with the federal land office itself. Unlike the government, however, the companies could charge whatever they liked for land made valuable by the access to transportation the railroad provided. Sometimes the companies waited to select their sections until they could see more clearly how settlement was proceeding. In the meantime, no one else could take up claims. Even after it had made a choice, the company might lease the land, refusing to sell until prices had risen. And because unsold railroad land was exempt from taxation, the burden of paying for local government shifted from giant corporations to middling farmers and ranchers. Later in the century Grangers and Populists would argue that society as a whole had a right to expect some return from the rising value of the lands. But during the 1860s the

Leland Stanford, c. 1880. Department of Special Collections, Stanford University Libraries.

government's concerns were short-range—the immediate transportation of men and supplies—and land grants did the trick. In the long run, society paid heavily, and a few men reaped rich rewards.

––––––

Prominent among the railroad millionaires were the "Big Four"—Collis P. Huntington, Mark Hopkins, Leland Stanford, and Charles Crocker—the founders of the Central Pacific. As the principal stockholders of this, the first of California's giant corporations, they grew fabulously wealthy, but their collective nickname came neither from their wealth nor power but from their collective bulk, weighing in at some 860 pounds. Each man hailed from modest roots in the Northeast, and each would later loudly proclaim the importance of Puritan virtues like diligence and thrift. But, as Crocker once admitted, "luck had a hell of a lot to do with it," as did their willingness to play hard and fast with the rules when necessary.[12]

All four were forty-niners. Huntington had come to California via Panama, where, like thousands of others, he was stranded for three months clamoring for passage up the coast to San Francisco. During that time, shrewdly buying and selling whatever he could get his hands on, he increased his initial grubstake of twelve hundred dollars by nearly 300 percent. His waking hours, and perhaps even his dreams, were dominated by an omnivorous sense of opportunity. When he arrived in the goldfields he immediately grasped the fact that fortune lay not in the gravel at the bottom of a pan but in the sale of the pan itself. Huntington opened a Sacramento miner's supply, charging what the market would bear. Crocker told a similar story.

After trudging cross-country in 1850, his few possessions "tied up in a cotton hand-kerchief," he worked briefly in the mines before he saw the light and became a partner in a general store. Hopkins and Stanford—the first an accountant with an unsurpassed talent for juggling numbers, the other a glad-handing lobbyist—had learned the same lesson before their overland treks, and both went west intending to become prosperous merchants in the gold region.[13]

In 1861, in an upstairs room of the Sacramento store jointly owned by Huntington and Hopkins, this group was called together by a zealot of a railroad builder by the name of Theodore Judah. It was not the first time Judah spread his plans, surveys, and dreams before potential investors. But the Big Four were the first to respond favorably, each pledging to buy fifteen thousand dollars of stock in the company for which Judah had drawn up the articles of incorporation. When Judah died unexpectedly, operations fell directly to the Big Four. Although they knew each other hardly at all—and would never become personal friends—they quickly developed a most effective division of labor. Hard-headed Crocker supervised construction, while inscrutable Hopkins kept the books; Huntington used his talents bidding for supplies in the East, while Stanford worked the state legislature and the halls of Congress, an assignment greatly advanced when, later that year, he won election as California governor on the Republican ticket. The Big Four were about to undertake one of the most spectacular construction projects of the age, yet as Crocker remembered, "none of us knew anything about railroad building."[14]

Not so the leader of the Union Pacific, who had won his spurs building eastern railroads before the war. Thomas C. Durant, chief manager of the UP, was trained as a physician but left medicine for a more lucrative career in finance, learning his business as construction manager for the Chicago & Rock Island line as it built across Iowa during the 1850s. Because every Iowan wanted to be as close to the rail line as possible, Durant threatened to bypass towns or counties that failed to buy sufficient bonds. There are stories of him laying out town sites, auctioning off lots to speculators, then shifting the line to cheaper adjoining land, and repeating the whole process. In 1858 Congress awarded the company a large land grant if it completed the Iowa project within ten years. Knowing that this was more than enough time, Durant slowed construction, reasoning that the longer the company took, the more valuable the land would become. Henry Farnam, president of the Chicago & Rock Island Railroad, later wrote that "Durant unfortunately yielded to the general spirit of speculation which had taken possession of so many railroad men of that time." It was a preview of what was to come with the construction of the Union Pacific.[15]

Durant's invention of a way of making fabulous profits for the Union Pacific on the construction of the road itself marked the highpoint of his financial "evil genius." He set up a subsidiary corporation, the Crédit Mobilier, wholly owned by the UP's principal stockholders. Through dummy third parties, he channeled all construction contracts to Crédit Mobilier, which in turn exaggerated expenses by double or triple. Though the accounts of the UP showed little profit, the Crédit Mobilier paid handsome dividends. It was one of the most ingenious swindles in American history. The con game was plain enough to see, but Durant also had an enormous slush fund that he used to keep official Washington from noticing. Republican congressman Oakes Ames, appointed head of Crédit Mobilier, distributed UP stock certificates, as he put it, "where they will do the most good for us." When the scandal finally broke into the open—with the publication in 1869 of an exposé in the *North American Review* by Charles Francis Adams, grandson of the nation's sixth president— the subsequent congressional investigation revealed that the entire Republican leadership, including the vice president and the chairmen of some of the most important House and Senate committees, had accepted Ames's bribes. Massachusetts senator George Hoar, one of the few Republicans untouched by the scandal, denounced the Union Pacific: "Every step of that mighty enterprise had been taken in fraud."[16]

The Crédit Mobilier was only one piece of a scandalous period. The Central Pacific had its own version of the same idea, the Credit and Finance Corporation, which charged ninety million for work worth only a third of that, but the Big Four avoided public exposure because their records just "happened" to be destroyed in a fire. Huntington distributed more than his fair share of graft, remaining confident in his own righteousness while performing magic with the company's millions. "If you have to pay money to have the right thing done, it is only just and fair to do it," he once wrote. Sometimes a man "won't do right unless he is bribed to do it." In his day Huntington corrupted office holders, lawmen, and regulatory commissioners, just as he pressured and blackmailed newsmen to manipulate public opinion. An acquaintance captured Huntington's spirit: "Tigerish and irrational in his ravenous pursuit, he was always on the scent, incapable of fatigue, delighting in his strength and the use of it, and full of the love of combat. If the Great Wall of China were put in his path, he would attack it with his nails."[17]

With financing in place, in 1865 the Union Pacific and Central Pacific began a frantic race to see which could build the fastest, get the largest subsidy, and engross most of the future commerce. Except for winters, when rough weather forced the suspension of construction, there were at least 20,000 men working constantly to build what Oakes Ames, without exaggeration, called "the greatest public work of this century." Supervising the project for the Union Pacific were the Casement brothers, sons of immigrant parents and experienced railroad contractors, though they were only in their thirties. Jack stood five feet four inches tall, his brother Dan "five feet nothing," but they were toughs who drove their workers demonically. American legend has it that the majority of those workers were Irish, and for the most part they were, al-

Temporary and permanent bridges at Green River, Wyoming. Photograph by A. J. Russell,
c. 1869. Beinecke.

though there were also ex-Confederate and Union soldiers, Mexicans, and former
African-American slaves.[18]

The Central Pacific at first had a harder time finding workers. The gold-rush
hordes had rushed elsewhere and labor in California was dear. Charles Crocker considered importing Mexicans but instead decided to give the abundant Chinese population a try. "I will not boss Chinese!" announced his superintendent of construction. "Who said laborers have to be white to build railroads?" Crocker shot back. "We
can't get enough white labor to build this railroad, and build it we must, so we're
forced to hire them." The Chinese soon impressed everyone with their persistence,
diligence, and courage, and they became the workers of choice. "Wherever we put
them we found them good," wrote Crocker, "and they worked themselves into our
favor to such an extent that if we found we were in a hurry for a job of work, it was

better to put on Chinese at once." Along some of the nearly impassable gorges of the Sierras, Chinese workers chipped away at solid granite walls with claw hammers, carrying off the rock by basket loads—a job so difficult that in spite of their numbers they were able to average only eight inches of laid rails per day. They became expert in handling the nitroglycerin used to blast through the mountains, although many died in the inevitable accidents. By 1867 Crocker was employing twelve thousand Chinese, 90 percent of his workforce.[19]

The Chinese received the same wages as white workers, but they shunned the board supplied by the company—salt beef, potatoes, and bread—and supplied their own food, a considerable savings for the Union Pacific. Independent contractors hauled in dried bamboo sprouts, mushrooms, cuttlefish, salted cabbage, rice, and peanut oil. Chinese workers drank tepid green tea, while white workers washed down their heavy meals with strong coffee or raw whiskey. Chinese workers might use opium on their days off, but they rarely drank booze. "You do not see them intoxicated with it," wrote one observer, "rolling in gutters like swine."[20]

His reference was to the debauchery common in the UP camps, which swarmed with whiskey vendors, gamblers, and prostitutes. "It fairly festered in corruption, disorder, and death," wrote journalist Samuel Bowles after visiting the village of vice at the end-of-track in 1868, "and would have rotted, even in this dry air, had it outlasted a brief sixty-day life. But in a few weeks its tents were struck, its shanties razed, and with their dwellers moved on fifty or a hundred miles farther [west] to repeat their life for another day." The most notorious was Julesburg, in northeastern Colorado, the temporary home for thousands of railroad workers, bartenders, gamblers, prostitutes, and assorted criminals. By a ratio of four to one, more Union Pacific workers died from exposure, violence, and disease in these "Hell-on-Wheels" tent towns than in the many industrial accidents. It was a brawling, whoring, drunken civilization that the railroad brought West.[21]

The Casement brothers may have left the UP workers to their own pleasures after hours, but they drove them furiously during the days. They perfected a highly efficient division of labor with not a single motion wasted. Three strokes to the spike, ten spikes to the rail, four hundred rails to the mile—they pushed the men to quicken the pace, offering time and a half for each mile-and-a-half day, double time for two. At the peak of construction in 1868 and 1869, the workers were whipped into a frenzy of six to seven miles of track per day. The CP, too, once it had blasted through the Sierras and reached the Nevada deserts, began to calculate its daily distance in multiple miles. Indeed, on one remarkable day in early 1869, the Chinese workers established an unbeatable world record by laying ten miles and fifty-six feet of track in a single twelve-hour period, winning Crocker a ten-thousand-dollar wager with Durant. But desperate for the extra miles, the two companies refused to agree on a meeting point for their lines. Advance parties of surveyors and graders actually passed

Chinese construction workers on the Central Pacific, c. 1868. Denver Public Library, Western History Department.

each other on the Utah desert and were working on parallel routes when President Grant demanded a halt to the foolishness, summoning company representatives to a White House summit and negotiating all night until at last the two companies picked a place of junction at Promontory, near Ogden, Utah.

There the symbolic joining of the rails was enacted on May 10, 1869. Dignitaries from both coasts joined railroad workers. "Grouped in picturesque confusion were men of every color, creed, and nationality," wrote one observer, "the Indian, the Mongolian, the Saxon, the Celt, and the half-caste Mexican, some arrayed in gorgeous costumes, and some innocent of any, mingling freely with American citizens and sol-

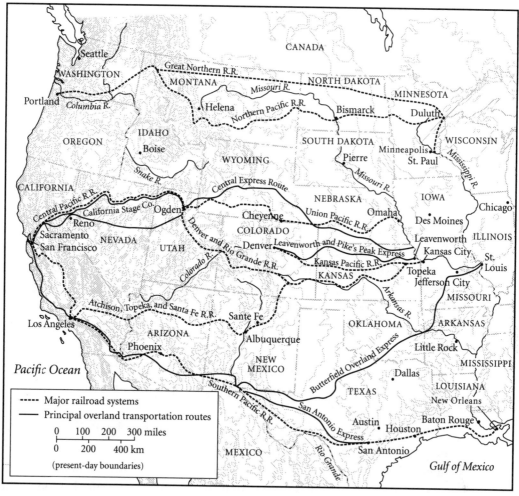

WESTERN RAILROADS

diers." A gang of Chinese workers laid the last few rails and drove all but the last spike, then were hustled off so as not to appear in the official photographs. As the band played and the crowd cheered, Leland Stanford came forward and set in place an eighteen-ounce golden spike, crowned with a large gold nugget. A telegraph wire was attached to the spike and another to the hammer in Stanford's hand, so that on impact the news would flash to a waiting world. Stanford took a weak little swing . . . and missed his mark. He shrugged in embarrassment and handed the hammer to Durant, who took his shot. He, too, missed. Realizing that the signal had not been sent, a telegrapher tapped out "DONE."[22]

But the work was *not* done. The race between the companies had taken precedence over careful construction. "I am very glad to learn that you have made up your mind to go in for quantity of road instead of quality," Huntington had written to Crocker in 1868. The result was shoddy work. Ballast had been improperly laid and roadbeds collapsed; curves had been engineered too sharply and trains derailed. Government specifications called for twenty-four hundred hardwood ties per mile, but UP records indicated that in some locations the contractor got by with fewer than half that number, all of them fabricated of soft cottonwood that rotted quickly. In 1869, while the Crédit Mobilier reported profits of sixteen million dollars, a government inspection of the line indicated that it would cost nearly ten million dollars to correct faulty construction.[23]

Regular transcontinental service began immediately anyway. First-class travelers paid a hundred dollars for the trip from Omaha to Sacramento, coach passengers seventy-five. It is hardly surprising that service was intermittent and amenities were few. The English writer Oscar Wilde complained of his six-day trip from Omaha to Sacramento that he was confined to "an ugly tin-kettle of a steam engine." Other travelers lambasted cramped quarters, stifling heat alternating with freezing cold, and insufferable food at the station stops. A Connecticut man described the dining halls as little more than "miserable shanties, with tables dirty, and waiters not only dirty, but saucy." Another passenger wrote of being offered "fried fish, fried mutton, fried eggs, fried mush (a great luxury), fried potatoes and fried pudding—all swimming in grease; bad coffee without milk, dough cakes without butter, and muddy water out of dirty glasses."[24]

But the inevitable complaints were less remarkable than the effusive praise. The public applauded the technological triumph of a transcontinental railroad as something little short of a miracle. Henry Varnum Poor, a hardboiled economist and publisher of *Poor's Manual of Railroads,* slipped into uncharacteristic rhapsody as he rode the first Central Pacific train across the summit of the Sierra Nevada. "The steam is shut off, the brakes put down, and, as the eagle sets his wing and floats noiselessly down, through the realms of air toward the earth from his eyrie among the clouds, we slide swiftly and smoothly down the acclivities of the mountains into the Great Basin of Nevada." For literary minds, romantic symbolism draped the road. In spite of the slipshod work, the tremendous costs, and the untested results, the transcontinental railroad was an old dream finally realized. "The crossing of the Sierra Nevada Mountains is the greatest achievement yet accomplished in civil engineering," Poor concluded. Having never found a Northwest Passage, Americans had fashioned one instead.[25]

In the thrall of railroad fever—even before the completion of the first transcontinental line—Congress offered huge donations of public land to three more companies. The Atchison, Topeka, and Santa Fe would follow the old Santa Fe Trail between Missouri and the new Southwest; the Southern Pacific (the successor to the CP, owned by the Big Four) would connect southern California to New Orleans; and the Northern Pacific would link the Great Lakes with the Columbia River. These companies banked their land grants, but none of their projects made much initial headway. The Santa Fe found itself stalled at the Raton Pass bottleneck into New Mexico, fighting off a competing line. The Big Four were content to devote their energies to constructing a maze of interconnecting lines that gave them monopoly control of California's transportation. "Without much trouble," Huntington clucked contentedly, "we ought to control the whole railroad system west of the Rocky Mountains." The Northern Pacific, the most ambitious of the new projects, failed to find adequate funding, despite energetic efforts by financier Jay Cooke, who had become something of a popular hero by masterminding the sale of Union bonds during the Civil War. The line got only as far as Bismarck, in Dakota Territory, before Cooke ran out of capital in 1873. The Northern Pacific went into receivership, forcing Cooke to close and lock the doors of his powerful Philadelphia banking house, bringing down the whole shaky financial structure of the western railroads. Within hours the New York Stock Exchange crashed, shut down, and remained closed for several weeks. The Panic of 1873 brought on the worst depression America had yet experienced; more than eighteen thousand businesses failed, most of the nation's railroads went bankrupt, and western railroad building ceased altogether for four years.[26]

Contraction is a necessary part of capitalist economics, and so the railroad companies consolidated and regrouped. Late in the decade they began a second round of construction. Finally reaching New Mexico, the Santa Fe constructed a line down the Rio Grande valley, where it linked up with the eastward-building Southern Pacific, opening the nation's second transcontinental route in 1881. The Big Four (actually the Big Three, Hopkins having died) were determined to keep California for themselves, but after armed confrontations with agents of the Santa Fe they finally allowed the line to build across northern New Mexico and Arizona into Los Angeles, while the Southern Pacific ran its track to El Paso, across Texas to San Antonio and Houston, finally terminating in New Orleans. Meanwhile, the Northern Pacific (under new ownership) reached Portland in 1883. The last of the great transcontinental railroads was James J. Hill's Great Northern, from Lake Superior to Puget Sound on a route paralleling the Canadian border. Although Hill was too late for federal land grants—Congress had second thoughts after 1873—he skillfully played the government for all the financial aid, direct and indirect, he could glean. When the Great Northern reached Seattle in 1893, five transcontinental lines linked the West with the rest of the country.

To the Indian people of the West, the railroad was a dagger penetrating their heartlands. The locomotives' fumes they likened to the acrid smoke of rifles, and they dreamed of the day they might blow their lungs free of them both. Sioux and Cheyenne war parties attacked and harassed workers at the UP's end-of-track but were beaten back by Pawnee warriors in a new all-Indian army battalion. The transcontinental lines made it possible for the army to rush troops and supplies to endangered areas. Native peoples understood this potential full well. Within months of the ceremonies at Promontory, Spotted Eagle, chief of the Sans Arcs Sioux, was sputtering in frustration that "he would fight the rail road people as long as he lived, would tear up the road and kill its builders." But it was too late. More to the point, perhaps, was Chief Red Cloud's lament upon the completion of the Union Pacific through the former hunting grounds of the Sioux: "The white children have surrounded me and have left me nothing but an island."[27]

In the Southwest, the Santa Fe and Southern Pacific lines encircled the territory of the troublesome Apaches. Most American army officers had great difficulty engaging these elusive warriors—perhaps the most brilliant guerrilla fighters in the history of mounted warfare—but with characteristic dogged determination, General George Crook finally defeated the Western Apaches, the largest of the six Apache tribes, and in 1875 moved them onto a reservation at San Carlos in southeastern Arizona. Employing the lesson learned from the use of Pawnees against the Sioux, Crook recruited reservation Apaches to assist in tracking down and defeating the "hostiles" from the other tribes.

The most feared of them was Geronimo of the Chiricahuas, famed among his people as a spiritual leader and a healer as well as a war chief. As a young man, Geronimo had a vision in which a spirit informed him that "no gun can ever kill you, and I will guide your arrows." From that moment he was completely without fear. "Not content to fight according to Apache custom, from behind rocks and greasewood bushes," in the words of one Indian agent, "he rushed into the open many times, running zigzag and dodging so that bullets from the soldiers rifles did not hit him." Pursued relentlessly by Crook's Apache scouts, Geronimo finally laid down his arms and brought his people into the San Carlos reservation in the late 1870s. They found it hard to live in this desolate and confining place, surrounded by strangers, and in 1885 Geronimo and forty-two of his Chiricahua warriors, along with several dozen women and children, escaped the reservation.

For more than a year these last unconfined Apaches eluded the army. Seventeen Arizona settlers died in Chiricahua attacks. "If he were seen by a civilian, it meant that he would be reported to the military and they'd be after us," one of the Apaches later explained, "so there was nothing to do but kill the civilian and his entire family. It was terrible to see little children killed. I do not like to talk about it. I do not like to think of it. But the soldiers killed our women and children, too. Don't forget that." There was panic in Arizona and alarm throughout the nation. Newspapers pro-

Apache chief Geronimo. Photograph by E. K.
Sturtevant, c. 1886. Beinecke.

claimed Geronimo the "wickedest Indian that ever lived." Finally, after months of being hounded, he accepted an American promise of a new reservation for his people.
But it was a lie. Once they had surrendered, all five hundred Chiricahuas were
hustled onto sealed railroad cars and shipped eastward across the continent to an
army prison in Florida. Without sanitation facilities or ventilation, their transcontinental journey was hellish. "When I think of that trip, even at this time, I get sea-
sick," wrote the officer in command. None of the Chiricahuas would ever return to
their native land.[28]

Union Pacific Depot, Omaha, Nebraska. From Frank Leslie's Illustrated Newspaper, *August 1877. Library of Congress.*

The same railroads that removed Apaches brought mining engineers and investment bankers to the new Southwest. They saw their opportunities and they took them. It was only after the arrival of the Santa Fe and the Southern Pacific in the 1880s that the large-scale mining of copper began in southern Arizona. Within a decade the copper companies were the largest employers in the Southwest. As William Robbins writes, "The railroad was the key instrument in transforming the area from preindustrial forms of economic activity to modern industrial technology." Railroad and mining companies—based in New York, Philadelphia, San Francisco, or other distant cities—exercised outside control over the Arizona economy and long dominated local and territorial politics. The railroad was a capitalist connection and it introduced a new version of colonialism.[29]

The wageworkers' frontier, the restless movement of the itinerant army of miners, harvesters, and construction workers around the West, was made possible by steel rails. Men seeking work rode inside and atop the freight cars and on the bolstering rods beneath. William Z. Foster, later a leader of the American Communist Party, recalled the experience. "The car rumbled over a switch, and the rod cleared the rails by hardly more than an inch or two. My heart popped into my mouth. I shivered at such a narrow margin and tried not to think of what would happen to me if the brakerod should come loose, bend down more, or break outright, or if we should run across one of those pieces of wire that are frequently to be found snagged in the ballast between the tracks. In any of these cases I should be instantaneously cut to pieces, as hundreds of hoboes had been before me." From 1901 to 1905 the railroads reported the accidental deaths of some twenty-five thousand itinerants.[30]

With the railroad the character of western settlement changed fundamentally. "Instead of a slowly advancing tide of migration, making its gradual inroads upon the circumference of the great interior wilderness," wrote Secretary of the Interior Jacob D. Cox in 1869, "the very center of the desert has been pierced. Every station upon the railway has become a nucleus for a civilized settlement, and a base from which lines of exploration for both mineral and agricultural wealth are pushed in every direction." Locomotives now hauled the products of western mines, farms, ranches, and forests directly to highly developed markets in the East, providing westerners with access to the latest eastern goods. Railroads encouraged specialization. Unlike the trans-Appalachian West, which had been occupied first by farmers producing almost exclusively for themselves or for local markets, the settlement of the Far West would proceed on a fully "business basis." Every farmer and rancher would be a competitor in a rapidly expanding world market. But this meant competing against giants, like the railroad companies, which conspired with one another to divide up territories and set shipping rates to the disadvantage of the small producer.[31]

"The locomotive is a great centralizer," wrote San Francisco journalist Henry George. "It kills little towns and builds up great cities, and in the same way kills little businesses and builds up great ones." No one could deny the power of the railroad. And no railroad company dominated more completely than the corporate spawn of the Big Four. Combined, this network was known as the "Octopus," with tentacles reaching into every nitch and corner of California. By the 1870s the Southern Pacific controlled more than 80 percent of the state's rail traffic. George raised the fundamental question of why railroads and other corporations should reap the benefit of the rising value of the land while society at large received so little. "Just think of it!" he wrote, "25,600 acres of land for the building of one mile of railroad. And this given to a corporation, not for building a railroad for the Government or the people, but for building a railroad for themselves; a railroad which they will own as absolutely as they will own the land—a railroad for the use of which both Government and people must pay as much as though they had given nothing for its construction."[32]

In the dusk of a July evening in 1873 a small band of men loosened a rail at a blind curve on the tracks of the Chicago, Rock Island and Pacific Railroad near Council Bluffs, Iowa. Within minutes an eastbound train hit the curve and derailed, killing

Jesse (left) and Frank James, c. 1875. Denver Public Library, Western History Department.

the engineer. The masked men clamored aboard the cars, guns drawn, and while some of them collected money and valuables from the passengers, others blew the express company safe and took two thousand dollars. Then, mounting their horses and waving their hats, they rode off into the night. The brothers Jesse and Frank James and their gang of outlaws—former bushwhackers who had ridden with Confederate guerrilla William Quantrill—had been robbing banks in western Missouri and Iowa since the end of the Civil War, but this was their first train robbery. For the next few years their holdups continued while detectives hired by the banks and the railroads pursued them fruitlessly. The end did not come until a member of the James gang, bribed by government authorities, shot Jesse in the back at his home in Saint Joseph in 1882.

To the western Missouri farmers who decried the monopoly of the railroad, the James brothers only preyed on the institutions that were preying on them. They were "bold highwaymen," declared the Kansas City editor John N. Edwards, exacting "tribute on banks and railroad corporations and express monopolies." The legend

Railroad strike of 1877 in Saint Louis. From Allan Pinkerton, Strikers, Communists, Tramps and Detectives *(New York, 1900). Yale University.*

of the American Robin Hood grew out of the passions people felt about the railroad and its capitalist conquest of the West. In the year Jesse died, people began to sing:

> Jesse James was a lad who killed many a man.
> He robbed the Glendale train.
> He stole from the rich and he gave to the poor,
> He'd a hand and a heart and a brain.

"While they were robbers and bandits, yet what they took from the rich they gave to the poor," echoed Nat Love, a black cowhand who claimed to have ridden for a time with the James brothers. "And if they were robbers, by what name are we to call some of the great trusts, corporations and brokers, who have for years been robbing the people of this country?" Two currents were flowing together here—the western antilaw tradition and newer protests against corporate industrial power.[33]

A greater challenge to the power of the road took place in 1877 when railroad workers staged a nationwide strike, shutting down the rail system. During the depression of the 1870s workers suffered a series of crippling wage cuts; by the middle of the decade, for example, for a grueling twelve-hour day brakemen were being paid only $1.75 ($22 in 1995 dollars), down from $2.50 ten years before. When, in the summer of 1877, the nation's four largest railroad companies adopted yet another 10 percent wage cut, eastern workers spontaneously left their jobs and seized control of switching yards and depots. President Rutherford B. Hayes sent in federal troops, there were armed confrontations, and during the two weeks of the strike more than a hundred people died in the violence. The managers of the western lines at first felt immune to the disorder. "Our people did not think that we would have serious trouble," a prominent San Francisco merchant later remembered, "the Central [Pacific] Railroad and the system having never had serious trouble with their operatives." In spite of his prediction, the strike spread westward, first to Saint Louis and Kansas City, where workers struck the Missouri Pacific and the Santa Fe, then to the Union Pacific yards at Omaha, across the plains to the Central Pacific facilities at Ogden, Utah, and finally to the Pacific coast.[34]

But old ethnic antagonisms would distract and dilute the protest. In San Francisco several thousand people gathered before City Hall to hear Dennis Kearney of the Workingman's Party of California harangue the Big Four. With one breath Kearney argued for popular power over the railroad—"the Central Pacific men are thieves and will soon feel the power of the workingmen"—then with his next appealed to the worst prejudices of his fellow Californians—"I will give the Central Pacific just three months to discharge their Chinamen, and if that is not done Stanford and his crowd will have to take the consequences." There followed three days of anti-Chinese rioting. Mobs attacked Chinatown, beat up Chinese men and women, and burned buildings. The railroad did not fire the Chinese in response to the demands of the Workingman's Party, but Congress took note of the anti-Chinese sentiment sweeping the West. The Burlingame Treaty with China, signed in 1868 while Chinese laborers were still hard at work on the transcontinental line, had pledged an open door for Chinese immigration. But in 1882, intoning that "the coming of Chinese laborers to this country endangers the good order of certain localities," Congress passed the Chinese Exclusion Act, suspending further immigration of "all persons of the Chinese race" for ten years. Thereafter it was repeatedly extended until it became permanent as part of the Immigration Restriction Act of 1924.[35]

Clamor from labor unions in California thus helped to produce national policy. Yet Chinese exclusion did not prevent Kearney's racist populism from rearing its head in dozens of western places in the coming decades. Perhaps the most barbaric incident took place in 1885 in the railroad town of Rock Springs, Wyoming, when the Union Pacific attempted to replace white workers with lower-paid Chinese. In a coordinated attack, workers invaded the Chinese section of town, shooting, burning, and looting, while a group of their wives and mothers stood to the side, laughing, cheering, and firing gunshots at fleeing Chinese. Chinatown was burned to the ground and twenty-eight Chinese died in the flames. In the aftermath of this massacre, there were attacks on Chinatowns all over the West.[36]

The Knights of Labor, the premier national labor organization of the 1880s, hailed the Exclusion Act, and they were implicated in the campaign of interethnic violence.

The inability to close ranks with workers of color would prove to be their greatest weakness. In 1885, in response to a wage cut, the Knights struck and shut down Jay Gould's Southwest System, which included the Wabash, the Missouri Pacific, and the Missouri, Kansas, and Texas. Caught off guard, Gould had no choice but to negotiate. In the wake of this success, workers all over the West flocked to the Knights. The following year, feeling their oats, Southwest workers struck the line again. This time Gould pulled out all the stops, hiring hundreds of Mexicans to run the trains and arming hundreds of deputies to clear the tracks. In Palestine, Texas, a posse of two hundred company men, armed with Winchester repeating rifles, took control of the rail yards, and in Fort Worth a gun-slinging marshal engaged in a shoot-out with strikers in which several men were killed.

With their defeat in the second Southwest strike, the Knights of Labor faded in the late 1880s. They were replaced by a new militant organization, the American Railway Union (ARU), founded by Eugene Debs. In one of its first actions, the ARU struck the newly completed Great Northern when that line attempted to put in place a lower wage scale. In the face of impressive worker solidarity the company was forced to accept a settlement, and with this success the new union soon had 150,000 members nationwide, with its strength in the West. In 1894, in support of striking workers at the Pullman Sleeping Car Company, the union called on its members to refuse to handle trains running Pullman cars. In a reprise of the events of 1877, President Grover Cleveland called out federal troops and there was an armed confrontation in Chicago that left thirteen strikers dead and fifty wounded. In the aftermath of this violence ARU members brought the nation's rail traffic to a halt. They shut down all the western lines except the Great Northern, which didn't run Pullman cars.

The Pullman strike proved to be the high point of western protests against the railroads. Strikers occupied and held the rail yards in Omaha, Ogden, Oakland, and Los Angeles; they burned bridges along the transcontinental line in Nevada. One of the most dramatic and memorable incidents took place on a hot and humid July Fourth in Sacramento. Local militiamen were ordered to the train station to disperse the strikers. They arrived to find hundreds of ARU members and sympathizers before the depot, waving American flags. People called out militiamen by name, urging them to put down their guns. "Frank, if you kill me you make your sister a widow," one man was heard calling out. Gradually the soldiers lowered their guns and wandered away to the shade, where ARU women served them lemonade and ice. Community support for the strike also ran high in Los Angeles, where again the militia was called out. "If we had to fight Indians or a common enemy there would be some fun and excitement," one soldier exclaimed to a reporter, "but this idea of shooting down American citizens simply because they are on a strike for what they consider their rights is a horse of another color." Public support for the strike in California finally eroded, however, after an incident of train-wrecking terrorism killed an engineer and four guardsmen near Sacramento.[37]

The national strike was finally broken, but it demonstrated the depth of western feeling about the railroad. To some the iron rails that stretched across the continent were the achievement of the age. Robert Louis Stevenson, an early passenger, likened its mythic qualities to those of ancient Troy itself. It was a monument to the perseverance and power of a people, and the men who built that monument were only a little lower than the gods. To others the railroad was not a monument but a monster, and the Frankensteins who created it were, in the words of the *Sacramento Union*, "cold-hearted, selfish, sordid men." To opponents of the railroad, the brave hearts were the wild boys who struck the lines, burned the bridges, and robbed the eastbound train, loaded with western plunder.[38]

FURTHER READING

Gunther Barth, *Bitter Strength: A History of the Chinese in the United States, 1850–1870* (1964)

William Deverell, *Railroad Crossing: Californians and the Railroad, 1850–1910* (1994)

Rhoda R. Gilman, Carolyn Gilman, and Deborah M. Stultz, *The Red River Trails: Oxcart Routes Between St. Paul and the Selkirk Settlement, 1820–1870* (1979)

Sarah H. Gordon, *Passage to Union: How the Railroads Transformed American Life, 1829–1929* (1997)

Oscar Lewis, *Big Four: The Story of Huntington, Stanford, Hopkins, and Crocker, and the Building of the Central Pacific* (1938)

Richard O'Connor, *Iron Wheels and Broken Men: The Railroad Barons and the Plunder of the West* (1973)

William G. Robbins, *Colony and Empire: The Capitalist Transformation of the American West* (1994)

David Roberts, *Once They Moved Like the Wind: Cochise, Geronimo, and the Apache Wars* (1993)

William A. Settle, Jr., *Jesse James Was His Name; or, Fact and Fiction Concerning the Career of the Notorious James Brothers of Missouri* (1966)

Carlos Arnaldo Schwantes, *Hard Traveling: A Portrait of Work Life in the New Northwest* (1994)

John Hoyt Williams, *A Great and Shining Road: The Epic Story of the Transcontinental Railroad* (1988)

Oscar Osburn Winther, *The Transportation Frontier: Trans-Mississippi West, 1865–1890* (1964)

10

Open Range

One hot summer day in 1883 Teddy Blue Abbott, trailing a herd of cattle from Texas to Montana, surmounted a hill, stretched tall in his saddle, and surveyed the Platte River country spreading before him. "I could see seven herds behind us," he remembered, "I knew there were eight herds ahead of us, and I could see the dust from thirteen more of them on the other side of the river." To Abbott "all the cattle in the world seemed to be coming up out of Texas." With access to eastern markets provided by western railroads, the cattle kingdom had expanded until it stretched high, wide, and handsome from Texas north to the Canadian prairies. Within a few years, however, the harshest winters in living memory would sweep down upon the plains, bringing a sudden end to the world in which Teddy Blue came of age. "Just when everything was going fine, and a cowpuncher's life was a pleasant dream," he later reminisced, "the whole thing went Ker Plunk, and we are now a prehistoric race."[1]

What Abbott lamented was the end of the open-range cattle industry and the extinction of the rambling cowboy, the most renowned of all America's folk heroes.

> As I was out walking one morning for pleasure,
> I spied a cowpuncher come riding along.
> His hat was throwed back and his spurs were a-janglin',
> And as he rode by he was singing this song:
>
> "Whoopee ti yi yo—git along little dogies,
> It's your misfortune, and none of my own.
> Whoopee ti yi yo—get along little dogies,
> You know that Wyoming will be your new home."

"Branding Cattle on the Prairies of Texas." Engraving based on a sketch by James E. Taylor, from Frank Leslie's Illustrated Newspaper, *June 25, 1867. The Library Company of Philadelphia.*

This colorful character—whose western yodel one commentator described as "a cross between the lonely howl of the coyote and the wild song of the plains Indians"—whoopee ti yi yo'd his way onto the American scene in the aftermath of the Civil War. According to the traditions of western history, his heyday lasted less than twenty years. Yet despite the end of the big trail drives, cowboying continued on countless ranches throughout the West, and more than a century later, the Great Plains states remain the largest producers of beef in the nation. Nor was the cowboy's appearance as sudden and abrupt as legend would have it. He was, in fact, the offspring of a history of frontier mixing and mingling as old as the European invasion of the Americas itself.[2]

The Spanish brought the first cattle to the New World. They also imported a tradition of open-range herding by horse-mounted drovers. As early as 1500, Spanish cowboys called *vaqueros* were raising cattle commercially in the Caribbean, where their techniques mingled with those of slaves who had herded cattle in their African homelands. Indeed, linguists believe that the word *dogie*—a term for the motherless calves that lingered in the drag of the herd—came from the Bambara language of west African slaves. Spanish stock from the Caribbean first crossed to the North American mainland with Cortés and the conquistadors. Well known is the terror his horses aroused among the native Mexicans; less known is the disgust Indians felt for the cattle that trampled and destroyed their fields, preparing the way for dispossession. Herding soon became an important part of the Mexican colonial economy, and later in the sixteenth century, when silver mines opened in the northern country, vaqueros followed with herds of cattle to supply the demand for beef.[3]

The tradition of raising cattle for meat, hides, and tallow in the American Far West began when Juan de Oñate's men trailed more than a thousand head into the Rio Grande valley in 1598. Mission friars later built large cattle herds in California and Texas, and by the end of the eighteenth century several million grazed on the thousand hills of the California coastal range and on the grasslands between the Nueces River and the Rio Grande in Texas. Where the stock ran wild for most of the year, nature selected for the hardy. The evolutionary result was the Texas longhorn, with horns that could span six feet, a wild glint in its eye, and a racy flavor to its meat. In the judgment of one nineteenth-century American, longhorns were "fifty times more dangerous to footmen than the fiercest buffalo." But vaqueros learned to manage them with a combination of superb horsemanship and skillful roping, and by the 1760s Tejanos were driving their cattle to market in New Orleans. Indeed, during the American Revolution, Spanish officials in New Orleans provisioned American pioneers in Kentucky with Texas beef.[4]

It was in Louisiana that Anglo Americans first encountered Hispanic traditions of cattle raising. Herding had long been an occupation in the backcountry of the colonial South. Settlers built "cow pens" many miles from their farms to corral their stock, leaving them in the care of African or mixed-ancestry slaves and indentured servants. Using dogs rather than horses to tend their shorthorned British breeds, these footsore herders, known as "cow-boys," pressed into the Appalachian foothills in pursuit of fresh grazing land, placing them in the westering vanguard. Daniel Boone himself was first guided over the Blue Ridge by an African-American cowherd named Burrell, who blazed a trail to the headwaters of the Tennessee River by following the meanderings of his master's cattle. About the time of the Louisiana Purchase, backcountry cowboys and Indian drovers leapfrogged the Mississippi floodplain, and soon both groups were learning and adapting the vaquero traditions of horsemanship and roping. The large number of Spanish loanwords in the lingo of western cattle raising—*lariat, lasso, rodeo, rancho*—testify to this process of cultural fusion.

Southwestern Louisiana was the proving ground for a composite backcountry-vaquero herding culture that became indelibly associated with Texas once Americans began filtering into that province in the 1820s. Herding rivaled cotton as the most important economic pursuit in the region, and ranchers shipped beef throughout the Caribbean. By the 1830s Anglo herders along the Gulf coast of Texas had grown proficient enough with horse and lariat to raid the ranchos of the Nueces

Strip, driving stolen stock north to spreads of their own along the Brazos or the Trinity rivers. After the Texas Revolution rancher violently replaced *ranchero* across the savannas of south Texas. Cattlemen shipped their stock to market by steamer from Brownsville or Galveston, or combined their herds and drove them northeast to Shreveport or New Orleans, following old Tejano trails. Some Texans, however, were lured further north in an attempt to tap eastern markets in the United States. Texans first trailed longhorns up what was known as the Shawnee Trail to Missouri in 1842, and by 1850 a sizable market for Texas beef had developed in Sedalia and Kansas City. But the Civil War brought to an end these early northern drives, just as the Union naval blockade closed off Caribbean markets. When Texans went off to fight for the Confederacy, their neglected stock scattered across the countryside, and by 1865 an estimated five to six million feral longhorns were grazing on the Texas range.

The drives to market recommenced after the war. With New Orleans a commercial wreck, cattle drovers turned their attention north to Missouri once again, but few longhorns, waylaid by former Jayhawkers, bushwhackers, and Indian Confederates-turned-bandits, reached their destination. Enterprising Texans soon discovered a new and more secure northern market, however, to the west of Missouri in Abilene, Kansas, where the Kansas Pacific Railroad established a stockyard and depot in 1867. That year 35,000 head of cattle arrived at the railhead, but over the next half decade Abilene shipped out more than 1.5 million Texas longhorns. The new western railroads badly needed this traffic, and cattle quickly became one of their most important cargoes. The Santa Fe line established competing market towns at Wichita and Dodge City, and soon thousands of western cattle were arriving by rail at distribution points in Kansas City, Saint Louis, and Chicago, where the huge Union Stockyard was capable of handling up to 21,000 cattle each day.

The railroad linked the western range to new consumer markets. Traditionally pork had been the most common meat on the American table, but faced with this new and abundant supply of beef, Chicago meat packers Philip Armour and Gustavus Swift quickly transformed the national diet. Rather than follow the standard practice of sending live cattle east to local slaughterhouses, they pioneered the practice of killing and butchering the animals on "disassembly" lines, then used refrigerated railroad cars to ship great quantities of dressed beef to eastern markets. Because salable meat constituted only about half a steer's body weight, this method produced dramatic savings in shipping costs and allowed the packers to undercut the price of locally butchered beef. Packers made their biggest profits, however, on the "waste": dried blood packaged as fertilizer, hooves and feet boiled into glue, bone carved for knife handles, and fat converted into margarine. Nearly everything else was ground up for sausage and stuffed into the entrail casings. What finally remained was

dumped into the Chicago River, producing a fetid stench so overpowering that on hot summer days people in the southern part of the city fell sick from just breathing the air. Not until Upton Sinclair's 1906 muckraking novel *The Jungle* would the unsanitary and corrupt practices of the packers be exposed, which resulted in the passage of federal inspection programs. In the meantime Swift and Armour invested heavily in advertising, turning the names of their firms into trusted national brands and fundamentally altering the choices of consumers around the country.

With the increased demand for beef, cattlemen found that a steer selling for ten dollars or less on the overstocked Texas range could bring twenty-five dollars or more at one of the Kansas railheads. After paying costs, a herd of two or three thousand longhorns could bring a tidy profit. With prices climbing to forty dollars a head and more in Chicago, stockdealers further up the food chain also made substantial profits. What the market created, of course, it could as easily destroy. When the bottom dropped out of the American economy in 1873, for example, hopeful drovers arrived in Kansas to find that prices had fallen below costs, leading one observer to note that "cattlemen, as well as cattle, are slaughtered every day." But until the 1880s prices generally favored the producer. The accountant's bottom line created the conditions for the great long drives of American legend.[5]

Driving a herd of some two thousand three-year-old steers several hundred miles north required the labor of ten or fifteen drovers, equipped with 100 to 150 horses, as well as a trail boss and a cook equipped with a chuckwagon stocked with flour, salt, sugar, and canned goods. Teddy Blue Abbott remembered the dust, thick as fur, on the eyebrows of the drag men and the black phlegm they coughed up for weeks after the drive. There were days of deadly dull work punctuated by moments of high drama: sudden stampedes of hundreds of steers, dry runs with animals bellowing from thirst, and infernal weather. In the evening men sang of their toils:

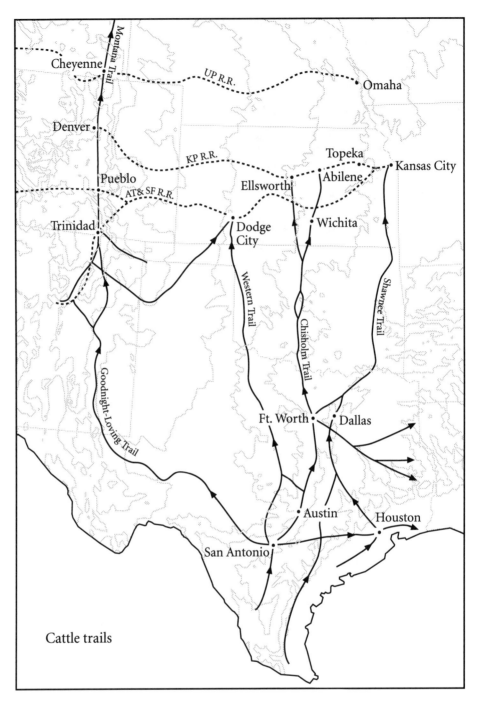

TEXAS CATTLE TRAILS

Oh, the cowboy's life is a dreary, dreary life,
All out in the midnight rain;
I'm almost froze with the water on my clothes,
Way up on the Kansas line.

Wichita, Kansas, 1870 and 1875. Kansas State Historical Society, Topeka.

Cowboys tended to be young, because just one or two trail drives were sufficient adventure for most men. "For a man to be stove-up at thirty may sound strange to some people," wrote veteran James McCauley, "but many a cowboy has been so bunged up that he has to quit riding that early in life."[6]

If headed for the stockyards at Wichita or Abilene, drovers took the Chisholm Trail, a path blazed before the war by an old métis trader named Jesse Chisholm. Later drives shifted to the Western trail leading to Dodge City, or the Goodnight-Loving Trail—named for gruff old Texas rancher Charlie Goodnight and his partner Oliver Loving—running west from central Texas to the Pecos River, then north to Denver and Cheyenne. Where the trail connected with the railroad, there was the cattle town, a bustling commercial center set down in the middle of nowhere. The town's business centered on the stockyards and the stockman's hotel, where cattlemen and beef dealers made their connections. Nearby was the bank—"as fat a thing as gold mines," according to one Wichita visitor—which might calculate a season's transactions in the millions of dollars. Then there were the mercantile establishments, Mayer Goldsoll's Texas Store in Abilene, or Jacob Karatofsky's Great Western Store in Wichita, many operated by Jewish businessmen. At the mercantile, wranglers often used their wages to replace their worn-out clothes for a brand-new set of duds. Standards quickly emerged: durable denim pants made by Levi Strauss of San Francisco, broad-brimmed hats by the John B. Stetson Company of Philadelphia, and hand-tooled boots by Joe Justin of Texas. After his first trail drive, Teddy Blue Abbott bought a fancy shirt and pants, a white Stetson, and hand-tooled boots. "Lord, I was proud of those clothes!" he remembered, and he traveled home to Nebraska just to show them off. But his sister took one look at him and declared, "Take your pants out of your boots and put your coat on. You look like an outlaw!"[7]

———

The reputation for cowboy outlawry came largely from the wild doings in the cattle town demimonde, brawling, hard-fisted meccas of vice and vulgarity, cousins to the end-of-track Sodoms and the mining camp Gomorrahs. In 1870 Abilene counted thirty-two saloons, more than a sufficient number for a town that had a permanent population of just five hundred but was consistently crowded with hundreds of drovers and gamblers all through the shipping season. Texan J. L. McCaleb remembered riding into Abilene when he was just a kid, fresh off the trail. "The first place we visited was a saloon and dance hall. We ordered toddies like we had seen older men do, and drank them down, for we were dry, very dry. . . . As I was drinking it a girl came up and put her little hand under my chin, looked me square in the face, and said 'Oh, you pretty Texas boy, give me a drink.'" Joseph Snell has tracked the histories of more than six hundred cattle town prostitutes who turned tricks from 1870 to 1885. Like their cowboy johns, nearly all were young (average age twenty-three), but there, Snell concludes, the generalizations end. They "were short or tall, fat or thin, pretty or homely. They came from good families and bad, which they left behind in the East, or in England, Ireland, Germany, France, the Indian Nations, or just about any place that produced girls. Prostitution was a melting pot where the only general criterion was possession of a female body." Cattle culture was diverse and motley in all its many ways.[8]

The volatile mix of unattached young men, alcohol, and firearms meant that the cattle towns were violent places. Dodge City of the 1870s, for example, had a homicide rate of 50 on today's Federal Bureau of Investigation scale (the number of killings per 100,000 persons), ten times higher than the rate in New York City during the same decade, twice as high as the famously violent American cities of the early 1990s. (The cattle towns were not the most violent places in the American West, however. Historian Roger McGrath has found that the California mining town of Bodie, in the High Sierras, had an astounding rate of 116.) Firearms were the principal cause of these deaths, but less than a third of the victims died in exchanges of gunfire. Most were gunned down unarmed. Even the mythic lawmen rarely fired their guns with mortal results. Wyatt Earp killed one man while serving as an officer in Wichita and Dodge City, but mostly he used his revolver to pistol-whip or "buffalo" rowdy, drunken cowpunchers into submission. When James "Wild Bill" Hickok was marshal of Abilene in 1871, he killed two men in a bloody confrontation, but one was his own deputy, accidentally shot. In spite of the thousands of "high noon" gunfights of

"Dodge City Peace Commissioners" in 1876 (clockwise from back left): W. H. Harris, Luke Short, Bat Masterson, Neal Brown, L. McLean, Wyatt Earp, Charles Bassett. Beinecke.

movie and television westerns, cattle town newspapers made no mention of duels fought in dusty streets.

Certainly many cowpunchers were armed with revolvers and an assumption that might makes right. A French traveler in cattle country, Baron Edmond de Mandat-Grancey, listened in on a group of drovers debating the value of friends and principles and overheard one man boldly concluding that what counted most in life was "a big revolver and self-reliance!" Western men, writes McGrath, "adhered to a code of conduct that required a man to stand and fight, even if, or perhaps especially if, it could mean death." But few wranglers went looking for trouble, and in fact few were even proficient with their six-shooters. Most gunshot wounds, it turns out, were accidental. Particularly dangerous were the new "double-action" revolvers introduced by the Colt Repeating Firearms Company in the late 1870s, guns that could be fired either by pulling the trigger or by cocking and releasing the hammer. "It is well known that most of the accidents with revolvers arise from the unintentional manipulation of the hammer," reported the *Dallas Weekly Herald*. "Either it receives a blow, or it is allowed to slip off the thumb in cocking, or it is caught against the clothing, and particularly when it is at full cock." Men shot themselves while working, while removing their guns from wagons or packs, even while undressing.[9]

Cowhands may not have been the gunslingers legend makes them out to be, but violence was built into the everyday life of handling cattle. They drove herds cruelly to the limits of the animals' endurance. At trail's end they forced steers into cramped railroad cars, prodding them forward with steel rods (hence the name "cow-puncher"). During the roundup ropers snagged calves by their hind feet as they nursed from their mother's udders, then dragged them kicking and bellowing to the branding fire. Veteran Reuben Mullins described the process. It took two men to hold the animal down "while the hot iron was pressed to its left side, causing the smoke and stink from the burning hair, skin, and flesh to create a horrible condition." Meanwhile another man was at work with his knife, dehorning the animal, cropping its ears, bobbing its tail, and, if the poor thing was male, carving out its testicles. "Then the calf, either a year or a day old, was turned loose and went staggering back to its mother." That these things were necessary did not make them any less brutal. Such hard and callous experiences can breed hard and callous men.[10]

Most cowhands were southwestern boys from Texas or Louisiana. The majority were white, but reflecting the diverse sources of cowboy culture, African Americans, Mexicans, and even Indians participated in the drives. George Saunders, president of the Old Time Trail Drivers Association, in 1925 estimated that one-third of all trail cowboys were African American, Mexican, or Indian. That may be a high figure, for close studies of west Texas suggest that the proportion of African American ranch hands there was low. But in the southeast portion of the state at least one in four cowboys was black, reflecting the southern origins of herding. Teddy Blue Abbott trailed north with a "mixed outfit" in 1879. "The Olives was mostly hard on Mexicans and Negroes," he wrote of his employers, "because being from Texas they was born and raised with that intense hatred of a Mexican, and being Southern, free black men was poison to them. But they hired them because they worked cheaper than white men." The wise trail boss hired a few Mexican vaqueros because they were so familiar with the tools and techniques of the trade. As Texas folklorist Américo Paredes writes, Mexicans "with some justice could feel superior to the Anglo when it came to handling horses and cattle." Like Anglos, vaqueros composed ballads, or *corridos*, celebrating their cattle trail experiences.

> Five hundred steers,
> All big and quick,
> And thirty Anglo cowboys
> Could not control them.

Nat Love. From The Life and Adventures of Nat Love . . . *(Los Angeles, 1907). Beinecke.*

Five Mexicanos rode up,
All wearing good chaps,
And in a few minutes,
Took charge of the cattle.

Those five Mexicanos
Round them up quickly,
And the thirty Anglos
Look on in amazement.[11]

The vaqueros remain mostly anonymous, but the names of a few African Americans found their way into the record. Monroe Brackins was born a slave in east Texas and learned to ride before he could walk. "I never had to hunt a ranch to work on," he told an interviewer late in his life, for "there was someone always ready for me on account of being a good cowhand." Former slave Bose Ikard helped Goodnight and Loving blaze their famous trail, then worked for years on Goodnight's JA Ranch. "He surpassed any man I had in endurance and stamina," the old cattleman testified. But racism was a fact of life on the range. "If it weren't for my damned old black face," swore Jim Perry, who for twenty years worked as a hand on the giant XIT spread in the Texas panhandle, "I'd have been boss of one of these divisions long ago." Perhaps best known was Nat Love, who trailed cattle for a time and later published a popular autobiography that included more than the usual portion of western braggadocio.[12]

Indian cowboys were also common on herds driven up from the Cherokee or Creek nations, but the prejudice against them was even stronger. "As a race they are absolutely devoid of all feeling and gratitude," one Indian-hating rancher snarled. "They are cruel, heartless, and treacherous as a coyote." But another cattleman judged Indian wranglers "the best in the world," and declared, "If I had a million head of cattle, I would place them all under Pawnee herders." Indian cowboys had long experience riding the range. In the colonial period stray stock were frequently claimed by southeastern Indians, and in the eighteenth century many natives became skilled herders. Traveling in Florida in the 1770s naturalist William Bartram encountered Seminoles trailing their "innumerable droves of cattle" to market. Colonial herders were soon following Indian trails through the pine barrens of southwest Georgia to the coastal plains of West Florida and Louisiana. Stock raising became an essential feature of Choctaw culture, writes historian Richard White, "and made pastoralists of many who had been hunters." With removal, the ranchers of the Five Civilized Tribes brought their herds to Oklahoma, but the tide of white settlement during the last quarter of the nineteenth century overwhelmed them.[13]

"DANCE-HOUSE."

Saloon in Abilene, Kansas. From Joseph G. McCoy, Historic Sketches of the Cattle Trade of the West and Southwest *(Kansas City, 1874). Beinecke.*

The motley groups of men on the trail enjoyed an earthy and ribald humor that early folklorists and historians unfortunately bowdlerized. Jack Thorp, an early collector of cowboy songs, made sure his material was "dry-cleaned for unprintable words." He must have sorted through a lot of dirty laundry. As one old hand told John Lomax, another famous folk-song collector, "in the singing about camp, a cowboy would often cut loose with a song too vile to repeat; great cheers and hurrays would usually follow and there would be calls for more."

> I opened the door, and stepped up to the bar,
> Says a dancing young beauty, "Will you have a cigar?"
> "You are a cowpuncher, and this I do know,
> Your muscles are hard from your head to your toe."
> She twisted my mustache, she smoothed down my hair;
> My ellick grew hard; it did, I declare.

"These songs were sung for other cowboys, usually at stag dances," old hand Riley Neal told song collector Guy Logsdon. Those stag dances were an important aspect of this lonely, all-male culture. "There were no maidens to add the feminine charm to the occasion," wrote an observer of a stag dance in 1885, but "a number of the bovine guardians agreed to don the female attire." A cattleman remembered a drunken ball at which two of his drovers danced together happily all night. "She ain't much for pritty," one of the hard-bitten hands exclaimed about the other, "but she's hell for active on the floor—so dod-burned active couldn't tell whether she was waltzin' or tryin' to throw me side-holts." It is unclear how much of this reassigning of sex roles spilled over into overt homosexuality. Sex research Alfred C. Kinsey, however, concluded that intimate contact "was probably common among pioneers and outdoor men in general, . . . groups that are virile [and] physically active. Such a background breeds the attitude that sex is sex, irrespective of the nature of the partner with whom the relation is had."[14]

"I suppose those things would shock a lot of respectable people," said Teddy Blue Abbott, "but we wasn't respectable and we sure didn't pretend to be." Yet after the ribaldry, men were likely to strike up some old-time church hymn or sing movingly of homesickness ("I'm a poor lonesome cowboy and a long way from home"), of lost love ("Just remember the Red River Valley / And the cowboy who loved you so true"), or of death ("I spied a dear cowboy wrapped up in white linen, / Wrapped up in white linen as cold as the clay"). Western novelist Wallace Stegner captured both sides in his recollection of a boyhood spent among wranglers on the northern plains. "Many things that those cowboys represented I would have done well to get over quickly, or never catch: the prejudice, the callousness, the destructive practical joking, the tendency to judge everyone by the same raw standard. Nevertheless, what they themselves most respected, and what as a boy I most yearned to grow up to, was as noble as it was limited. They honored courage, competence, self-reliance, and they honored them tacitly. They took them for granted. It was their absence, not their presence, that was cause for remark. Practicing comradeship in a rough and dangerous job, they lived a life calculated to make a man careless of everything except the few things he really valued."[15]

In April 1871 Mrs. A. Burks, riding in a little buggy, accompanied her rancher husband and his Mexican vaqueros on the drive from Nueces County, Texas, to Ellsworth, Kansas. They experienced frightening thunderstorms and tough river crossings because of the high water. They lost cattle to stampedes and to rustlers. They found disappointingly low prices at the railhead. But in spite of these difficulties, she found the trip invigorating, and her account suggests that she enjoyed the attention that came with being the only woman in camp. "The men rivaled each other in attentiveness to me," she wrote, "always on the lookout for something to please me, a surprise of some delicacy of the wild fruit, or prairie chicken, or antelope tongue." One day, as the company was taking the midday meal, the foreman told her: "In the heat of the day when I am riding behind my cattle, I think of you and am sorry for you. But when I see your smile of happiness and contentment I know all my sympathy is wasted." His comment tickled her. "For what woman, youthful and full of spirit and the love of living,

The Becker sisters on their ranch in the San Luis Valley of Colorado, c. 1910.
Colorado Historical Society.

needs sympathy because of availing herself of the opportunity of being with her husband while at his chosen work in the great out-of-door world?"[16]

Most women remained back at the ranch, but they displayed the same spunky spirit as Burks, taking over day-to-day management of the operation in their husbands' absence. Cora Slaughter, who ran the home place during the annual cattle drives, found "real pleasure" in ranch work. "I loved to work with cattle," she wrote late in her life, "and spent a good deal of my time on the range." Not all ranchwomen loved "outdoors work," of course, but all were accustomed to it. In 1881 young schoolteacher Angeline Mitchell of Kansas spent a season boarding with a ranch family in the arid countryside west of Prescott, Arizona. "For the first time in my life I know what it is to feel utterly cast away & homesick," she wrote in her diary. "This is desolation itself here." Soon after her arrival she met a tall cowboy. "My little lady," he greeted her, "where on earth did a dainty bit of humanity like you drop from?" As Mitchell soon learned, dainty didn't do in Arizona. Late one night the sound of a stampede awakened her. With the men off trailing cattle, only women and children were at home. Rushing for the door, they saw a thundering herd heading straight for the ramshackle cabin. Without hesitation the women burst outside, waving sheets, beating tin pans, and yelling at the top of their lungs. "Such an awful pow-wow was too much for the cattle & they swerved passed each side of us & our house, so close they nearly grazed us." Few men figure in Mitchell's colorful account, but it is filled with vivid portraits of proud, capable women who knew how to run cattle as well as their kitchens.[17]

Widows frequently took over the ranch on the death of their husbands. Ella Bird-Dumont, whose husband died and left her a dusty spread in the Texas panhandle, remembered that a little income from embroidering vests, gloves, and other clothing for cowboys "made us very comfortable living until the increase or revenue from my cattle began coming in." Even in her old age she remained proud that she had been able to provide a "safe and secure" living for herself and her children and that she developed "confidence in myself." Bird-Dumont hired a foreman to run her ranch, but other widows took over the management themselves. According to the recollection of a friend, ranchwoman Ann Bassett "could fit right in the toughest cow camp, [and] take her place in the saddle with the rest, and live the life they lived, doing with equal skill her share of the work on the range." Bassett was one of a number of western women who earned the title "cattle queen." The most famous was Elizabeth Collins, who took over the operation of a large ranch when her husband fell ill, made a fortune as a shipper, and published her recollections under the title *The Cattle Queen of Montana*.[18]

Girls who grew up on western ranches usually worked outside with their fathers. In her memoir of growing up on a ranch in Lincoln County, New Mexico, Lily Casey wrote of learning "to ride, rope, brand, and perform the various functions of a cowboy," and in the nearby Hispano community Prudencia Miranda developed into such a good horsewoman that she joined the boys in the sport known as *correr el gallo*, "running the cock," in which competing riders raced to grab the head of a rooster, buried up to its neck in the sand. Many ranch daughters remembered family conflicts about "outdoors work." Marie Jordan Bell grew up at the turn of the century on a ranch near Laramie. When her grandmother came to visit she would scold Marie's mother because the girl was always outdoors riding with the boys. "She told Dad that she thought he was making a boy out of me; she didn't think it was very proper." Her father fumed. "He said that I was his daughter and he would raise me the way he saw fit. That ended that."[19]

Bell's great niece, the western writer Teresa Jordan, also grew up on a Wyoming ranch. For her wonderful book *Cowgirls* (1979), she interviewed dozens of ranchwomen and as a result probably understands their lives better than just about anyone else. She found that most "cowgirls" identified with their fathers and from a young age wanted to be outside, among the men. Fern Sawyer, who was born and raised on a New Mexico ranch in the early twentieth century and later became a big star in women's rodeo, recalled what her father told her when she was just a kid. "You don't have to ride," he said. "You can either help me, or you can go help your mother in the house. That's your choice. But if you go with us, you are going to be treated just like one of the cowboys. You don't quit. You are just one of them." Sawyer chose the outdoors and "was never sorry." But whether daughters chose the indoors, the outdoors, or both, there seems little doubt that growing up on a ranch helped to develop women of strong and independent character. On a trip through Texas, English novelist Anthony Trollope encountered ranchwomen "sharp as nails and just as hard"—the type likely to strike a sassy pose with their husbands. "They know much more than they ought to," Trollope wrote, tongue in cheek. "If Eve had been a ranchwoman, she would never have tempted Adam with an apple. She would have ordered him to make his own meal."[20]

In his memoirs, William Tecumseh Sherman, commanding general of the army, pointed to the expansion of the open-range cattle industry as a decisive factor in the conquest of the Far West for the United States. "This was another potent agency in producing the result we enjoy to-day," he wrote, "in having in so short a time replaced the wild buffaloes by more numerous herds of tame cattle, and by substituting for the useless Indians the intelligent owners of productive farms and cattle-ranches." Sherman was right about the succession on the range—cattle replaced buffalo and cowboys replaced Indians—but wrong about the agency, for although cattlemen profited from the elimination of the great buffalo herds, they had little to do with the work of destruction. That was something accomplished by buffalo hide hunters, aided and abetted by the frontier army and Sherman himself.[21]

Plains Indians had long hunted the buffalo, and the level of their hunting greatly increased with the development of the equestrian Indian tradition in the eighteenth century. From a peak of perhaps thirty million, the number of buffalo had declined to perhaps ten million by the mid-nineteenth century, partly as a result of commercial overhunting by Indians, but also because of environmental competition from growing herds of wild horses and the spread of bovine diseases introduced by cattle crossing with settlers on the Overland Trail. By overgrazing, cutting timber, and fouling water sources, overland migrants also contributed significantly to the degeneration of habitats crucial for the health and survival of the buffalo. The confluence of these factors created a crisis for buffalo-hunting Indians by the 1860s. Tribal spokesmen protested the practice of hunters who killed for robes, leaving the meat to rot on the plains. "Has the white man become a child," the Comanche chief Santana complained to an army officer in 1867, "that he should recklessly kill and not eat?" But it was less a case of childish whim than cynical guile. "Kill every buffalo you can!" Colonel Richard Dodge urged a sport hunter in 1867. "Every buffalo dead is an Indian gone."[22]

The extension of railroad lines onto the Great Plains and the development in 1870 of a technique for converting buffalo hide into commercial leather sealed the buffalo's fate. Lured by the profits to be made in hides, swarms of hunters invaded western Kansas. Using a high-powered rifle, a skilled hunter could kill dozens of animals in an afternoon. And unlike the hunter of buffalo robes, who was limited to taking his catch in the winter when the coat was thick, hide hunting was a year-round business. General Philip Sheridan applauded their work. "They are destroying the Indians' commissary," he declared. "Let them kill, skin, and sell until the buffaloes are ex-

"Shooting Buffalo on the Line of the Kansas-Pacific Railroad." From Frank Leslie's Illustrated Newspaper, *June 3, 1871. The Library Company of Philadelphia.*

terminated." As the buffalo hunters did their work, Indians also accelerated their kills, attempting to capture their share of the market. At the Santa Fe depot in Dodge City mountainous stacks of buffalo hides awaited shipment to eastern tanneries. Historians estimate that in the five years between 1870 and 1875 five or six million buffalo died on the southern plains, wiping out the southern herds. The war on the animals then shifted to the northern plains, following the advancing tracks of the Northern Pacific. "If I could learn that every Buffalo in the northern herd were killed I would be glad," Sheridan declared in 1881. "Since the destruction of the southern herd . . . the Indians in that section have given us no trouble." His hopes were soon fulfilled. "It was in the summer of my twentieth year (1883)," the Sioux holy man Black Elk later testified, that "the last of the bison herds was slaughtered by the Wasichus," the Lakota term for white men. With the exception of a small wild herd in northern Alberta and a few remnant individuals preserved by sentimental ranchmen like Charlie Goodnight, the North American buffalo had been destroyed. "The Wasichus did not kill them to eat," said Black Elk incredulously. "They killed them for the metal that makes them crazy, and they took only the hides to sell. . . . And when there was nothing left but heaps of bones, the Wasichus came and gathered up even the bones and sold them." This shameful campaign of extinction remains unmatched in the American annals of nature's conquest.[23]

To most westerners, the disastrous effect on the Indians was a prime justification for and a happy result of the buffalo's slaughter. Missionaries and other humanitar-

A mountain of buffalo bones, c. 1880. Burton Historical Collection, Detroit Public Library.

ians who wished to salve their consciences argued that now Indians would have to cease their nomadic hunting and settle on the reservation, becoming Christians and farmers, and learn to like the white man's beef. Reservation Indians became dependent on deliveries of government beef. A great deal of the cattle driven up from Texas went to feed reservation Indians.

> Oh, you'll be soup for Uncle Sam's Injuns;
> "It's beef, heap beef," I hear them cry.
> Git along, git along, git along, little dogies,
> You're going to be beef steers bye and bye.

The cattlemen hardly objected, for they got good prices from the government and sent the worst of their animals to the reservations. Who would care? Certainly the Indians were in no position to object.[24]

Soon the range where the buffalo had roamed was being stocked with Texas longhorns. Cattlemen bought heifers and bulls in Texas and drove them north, where they opened new ranches along the watercourses. In 1880 buffalo in Montana far outnumbered the 250,000 cattle; three years later the buffalo had disappeared and the range stock had increased to 600,000. It was, in the words of cultural geographer Terry Jordan, "one of the most rapid episodes of frontier advance in the Euroamerican occupation of the continent." The transition had an unfortunate ecological effect that was not immediately apparent. In the natural cycle the buffalo ate the grasses, produced manure for new plant life, and in death returned nutrients to the earth. The cattle, however, after fattening on the plants of the plains, were transported long distances for slaughter at maturity. Their blood and unused remains were dumped in rivers, and their flesh went even farther afield. The natural cycle of life on the plains was thus broken.[25]

A year or two after the last of the northern buffalo herds had been hunted to extinction, Teddy Blue Abbott was tending cattle near the Yellowstone River in Montana when he ran into a small group of Sioux hunters. They made a friendly greeting, shared a bottle, and soon the Indians were reminiscing about old times. One of the men told Abbott of "the way they used to live before the white man came. They would go down a creek and camp where there was good grass and water, run a bunch of buffalo down and skin them and get the meat—then when the grass got a little short they would just move on to a place where there was new grass, and keep that up, no troubles or worries." Later in the day, after he'd parted company with the Sioux, Teddy met up with his friend Charlie Russell. Russell would later become a famous western artist, but in those days he was just one of the boys. "God, I wish I'd been a Sioux Indian a hundred years ago," Abbott exclaimed after telling Russell of his encounter. "Ted, there's a pair of us," Russell replied. "They've been living in heaven for a thousand years and we took it away from 'em for forty dollars a month."[26]

An experienced wrangler of the late nineteenth century could expect to earn the same pay as Abbott and Russell, about thirty or forty dollars a month. That converts to about five or six hundred in today's dollars, just about what ranch hands are paid today. Obviously no one took up cowboying to get rich but because of a love of horses, the great outdoors, and the company of good old boys. But wages have remained flat for a century also because ranchers have consistently enjoyed a labor surplus, which has allowed them to reinforce the class distinction between employer and working man.

> When I got to the boss and tried to draw my roll,
> He had me figured out nine dollars in the hole.
> I'll sell my outfit as soon as I can
> And I wouldn't punch cows for no damned man.

As this verse from the "Old Chisholm Trail" suggests, the poor pay and the seasonal nature of the work made it unlikely that many cow*boys* could ever rise into the ranks of cattle*men*.[27]

During the 1880s, however, plenty of investors expected to get rich from the cattle business. Profits were high and well publicized. James Brisbin's *Beef Bonanza, or How to Get Rich on the Plains* (1881) carried the message widely, telling a simple story as dazzling as a gold strike. By keeping his costs low, an investor could expect a profit of 25 to 40 percent a year. Capital poured in from New York, London, and Edinburgh. Theodore Roosevelt was one of many easterners who turned to ranching for fun and profit, investing $82,500 in a Badlands ranch in Dakota Territory. In 1883 Scots investors dumped $2.5 million ($33 million today) into the huge Swan Land and Cattle Company, which controlled more than six hundred thousand acres of Nebraska and Wyoming range. Another Scots firm, the Espuela Cattle Company, opened a half-million-acre spread in Texas called the Spur Ranch. British investors financed Charlie Goodnight's huge JA Ranch in the Palo Duro Canyon of Texas. A movement of consolidation swept over the cattle country, inaugurating the brief ascendancy of what historian J. C. Mutchler calls the "super ranch." Sprawling over three million acres in ten Texas panhandle counties was the XIT (which stood for "Ten in Texas"). Richard King, owner of the enormous King Ranch of south Texas, employed three hundred vaqueros to work his sixty-five thousand cattle. On John Chisum's "Rancho Grande," a massive spread straddling the Texas–New Mexico border that covered a territory the size of southern New England, wranglers branded eighteen thousand calves in a single season in 1884.[28]

Cowhands increasingly found themselves working in what was truly a cattle *industry*. "No class is harder worked, none so poor paid for their services," a wrangler named Broncho John told Eleanor and Edward Aveling, daughter and son-in-law of Karl Marx, on a tour of the United States investigating labor conditions. Some cowboys tried to organize. At the same time that the Knights of Labor were signing up railroad workers they were also active among cowhands, and there were cowboy locals and strikes for higher pay and better working conditions throughout the cattle kingdom just as there were elsewhere in industrializing America. In the spring of 1883 the *Denver Republican* reported that a demand for a wage increase to fifty dollars per

Cowboys awakening the relief watch, c. 1880s. Library of Congress.

month had resulted in "an extensive strike among the cowboys" on the largest outfits in the Texas panhandle, including Goodnight's JA Ranch and the XIT. Three hundred men held out for more than a year against paid gunmen and Texas Rangers but lost in the end when cattlemen replaced them with scabs. In 1886 a strike in Wyoming was more immediately successful at restoring a wage cut, but the leaders were all subsequently blacklisted. Historian Jack Weston points to many other instances of "slowdowns, threats, intimidating behavior, and collective defiance among cowboys displeased with their pay, bosses, or work conditions." Cowhands organized the Northern New Mexico Small Cattlemen and Cowboys' Union in the mid-1880s, declaring that "the working season of the average cowboy is only about five months, and we think it nothing but justice that the cowmen should give us living wages the year around." But cattlemen broke this and all other unionization efforts by organizing powerful stockmen's associations.[29]

The expansion of the cattle industry also brought ranchers into conflict with sheepmen, a struggle with ethnic dimensions. Hispanos and Navajos had been herding sheep in New Mexico since the seventeenth century, but in the 1870s ranchers began to compete with them for access to grass and water. "You cannot go ten miles on any road without seeing the covered wagons with from six to sixteen tow headed children aboard," reported an observer in Lincoln County, in the southeastern portion of New Mexico Territory. Violence was the predictable result of the rancher's belief that, as one Texan put it, "cattle cannot thrive on the same range with sheep." The first shooting took place in Lincoln County when constable Juan Martínez tried to arrest a group of drunken and rowdy cowboys in December 1873; guns blazed and four men, including Martínez, fell dead. Headlines in the *Santa Fe New Mexican* decried this "unfortunate war between the Texans and the Mexicans." Over the next few months at least thirteen men died in the ethnic fighting. Most western historians have preferred to focus on the next phase of the "Lincoln County War," from 1878 to 1880, when competing factions of Anglo ranchers (one of which included the infamous gunman William "Billy the Kid" Bonney) fought each other for political control of the county. But the more enduring conflict pitted Anglo cattlemen against Hispano sheepmen. According to New Mexico's territorial governor Edmund Ross, "native inhabitants who have long been in possession" were being "ousted from their homes" by ranchers. "I understand very well, and so do you," he wrote to a rancher in 1886, "what a cow-boy or cattle herder with a brace of pistols at his belt and a Winchester in his hands, means when he 'asks' a sheepherder to leave a given range." From 1860 to 1890, as the population of Lincoln County grew from eighteen hundred to more than seven thousand, the proportion of Hispanos dropped from more than 80 to less than 50 percent, and cattle ranchers prevailed over sheepherders. Lincoln County became known as "Little Texas."[30]

Hispano sheepherders were more successful in defending against the invasion of cattle in San Miguel County, in northeastern New Mexico. In the early 1880s ranchers began to fence off large tracts of grassland that Hispano communities had traditionally considered part of their common pasture (*tierra de pasto*). The vigilante group Las Gorras Blancas (The White Caps) rode out at night to cut the fences and torch the haystacks of offending ranchers. Authorities condemned these nightriders as "lawless mobs," but as one federal judge wrote, their actions were, in fact, "the protests of a simple, pastoral people against the establishment of large landed estates, or baronial feudalism, in their native territory." Las Gorras Blancas fought the ranchers to a stalemate in San Miguel County. One of their leaders, Juan José Herrera, was also an organizer for the Knights of Labor, the union that had been active among cowboys, and in 1889 fifteen hundred members of the vigilance group became a Knights' local assembly. Here the Knights were able to overcome the racial exclusion that marred their work elsewhere in the West.[31]

There were even bigger troubles ahead for ranchers. During the 1870s and 1880s American farmers began to colonize the eastern fringes of the Great Plains. "Civilization and cattle trailing were not congenial," wrote cattleman Baylis John Fletcher. "We had constantly come in collision with the farmer, who wanted the grass for their domestic animals." The town of Abilene was one of the first flashpoints for this legendary confrontation between cowpunchers and sodbusters. In 1871 thousands of longhorns awaiting shipment overran dozens of newly settled farms on the town's

Four men reenact the cutting of a rancher's barbed-wire fence. Photograph by Solomon D. Butcher, 1885. Nebraska State Historical Society.

outskirts. One settler appealed to a group of cowboys to spare his meadow, but they told him to "go to hell" and laughed as their cattle feasted on his grass. When Jacob Schopp's cornfield was destroyed by steers, he captured some of the drovers' horses and held them in lieu of damages. An armed standoff ensued, but finally, commending Schopp's grit, the Texans relented and paid him fifty dollars. In an attempt to avoid such troubles, most cattlemen trailed their herds further west in subsequent years, but the same conflict eventually recurred in Wichita, Dodge City, and elsewhere. Farmers grew increasingly aggressive, using barbed wire—patented in 1874—not only to protect their fields but to block trails and fence off watering holes. Also at issue was splenic or Texas fever, a tick-borne parasitic disease carried by longhorns; the tough Texas breed was immune, but the disease wiped out domestic short-horn stock. Pressured by farmers, the Kansas state legislature created quarantine districts into which Texas cattle could not be driven. When these blanket quarantine laws were ruled unconstitutional in the 1880s, rigorous inspection regulations took their place. In 1885 state inspectors along the Kansas border were so thorough that the resulting traffic jam backed up more than a hundred thousand head on the Western Trail.[32]

For cattlemen, the destruction of the buffalo and the opening of the western plains seemed to come at precisely the right moment. With investors throwing money at them, there was plenty of incentive to expand, and in those arid regions they did not have the competition of hostile farmers to fear. But a combination of market and natural forces proved their comeuppance. In the first place, ranchers stocked the western range with far too many cattle, inevitably driving prices down by the mid-1880s. Determined to wait out the market slump, stockmen's associations kept tens of thousands of steers off the market. Soon the grasslands were overgrazed. Everyone knew that this would mean weak cattle and a die off in the winter, but the expansion of open-range herding had taken place during an extended period of unusually wet and mild conditions on the Great Plains, and based on the expectations cattlemen built up over the previous decade, they believed they could take the loss. That's when nature returned to the more typical pattern of arid summers and frigid, stormy winters. First, drought struck the overstocked ranges. Fearing the starvation of their herds, many cattlemen drove their stock north to the still-lush meadows of Montana. But this exposed even more cattle to the harshest of the winter blizzards. It was a vicious cycle. "Animals quickly learn to 'rustle' through the snow to the sweet hay beneath," a Montana newspaper reassured its readers. It was little more than wishful thinking, but there was plenty of that in good supply. "Never in the history of the cattle business of the West has the future of this industry looked brighter and more promising than at the present time," wrote the author of yet another promotional tract.[33]

Losses from the one-two punch of drought and freeze already had many ranchers on the ropes when they were clobbered by the brutal winter of 1886–87, the worst on record. "Poor old bovines," wrote cowboy Reuben Mullins, "they would just drift with the storm and bellow until they could go no further; then they'd lie down on the trail and freeze to death. The following spring if a man should ride along any trail, he could count dead cattle by the thousand. . . . The stench from the decomposing cattle was fearful, and one couldn't get away from it." Losses varied, but in the northern plains they reached as high as 90 percent. "The fact we must now face," wrote the *Rocky Mountain Husbandman,* is that "range husbandry is over, is ruined, destroyed, and it may have been by the insatiable greed of its followers.[34]

Waiting for a Chinook. *Watercolor by Charles M. Russell, 1886. Montana Stockgrowers' Association and the Montana Historical Society.*

The "great die up," as the winter of 1886–87 became known, made large cattlemen aware of just how precarious their business was. Eastern and foreign investors bailed out, cutting their losses. Some ranchers moved toward smaller, fenced spreads, on which they could confine their cattle, improve their stock through selective breeding, and make a profit by selling high-quality beef. These ranchers planted fields of hay for winter feeding. "Things were changing fast," one rancher wrote. "New people began coming in to file for homesteads wherever there was water, or to buy up any little piece of patented land available. The old-timers who had used the range lands for most of a lifetime were dismayed to find many of their water holes fenced off, with No Trespass signs nailed to nearby trees." Many big ranchers resisted these innovations, attempting to hold on to their crumbling open-range empire. The old system would make its last stand in a conflict between big and small ranchers known as the Johnson County War.[35]

In Wyoming many of these start-up ranches were concentrated in isolated Johnson County, where the grassy valleys of the Powder River meet the Bighorn Mountains. The Wyoming Stock Growers' Association—representing the established cattlemen—thought of these newcomers as interlopers and accused them of building their herds by rustling "mavericks" from the open range. Mavericks—named for an antebellum Texas cattleman who neglected to brand his cattle—were calves and yearlings that had missed being marked during the official semiannual roundups. The politically powerful association got the territorial legislature to pass a Maverick Law, which declared every unbranded calf on the open range to be association property. There is little doubt that many small ranchers were engaged in rustling. Reuben

Mullins, who cowboyed in Wyoming during this period, knew "some mighty fine boys carrying little irons" that they used to put their own brand on mavericks. In spite of the law, many cowboys believed that this was only fair play. Hadn't the early ranchers done the same thing in Texas? Although Mullins claimed that he "never indulged in this questionable game," he sympathized with the rustlers, pointing out that the cattle barons "had cut off every avenue for advancement." In the words of an old cowboy adage, "If you stole a few cattle you were a rustler. If you stole a few thousand you were a cattleman." Such views were widely held. When the association's "stock detectives" brought accused rustlers into court, juries of local citizens refused to convict them.[36]

In fact, the rustling charges were really just a cover for the association's attempt to eliminate competition. "The rustler," wrote Asa Mercer in his classic history of the conflict, "is the cattle baron's convenient scarecrow." Failing in the courts, the cattlemen turned to violence. Their first strike came against James Averell and his lover, Ella Watson, who were living on homestead claims that the association considered part of the "open range." The cattle barons first tried to force them out by spreading rumors that Averell was the leader of a rustler band, and that Watson, known as "Cattle Kate," was a notorious prostitute who had built her fine herd by accepting steers for sexual services. Historians still dispute the truth of the charges. The pair refused to be intimidated, however, and Averell published angry denunciations of "land monopolists" in the newspaper. Finally, in 1889 a group of vigilante cattlemen invaded their ranch and lynched the couple. Although the murderers were well known, they walked free when the witnesses to the crime mysteriously "disappeared."[37]

The lynching of Averell and Cattle Kate stirred up animosity toward the cattlemen. The small ranchers organized a competing organization, the Northern Wyoming Farmers and Stockgrowers Association, and in 1892 they arranged to drive—rather than ship—their cattle east, avoiding the big interests and their railroad connections. Nathan Champion, a trail boss with a tough reputation, was to lead the drive. The big interests responded by sending fifty gunmen into Johnson County, where they killed three men and besieged Champion in a cabin along the Powder River. He held them off for twelve hours before the invaders burned him out and murdered him. Outraged Johnson County citizens organized into a vigilante mob of their own and surrounded the invaders, determined to hang them all. But the screams of the cattle magnates were heard as far away as Washington, D.C., and President Benjamin Harrison sent in United States troops to restore order. It is debatable whether federal intervention brought law and justice, for the cases against those who killed Champion and his friends were quietly dropped when the witnesses again disappeared. In the Johnson County War the most powerful political forces in Wyoming stood in opposition not only to the rustler but to any cowboy individualistic enough to remain on his own.

The Johnson County invaders, 1892. American Heritage Center, University of Wyoming.

With this fiasco the days of the western open range came to an end, just twenty-five years after the first trail drives to Abilene. Even big ranchers began to adopt newer methods. Ranch hands now had to leave the saddle to make barbed-wire fences or cut hay. Before cattle were shipped to market, they were fed grain to increase fat and flavor. State and federal officials got involved with control measures for epidemic maladies like foot-and-mouth disease. Production and capital costs mounted, but the price for beef remained low. Then during World War I prices rose to unprecedented levels and ranchers expanded their herds, only to face catastrophe with the inevitable postwar bust. In the 1920s thousands of small producers were forced out of business. Yet how could the remaining ranchers complain? By the 1920s—with a craze for hamburgers sweeping the country—Americans were eating more beef than ever.

Perhaps the most telling sign of change was the introduction of blooded Angus, Hereford, and Brahmin bulls and careful experiments in breeding. Soon the ubiquitous longhorns of myth became an endangered species. When Congress passed legislation to establish a national herd of longhorns in 1927, the United States Forest Service could find only three bulls and twenty cows. Rangers relocated a few animals to the Wichita Mountains Wildlife Refuge in Oklahoma, where they gradually built up a reproducing herd on range shared with some of the country's few remaining buffalo.

According to Teddy Blue Abbott, most of the "prehistoric" trail hands shared the same fate as the longhorn and the buffalo. But Abbott himself was one of the minority who successfully made the transition from cowboying to ranching. In the 1890s he fell in love with Mary Stuart, daughter of pioneer Montana rancher Granville Stuart. "I had always blowed my money as fast as I made it or a lot faster," Abbott wrote, "but now I made up my mind to get enough for a start in life and a nice little home of our own." After they were married, the couple homesteaded a small ranch near Miles City, where they built up a herd and even farmed a little, in addition to raising a passel of children. "We got a little better off year by year," he recalled shortly before his death in the late 1930s. During World War I, when the price for beef was high, he made a bundle, but hard times followed. "In 1919 I was $50,000 to the good. But you know what happened when that boom bust. I lost most everything. Such is life in the Far West."[38]

FURTHER READING

E. C. "Teddy Blue" Abbott and Helena Huntington Smith, *We Pointed Them North: Recollections of a Cowpuncher,* edited by Ron Tyler (1991)
David Dary, *Cowboy Culture: A Saga of Five Centuries* (1981)
Robert R. Dykstra, *The Cattle Towns* (1968)
Teresa Jordan, *Cowgirls: Women of the American West, An Oral History* (1982)
Terry G. Jordan, *North American Cattle-Ranching Frontiers: Origins, Diffusion, and Differentiation* (1993)
Winifred Kupper, *The Golden Hoof: The Story of the Sheep of the Southwest* (1945)
Guy Logsdon, ed., *"The Whorehouse Bells Were Ringing" and other Songs Cowboys Sing* (1989)
Roger D. McGrath, *Gunfighters, Highwaymen, and Vigilantes: Violence on the Frontier* (1984)
Robert J. Rosenbaum, *Mexicano Resistance in the Southwest: "The Sacred Right of Self-Preservation"* (1981)
William W. Savage, Jr., ed., *Cowboy Life: Reconstructing an American Myth* (1975)
Richard W. Slatta, *The Cowboy Encyclopedia* (1994)
___ , *Cowboys of the Americas* (1990)
Don D. Walker, *Clio's Cowboys: Studies in the Historiography of the Cattle Trade* (1981)

11

The Safety Valve

Most mid-nineteenth-century Americans were believers in the Jeffersonian promise that ordinary citizens—armed only with courage, stamina, and self-reliance—could move West, stake modest claims to the land, and make a success of it. The promise depended on the availability of western land, boundless, fertile, and cheap, and in post–Civil War America it was underwritten by the Homestead Act. Congress passed this historic legislation in the spring of 1862, as Union and Confederate troops fought and died for control of western Virginia and Tennessee, earlier Wests. But homestead enthusiasts would not allow the dying to spoil their legislative achievement. "We doubt whether any endowment on so magnificent a scale has ever been conferred on the moneyless sons of labor," read one rhapsodic editorial; the Homestead Act would shape American society "upon ages to come, when the battles on the Potomac and Tennessee will be regarded as mere incidents in history."[1]

Before the Homestead Act, the principles of American land policy were embodied in a sequence of emendations and elaborations to the foundational Land Ordinance of 1785, which opened the western public domain to settlers—but at a price, for the sale of public lands was to constitute a principal source of federal revenue. Over the next fifty years, in response to citizen complaints that the land law favored capitalists and speculators over actual settlers, Congress gradually lowered the price to $1.25 per acre and reduced the size of the minimum purchase from 640 to 40 acres.

But what settlers most wanted was the legalization of squatting: the right to select and improve lands anywhere on the public domain—even before they were surveyed—with the guarantee that when the land was officially "opened" they would be granted the opportunity to buy at the minimum price. In the American vernacular this right became known as "preemption." Representative Balie Peyton of Tennessee presented the plight of the squatter to Congress in 1835. "He had chosen that spot as the home of his children. He had toiled in hope. He had given it value, and he loved the spot. It was his all. When the public sales were proclaimed, if that poor man attended it, he might bid to the last cent he had in the world, and mortgage the bed he slept on to enable him to do it. He might have his wife and children around him to see him bid; and when he had bid his very last cent, one of those speculators would stand by his side and bid two dollars more. And thus he would see his little home, on which he had toiled for years, where he hoped to rear his children and find a peaceful grave, pass into the hands of a rich moneyed company." A New York editor, by contrast, declared that preemption amounted to "granting bounties to squatters engaged in cheating the government out of the best tracts of land." During the presidential election of 1840, however, both the Whig and Democratic platforms endorsed a preemption law, and in 1841, soon after the election of William Henry Harrison ("Old Tippecanoe") to the presidency, Congress passed what was known as the "Log Cabin Bill," granting preemption rights to all Americans. The land was still not free, however, for sooner or later squatters, like everyone else, had to pay for the acres they tilled.[2]

The passage of the Log Cabin Bill set Americans to arguing whether the time had not come for dropping the revenue principle altogether and providing *free* land for settler families. The most vocal proponent for such a "homestead" law was labor leader George Henry Evans, editor of the New York *Working Man's Advocate*. Urging the laboring man to "Vote Yourself a Farm," Evans proposed a federal program to grant 160 acres of the public domain in the West to any citizen who was willing to improve it. Free land, he believed, like the "safety valve" on a steam boiler, would "carry off the superabundant labor [of eastern cities] to the salubrious and fertile West." Like many other nineteenth-century reformers, Evans was disturbed by the increasing concentration of land in the hands of wealthy Americans—what his contemporaries referred to as "land monopoly." Evans urged that strict legal limits be placed on the quantity of public land an individual could acquire. Even more radical proposals to eliminate land monopoly were circulating. Firebrand labor leader Thomas Skidmore argued that the government should confiscate large landed estates and redistribute them to ordinary workingfolk. Horrified capitalists denounced both Skidmore and Evans as "agrarians"—a term conservatives had previously used to deride the Shays rebels in late eighteenth-century Massachusetts.[3]

Evans's proposals were rescued from the political fringe by another New Yorker, Horace Greeley, editor of the nationally distributed New York *Weekly Tribune,* the most influential newspaper in nineteenth-century America. Greeley spoke to a wide constituency that included merchants and manufacturers. "Every smoke that rises in the Great West," he reminded them, "marks a new customer to the counting rooms and warehouses of New York." Western expansion was good for eastern business. Greeley, too, was an avid believer in the notion of a western safety valve, emphasiz-

Horace Greeley, 1872. Beinecke.

ing the benefits that free land would have for employers: strikes, he argued, "will be glaringly absurd when every citizen is offered the alternative to work for others or for himself, as to him shall seem most advantageous."[4]

Editorials in the *Weekly Tribune* kept the homestead issue at the top of the political agenda during the 1850s, and in the minds of millions of Americans Greeley's name became indelibly linked to the promise of free western lands for settlers. "I turned my face westward with the spirit of Horace Greeley," wrote African-American homesteader Oscar Micheaux more than a half-century after the passage of the Homestead Act, "his words 'go west, young man,' ringing in my ears." Fact was, Greeley did not coin this famous phrase, so identified with him, but quoted it from an Indiana newspaper. Tell that to the thousands of pioneers like Micheaux who located the source of their westering inspiration in the New York editor who made the homestead law his crusade.[5]

In the mid-1850s the new Republican Party embraced the homestead program as part of its effort to build an alliance between northeastern and western politicians. In exchange for eastern votes for homestead legislation, westerners would support higher tariffs to protect "infant industries" like textiles and iron. Under Republican auspices the homestead program took on an antislavery cast. "A country cut up into small farms, occupied by many independent proprietors who live by their own toil," George Washington Julian of Indiana told his fellow congressmen, would present a "formidable barrier against the introduction of slavery." Southern legislators, fearing that the agitation for free land inevitably would lead to "Free Soil"—the political movement to bar slavery from the territories—became implacable opponents of the homestead bill. One Alabama senator warned that the plan was "tinctured with abolitionism." In 1859 the Republican coalition succeeded in pushing the legislation through Congress, only to have it vetoed by Democratic President James Buchanan, deeply in debt to southern supporters. The issue immediately became fodder for the presidential campaign of 1860. "Does any one suppose that Abraham Lincoln would ever veto such a bill?" Greeley editorialized.[6]

The secession of the southern states and the mass departure of southern congressmen from Washington after the Republican electoral triumph of 1860 removed the final obstacle to the passage of the "Act to Secure Homesteads to Actual Settlers on the Public Domain." It took effect on January 1, 1863, the same day as the Emancipation Proclamation. Persons over the age of twenty-one—both men and women, citizens and immigrants who had declared their intention to become citizens—were eligible to file for up to 160 acres of surveyed land on the public domain. Homesteaders had to cultivate the land, improve it by constructing a house or barn, and reside on the claim for five years, after which they would receive full title, paying only a $10 fee. Alternately, after only six months of residence they could exercise a "commutation clause," allowing them to purchase the claim at the minimum cash price

A homesteading family on the plains, c. 1880s. Nebraska State Historical Society.

of $1.25 per acre. The dream of free land had become law. Americans were encouraged to believe, as President Franklin D. Roosevelt would later express it, that "at the very worst there was always the possibility of climbing into a covered wagon and moving west, where the untilled prairies afforded a haven for men for whom the East did not provide a place." By 1935, when Roosevelt issued an executive order finally putting an end to the program, the Homestead Act had created farms for more than four hundred thousand families.[7]

Those homesteaders received 285 million acres, an achievement of historic proportions, but one that needs to be put in perspective. Over the same seventy-year period more than 700 million acres passed from the public domain to private hands through *purchase* rather than grant. In other words, for every 160 acres of western land given away, another 400 were sold. Most western settlers, it turns out, were not homesteaders. A large proportion took up public land under the terms of the Log Cabin Bill of 1841. Because only surveyed land was open to homesteading, and government surveys of the vast West proceeded at a snail's pace, the odds were great that to get the land they wanted settlers had to squat, establish a preemption claim, and buy the land later. Furthermore, homesteading was not permitted on lands taken from the western Indian nations (approximately 100 million acres after 1862), lands given to the states to support "land grant colleges" (140 million acres), or lands in the alternating sections the government retained along the routes laid out by the railroads. Lands in these categories, with minor exceptions, were available by cash purchase only. Most important, the federal government granted 183 million acres to the western railroads—an area larger than the state of Texas—and all that land was sold at top dollar. Lands along the rail lines, of course, were the most attractive of all, since by definition they offered access to transportation, without which western farming was not feasible.

On the tenth anniversary of the Homestead Act in 1873 the federal government circulated a pamphlet boasting that the law had "prevented large capitalists from absorbing great tracts of the public domain." It was a barefaced lie. Disregarding the advice of Evans and Greeley, the Republican Congress refused to enact limitations on the amount of public land individuals could acquire. The Homestead Act thus failed to realize reformers' hopes of forestalling land monopoly in the West. Speculators were able to amass large holdings by purchase from railroads or states, both only too happy to lower prices for big buyers. As a result, speculators grabbed the best farming land in the West before any of it was available to homesteaders. Almost all the land remaining was distant from rail lines, putting homesteaders at a distinct disadvantage.[8]

Then there were the notorious strategies unscrupulous men devised to defraud the government and frustrate the intentions of the legislation. "Dummy" homestead entries became so common that they were standing jokes in late nineteenth-century America. Working at the bidding of speculators, hired men set up tiny prefabricated shacks on 160-acre quarter-sections to satisfy the minimum legal requirements of "improvement," paid the minimum cash price after the required six months of residence, then signed over the deed to their employers. Cattlemen and lumbermen were able to acquire tens of thousands of acres by using such methods. In one shocking episode, uncovered by federal investigators at the turn of the century, the California Redwood Company rounded up foreign sailors in San Francisco, marched them to the courthouse to file citizenship papers, then to the land office to take out timber claims, then to a notary public to sign blank deeds transferring title to the company, and finally to paymasters who gave them each fifty dollars. "Immense tracts of the most valuable timber land," wrote the commissioner of the General Land Office in 1901, "have become the property of a few individuals and corporations." After a detailed study, historian Fred Shannon estimated that between 1862

Homesteader fraud: a house "twelve by fourteen." From Albert D. Richardson, Beyond the Mississippi . . . *(New York, 1867). Beinecke.*

and 1900 half of all homestead entries were fraudulent. The fact was, the engrossment of land was more prevalent after the Homestead Act than before.[9]

Meanwhile, 49 percent of all genuine homesteaders failed to patent, or "prove up," their claims. The land may have been free, but the cost of equipment, seed, and supplies for the first year or two was often more than families could manage. Others found themselves unable to stick it out in isolated locations for the required residency period. Still others failed to make their acres pay commercially because of the poor quality of their land and its distance from the railroad. Thus small western farmers still became, as often as not, tenants on land owned by others. The homestead program, George Washington Julian lamented in 1879, had become "a cruel mockery."[10]

Although railroads and land developers continued to promote the post–Civil War West as a haven for the working man, the whole idea of the "safety valve" was a farce. At a time when the cost of a railroad ticket for a family of five was the equivalent of half a year's wages, few working men could afford to take Greeley's advice and "go west." Without farming skills, most of the urban easterners who headed West settled not in the country but in western towns and cities, trading industrial work in places like Buffalo, New York, for industrial work in places like Butte, Montana. Indeed, the dominant population trend in the late nineteenth century was the movement from farm to city, not city to farm. Far more Americans followed Greeley's example—he had moved from his rural birthplace to New York City—than his advice. "For every city laborer who took up farming, twenty farmers flocked to the city to compete for his vacated job," Fred Shannon wrote in 1945. "This is not the way that safety valves are supposed to operate." It is far more accurate, Shannon concluded, to say that the city "was a safety valve for *rural* discontent."[11]

Nevertheless, by purchase and grant from the public domain, Americans opened more farmland during the last third of the nineteenth century than in all of the nation's previous history. The most productive of these were the prairie lands of Minnesota, Iowa, eastern Nebraska, and Kansas, where adequate rainfall nourished tall and luxuriant grasses and loamy top soils several feet deep. Here settlers found it possible to transplant the "corn and hog" farm economy of the Mississippi valley. "When the corn is in the ear," wrote Englishman Rudyard Kipling, traveling across these prairies, "the wind chasing shadows across it for miles on miles breeds as it were a vertigo in those who must look and cannot turn their eyes away." Observers never tired of comparing the plains with the ocean—an unbroken "sea of grass" across which prairie schooners sailed. [12]

Had Kipling traveled further west, beyond the ninety-eighth meridian, where erratic rainfall totaled fewer than twenty inches a year, his vertigo might have touched on madness. There the undulating prairie grasses gave way to a short, tough cover of bluestem and buffalo grass. Rivers ran across the high plains from the Rockies to the Mississippi, but they were separated by hundreds of miles of arid plains. The high mountains squeezed most of the moisture from the clouds and left the winds dry and pitiless. This was Major Stephen Long's "Great American Desert," and from what Americans had learned from their school atlases, as well as from what they could see with their own eyes, it is little wonder that they thought better of attempting to settle here. "The people now on the extreme frontiers are near the western limit of the fertile portions of the prairie lands," army explorer Gouverneur K. Warren wrote in 1858. "They are, as it were, upon the shore of a sea, up to which population and agriculture may advance, and no further."[13]

In *The Great Plains* (1931)—one of the most influential books ever written about the American West—Texas historian Walter Prescott Webb argued that before Americans could successfully settle the plains they had to find a means to adapt to its environment. The ninety-eighth meridian was "an institutional *fault* (comparable to a geological fault)," Webb wrote, and "at this *fault* the ways of life and of living changed." In the timbered East the ax had been the essential pioneer tool, felling trees for cabins and splitting rails for fences; on the treeless plains the ax was of little use, yet farmers still needed material for homes and fences. Rainfall was abundant in the East, but drought characterized the plains. Webb pointed to a sequence of adjustments to these difficulties. Settlers took to building shelters of sod and to burning buffalo dung, or "chips," for heat and cooking. Barbed wire—invented in 1874 by

Joseph Glidden, a farmer in De Kalb, Illinois—could make a fence that was "bull strong and hog tight." It was a godsend for western settlers, and by 1880 they were buying more than eighty million pounds of it each year. Improved drilling equipment made it possible to sink wells hundreds of feet, drawing water up from underground aquifers through the use of prefabricated windmills powered by the prevailing currents that reliably swept across the plains. Windmills provided water for drinking, irrigating gardens, watering stock, even maintaining lawns. In the isolated expanse of the plains one observer was struck by "the sight of a sod house with flower beds and a lawn sprinkler." Windmills "enabled the homesteader to hold on when all others had to leave," Webb wrote. "It made the difference between starvation and livelihood." By the turn of the century the windmills had become the ubiquitous symbol of plains farming, looming over farmers' homesteads like ancient totems.[14]

The American settlement of the arid plains also required a shift of attitude. The idea of the "Great American Desert" had to be replaced by what Henry Nash Smith called "the myth of the garden." In part this was simply the result of risk-taking pioneers testing the limits of expansion. As early as the 1840s settlers along the Santa Fe Trail were telling trader Josiah Gregg that "droughts are becoming less oppressive in the West." In the 1850s and 1860s some people speculated that more abundant rainfall might be produced by the "atmospheric friction" of locomotive wheels on steel rails or electrical currents surging through telegraph wires. But in the post–Civil War West these folk beliefs were taken up by respected authorities and transformed into propositions backed with Victorian scientific certitude. The very act of farming arid land, it was proposed, would transform the climate. "The settlement of the country, has already changed for the better the climate of that portion of Nebraska lying along the Missouri," geologist Ferdinand V. Hayden of the University of Pennsylvania wrote in 1867 after a survey of the state. Pure poppycock—but music to the ears of western state bureaucrats, land speculators, and railroad executives who stood to gain by increased settlement. The connection between science and speculation was most blatant in the case of amateur climatologist and Nebraska town-site developer Charles Dana Wilbur. "By the sweat of his face, toiling with his hands, man can persuade the heavens to yield their treasures of dew and rain upon the land he has chosen for his dwelling place," he insisted in 1881, and concluded with the inspired slogan of a practiced pitchman: "Rain follows the plough." This became the pseudoscientific watchword of thousands of settlers, as beguiling as a dowsing fork.[15]

Dana had the good fortune to write near the beginning of one of the periodic wet cycles that punctuate the climate history of the Great Plains. During wet years grasses cover the rolling plains. But dry years follow, the grasses die, and the wind picks up the thin top soil, exposing sand hills and dunes. "We like to think of whatever climate we're in as normal," says Daniel Muhs of the U.S. Geological Survey, "and our natural assumption is that it will keep on that way—that's a very tenuous assumption."

A Nebraska family poses with its new windmill, c. 1890. Nebraska State Historical Society.

During the early nineteenth century, when Pike and Long explored the continental interior, the plains were in the midst of a dry cycle. But from the late 1870s to the mid-1880s rainfall was relatively abundant, creating conditions for one of the greatest land booms in American history. Thousands of farmers left the sea of grass behind and pushed out onto the arid country of West Texas and the high plains of western Kansas and Nebraska or eastern Colorado. Considered a desert just a few years before, the area was now one of the fastest-growing farm regions of the country.[16]

In 1886, as surely as night follows day, the wet years gave way to a drought that continued until the mid-1890s. What the drought did not kill, the hot winds and the chinch bugs did. Stephen Crane, reflecting on this period, wrote of it as an agricultural apocalypse. "The farmers helpless, with no weapon against this terrible and inscrutable wrath of nature, were spectators at the strangling of their hopes, their ambitions, all that they could look to from their labor. It was as if upon the massive altar of the earth, their homes and their families were being offered in sacrifice to the wrath of some blind and pitiless deity. The country died." Between 1888 and 1892 half the population of western Kansas and Nebraska pulled up stakes and moved back east to Iowa and Illinois; a reporter in Omaha estimated that in 1891 eighteen thousand prairie schooners had crossed the Missouri River headed for Iowa. Times were hard, but in frontier fashion some people found the ability to laugh in the face of disaster. People told a story of two farmers meeting on a dusty trail, one headed east, the other west. "This would be a fine country if we just had water," said Mr. Westbound with a touch of hope in his voice. "Yes," Mr. Eastbound replied wearily, "and so would hell."[17]

The drought finally ended in the late 1890s, ushering in another wet cycle, and with it yet another mass migration to the plains. The single biggest land boom in North American history took place from 1900 to 1909. Thousands of families purchased railroad land and took up homestead claims in the western Dakotas and eastern Montana as well as the prairie provinces of Canada (which had passed the Dominion Land Act in 1872, offering terms almost identical to the Homestead Act). Most settlers came determined to practice the techniques of "dry farming," one of the most important of the adaptations to arid conditions. Rather than raising corn, they turned to drought-tolerant crops like "Turkey Red" wheat, introduced to the southern plains in the 1870s by Mennonite immigrants from the arid Crimea region of Russia, or durum wheat, imported to the Dakotas from drought-prone Turkistan at the end of the century. In an attempt to store up the moisture in the soil, farmers allowed their fields to lie fallow in alternate years. Many people were converts to the dry-farming faith of agricultural journalist Hardy Campbell of Nebraska, who argued that the trick to farming the plains was deep plowing, soil packing to conserve moisture, and surface harrowing to create a "dry mulch" preventing evaporation. Like Charles Dana Wilbur, Campbell employed the rhetoric of science, but his advice consisted mostly of unsupported assertions later disproved by soil scientists. His techniques worked well enough during the wet years, but when drought inevitably returned to the high plains in 1910, crops again withered and died. The soil dried out to the depth it had been plowed, was picked up by the hot winds, and was blown away. One Dakota settler expressed his frustrations in poetry:

> Oh but I'm weary of case hardened skies,
> Scorching south winds and land agents' lies.
> I am tired of "dry farming" with its plowing so deep,
> And I'm weary of sowing where no one can reap.

Dust storms blew throughout the region and settlers again migrated eastward by the thousands.[18]

The pioneer experience on the high plains suggests that Walter Prescott Webb exaggerated the importance of the adaptations settlers made crossing the "fault line" of aridity. Barbed wire and windmills were useful tools, but insufficient to master the plains environment. "Dry farming" was an important advance, but even that technique could not withstand drought. As an agricultural expert testified in 1911, twenty-five years of experience had failed to solve the problem. It was a misconception, he wrote, "that any definite 'system' of dry-farming has been or is likely to be established that will be of general applicability to all or any considerable part of the Great Plains area." Yet a return to adequate rainfall on the plains, combined with the enormous demand for farm products during World War I, provided all the incentive needed for farmers to plow up millions of additional acres of the Great Plains before the end of the 1920s.[19]

Farm mechanization was the most powerful adaptation of all. In the years following the Civil War a long line of improvements appeared one after the other. Steel replaced wood and iron in the manufacture of plows; new riding plows allowed farmers to sit and drive their teams, and soon horses were pulling "gang plows" that turned over several rows simultaneously. Horsepower was also put to use with new hay mowing, raking, and loading machines. A ton of hay could be loaded from the field in just five minutes. The "McCormick 'Old Reliable' Automatic Self-Rake Reaper" of 1867 cut wheat and swept it aside for binding. It was not long before an inventive westerner perfected an automatic binder that gathered the shocks, tied them with a length of twine, and kicked them free. Power threshers appeared, the early ones using horsepower, later models driven by coal-fired steam boilers. In 1880 harvesting and threshing were for the first time joined in the "combine" machine, and within a few years giant steam combines were producing up to eighteen hundred sacks of grain each day. By the end of the century wheat farming was eighteen times more productive than it had been before the Civil War.

Mechanization made possible the giant "bonanza farms" of the northern plains and the great central valley of California. Many of these farms grew from the corporate design of the railroads. After the Panic of 1873, the Northern Pacific attempted to fend off bankruptcy by offering its far-flung acres in exchange for its own depreciated securities. Within two years the railroad had sold off 483,000 acres in the Red River Valley of Dakota Territory at five dollars an acre, with just twenty-three buyers accounting for two-thirds of the acreage. They divided the land according to the most modern principles of efficient production and hired the best foremen and managers they could find. An average of 250 farmhands labored on every ten thousand acres. The most famous of the bonanza farms was the thirty-four thousand acres a few miles west of Fargo managed by Oliver Dalrymple, an experienced grain

Combined reaper-thresher harvests prairie wheat on a bonanza farm. Photograph by the Keystone View Company, c. 1890. Beinecke.

farmer from Minnesota. One of Dalrymple's rippling wheat fields stretched for thirteen thousand unbroken acres. Separate gangs working on distant corners of the farm might not see each other for the entire season. According to one tall tale, a plowman would set to work in the spring and cut a straight slice across the farm until fall; then he would turn around and harvest his way back. In California, where huge estates were carved from the land grants of the Central Pacific, the largest farms stretched over sixty-six thousand acres and produced more than a million bushels annually. By 1880 California had become the biggest wheat-producing state in the nation. Whether in the Dakotas or in the San Joaquin valley, these farms embodied the vital components of industrial capitalism—the application of machinery to mass production, absentee ownership, professional management, specialization, and proletarian labor.

The farms of the thousands of emigrants who found their way to the Great Plains in the late nineteenth century could not have provided a more striking contrast with those bonanza operations. Authorities in the Department of Agriculture recommended that settlers have at least a thousand dollars in capital—for even assuming free homestead land, there were the costs of moving, fencing, seed, livestock, and the purchase of equipment—but most newly arriving families probably had less. Most were poor and probably undersupplied. In the words of a doleful ballad of the time:

> How happy I am on my government claim,
> Where I've nothing to lose and nothing to gain,
> Nothing to eat and nothing to wear,
> Nothing from nothing is honest and square.
>
> But here I am stuck and here I must stay,
> My money's all gone and I can't get away;
> There's nothing will make a man hard and profane
> Like starving to death on a government claim.

Poor tenant farmers and hired hands came from the states of the Old Northwest and Old Southwest, hoping to climb the agricultural ladder to farm ownership by investing their labor in free or cheap land. Thousands of former slaves came from the Black Belt cotton lands of Tennessee, Mississippi, Alabama, and Louisiana, intending to take up homesteads in Oklahoma and Kansas. Millions of immigrants came from Europe, toting a few treasured heirlooms but relatively little capital. By end of the century Germans made up a third of the population of Texas, and so large were the numbers of Swedes, Norwegians, and Russians in the population of the northern plains states that according to the census of 1890 the region had the highest proportion of foreign-born people in the country.[20]

Many of these settler families built their houses from the earth itself. Arriving at their claims, families worked together slicing the tough, grassbound sod into bricks about a foot wide and three feet long. Then they placed them end to end to form walls three feet thick to make an enclosure about eighteen by twenty-four feet. Two forked tree trunks held the ridgepole. Over the rafters went tar paper—if the builder was lucky enough to afford it—then a layer of sod bricks, from which eventually grass and sunflowers would flourish. Because of its insulation, the room was cool in summer and warm in winter—warmer, that is, than the blizzards raging outside. The "soddy" offered cheap accommodations, but it often sheltered hardship incarnate. With one window and one door there was little light and little ventilation. Dirt showered down from the ceiling and the soggy roof was in constant danger of caving in. Novelist and historian Mari Sandoz wrote of the time before her birth when her father, "Old Jules," brought his Swiss bride to a soddy in Nebraska. Toward morning of their first night it rained. "The roof leaked a little at first, then more. Soon every-

Nebraska homesteaders pose in front of their soddy. Photograph by Solomon D. Butcher, c. 1880. Solomon D. Butcher Collection, Nebraska State Historical Society.

where. Henriette sat on the wet straw tick all the next day with a purple umbrella over her head, crying noiselessly."[21]

Soddies were common in the 1880s, but in later decades the tar-paper shack, made of third-rate lumber and insulation paper, was more typical. Edith Ammons, who homesteaded a South Dakota claim with her sister, Ida Mary, described their home as a "none too substantial packing-box tossed haphazardly on the prairie, which crept in at its very door." The tar paper that covered the cracks and kept out some of the weather came in two grades. "The red was a thinner, inferior quality and cost about three dollars a roll," Ammons remembered, "while the heavy blue cost six. Blue paper on the walls was as much a sign of class on the frontier as blue blood in Boston." A few months after their arrival the two women experienced their first plains blizzard. "The howling of the wind and the beating of the snow against the shack made it impossible to hear any other sound. Cowering in that tiny shack, where thin building paper took the place of plaster, the wind screaming across the Plains, hurling the snow against that frail protection, defenseless against the elemental fury of the storm, was like drifting in a small boat at sea, tossed and buffeted by waves, each one threatening to engulf you."[22]

The bonanza farms used the most mechanized equipment, but historian Paula

Nelson, in a detailed study of settlement in western South Dakota, finds that it was too expensive for most pioneers. "It was quite literally strong backs and hands that made homes, barns, fences, and fields," she writes. An example is the family of William and Carrie Miller, who in 1906 left Wisconsin to homestead a western claim on land the Sioux had hunted only a generation before. They brought with them a wagon, a set of hand tools, and an old walking plow. While Carrie and the children planted and tended a garden, William plowed a field and sowed it with oats for the horses and exchanged his labor with a neighbor for the loan of a horse-drawn mower to make winter hay from the prairie grasses. Their cash income for the first few years came from the sale of Carrie's butter and eggs. It was only after several seasons of hard work and saving that William was able to purchase a self-binding reaper and began to produce grain for the market. The Millers were laid low by the drought of 1910–11, which struck right after a disastrous fire that consumed their barn and destroyed most of their stock and equipment. While Carrie and the children struggled through by hauling water from a distant stream to irrigate the garden, William found temporary work on a bonanza farm up north. Their experience is testimony to the persistence of the traditions of self-sufficiency that had sustained frontier settlers from the beginning of westering in the eighteenth century. The only thing unique about the Millers was their stubbornness; they stuck it out when drought, blizzards, and grasshopper plagues drove most of their neighbors back east. As one of the Miller children wrote years later, "So many families moved away that there weren't enough children to keep a school open."[23]

The ability of farm families to hunker down to bare subsistence gave them an advantage over the bonanza farms, whose managers always had the bottom line to face. Corporate agriculture on the Great Plains was eventually driven out of business by pestilence and drought. Absentee owners reinvented themselves as land speculators and attempted to recoup their capital on the increased value of the land itself. But despite slim pickings, there would always be sodhouse or tar-paper farmers like the Millers persisting on the land.

The Homestead Act allowed women to apply for land under the same conditions as men, requiring only that they be at least twenty-one and unmarried (single, divorced, widowed, or otherwise the head of a household). The records of the General Land Office reveal that a significant number of women took advantage of this provision. Case studies of various western locales demonstrate that single women made up from 5 to 15 percent of all homestead entries before 1900, with the proportion rising to 20 percent in the early twentieth century. Women proved up at a similar or better rate than men. "These numbers are significant, if not overwhelming," writes Sherry L. Smith, "since taking up homesteads, at least in the popular perception, re-

Women homesteaders pose outside their tar-paper shack in South Dakota, c. 1910. South Dakota Historical Society.

mains an activity associated with men." Thirty to forty thousand is a reasonable estimate of the number of homesteading women who gained title to western land in their own names.[24]

The most famous of them was Wyoming ranchwoman Elinore Pruitt Stewart, whose *Letters of a Woman Homesteader* was greeted with considerable acclaim when it was published in 1914, then revived as a classic of western women's history in the 1970s. (It also inspired the beautiful film *Heartland* [1979].) Stewart's charming account detailed her efforts to homestead an arid quarter-section in Sweetwater County, Wyoming. Homesteading, she argued, offered an important means by which women could achieve economic independence. "Any woman who can stand her own company, can see the beauty of the sunset, loves growing things, and is willing to put in as much time and careful labor as she does over the washtub, will have independence, plenty to eat all the time, and a home of her own in the end." Popular interest in Stewart's theme stimulated the creation of what Dee Garceau calls the "woman homesteader genre." Mass-circulation magazines such as *Atlantic* and *Collier's* published essays and stories by numerous western women, offering homesteading as a way for single women to improve their lot.[25]

Recent research into the details of Stewart's life, however, discloses that she departed significantly from the facts in her narrative. She wrote of her journey to Wyoming to keep house for widowed rancher Clyde Stewart, detailed her decision to homestead the tract adjoining his, and much later in the book noted their decision to marry. What got obscured in this telling was that Elinore and Clyde married only a week after she made application for her homestead. As Sherry Smith puts it,

Stewart's "days as a single woman homesteader were clearly limited." But rather than disqualifying Stewart's story as a historical source, an understanding of this background actually strengthens its interest and importance. Dee Garceau, who studied the General Land Office records for Sweetwater County, notes that many (if not most) of the single women who filed claims there did so as part of a strategy to enlarge an existing family ranch. It took substantial acreage to pasture a herd of cattle, and deceptions like those of the Stewart family were attempts to work around the provisions of the law. Homesteading was not something easily accomplished by lone individuals—whether men or women—but required the cooperative work of the whole family.[26]

This perspective also suggests that stories of single women homesteaders ought not be read as strictly true but rather as compelling metaphors of women's independence. The American West has always been a site for symbolic masculine achievement. Women probably meant these stories to be read in the same way. Proving up meant more than simply meeting the legal requirements—it meant proving oneself. In the early twentieth century, stories of women homesteaders offered a western version of the "New Woman." As historian Sherry Smith writes, they were the "feminine version of the popular safety-valve myth."[27]

"The American farmer of today is altogether a different sort of man from his ancestor of fifty or a hundred years ago," William A. Peffer, editor of the *Kansas Farmer*, wrote in 1891. "The farmer thrashes his wheat all at one time [and] he disposes of it all at one time. He sells his hogs, and buys bacon and pork; he sells his cattle, and buys fresh beef and canned beef or corned beef, as the case may be; he sells his fruit, and buys it back in cans. . . . He buys nearly everything now that he produced at one time himself, and these things all cost money." Western farmers might practice subsistence during the pioneer days or to survive the pinch of hard times, but ultimately they had to find their place in the market economy. Success had to be measured in dollars, and the disturbing truth was that from the end of the Civil War to the end of the century the prices for farm commodities did nothing but fall. The wholesale price index of farm products (in which the 1910–14 average is arbitrarily assigned the value of 100) fell steadily from a century high of 162 in 1864 to a low of 56 in 1896; only once in American history, during the depression that followed the Panic of 1837, had farm prices been lower. Wheat that sold for a dollar a bushel in 1870 was down to eighty cents by 1885 and only half a buck ten years later. These are government figures; the prices offered by grain dealers at the railhead were lower. Dakota farmers of the 1890s, for example, were getting only thirty-five cents a bushel for wheat that cost them at least fifty cents to produce.[28]

Individual farmers responded in the only way they could, by attempting to pro-

duce more and produce it more efficiently. It was a losers' strategy. The steadily increasing flow of farm commodities onto the market simply accelerated the downward pressure on prices. Thousands of farmers borrowed heavily to buy more land
or mechanized equipment, mortgaging their farms, their livestock, even their belongings. They were encouraged by the boomers and boosters. "Do not be afraid of
going into debt," advised the editor of the *Belle Plaine News* of Kansas; "double,
treble, quadruple your expenditures." Fred Shannon estimated that by 1890 there
were more mortgages in the high plains states than there were farm families. Without adequate returns, farm indebtedness led inevitably to foreclosure. A Kansas song
warned that

> A chattel mortgage in the West
> Is like a cancer on your breast;
> It slowly takes your life away,
> And eats your vitals day by day.

As a result of falling prices and massive indebtedness, approximately 45 percent of
Kansas farmers were in default by the early 1890s. There were farmers in the Dakotas, it was said, who could not even leave the state because of mortgage liens against
their horses.[29]

Western farmers tended to identify the East as the source of their problems. The
two most important symbols of eastern colonialism were the railroads and the
banks. Freight rates in the West (and in the impoverished South) were frequently two
or three times those for comparable distances in the East. West of the Mississippi the
Burlington line, for example, charged four times what it levied to the east. Railroad
companies, it is true, encountered special problems in the West, a region that by the
nature of its extractive economy exported far more raw materials and crops than it
imported manufactured goods. During peak harvest times railroad executives complained that they were forced to send empty cars westward to handle the huge grain
shipments. But the main reason for the high rates was an absence of western competition and the drive to maximize profits where possible. High rates in the sparsely
settled West paid for eastern losses—from rebates to favored shippers, from competitive rate wars, from free passes for sympathetic judges and public officials. When
the farmer groaned that he was paying the value of one whole bushel of corn or wheat
in order to get a second bushel to market, he was not exaggerating.

Another cause of western suffering was the country's banking and monetary system. During the Civil War Congress had, in large measure, financed the war by authorizing the issue of $432 million in paper notes. These "greenbacks"—so called be-
cause of the distinctive color of the ink on their reverse side—were declared "legal
tender" for all public and private transactions but could not be redeemed at the
United States Treasury for gold or silver. It was the first issue of federal "fiat money,"

currency backed not by precious metals but only by the authority of the federal government. By war's end the circulation of greenbacks had resulted in inflation that cut the value of the dollar in half, and the Republican congressional majority ordered that the country gradually retire most of the greenbacks in circulation and return to a metallic standard. The resulting contraction in the supply of money was great news for capitalists and creditors, whose investments increased with every uptick in the dollar's value, but awful news for farmers and debtors, who not only received less for their products because of deflation but also had to repay their loans with dollars worth a good deal more than the dollars they had borrowed. Combine depressed prices with annual rates of interest that often climbed as high as 25 percent in the West, and it is easy to understand the growing hostility of westerners to banks and bankers. Many were attracted to the political argument of the Greenback Party, that a growing industrial economy needed an expanding money supply. Other westerners, especially those from mining states and regions, demanded the unlimited minting of silver coin, another measure which would have had a significant inflationary impact on the economy by increasing the amount of money in circulation.

The image of the westerner besieged by economic forces beyond his control became a cultural commonplace of the late century. Hamlin Garland, raised in rural Wisconsin, recounted some of the sad details in "Under the Lion's Paw," one of a number of short stories in his *Main-Traveled Roads* (1891). Farmer Haskins rents a place he could have bought for three thousand dollars had he the money. Husband, wife, and son work for two long, dreary years and by scraping and saving build the place up and save the original purchase price. But when the owner sees the improvements, he jumps the price of the farm to five thousand dollars. Haskins must go into debt to purchase the value that the family's sweat has added to the land. Ready to kill the owner, he swallows his anger and returns to his newly mortgaged acres. Western farmers could not escape from the grip of the capitalist paw.

Western farmers did not simply respond as individuals. Through their hardships and struggles they developed a powerful collective consciousness. They read their own newspapers and journals—publications with names like the *Kansas Farmer* or *Western Rural*—and they started their own organizations. The first one of national importance was the National Grange of the Patrons of Husbandry, founded shortly after the Civil War. By 1875 it counted 850,000 members in hundreds of local chapters or "Granges" (an old word for a farmer's house). At meetings and picnics men swapped yarns and women exchanged recipes, but mostly Grangers talked politics, though the organization had pledged itself to be "non-political." Together they exerted sufficient pressure on state legislatures to win regulations governing railroads and grain elevators. Challenged by the railroads and the wholesalers, the Supreme

Farmers bring their wheat to the grain elevator at Wausa, Nebraska. Photograph by Lynn and Johnson, 1904. Nebraska State Historical Society.

Court finally upheld these laws in the landmark case of *Munn v. Illinois* (1876), which declared that such facilities were "clothed with a public interest." The principle of government commercial regulation—the Grangers' legacy—eventually led to the passage of the Interstate Commerce Act of 1887, the first federal attempt to regulate the railroads.

The Grange was strongest in the Midwest. Elsewhere the preeminent organization was the Farmers' Alliance, a group that took shape in Texas during the mid-1870s and within a decade mushroomed into hundreds of local groups spread throughout the rural South, the Great Plains, and the Rocky Mountain states with a membership of several million. Like the Grange, the Alliance responded to the social as well as the political needs of farm families, organizing picnics, camp meetings, and educational institutes. From their isolated homesteads families packed into wagons heading for Alliance meetings, frequently joining in long trains to demonstrate their solidarity. "I watched the procession as it paraded from the city to the picnic ground," wrote a reporter for a Kansas newspaper and added, with a sense of history, that "nothing like this has happened since 1856, when the old Whig party disintegrated and voted for the old pathfinder Frémont." The essential appeal of the Farmers' Alliance was its affirmation of American values and images. Familiar hymns took on new political meaning:

> God hears the cry of millions
> Who labor and toil, who have reaped down the grain.

Their cries, saith the Lord of the Sabbath,
Shall not go unheeded, shall not be in vain.[30]

At first the Alliance sought to create cooperative grain elevators, trade exchanges, and buying clubs for farm men and women that would cut out middlemen and pass on the savings. When these failed—largely because of the active opposition of merchants, brokers, and railroads—the Alliance moved directly into politics. In the early 1890s it helped found the Peoples' Party, whose followers became known as the Populists, aligning the farmers' movement with the western Knights of Labor, Greenbackers, and "silverites." "We meet in the midst of a nation brought to the verge of moral, political, and material ruin," Ignatius Donnelly of Minnesota declared in the keynote address at the founding Omaha convention in 1892. "We seek to restore the Government of the Republic to the hands of the 'plain people' with whom it originated." The party platform, written largely by Donnelly, was a remarkable document, calling for a series of reforms that appealed to both farmers and workers: government ownership of the nation's transportation and communications systems; expansion of the homestead program by returning to the public domain all unsold lands granted to the railroads; creation of a national system of warehouses (called the "sub-treasury"), where farmers could store their crops in exchange for government loans; commitment to a flexible national currency based not only on gold but on silver and "fiat money" as well; the establishment of a graduated income tax; and the eight-hour day. James B. Weaver, the party's candidate for president, was the child of a settler family who worried about the widening chasm between the haves and the have-nots. Initially hoping only to make a showing, the Populists were thrilled when Weaver polled over a million votes in the 1892 election, winning the states of Kansas, Colorado, Idaho, and Nevada outright and a plurality in North Dakota. The Populists elected three governors and sent ten representatives and five senators to Congress, including William A. Peffer of Kansas. Soon thereafter the depression of 1893 firmly cemented sentiments. The Populist revolt had begun.

In addition to Donnelly and Weaver the Populists brought a colorful crew of western advocates to national attention. They included Kansas cattleman Jeremiah Simpson, who became known as "Sockless Jerry" to his supporters by turning to advantage an opponent's sarcastic comment that Simpson was so "country" he wore no socks. But no one better represented the Populists than Mary Elizabeth Lease, a former homesteader and one of the first women to practice law in Kansas, who became famous for a speaking style that combined biblical imagery, frontier wit, and agrarian radicalism in equal measure. "The land, which is the heritage of the people and the source of all wealth, has passed into the hands of a few who toil not, neither do they spin," she preached in her deep contralto. What the country needed was "the enactment into law of the truths taught by Jesus." Attempting to discredit Lease, a hos-

Populist orator Mary Lease, c. 1890. Kansas State Historical Society, Topeka.

tile reporter once attributed to her the comment that farmers should "raise less corn and more hell," but the phrase endeared her all the more to her supporters and it became the slogan of the day. "This is a nation of inconsistencies," Lease once declared. "The Puritans fleeing from oppression became in turn oppressors. We fought England for our liberty and put chains on four million blacks. We wiped out slavery and [then] by our tariff laws and national banks began a system of white wage slavery worse than the first." An oversimplification, perhaps, but her history rang true to enthusiastic audiences in the West.[31]

Lease was but one of a number of remarkable women who helped to lead the Grange, the Farmers' Alliance, and the Populist Party. These organizations were unusual among their nineteenth-century counterparts in allowing women to take part as members, officers, and convention delegates. Indeed, women's participation in the western reform movements of the late nineteenth century seems to have been critical in the early victory of woman suffrage in the West. Of the fifteen states that enacted equal suffrage laws before the passage of the Nineteenth Amendment to the Constitution in 1919, thirteen were in the trans-Mississippi West. Support for woman suffrage, argues historian Elizabeth Jameson, "seems to have come less from the genteel upper classes than from farmers and miners who endorsed political philosophies that supported equality."[32]

To conservatives, the Populist platform seemed salted with radicalism, especially in its call for the nationalization of the railroads and a progressive income tax. In fact, a diluted form of Marxism became popular among many Americans during the 1880s and 1890s. Laurence Gronlund's influential *The Cooperative Commonwealth* (1884) offered an American primer on the principles of socialism, and Edward Bellamy's *Looking Backward* (1888) described a socialist America of the future and spawned hundreds of "Nationalist Clubs." Gronlund and Bellamy wrote for an urban public, and though they stirred Boston, New York, and San Francisco they found little following among western farmers. The radical doctrines of California journalist Henry George did make some headway in the country. In *Progress and Poverty* (1879), his homegrown indictment of American capitalism, George shook a generation of Americans by arguing that the only way to break up the great monopolies that were strangling the American worker was to tax away the increase in land values (what he termed the "unearned increment"). Under George's scheme the railroads would pay plenty for what they had reaped in land speculation. Jerry Simpson and Hamlin Garland both championed George's "single tax."

The Populists were anxious for electoral victory, however, and in 1896 they rejected these more radical ideas for "fusion" with the Democratic presidential candidacy of William Jennings Bryan of Nebraska. Bryan's most radical proposal was his opposition to the monetary gold standard and his support for the free coinage of silver, a measure designed to break the deflationary back of the depression. "You shall not press down upon the brow of labor this crown of thorns, you shall not crucify mankind upon a cross of gold," he thundered famously in his acceptance speech. This position insured Bryan's popularity in western mine communities. To be sure, "silver" was more symbol than substance, standing for federal intervention in the economy and the quest for greater reforms. But Bryan's rhetoric also underlined the fact that, in the end, the Populists spoke for rural America. "Burn down your cities and leave our farms, and your cities will spring up again as if by magic," he orated, "but destroy our farms and the grass will grow in the streets of every city in the country."[33]

Bryan waged a fighting campaign and captured the states of the South and interior West, but he failed to carry the critical states of the Pacific coast and the Midwest, thus losing to Republican William McKinley. The Populist challenge faded with the decline of the Democrats into the status of a regional party based in the South, a pattern that would prevail for the next thirty years. In the end western farmers and miners had been unable to convince industrial workers of the merits of their cause. The interests of workers and farmers sometimes clashed. Low prices for wheat translated into cheap flour used to bake cheap bread for hungry workers in hundreds of new industrial bakeries, and urban workers feared that inflation would raise the price of basic commodities.

Many of the Populist proposals would be taken up by the Progressives of the early twentieth century, although in a distinctly more urban style, with little of the rural flair of a Jerry Simpson or a Mary Elizabeth Lease. Later they would inspire the New Deal, many of whose programs, wrote westerner Thurman Arnold in 1942, could be traced directly back to "the general philosophy and specific ideas" of the Grangers, the Greenbackers, and the Populists of the late nineteenth-century West.[34]

Some historians argue that the western agrarian movement also had important consequences for the development of American foreign relations. One response to the crisis of overproduction was a western push to expand overseas markets. "Our crops are now far beyond the requirements of our home consumption," asserted a representative from Texas. "We must either have the foreign market or none." During the 1870s, in response to warfare and failed harvests in Europe, American agricultural exports increased enormously. By the end of the decade shipments of meat and wheat abroad nearly doubled over what they had been ten years before. But the export bonanza collapsed when European harvests returned to normal and governments began to raise tariff barriers in an attempt to protect their farmers. Western congressional representatives were prominent among those demanding that the United States pry those markets open again.[35]

There was also the lure of Asian commerce, an old dream of American expansionists. In 1869 Ignatius Donnelly defended William Henry Seward's purchase of Russian America by arguing that America's "destiny is to grasp the commerce of all the seas." Alaska, he argued, was simply "one of the necessary steps" to bring the nation "face to face with the four hundred millions of the Chinese empire and with the other vast populations of India and Japan." The attempt of the United States to expand foreign markets was, in part, designed to quiet the protests of farmers. Broad western support for commercial expansion in the Pacific was premised on the hopes of opening huge new markets. "Hawaii is the key to the whole commerce of the Pacific Ocean," the editor of the *Pacific Rural Press* wrote in support of annexation of the islands in 1893. Western representatives argued for a form of overseas expansion that contrasted with old-style European colonialism. What they wanted was to see freedom—American freedom of trade anyway—extended everywhere on the globe. This was the formula invoked during the Spanish-American War of 1898: America would expel the Spanish imperialists from Cuba and guarantee the political independence of the island in exchange for economic privileges that would expand the marketplace for American farmers. William Appleman Williams has argued that "the roots of the modern American empire" grew out of an agreement on expansion proposed by the agrarian West and accepted by the industrial East.[36]

––––––

In 1896 depression began to loosen its grip on the nation's economy. The same year saw the end of the long drought on the plains. Leaving the previous quarter-century of hard times behind in the dust, the American farm economy took off in a sustained boom that would carry it through World War I. For the first time in more than a generation farmers were able to secure credit at reasonable rates and make a decent profit on their products. By 1910 the price of a bushel of wheat had risen to nearly a dollar and the demand associated with the European war that began in 1914 drove farm prices to unprecedented heights. This would long be remembered as the "golden age" of American agriculture, when the prices for farm and industrial goods were in good balance. Indeed, when New Deal legislation instituted a program of federal price supports for farm commodities, the farm prices of the period 1909–14 would be enshrined as the norm.

But with prosperity came a great deal of structural change in western agriculture: the consolidation of small farms into larger units, a dramatic turn toward mechanization and specialization, and a considerable increase in capital requirements. By 1910 the best homestead land in both the United States and Canada had been taken up, and authorities began to advise potential settlers that the costs of starting a farm would now require a minimum of fifteen hundred dollars, the equivalent of twenty thousand dollars in 1995. The increasing capital cost of farming was accompanied by a disturbing increase in the number of farm tenants in the West. Agricultural experts had noted this trend since the 1880s, but optimists had argued that most renters were young farmers about to move up the agricultural ladder to ownership. As the rates of tenancy continued to skyrocket, however, tenants came to be seen as the sign of shrinking rather than expanding opportunity. In Texas the proportion of tenants in the agricultural workforce grew from 38 percent in 1880 to more than 60 percent in 1920. Many of these encumbered farmers were African-American sharecroppers, forced back into quasi-slavery after the failure of Reconstruction. But the most shocking increase in tenantry was among the white farmers of the Great Plains states, where the number of new tenants outstripped the growth of independent farm ownership. By 1920 tenants made up more than 40 percent of the agricultural workforce in the northern plains. For families without capital, renting land had become the only alternative to migration to the cities. People had long worried that the agricultural ladder was rickety, but there was now a growing consensus that the rungs were broken.

Another sign of transformation in western agriculture was the enormous increase in the number of wageworkers in the countryside. Western agriculture had long depended on hired labor, but in earlier decades most farmworkers were poor homesteaders who labored for their more prosperous neighbors in order to raise money to improve their land or buy equipment. By the late nineteenth century, however, an estimated two hundred thousand migrant farmworkers were harvesting wheat on the plains, moving from Texas in late May or early June to western Kansas and Nebraska in midsummer, and finally to the prairie provinces of the Canadian West in the fall. Elizabeth Gurley Flynn, who spent several years working as a labor organizer among these migrant workers, learned a great deal about them. "The majority were American-born Eastern youth of adventurist spirit who had followed Horace Greeley's advice: 'Go West, young man and grow up with the country!'" But they came West after the best homestead land had been taken up. "They became floaters," wrote

Harvest workers near Moro, Oregon, c. 1910. Oregon Historical Society.

Flynn, "without homes or families." Western farming was now tied to the restless wageworkers' frontier, a labor system with its roots in the California gold rush. There was little opportunity for harvest workers to settle down on western homesteads.[37]

As hopes of farm ownership evaporated with the rising price of land and equipment, migrants turned toward unionization. Bill Haywood, the former western miner who now led the Industrial Workers of the World, announced a campaign to organize harvesters into a new "Agricultural Workers Organization," a union affiliated with the Wobblies. Farm income had increased, Haywood argued, but farm wages remained stagnant. Farmers were improving their homes as well as their farms, adding indoor plumbing and steam heat, but hired men continued to sleep in damp old soddies or filthy chicken coops. "The farmer looked at me, his hired hand, as if I was just another work horse," one worker complained. IWW organizers rode the rails with harvesters and camped with them in the "hobo jungles" on the outskirts of prairie towns. They argued for adequate board, good places to sleep, and a minimum daily wage of three dollars, with an additional fifty cents for every hour worked over ten in a single day. Harvesters were attracted to the spirit and enthusiasm of the young organizers, who were famous for singing from the little red songbooks organizers distributed "to fan the flames of discontent."

I.W.W. cartoon, c. 1910. Yale University.

> It is we who plowed the prairies;
> Built the cities where they trade.
> Dug the mines and built the workshops,
> Endless miles of railroad laid.
> Now we stand outcast and starving,
> 'Midst the wonders we have made.
> But the Union makes us strong.[38]

From 1914 to 1917 the AWO signed up more than eighteen thousand harvesters from Oklahoma to the Dakotas. In some areas farmers negotiated labor agreements. The Non-Partisan League of North Dakota, one of the few organized remnants of the old Farmers' Alliance, worked out a schedule of wages, hours, and working conditions for harvesters. But most farm owners reacted in fear and anger, and in many communities migrant workers and labor organizers were harassed, jailed, and in some cases murdered. The IWW reported that groups of men were arrested because "they kicked on the grub they had for breakfast," or "for refusing to work after

6 o'clock at night." After the United States joined the war in Europe in 1917, the Wobblies, who opposed American participation, became the target of government repression, and the AWO collapsed. [39]

There were also structural reasons, however, for the failure of unionism in the western countryside. Employing a narrow Marxist definition of the working class, the IWW classified all farmers as capitalists and refused to organize tenants. Yet this growing segment of the rural population was potentially the most radical of all. In Oklahoma in 1917 tenant farmers adopted collective and direct action against landowners, but IWW-organized hired hands stood aside. The tenants were crushed by state authorities in an episode known as the Green Corn Rebellion and their energy was thus lost to the Wobblies.

Perhaps even more important were new forms of mechanization—the most important of which was the gasoline-powered tractor—aimed at making the farmer self-sufficient in labor. "When money is paid to hired help it is gone," read an advertisement in a regional newspaper, but "when money is put into labor-saving machinery, the machinery remains, to give help and save time and labor for the rest of your life." Assisted by the smaller combines marketed after the war, a farmer with large acreage needed only two or three men to help with the harvest rather than the eighteen or twenty that had been common before the war. It all pointed to the end of the wageworkers' frontier in the West. "The decline of the IWW as an organization," wrote organizer William Z. Foster, who worked as a migrant laborer in the West, "kept pace with the diminishing role of the floating workers in the West through the introduction of farm machinery, the completion of the building of the railroads, and the tendency of workers to settle down."[40]

Migrant labor was also an essential feature of the intensive agricultural districts—specializing in the production of vegetables and fruit—cropping up throughout the Far West, including the "Winter Garden" area along the lower Rio Grande in Texas, the Gila and Salt river valleys in southern Arizona, and the Yakima valley in Washington. Most important were the fertile valleys of California, which by the turn of the century were producing most of the fruits and vegetables being canned, dried, and shipped fresh to markets around the country. Chinese immigrant farmers had been the first to introduce intensive methods of cultivation in the mid-nineteenth century. "The ant-like Chinese have transformed the sterile sand into the most fertile black earth," wrote a visitor to the Bay Area shortly after the Civil War. "All the fruits and vegetables, raspberries and strawberries, under the care of the Chinese gardeners grow to a fabulous size. I have seen strawberries as large as small pears, heads of cabbage four times the size of European heads, and pumpkins the size of our wash tubs." Soon landowners were paying "wheelbarrow brigades" of Chinese workers to

Chinese field workers in southern California, c. 1880. The Huntington Library, San Marino, California.

build dikes, dig irrigation canals, and introduce row crop agriculture to the delta region of the state's Central Valley. A commentator in California's *Overland Monthly* noted in 1869 that "the descendants of the people who drained those almost limitless marshes on either side of their own swiftly-flowing Yellow River, and turned them into luxuriant fields, are able to do the same thing on the banks of the Sacramento and the San Joaquin." Chinese tenants in the delta were the first farmers in the West to produce and market commercial crops of potatoes, asparagus, strawberries, and sugar beets, leading the way in the transformation of California's wheat fields and cattle ranges into orchards, vineyards, and spreading acres of row crops.[41]

Harvesting these diverse crops demanded an army of nearly two hundred thousand migrant workers. Thousands of men tramped from place to place, following routes determined by the pattern of ripening crops, beginning perhaps by picking winter lettuce in the irrigated fields of the Imperial Valley near the Mexican border, moving to the navel orange groves of the southern California citrus belt, then to the pea fields of the Bay Area in the spring, the berry and fruit orchards of the Salinas valley in summer, the vineyards of the humid Sacramento valley in September, finally ending the year picking cotton in the arid fields of the San Joaquin valley in October and November. Chinese men originally made up about half of this migrant army, but the radical decline in immigration from China after the passage of the Exclusion Act forced growers to search elsewhere for workers. After the Spanish-American War of 1898 thousands of immigrant farmworkers began to arrive from the Philippines, the Hawaiian Islands, and especially from Japan and Mexico. By the eve of World War I, Asian and Mexican workers made up about half of the migrant farm laborers in California.

The IWW sought to organize the migrant workers of California just as they did the harvesters of the Great Plains. In 1913, in the Sacramento valley town of Wheatland, an armed posse of growers and sheriff's deputies attacked striking hop pickers and Wobbly leaders; in the resulting melee four men were killed, two strikers, a sheriff, and the county attorney. In a climate of fear and repression, the IWW called on farmworkers to "depend on [your] own individual action to make every kick count." Growers reported numerous incidents of "labor sabotage," from fruit trees killed with poison spikes to barns and outbuildings torched and burned. The IWW, declared California's governor, was "an organization that has for its purpose the destruction of property, of crops, of human life, and of the government itself." The federal campaign of repression against Wobbly leaders in 1917 was highly effective in enforcing a decade of "labor peace" in the California countryside.[42]

Growers were convinced that the best way to defeat such organizing was to increase the proportion of immigrant workers in their fields. Because of immigrants' subordinate place in the ethnic and racial hierarchy, growers got away with paying them substandard wages and subjecting them to horrible working conditions. This "dual labor system" was a critical part of the institutional social structure of the West. One San Joaquin valley employer candidly explained his preference for Mexican hands. "We can control them at night behind bolted gates," he declared, and "make them work under armed guards in the field." In short, he asserted, "we want Mexicans because we can treat them as we cannot treat any other living men." In 1917 the administration of President Woodrow Wilson agreed to suspend the head tax and literacy test for Mexicans crossing into the United States and at the urging of western growers added provisions for Mexican contract labor to the Immigration Act of the same year. Already thousands of Mexicans were fleeing the revolutionary violence that had been tearing their country apart since 1910. During the years of World War I alone, more than a hundred thousand Mexicans entered the United States.[43]

One of them was nine-year-old Francisco Chico, who crossed at El Paso with his refugee family in 1918. A few weeks later, in a crowded immigrant camp on the Rio Grande, his mother became one of the thousands of victims who died in the great influenza pandemic of that year. His father was able to find work in an Arizona copper mine, but he was killed two years later in an industrial accident. At age twelve Francisco suddenly was thrust into the role of breadwinner for his grandparents and three younger siblings. Together they hitched a ride across the desert to southern California, where the boy found work picking oranges for a dollar a day. For immigrants like the Chicos, the American West was once again operating as a "safety valve"— but in ways that Horace Greeley could scarcely have imagined.

FURTHER READING

Sucheng Chan, *This Bittersweet Soil: The Chinese in California Agriculture, 1860–1910* (1986)
Cecilia Danysk, *Hired Hands: Labour and the Development of Prairie Agriculture, 1880–1930* (1995)
Gilbert C. Fite, *The Framer's Frontier, 1865–1900* (1966)
Dee Garceau, *The Important Things of Life: Women, Work, and Family in Sweetwater County, Wyoming, 1880–1929* (1997)
Michael Kazin, *The Populist Persuasion: An American History* (1995)
Don Mitchell, *The Lie of the Land: Migrant Workers and the California Landscape* (1996)
Paula M. Nelson, *After the West Was Won: Homesteaders and Town-Builders in Western South Dakota, 1900–1917* (1986)
Jeffrey Ostler, *Prairie Populism: The Fate of Agrarian Radicalism in Kansas, Nebraska, and Iowa, 1880–1892* (1993)
Nigel Anthony Sellars, *Oil, Wheat, and Wobblies: The Industrial Workers of the World in Oklahoma, 1905–1930* (1998)
Fred A. Shannon, *The Farmer's Last Frontier, Agriculture, 1860–1897* (1945)
Henry Nash Smith, *Virgin Land: The American West as Symbol and Myth* (1950)
Elinore Pruitt Stewart, *Letters of a Woman Homesteader* (1914)
Walter Prescott Webb, *The Great Plains* (1931)
William Appleman Williams, *The Roots of the Modern American Empire: A Study of the Growth and Shaping of Social Consciousness in a Marketplace Society* (1969)

12

A Search for Community

Americans have always had itching feet. The movement of people from one place to another is one of the most important factors in our history. By the time of the Revolution the pressing desire for *elbow room* was so strong that in typical American communities in all regions of the country at least four of every ten households packed up and left every ten years. High rates of geographic mobility have continued to characterize our national life ever since.

"Many of our neighbors are true backwoodsmen, always fond of moving," John Woods of southern Illinois noted in 1820. Among these "extensive travelers, to have resided in three or four states, and several places in each state, is not uncommon." His observation is borne out by the migration histories of the residents of Sugar Creek, a pioneer community in central Illinois founded in the second decade of the nineteenth century. Eighty percent of arriving families had made at least one previous move across state lines, 35 percent two or more. Similarly, eight in ten of the families who traveled the Overland Trail to Oregon and California had already made at least one interstate move, many had made several, and a substantial minority had been almost continuously in motion.[1]

What kinds of communities could form in the West with so many men and women moving in and out? On the frontier, wrote Timothy Flint, Yankee minister and longtime western observer, "everything shifts under your eye. The present occupants sell, pack, depart. Strangers replace them. Before they have gained the confidence of their neighbors, they hear of a better place, pack up, and follow their precursors. This circumstance adds to the instability of connexions." But there was considerably more social continuity than the raw statistics of mobility suggested. In the Sugar Creek community, for example, a quarter of the early settlers were what western writer Wallace Stegner calls "stickers," laying down roots and living out their lives in the area. Three-quarters of their children and grandchildren also made permanent homes in the community, most marrying the descendants of other sticker families. Quietly, people were weaving kinship connections and consolidating their lands. By 1860, four decades after its founding, community life in Sugar Creek was dominated by this interconnected group of sticker families.[2]

The riddle of community in the American West is solved by recognizing the coexistence of both the movers, a transient majority who farmed for a time before pushing on, and the stickers, a minority of men and women who persisted in the area, intermarried, and passed farm land down to their descendants. The settlers "are not always in motion," wrote the early western writer James Hall in the 1830s. "They remain for years in one spot, forming the mass of the settled population, and giving a tone to the institutions of the country; and at each remove, a few are left behind, who cling permanently to the soil, and bequeath their landed possessions to their posterity." Posterity and landed possessions—family and land—played a role equal to migration in shaping the character of western communities.[3]

Rural life in the great open spaces of the trans-Mississippi West was filled with hard work, monotony, and often stultifying isolation. What romantic travelers might describe as boundless skies, billowing grain, and the soft warmth of a kitchen fire could appear quite different to men and women laboring under the hot sun, battling to save their crops from drought and grasshoppers, or toiling long hours over a hot stove. Nowhere were the physical hardships more starkly revealed than in the lives of pioneer women. Hamlin Garland, raised on an Iowa homestead, looked upon his graying, wrinkled mother, old long before her time, and thought back over her frontier life. "My heart filled with bitterness and rebellion, bitterness against the pioneering madness which had scattered our family, and rebellion toward my father who had kept my mother always on the border, working like a slave."[4]

It was social isolation, however, not movement per se, that took the greatest toll on women. On earlier frontiers the distance between farms had been an obstacle to community, but on the Great Plains it became an overwhelming problem. "There were few settlers in the valley at that time," one woman recalled of her early years in west Texas, "and it would be two or three months at a time that Mother and I would not see another white woman." Farm or ranch wives might be surrounded by husbands, children, and hired hands, but the companionship of other women was hard to come by. "I feel quite lonesome & solitary," one woman confided to her diary. "My spirits are depressed. I have very little female society." Journalist Eugene Victor Smalley was appalled by the isolation of homesteaders on the northern plains in the 1890s: "Each family must live mainly to itself, and life, shut up in the little wooden farmhouses, cannot well be very cheerful." The loneliness affected the children, too.

Farm cooks on the Odegaard Ranch near Quincy, Washington. Photograph by O. H. Henderson, 1912. Historical Photograph Collections, Washington State University Libraries.

"Mamma, will we always have to live here?" a young boy of southwestern Kansas asked his mother. She shook her head yes, and he cried out desperately, "and will we have to die here, too?"[5]

The struggle to make and sustain connections between isolated western households—the work of constructing a community—was perhaps the most difficult of all pioneer tasks. Communities drew energy from numerous connections. Neighbors exchanged work and participated in barn raisings or harvesting, women sewed and quilted together, and men worked on road crews, played on local baseball teams, or joined voluntary organizations—all face-to-face ties that bind. One of the first tasks, strikingly consistent and everywhere compelling, was organizing a school. Teachers were most frequently young women, one of the few occupations open to them. Doris Elder Butler of Oregon remembered that "when a girl finished high school, if she had no other definite plans"—getting married, she meant—"it was expected that she would go out into the country to teach school, and it seemed that everyone even remotely concerned took it for granted that I would follow that custom." She did. Schoolmarms not only instructed the children but played a role as community organizers. The one-room schoolhouse often did joint duty as a community center.[6]

Schoolteacher and students on the plains, c. 1880. National Archives.

Groups of like-minded families might use the schoolhouse as a meeting place for religious services. Little ecumenical congregations formed, bringing together people of various Protestant views, and sometimes even included Catholics. Eventually the most popular denominations founded churches of their own. Building and running churches brought experience in getting things done, and common beliefs and rituals helped to build sustaining bonds of affection. Religion was the greatest ally of the pioneers in the formation of western communities.

American denominations turned their attention to the frontier in the first years of the new nation. The Presbyterians and the Congregationalists, the two largest organizations of the Revolutionary era, joined forces in 1801 in a "Plan of Union," designed to coordinate the western expansion of their churches. But their seminaries were never able to supply the demand for ministers to the rapidly growing West, and their missionaries were easily scandalized at unsettled frontier conditions, quick to moralize about violence, drinking, and gambling—making it difficult for them to win western hearts and minds. Other sects were more adaptable. Although the Baptists believed that an educated ministry was a good thing, they hardly considered a college degree a prerequisite to godliness, and the church authorized the use of untrained and unsalaried lay preachers. This army of organizers founded hundreds of Baptist congregations throughout the West. The Methodists were also particularly effective. Francis Asbury, the first Methodist bishop in the United States, invented the institution of the "circuit rider," a preacher who sallied forth with his Bible to do battle with frontier irreligion and isolation. As a result the Methodists became the

Kansas baptism, c. 1870. Kansas State Historical Society, Topeka.

fastest-growing denomination of the early Republic, expanding from fewer than a thousand members at the time of the Revolution to more than a quarter-million by the Civil War.

The conversion of the West largely depended on the work of such itinerant preachers, men who understood and sympathized with pioneer conditions, who "endured extreme hardships, gained little gratitude for their sacrifices, and frequently found an early grave," writes historian David Kimbrough. The archetypal western circuit rider was Peter Cartwright, who was converted to Methodism when he was a teenager at the opening of the nineteenth century, then rode the circuits throughout the Old Northwest until his death in 1872. The established eastern denominations, Cartwright believed, "had no adaptation to the country or people" of the West. "The great mass of our Western people wanted a preacher who could mount a stump, a block, or old log, or stand in the bed of a wagon, and without note or manuscript, quote, expound, and apply the word of God to the hearts and consciences of the people." In Cartwright's mind religious and civic responsibility were indistinguishable. "Yes my friends," he declared near the end of his long life, "for seventy long years, amid appalling difficulties and dangers, I have waged an incessant warfare against the world, the flesh, and the devil and all other enemies of the Democratic party."[7]

The fire of religious enthusiasm in men like Cartwright was first sparked in 1801 at a place called Cane Ridge in central Kentucky. At this "Great Revival" a crowd of some twenty thousand country folk came together to pray, sing, and get saved in the open air. It was the prototype for thousands of "camp meetings," ubiquitous in the nineteenth-century West. In late summer—after the crops had been "laid by" and before the intense activity of the harvest—dozens of families converged on some shady grove, many prepared to stay for several days or even weeks. "A camp meeting," one observer wrote, "is the most mammoth picnic possible. As at a barbecue, the very heart and soul of hospitality and kindness is wide open and poured freely forth." But something more important than mere socializing was going on, something special and awe-inspiring. As one frontier preacher wrote, the occasion offered an opportunity "for the mind to disentangle itself of worldly care, and rise to an undistracted contemplation of spiritual realities." The milling crowds, the campfires casting an eerie light through the grove at evening, the preaching, the singing, the enthusiastic reaction of those being saved—all heightened the sense of the extraordinary that suffused the successful camp meeting. It was an occasion for binding together groups of people, a sacred process of community organizing.[8]

As churches formed the founding members often signed covenants that formally bound them together. The covenant of the Buck Run Church in Kentucky, for example, spoke the language of *communitas:* the members solemnly agreed to "watch over each other in brotherly tenderness," to edify one another, to succor the weak, to bear each other's burdens, and to hold in common all "hands and hearts." These were the strongest bonds a community could claim. The ideal of the small, close-knit community was carried deep in the minds of most settlers, and a covenanted community was a sacred enterprise, reaching down to the smallest detail of helping one's neighbor when in trouble or gone astray.[9]

The strongest example of a covenanted community in the trans-Mississippi West was the Church of Jesus Christ of Latter-day Saints, a group better known as the Mormons. Their epic exodus of the late 1840s took them from Illinois to the shores of the Great Salt Lake, where they planted several dozen communities. They were strongly driven by a theological principle they knew as "the Gathering," the imperative to build a new Zion, a communal utopia, in the American wilderness. In order to build the largest possible gathering in the desert, Mormon leader Brigham Young and his advisers dispatched missionaries to the East and across the Atlantic to the industrial towns of England and the farms of Scandinavia. Their preaching was spectacularly successful, and communal dreams were soon pulling thousands of converts to Salt Lake. So heavy was the migration, and so short the supply of mules and wagons, that Young even organized a series of "handcart brigades," with emigrants themselves pulling inexpensive carts loaded with their possessions. In 1859 two of these brigades were caught in early winter blizzards and at least two hundred people froze to death, the single worst disaster in the history of the Overland Trail. The handcart brigades were discontinued, but the migration to Salt Lake continued unabated. By 1880 some one hundred thousand Mormons were living in more than 350 communities scattered across the inland desert. Brigham Young envisioned the creation of a Mormon empire called "Deseret," stretching from Idaho to Arizona, from Utah to the California coast.

One of those communities was the little town of Alpine, founded in 1860 in the western foothills of the Wasatch Mountains, south of Salt Lake City. Most of its settlers came from England, urban workers whose lives had been torn asunder by the upheaval of the Industrial Revolution. In Alpine they created a close and supportive rural community, huddling their homes beside a great common field where the people labored in common. The community of Alpine, writes historian Dean May, "drew nearly all adults into some type of voluntary activity that caused them almost daily to talk to, work with, contend with, and in time form enduring ties to others in the settlement." Whereas other western places had difficulty holding on to their residents for more than a few years, Alpine was a sticker community. At the turn of the century, forty years after its founding, representatives of every one of its founding families still lived in the village.[10]

The Mormons were not only communal but strongly practical. Most of Brigham Young's divine revelations, and certainly his leadership, concerned economic matters. Joseph Smith's early doctrines of stewardship and consecration were coupled with a Horatio Alger ideal: every herdboy expected to become a prosperous patriarch. The Mormons' economic system was in fact a bootstrap operation. There was no foreign or eastern capital available for development, but the church devoted its own resources to setting up sugar beet factories and mining smelters, assigning new recruits to work in those industries. The church became the owner of mercantile outlets, sugar and woolen factories, and a bank and a life insurance company, as well as a major stockholder of railroads. The Mormons succeeded spectacularly, proof to them of God's blessings. Communitarian theology was happily wedded with economic development.

The federal government created the territory of Utah and appointed Brigham Young governor. But federal officials sent to administer the territory found to their chagrin that the Mormon church retained the real power and that nonbelievers ("gentiles" in Mormon parlance) were excluded. They accused the Mormons of running a "theocracy," and they were partly right. Before his murder, Joseph Smith himself had termed the Mormon system a "theo-democracy," in which voters were asked to confirm God's will as revealed to the church hierarchy.

The conflict between Mormons and gentiles increased greatly in 1852 when the church announced that one of its fundamental tenets was "plural marriage." Rumors of this practice had been one of the causes for the Mormon troubles in Illinois,

Mormon family in Utah. Photograph by A. J. Russell, c. 1869. Beinecke.

and this acknowledgment that the church indeed encouraged polygamy produced another firestorm of controversy that would burn for half a century. Americans focused on the extraordinary cases—like Brigham Young's marriage to twenty-seven women and his paternity of fifty-six children. But he was hardly a typical Mormon. In its heyday no more than 15 percent of Mormon families practiced polygamy, and two-thirds of these plural marriages involved just two wives. The extent of polygamy among the Mormons has been greatly exaggerated. Still, plural marriage was woven into the fabric of the Mormon community, part of the Saints' conception of their distinctive way of life.

In 1856 polygamy went onto the nation's political agenda when the newly formed Republican Party included in its political platform a condemnation of "those twin relics of barbarism—polygamy and slavery." The next year, concluding that the federal territorial government was a sham—that real power was located within the hierarchy of the Mormon church—President James Buchanan ordered a federal military expedition to Utah to bring the Saints into line. With the memory of persecutions in Missouri and Illinois still fresh, the Mormons prepared to burn Salt Lake City and flee into the desert. At the last minute negotiators for both sides narrowly avoided armed conflict, but not before an agitated group of Mormon vigilantes attacked a wagon train of troublesome Missourians at a spot in Utah called Mountain Meadows, killing 120 men, women, and children. Eventually the vigilante leader, John D. Lee, was executed by federal authorities.

The controversy over polygamy continued, however. After the Civil War, feminist advocates of woman suffrage argued that the Mormons presented a case study in the consequences of women's disenfranchisement. If only Mormon women had the vote, they argued, surely they would "do away with the horrible institution of polygamy." Catching wind of this, Brigham Young sensed immediately that he could turn it to Mormon advantage. In 1870 the Utah territorial legislature passed the first universal woman suffrage bill in the nation. Feminists were overjoyed, and Susan B. Anthony and Elizabeth Cady Stanton traveled to Utah to congratulate Mormon women. But the mood shifted as Mormon women, in election after election, voted exactly as Mormon men did. Gradually plural wives stopped being seen as victims and began being portrayed as dupes. Proclaiming that "woman suffrage in Utah means only woman suffering," the opponents of votes for women seized the issue as a cautionary tale—married women were incapable of being independent, and votes for women inevitably degraded the electoral process. It was years before the woman suffrage movement recovered from this public relations disaster.[11]

Although federal laws proscribing polygamy were passed in 1862 and 1874, the Edmunds Act of 1882 was the first legislation to stipulate severe penalties for polygamists. Armed with this statute, federal authorities began arresting Mormon men for "unlawful cohabitation," imprisoning more than a thousand of them over the next decade. But the Mormon hierarchy refused to relent. In 1887 Congress turned up the heat yet again by passing legislation disincorporating the Mormon church, confiscating its real estate, and abolishing women's suffrage in Utah. The struggle against polygamy widened into a war against "theo-democracy" in Utah. Facing institutional collapse, in 1890 the Mormon hierarchy agreed to the abolition of polygamy in practice (though not in theory), and in 1896 Congress finally voted to admit Utah to the union of states. It had been a long and bitter struggle, which the Mormons would always regard as one more evidence of implacable hostility toward their religious beliefs and their communitarian experiment.

In 1879 yet another mass exodus to the western promised land took place, this one by thousands of African Americans from the Old Southwest. The background of this dramatic episode lay in the failure of southern land reform after the Civil War. "Forty acres and a mule"—land and the means to work it—was the cry that echoed throughout the communities of former slaves in the South. In 1866 Congress passed a Southern Homestead Act, extending the terms of the western bill to freedmen and women in the South, but what little remained of the public domain there was swampy, barren land, far from transportation links, and in the end only a few thousand people benefited from this program. Real land reform would require the confiscation of large plantations and the redistribution of land to the men and women

The Spees family, homesteaders near Westerville, Colorado, c. 1880. Denver Public Library, Western History Department.

who had worked the land for years without compensation. "Perhaps never in American history," writes V. Jacque Voegeli, "has the federal government had a better opportunity both to mitigate racial intolerance in the South and to emancipate the freedmen from the heritage of slavery." But neither Congress nor the southern reconstruction governments were willing to commit themselves to such a radical violation of private property rights. After Republican reconstruction governments gave way to Democrat "redeemer" regimes, followed by the final withdrawal of federal troops from the South in 1877, many African Americans in the Old Southwest began to look west for a better future.[12]

Freedmen and women would have to "repeat the history of the Israelites," declared one assembly of black Alabamians, and "seek new homes beyond the reign and rule of Pharaoh." Benjamin Singleton, a former Tennessee slave, led a group of African Americans to an agrarian colony in western Kansas in 1875, and three years later he circulated broadsides throughout the Old Southwest exhorting other freedmen and women to join him in an even bigger venture. Singleton's plan called for the orderly migration of several hundred families, but the word of mouth soon grew into wild rumors—that there was free land for ex-slaves in Kansas and that the federal government would provide free transportation and supplies. Suddenly, in the spring of 1879, thousands of African Americans throughout the Old Southwest packed up and headed for the fabled land of John Brown—by steamboat, wagon, and foot. "I am anxious to reach your state," one black Louisianian wrote to John Pierce St. John, the governor of Kansas, "because of the sacredness of her soil washed by the blood of humanitarians for the cause of freedom." Within a few short weeks more than twenty thousand "Exodusters," as they called themselves, flooded into the state. Kansans rose to the occasion. "Kansas has a history devoted to liberty," proclaimed Governor St. John, and its citizens would not deny the freedmen and women in their hour of need, for "when the life of the Nation was in danger, the blood of the negro mingled with our blood to sustain the Union." A hurriedly organized state relief association assisted several thousand Exodusters to settle a dozen communities in western Kansas and several more in Indian Territory (what would later become the state of Oklahoma). Eventually some forty black towns were established on the southern plains.[13]

One of the best known was Nicodemus, on the upper Solomon River, where some 150 black families had built a community by the mid-1880s. Like most settlers, the people of Nicodemus found themselves poorly prepared for the arid conditions of the western plains, and many moved on during the drought and economic hard times at the century's end. A group of stickers, however, found jobs on the railroad or took work with neighboring white farmers as hired hands, and the community survived into the twentieth century. Grant Cushinberry, born and raised there, remembered that the heart of the community was the African Methodist Episcopal church. "Momma didn't allow us to dance or play no music on Sunday," he told an interviewer, "every living soul had to go to church." After the service his mother "always brought some old preacher home for dinner." At these gatherings the family would retell stories of the suffering that had forced them out of Egypt. Cushinberry vividly recounted a family tale of the Ku Klux Klan coming to the cabin of an uncle late one night. Dragging the man's pregnant wife into the yard, they strung her up by the heels and "cut the baby out of her stomach." Her husband grabbed his shotgun and blasted the nightriders to kingdom come, "then he ran all day and all night until he got to Kansas." Such stories are powerful agents of community.[14]

Rather than homestead the dry prairies, most Exodusters elected to remain in one or another of the previously settled Kansas towns, where they found work as laborers or domestics. By the mid-1880s, for example, more than three hundred African Americans were living "across the tracks" in the town of Manhattan. "We were all pushed back over there," remembered Dorothy Fulghem, a longtime black resident. But segregation had its benefits, she recalled. "We had our own churches"—three African-American congregations that provided a rallying point for community life—and "we were raised in the church," Fulghem remembered. "We were sort of like one family," said another black woman, "We just all stuck together." The black congregations led the unsuccessful opposition to a school board plan to segregate the town's public schools. "Compel us to associate with the negro," warned one white resident, "and we become a slave in turn." Soon Frederick Douglass School opened for the black children across the tracks.[15]

In spite of their historic "devotion to liberty," turn-of-the-century Kansans joined the rest of the country in establishing separate and unequal institutions for minorities. This was the world into which writer, photographer, and filmmaker Gordon Parks was born in 1912. Nearly all of the public facilities in his hometown of Fort Scott, Kansas, were segregated. "The grade school was segregated but the high school wasn't," Parks writes in his autobiography, "mainly because the town fathers couldn't scrounge up enough money to build a separate one. But even inside those walls of meager learning, black students had to accommodate themselves to the taste of salt. The class advisers warned us against seeking higher education, adding, 'You were meant to be maids and porters.'" Even after achieving great success in his profession, Fort Scott remained for Parks "the place I attack in dreams." Parks later wrote a poem in which he tried to summarize his ambivalent feelings about his birthplace.

> I would miss this Kansas land that I was leaving.
> Wide prairie filled with green and cornstalk; the flowering apple,
> Tall elms and oaks beside the glinting streams,
> Rivers rolling quiet in long summers of sleepy days
> For fishing, for swimming, for catching crawdad beneath the rock. . . .
> Junebugs, swallowtails, red robin and bobolink,
> Nights filled of soft laughter, fireflies and restless stars. . . .
> Yes, all this I would miss—along with the fear, hatred and violence
> We blacks had suffered upon this beautiful land.[16]

In 1985 the Native Sons and Daughters of Kansas selected Parks as "Kansan of the Year." During the presentation ceremony in Topeka, sitting with the governor and one of the state's United States senators, Parks listened as the master of ceremonies read his Kansas poem aloud. But the reading stopped short, omitting the crucial last two lines. "My heart quailed and filled with governable fury," Parks wrote afterward. He arose, walked to the podium, and read the deleted lines to a thunderstruck audience. Going back to Kansas was "like returning to a battlefield where a truce has been signed," he mused. "It will always be the identity of my brutal past."[17]

———

Persecution drove the flight of the Mormons and the Exodusters, yet they were both migrations of hope. The West, however, was also the site of forced removals and relocations—migrations of terror. The Cherokees' Trail of Tears was repeated many times, not only for eastern Indians like the Seminoles or the Sauks but for the native peoples of the plains and mountains, forced to relocate to godforsaken corners of In-

Chief Joseph of the Nez Percé. Photograph by William H. Jackson, c. 1880. Special Collections Division, University of Washington Libraries.

dian Territory or squeezed onto small "reserved" portions of their former home-lands. One memorable migration of terror took place in the Pacific Northwest in the fall of 1877, when the federal government insisted that all the Nez Percé Indians re-locate to a confined reservation. About a quarter of them refused, a group of young warriors led a bloody raid on nearby settlers, and the army attacked. At that point the Nez Percé chiefs decided that their only alternative to destruction was flight. They led fifty fighting men and three hundred women and children over a desperate trail of more than thirteen hundred miles through the rugged mountains of Idaho, Wyoming, and Montana, in the hope of reaching Canada, and successfully beat back three full-scale army attacks. Just fifty miles from freedom they were surrounded. Af-ter five days of watching his people freeze and starve, Chief Joseph, the only surviv-ing leader, surrendered. From the depth of feeling, he offered a moving eulogy to three centuries of warfare: "Hear me, my chiefs. I am tired; my heart is sick and sad. From where the sun now stands I will fight no more forever."[18]

The end of three centuries of warfare found western Indians confined to a series of reservations. These reservations were thought to be temporary expedients, not

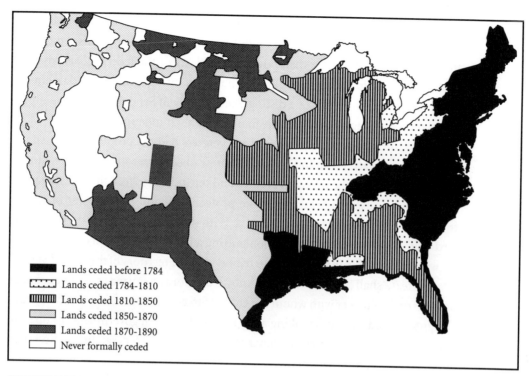

Lands ceded before 1784
Lands ceded 1784-1810
Lands ceded 1810-1850
Lands ceded 1850-1870
Lands ceded 1870-1890
Never formally ceded

INDIAN LAND CESSIONS

permanent institutions. Late nineteenth-century Indian policy was premised on the assumption that Indians would become farmers, Christians, and citizens. The task, as Sioux agent Thomas J. Galbraith put it, was "to make white men of them." He provided a succinct summary of federal goals for Indians during the era that stretched from the 1870s to the 1930s: "weaken and destroy their tribal relations and individualize them by giving each a separate home and having them subsist by industry." The goal of federal policy, according to Galbraith, was "to break up the community system." At the same time that western pioneers were building new communities in the West the federal government was using its power to destroy ancient ones.[19]

The first step was the elimination of all vestiges of Indian sovereignty. The limited sovereignty of Indian nations had been the foundation of federal policy since the first days of the Republic, enacted into law in the Indian Intercourse Act (1790) and confirmed by the Supreme Court in the famous case *Worcester v. Georgia* (1832). This was all to be swept away. Ely Parker, commissioner of Indian Affairs during the presidency of Ulysses S. Grant, condemned the treaty system for falsely impressing the Indians with notions of their own independence. The time had come, he wrote, when "this idea should be dispelled, and the government cease the cruel farce of thus dealing with its helpless and ignorant wards." Indians had never been citizens of the

Republic but constituents of their own tribes or nations, subject to government, law, and custom administered by their own authorities. Without institutions of their own they became nothing more than powerless subjects of the federal government—"helpless wards," in Parker's apt phrase. The sad irony here was that Parker himself was an Iroquois, a member of a distinguished family of Senecas, and he quietly ignored the long struggle of his people to maintain their independence.[20]

In 1870 the Supreme Court ruled that Congress had the power to supersede or even to annul treaties with Indian tribes. As one observer wrote at the time, the decision "emboldened the whites to predict, and the Indians to fear, that the new principle would be used to break down the protection found in the terms of Indian treaties." That is precisely what happened. With this green light from the Court, the next year Congress passed a resolution putting an end to the system of treaty-making with Indians. "No Indian nation or tribe within the territory of the United States," read the text, "shall [henceforth] be acknowledged or recognized as an independent nation, tribe, or power with whom the United States may contract by treaty." In 1885 Congress passed legislation taking away the right of tribal governments to operate under their own traditional, customary law and extended federal jurisdiction over serious crimes committed on reservations.[21]

The legal niceties arranged, there followed an unprecedented federal assault on Indian autonomy. "The preservation of good order on the reservations," declared the commissioner of Indian Affairs, "demands that some active measure should be taken to discourage and, if possible, put a stop to the demoralizing influence of heathenish rites." Federal Indian agents were directed to undertake a sustained campaign of forced cultural modification—outlawing Indian customs they considered "savage and barbarous," like the Sun Dance of the Plains Indians or the "pagan, horrible, sadistic, and obscene" rituals of the Pueblos. The United States was doing precisely what other imperial powers had done to their colonial subjects. In their Pacific island colonies, for example, the French outlawed singing and dancing at native religious ceremonies, while in southern Africa the British imprisoned "witch doctors." Colonial authorities, stated a manual of the British colonial service in 1861, "have the right—in virtue of the relative position of civilized and Christian men to savages—to enforce abstinence from immoral and degrading practices [and] to compel outward conformity to the law of what we regard as better instructed reason." These similarities were acknowledged at the time. The United States was "a great colonial power," wrote Harvard history professor Albert Bushnell Hart, and "our Indian agents have a status very like that of British in the native states of India."[22]

Cultural imperialism was also notable in the curriculum of reservation schools. "If Indian children are to be civilized they must learn the language of civilization," ruled the secretary of the interior, and the Indian Bureau issued regulations that "no textbooks in the vernacular [the local native language] will be allowed in any school."

A group of Chiricahua Apache students on their arrival at Carlisle Indian School and four months later, c. 1890. The Huntington Library, San Marino, California.

This, too, was a familiar colonial practice. In a similar vein a British official in South Africa wrote that "primitive customs and taboos must go [and] with them must also go the native mode of life and probably the language which was adapted to that life." Even more severe was the practice of sending children to Indian boarding schools, most famously Carlisle Indian School in Pennsylvania, founded in 1879 by Richard Henry Pratt, a former commander of Indian scouts. The girls were given Anglo-American names, dressed as Victorian ladies, and taught to play the piano. The boys were organized into military companies and drilled in uniforms.[23]

"They told us that Indian ways were bad," Sun Elk, a resident of Taos Pueblo, remembered years later of his boarding school experience. "They said we must get civilized. . . . The books told how bad the Indians had been to the white men—burning their towns and killing their women and children. But I had seen white men do that to Indians. We all wore white man's clothes and ate white man's food and went to white man's churches and spoke white man's talk. And so after a while we also began to say Indians were bad. We laughed at our own people and their blankets and cooking pots and sacred societies and dances." After seven years of education Sun Elk came home. "It was a warm summer evening when I got off the train at Taos station. The first Indian I met, I asked him to run out to the pueblo and tell my family I was home. The Indian couldn't speak English, and I had forgotten my Pueblo language."[24]

On the reservation itself, said one federal official, Indians were to be placed "in positions where they can be controlled and finally compelled by sheer necessity to resort to agricultural labor *or starve*." By design the government supplied only basic necessities. Indeed, the goods issued to reservation Indians—who had been deprived of their ability to hunt—were the equivalent of only half the daily rations distributed to American troops in the field. Hunger and poverty became constant facts of reservation life. But necessity did not transform Indians into farmers. Most reservation land was too barren or too arid to support agriculture. And there was significant resistance from Indians who had been accustomed to a completely different way of life. "The whites were always trying to make the Indians give up their life and live like white men," said the Sioux chief Big Eagle, "go to farming, work hard, and do as they did—and the Indians did not know how to do that, and did not want to anyway."[25]

The most destructive blow to Indian communities, however, was administered by reformers, men and women who thought of themselves as "Friends of the Indians." Their solution to "the Indian problem" was a program called "allotment in severalty." Collective ownership of land—the material base of Indian communities—would give way to individual ownership. Reservations would be divided up and "allotted" in small parcels to each Indian head of household. Once the family had demonstrated its responsibility by improving its property, they would become naturalized

American citizens. "Selfishness," declared Senator Henry Dawes of Massachusetts, "is at the bottom of civilization. Till this people will consent to give up their lands, and divide them among their citizens so that each can own the land he cultivates, they will not make much more progress." After allotment, reformers believed, tribes would wither away and Indians would be absorbed into the nation as individuals.[26]

The popular writer Helen Hunt Jackson greatly strengthened the reform cause. Widowed and bereaved by the loss of her two sons while still a young woman, Jackson removed for her health in the 1870s to Colorado, where she met and married a Quaker banker and began publishing poems and stories. Struck by the wretched plight of western Indians, Quakerly concern motivated her to research and write an angry exposé, *A Century of Dishonor* (1881), which detailed a history of unjust treatment and broken treaties by the United States. This polemic was followed by her best-selling novel, *Ramona* (1884), a romantic yet tragic tale of the destruction of California's Indians. Jackson's books fueled a growing movement for the reform of Indian policy. Although she died in 1885, her legacy was the Allotment Act, passed by Congress in 1888.

A majority of Indian tribes opposed allotment. The chiefs were interested in "keeping the Indian as he is," wrote Herbert Welsh, president of the Indian Rights Association, "his tribal relations untouched, his reservations intact." Indian leaders, went the conventional wisdom, didn't know what was good for their people. But a majority of western congressmen were enthusiastic supporters of the legislation. The reason was simple. After reservations had been allotted in parcels of 160 acres to Indian families, there would be tens of thousands of acres of "surplus lands," and those would be opened to white settlers. It was a corrupt bargain. Senator Henry M. Teller of Colorado was one of the few who spoke out against the bill. "I want to put upon the record my prophecy in this manner," Teller told his Senate colleagues. "When thirty or forty years shall have passed, and these Indians shall have parted with their title, they will curse the hand that was raised professedly in their defense." The devastating results of allotment were just as Teller had foretold. In 1888 Indian tribes held 138 million acres. By 1934 this domain had been reduced to 47 million.[27]

With armed resistance impossible and their cultures and communities under attack, the Indian people of the West responded with an outburst of visionary religious energy. The Ghost Dance was the final flame of hope before a long period of resignation. This movement recalled the religious resurgences of earlier Indian holy men—the Delaware Prophet Neolin, who inspired Pontiac's Revolt, and Tenskwatawa, the Shawnee Prophet, brother of Tecumseh. The Ghost Dance emerged from the vision of Wovoka, a shaman among the Paiutes of Nevada, who felt himself inspired by the Great Spirit to speak to all Indians. We must act as brothers and

never resort to violence, Wovoka preached. If Indians gave up alcohol, lived simple lives, and dedicated themselves to meditation and prayer, the Great Spirit would restore control of their lives and lands. Wovoka foresaw a day when the white man would disappear, along with his implements—guns, whiskey, and manufactured goods. Dead Indians would then rejoin the living and brothers and sisters would live together in a world "free from misery, death, and disease." Wovoka's followers developed his message into a ritual that included five days of worship by slow dancing and meditation. Impractical and illusory, yet beautiful in its simple pathos, rich in spirituality, and empowered by ethnic memory, Wovoka's was a message of community flowering from the depths of despair. It spread rapidly among the tribes throughout the Far West, suggesting yet again the power of religion as a powerful sustaining bond of community.[28]

Sitting Bull, still an important communal leader of the Sioux, sent emissaries to meet with Wovoka, and they returned to the northern plains in the summer of 1890, inspired by his message. Traditional Sioux people and their chiefs—men like Sitting Bull at the Standing Rock Reservation and Big Foot at Cheyenne River—transformed Wovoka's pacifist message into something far more militant and confrontational. Sioux men, women, and children came together for rituals lasting for several days and nights, singing and dancing themselves into trances. Anthropologist James Mooney, whose century-old study of the movement remains a vital document, translated a Sioux song that he believed "summarized the whole hope of the ghost dance."

> The whole world is coming,
> A nation is coming, a nation is coming,
> The Eagle has brought the message to the tribe.
> The father says so, the father says so.

Over the whole earth they are coming.
The buffalo are coming, the buffalo are coming.
The Crow has brought the message to his tribe,
The father says so, the father says so.

To Indian agents who had been working hard for years to suppress all traces of "pagan" ritual among the Sioux, the Ghost Dance was terrifying. "Indians are dancing in the snow and are wild and crazy," one agent telegraphed his superiors. *"We need protection and we need it now."*[29]

In response the Seventh Cavalry—Custer's old regiment, eager for vengeance—hurried to the reservation, but Sioux ghost dancers, led by Chief Big Foot, took refuge in the unmapped region known as the Bad Lands, in the northwest corner of the Pine Ridge Reservation. Frustrated, federal officials ordered the arrest of all the traditional chiefs. "Let the soldiers come and take me away and kill me," Sitting Bull responded defiantly when told he was to be arrested, but it was Sioux reservation police who came to his door. "We are of the same blood, we are all Sioux, we are relatives," Sitting Bull said, trying to shame them. "If the white men want me to die, they ought not to put up the Indians to kill me." Sitting Bull's friends and family tried to protect him, but in the subsequent skirmish eight men were shot, and afterward Sitting Bull and his seventeen year-old son lay dead on the cold ground.[30]

A few days after Sitting Bull's death, in late December 1890, the Seventh Cavalry caught up with Big Foot and his band of ghost dancers at an encampment on Wounded Knee Creek. A few miles away, in the main Sioux settlement on the Pine Ridge Reservation, a young man named Black Elk learned that the dancers had been surrounded. "I felt that something terrible was going to happen," he later remembered, and "that night I could hardly sleep at all." Early the next morning he awoke to the sound of distant gunfire, "sounds [that] went right through my body," and he and several other young men jumped on their horses and galloped toward Wounded Knee. Reaching a ridge, Black Elk looked down and saw an unforgettable sight—one that will forever haunt Americans of goodwill. "What we saw was terrible," he remembered. "Dead and wounded women and children and little babies were scattered all along there where they had been trying to run away. The soldiers had followed along the gulch, as they ran, and murdered them in there."

Sometimes they were in heaps because they had huddled together, and some were scattered all along. Sometimes bunches of them had been killed and torn to pieces where the wagon-guns hit them. I saw a little baby trying to suck its mother, but she was bloody and dead. . . . Men and women and children were heaped and scattered all over the flat at the bottom of the little hill where the soldiers had their wagon-guns, and westward up the dry gulch all the way to the high ridge, the dead women and babies were scattered. When I saw this I wished that I had died too,

Burial of the dead at Wounded Knee. Photograph by George Trager, 1890. Nebraska State Historical Society.

but I was not sorry for the women and children. It was better for them to be happy in the other world, and I wanted to be there too.

The soldiers had been disarming the Sioux when a gun accidentally went off. Trigger-happy troops raked the Indian camp with the murderous fire of four machine guns while the Sioux fought back as they could. The fire left 146 Indians, including 44 women and 18 children, dead on the battlefield. The Seventh Cavalry lost 25 soldiers, most probably killed by the crossfire of their own guns. After the battle a blizzard swept down upon the scene, covering the bodies and freezing their macabre death gestures.[31]

At Wounded Knee the work of community destruction was revealed in all its ghastly horror. "Here in ten minutes an entire community was as the buffalo that bleached on the plains," wrote the western writer Mari Sandoz. "There was something loose in the world that hated joy and happiness as it hated brightness and color, reducing everything to drab agony and gray." In 1903 the Pine Ridge Sioux erected a monument over the mass burial of the Wounded Knee martyrs, a site that for them—indeed for many Americans—has become a shrine to the Indian victims of colonization.[32]

During the second half of the nineteenth century, on the lands confiscated from the Sioux and other Indian communities in the West, immigrants from Europe founded hundreds of new rural communities of their own. "European immigrants are the forgotten people of the American West," writes historian Frederick C. Luebke. In American myth, the frontier was supposed to transform immigrants into generic Americans. But aside from the English and the Canadians—who preferred to fill in the country as individual families, perhaps because they felt comfortable as English-speakers—European immigrants tended to settle the West in groups. Retaining many of their ethnic traditions through the second generation, they didn't fit expectations and were left out of the frontier story. These immigrant villages were also "covenant communities," for in nearly all of them the immigrant church became what historian Kathleen Neils Conzen calls an "institutional rallying point." "Nobody made us build them, and they weren't put up with tax money," Norwegian immigrant farmer Carl Hanson remarked about the Lutheran churches that appeared on the landscape of the northern plains. "We scraped the money together for them, not from our surplus, but out of our poverty, because we needed them." The immigrant church was the institution charged with the responsibility of upholding values and preserving continuity with the premigration past. It offered the first and often only defense against the rapid and total assimilation of immigrant children. Here, too, religion formed the heart of the community.[33]

The Irish offer one example. Often they came West to find work as miners, clustering in the mining districts of states such as Montana, Wyoming, and Nevada, where the proportion of Irish-born greatly exceeded the national average. At the end of the nineteenth century the copper center of Butte was the most Irish city in America. Under the management of Marcus Daly, himself an Irish immigrant, the Anaconda mining operation favored the employment of Irishmen. Butte miners told the joke of the Irishman who sent a letter back home encouraging his brother to come over. "Don't stop in the United States," he wrote, "come right on out to Butte." The Irish community in Butte was rooted in strong kinship ties, ethnic associations such as the Ancient Order of Hibernians, and, most important, the Catholic parish, staffed almost entirely by Irish priests.[34]

German immigrants arriving in Lincoln, Nebraska, c. 1895. Nebraska State Historical Society.

Germans in the West also tended to cluster into ethnic enclaves. Hessians began arriving in Texas during the 1830s, soon after they obtained a grant of land from Stephen Austin. By 1860 more than thirty thousand of them made up the majority in the picturesque Texas hill country, clustered in little farming communities with a Lutheran church nearly always at the center. One can still see the stone churches, houses, and meandering walls they built and on occasion still hear German being spoken by residents in the vicinity of New Braunfels, south of Austin. Other common German destinations were Wisconsin, Minnesota, the Dakotas, and Nebraska, where Catholic Rhinelanders began settling in the 1850s. These were communities of stickers, with remarkable rates of persistence well into the twentieth century. A second-generation German American later recalled how he ended up staying on the family farm in Minnesota. "Dad said, 'I am getting old and I cannot work the farm anymore.' That's how I was hooked with it; I couldn't say no and leave them sit alone. I could have gotten a job somewhere, gone away. But I couldn't do that to my parents." Thousands of other rural sons, of course, had little difficulty saying "no" and leaving the home place for a farther frontier, perhaps an urban one. But the strong sense of kinship and community among these German Americans made the difference.[35]

After the Civil War each of the states and territories of the upper Midwest and northern plains pursued active immigrant recruitment policies, publishing guides in the languages of target groups and sending agents across the Atlantic to pitch the advantages of their lands. They were remarkably successful, for in much of rural Europe a process of agricultural consolidation was throwing tens of thousands of families off their farms. During the last quarter of the nineteenth century from a third

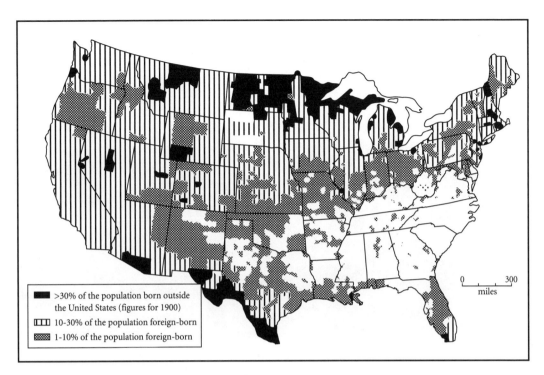

THE FOREIGN-BORN POPULATION IN 1900

to a half of the population of the northern plains was foreign-born, the highest proportion of any region in the nation. The countryside was a patchwork of culturally homogeneous communities of Germans, Czechs, Poles, Russians, Hungarians, and especially Scandinavians.

According to historian Robert Ostergren, church affiliation among the nineteenth-century immigrant communities of rural Minnesota was very high. In Isanti County, fifty miles north of Minneapolis–Saint Paul, more than seven hundred Swedish households made up seven distinct communities, each with its own Lutheran church and pastor. The role of the church as a conservative force cannot be underestimated. Through its ceremonies and its holidays it helped perpetuate the old customs of the homeland. A pastor, newly arrived from Sweden, wrote of how impressed he was "to see the people coming to Church in festive array, with clothes cut according to the ancient style, the man dressed in the leather apron, the woman with the short waist, red stockings, and large shoes." Church-run "Swede schools" supplemented public education, teaching children to sing Swedish songs and to read the Swedish Bible, Swedish history, and Swedish literature. The church also presided over a pattern of in-marriage. Ostergren's research shows that eight of ten marriages in these communities were between men and women of the same congregations. Similar patterns were present within other rural immigrant communities.[36]

Well into the second generation homeland languages continued to be the primary

Norwegian American singers in costume at the Minnesota State Fairgrounds, 1925.
Minnesota Historical Society.

means of communication within these ethnic communities. Compare this with the experience of Scandinavian Mormon converts in Utah. The Mormons frowned on ethnic distinctions, which they thought would fracture their communal unity, and without an immigrant church to perpetuate old cultural traditions, virtually all second-generation Mormon converts spoke English, regardless of their immigrant background. The difference between Utah and the upper Midwest was highlighted by the experience of Mad Anderson, a Mormon missionary of Swedish background, assigned to proselytize among rural Swedes in Minnesota. Missionary work was slow, he wrote home in 1884, because of the "downright shame that young missionaries of Scandinavian descent often are unable to speak the language of their parents and thus are handicapped."[37]

The ability to retain their cultural heritage while becoming American citizens was one of the things that attracted these immigrant communities. As historian Jon Gjerde puts it, they developed a "complementary identity that pledged allegiance to both American citizenship and ethnic adherence." Cultural homogeneity characterized these ethnic communities until the early twentieth century, when to the chagrin of church elders, who associated cultural change with spiritual loss, the third generation began to move more decisively in the direction of assimilation. Swedish congregations in rural Minnesota engaged in a prolonged and divisive debate over whether God could hear prayers in English. During the "Americanization" frenzy of

World War I—when a number of midwestern governors issued proclamations forbidding the public use of any language but English (even on the telephone!)—Swedish churches finally began to hold their worship services in English.[38]

The declining use of homeland languages was a symbol of other assimilative trends, including increased rates of out-migration and intermarriage. One of the most voluble critics of assimilation was Ole Rölvaag, who immigrated from Norway as a young man in 1896, attended St. Olaf College in Minnesota, was tenured as professor of literature there in 1907, and became a famous novelist with the publication of *Giants in the Earth* (1927). In the drive to become "American," he warned fellow Norwegians, they risked losing the "intimate spiritual association with our own people." Lecturing to a class on immigration history he urged his students to "show the greatest faithfulness to your race, to the cultural and spiritual heritage which you have received and which you may receive in still larger measure. You must not erase your racial characteristics in order to become better Americans. You must deepen them if possible." Rölvaag believed that American culture had little to offer except a preoccupation with material success. "I have met with none but crippled souls," he wrote of his encounters with farmers in the Minnesota countryside. "They are dead, dead, living dead! Their highest interests are hogs, cattle and horses. The spiritual life, received of God as the most precious gift, is dead. The sense of beauty, with which they might perceive the wonders and glories of nature, and the beauty in life, has been killed by the cold hand of materialism." In his last novel, *Their Fathers' God* (1931), Rölvaag foresaw a bleak future: "If this process of leveling down, of making everybody alike by blotting out all differences is allowed to continue, America is doomed to become the most impoverished land spiritually on the face of the earth; out of our highly praised melting pot will come a dull, smug complacency, barren of all creative thought and effort. Soon we will have reached the perfect democracy of barrenness."[39]

The barren sameness of western community life was most famously critiqued in novelist Sinclair Lewis's *Main Street* (1920). When Carol Kennicott, Lewis's main character, arrives at Gopher Prairie, it seems scarcely more impressive than a hazel thicket: "There was no dignity in it, nor any hope of greatness. . . . It was a frontier camp. It was not a place to live in, not possibly, not conceivably." Feeling its plainness and flimsiness, Carol walks its length and breadth in just thirty-six minutes. The residents, she concludes, were as "drab as their houses, as flat as their fields." Lewis had grown up in a small prairie town, and he fashioned Gopher Prairie to stand for dozens of similar places, from Peoria to Petaluma. "Main Street," he wrote, "is the culmination of Main Street everywhere." The identical grid pattern, ignoring the terrain, borrowed from Philadelphia because it was regular and sensible. The same false

Main Street, Sioux City, Iowa. Photograph by B. H. Gurnsey, 1869. Beinecke.

fronts dressed up the dry-goods store and the post office, the saloon and the livery stable, the schoolhouse and the church. From the Mississippi valley to the Pacific coast, these towns were like little corn hills—some tall, some short, some with more ears and kernels than others, but from a distance indistinguishable.[40]

For decades Americans had professed to believe that small towns were the best the nation had to offer. Novelist Zona Gale looked back on her Wisconsin hometown with quiet affection. The main street of *Friendship Village* (1908) held memories of tulip beds and twilight bonfires, with people concerned enough to help one another through illness and hard times. For Gale the essence of small town life was fellowship. "In this simple basic emotion," she wrote, "lies my joy in living in this, my village." But Gale's nostalgia seemed terribly old-fashioned in the aftermath of World War I. Lewis's *Main Street*—published the same year the Census Bureau announced that the population of urban America outnumbered rural America for the first time—conveniently marks an attitudinal sea change. Not that Lewis was the first. Preceding him had been Hamlin Garland's realist stories of hard-bitten western farm families in *Main-Traveled Roads* (1891) and Edgar Lee Masters's *Spoon River Anthology* (1914), verses depicting the crimped lives of small town residents. But with *Main Street* the cynical view became mainstream.[41]

The myth of small town life had pictured a homogeneous, classless society in which anyone with ambition, thrift, and diligence could easily move upward. But in fact class was everything in the small town. It was true that during their earliest years class lines were indefinite and social mobility was noticeable. The initial surge of economic expansion into Trempealeau County, Wisconsin, in the 1850s, for example, opened opportunities on every side. By the end of the Civil War, however, those doors had nearly closed. Rigid class lines appeared early nearly everywhere, even in the supposedly wide-open cattle towns of the Great Plains, where within a few years of their founding the richest 20 percent of the population controlled more than 80 percent of the real estate. The working classes were divided between craftworkers, transients, and drifters. African Americans, Mexicans, Asians, and occasionally a few Indians were isolated at the bottom of the social ladder.

Toward the end of the nineteenth century the atmosphere in small western towns seemed increasingly uneasy. The industrial promise of links between farm and market had not been fulfilled; clearly, the railroads served eastern capital. Conflicts within the community grew more overt, especially as the quarter-century of depression from 1873 to 1898 exposed the vulnerability of the poor. The hardening of class lines bred dissatisfaction, and small town newspaper editors had to admit the existence of discord. Social conflict became the rule rather than the exception, and cohesiveness degenerated into narrow morality. Frederick Russell Burnham, who lived in a Midwest small town in the 1870s, thought that most people spent half their time trying to reform someone else in a quiet fervor of "intolerant religiosity." This oppressive, narrow morality—peeping through keyholes—was the cause of Carol Kennicott's rebellion in *Main Street*. Intellectuals fled to the cities and began to describe their former environment as smug, prejudiced, sterile, and joyless.[42]

Much of the trouble stemmed from small town America's resistance to change. Dedicated to prudential virtues and "the good old days," townspeople saw corruption in industrial values and sighed, in the words of poet Vachel Lindsay, "for the sweet life wrenched and torn by thundering commerce, fierce and bare." True, towns often courted small-scale industry in the hope of creating more jobs and revenue in their own precincts. But monopolies beyond their control, large-scale corporations, and intervention by the federal government corroded community autonomy. Turning inward, the residents of small western towns developed intense localism as a shield against unwelcome change. Confronting fears that the "end of the frontier" would bring an end to the assimilation of foreigners, the white middle class of the small town lashed out against "un-American" immigrants. Fear and loathing marked the end of one West and the creation of another.[43]

———

In the American West of the late nineteenth and early twentieth centuries, no immigrants faced more prejudice and hostility than the Chinese and the Japanese. In 1878 a federal judge in California ruled that Chinese immigrants could not become naturalized citizens because they were not "white persons" within the meaning of the Naturalization Act of 1790, a decision extended to the Japanese by the Supreme Court in 1922 and not repealed by legislation until after World War II. Throughout the West, states and localities passed laws denying Asians the right to vote, forbidding their employment by public agencies, and restricting them to residential ghettos. But with the same dream of land ownership and prosperity that motivated other settlers, there were many Asian stickers who raised families and built communities. At least their children became citizens by birth.

Permanent Chinese communities began to appear in the California countryside in the 1860s wherever Chinese workers toiled in the fields and orchards, the first in the extensive delta region of the Sacramento River. "They form little communities among themselves, do their own cooking, live in little camps together," wrote one landlord. "If you can get them this year you can get them next year and the year after. They become attached to your place and they stay with you." Similarly, in the 1870s growers in the citrus belt of southern California began employing Chinese men in their groves and packinghouses. They perfected what became known as the "China pack"—each piece of fruit individually wrapped in tissue paper then carefully packed into a crate, tighter at the edges than at the center, creating a fecund and appealing bulge. It was like a work of art, one grower remembered, "every wrapper smooth, not a wrinkle, and the tissue triangled to a point on top so that when the box was opened it was something to display in a grocer's window." Citrus growers came to depend on the industry and careful work of the Chinese, and soon every town in the citrus belt had its own "Chinatown," usually on the poor side of the tracks.[44]

By the 1870s Chinese workers made up half of California's agricultural workforce. Although they were appreciated by the growers, there were waves of anti-Chinese violence during periods of economic depression. In 1873 white farmworkers in California held rallies demanding the discharge of Chinese laborers. Vigilantes invaded Chinese communities in the delta of the Sacramento valley, forced families to pack up and leave, then burned their homes. The old pioneer John Bidwell, who employed Chinese on his ranch, had his buildings burned after ignoring a threatening note: "You are given notice to discharge your Mongolian help within ten days or suffer the

Anti-Chinese riot in Denver, 1880. Denver Public Library, Western History Department.

consequences." The arsonists were tracked down, convicted, and sentenced, and Bidwell rebuilt. But the night before he was to reopen his operation his buildings were again burned to the ground. In Chico, five Chinese tenant farmers were shot to death and their bodies burned in their cabins. Another episode of violence against the Chinese took place during the terrible depression year of 1893. In several San Joaquin valley towns armed mobs intimidated Chinese workers with pistol shots, and dozens of Chinese men were driven to the railroad station, where they were forced onto departing trains. In the citrus town of Redlands, east of Los Angeles, vigilantes swept into Chinatown one evening in September, looting, burning, and beating residents. Growers denounced the rioters as "hoodlums" and argued that they could not "afford to pay the wages demanded by the whites." But Senator John Miller argued that Chinese workers "can dispense with the comforts of shelter and subsist on the refuse of other men, and grow fat on less than half the food necessary to sustain life in the Anglo-Saxon." Chinese Americans remember this period as "the driving out." By the turn of the century most had relocated to the Chinatowns of the largest western cities, where they found an uncertain refuge.[45]

"Now that the Chinese have been excluded," Methodist missionary Merriman Harris wrote from California in 1888, "there is a demand for cheap labor and it is probable that Japanese laborers will be brought over to supply the demand." He was right. The Japanese government did not allow emigration until the end of the century, so it was not until the 1890s that Japanese men began arriving to seek work on the railroads and especially on the commercial farms of the West. In 1900 Harris reported "an unusually large influx of Japanese to the Pacific coast" and noted that they "go into the country districts and readily find work in the fruit orchards and on the ranches." By 1910 there were more than thirty thousand Japanese farmworkers in California, the single largest ethnic group toiling in what California journalist Carey McWilliams would later call the "factories in the field."[46]

Japanese workers evoked a familiar response from racist westerners. Senator James Phelan, former mayor of San Francisco, declared that white men could not compete with the Japanese because "they know no rest and respect no standards," and he warned his constituents that the Japanese were "rapidly acquiring the most productive lands." Some commentators saw the Japanese as an even greater threat than the Chinese because many of them leased or purchased land of their own. Japanese growers were soon supplying most of the vegetables and much of the fruit sold in the urban markets of California. Reacting to pressures from exclusionists, in 1908 President Theodore Roosevelt negotiated the so-called Gentleman's Agreement with the Japanese government, ending the immigration of Japanese men to the United States. And in 1913 the California legislature prohibited the ownership or long-term leasing of land by aliens of Asian descent, legislation imitated by several other western states. But Japanese immigrants (who called themselves Issei—the first generation in America) were soon shifting the title of their farms to their American-born children (the Nisei), who were citizens, not aliens. By 1920 Japanese farmers, in control of only 1 percent of California's agricultural land, were raising and marketing crops equal to 10 percent of the total value of the state's production. In response the California legislature strengthened the anti-Asian leasing law in 1923, but no constitutional law could prohibit landownership by Nisei.[47]

The Gentleman's Agreement had permitted the continued immigration of wives of Japanese men already residing in the Pacific states, and during the dozen years between 1908 and 1924—when all Japanese immigration was ended as part of the comprehensive Immigration Restriction Act of 1924—approximately sixty thousand Japanese women entered the country. Perhaps half that number were what were known as "picture brides," women whose families arranged for their marriage-by-proxy to immigrant Japanese men in America. "When you think about it, my god" one Issei remembered, "those girls were only eighteen or nineteen and came across to meet somebody they didn't even know. They had guts." Women meant families, a point not lost on California's Senator Phelan. "The rats are in the granary," he declared when asked about the immigration of Japanese women. "They have gotten in under the door and they are breeding with alarming rapidity." Nisei children would add to "the horde of nonassimilable aliens who are crowding the white men and women off the land. If this is not checked now it means the end of the white race in California." In 1919, when Phelan issued his warning, the Japanese made up less than 3 percent of the state's population.[48]

Most of them lived in the countryside in isolated communities. There were a number in California's fertile San Joaquin valley. Typical was the Japanese community that developed in the town of Del Rey, which one local Nisei told an interviewer was "20 miles south of Fresno, 200 miles from San Francisco or Los Angeles, and 100 years from Japan." Del Rey, a center of California raisin growing, began attracting Japanese laborers at the turn of the century, and within a decade Japanese farmers had begun leasing and buying land in the names of their Nisei children. The town was multiethnic, with Armenians, Mexicans, Chinese, and Japanese each in their own enclaves. "Japtown," as the Del Rey Japanese community was locally known, was like a little neighborhood in Tokyo, its wooden buildings packed tightly together, opening onto courtyards with fish ponds and ornamental trees.[49]

Historian Valerie Matsumoto studied another Japanese community of the San Joaquin valley, the Cortez Colony of Merced County, established by Japanese Christians in 1920. One of their first priorities was the founding of a church, like the pioneers of an earlier West. "May the Cortez Colony expand," they prayed at their first official service, "and may the colonists find unity in Christ and be able to move forward in faith, hope and love to accomplish God's will." The church, Matsumoto writes, "cemented the bonds of friendship and support" within the community. At Del Rey, where Japanese farmers were evenly divided between Christians and Buddhists, the center of the community was the nonsectarian *kyowakai,* or community club. "Everybody that's Japanese in Del Rey, they had to join *kyowakai,* an automatic member," one longtime resident recalled. The kyowakai building, known as Del Rey Hall, was the location for meetings of both the Christian and Buddhist congregations, for children's Japanese-language classes, and for community gatherings. "The Del Rey Buddhist Church was a very important part of my growing experience," a Nisei resident of Del Rey remembered. "it made a very positive, a big difference in me." Painfully aware of the prejudice against them in the larger world, the Japanese of Del Rey tried to keep to themselves. "We always stood together, whether we liked it or not. . . . That's why the community remained so important."[50]

There was a rise in nativist sentiment after World War I, and Japanese communities in the West found themselves under attack. In Oregon's Yakima valley a politically ambitious attorney led a local movement to evict Japanese farmers from their leaseholds on Indian reservation land, which was under federal control and thus exempt from the state's anti-Asian leasing law. "THE JAP MUST GO," he declared in a manifesto claiming that Japanese farmers were "slowly but surely" acquiring all the best land in the valley. When the economy went sour in the 1930s the verbal attacks turned violent. Terrorist bombs destroyed the homes and property of two Japanese farm families. "All our forefathers, yours and ours, came across the oceans," the Japanese American Citizens League appealed to valley residents, and "we should all have the same equal rights." Their entreaty was answered by the explosion of two more dynamite bombs on a Japanese farm. "We're charged with wanting to get rid of the Japs for selfish reasons," a farmer from California's Central Valley told a reporter. "We might as well be honest. We do. It's a question of whether the white man lives on the Pacific Coast or the brown man."[51]

There was also violence directed against Japanese farmers in the Salt River valley of Arizona. Out of the more than 4,000 farm families in the district only 120 were Japanese, but there was widespread resentment at the way the immigrants had worked around the state's anti-Japanese Alien Land Law by shifting title to their Nisei children. "Let it be suggested that the newcomers depart quietly while they are still safe and before a war starts," a local newspaper warned. "Unless something like this is done at once—look out!" In August 1935 fifteen hundred white farmers drove through the streets of Phoenix carrying banners proclaiming, "We Don't Need Asiatics," and "Get Out Or Be Put Out." Before the movement sputtered out a few months later, there were sixty-nine violent incidents, including dynamite attacks on Japanese homes and drive-by shootings of Japanese men and boys working in their fields. Fortunately, no one was killed. A group of Japanese farmers suggested negotiations. "We don't care to hear them talk," answered a leader of the expulsion movement. "All we want is to see them walk."[52]

Chinese immigration to the American West all but ceased with the Exclusion Act of 1881, and Japanese migration was severely restricted by the Gentleman's Agreement of 1908. But in the early twentieth century there was an explosive increase in Mexican immigration to the western United States. Official government statistics record the entry of 728,171 Mexicans between the turn of the century and 1930, but historians who have studied this migration estimate that perhaps that many more crossed the border illegally, which would place the total immigration at about 10 percent of the entire population of Mexico. This was yet another of the mass migrations that characterized the history of the American West.

Many of these immigrants were refugees of the revolution in Mexico that followed the overthrow of the dictator Porfirio Díaz in 1911 and engulfed the country for nearly ten years. Some of the bloodiest fighting took place in Mexico's northern states, and thousands of war-torn civilians looked toward the United States for their safety. During one week in 1916 United States immigration agents counted nearly five thousand Mexicans attempting to cross the Rio Grande at El Paso. Unable to cope with such numbers, officials closed the border crossing, but refugees were soon coming over illegally downriver, in the city's eastern section.

Revolutionary sentiment spilled over the border with the refugees. In the Rio Grande valley of Texas, farmers from the Midwest and South had been buying up large tracts, introducing irrigation, and growing cotton and vegetables with the labor of Mexican migrants. The traditional ranchero world of south Texas was giving way to commercial agriculture. In spite of the Tejanos' determined resistance, commercial farmers took over county governments and instituted laws segregating public accommodations and schools. Texas enacted a statewide poll tax in 1902 that effectively constrained thousands of poor blacks and Tejanos from participating in electoral politics. It was not long before frustrations erupted into violence. In 1915 a group of Tejano rancheros and businessmen met in the small town of San Diego on the Nueces River—not far from the spot where the Mexican War had begun seventy years before—and issued a proclamation calling for armed insurrection by a "Liberating Army" of the oppressed castes of the Southwest—Hispanics, Asians, African Americans, and Indians. Several hundred (perhaps several thousand) Tejanos pledged themselves to *El Plan de San Diego*, as this quixotic manifesto was known. Armed and mounted Tejano raiders attacked farms and railroads, burned bridges, and sabotaged irrigation systems, in the process killing several dozen Anglos.[53]

Texas authorities responded with what historian Walter Prescott Webb described

Texas Rangers pose with the corpses of Mexican raiders near the Rio Grande. Photograph by Robert Runyon, 1915. Robert Runyon Photograph Collection, Center for American History, University of Texas at Austin.

as "an orgy of bloodshed." Anglo vigilance committees lynched suspected insurrectionists while the Texas Rangers conducted punitive raids against Tejano communities. According to longtime resident Emma Tenayuca, the Rangers invaded "villages in the border country, massacred hundreds of unarmed, peaceful villagers and seized their lands." Webb estimated that as many as five thousand Tejanos and Mexicans were killed. Soon Mexican supporters were retaliating from across the Rio Grande, terrorizing Anglo communities in Brownsville and other south Texas towns. In 1916 Francisco "Pancho" Villa and his northern Mexican vaquero army threatened an invasion of the city of El Paso, then shifted west to loot and burn the border town of Columbus, New Mexico. President Woodrow Wilson sent an American army on a "Punitive Expedition" across the border, and for the next several months the troops exhausted themselves chasing Villa's forces around the deserts of Chihuahua. It was in the context of border warfare that Americans first learned of the infamous "Zimmerman Telegram," a message sent by German foreign secretary Arthur Zimmerman to his ambassador in Mexico but intercepted and decoded by American intelligence agents. Zimmerman proposed a deal in which Mexico would agree to declare war on the United States and in exchange Germany would support the return of "lost territory in New Mexico, Texas, and Arizona." Given the violence along the border, the threat seemed all too real, and the Zimmerman Telegram was an important factor in America's entry into World War I.[54]

Revolutionary violence may have *pushed* refugees across the border, but migrants were also *pulled* by the growing demand for labor in the orchards and fields of the new Southwest. "The cry of the hour is continually for more dependable labor," reported the *El Paso Daily Times* in 1912. Encouraging Mexican immigration—and thus increasing the supply of labor and lowering wages—was clearly in the interest of the powerful farmers' associations of the Southwest, who were engaged in a fierce struggle with IWW organizers. City officials of El Paso and other border towns equally overwhelmed with immigrants appealed to the federal government to stem the tide, but the growers opposed every attempt to restrict the Mexican exodus. By the 1920s Mexican migrants made up about three-quarters of the more than one million farm laborers in the American West.[55]

The proximity of Mexican migrants to their communities of origin made them unique among the immigrant groups who settled the American West. When Mexico ceded the territory to the United States many Latino families were divided, and there was regular movement back and forth across the untended border. Thus began a pattern of continuous cross-border migration. A typical Mexican farmworker of the early twentieth century might follow the harvest cycle through the irrigated fields of the Southwest, then return to his Mexican village for the winter. Early in the century an inspector interviewing Mexicans at the border found that 69 percent had been to the United States at least once before. During the mass exodus of the Mexican Revolution, however, thousands of families decided to settle permanently in the United States. They founded new *colonias* in the dozens of farm towns servicing the intensive agricultural districts—usually on the rough side of the tracks, often on the site of former Chinatowns, abandoned during earlier bouts of vigilante violence. Newcomers headed for *tenemos familiares,* places where extended family or former neighbors resided; colonias often had strong links with one or two villages back home. These strong connections encouraged migrants to think of themselves as members of what historian Sarah Deutsch calls a "regional community." In the words of a federal immigration study of 1922, "The psychology of the average Mexican alien unskilled worker from Mexico is that he is only upon a visit to an unknown portion of his own country." *Sin fronteras*—a world without borders—that was the Mexican migrant's watchword.[56]

Growers were fond of assuring themselves that this pattern of continued loyalty to Mexico operated in their favor. As a spokesman for California growers put it, the Mexican was "a 'homer'—like a pigeon, he goes back to roost." Another grower condescended that "the Mexican likes the sunshine against an adobe wall and a few tortillas, and in the off season he drifts across the border where he may have these things." In other words, Mexicans were simple peasants, grateful for the employment that growers provided, unlikely to cause labor trouble. Although it is true that most Mexicans remained loyal to the country of their birth and that they had one of the lowest rates of naturalization of any immigrant group in American history, equating this ambivalence about citizenship with docility was wishful thinking. Consider how one immigrant responded when asked whether he planned to become an American citizen: "I would rather cut my throat before changing my Mexican nationality. I am only waiting until conditions get better, until there is absolute peace before I go back." Not the words of a quiescent man. For many Mexican immigrants, memories of their native land were interwoven with family traditions of militancy. Children were taught to admire grandfathers who had fought with Benito Juárez, fathers who had stood with Emiliano Zapata, mothers who had been *soldaderas* in the army of Pancho Villa. Indeed, most migrants came from precisely those areas where the Mexican Revolution had been most intensely argued and fought, and many had participated in peasant rebellions or union struggles. According to historian Devra Weber, for thousands of Mexican migrants "the image of the Mexican Revolution became a model of collective struggle."[57]

Working conditions in the fields and orchards of the Southwest tested loyalty to those traditions. The growers considered us slaves, remembered one migrant Mexican worker; they "treated the horses and the cows better than the farm workers. At least they had shelter, but we lived under the trees." According to a report of the California Department of Immigration and Housing, most migrant farmworkers were forced to provide their own accommodations; some had their own tents, but others "fix a rude shelter from the limbs of trees." Grower-owned labor camps were little better. California investigators found "filth, squalor, and entire absence of sanitation." Of some three hundred facilities inspected in 1934, for example, 3 percent were in compliance with the standards set by law, 25 percent violated one or more regulations, and 72 percent were judged dangerous to the workers' health and safety. To make matters worse, the wages of farmworkers began to fall in the mid-1920s and kept falling during the depression years. In 1935 a typical migrant worker earned only $280 per year (the equivalent of about $3,000 in today's values). Belying their reputation as docile and submissive, Mexican farmworkers responded by organizing unions and battling growers for better working conditions and higher wages. "We would have starved working," declared one organizer, "so we decided to starve striking."[58]

Historians have documented 160 major farm labor strikes in California alone during the 1930s, most of them prominently featuring Mexican workers and organizers. High tide came in 1933, when growers were hit with 37 strikes involving forty-eight

Mexican cotton pickers on strike in California's San Joaquin Valley, 1933. Bancroft Library, University of California, Berkeley.

thousand workers and affecting two-thirds of the state's agricultural production. In the words of Carey McWilliams, who served as chief investigator for California's Department of Immigration and Housing in the late 1930s, these strikes were "the most extensive in the farm labor history of California and the United States; in scale, number, and value of crops affected, they were quite without precedent." Organized by the Cannery and Agricultural Workers Industrial Union, the actions began in April among pea pickers in the Bay Area, spread to the berry fields of southern California in June, to the fruit orchards and vineyards of the central valleys in late summer, and concluded with a massive strike of fifteen thousand cotton pickers in the southern San Joaquin valley in October. Forcibly evicted from grower-owned camps, strikers set up their own encampment communities on unoccupied land, including a huge tent city housing three thousand near the dusty valley town of Corcoran. A traveling troupe of Mexican actors known as Circo Azteca raised a platform near the center of camp and staged reenactments of radical events from Mexican and American history. Many of the strike organizers were veterans of the Mexican Revolution.[59]

These attachments to Mexico could inspire, but they could also be a barrier to progress. This was something migrant Mexican workers began to realize during the struggles of 1933. When the strikes were broken, as all eventually were, it was not because of the absence of worker resolve, for there was an abundance of that, nor because of grower violence, although there was plenty of that, too, including three strikers shot dead and many more wounded during the cotton strike. No, most of the strikes were ended by the intervention of Mexican consular officials who arranged meager deals with growers under the assumption that the Mexican state represented the interests of Mexican migrants. Union organizers were infuriated by this violation of the principle of solidarity, but the Mexican government had decided that the continuation of these strikes was not in Mexico's interests. "The Mexican consul played a major role in California's labor struggles of the 1930s," writes historian Gilbert Gonzáles, "providing a prominent bulwark against working class radicalism." It was an important lesson, encouraging Mexicans to stop thinking of themselves as movers and to start considering the implications of becoming stickers, to be Mexican Americans.[60]

FURTHER READING

John Mack Faragher, *Sugar Creek: Life on the Illinois Prairie* (1986)

Jon Gjerde, *The Minds of the West: Ethnocultural Evolution in the Rural Middle West, 1830–1917* (1997)

Gilbert G. Gonzáles, *Labor and Community: Mexican Citrus Worker Villages in a Southern California County, 1900–1950* (1994)

Robert V. Hine, *Community on the American Frontier: Separate But Not Alone* (1980)

Frederick C. Luebke, ed., *Ethnicity on the Great Plains* (1980)

Valerie J. Matsumoto, *Farming the Home Place: A Japanese American Community in California, 1919–1982* (1993)

Dean L. May, *Three Frontiers: Family, Land, and Society in the American West, 1850–1900* (1994)

Sandra L. Myres, *Westering Women and the Frontier Experience, 1800–1915* (1982)

T. Scott Miyakawa, *Protestants and Pioneers: Individualism and Conformity on the American Frontier* (1964)

James Mooney, *The Ghost-Dance Religion and the Sioux Outbreak of 1890* (1896)

John G. Neihardt, *Black Elk Speaks: Being the Life Story of a Holy Man of the Oglala Sioux* (1932)

Robert C. Ostergren, *A Community Transplanted: The Trans-Atlantic Experience of a Swedish Immigrant Settlement in the Upper Middle West, 1835–1915* (1988)

Nell Irvin Painter, *Exodusters: Black Migration to Kansas After Reconstruction* (1976)

Devra Weber, *Dark Sweat, White Gold: California Farm Workers, Cotton, and the New Deal* (1994)

13

The Urban Frontier

The historic West of popular imagination is a region of scattered populations and rural isolation, an "area of free land" whose settlement the historian Frederick Jackson Turner famously identified as "the really American part of our history." Turner was beginning his career at the University of Wisconsin when he declared this "frontier thesis" in 1893. Only six years later another young historian, Adna Weber of Columbia University, published a study that fundamentally challenged Turner's ruling assumption. "In the Western states a larger percentage of the people dwell in cities," Weber demonstrated, "than in any other part of the nation except the North Atlantic states." The West was more urban than rural. That scholars had not previously noticed this demographic fact was "astonishing," Weber allowed, but the fact was, in the West of the late nineteenth century, "the cities have grown entirely out of proportion to the rural parts."[1]

Weber's revelation was provocative. But his book sunk into undeserved obscurity, its author pursuing a long career as statistician for New York State. Frederick Jackson Turner, meanwhile, became one of the nation's most distinguished historians, and his thesis rose to the status of orthodoxy. It didn't take a scholar to see that the twentieth-century West was increasingly urban and included the fastest-growing cities in the country, but this fact was taken as confirmation of Turner's assertion that the "close of the frontier" at the end of the nineteenth century marked the end of one era and the beginning of another. The modern regional West might be predominantly urban, but westering had been predominantly rural, as was nearly all the history written under the influence of the frontier thesis.

More recently western historians have taken another look and found that long before Adna Weber published his study many eyewitness participants had noted the importance of cities in the westward movement. "Without transition you pass from a wilderness into the streets of a city, from the wildest scenes to the most smiling pictures of civilized life," remarked Alexis de Tocqueville after traveling through the trans-Appalachian West in the early 1830s. A Scots farmer in Illinois wrote to his family, "Here it is not uncommon to have large cities spring up in a few years." The urban character of westering intensified in the trans-Mississippi West, where the aridity dictated a low density of rural population, and the extractive economy encouraged the development of industrial urban centers. It all confirmed an old American pioneer proverb: "Give me a rich country, and I'll soon give you a large city!"[2]

Towns and cities were a critical part of the first frontier of the United States, the trans-Appalachian West. Townbuilders platted Lexington and Louisville in Kentucky during the American Revolution, years before the great postwar migration that filled the Ohio valley with American settlers. Even as American armies continued to battle the confederated Indian tribes for control of the region, eastern developers laid out the town of Cincinnati as the administrative capital of the Old Northwest. In the Old Southwest, the entrepôts of Nashville, Natchez, and Memphis were essential to the development of the planter economy. These towns "were the spearheads of the frontier," writes historian Richard Wade. "Planted far in advance of the line of settlement, they held the West for the approaching population." A great deal of ink has been spilt debating Wade's "spearhead" thesis, and the controversy has devolved into one of those tiresome chicken-or-egg arguments. Less important than whether the settlement of town or country came first is an acknowledgment of the essential role of cities in westering from the beginning of our national history. "Urbanization was a development correlative with the expansion of the frontier," writes the distinguished urban historian Bayard Still, and was "often an integral part of it."[3]

These incipient western cities were ruthless competitors for the trade of the extensive agricultural hinterland of the Mississippi valley. Urban merchants sought to capture the business of thousands of farmers who were moving beyond subsistence and devoting more of their time and energy to the production of a "surplus" for market. What Wade calls "urban imperialism"—the ceaseless and constant competition among towns for new rural markets—was a powerful stimulus to the expansion of commercial and industrial enterprise.[4]

The first clear victor in this struggle for western urban supremacy was Cincinnati, founded in 1789 and grown into an important market center by 1800. "I could scarcely believe my own eyes," a visitor from New Jersey wrote home, "to see the number of people and wagons and saddle horses and the quantities of meat, flour, corn, fish, fowl, and sauce [preserves and jams] of all kinds that were offered and actually sold." It was the steamboat, however, that made Cincinnati a regional power. In 1816

Henry M. Shreve, a Pittsburgh keelboat captain, launched the *Washington,* a double-deck, shallow-hull side-wheeler able to carry heavy cargoes in the relatively shallow waters of the upper Ohio. Taking advantage of its location at the center of the nineteenth-century "corn belt," Cincinnati's merchants concentrated on the slaughter and packing of pork ("corn on four legs") for shipment downriver to New Orleans, from where it was distributed to butchers along the Atlantic coast. Lard they exported by the hundredweight for use as cooking fat in the Caribbean and South America. By the late 1820s Cincinnati had become the nation's unrivaled meat-packing champion, crowned "queen city" of the Ohio by local boosters but better known as "Porkopolis." Pork packers contracted for hogs not only in Ohio and Indiana but deep into Kentucky and far down the Ohio River, stealing business from Lexington and Louisville, and by the 1840s they were processing an estimated four hundred thousand hogs a year.[5]

From the mountains of slaughterhouse refuse, enterprising capitalists created new industries—producing leather, brushes, glue, soap, and chemicals—and on this economic base Cincinnati rose to become the first industrial city west of the Appalachians. At midcentury some twenty thousand workers were manufacturing clothing, furniture, building materials, and cooking stoves, as well as such capital goods as steam engines and mills. "The city's smokestacks," writes historian Carl Abbott, "emitted a perpetual blanket of smoke as dense and black as that over the mill towns of England." Cincinnati also triumphed as the cultural center of the early trans-Appalachian West, with numerous academies and "commercial colleges," scores of magazines, dozens of newspapers, and publishing houses that printed and distributed hundreds of books. It was a Cincinnati firm that published the famous McGuffey Eclectic Readers, the most common texts in western schools during the nineteenth century. All this development was based on the close relation between city and country. "The pride and support of Cincinnati is her rich and extensive back country," wrote an editor of one of the city's papers, "and the people of that country should never forget how much the value of their lands and the profits of their industry depend upon her welfare and commercial relations."[6]

Another western metropolis developed in Saint Louis, founded by French traders from New Orleans in 1762 at the strategic junction of the Missouri and Mississippi rivers. The town long served as the headquarters of the Rocky Mountain fur trade, but it was the trade in lead—essential for ammunition—that accounted for its rise as one of the great cities of the Mississippi valley. During the territorial period Moses Austin and other businessmen opened a number of successful lead mines in eastern Missouri, giving the city its start in the business. When steamboats began operating on the Mississippi, after the War of 1812, experienced lead traders from Saint Louis were able to seize control of the commerce of the mining district upriver at Galena, Illinois. Control of the nation's lead trade enabled Saint Louis to free itself from the

The busy Mississippi River levee at Saint Louis. Photograph by Boehl and Koenig, c. 1875. Beinecke.

economic dominance of Cincinnati, establishing a hinterland of its own along the Mississippi corridor north of the city. By 1830, according to Thomas Ford, who served a term as governor of Illinois, "nearly the whole trade of Illinois, Wisconsin, and the Upper Mississippi was concentrated at Saint Louis."[7]

Cincinnati and Saint Louis were the urban success stories of the early nineteenth century. But the competition for hinterlands was more frequently a destroyer rather than a builder of towns. Consider the fate of Alton, Illinois, upstream and across the river from Saint Louis. Illinois leaders, chagrined to find the commerce of their lead district in the hands of Missourians, arranged for the state bank to finance a plan by Alton businessmen to recapture that trade. But Saint Louis merchants, leveraging their commercial dominance, were able to prevent their Alton competitors from chartering enough steamboats, driving them into bankruptcy. Alton hung on as a second-class river town, but ruthless competition drove dozens of other aspiring cities to ruin. On a trip down the Ohio, landscape architect Frederick Law Olmsted was startled by the number of forlorn and abandoned towns he saw. "Each had its hopes," he wrote, "of becoming the great mart of the valley, and had built in accordant style its one or two tall brick city blocks, standing shabby-sided alone on the mud-slope to the bank, supported by a tavern, an old storehouse, and a few shanties. These mushroom cities mark only a night's camping-place of civilization." Western writer James Hall reminded his readers of the hundreds of town sites that had become "the residence only of frogs and mosquitoes."[8]

What explained the rise of some western cities and the fall of others? There were as many theories as there were local boosters with predictions of why their towns were "destined" to rise to greatness. S. H. Goodin of Cincinnati argued that his city had risen to dominance in the Ohio valley because of what he termed the urban "law of gravitation." Once a city achieved critical economic mass, as Cincinnati had, other towns were inevitably drawn within its orbit. But what would the continued progress of western expansion mean for Cincinnati's future? Goodin predicted the rise of a "grand centre" where the entire commerce of the continental interior would converge, "a city which shall have all [other] cities as satellites or outposts." Not surprisingly, he believed that Cincinnati would be the site of that future megalopolis.[9]

Saint Louis produced its own urban theorist, newspaper man William Gilpin, a political disciple of Missouri's Senator Thomas Hart Benton. Like Benton, Gilpin was a believer in the heliotropic theory of the westward progression of empires, and he worked to fit this ancient dogma to the requirements of urban boosterism. The "immortal fire of civilization," he declared, had been moving in a western direction for centuries along what he termed the "Isothermal Zodiac," a temperate band of latitude circling the globe in the northern hemisphere. Over previous millennia the site of the world's leading city had been steadily moving west, from Athens to Rome, to Paris, to London, and finally to New York City. Inevitably this continuing migration would settle next on . . . why, Saint Louis, of course. "Just look at her position on the map of North America," Gilpin gushed, "exactly in the center of the Union, where the navigable arteries unite." Gilpin's science—supported by highfalutin rhetoric and mind-numbing statistics—had at least the advantage of flexibility. When he moved to the western town of Independence to assume the editorship of another paper, he took a second look at his data and decided that the next "world city" would be built at Kansas City, the vicinity of his new home. Later, when President Lincoln appointed him governor of Colorado Territory, Gilpin recalculated his statistics a final time and announced that Denver would be the site of "Centropolis."[10]

Goodin, Gilpin, and other western urban boosters believed in the "doctrine of natural advantage," a version of geographic determinism. As one booster put it, "God has marked out by topography the lines of commerce." But the truth was, the "great tracings of the Almighty's finger" played a far less significant role than the "invisible hand" of eastern capital. The rise of Saint Louis was made possible by New York and Boston investors, attracted by the profits being made by local entrepreneurs in the shipping business. "It requires no gift of prophecy," wrote one easterner, "that it will ultimately become the largest city in the western world." Many capitalist firms from the East established branch offices in the city. "The counting-rooms, the stores, the mills, and the machine shops," wrote a reporter in Saint Louis, were "filled by New Englanders and New Yorkers." The city's commercial future was determined not by God but by Wall Street and State Street bankers.[11]

The importance of eastern control became clear during the mid-1850s, when Saint Louis was thrown into turmoil by the border war that broke out over the future of slavery in Kansas. Proslavery mobs threatened eastern merchants, and in 1856 several incoming shipments of goods were destroyed in a desperate search for rifles being sent to free-soil forces. These attacks were front-page news in the East. In a powerful series of editorials, William Cullen Bryant of the *New York Post* discouraged his readers from further investments in Saint Louis. "Men who have no regard for the rights of others," he warned, "cannot be expected to pay their debts." Francis Hunt, a Bostonian doing business in Saint Louis, admonished his local associates that unless the attacks ceased, the "source of their prosperity shall be cut off and driven to a northern route." With the open hostility toward "Yankees" unabated, Hunt soon closed his doors and joined the flight of eastern businessmen from the city. Almost overnight the city's economy collapsed.[12]

The controversy over slavery crippled Saint Louis at precisely the moment of its greatest challenge by the upstart city of Chicago. Little more than a swampy outpost on the southwestern shore of Lake Michigan in the 1830s, Chicago was the creation of eastern capitalists in collaboration with the state of Illinois. While speculators invested in unimproved city lots, driving up property values, the state undertook an ambitious program of lakeshore harbor improvements and canal construction, connecting Chicago with both eastern markets and the surrounding countryside. During the 1840s the city was able to capture the grain trade of northern Illinois and southern Wisconsin. Chicago's fortunes boomed just as eastern investors were pouring capital into railroad construction, and by the early 1850s a number of eastern railroad companies had selected Chicago as their western terminus, while several western companies were constructing lines radiating outward from the city into the adjacent countryside. One of the most important was the westbound Chicago and Rock Island, which ambitious Chicago businessmen hoped would give them the wherewithal to capture the lead trade of Galena from the control of Saint Louis merchants. The Rock Island line reached the Mississippi in 1854 and during its first season of operation succeeded in diverting half the output of the lead mines to Chicago. Two years later the Rock Island became the first railroad to bridge the Mississippi.

"The faces of the men of business of the valley of the Upper Mississippi, who have heretofore looked Southward and downward, will now look upward and Eastward," crowed Chicago's *Daily Democratic Press*. "How can they resist it?" When in 1856 a Saint Louis steamboat crashed into the Rock Island bridge and exploded in flames, its owners sued the bridge company and the railroad. The suit was a showdown be-

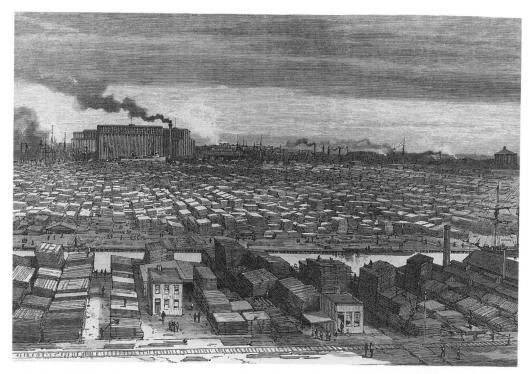

The Chicago lumber district. From Harper's Weekly, *October 20, 1883. Beinecke.*

tween the two cities. "If we are beaten," warned the Saint Louis Chamber of Commerce, "the commercial position of Saint Louis, which is now the pride and boast of her citizens, would be counted among the things that were." And so it was. Abraham Lincoln, then an Illinois attorney in private practice, effectively argued in federal court that the railroad bridge represented the best hopes of a developing West. The jury deadlocked, the judge dismissed the suit, and Saint Louis was forced to concede the loss of the upper Mississippi. A reporter saw the evidence of Chicago's victory on a visit to a mercantile establishment in Omaha. "The ancient store boxes in the cellar have 'Saint Louis' stenciled on them; those on the pavement, 'Chicago,'" he wrote. "Omaha eats Chicago groceries, wears Chicago dry goods, builds with Chicago lumber, and reads Chicago newspapers." Chicago's triumph did not result simply from the "natural advantage" of its geography. Rather, it was the combined result of location, savvy investing, an innovative new mode of transportation, cutthroat competition, and the political crisis that marked the coming of the Civil War.[13]

―――――――――

Chicago emerged as the dominant western metropolis, the city with the strongest links to eastern markets, just as the explosive settlement of the trans-Mississippi West got under way. Chicago became what geographer Andrew Frank Burghardt calls a "gateway city," the link between the settlements and resources of the West and the cities, factories, and commercial networks of the Northeast. Within a few years the competition of the transcontinental railroad opened an undeveloped hinterland of unprecedented size, one stretching from the Great Lakes to the Rocky Mountains and beyond. "The range of the trade of Chicago," wrote an economist for the federal government in 1881, "embraces an area constituting more than one-half of the territorial limits of the United States." Historian William Cronon has detailed the city's role as headquarters for the late nineteenth-century colonization of the trans-Mississippi West. Chicago lumber merchants set thousands of men to work cutting the pine forests of the Great Lakes and shipped westward the billions of board feet of lumber needed for the construction of the railroad system as well as for countless homes, towns, and cities on the Great Plains. Chicago entrepreneurs built dozens of grain elevators and devised the practice of commodity trading on the city's Board of Trade, providing a world market for the thousands of farmers who converted the grassland into a fruited plain. Chicago meatpackers financed the western cattle industry, and the southside stockyards became the city's largest employer, drawing tens of thousands of immigrant workers from Ireland, Germany, Bohemia, Poland, and Slovakia. Much of the fabulous wealth produced by this western empire went into the hands of the eastern investors who bankrolled the system. But great accumulations also built up in the accounts of Chicago's capitalists, who used them to build an urban industrial economy that by 1880 had made theirs into the nation's "second city."[14]

By that time Chicago stood atop a western urban hierarchy that included some two dozen cities in the trans-Mississippi West, each with its own immediate commercial hinterland, but each also in a tributary relationship to Chicago. The "railroad capitalism" of the late nineteenth century concentrated decision making in great urban centers, ordering lesser cities into a pecking order. As Adna Weber pointed out in his prescient urban study, commerce "favors the great centers, rather than the small or intermediate ones." For the West, that great center was Chicago. This interconnected urban system, writes Gilbert Stelter, "reflected the basically colonial nature of western life."[15]

William "Buffalo Bill" Cody told a story that illustrates the point. As a young buffalo hunter supplying meat for construction crews on the Kansas Pacific in the 1860s, Cody and a friend went into partnership to develop a town they called Rome at a spot on the prairie where the railroad had announced it would locate its repair shops. The partners staked out lots, and soon merchants, saloon-keepers, and ordinary settlers arrived and built on them. But returning from a hunt one afternoon, Cody discovered that "the town was being torn down and carted away. The balloon-frame buildings were coming apart section by section. I could see at least a hundred teams and wagons carting lumber, furniture, and everything that made up the town over the

A deserted railroad town in Kansas. From Harper's New Monthly Magazine, *February 1874.*
Library of Congress.

prairies to the eastward." Officials in some far-flung corporate office had decided to relocate the repair facilities to Hays City, and Rome was unbuilt in a day.[16]

Denver narrowly avoided duplicating Rome's sudden fall. When the Union Pacific bypassed the town in 1867, many of Denver's businessmen panicked and rushed north to Cheyenne on the rail line. A number of the city's more determined and optimistic citizens, however, organized a railroad company of their own called the Denver Pacific, used their Washington connections to win a land grant and subsidy from Congress, and ran tracks north to link up with the transcontinental line. Claiming a place of prominence in the emerging urban system demanded aggressive promotion. Consider the case of the neighboring towns of Leavenworth and Kansas City, both aspiring to the status of regional metropolis. The business and political community of Kansas City unified behind a plan to win a rail connection and offered choice city lots to influential railroad men, but Leavenworth's citizens fell to quarreling over the financing of a bond issue. Kansas City beat its rival to the punch, was first to bridge the Missouri, and Leavenworth became a tributary of its neighbor. There is a similar story about the rivalry between the Texas towns of Houston and Galveston. Feeling secure with their fine bay and harbor, Galveston's leaders wasted precious time squabbling over which railroad they should invite into the city, pro-

Temple Square, Salt Lake City, 1889. Utah State Historical Society.

viding Houston's inland elite with time to construct an ambitious canal to the Gulf, dredge a deep harbor at Buffalo Bayou, and finance a railroad of their own, linking them to the national transportation system. Grabbing the advantage, Houston had captured a vast Texas hinterland by the turn of the century. Galveston continued to pout for years, teaching local schoolchildren that crass, commercial Houston had stolen their natural port.

In the Great Basin, the Mormons at first sought to remain apart from the developing urban system of the West. Warned by Brigham Young "not to have any trade or commerce with the gentile world," the leadership attempted instead to develop an exclusive hinterland along the "Mormon Corridor," a series of ninety-six outposts extending southwest from Salt Lake City to San Bernardino and San Diego on the Pacific Ocean. The Mormon church assisted in settling more than seventy thousand emigrants on mostly self-sufficient farms and ranches along this corridor. But Salt Lake City's role as a bustling way station to the Far West also attracted hundreds of gentiles who did not hesitate to set up businesses with links to the national capitalist economy. It soon became clear to the Mormon leadership that their policy of isolation would simply prevent them from having any say in the development of their region. When the transcontinental Union Pacific line was built north of Salt Lake City in 1869, the church financed a line connecting the city with the depot at Ogden,

An oil field near Houston, c. 1905. Houston Public Library,
Houston Metropolitan Research Center.

and over the next decade the Mormons undertook a program of industrial development. By the mid-1870s manufacturing had become important enough to the local economy that the editor of a local magazine could write that Salt Lake City was "eminently a manufacturing community."[17]

By the end of the nineteenth century a handful of western cities had developed as industrial and financial powers in their own right. The twin cities of Minneapolis and Saint Paul, for example, took advantage of the cheap waterpower available at the Falls of Saint Anthony on the Mississippi River and built an energetic lumber and flour milling industry. Using their own capital, local millers helped finance the construction of rail lines into the Dakotas and western Canada to capture the wheat and

A panorama of San Francisco. Photograph by Eadweard J. Muybridge, 1877. Beinecke.

lumber trade. By 1880 the combined output of Minneapolis companies such as Pills-bury outpaced Milwaukee, Saint Louis, and Chicago in the production of flour. In Denver, local capitalists invested in smelting, processing the ores produced by the region's many mines. In 1870, when the population numbered just 5,000, the city's annual industrial output was only $250,000, but thirty years later Denver's 134,000 residents were producing commodities valued at more than $50 million—not only a huge increase in volume but an eightfold growth in productivity. "Our smelter business has no parallel in any other state," a local business journal boasted. As a rising regional power, Denver was able to circumvent Chicago and establish direct connections with New York financiers, becoming a regional command post for great mining interests controlled by the Rockefeller and Guggenheim families.[18]

Houston followed a similar trajectory of building on local advantage. In the late nineteenth century the city became the center for the distribution of lumber from the piney woods of east Texas and cotton from a hinterland stretching as far north as Arkansas. "We moved to Houston because Houston was the little end of the funnel that drained all of Texas and the Oklahoma territory," explained one cotton broker. But Houston's remarkable rise as one of the great cities of twentieth-century America dates from the huge oil gusher unloosed in 1901 at Spindletop, in nearby Beaumont. Spouting two hundred feet high, it blew off a hundred thousand barrels a day for ten days, creating a huge oil lake that caught fire and burned for weeks. Within months engineers tapped other vast oil fields along the Gulf coast. Local companies with the now-familiar names of Gulf, Texaco, Shell, and Humble (later Exxon) built refineries and established headquarters in Houston. With federal funding the city deepened the channel at Buffalo Bayou, permitting access for huge oil tankers. Petroleum became the foundation for a diversified industrial economy as other enterprises were drawn to the area: chemicals, machine tools, and warehousing. Houston banker Jesse H. Jones predicted that the city would become "the in-

evitable gateway through which the products of this growing southern and western empire can best reach the markets of the world." Indeed, historian David McComb shows that by 1910 Houston's economy had moved into the stage of self-financed growth. The success of Houston, Denver, Salt Lake, and Minneapolis did not alter the basic configuration of power between the urban and rural West—command and control continued to be concentrated in a small number of metropolitan areas. But the increasing importance of regional cities did mean serious competition for Chicago, which by 1900 had relinquished the status of "gateway city" of the West.[19]

San Francisco was the first regional city of the trans-Mississippi West to achieve first-class status, although like all western cities it began as a colony of the East. The population of gold rush California was drawn from many quarters, with a majority from the rural Mississippi valley, but the residents of early San Francisco hailed preponderantly from the urban Northeast. During the city's first decade nearly all the principal merchants and bankers were agents or associates of Boston and New York firms, and a survey of the city's lawyers found that 40 percent had been licensed to practice by the New York State bar. But the fabulous wealth of the mines led to the early creation of a powerful group of local capitalists, providing an opportunity for independence that other western cities could only envy. Perhaps the event signaling San Francisco's arrival as one of a handful of elite American cities was the capture, by its bankers and Silver Kings, of the unprecedented wealth of the Comstock Lode in the late 1860s. From their headquarters on San Francisco's Nob Hill, writes historian Rodman Paul, "Comstock millionaires underwrote many a new venture in the American West and abroad."[20]

Henry George, San Francisco's radical journalist, was one of the first to note the city's rise to "gateway" status. "Not a settler in all the Pacific States and Territories but must pay San Francisco tribute," he wrote. "Not an ounce of gold dug, a pound of ore smelted, a field gleaned, or a tree felled in all their thousands of square miles, but must add to her wealth." By 1880 San Francisco's commercial hinterland stretched from Panama to Alaska, from the sugar plantations of the Hawaiian Islands to the mining districts of northern Idaho. It was also the first industrial city in the trans-Mississippi West. In 1880 approximately thirty thousand workers produced output valued higher than the combined total of all the other urban centers of the West. "San Francisco dwarfs the other cities," the English scholar and diplomat James Bryce observed in 1888, "and is a commercial and intellectual centre and source of influence for the surrounding regions, more powerful over them than is any Eastern city over its neighborhood. It is a New York which has got no Boston on one side of it, and no shrewd and orderly rural population on the other, to keep it in order."[21]

In the 1870s San Francisco investors began to buy up thousands of arid acres in the undeveloped southern portion of the state. With a population of only ten thousand, Los Angeles was "still a mere village—mostly Mexican," wrote visitor David Starr Jordan, "and the country round was practically a desert of cactus and sagebrush." But San Franciscans were betting on an explosion of interest when the Southern Pacific and the Santa Fe linked L.A. to the national rail network in the 1880s. The boom came with the completion of the two rail lines in 1887, provoked by a fare war between them that drove down the price of a ticket from Saint Louis to as little as five dollars. That brought an estimated two hundred thousand tourists, curiosity-seekers, and land speculators. They thrilled to the pitch of boosters, as had generations of previous westering dreamers. Like Kentucky and Texas in earlier times, Southern California was a land unmatched for its fertility and beauty. "There are calla lilies by the acre," read one typically overblown guidebook, "and tall enough to be picked by a man on horseback; hedges of geraniums, fifteen feet high; rods and rods of carnations and pinks; heliotrope grown into trees, forty feet high; roses of a thousand varieties, by the million, it being no rare thing to see a hundred thousand, two hundred thousand, or more, buds and blossoms and full blown roses on a single bush at the same moment." One visitor wrote home: "I apparently have found a Paradise on Earth."[22]

The resulting frenzy of buying and selling sent real estate prices through the roof, and in a little less than two years southern California developers laid out more than sixty new towns on nearly eighty thousand acres. The smart money got out before the inevitable bust of 1889, which destroyed thousands of paper fortunes. "I had a half a million dollars wiped out in the crash," cried a character in Theodore Van Dyke's novel of the boom, *Millionaires of a Day* (1890), "and what's worse, $500 of it was cash." Yet the episode left Los Angeles with a population of more than fifty thousand and whetted the expectations of the local business elite. Few would have disagreed with the vice president of the Santa Fe Railroad who predicted that "people will continue to come here until the whole country becomes one of the most densely populated sections of the United States."[23]

Before that could happen, however, there were severe constraints to be overcome. Los Angeles had no adequate harbor along the nearby Pacific coast, and without one, a local booster warned, the city was destined to "become a backcountry to San Diego." Moreover, southern California lacked sufficient water to support the swelling masses of a great city. Indeed, so unpropitious was the location, many have wondered why a city was being built here at all. "It is difficult to find any really good reason why the city of Los Angeles should have come into existence," the ecologist Raymond Dasmann once wrote, reflecting the opinion of many of his fellow San Franciscans. But in the twenty years following the initial boom, the leaders of Los Angeles took on these problems and solved them. The harbor question was taken to Washington, D.C., and after a concerted campaign Congress voted in 1897 to "improve" the anchorage at the village of San Pedro, a part of greater L.A. Over the next decade the U.S. Army Corps of Engineers invested millions, in the words of historian Robert Fogelson, "to duplicate at Los Angeles what nature created gratuitously at San Francisco," converting San Pedro into one of the world's great ports. Not coincidentally, many of the leaders of this project made fortunes speculating in valuable waterfront property.[24]

Meanwhile, the city's establishment was on the prowl for new sources of water. In 1905 and 1907 the L.A. Board of Water Commissioners proposed, and the voters approved, more than twenty-five million dollars in bonds to finance the construction of an aqueduct diverting the flow of the Owens River, some two hundred miles northeast on the flank of the Sierra Nevadas, and channeling it to the city. This project was one of the most massive engineering projects in American history, comparable to the construction of the Erie Canal or the transcontinental railroad. The water arrived in 1913, providing Los Angeles with more than enough capacity to quench the thirst of its approximately 350,000 residents, enough indeed to sustain a population numbering in the millions. What L.A.'s citizens had not been told, however, was that a syndicate of wealthy citizens—including government insiders—had previously bought up more than one hundred thousand acres in the adjacent San Fernando valley, where Owens River water was stored in reservoirs. "Anyone who knew this, and bought land in the San Fernando valley while it was still dirt-cheap," writes historian Marc Reisner, "stood to become very, very rich." The syndicate made an estimated profit of one hundred million dollars. In an era of aggressive western promotion, the elite of Los Angeles set a new standard for urban buccaneering.[25]

One of the most prominent members of that elite was Henry E. Huntington, nephew and heir of Collis P. Huntington of the Southern Pacific railroad, one of the legendary Big Four. Huntington invested his abundant family capital in Los Angeles trolley companies and real estate, and by 1900 he had become southern California's single largest landowner and majordomo of the interurban rail system known as the

A crowd celebrates the arrival of Owens River water in Los Angeles County, 1913. Los Angeles Department of Water and Power.

Pacific Electric. Huntington built dozens of new trolley lines, connecting his undeveloped tracts to the city center. "Railway lines have to keep ahead of the procession," he instructed his lieutenants. They "must anticipate the growth of communities and be there when the homebuilders arrive—or they are very likely not to arrive at all." Leaving nothing to chance, Huntington had his land subdivided into lots and planted with pepper trees from Peru, jacarandas from Brazil, and palm trees from Asia and Africa, had the streets surveyed and paved, and even the utilities laid out in advance of building. He thus helped create the conditions for what became the southern Californian preference for detached single-family homes with private landscaped yards—decades before this became the ideal elsewhere in the country. Huntington helped invent a new kind of dispersed urban landscape, what a later generation would call *sprawl*. "As much as any single person," writes historian Kenneth T. Jackson, Huntington "initiated the southern California sprawl that still baffles visitors."[26]

Thus Los Angeles was ready-made for the automobile and became the first city in the nation to enthusiastically embrace car culture. The country's first filling station appeared there in 1909, the same year that California became the first state to authorize a bond issue for a paved state highway system. Autos accelerated the process of decentralization that Huntington began. In the 1920s builders developed some thirty-two hundred new subdivisions with 250,000 new homes in outlying areas. Los Angeles, as journalist Carey McWilliams famously observed, has from its beginnings been "a collection of suburbs in search of a city."[27]

Early twentieth-century L.A. was primarily an urban service center for the booming agricultural hinterland of southern California. The production of citrus fruit, for example, was spread widely throughout the foothills and valleys of the southland, but the association that organized the picking, packing, and national distribution of "Sunkist" oranges was located in the city. "The center of power in the industry is not to be found in the elegant residences on Smiley Heights in Redlands," wrote McWilliams, "but in the offices of the California Fruit Growers Exchange in Los Angeles." Real estate and tourism provided other sources of economic strength. But the low level of industrialization in early twentieth-century L.A. was remarkable. James M. Cain, who moved to the area in the 1920s to work as a Hollywood screenwriter, was appalled at "the piddling occupations" of his neighbors, and in *The Postman Always Rings Twice* (1934), his classic *noir* novel of southern California, one of his characters remarks that the "whole goddam country lives selling hot dogs to each other."[28]

Southern California leaders such as Huntington, however, were empire builders, and they anticipated a great future for their city. "Los Angeles is destined to become the most important city in this country, if not the world," Huntington wrote. "It can extend in any direction as far as you like; its front door opens on the Pacific, the ocean of the future. The Atlantic is the ocean of the past. Europe can supply her own wants. We shall supply the wants of Asia." Huntington stood at the modern end of a long line of westering prophets.[29]

During the second half of the nineteenth century the direction of American expansion shifted from the countryside to the city. During the farm crises of the 1870s and the 1890s tens of thousands of families abandoned their farms and ranches and headed for urban areas. But even prosperity produced out-migration in the countryside. As pioneers settled rural districts, eventually the number of farms or ranches approached the maximum number the land would support. Landowners sought to increase their productivity through mechanization, and those who were successful invested their returns in the purchase of additional land and equipment, expanding their holdings by buying the farms of less fortunate neighbors, who moved on. Compare this pattern of economic development to that of the city, where innovations in manufacturing led to the creation of new opportunities and new jobs, what economists call a "multiplier" effect. But in the countryside, economic development inevitably meant depopulation. Rural townships in the Midwest had begun to lose population by the 1880s, and over the next half-century most of the rural West was overtaken by this trend. The city had always been an important part of westering, but these patterns exaggerated the importance of the city in the trans-Mississippi West of the twentieth century. For every industrial worker who became a farmer, twenty farm boys rushed to the city to compete for his job.

This movement from farm to city is relatively well known. Less so is the fact that for every twenty farm boys, as many as twenty-five or thirty farm girls moved from the rural West to the cities. In the words of a Census Bureau report in 1920, "The farmer's daughter is more likely to leave the farm and go to the city than is the farmer's son." This amounted to a stunning reversal of the traditional pattern of western settlement, which featured the presence of many young, unattached men among the migrants but almost no single women. One historical study of rural households in late nineteenth century Illinois, Iowa, and Minnesota details the "defeminizaton" of the countryside, with six in ten daughters of typical families leaving the area while seven in ten sons remained. Many of these young women, of course, married farmers from some other community, but more of them headed for the cities. There is evidence for this at the urban end of the trail where, by the 1880s in most western cities, native-born young women had begun to outnumber native-born young men. Over the next half-century the proportion of young women in the urban population continued to rise.[30]

What explains the greater rates of female migration to the city? In the opinion of many contemporaries, young women were pushed out of the countryside by constricted opportunities and the lingering legacy of patriarchy. "I hate farm-life," declares a disillusioned bride in Hamlin Garland's Main-Traveled Roads (1891). "It's nothing but fret, fret, and work the whole time, never going any place, never seeing anybody but a lot of neighbors just as big fools as you are. I spend my time fighting flies and washing dishes and churning. I'm sick of it." Around the turn of the twentieth century the theme of women's drudgery came to dominate discussions of rural life. In order to assess the views of country women themselves, in 1913 the Department of Agriculture surveyed several thousand farm wives. The results confirmed the worst. The consensus among women was that they were overworked, that they

A young Colorado emigrant in Los Angeles, c. 1925. Private collection.

had limited educational and vocational options, and that "old fashioned" male attitudes kept them at home and prevented their full participation in public and community life. "Isolation, stagnation, ignorance, loss of ambition, the incessant grind
of labor, and the lack of time for improvement by reading, by social intercourse, or
by recreation of some sort are all working against the farm woman's happiness," one
woman wrote.[31]

Women may also have been fleeing male violence. Historian David Peterson del
Mar finds a good deal of provocative evidence in the records of the divorce courts in
rural Oregon. One man, defending himself against the charge of battering his wife,
explained to the judge that he beat her because "a man should rule over his wife in
everything except religion." Another man argued that he had used only the violence
"necessary and reasonable to enforce rightful obedience" and swore he would hit his
wife again "if she did not do to suit." A father, testifying on behalf of his daughter,
told the court that he had seen evidence of her husband's abuse many times. "I saw
her with a very black eye," he told the judge of his last visit, and continued that when
he asked his girl about it, she told him, "Pa, the world will never know what trouble
I have seen." Del Mar concludes that "husbands commonly used physical force on
their wives." His documentation comes from only a single state, and divorce records
typically tend to emphasize the worst, but other kinds of evidence suggest that domestic violence was commonplace in the West. Readers of Mari Sandoz's biography
of her homesteader father, *Old Jules* (1935), are shocked at his violent treatment of

women. When Sandoz's mother asks Jules to help her with the work around the farmyard, he rages—"You want me, an educated man, to work like a hired tramp!"—and throws her against a wall. Yet Sandoz makes it clear that her father was no different from the other men she knew growing up in Nebraska. A woman was something to exploit, to work and bear children.[32]

Many young women fled to the city to avoid such a fate, some in desperation because they had experienced male abuse firsthand. According to historian Joanne Meyerowitz, the records of welfare agencies in early twentieth-century Chicago are filled with stories of rural women who came to the city to escape abusive male relatives. One such girl sought protection from Traveler's Aid when she arrived at Union Station late one evening in 1912. "Her stepfather had been making improper advances toward her for some time," read the case record, "but so far she had been able to resist them. Her life was threatened if she told her mother. But the importunities of the man had become so insistent that the girl was afraid to remain longer and she fled." Another young migrant reported heated arguments with her father about dating. "We kept having fights back and forth about the boys I went out with and the hours that I kept," she explained to the social worker. "He even accused me of wanting to do things which I'd not even thought of doing up to that time." She resolved to leave home when her father threatened to whip her. "I was always willing to stand up for my rights," she told the social worker. Of course there is no way of knowing how common such experiences were.[33]

Probably most women came to the city with high hopes. One rural mother wrote that her country daughter left the countryside in pursuit of greater economic freedom. "She isn't going to 'stay put,' but will get out where she can earn some money of her very own, to buy the little things so dear to the hearts of girls." The city pulled young women out of the country. Urban employment offered them a means of determining their own affairs, of providing them with incomes of their own—something hard to come by in the country, where just about the only paid work for women was teaching school. As early as the 1890s there were reports of working girls in western cities spending substantial sums on clothing, makeup, and amusements. After a ten-hour day working in shops, restaurants, or factories, young women sought excitement at dance halls, the theater (a few years later at the movies), or simply strolling the streets with their companions and enjoying the city scene. "Dallying in front of display windows, women announced themselves as independent wage-earners and consumers," writes Mary Murphy, who studied young women in early twentieth-century Butte, Montana. "Their dress, their assertive presence on the sidewalk, and their flirtatious manners proclaimed their right to share the street—and by extension movie theaters, dance halls, restaurants, and nightclubs—with men and do so on their own terms."[34]

Although most unmarried working women in western cities continued to live with parents or relatives, the number living on their own greatly increased as thousands of young migrants flooded in during the early twentieth century. Many newcomer women first found residence in the group homes of charitable organizations like the Young Women's Christian Association, but few chose to live there for long. Regulations about "lock-up" and "lights-out," as well as limitations on visitors, alienated many young women, who were unwilling to trade the rules of their parents for those of social workers. "After I know the city better and as soon as I get a raise," a woman at a YWCA home told an investigator, "I'm going to take an apartment and run my own affairs. Then I won't miss out on a meal if I'm late. Neither will I have to observe rules, and I can entertain my friends when and how I please." Few single working women, however, could afford apartments of their own. Most settled for a "furnished room," a place—in the words of one young migrant of the 1920s— "where we can unpack our trunk, anchor our electric iron, and hang our other blouse over the chair." The demand for freedom and independence in living arrangements led to the growth of rooming house districts in many cities. Often these became the location of urban "bohemias," where artists, intellectuals, and political radicals filled the air with excitement.[35]

Historians have neglected the fascinating and important story of these female migrants. Concentrating on the changing "manners and morals" of middle-class women during the early twentieth century, they have ignored the fact that it was mostly urban working women—many of them fresh from the country—who as early as the 1890s were charting a course for "the new woman," one that included a measure of economic independence and the possibilities for life apart from family. Why does the country girl come to the city? asked Chicago social worker Frances Donovan in 1920. Because "it is her frontier, and in it she is the pioneer." These young women should be given their appropriate place as urban pioneers, side by side with the forty-niners and migrating families in the drama of the moving American.[36]

Western cities also attracted thousands of immigrants from abroad. In 1880 foreign-born residents made up a third or more of the populations of Salt Lake City, Portland, Sacramento, and Omaha. These were immigrant cities quite as much as eastern places like Cleveland, Buffalo, or Scranton. Indeed, in 1880 San Francisco had the highest proportion of foreign-born (45 percent) of any city in the nation, more than either New York (40 percent) or Chicago (42 percent). An early visitor was struck by the astounding ethnic diversity: "French, Germans, Mexicans, English, Americans, Irish, and even Chinese, white, black, yellow, brown, Protestants, Catholics, atheists, thieves, convicts, assassins—behold the population of San Francisco." During the first decades immigrant groups carved out neighborhoods along the crowded, hilly streets. Several thousand French residents lived on or near Commercial Street. Up Montgomery, beyond Pine, were the Germans, and a few blocks further north the substantial neighborhood of German Jews. The Irish, the city's largest ethnic group, lived on the slopes of Telegraph Hill along with many Mexican Americans and African Americans, while the Italians clustered along Broadway and in North Beach.[37]

The European immigrants in San Francisco have a history that resembles few other American cities. According to historians William Issel and Robert Cherny, "No white group found itself excluded from the ladder of economic and social mobility." Consider the Italians. In a city with little manufacturing, they moved into fishing, skilled craftwork, and small business. Italian workers rose to leadership in the city's powerful labor movement, and Italian names were prominent in the city's business community. Amadeo Peter Giannini, a lumbering deep-voiced, stubborn tyrant of a man, spent his early years in the family wholesale produce business, selling crates of lettuce and peaches in San Francisco's foggy predawn light. But in his thirties he switched to banking, opening the Banca d'Italia in North Beach. After the devastating earthquake of 1906 he carted out of the burning city eighty thousand dollars hidden under the fruit crates of his old produce firm, and while the city smoldered he was the first banker to reopen for full operations. In an era when banks were austere places frequented only by capitalists and businessmen in their dark suits and starched shirts, Giannini invented the idea of consumer banking, offering small loans to ordinary people at reasonable rates of interest and opening friendly "branch banks" in urban and ethnic neighborhoods. In 1930, the year he renamed his institution Bank of America, he claimed some 280 branches scattered throughout the West.[38]

The most unusual of San Francisco's ethnic communities—and the one most distinctively western—was Chinatown, a place the English writer Oscar Wilde described as "the most artistic town I have ever come across." It was a bustling district of tenements, boardinghouses, small factories, restaurants, and shops, "stocked with hams, tea, dried fish, dried ducks, and other Chinese eatables," in the words of one visitor. "Suspended over the doors were brilliantly-colored boards covered with Chinese writings, and with several yards of red ribbon streaming from them; while the streets thronged with Celestials, chattering vociferously as they rushed about from store to store." In the 1880s approximately twenty-five thousand Chinese, nearly 10 percent of the city's population, squeezed into Chinatown's eight or twelve city blocks in the shadow of the millionaire enclave on Nob Hill.[39]

By rigid custom, San Francisco's Chinese were not permitted to live outside Chinatown. At the margins of their neighborhood Chinese men and women were greeted by the singsong taunts of children: "ching-chong-Chinaman." According to one longtime resident of Chinatown, "If ever you passed the boundaries, the white kids would throw stones at you." Chinese fishermen, whose walk to the wharves took

Ross Alley, in San Francisco's Chinatown.
From Arnold Genthe, Pictures of Old
Chinatown *(New York, 1908). Beinecke.*

them through Irish or Italian neighborhoods, were frequent targets of abuse. In 1868, as he walked home with a basketful of crabs, one Chinese man was attacked by hooligans who beat him senseless with hickory clubs, branded him with a hot iron, and left him for dead. But anti-Chinese violence was even more widespread in the rural West, and during the late nineteenth century most Chinese fled to the cities. They concentrated in Chinatowns like San Francisco's, where at least they could practice their own customs and enjoy a certain security in numbers. They were protected by the powerful "Six Companies," a merchant-dominated directorate of clan associations that governed the Chinese community.[40]

During the first three decades of San Francisco's history Chinatown's children were excluded from city schools. "The prejudice of caste and religious idolatry are so indelibly stamped upon their character," declared the city's school superintendent, that educating them was "almost hopeless." Then in 1884 a Christian Chinese couple, Mary and Joseph Tape (themselves educated in foreign mission academies), sued the Board of Education to admit their daughter to the local elementary school. "Is it a disgrace to be born Chinese?" the mother wrote in a remarkable letter to the board. "I will let the world see, sir, what justice there is when it is governed by the race prejudice men!" The Tapes won their suit, the court deciding that discrimination in education was unconstitutional, but the city circumvented the ruling by establishing a separate school for Chinese children in Chinatown. Educational discrimination would continue to harm them for decades to come. Esther Wong, a Chinatown schoolgirl in the 1920s, remembered a time when her teacher instructed her to read aloud. "Well, I read for her, and there were no mistakes," Wong told an interviewer, and then the teacher said, very slowly, "Well, you read all right, but I don't like you. You belong to a dirty race."[41]

Most Chinese failed to benefit from the city's prosperous economy. During the late nineteenth century San Francisco's immigrant working class succeeded in organizing one of the most powerful labor movements in the country. Job security and good wages facilitated upward mobility, and working-class families began to move out of their old ethnic communities and into new neighborhoods on the west side of the city or to newly developed suburban towns to the south. But one of the fundamental principles of western labor solidarity was the exclusion of the Chinese from the unions. And because many of the male workers in Chinatown had been fraudulently admitted to the country as the "paper sons" of wealthy merchants (the only group allowed to bring over family members by the terms of the Exclusion Act), they found themselves without any legal protection and became prime targets for exploitation and abuse by those same businessmen. Representatives of the Six Companies cut deals with city officials that allowed them to circumvent zoning and labor laws. About half the city's manufacturing labor force was Chinese, but Chinatown was the center of the city's sweatshop district. Segregated and excluded from the mainstream, the Chinese in San Francisco lived in a world of their own, one of the least assimilated immigrant groups ever to exist in America. Chinatown was a city within the city.

In contrast to San Francisco, relatively few European immigrants settled in early twentieth-century Los Angeles. The white population was drawn mostly from the Midwest and plains, from the farms and small towns of Indiana, Illinois, Nebraska, Iowa, and Kansas. A large proportion of these emigrants were elderly, "retired farmers, grocers, Ford agents, [and] hardware merchants," wrote Louis Adamic, author of an early debunking history of the City of Angels. "They sold out their farms and businesses in the Middle West or wherever they used to live, and now they are here in California—sunny California—to rest and regain their vigor, enjoy the climate, look at pretty scenery, live in little bungalows with a palm-tree or banana plant in front, and eat in cafeterias. Toil-broken and bleached out, they flocked to Los Angeles, fugitives from the simple, inexorable justice of life, from hard labor and drudgery, from cold winters and blistering summers of the prairies." Go west, *old* man. "As New York is the melting-pot for the peoples of Europe," wrote novelist Sarah Comstock, "so Los Angeles is the melting-pot for the peoples of the United States." Actually, there was relatively little melting. Many emigrants, lonely for their old homes, joined other lonesome folks in one or another of the several dozen "state societies" of southern California. Thousands joined the Pennsylvania Club and the Illinois Association, and crowds estimated at 150,000 people or more attended the annual Iowa Society picnic.[42]

After World War I the character of emigration to Los Angeles changed, as the city began a period of rapid industrialization. Stimulated first by the enormous expansion of federal spending during the war, the industrial revolution in southern California moved into high gear, fueled by the discovery of vast local petroleum fields. Oil was discovered in the 1890s, but the really big fields were opened after the war, the first in 1920 at Huntington Beach (one of Henry Huntington's many developments), followed by several more in quick succession. Almost overnight the region was supplying nearly 10 percent of the nation's fuel oil and gasoline. In California, as in Texas, local capital financed petroleum development, supplying one of the most important early examples of western industrial development. California overtook Texas and Oklahoma as the largest oil-producing state during the 1920s, and by 1930 refining was the state's largest industry. The "multiplier effects" of the petroleum industry were remarkable. Between the wars Los Angeles rose to become the West's largest industrial center—the nucleus of the nation's oil equipment and service industry, the second largest tire-manufacturing center, and the largest producer of steel, glass, chemicals, aircraft, and automobiles in the West. Perhaps the most visible sign of economic development was the fabulous growth of the motion picture industry, which by the end of the 1920s was employing more than fifteen thousand.

As word of L.A.'s economic miracle spread eastward, the city began to experience unprecedented population growth. More than a hundred thousand new residents arrived each year during the early 1920s, part of the massive national relocation taking millions from farms to cities. From states like Arkansas, Oklahoma, and Texas came thousands of poor folks in search of work. "Like a swarm of invading locusts," wrote essayist Mildred Adams, "migrants crept in over the roads. They had rattletrap automobiles, their fenders tied with string, and curtains flapping in the breeze; loaded with babies, bedding, bundles, a tin tub tied on behind, a bicycle or a baby carriage balanced precariously on top. Often they came with no funds and no prospects, apparently trusting that heaven would provide for them. They camped on the outskirts of town, and their camps became new suburbs."[43]

The migration to southern California included thousands of African Americans, Mexicans, and Japanese, who by 1930 made up approximately half of the unskilled workforce at the base of the region's industrial economy. The rapid rise in the proportion of these groups in the population—from 6 percent in 1910 to nearly 15 percent in 1930—caused considerable alarm among many of the county's white residents. Overt hostility was widespread. "Negroes: We Don't Want You Here," screamed the headline in one local paper in 1922. "Now and forever, this is to be a white man's town." Local chapters of the Ku Klux Klan staged nighttime rallies in

Restricted housing tract, Los Angeles, c. 1940.
Southern California Library for Social Studies and Research.

public parks and organized auto caravans through minority neighborhoods, "to put us in our place," as one Mexican immigrant told his son. In the area surrounding the downtown campus of the University of Southern California, homeowners formed the Anti-African Housing Association (later renamed the University District Property Owners Association), and black newcomers who had dared to cross the color line separating neighborhoods were greeted by burning crosses on their lawns. White residents harassed Japanese families moving into white areas, and in one particularly frightening case vigilantes burned one Japanese family out of its home. Even more effective, however, were the silent "restricted covenants" written into the deeds of homes in most sections of the city, excluding "Negroes, Mongolians, Indians, and Mexicans" from occupancy. By the 1920s, 95 percent of the city's housing had been declared off-limits to racial minorities. Minority home buyers brought suit to challenge the legality of these deed restrictions, but local courts continued to uphold them until 1948.[44]

The African-American population of Los Angeles—which grew from eight thousand in 1910 to nearly forty thousand in 1930, making it the largest in the West—was confined to an area along Central Avenue in the southern section of the city and to a rural district further south initially known as "Mudtown." The writer Arna Bontemps, who attended school in Los Angeles in the 1920s, remembered "an aspect of savage wildness" about the area, with dusty, unpaved roads, grazing farm animals, and "on the air a suggestion of pigs and slime holes." Most of the black residents there had emigrated from Louisiana, Arkansas, and Texas, and "Mudtown," Bontemps wrote, "was like a tiny section of the deep south literally transplanted." After World War I the area was renamed "Watts," for real estate agent C. H. Watts, who developed tracts of cheap bungalows for black families. By the late 1920s, writes historian Gerald Horne, Watts was "a black island in an otherwise white sea," surrounded by lily-white suburbs like South Gate, Bell, Compton, and Lynwood, which advertised itself as "the friendly Caucasian city."[45]

Segregation was an everyday fact of life in southern California—in public education and transportation, at parks, swimming pools, hotels, restaurants, and theaters. Edward Roybal, a social worker who in 1949 became the first Mexican American elected to the Los Angeles City Council, remembered that during the 1930s it was common to see signs in the city's establishments warning, "No Mexicans or Negroes Allowed." Los Angeles, of course, was not unique in this. In the western states of Texas, Oklahoma, and Arizona, segregation was written into law. "Nowhere in the United States did minorities enjoy complete equality and integration," writes historian Robert Fogelson. "But in Los Angeles, where they were distinguished by race rather than nationality, the majority subjugated and excluded them even more rigorously." Dwight Zook, for many years a member of the county's Fair Employment Practices Commission, put it more boldly in an interview in 1965. Los Angeles, he declared, was "probably the most segregated city in the U.S."[46]

Mexican Americans made up the largest and fastest growing of the minority communities in Los Angeles, climbing from only six thousand in 1910 to nearly one hundred thousand in 1930. Their experience illustrates another dimension of the centuries-long conflict over acculturation and assimilation that lies at the heart of the history of the American West. The Mexican immigrants arriving in the city during the 1910s and 1920s first settled in the old city center, near the nineteenth-century Catholic cathedral. But as that area filled up, they began spilling eastward, over the Los Angeles River and into the area that has since become known as East L.A.—Mexican-American capital of the West. By the late 1920s East L.A. was developing into a stable community, a place where, as historian George Sánchez discovered, 44 percent of Mexican families owned homes. "Home ownership," Sánchez writes, "symbolized adaptation: permanent settlement in the city."[47]

The prosperity of the 1920s was short-lived. The Great Depression hit Los Angeles hard, and with a third or more of the county's workforce unemployed by 1931, there was growing clamor in the city for the deportation of Mexicans, who, in the

Mexicans await repatriation at a Los Angeles railway station, 1932. Herald Examiner Collection, Los Angeles Public Library.

words of President Herbert Hoover, "took jobs away from American citizens." This was pure bombast, of course, but Hoover nevertheless ordered the roundup of illegal aliens. In several neighborhoods of the Los Angeles barrio, immigration agents went door to door, demanding that residents produce papers proving their legal residency, summarily arresting and jailing those unable to do so, many American citizens among them. "It was for us the day of judgment," one resident wrote in 1931 in the pages of the local Spanish-language newspaper, *La Opinión*. "The *marciales*, deputy sheriffs, arrived in late afternoon when the men were returning home from working the lemon groves. They started arresting people. . . . The deputies rode around the neighborhood with the sirens wailing and advising people to surrender themselves to the authorities. They barricaded all the exits to the *colonia* so that no one could escape. . . . We the women cried, the children screamed, others ran hither and yon with the deputies in hot pursuit yelling at them that their time had come and to surrender."[48]

Raids like this one frightened many Mexicans into joining a voluntary program of repatriation organized by officials of Los Angeles County, and between 1930 and 1933 tens of thousands of Mexican citizens boarded buses and trains transporting them to the border. "The men were pensive and the majority of the children and mothers were crying," one *repatriado* told an interviewer years later. "From Los Angeles to El Paso some sang with guitars trying to forget their sadness."

> Good bye dear countrymen
> They are going to deport us
> But we are not bandits
> We came to toil.

There are no reliable statistics on the total number of Mexicans deported from Los Angeles, but in their authoritative study, Francisco E. Balderrama and Raymond Rodríguez estimate that at least a million Mexican citizens from the Southwest were repatriated during the 1930s.[49]

George Sánchez argues that the trauma of deportation marked an important step in the transition from Mexican to Mexican American in California. "What had been largely an immigrant community before the Depression became one dominated by the children of immigrants." While maintaining their identity as Mexicans, these children had grown up in the states, absorbing the values of American culture. The conflict between the generations often focused on gender. "Here the old women want to run things," grumbled one Mexican immigrant, "and the poor man has to wash the dishes while the wife goes to the show." One young woman, pointing out that her parents had been "born in old Mexico," complained to an interviewer that "as soon as I was sixteen my father began to watch me, and would not let me go anywhere or have my friends come home." Another boasted that the first thing she did when she left home was bob her hair in the fashion of the day. "My father would not permit it and I have wanted to do it for a long time. I will show my husband that he will not boss me the way my father had done all of us."[50]

Many young Mexican Americans, impatient with their immigrant parents, yet outraged by racism and segregation, became *pachucos,* a defiant cultural style that included slang speaking in a distinctive "Span-glish" argot, dressing in the long coats and pegged pants of the zoot-suiter, joining gangs, and "rumbling" in the streets. During World War II there was growing public controversy over these pachuco gangs, and in 1943 hundreds of sailors from the port of Long Beach invaded East L.A., assaulting young Mexican Americans and African Americans, stripping them of their clothes, and beating them senseless as the police stood by and white bystanders cheered. As sociologist Alfredo Guerra Gonzales suggests, what have been called the "Zoot-Suit Riots" should actually be remembered as "Serviceman's Riots." For the Mexican-American community, which sent its sons to fight in the war in greater proportion than any other group in the West, these riots would remain a bitter memory. A young Mexican American, arrested in 1943 as a public nuisance, eloquently expressed the feelings of his generation to the judge. "Pretty soon I guess I'll be in the

Mexican Americans demonstrate in support of striking streetcar workers in Los Angeles, 1941. Hearst Newspaper Collection, Department of Special Collections, University of Southern California Library.

army and I'll be glad to go. But I want to be treated like everybody else. We're tired of being pushed around. We're tired of being told we can't go to this show or that dance hall because we're Mexican, or that we better not be seen on the beach front, or that we can't wear draped pants or have our hair cut the way we want to. . . . I don't want any more trouble and I don't want anyone saying my people are a disgrace. My people work hard, fight hard in the army and navy of the United States. They're good Americans and should have justice."[51]

Justice for Americans. The violation of this principle was most evident in the history of the Japanese-American community in Los Angeles. Crowded into "Little Tokyo" in the downtown section of the city, the immigrant Issei and their Nisei children seemed willing to ignore discrimination and dedicate themselves to hard work and prosperity in the American style. "Scratch a Japanese American," writes scholar Harry Kitano, "and find a white Anglo-Saxon Protestant." Until the 1920s most signs seemed to point to assimilation and a weakening identification with Japan, but the passage of the Immigration Restriction Act of 1924, completely barring Japanese immigration, "was a stinging rejection of their hopes for economic and social assimilation," according to historian Brian Masaru Hayashi. "We are not whole-heartedly accepted by the country we reside in," one Nisei concluded. "True, we are American citizens, but only in a statutory sense. Socially we are just another foreigner, compelled to huddle into a small quarter of our own, unable to take part in American social activities, and above all denied positions in American firms, simply because of our race."[52]

During the 1930s, the aggressive campaign of expansion by Japan in China sparked considerable controversy within the Japanese-American community. Nisei Monica Sone later remembered bitter debates with her Issei parents. "I used to criticize Japan's aggressions in China and Manchuria while Father and Mother condemned Great Britain and America's superior attitude toward Asiatics and the interference with Japan's economic growth," she wrote. "During these arguments, we eyed each other like strangers, parents against children. They left us with a hollow feeling at the pit of the stomach." The Japanese American Citizens League, a Nisei organization formed in 1930 to promote assimilation, was critical of Japan. But this was not simply a generational conflict, for other Nisei publicly supported the empire. "I cry for joy over the Imperial favor that is now extending to the 400 million Chinese people," wrote a Japanese leader in Los Angeles. Another Nisei condemned the idea that "American culture was the only possible lifestyle" for what he called the coming "Era of the Pacific" and argued for less "Americanization" of the Japanese and more "Pacific-ization" of Americans.[53]

The loyalty of Japanese to their homeland was not unique. There were German Americans active in the Nazi Bund Party and Italian Americans who applauded Mussolini. But Japanese-American citizens were the only ones subjected to mass incarceration during World War II. Two months after the attack on Pearl Harbor, President Franklin D. Roosevelt signed Executive Order 9066, suspending the civil rights of both citizens and aliens of Japanese background in the western states, authorizing the confiscation of their property, and the "removal" of families from their homes and communities. The order was defended on the grounds of "military necessity," a justification upheld by the Supreme Court in 1944, although in 1982 a federal commission concluded that the United States government had possessed no evidence linking West coast Japanese Americans with espionage and that internment was the result of "race prejudice, war hysteria, and a failure of political leadership." The residents of L.A.'s Little Tokyo were rounded up and sent to one of the ten camps set up across the trans-Mississippi West. Many ended up at Manzanar in the Owens valley, left an arid waste by the diversion of water for urban Los Angeles. Manzanar was "the scene of a triple tragedy," says Richard Stewart, a Paiute Indian who leads tours around the abandoned site of the camp. First native Paiutes and Shoshones lost their homes, then farmers and ranchers lost their water, and finally Japanese Americans lost their rights. A total of 120,000 people were held in these detention camps for up to three years.[54]

"The evacuation and establishment of relocation centers were actions without precedent in American history," wrote Dillon S. Myer, director of the War Relocation Authority, in charge of the operation. What would the Cherokees or the Creeks, the Shawnees or the Nez Percé say to such an assertion? Was it mere coincidence that Myer found many of his lieutenants among the bureaucrats of the Bureau of Indian

Japanese Americans assemble for internment, Bainbridge Island, Washington. From Seattle Post-Intelligencer, *March 3, 1942. Yale University.*

Affairs or that the camps so closely resembled Indian reservations? "Has the Gestapo come to America?" one Japanese American wondered in 1942. No, this was not some alien idea invading America but the culmination of an old American fear of the other, the alien, the redskinned savage, the greaser, the Chink, and the Jap. "A Jap's a Jap," declared General John L. DeWitt of the Western Defense Command. "It makes no difference whether he is an American."[55]

Jeffrey S. Adler, *Yankee Merchants and the Making of the Urban West: The Rise and Fall of Antebellum St. Louis* (1991)

Francisco E. Balderrama and Raymond Rodríguez, *Decade of Betrayal: Mexican Repatriation in the 1930s* (1995)

Gunther Barth, *Instant Cities: Urbanization and the Rise of San Francisco and Denver* (1975)

William Cronon, *Nature's Metropolis: Chicago and the Great West* (1991)

Robert M. Fogelson, *The Fragmented Metropolis: Los Angeles, 1850–1930* (1967)

David Hamer, *New Towns in the New World: Images and Perceptions of the Nineteenth-Century Urban Frontier* (1990)

Brian Masaru Hayashi, *"For the Sake of Our Japanese Brethren": Assimilation, Nationalism, and Protestantism Among the Japanese of Los Angeles, 1895–1942* (1995)

Timothy R. Mahoney, *River Towns in the Great West: The Structure of Provincial Urbanization in the American Midwest, 1820–1870* (1990)

Earl Pomeroy, *The Pacific Slope: A History of California, Oregon, Washington, Idaho, Utah, and Nevada* (1965)

George J. Sánchez, *Becoming Mexican American: Ethnicity, Culture, and Identity in Chicano Los Angeles, 1900–1945* (1993)

Carey McWilliams, *Southern California Country: An Island on the Land* (1946)

Joanne J. Meyerowitz, *Women Adrift: Independent Wage Earners in Chicago, 1880–1930* (1988)

Judy Yung, *Unbound Feet: A Social History of Chinese Women in San Francisco* (1995)

Richard Wade, *The Urban Frontier: The Rise of Western Cities, 1790–1830* (1959)

Adna F. Weber, *The Growth of Cities in the Nineteenth Century: A Study in Statistics* (1899)

14

Plunder and Preservation

"The heavens are alive with pigeons!" The call echoes through the clearing where the pioneers have built their cabins. Men, women, and children pour from their homes and look skyward. Great flocks of passenger pigeons veer and ripple in masses of blue and purple as they migrate north from their winter roosts. "You may look an hour before you can find a hole through which to get a peep at the sun." With rifles and pistols the pioneers commence their attack on the birds, and feathery masses begin tumbling to the field, but so preoccupied are the hunters with the slaughter that none bother about the kill. Two men even deploy a little cannon and, loading it with shot, fire haphazardly into the sky, bringing down pigeons by the dozens with each report.

At the edge of the carnage stands an old scout clad in buckskin, the very man who years before had blazed the first trail to this valley. His rifle hangs on his arm, his dogs cower by his side, as if sensing their master's horror. "This comes of settling a country." Old Leatherstocking spits out the words in disgust, directing them at Judge Marmaduke Temple, the leader of this backwoods community. "Here have I known the pigeons to fly for forty long years, and till you made your clearings there was nobody to skear or to hurt them. I loved to see them come into the woods, for they were company to a body, hurting nothing." It's wicked, he murmurs, wicked. Moved by the old man's words, the judge responds. "I begin to think it time to put an end to this work of destruction," but Leatherstocking quickly reproaches him. "Put an ind, Judge, to your clearings," he insists. "An't the woods His work as well as the pigeons? Use, but don't waste. Wasn't the woods made for the beasts and birds to harbour in?" And shouldering his rifle, he walks sadly into the woods, taking care not to tread on the quivering birds that litter his path. "I wouldn't touch one of the harmless things that kiver the ground here, looking up with their eyes on me as if they only wanted tongues to say their thoughts."[1]

"Shooting Wild Pigeons in Iowa." From Frank Leslie's Illustrated Newspaper, *June 3, 1871. The Library Company of Philadelphia.*

This scene—one of the more celebrated in American literature—appears in James Fenimore Cooper's *The Pioneers* (1823), the novel that introduced the American reading public to Leatherstocking, the tragic frontier character who leads the settlement of the wilderness, bringing on the destruction of the world he loves. Cooper's depiction of the war waged upon the passenger pigeon, however, was no fiction. He set his novel in a backwoods community much like the frontier village of Cooperstown, New York, where he had grown up. In an early review of the book, a local newspaper editor vouched for the accuracy of Cooper's depiction of the pigeon shoot, "having ourselves witnessed similar sport upon the same favoured spot." In the nineteenth century billions of these birds inhabited eastern North America, and "market hunters" slaughtered them by the tens of thousands, selling them as squab for thirty to fifty cents a dozen. Naturalist John Jacob Audubon, who included a beautiful watercolor of a cooing pair in his *Birds of America* (1827–38), wrote of meeting a man who claimed to have killed as many as six thousand pigeons in a single day. In the spring the birds congregated in vast forest colonies, filling the trees with fragile nests jointly tended by male and female. Discovering such a site, market hunters would converge from all sides, knocking fledglings from the nests with long poles and shooting the anxious adults as they flew about in concern for their young. Serious declines in pigeon population were noted as early as the 1850s, and by the end of the century the species had been driven to extinction in the wild. The last known representative—an ancient female known to her keepers as "Martha"—died in the Cincinnati Zoo about midday on September 1, 1914.[2]

The record of the passenger pigeon's demise is unusually detailed. Historians are less well informed about the extinction of other indigenous North American species. Scientists have, however, compiled a list of approximately seventy known to have gone belly-up over the past two centuries, including the Labrador duck, the New England heath hen (a relative of the prairie chicken), and the Carolina parakeet (valued for its colorful plumage), the eastern sea mink and the eastern elk, the Wisconsin cougar and the Great Plains wolf. By the early twentieth century the only California grizzly left in California was the one on the state's bear flag. The beaver disappeared from most of its habitat by the 1840s, although it managed a revival after beaver hats went out of fashion. The sea otter and the fur seal of the Northwest coast were on the verge of extinction when saved by an international ban on commercial hunting early in the twentieth century. The buffalo perished by the tens of millions, of course, and by 1890 just eight hundred remained in several isolated herds. Less well known is the radical decline in the numbers of other game animals in the West. Nature writer Ernest Thompson Seton estimated in the 1920s that the number of western mule deer, antelope, and bighorn sheep, once counted in the millions, had fallen by 95 to 99 percent. Americans blasted their way across the continent, says Donald Worster, leaving in their wake "a landscape littered with skulls and bones, drenched in blood."[3]

Wildlife perished not only by gun or trap but more insidiously by the destruction of habitat. Wetlands were drained and woodlands cleared. James Fenimore Cooper was one of the first Americans to worry over such losses, and the popularity of his books suggests that many readers shared his concern. "I call no country much improved that is pretty well covered with trees," declares a boisterous woodchopper in *The Pioneers;* "to my eyes, they are a sore sight at any time, unless I'm privileged to work my will on them." But Leatherstocking decries the work of settlement that turns "good hunting grounds into stumpy pastures" and asserts his belief that "the garden of the Lord was the forest." In his heyday a hunter such as Leatherstocking could walk through stands of beech and maple stretching so broad and so deep that he might not see the sun for days on end. But by the early nineteenth century, when Cooper wrote, the great trans-Appalachian deciduous and evergreen forests were dwindling under the attack of civilization. Farmers by the hundreds of thousands had set about with sweat and determination to girdle, chop, and burn the trees from the fields of trans-Appalachia. The pungent smell of burning wood was to them the sweet perfume of "improvement." Eventually the woodlands east of the Mississippi were reduced to only about 2 percent of their former extent.[4]

The timber of the great woods also fed hundreds of small sawmills and pulp mills scattered throughout the West. By midcentury the construction of a national rail network and the rise of Chicago as a distribution center led to the industrialization of logging. The greatest timber volume and value came from the forests of the Great

Lake states. Some logging companies purchased huge stands of white pine from state and federal governments, but others perpetrated enormous frauds by paying their employees to enter phony homestead claims. "In all the pine region of Lake Superior and the Upper Mississippi where vast areas have been settled under the pretense of agriculture," the commissioner of the General Land Office reported in 1876, "scarcely a vestige of agriculture appears." In the vicinity of Duluth, Minnesota, for example, more than 4,300 homestead entries had been filed and completed, but an investigation found that only a hundred settlers were actually living and working on farms. The great bulk of the land had been logged and simply abandoned. Loggers systematically cut over huge areas, floating great rafts of logs downriver to giant steam-powered sawmills and leaving forests of stumps stretching for hundreds of miles—Leatherstocking's worst nightmare. The remaining "slash cover" of dead wood and brush provided fuel for terrifying fires that not only consumed millions of acres of forest each year but destroyed the humus in the already poor soil. In 1871 an inferno raging through the woods of Wisconsin destroyed the town of Peshtigo and killed more than 1,500 people, far more than the number that perished in the great Chicago fire of the same year. A Minnesota conflagration in 1894 incinerated five towns and claimed 413 lives. By that time the logging industry had about used up the available timber of the Great Lake region and was moving on to the South and to the old-growth forests of the Pacific Northwest.[5]

"The great American nation," wrote the English writer Rudyard Kipling after a visit to the West in the 1880s, "grasps all it can and moves on." Mining supplied another example of just how destructive the grabbing could be. The use of high-pressure water jets to wash down mountains of deposits, so that the gold could be separated from the rubble, was cheap and effective, but it took no account of the havoc wrought to streams and the valleys below, as tons of mud and rocks buried plant life, including crops, like a chronic avalanche. Farmers with clogged irrigation systems and inundated crops fought bitter legislative battles against mining companies. But by the time a federal judge declared hydraulic mining a public nuisance and issued a permanent injunction in 1884, an estimated twelve billion tons of earth had been eroded away, and the resulting silt had reduced the depth of San Francisco Bay by three to six feet. Even greater destruction to the bay came from the mercury mines in the foothills surrounding the town of San Jose. Mercury was essential in separating gold from quartz rock, and those mining operations dumped tons of the stuff into the streams that fed the bay, leaving a legacy that poisons the fish to this day.[6]

Petroleum drilling also could be powerfully destructive. The oil spills from gushers polluted soil and water and, catching fire, sent heavy clouds of acrid smoke drifting across the countryside. One Texas gusher of 1911 spewed out 116,000 barrels a day for nine days before it was capped. Plunder and pollution were component parts of the frontier economy, attributable to the desire for rapid exploitation, an economic

Oil gusher, Maricopa, California, c. 1905. San Francisco Museum of Modern Art. Gift of Stephen White.

system that awarded the highest premium to the fiercest competitor, and a laissez-faire government thoughtless of the common good. Above all, the American people adhered to what naturalist William Vogt, in an early environmentalist jeremiad, called "the cornucopian faith" of ceaseless abundance. North America was indeed rich in resources—rich enough to double the world's annual production of gold in 1849, rich enough to grow wheat sufficient to feed the world. Fish, furs, timber, oil—all were available in unending supply, it seemed. There was no need to worry.[7]

Americans began to challenge the myth of inexhaustibility in the mid-nineteenth century. The first to note the disappearance of fish, birds, and animals were sportsmen—and they were also the first to do something about it. This may come as news to today's environmentalists, some of whom accuse hunters of "animal murder," but as John Reiger puts it in his study of the origins of the conservation movement, "sportsmen led the way." Traditionally Americans hunted for the practical purpose of procuring meat or skins, but by the middle of the nineteenth century sport hunting had became popular, especially among men of the American upper class. What distinguished sport hunting from traditional hunting was its focus on means rather than ends. According to the "sportsman's code"—standards drawn from the hunting traditions of the English aristocracy—it was not the kill itself but the manner of killing that mattered. There were fair and foul ways of taking game. Sport hunters were outraged, for example, by the continuing war of market hunters on the passenger pigeon. On a number of occasions groups of sportsmen attempted to prevent the attacks of market hunters on large nesting colonies of pigeons; there were armed confrontations, and occasionally even exchanges of gunfire, but it did little good. Eventually the depletion of favorite trout streams and hunting ranges pushed sportsmen to organize, pressing state legislatures for laws limiting and regulating the take of wildlife. The campaign for hunting laws began after the Civil War, and by the end of the nineteenth century a majority of states and localities had established fish and game commissions, defined fishing and hunting seasons, and set licensing requirements and bag limits. These were the first modern organized efforts to regulate the use of the environment.[8]

A prominent leader of the national sportsmen's movement was George Bird Grinnell, a patrician New Yorker who earned a doctorate in zoology from Yale University, toured the West on scientific and hunting expeditions, and made friends with the Cheyenne Indians—which resulted in several magnificent books on native life and culture. In 1880 Grinnell became editor of *Forest and Stream,* one of a number of sportsmen's magazines founded in the late nineteenth century, and he used its pages to condemn the destruction of the buffalo as "mercenary and wanton butchery" and to decry the "corruption" of hunting by "the mighty dollar." In 1887 Grinnell and fellow New Yorker Theodore Roosevelt called together a group of wealthy sportsmen to establish a national society for the promotion of sports hunting. The Boone and Crockett Club—named for two of the nation's legendary backwoodsmen—sought to perpetuate the traits of "energy, resolution, manliness, self-reliance, and a capacity for self-help." The frontier experience had cultivated a "vigorous manliness" among Americans, Roosevelt wrote, and "unless we keep the barbarian values, gaining the civilized ones will be of little avail." The Boone and Crockett Club quickly became the nation's most influential environmental lobby, working for the protection of threatened species and the creation of a system of wildlife refuges.[9]

A second and complementary interest in the environment originated in romanticism, the dominant intellectual and aesthetic movement of the nineteenth century. Like Roosevelt, the romantics worried over the limiting and corrupting effects of too much civilization, and they celebrated the restorative power of immersion in nature. "The further we become separated from pristine wildness and beauty," wrote the artist George Catlin, who dedicated his career to preserving images of American Indians on canvas, "the more pleasure does the mind of enlightened man feel in recurring to those scenes." This sentiment ought to sound familiar, for it remains the most prominent rationale for the preservation of wilderness. In 1832 Catlin proposed setting off the grasslands of the Great Plains "in a magnificent park, where the world could see for ages to come, the native Indian in his classic attire, galloping his wild horse, with sinewy bow, and shield and lance, amid the fleeting herds of elks and buffaloes. What a beautiful and thrilling specimen for America to preserve and hold up to the view of her refined citizens and the world in future ages!" Catlin's proposal was flamboyant and impractical, and his conflation of Indians with elks and buffalo spoke volumes about the narrow ethnocentric assumptions of American romantics. But the notion of a national park where protected natural wonders might refresh the spirits of the overcivilized was an idea whose time would come.[10]

The physical drama, the sheer grandeur of western mountains and rivers, argued for protection, for some effort to keep their primeval beauty intact for later generations. The first serious proposal concerned the glacier-carved Yosemite Valley in the central Sierra Nevada of California. The valley vista was "discovered" in 1851 when gold miners attacked the villages of the native Yosemite people, driving them from the site the Indians knew as "Ahwahnee"—place of deep grass. Within a few years hearty tourists were trekking into the area, and their published accounts and drawings brought the spectacular scenery to national attention. The combination of granite cliffs, lofty waterfalls, verdant meadows, clear streams, and huge redwoods made Yosemite the perfect subject for romantic art of the sublime and picturesque, exemplified in the awe-inspiring paintings of the valley by Albert Bierstadt, which were widely distributed as engravings and chromolithographs. In 1864 a group of prominent citizens, including Frederick Law Olmsted, designer of New York City's

Yosemite Valley. *Painting by Albert Bierstadt, c. 1875. Yale University Art Gallery. Gift of Mrs. Vincenzo Ardenghi.*

Central Park, persuaded Congress to grant the valley to the state of California for "public use, resort and recreation." The reservation was small, only ten square miles; no thought was given to preserving the ecosystem, just the monumental scenery. Soon tourist facilities cluttered the valley floor. But at least Yosemite was saved from the destructive livestock grazing that depleted the deep grass and led to the serious erosion of other Sierra locations. To prevent such "destruction by settlement" of other spectacular sites in the West, a number of writers began to call for the creation of more "nature reserves." These proposals gained powerful support when the Southern Pacific Railroad noted a significant increase in tourist traffic along the rail lines leading to Yosemite.[11]

Railroad tourism dated from the advent in the late 1860s of Pullman sleeper cars—rolling hotels, paneled in mahogany, lights shaded with Tiffany glass—which could bring travelers comfortably to the great western tourist destinations. Western railroad interests thus became interested in the creation of federal parks, the first in the headwater region of the Yellowstone River, high in the Rocky Mountains. Long treasured by Indians as a rich hunting and fishing ground, Yellowstone was legendary among fur trappers for its iridescent pools, cobalt-encrusted springs, roaring waterfalls, and mirror lakes reflecting peaks between glistening glaciers. The descriptions of mountain men were at first considered western tall tales—geysers whose heads bumped the clouds, icy lakes adjacent to steaming pools where a fish dinner could be boiled while still on the hook—and no skeptical easterner took them seriously until a party of scientists and local boosters hiked into the area in 1870 and confirmed the existence of Yellowstone's "curiosities" and "wonders." The next year University of Pennsylvania geologist Ferdinand V. Hayden, founder of the United States Geological Survey, led a scientific survey that included pioneer western photographer William Henry Jackson and landscape artist Thomas Moran. Hayden's report—and particularly Jackson's photographs and Moran's watercolors—generated considerable interest. But things didn't really begin to happen until financier Jay Cooke, mindful of the profits that tourist traffic would generate for his Northern Pacific Railroad, proposed that Congress declare Yellowstone "a public park forever—just as it has reserved that far inferior wonder, the Yosemite Valley." His rhetoric marked the beginning of competition among railroads for the western tourist dollar.[12]

Unlike Yosemite, however, Yellowstone was located in federal territory (not until 1890 were Wyoming, Montana, and Idaho granted statehood), and hence this reserve would have to be a federal creation. Assured that the area was too high and too cold for agriculture and that consequently its designation would do "no harm to the material interests of the people," in March 1872 Congress designated more than two million acres on the Yellowstone River as "a public park or pleasuring ground for the benefit and enjoyment of the people," stipulating that all the timber, minerals, wildlife, and "curiosities" therein be retained "in their natural condition." Setting aside lands as "pleasuring grounds" was unprecedented, and the measure provoked vociferous opposition. One congressman protested that commercial development was being made to yield to "a few sportsmen bent only on the protection of a few buffalo," and another snorted at the proposed entrance of the government into "show business." Fortunately the majority followed the Missouri senator who asserted the benefits of a "great breathing-place for the national lungs." Yellowstone remained the only national park until 1890, when the Southern Pacific successfully lobbied for federal legislation creating a wilderness sanctuary in the area surrounding the Yosemite Valley and another to protect the groves of huge sequoias in the southern Sierra Nevada.[13]

The first national parks thus had everything to do with commerce and enterprise. In the public mind, however, one man was most responsible for these developments—John Muir, an American original and the country's most effective propagandist for wilderness. Born in Scotland and raised on a hardscrabble Wisconsin farm, Muir suffered through the domination of his strict Presbyterian parents. Finding his refuge in books and in nature, Muir left home at a young age for a lifelong study of the natural environment in the field. He tramped from Canada to Mexico and sailed from Alaska to the South Seas, writing about his experiences. A fervent disciple of Transcendentalism, Muir once invited Ralph Waldo Emerson, who was touring California, to "worship" with him at Yosemite. Emerson accepted but, instead of sleeping with Muir under the stars, chose to bunk in one of the park's tourist

A tourist and a resident of Yellowstone National Park, c. 1935. Denver Public Library, Western History Department.

hotels, explaining that the wilderness was "a sublime mistress, but an intolerable wife." For Muir, nature was all—wife, mistress, offspring, even God, though quite unlike the God of his strict Presbyterian fathers. The forests, he wrote in one of his first published essays, were "God's first temples." Muir's wilderness philosophy was anchored on the romantic contrast between sacred nature and what he called, perhaps remembering his father's discipline, "the galling harness of civilization."[14]

In truth there was no such clear line of demarcation between wilderness and civilization. From the beginning the national parks were exercises in compromise. Tourism demanded the construction and maintenance of roads, trails, and buildings; park visitors required hotels, restaurants, campgrounds, and garbage dumps, water, sewage, and power systems. Moreover, the mandate to retain the parks' "natural conditions" was interpreted to mean the cultivation of landscapes that conformed to the public's notion of wilderness. Officials at Yellowstone worked hard to encourage what one park superintendent called "the type of animal the park was for." To protect browsing herds of elk, moose, deer, and bighorn sheep, park managers went to war against wolves, mountain lions, and coyotes. To save the last bison herd from extinction they created a ranch where the animals were fed park-grown hay. To improve the fishing they introduced brook and rainbow trout in the streams. And to protect this concocted "wilderness," they struggled to suppress the forest fires that were a normal part of nature's cycle. This was what critic Alston Chase would later characterize as "playing God in Yellowstone." The dilemma has been a part of the entire history of the national parks.[15]

While John Muir cultivated an eccentric image—letting his hair and beard go untrimmed, living in the woods, and dedicating himself totally to "nature"—he understood better than most the practical side of the national parks. Without hesitation he joined himself to the efforts of the railroads to generate more tourist business. He worked with the Northern Pacific, lobbying for the creation of Mount Rainier and Glacier national parks in 1899, and with the Southern Pacific in 1906 to convince California to cede Yosemite Valley back to federal jurisdiction. To monitor federal administration of the parks and counter new threats to the mountain environment, in 1892 he organized the Sierra Club—an organization that would "be able to do something for wildness and make the mountains glad"—and served as its president for the next twenty-two years. Muir was an idealist and a romantic. But he was also an environmental politician.[16]

Curtailing the massive assault on the nation's forests by loggers proved more difficult than creating national parks. The first expression of official concern came when the report of the 1870 census documented the appalling deforestation that had taken place in the Great Lakes region. "The rapidity with which this country is being stripped of its forests must alarm every thinking man," declared Interior Secretary Carl Schurtz. "It has been estimated by good authority that, if we go on at the present rate, the supply of timber in the United States will in less than twenty years fall considerably short of our home necessities." But in the 1870s—the heyday of expansion in the trans-Mississippi West—Congress was in no mood to restrict access to western resources. Instead it passed the Timber Cutting Act of 1878, which made it even easier for private citizens and companies to cut timber on federal land. The legislation amounted to what one disapproving congressman called a "license for timber thieves on the public domain."[17]

To be fair, Congress also called for "further study" of the nation's forests. Those federal studies—half a dozen fat volumes stuffed with statistics, maps, and yet more warnings about deforestation—had little impact on the lawmakers but aroused many in the nation's intellectual community. Scientists were beginning to consider the web of connections among living things—a subject already known as ecology—and the impact of human action on the ecosystem. An important contribution to this thinking was the book *Man and Nature* (1864), written by American diplomat and amateur scientist George Perkins Marsh. Marsh was particularly interested in the problem of deforestation, which he had witnessed first in his boyhood home in the Green Mountains of Vermont and then in the Mediterranean hills of Turkey and Italy. Without forests to root the thin mountain soil, rains produced torrents that swept down hillsides, washed away topsoil, destroyed undergrowth, drove away wildlife, and flooded agricultural valleys. "We have now felled forest enough everywhere," Marsh wrote, "and in many districts far too much." Deforestation and erosion, he implied, had contributed to the fall of Old World civilizations and might produce the same result in America. By the 1880s other Americans were repeating his warnings. "We are following the course of nations which have gone before us," admonished the author of a federal report of 1882. "The nations of Europe and Asia have been as reckless in their destruction of the forests as we have been, and by that recklessness have brought themselves unmeasurable evils, and upon the land itself barrenness and desolation. The face of the earth in many instances has been changed as the result of the destruction of the forests, from a condition of fertility and abundance to that of a desert." By the end of the decade the American Forestry Association (founded in 1875) was calling for a moratorium on the sale of all public forest lands.[18]

The fledgling forestry movement found itself in a race with loggers, who were rapidly moving the center of their operations from the Great Lakes states to the Pacific coast. By 1890 the easily accessible forests of Douglas fir, spruce, and redwood along the California, Oregon, and Washington coasts had already fallen to the ax, their ancient logs sawed into boardwood and shipped to San Francisco or Los Angeles for the booming home construction market. Loggers had penetrated the mountainous backcountry, using large tractors called "steam donkeys" to open hauling trails, clear-cutting huge patches of forest, and shipping out the harvest of logs on precarious narrow-gauge railroads. In regions too rugged or isolated for rails, they built mountain "splash dams" where they dumped their logs and, when the ponds were full, blasted the dams to kingdom come, producing floods that washed the logs downstream to the sawmills. Imagine the environmental destruction! The scream of the power saws was heard night and day, and in summer and fall a smoky haze hung perpetually over the region, the product of the "wigwam burners" that disposed of mountains of sawdust. Inevitable forest fires fed on the slash left by logging operations. While noting with approval talk of the "exhaustion" of the Great Lakes states—which meant prosperity for the Northwest—the editor of the Portland *Oregon Telegram* could not help but wonder "how long will it be before we shall be making a similar report."[19]

Responding to considerable public concern that the Northwest would suffer the same fate that had befallen the Great Lakes states, Congress undertook a complete revision of the nation's land laws in 1891. They did a poor job of it, repealing some programs, extending others, and in the end failing to address adequately the worries

Lumberjacks fell a giant spruce in Washington. Photograph by C. Kinsey, c. 1900. Beinecke.

about deforestation. At the last minute, however, friends of forest reform slipped in an amendment—later known as the Forest Reserve Act—providing the president with the authority to carve "forest reserves" from the public domain. The expectation seemed to be that this power would be used sparingly, but over the next decade Presidents Benjamin Harrison, Grover Cleveland, and William McKinley used it to withdraw more than forty-seven million forested acres. Preservationists hoped—

and loggers feared—that these reserves would be closed forever to commercial exploitation. This is precisely what John Muir and the Sierra Club proposed. But following the advice offered by a special Forestry Commission, Congress in 1897 made it clear that the reserves were intended not for the preservation but rather the use of the forests. The Forest Management Act declared that the reserves should "furnish a continuous supply of timber for the use and necessities of citizens of the United States." The executive branch was directed to establish regulations for the management of the reserves, auctioning to the highest bidder the right to harvest timber in them.[20]

This legislation was a triumph for the energetic leader of the Forestry Commission, Gifford Pinchot. Born to a wealthy family, Pinchot was interested in woodcraft from a young age. His classmates at Yale described him as "tree mad." After graduation he went to Germany and France to pursue advanced studies in forestry, then returned to spend several years as the forester at Biltmore, the huge Vanderbilt family estate in the North Carolina hills, where he developed innovative techniques in reforestation of cutover lands. This work earned him the appointment to the Forestry Commission, and that success brought him to the attention of President McKinley, who named him chief forester of the United States in 1898 at the age of just thirty-three. When Theodore Roosevelt became president in 1901, Pinchot quickly became his closest adviser on environmental policy. They had much in common. Both men were members of the Boone and Crockett Club, outdoorsmen, and lovers of what Roosevelt called "the strenuous life." Both were boxers who enjoyed putting on the gloves and sparring with each other for a few rounds. And both were controversialists, men willing to take the heat for a policy of government environmental management.

"Conservationism," the name Roosevelt and Pinchot choose for their approach to the environment, was an ideology for postfrontier America. "When the American settler felled the forests he felt there was plenty of forest left for the sons who came after him," Roosevelt lectured. "The Kentuckian or the Ohioan felled the forest and expected his son to move west and fell other forests on the banks of the Mississippi." But, he argued, the frontier era had ended. Like many other Americans, Roosevelt believed that America was filling up, and old thinking had to change. No longer could the nation allow "the right of the individual to injure the future of us all for his own temporary and immediate profit." The nation now required an activist federal state to manage the western environment.[21]

The Roosevelt administration featured an unparalleled array of environmental activity. The president encouraged Congress to create several new national parks, and he used his presidential power to declare national monuments to set aside sixteen areas of unique natural and historical value, including Devil's Tower in Wyoming, the Olympic peninsula in Washington, and the Petrified Forest and

Grand Canyon in Arizona. He established more than fifty wildlife preserves and refuges and sponsored legislation creating the Bureau of Fisheries and the Bureau of Biological Survey. He withdrew oil, coal, and phosphate lands from the public domain in order to forestall, at least temporarily, their engrossment by corporate monopolies. Perhaps Roosevelt's most important action came in 1905, when he engineered the transfer of the forest reserves (renamed "national forests") from the Department of the Interior to Pinchot's National Forest Service in the Agriculture Department. In his first directive to the agency, Pinchot laid out the "wise use" environmental perspective that he shared with Roosevelt: "All the resources of forest reserves are for *use*, and this use must be brought about in a thoroughly prompt and businesslike manner, under such restrictions only as will insure the permanence of these resources. . . . You will see to it that the water, wood, and forage of the reserves are conserved and wisely used for the benefit of the home builder first of all." Pinchot's words remain Forest Service gospel to this day, what historian Samuel P. Hays calls the "gospel of efficiency"—rational planning to promote the efficient development and use of natural resources without waste.[22]

The approach of "utilizers" such as Roosevelt and Pinchot differed considerably from "preservationists" like John Muir. The president once joined Muir on a camping trip into Yosemite. The two men slept under the stars, waking to a blanket of fresh snow, and in his enthusiastic way Roosevelt declared it to be "the grandest day of my life." But later, around the camp fire, Muir challenged the president's love of hunting—"when are you going to get beyond the boyishness of killing things?" Muir communed with nature, but Roosevelt wanted to ride it like a bucking bronc. Another time Pinchot toured the western forests with Muir. "I took to him at once," Pinchot remembered, finding his companion "a most fascinating talker." As they conversed, however, their differences emerged. Muir challenged the federal policy of allowing sheep ("hoofed locusts") to graze on the public domain, and when Pinchot allowed that he held no animus toward sheep, Muir lost his patience. "Then . . . I don't want anything more to do with you," he sputtered. For Muir, "the hope of the world" was "fresh, unblighted, unredeemed wilderness." Compare this to Pinchot's favorite aphorism: "wilderness is waste." The distinction between conservation and preservation goes back to the beginnings of national environmental policy.[23]

The truth is, neither Roosevelt nor Pinchot spent much time worrying about their differences with Muir; they were too busy putting their conservation programs into operation and fending off more dangerous attacks from critics who wanted to dismantle federal authority over the forests. They found their most important allies in the large logging companies, which saw distinct advantages in establishing a cozy relationship with the National Forest Service. By the early twentieth century these corporations had gained control of nearly 50 percent of the nation's standing timber,

President Theodore Roosevelt (center) stands with Gifford Pinchot (left) and John Muir (right)
at Sequoia Grove in California's Sierra Nevadas, 1903. Keystone-Mast Collection, UCR/
California Museum of Photography, University of California, Riverside.

and locking up an additional 35 percent in the national forests suited them just fine,
for it froze out the competition of smaller loggers. In exchange for federal encouragement of combination in the logging industry, Pinchot expected companies to apply the principles of scientific management to their forests. The Weyerhaeuser Company—the world's largest private owner of standing timber, controlling resources
equal to half the national forest system—instituted impressive programs of reforestation. William Robbins persuasively argues that corporate lumbermen used the

Forest Service "as a tool to achieve stability," to avoid overproduction, glutted markets, and low prices in their industry. But on the positive side they rejected the old logging practice of "cut and get out."[24]

It was the small loggers—and there were a great many of them—who opposed federal regulation. "Czar Pinchot" constricted their opportunities with the creation of national forests and bureaucratic regulations. Although big logging companies had more land, small loggers had more political power, and in 1907 they won congressional repeal of the president's authority to declare national forests by executive order. Before Roosevelt signed the legislation, however, he and Pinchot pored over maps of the West and selected more than 16 million acres of new forest reserves. Independent loggers were outraged by these "midnight reserves," which increased the size of the national forests to more than 150 million acres, but Roosevelt and Pinchot were not deterred. In 1908 they convened a White House conference of the nation's governors, congressmen, Supreme Court justices, and leading scientists to consider the future needs of environmental policy, which Roosevelt described as "the weightiest problem before the nation."[25]

Pinchot stayed on at the Forest Service when Roosevelt left office in 1909, but he found the administration of President William Howard Taft far less friendly to conservation. Interior Secretary Richard Ballinger, a former mayor of Seattle, represented western anticonservation interests who wanted federal resources transferred to the states to facilitate their private development, a policy antithetical to the chief forester's plan of rational development under federal management. The two men tangled, and when Pinchot publicly accused Ballinger of a conflict of interest in 1910, Taft dismissed him. By the time he left office, however, Pinchot had built the Forest Service into a proud organization of more than fifteen hundred employees.

———

To the American public the Forest Service was personified by the forest ranger, the mounted officer who supervised the harvest of timber, enforced regulations against illegal loggers and hunters, and heroically battled forest fires. The word *ranger* has a long history in American English, in the seventeenth century designating gamekeepers, then gradually acquiring the military meaning of light infantry who "ranged" over the country, matching the guerrilla tactics of Indian fighters. Most famous in the history of the West, of course, were the Texas Rangers, the irregular fighting force first organized during the Mexican War, later designated the official constabulary of the Lone Star State. A good deal of this historical cachet was inherited by the rangers of the Forest Service, not least by their adoption of the uniform of the U.S. Army soldiers who in the late nineteenth century had been in charge of the national parks and forests: khaki shirts and jodhpurs, knee-high riding boots, and the flat-brimmed Stetson "campaign" hats that have since become the rangers' most notable symbol. In 1916, after Congress created the National Park Service to administer the growing system of national parks, a similar force of park rangers replaced federal troops, and they, too, adopted this military uniform.

The American public quickly fell in love with the hearty masculine figure of the ranger. Vivid stories were told about their battles against forest fires. There was the tale of Ranger Edward Pulaski and his crew, caught between two approaching fire lines during a massive fire in the rugged mountains of Idaho and Montana in 1910. An old hand, Pulaski knew of an abandoned mine shaft nearby, and rushing his men to the spot he led them inside. Soaking an old blanket in the water dripping from the wall, he held it over the mouth of the shaft in an attempt to keep out the smoke and fumes. The roar of the approaching conflagration threw the inexperienced men in the group into a panic, and Pulaski literally had to fight them off as they attempted to bolt from the mine. It took only a few minutes for the fury to sweep past, but Pulaski was badly burned and collapsed into unconsciousness. His men huddled around him. "Too damn bad," one ranger solemnly proclaimed, "he's dead." Pulaski stirred, opened one eye slightly, and murmured, "Like hell he is!" Such men were the embodiment of what President Roosevelt extolled as "the great virile virtues—the virtues of courage, energy, and daring; the virtues which beseem a masterful race— a race fit to fell the forests, to build roads, to found commonwealths, to conquer continents, to overthrow armed enemies." Now they were to guard the forests. Rangers offered a modern substitute for frontier heroes such as Boone and Crockett.[26]

The romance and goodwill the image of the manly ranger generated for the federal agencies managing the nation's parks and forests proved a most valuable asset. Both agencies developed what might be described as masculine institutional cultures, and it comes as no surprise that until the 1970s the Forest Service had a policy against hiring women as forest rangers. Nor is it surprising that it took a federal suit by female employees in 1981 to convince the agency to institute an affirmative action plan to advance women up the ranks. What *is* surprising, however, is the evidence dug out of the archives by Polly Welts Kaufman demonstrating that in its very early years the Park Service *did* employ women as park rangers.

Horace Albright, the first civilian superintendent at Yellowstone, hired at least ten women for his force of rangers. The first was Isabel Bassett, a nature lover with a degree in biology from Wellesley College, who came to the park looking for work about the same time Albright assumed his duties in 1919. "I am to be a government ranger in Yellowstone Park," she wrote excitedly in a letter home after Albright had offered her the job. "You never heard of a woman ranger? Well, neither have I." Another of Albright's early recruits was Marguerite Lindsley, the daughter of a former Yellowstone superintendent, born and raised in the park. She came home after earning an M.S. in biology and Albright hired her on the spot. No one knew the park better, or with more scientific understanding, something she amply demonstrated in the more

Naturalist Herma Albertson Baggley (third from left) poses in ranger uniform with coworkers at Yellowstone National Park, 1933. National Park Service History Collection.

than fifty articles on local flora and fauna she published in *Nature Notes*, the Park Service newsletter. Lindsley was also a genuine character. During the winter of 1925 she and a female friend made the complete 143-mile transit of the park on cross-country skis. And one summer she bought a secondhand Harley with a sidecar, and, disguised as men, she and her friend took a cross-country road trip, riding through "hail, sleet, mud, and washouts," camping along the way. [27]

When the chief inspector of the Interior Department came to Yellowstone in 1926 he was shocked at the number of female rangers Superintendent Albright had hired. Nosing around, he found male rangers who complained about these "posy pickers" and "tree huggers." But Albright forthrightly defended his policy. "Women can do just as well or better than men," he wrote, although he allowed that there were male rangers who "did not like the idea of having a woman on what everyone likes to think of as a 'he man' force. There is a certain romance and glamour to the title 'ranger' which seems lost when a woman occupied the position." Nevertheless he found that women did a much better job of interacting with the public. Not a man on his force could give a lecture, "even if his life depended on it." In spite of Albright's defense, the inspector's report caused a stir in Washington, D.C., and resulted in a director's decree that the Park Service would no longer hire women as rangers. At almost the same moment, *Sunset Magazine* published an adoring profile of Marguerite Lindsley and her exploits entitled "She's a Real Ranger." Lindsley received dozens of letters from young women asking for her advice on becoming a ranger, and she was forced to write back with the news that for the foreseeable future "the ranger staff will be made up entirely of men." The next year Lindsley resigned from the agency to marry another ranger.[28]

In 1929 Albright was elevated to the directorship of the National Park Service. Vindicated, he revoked the previous order and from his Washington desk tried his best to encourage his superintendents to adopt his open attitude about women. But Albright's retirement in 1933 marked the end of this bold experiment. Within a few years the Park Service was looking back on the days of the female ranger with considerable loathing. The employment of women, one official believed, had resulted in rangers being ridiculed as "pansy pickers and butterfly chasers." It was important for the service, insisted another, that rangers maintain their image as "the embodiment of Kit Carson, Buffalo Bill, Daniel Boone, the Texas Rangers, and General Pershing."[29]

By 1920 the great assault on the forests had moderated. The forested area of the United States stabilized at around 730 million acres, approximately 32 percent of the nation's land, about where it has remained in the years since. Although the production of lumber and wood products continued to rise with each passing decade, the much-feared "timber famine" never materialized. A great deal of the credit must go to Roosevelt and Pinchot—for preventing the reckless exploitation of millions of acres of national forest, instituting effective fire control, encouraging more efficient methods of logging, and promoting the concept of sustainable logging through reforestation. As Charles Wilkinson writes in his survey of western environmental law, theirs was "one of the greatest and most daring achievements in conservation history." To be sure, "cut and get out" practices continued among many of the small logging outfits of the Northwest, and there was insufficient attention to reforestation, even among the giants of the industry. Later generations of Americans would become alarmed over the loss of habitat and genetic diversity with the continued destruction of old-growth forests. Pinchot himself grew frustrated with the limitations of the system he had helped to create and argued for the extension of federal regulation over private forests, but that was something Congress refused to consider.[30]

Conservation had an important—if limited—effect on helping to stabilize the area of forested land in the United States in the twentieth century. But it was not the most important factor. The primary reason for the stabilization of the country's forests was the nation's declining need for farmland. The proportion of land devoted to growing crops had grown from five percent in 1850 to 20 percent in 1920, and at least half of this increase had come at the expense of forest clearing. By the second decade of the twentieth century, however, American agriculture was well into a mighty transformation characterized by the development of high-yield hybrid crops, the use of chemical fertilizers, and the introduction of labor-saving machinery. So great were the increases in agricultural productivity that there was little need for opening additional land. Consider just one aspect of this transformation, the shift from draft animals to internal-combustion engines. Before World War I more than a quarter of the nation's cropland was devoted to producing feed and fodder for mules and horses; by the end of World War II the replacement of livestock by tractors had freed up all this land, seventy million acres, for growing marketable crops.

The continuing progress of American agriculture confronted the nation with new problems—a surplus of crops and a surplus of farmers—that would require new ways of thinking. Yet Theodore Roosevelt and Gifford Pinchot—despite their progressive attitudes—continued to focus on the problem of scarcity, not surplus. This was most evident in another environmental program adopted during the Roosevelt administration, the federal support for western irrigation that would fundamentally reshape the twentieth-century West. During the last third of the nineteenth century there was considerable interest in irrigation, and by 1900 public and private projects were watering some eight million acres in the western states. It was clear, however, that further development would require massive dams, substantial reservoirs, and long-distance canal systems, investments beyond the means of corporations, municipalities, or even the states. "Great storage works are necessary," Roosevelt declared in his first presidential message to Congress, but "their construction has been conclusively shown to be an undertaking too vast for private effort. The [federal] Government should construct and maintain these reservoirs as it does other public works." In the debate over federal legislation, a few congressmen had the temerity to question the country's need for more farmland, but the winning arguments harked back to the nineteenth-century ideal of the yeoman farmer. Federal support for irrigation would open new lands and "furnish homes for the homeless and farms for the farmless," declared one congressman; such a plan would be "a great pacificator," promised another, offering a safety valve in times of "great social disturbances in the great cities." Not only was this nonsense, it was old nonsense; but it remained politically potent nonsense.[31]

In 1902 Congress passed the Reclamation Act, which established a new agency in the Interior Department—the Bureau of Reclamation—to administer a massive federal effort in the states of the trans-Mississippi West. Reclamation would make the deserts bloom. "Reclamation" is a curious term, since the West was naturally arid, and the lands were not really being *re*-claimed at all but transformed. Traditionally the word had a religious meaning. As one minister sermonized, "It is meet that God should be glad on the reclamation of a sinner." Not until late in the nineteenth cen-

*The All-American Canal moving Colorado River water to California's Imperial Valley.
Photograph by Carl Trulsen, 1992. Bureau of Reclamation, Department of the Interior.*

tury did it develop its environmental usage. The adoption of a synonym for Christian conversion to describe the technique of transforming barren into arable land is suggestive. That little prefix seemed to imply that the deserts were destined to bloom, suggesting that just as God rejoiced on the salvation of a backslider, so he smiled on "the salvation of the land"—a popular phrase of the day. As the preacher helped redeem the backslider, so the irrigator helped redeem the land, transforming waste to a state of grace.[32]

Thus were the irrigation projects of the twentieth-century West glossed with both populist ideology and Protestant sentiment. But projects of desert reclamation dis-rupted many rural westerners as they uplifted others. Water development often involved the destruction of traditional ways of life that had served residents for generations. Elephant Butte Dam on the Rio Grande in central New Mexico created a system of modern reservoirs and canals that replaced the ancient complex of *acequias* (ditches) that had watered hundreds of Hispano subsistence farmers and now forced them to become agricultural laborers. Western water projects also ran roughshod over Indians. In 1908 the Supreme Court ruled that a reclamation project on the Milk River in Montana was illegally diverting a river that ran through the reservation of the Gros Ventre and Assiniboine tribes. Indians, the Court announced, retained an inviolable right to the waters of their homelands. Yet over the next half-century the Interior Department—the very agency entrusted with protecting Indian rights—approved dozens of projects that flooded reservation lands and drained reservation rivers but provided little or no benefit to reservation people.

Perhaps this was to be expected. But the positive effects of reclamation on the lives of white farmers is also debatable. The Reclamation Act included provisions restricting the use of irrigation water to resident (not absentee) farmers with plots of 160 or fewer acres. From the program's beginning, however, bureaucrats found it inconvenient to enforce these limitations and generally ignored, waived, or overrode them. Agribusiness, not the small farmer, was the big beneficiary of federal irrigation. The men and women laboring in the reclaimed fields and orchards were not independent proprietors but migrant farmworkers. Moreover, reclamation projects meant to benefit rural residents were sometimes hijacked by urban interests, most famously when the city of Los Angeles commandeered the Owens River project that was supposed to benefit local farmers. "It is a hundred or thousandfold more important and more valuable to the people as a whole," Roosevelt avowed when he announced federal funding for L.A.'s plan, if water was "used by the city than if used by the people of the Owens Valley." As she watched the Owens River run dry, turning the farms and orchards around her to desert sands, western writer Mary Austin wondered, "is all this worthwhile, in order that Los Angeles should be just so big?"[33]

Frequently rivers were dammed and valleys flooded with little concern for the loss of ecosystems or natural wonders. The most infamous example was the Hetch Hetchy Valley in Yosemite National Park, whose sharp glacial walls and meadowed floor John Muir described as "a grand landscape garden, one of Nature's rarest and most precious mountain temples." Some two hundred miles to the west San Francisco engineers in search of a dependable urban water supply fastened on Hetch Hetchy as the best place to impound city water. The case sorely tested the priorities of the Roosevelt administration. When the city first approached the federal government for approval in 1903 the immediate reaction was that the plan was incompatible with the valley's "wonderful natural conditions and marvelous scenic interest."

But Roosevelt soon decided that "domestic use, especially for a municipal water supply, is the highest use to which water and available storage basins can be put." Muir went on the attack, characterizing his opponents as "temple destroyers" and "devotees of ravaging commercialism," and composed an essay containing what were perhaps the most famous lines of his career as a wilderness polemicist: "Dam Hetch Hetchy! As well dam for water-tanks the people's cathedrals and churches, for no holier temple has ever been consecrated by the heart of man." Roosevelt vacillated, passing the matter on to his successors when he left office. Finally, in 1913, the project won approval by the Wilson administration. It would be Muir's last stand. He died a year later, deeply saddened by his defeat. "We may lose this particular fight," he wrote shortly before his death, "but truth and right must prevail at last." The granite temple of Hetch Hetchy would disappear under hundreds of feet of water, but preservationists would never forget this cautionary tale.[34]

These negative impacts should be weighed against the success of the Reclamation Bureau, which during its first three decades completed twenty-two western projects. By that time irrigation was watering some fourteen million acres of western land, on which were grown major portions of the nation's fruits and vegetables, sugar beets, alfalfa, and cotton. Yet that very success was, in a way, the program's greatest weakness, for reclamation only added to the growth of agricultural surpluses. This was not immediately apparent. The industrial expansion of the early century and the extraordinary demand of World War I kept farm prices high, encouraging large farmers to mechanize their production and irrigators to invest in expensive water distribution systems. But following the war, when demand shrank and farm prices plummeted, not only did farmers have a tough time servicing the debts they had assumed to buy equipment, but many irrigators found it impossible to pay their obligations for construction costs and water fees. Individual farmers responded to lower prices the only way they knew how, by growing more in the hope of increasing their revenue. Western irrigators planted more sugar beets and alfalfa, wheat farmers plowed up millions of acres of raw prairie, and ranchers overstocked the range with cattle and sheep. Predictably, this drove the price of farm commodities further downward. By 1929 average farm income had fallen to 64 percent of its level ten years before, and this was *before* the stock market crash and the onset of the Great Depression. When the nation's industrial economy went into a tailspin, agricultural markets collapsed. By 1932 farm income was a mere fifth of its postwar high. What future was there in a program designed to increase the nation's cropland when the nation could not market the crops it was already producing?

———

In the late 1920s Congress passed legislation empowering the federal government to purchase surplus crops as a way of pushing up prices, but President Calvin

Coolidge vetoed it and President Herbert Hoover indicated that he would do the same. The victory of Franklin D. Roosevelt in the presidential election of 1932, however, brought to the White House a leader committed to tackling the farm problem. In one of his first acts, Roosevelt signed the Agricultural Adjustment Act, passed by the New Deal Congress, authorizing the government to fix production quotas, purchase surplus crops at a guaranteed price (based on the "parity" between industrial and agricultural purchasing power during the prosperous years 1909 to 1914), and store those surplus commodities in government granaries for sale during years of crop failure. It was a version of the program western populists had proposed a half-century before, and it would remain the foundation of federal agricultural policy for the rest of the twentieth century. Gradually farm prices climbed back to profitable levels. Yet the program only assisted farmers with large operations. It did little or nothing for small producers, who continued to lose their farms at an alarming rate. And it had the effect of tossing tenants and sharecroppers off their rented land, because those plots were frequently the very ones landlords retired from production. "I let 'em all go," a Texas farmer told a sociologist who inquired about his tenants. "I bought tractors on the money the government give me and got shet of my renters. You'll find it everywhere all over the country that way. I did everything the government said—except keep my renters. The renters have been having it this way ever since the government come in. They've got their choice—California or WPA." A displaced Oklahoma tenant described his family's options more starkly: "move or starve."[35]

The turmoil of farm bankruptcy and tenant eviction created another epic western migration, but this time with pioneers traveling by automobile rather than covered wagon, as does the Joad family in John Steinbeck's vivid period novel *The Grapes of Wrath* (1939). California seemed a new promised land. "By God, they's grapes out there, just a-hangin' over inta the road," says Steinbeck's Grandpa Joad. "I'm gonna pick me a wash tub full a grapes, an' I'm gonna set in 'em, an' scrooge aroun', an' let the juice run down my pants." But instead of an agrarian dream the family finds an industrial nightmare, California's factories in the field. Like the Joads, tens of thousands of "Okies" and "Arkies" found work as fruit or vegetable pickers, but even more joined the ever-increasing human flood into greater Los Angeles and other western urban centers.[36]

The states of the Pacific coast received more than 750,000 migrants during the 1930s. They came not only from Oklahoma and Arkansas but from the Dakotas, Kansas, and Texas, all areas where the agricultural crisis of the Great Depression was compounded by the extraordinary environmental crisis known as the Dust Bowl. Drought gripped the entire nation during the 1930s, but had its worst effects on the Great Plains. Huge dust storms began sweeping across the prairies in the early spring of 1932. The next year the dust rose so high that it was sucked up by the jetstream and

"Farmer and Sons Walking in the Face of a Dust Storm, Cimarron County, Oklahoma."
Photograph by Arthur Rothstein, 1936. Library of Congress.

came down like snow on Chicago, Washington, D.C., and even ships in the Atlantic. With each passing year the storms grew fiercer. The worst year was 1935. The storms began in February and reached a terrible climax on April 14, "Black Sunday," when a huge duster enveloped nearly the entire state of Kansas. It was "the greatest show since Pompeii was buried in ashes," wrote Kansas newspaper editor William Allen White. Gradually the drought loosened its grip, the rains returned, and the dust storms subsided, but the whole region was left reeling. Drought recurs naturally on the plains, and there had been small dust storms during the previous dry cycle in the late nineteenth century, but nothing in recorded history approached the ferocity of the Dust Bowl. The difference was the extent of the grassland lost since the 1890s, especially the excessive plowing and grazing of the 1920s that denuded millions of acres of their natural vegetation. Dry prairie winds scoured the unprotected topsoil, turning some twenty-four million acres into barren desert by 1938. Renowned environmental scientist Georg Borgstron ranks the Dust Bowl as one of the three worst ecological blunders in world history. But unlike the other two—the deforestation of

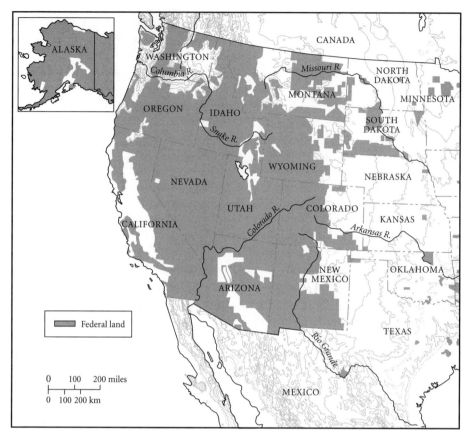

FEDERAL LANDS IN THE WEST

China's uplands in the third millennium B.C.E. and the erosion of Mediterranean hills by overgrazing sheep two thousand years ago—this disaster took only half a century to accomplish.[37]

The rural West thus faced not only economic collapse but environmental catastrophe. Franklin Roosevelt responded with the most environmentally oriented administration since that of his distant cousin Theodore in the early century. "Long ago, I pledged myself to a policy of conservation," FDR told a campaign crowd in 1932 and promised that he would "guard against the ravaging of our forests, the waste of our good earth and water supplies, the squandering of irreplaceable oil and mineral deposits, the preservation of our wildlife, and the protection of our streams." For interior secretary (or secretary of the West, as some called the position), he appointed Harold Ickes, a lifelong Republican who first entered politics in support of Teddy Roosevelt, became a committed conservationist, and during the 1932 campaign year led a movement to replace Hoover with Gifford Pinchot as the Republican nominee. When that quixotic effort failed he jumped parties to support Roosevelt. "We have reached the end of the pioneering period of 'go ahead and take,'" Ickes declared upon assuming his duties at the Interior Department, "we are in the age of planning for the best of everything for all." Ickes and Roosevelt moved on several fronts to establish better environmental management of the Great Plains. Thousands of young men in the Civilian Conservation Corps were set to work planting trees by the hundreds of millions in "shelterbelts," designed to provide windbreaks, retard soil erosion, and create habitat for wildlife. The Taylor Grazing Act of 1934 brought the public range lands under the regulation of a new agency, the Grazing Service (renamed the Bureau of Land Management in 1946), with the mandate of preventing overgrazing. The Soil Conservation Service, established the following year, targeted seventy-five million acres of plains cropland that should be retired from production, and though Congress failed to provide funding sufficient to meet that goal, the administration returned more than eleven million acres to grass.[38]

Environmental historian Donald Worster, author of a thought-provoking history of the Dust Bowl, argues that these were half measures and reflected "no fundamental reform of attitudes." He may be right. Still, the New Deal marked a watershed in the history of the West. Theodore Roosevelt was the first president to understand the necessity of moving beyond the old frontier myth of inexhaustible resources and inventing new ways of managing the western environment. Franklin Roosevelt completed that transition. "Our last frontier has long since been reached and there is practically no more free land," he declared during the campaign of 1932. "There is no safety valve in the form of a Western prairie to which those thrown out of work by the eastern economic machines can go for a new start." Now Americans were faced with "the soberer, less dramatic business of administering resources . . . , of distributing wealth and products more equitably." No president had ever said such a thing. In 1935 Roosevelt made good on this declaration with an executive order withdrawing all remaining public lands from entry and placing them under federal conservation authority. The termination of the federal policy of selling off or giving away the public domain—a program that began with nation's first Land Ordinance in 1784—truly marked the passing of the nation's long era of frontier settlement.[39]

According to Roosevelt, the frontier era was over. But the West had been left an economic basket case. During the 1930s westerners Bernard De Voto and Walter Prescott Webb again voiced the old western complaint of colonial exploitation in powerful statements. In his influential jeremiad of 1934 in *Harper's*, "A Plundered Province," De Voto argued that the East had created the West as a colonial dependency, had plundered its natural resources, and didn't give a damn for its economic development. A few years later Webb published the angry *Divided We Stand: The Crisis of a Frontierless Democracy* (1937), which argued further that the Great Depression was largely the result of the close of the frontier and the uneven economic development of the West and South. The New Dealers largely agreed with this analysis. "Economic disadvantage creates a backward country," wrote Thurman Arnold, a lawyer from Laramie who served in the Justice Department. The Northeast and the Midwest had developed into economic powerhouses, but the rural West and South remained essentially colonial economies. "The West ships raw materials three thousand miles East," as another New Dealer put it, "then gets the finished products from those materials shipped back three thousand miles." Only by building up the whole country could the nation avoid catastrophe. One of the most enduring legacies of the New Deal was Roosevelt's decision to build an industrial infrastructure in these underdeveloped regions. The New Deal's program of public investment was unlike anything seen previously in American history, and it transformed the West.[40]

The New Deal program focused on multipurpose river development. Reclamation concentrated on irrigation, but during the 1920s many westerners began arguing for river projects that would also provide hydroelectric power. Wherever electricity was cheap and plentiful, prosperity seemed to follow. Electric utilities and companies manufacturing electrical appliances were two of the fastest growing sectors of the economy in the 1920s. Republicans placed their faith in private utilities, but although these companies spent billions wiring the cities and suburbs, they failed to see a market in rural electrification. By the end of the 1920s only about 10 percent of the nation's farmers and ranchers enjoyed electricity for their homes or work, and vast districts of both the rural West and South remained unconnected to the nation's growing power grid, essentially blocked from economic development. In 1928 a coalition of southern Democrats and western Republicans ("the alliance of cotton and corn") passed the first multipurpose river bill—a huge dam and hydroelectric complex at Boulder Canyon on the Colorado River, designed to provide irrigation, flood control, public water supplies, and hydroelectric power to Arizona, Nevada, and California. They next attempted to secure federal funding for projects on the Tennessee and Columbia rivers but were blocked by the Hoover administration.

Roosevelt, however, was an enthusiastic supporter of multipurpose river development. During his campaign for the presidency he came out in favor of the Columbia project. "Vast water power can be of incalculable value to this whole section of the country," he told a crowd in Portland. "It means cheap manufacturing production, economy, and comfort on the farm and in the household." Massive infusions of federal investment could provide the spark to ignite regional economic growth. Even before he took office, Roosevelt announced the model New Deal river project, the Tennessee Valley Authority (TVA). Congress approved the TVA in the spring of 1933, and over the next several years New Dealers in Congress won approval of similar projects for the Columbia, the Sacramento and San Joaquin in California's Central Valley, and dozens of smaller rivers throughout the West. Congressman Sam Rayburn of Texas sponsored the Rural Electrification Act, which connected tens of

Hoover Dam with Lake Mead in the background. Photograph by Andy Pernick, 1996. Bureau of Reclamation, Department of the Interior.

thousands of rural households to the nation's power grid. "I want my people out of the dark," Rayburn told his colleagues. "Can you imagine what it will mean to a farm wife to have a pump in the well and lights in the house?" With identities as both southerners and westerners, Rayburn and other Texas Democrats were enthusiastic congressional leaders for Roosevelt's program of development for the South and West.[41]

The projects themselves employed tens of thousands of workers and helped launch some of the West's biggest corporations. A consortium of western contractors known as the Six Companies built Hoover Dam on the Colorado, which Joseph Stevens describes as "the most ambitious government-sponsored civil engineering task ever undertaken in the United States." The contracting companies were led by Henry J. Kaiser, an energetic, smiling German American known as the New Deal's "favorite businessman." This able and ambitious industrialist went on to build the superstructure at Grand Coulee Dam on the Columbia (three times the size of Hoover Dam) and the gigantic cement pilings for the San Francisco Bay Bridge. When he failed to win the contract for the construction of Shasta Dam on the Sacramento, Kaiser successfully bid to supply the cement, then in just six months constructed his own cement plant, the largest in the world. Kaiser and other New Deal contractors in the West were largely financed by San Franciscan A. P. Giannini's Bank of America, which in turn was funded by the New Deal's Reconstruction Finance Corporation. By 1939 the Bank of America operated more than five hundred branches in the West.[42]

Historian Jordan Schwarz calls this arrangement "state capitalism," and he argues that "nothing was more responsible for western industrial development." The federal government invested more in development projects in the West than in any other region. Adding up both federal expenditures and loans, "the big winner in the New Deal was the West," Schwarz concludes. The river projects proved enormously successful, generating far more power than anyone anticipated and sharply lowering energy prices throughout the country. Cheap electricity from government-built dams stimulated the industrialization of the Tennessee and Columbia basins and propelled California forward as the nation's leading industrial state during World War II. Indeed, it is arguable that victory in the war was made possible by the New Deal strategy of industrial development. New western aluminum and steel mills provided the materials needed by western shipyards and aircraft plants. Nuclear weapons were developed at industrial complexes supplied by power generated by dams on the Tennessee, Columbia, and Colorado rivers. In short, the New Deal transformed the West into a powerful industrial economy.[43]

The New Deal conviction that the frontier era had ended was also reflected in its Indian policy. Another feature of frontier economics was the consistent attempt to secure Indian resources for private exploitation and development. The Allotment Act of 1888 was proposed as a departure from this pattern, but in fact allotment accelerated the assault on Indian lands. A study conducted in 1928 by Lewis Meriam of the Brookings Institute (a Washington think tank funded by the Rockefeller Foundation) concluded that allotment had "resulted in much loss of land without a compensating advance in the economic ability of the Indians." In Oklahoma tribes such as the Cherokees were stripped of 40 percent of their homelands, while the rest was distributed in small parcels to Indian families. The holdings of the Sioux were reduced by a third, the Ojibway estate by fully 80 percent. The total Indian land base stood at forty-seven million acres—only a third of what it had been when allotment was proclaimed the solution to further Indian dispossession. Moreover, the report declared, the policy of assimilation had been nothing more than an attempt to "crush out all that is Indian" and had demoralized many tribes. Indians had become the most impoverished group in the United States.[44]

The Meriam Report was the product of a profound intellectual movement in America that rejected the concept of assimilation and endorsed the ideal of "cultural pluralism," a term coined in 1915 by the Harvard philosopher Horace Kallen. America, Kallen argued, was best understood as a "federation or commonwealth of national cultures," a "democracy of nationalities, cooperating voluntarily and autonomously through common institutions in the enterprise of self-realization through the perfection of men *according to their kind*." That last phrase was the key one, the essence of the position taken by pluralists. Assimilationists had based their thinking on an assumption of the superiority of Anglo-American culture. The pluralists, by contrast, were strongly influenced by new perspectives in anthropology being advanced by Franz Boas of Columbia University and his students Ruth Benedict, Robert Lowie, and Margaret Mead, all of whom had studied the Indians of North America. Impressed by the enormous diversity among cultures, the pluralists argued that each should be considered from within the framework of its own values and assumptions.[45]

Sitting in on classes at Columbia was John Collier, a young man from Atlanta who came to New York City early in the twentieth century and after a few years of course work became a social worker in the city's settlement houses. But the pluralist perspective he had imbibed at Columbia inevitably clashed with the paternalism he found characteristic of his profession. By 1920 Collier had relocated to Taos, New Mexico, where he became a great admirer of the communal culture of the Pueblo Indians. Most impressive to him was the Pueblos' determination to preserve their values and traditions against the attacks of assimilationists, including the campaigns of the Bureau of Indian Affairs (BIA). This continuing effort was part of the same crusade against Indian cultural expression that had resulted in the massacre of Ghost Dancers at Wounded Knee in 1890. When the Pueblos became involved in a fight to defend their land and water rights, Collier eagerly jumped to their support, organizing a powerful support network among reformers around the country. Eventually this network grew into the American Indian Defense Association, and Collier

John Collier (second from left) meets with a group of Oglalas at the Pine Ridge reservation, 1933. Beinecke.

became a nationally known critic of Indian policy. One of the charter members of Collier's association was Harold Ickes, and when Ickes took the job as Roosevelt's interior secretary in 1933 he asked Collier to join the administration as the new commissioner of Indian affairs.[46]

His policies, Collier announced at his swearing in, would focus on "ending paternalism and extending civil rights" to Indian people. "Indians, whose culture, civic tradition, and inherited traditions are still strong and virile, should be encouraged and helped to develop their life in their own patterns." Collier set to work drafting a set of reforms, the Indian Reorganization Act, that Congress passed in 1934. His implementation of this legislation, which historians call the "Indian New Deal," represented the most radical shift in Indian policy in American history, one that fundamentally affected the lives of tens of thousands of Indians. In the first place it put an end to the government campaign of repression and inaugurated an unprecedented era of Indian cultural freedom. Early in his tenure Collier issued a directive to Indian agents proclaiming religious freedom on all reservations. "There have existed tribal religions which have been forged out through thousands of years of endurance," he wrote, "which contain deep beauty and spiritual guidance, consolation, and disciplinary power." An Indian agent on the Oglala reservation at Pine Ridge, South Dakota, later remembered communicating Collier's directive to Bert Kills Close, a traditional spiritual leader. "Bert sat there, stroked his braids, looked off into the distance, and then said in Lakota, 'Well, I'll be damned.'" It was a common reaction, for

Apache cowboys on a roundup in Gila County, Arizona. Photograph by Gilbert Campbell, 1941. Arizona Collection, Arizona State University Libraries.

words like those had never before passed the lips of a commissioner of Indian affairs. Under Collier's leadership boarding schools were phased out and replaced by reservation day schools in which Indians had a much greater impact in the determination of the curriculum. The bureau sponsored the publication of bilingual textbooks printed in both English and native languages and encouraged teachers to adopt them. Indian people also began to take a more prominent role in the running of the BIA. From an insignificant few before the New Deal, the number of Indian employees at BIA had increased to several thousand by the early 1940s.[47]

The Indian New Deal also ended the policy of allotment. Remaining unalloted reservation lands were reconsolidated and placed under the control of tribal corporations. Individual Indians who had been awarded allotments were encouraged to exchange those lands for shares of common stock in Indian corporations. The BIA also established a fund from which tribes might borrow in order to purchase reservation lands from non-Indian owners, for example, or to pursue projects of economic development.

The Meriam Report had suggested that stockraising seemed to offer the most promise for the economic renewal of western Indians. "Not only does the average Indian show considerable aptitude for this work, but enormous areas of Indian land, tribal and individual, are of little value except for grazing," the report concluded. Encouraged by Collier's BIA, the number of Indian cattle ranchers doubled and the value of Indian cattle sales increased more than tenfold, reaching three million dollars by 1939. One of the most successful examples was the San Carlos Apache tribe, whose reservation is located in the Gila Mountains of southeastern Arizona. By 1940 the tribe's twenty-eight thousand head of registered Herefords had become the largest in the Southwest. "The cattle industry is undoubtedly a fortunate choice for the reservation," wrote an anthropologist studying the tribe. "Indians I have known like the idea of cattle work, for they feel it is something worth a man's effort. They like an occupation which supplies action and at present when the cowboy is so idolized in the West, the idea of being one is attractive to young men." Young Indian men took to dressing in boots, spurs, and Stetsons. But as historian Peter Iverson notes, their mastery of ranching "increased rather than decreased their identity as San Carlos Apaches. Being cowboys had allowed them to be Indians."[48]

Such successes were possible only when Indian people were allowed to exercise sovereignty over their affairs. Under the auspices of the Indian Reorganization Act, 181 tribes voted to organize new forms of representative self-government, and during Collier's tenure about half of those tribes adopted written constitutions and elected leaders. To be sure, the BIA continued to have extraordinary authority in the affairs of reservation Indians, retaining veto power over the decisions of tribal councils and supervising the fiscal and economic arrangements of Indian nations. Indian agents and reservation superintendents continued to dole out jobs and funds, and many tribal councils acted as little more than rubber stamps. Nevertheless, the New Deal was the first administration in American history to declare that tribal governments had the right to exercise what the chief legal adviser to the Interior Department called "internal sovereignty." Except in cases where tribal jurisdiction had been limited by the express action of Congress—as it did in 1885 when it extended federal jurisdiction to such felony offenses as murder, rape, and robbery committed on reservations—Indian nations were to enjoy all their "original sovereignty." Over the next several decades the federal government itself would frequently violate this directive, and it was rarely as attentive as it should have been to its responsibility to protect Indian nations from legal encroachments by the states. But the legal principle enunciated by the New Deal established an extremely important precedent. Upheld by a series of important federal court decisions after World War II, Indian sovereignty would assume importance as the most fundamental principle of Indian law in the second half of the twentieth century.

Sovereignty meant that Indians were to be directly involved in setting up and running their new governments. This sometimes led to striking contradictions. The Tohono O'odam (Papagos) of southern Arizona, for example, simply had no words in their language for "representative" or "budget." Imagine the difficulty of convincing them to give up their traditional forms of leadership for a political system they could not explain to themselves. There were also longstanding political disagreements within Indian communities between progressives and traditionalists, assimilationists and separatists, mixed-bloods and full-bloods. Among the most acculturated Indian people—many of whom had accepted allotments and now operated farms or ranches—there were fears that the reorganization of Indian policy might threaten their title. Other acculturated Indians criticized what they thought was Collier's sentimental and romantic attachment to traditional Indian culture. These critics argued that the Indian New Deal was a "back to the blanket" program that would retard progress and condemn Indians to perpetual poverty and subjugation. The Iroquois leader Alice Lee Jemison, for example, argued that "reform only meant the strengthening, not the diminishing of bureaucratic control in the lives of American Indians."[49]

On the other hand, among those Indians who continued to believe in the viability of traditional forms of tribal government, there was considerable opposition to the establishment of democratically elected tribal councils and chairmen. Many traditionalists feared that these councils would be dominated by assimilated Indians educated in boarding schools. At Pine Ridge, for example, a representative council replaced the traditional self-selected one in an election in which most traditionals refused to participate. Democratic government "fits your way of living and style of thought," traditional Oglala leader Robert Bad Wound told congressmen at a hearing in 1939, "but it does not fit us at all. We do not understand it. It is not the proper thing for us work under." Disagreements over Indian reorganization among Indians themselves fueled the fires of factionalism that existed on nearly every reservation in the country. Although most Indian tribes and communities accepted the Indian New Deal, seventy-seven tribes rejected it. Among the rejectionists were the Iroquois and the Navajos—two of the most influential Indian nations in the country. Both already had traditional council governments of their own. The Iroquois feared that acceptance would compromise the hardline position they had taken on the question of sovereignty for more than a century. In 1924, when Congress passed the Indian Citizenship Act, declaring for the first time that Indians were United States citizens, the Iroquois council had rejected it, declaring that Iroquois people were already citizens of the Iroquois Nation.[50]

Collier himself had nothing to do with the Iroquois decision, but he was implicated in the rejection of reorganization by the Navajos, a case that illustrated the continuing conflicts of the federal relationship to Indian people. According to federal studies of the multipurpose development project on the Colorado River, herds of Navajo sheep were overgrazing grasslands and causing serious erosion, and the soil carried down to the river threatened to silt up the reservoir behind Hoover Dam. "Down there on the Colorado is the biggest, most expensive dam in the world," Collier told a meeting of the Navajo council in 1934, "which will furnish all southern Cal-

Navajo shepherds with their flock. Photograph by Edward S. Curtis, c. 1905. Beinecke.

ifornia with water and with electric power." The Navajos were grazing too many animals on too little grass. The government would "never use compulsion on the Navajo tribe," he promised, but Collier later admitted that federal agents had bullied and intimidated Navajo stockraisers to accomplish the slaughter of tens of thousands of sheep and goats. The Navajo stock-reduction program had disproportionately negative effects on the smallest and most economically vulnerable Indian herders and devastated thousands of native families, reducing them to dependency on the federal dole. Collier and the BIA became anathema to most Navajos, and the resentment over stock reduction resulted in a protest vote that killed the new constitution.[51]

In the name of reclamation, John Collier, passionate defender of Indian ways of life, nearly destroyed one of the few remaining viable Indian economies in the West. Indians might continue to be exploited and pushed aside even as the West developed a powerful industrial economy.

FURTHER READING

Samuel P. Hays, *Conservation and the Gospel of Efficiency: The Progressive Conservation Movement, 1890–1920* (1959)
Norris Hundley, Jr., *The Great Thirst: Californians and Water, 1770s–1990s* (1992)

Peter Iverson, *When Indians Became Cowboys: Native Peoples and Cattle Ranching in the American West* (1994)

Polly Welts Kaufman, *National Parks and the Woman's Voice: A History* (1996)

Roderick Nash, *Wilderness and the American Mind,* 3d ed. (1982)

John F. Reiger, *American Sportsmen and the Origins of Conservation,* rev. ed. (1986)

William G. Robbins, *Lumberjacks and Legislators: Political Economy of the U.S. Lumber Industry, 1890–1941* (1982)

Jordan A. Schwarz, *The New Dealers: Power Politics in the Age of Roosevelt* (1993)

Richard West Sellars, *Preserving Nature in the National Parks: A History* (1997)

Richard White, *The Roots of Dependency: Subsistence, Environment, and Social Change Among the Choctaws, Pawnees, and Navajos* (1983)

Michael Williams, *Americans and Their Forests: A Historical Geography* (1988)

David M. Wrobel, *The End of American Exceptionalism: Frontier Anxiety from the Old West to the New Deal* (1993)

Donald Worster, *Dust Bowl: The Southern Plains in the 1930s* (1979)

The Myth of the West

In the year or two preceding Daniel Boone's death in 1820 at the age of nearly eighty-six, a steady stream of visitors beat a path to the door of his home on Femme Osage Creek in Missouri. When the old man saw strangers approaching, one of his sons later recalled, he would "take his cane and walk off to avoid them," but if cornered he would sit and talk with them. "Though at first reserved and barely answering questions," one visitor remembered, Boone soon "warmed up and became animated in narrating his early adventures in the West." Frequently visitors brought personal copies of *The Adventures of Col. Daniel Boon* (1782), the account written by Kentucky promoter John Filson that had made Boone famous. Filson claimed to have used the authentic first-person voice of Boone himself, although comparing the text with surviving Boone letters suggests that few of the words were actually his. It never seemed to bother him. Although never shy about complaining of those whom he thought misrepresented his life or deeds, for Filson's account Boone had nothing but praise. "All true! Every word true!" the old man exclaimed after one of his visitors read a portion aloud. "Not a lie in it."[1]

Filson's text had made Boone into a household name. Appearing in at least a dozen American editions before Boone's death, it has rarely been out of print in the more than two centuries since its publication. In English, Irish, German, and French editions it created a minor sensation among European intellectuals, who celebrated Boone as an American original, a "natural man" of the wilderness. Filson's Boone was the archetypal frontier hero, the leading man in a unique narrative tradition that would come to be known as the "western." He is a man most at home in the wilderness, a world he understands and loves as the Indians do. And Boone's intimate knowledge of the Indians enables him to confront and defeat them.

This was the story old Boone's admirers had imbibed from childhood, and the old

COL. DANIEL BOON.

Daniel Boone in Missouri, eighty-five years old. Engraving by James Otto Lewis, 1820, based on a lost portrait by Chester Harding. Missouri Historical Society.

man delighted in the honor it brought to the family name. Yet he did not hesitate to confront his visitors with the fact that in the years since the Revolution his life had taken some disappointing turns. He had taken up surveying, opened a general store, and planned to settle his children and grandchildren on nearby plots of land. "But alas!" he lamented, "it was then my misery began." As recompense for patriotic service to the country "I thought I was entitled to a home for my family," but "another man bought the land over my head." Boone became involved in legal squabbles over title, was forced to defend himself in court, and eventually lost both his lands and his business. Disappointed and downhearted, "I determined to quit my native land," moving the family to Spanish Missouri, where authorities granted them a generous estate. But "my misfortune did not end," he continued, for when the United States acquired the territory with the Louisiana Purchase, in came the lawyers and the speculators, and eventually his Spanish grants also were declared null and void. "I have lived to learn," Boone concluded with a world-weary sigh, "that your boasted civilization is nothing more than improved ways to overreach your neighbor."[2]

And through all his trials, Boone asked, who do you suppose turned out to be my most constant friends? Why, the Indians, the very people I helped to dispossess. Boone had never been an Indian hater, maintaining that he always "fought the Indians fairly" and "respected the rights of the preemptor of the soil." He disliked recounting war stories and refused to count scalps. Legend portrayed him as "a wonderful man who had killed a host of Indians," and, he allowed, "many was the fair fire I have had at them." But "I am very sorry to say that I ever killed any," Boone avowed, to the shock of his visitors, "for they have always been kinder to me than the whites." In fact, during his last years in Missouri, Boone frequently hunted with old Indian friends. A descendant told of watching old Boone and his Indian friends rehearsing their former adventures around a campfire. If forced to choose, Boone concluded, he would "certainly prefer a state of nature to a state of civilization." This admission was embarrassing to partisans of the "Indian-hating school" of frontier history. Perhaps senility had contributed to such sentimental and "weak" feelings toward the Indians, one critic suggested, and hoped that Boone's controversial statements be allowed to "quietly sleep in the newspaper where it was printed."[3]

Boone's life story, appearing as it did during the formative years of the early Republic, was one of the foundation stones for what Richard Slotkin calls "the myth of the frontier." In our debunking age the word *myth* has become a synonym for erroneous belief. Slotkin, however, employs the term in an anthropological way to mean the body of tales, fables, and fantasies that help a people make sense of their history. The myth of the frontier has always promised authenticity—"Every word true!"— and it is right to be skeptical of such claims. But a myth is not necessarily false; some legends, in fact, may be accurate in most details.

Myth, like history, interprets and attempts to find meaning in past events. But when transformed into myth, history is reduced to its ideological essence. The western—the characteristic story form of the frontier myth—is essentially a tale of progress, a justification of violent conquest and untrammeled development. Boone's story—as the frontier pathfinder for American civilization—was a prominent piece of that triumphal tale. Yet the stories Boone told in his last years raised troubling questions. If the western country had been wrested from the Indians by men like him, why had the rewards been swept up by the merchants and lawyers? Why were poor backwoodsmen dispossessed of their lands, just as the Indians had been? Was that the real meaning of the term *civilization?* Because myth is composed in the figurative language of metaphor and symbol rather than the logical language of analysis, it may incorporate such doubts without confronting them. As Slotkin writes, "The most potent recurring hero-figures in our mythologies are men in whom contradictory identities find expression." Thus the progressive narrative of the western is consistently subverted by the presence of pathfinders who are also critics of civilization, outlaws who are Robin Hoods, and whores who have hearts of gold. Americans are drawn to characters of paradoxical impulse, to "good-badmen," or army scouts who identify with the Indian enemy. Things are simple in the western, but not always as simple as they seem. It is an example of what the critic Stuart Hall calls the "double-stake in popular culture, the double movement of containment and resistance."[4]

During the generation following Boone's death the character of the frontiersman became a ubiquitous presence in American culture. Of primary significance was the work of American novelist James Fenimore Cooper, who created an enduring literary version of the Boone character—variously identified as Leatherstocking, Hawkeye, or Deerslayer—in a series of five novels known as "The Leatherstocking Tales." An early review of Cooper's first western, *The Pioneers* (1823), noted that Leatherstocking was "modeled from the effigies of old Daniel Boone." The association was strengthened when, in the opening pages of his third tale, *The Prairie* (1827), Cooper explicitly linked his character with "Colonel Boone, the patriarch of Kentucky, . . . hardy pioneer of civilization." From its beginnings the western has insisted on the authenticity of its presentation as a story drawn from life.[5]

Cooper did not, however, intend Leatherstocking as the hero. According to the literary conventions of the day, heroes had to be men of genteel birth. Thus Cooper's plots feature well-bred officers romancing pale ladies, the kind likely to swoon when the going gets rough. Most readers have little interest in the leading characters of *The Last of the Mohicans* (1826). It is the supporting cast that fascinates: strong and resourceful Cora, condemned by her heritage of mixed blood; noble Indian warrior Uncas, instinctively understanding Cora's worth and loving her for it; brave and honest Hawkeye, nature's aristocrat.

The two groupings of characters, however, allowed Cooper to stage a conflict between civilized restraint and natural freedom. On the surface, his novels offer a progressive reading of America's frontier history and make a case for "the march of our nation across the continent." Judge Temple in *The Pioneers* is a visionary, patterned on Cooper's own father, the founder of Cooperstown, New York. "Where others saw nothing but a wilderness," the judge sees "towns, manufactories, bridges, canals, mines, and all the other resources of an old country." Nonetheless Cooper allows Leatherstocking to make a powerful argument against civilization. "The garden of the Lord was the forest," declares the old hunter, and was not patterned "after the miserable fashions of our times, thereby giving the lie to what the world calls its civilizing"—a paraphrase of one of old Boone's lines. Cooper's sentimental attachments lie with "forest freedom," compelling his readers to dwell on the price of progress. Francis Parkman, the great nineteenth-century romantic historian, proposed this summary of Cooper's message: "Civilization has a destroying as well as a creating power" and "must eventually sweep before it a class of men, its own precursors and pioneers, so remarkable both in their virtues and their faults that few will see their extinction without regret. Of these men Leatherstocking is the representative." Cooper's ambivalence about progress resonated with a deeply felt American regret about the loss of the wilderness as an imagined place of unbound freedom.[6]

The frontiersman entered the broader realms of American popular culture in the 1830s. In his popular play *The Lion of the West* (1830), James Kirk Paulding featured the character of Nimrod Wildfire, a bragging, buckskin-clad frontiersman who had come to Washington, D.C., as a congressman. Obviously based on real-life David Crockett of Tennessee, Wildfire's apotheosis came the evening Congressman Crockett attended a performance and the audience called him to the stage to take a bow with the company, an early example of the indiscriminate mixing of fact and fancy in the western. Knowing a good thing, Crockett published his own story, *A Narrative of the Life of David Crockett of the State of Tennessee* (1834), the first autobiography of a western American. Although the book considerably stretched the truth, it was written in Crockett's authentic voice and introduced frontier tall tales to a wide popular audience.

Soon there were many imitations, including a long-running series of the *Davy Crockett Almanac,* supposedly recounting his ongoing feats in his own words, although Crockett himself had no connection with the publications, which saw their heyday long after their protagonist had been killed at the Alamo. "I can outlook a panther and outstare a flash of lightening; tote a steamboat on my back and play at rough and tumble with a lion," thunders the Davy of the almanacs. "I can walk like

Dime novel hero Seth Jones. From Edward S. Ellis, Seth Jones, or, The Captives of the Frontier *(New York, 1860). Beinecke.*

an ox, run like a fox, swim like an eel, yell like an Indian, fight like a devil, and spout like an earthquake, make love like a mad bull, and swallow a nigger whole without choking if you butter his head and pin his ears back." This ribald character violates all the standards of polite society, observes Carroll Smith-Rosenberg. "Crockett denied the naturalness, the desirability, and the inevitability of bourgeois values and class distinctions." Crockett's over-the-top shenanigans, she argues, offered a subversive alternative to Victorian convention.[7]

Crockett was also a character in the first of the "dime novels," cheap paperbacks with sensational themes, that began appearing with the invention of the steam-powered printing press in the 1840s. It was the publishing house of Beadle and Adams, however, that first began issuing them in large numbers. In 1860 Erastus and Irwin Beadle, with their partner Robert Adams, set out to apply the techniques of mass production to publishing. Their first great success came almost immediately. *Seth Jones; or, The Captives of the Frontier* (1860), by Edward S. Ellis, tells the story of a white girl captured by Mohawks on the frontier of late eighteenth-century New York—a locale familiar to Cooper's readers. In a stirring finale, she is rescued by Seth Jones, a lovable scout in buckskin, who knows the wilderness and its native inhabitants as he knows the back of his hand. Ellis reveals Seth to be a gentleman in disguise, thus neatly combining the roles of frontier scout with well-born hero, suggesting the gradual democratization of American cultural forms. The book sold 450,000 copies in just six months and established Beadle and Adams as a publishing powerhouse.

Although the frontier was not the only setting for their stories, it was by far the most popular, with more than two-thirds of the 3,158 titles they published between 1860 and 1898 set in the West. Hunter-scouts like Seth Jones gradually gave way to outlaw, ranger, and cowboy heroes, and the requirement of genteel parentage was eventually dropped.

Novel followed novel, with Beadle's corps of writers churning out copy at the astounding rate of a thousand words per hour, a complete story every three days. Prentiss Ingraham, champion of the dime writers, was said to have delivered a thirty-five-thousand-word story to his publisher after a single marathon writing session lasting a day and a night. Literary historian Henry Nash Smith calls this "automatic writing." Forced to suspend any pretense of literary creativity, Smith suggests that dime novelists met their deadlines by identifying with the preoccupations of their readers, producing works he characterizes as "an objectified mass dream." It is an intriguing idea, if a difficult one to prove. But assuming that dime novels did map the fixations of their readers, it was a terrain both familiar and exotic. In the standard plot, savage redskins, vicious greasers, or heathen Chinee were laid low by conventional white heroes. By this point the relatively genteel Boone and even the more lascivious Crockett had given way to excessively violent characters—Indian-fighting Kit Carson, or big Jim Bowie, with a chip on his shoulder to match the massive knife in his belt. The stories also took subversive turns. In the early 1880s the James gang, then terrorizing banks and railroads on the Missouri border, became a favorite subject. Week after week Jesse and Frank defied the law and got away with it in the dimes—until respectable outrage finally forced the postmaster general to ban the series from the mails.[8]

Female characters were central to many recurring dime novel fantasies. The first Beadle and Adams novel, *Malaeska: The Indian Wife of the White Hunter* (1860), by Ann Sophia Stephens, retold America's oldest frontier legend—the Pocahontas story. Stephens's tear-jerker recounts the tragic tale of an Indian maiden who, against the wishes of her own people, rescues a white frontiersman, marries him, and bears his child, is exiled from her own land, and suffers a lonely death in an urban slum. As folklorist Rayna Green notes, "The Indian woman finds herself burdened with an image that can only be understood as dysfunctional." True enough. On the other hand there is no way that this could be characterized as a triumphal narrative of progress. Yet *Malaeska* sold three hundred thousand copies, and Stephens followed her success by writing three more romances with native women as protagonists. Another persistent dime novel fantasy was the "woman with the whip"—the western gal who acts a man's part but is all the more alluring for it. Frederick Whittaker's *The Mustang-Hunters; or, The Beautiful Amazon of the Hidden Valley* (1871) features a cross-dressing heroine, "a marvelous mixture of feminine gentleness and masculine firmness."[9]

Calamity Jane, the first dime novel heroine. From Edward L. Wheeler, Deadwood Dick in Leadville; or, A Strange Stroke for Liberty *(Cleveland, 1908). Beinecke.*

Dozens of similar dime-novel "she-males" followed, most famously Calamity Jane, introduced in Edward L. Wheeler's *Deadwood Dick on Deck; or, Calamity Jane, the Heroine of Whoop-Up* (1878), based on the life of a real western woman, Martha Jane Canary. Beadle's writers loved using real westerners as subjects. Edward Ellis could write about Seth Jones one week, Daniel Boone, Davy Crockett, or Kit Carson the next. In dime novels the fact and the fancy came indiscriminately mixed. But Beadle warned his authors to avoid "repetition of any experience which, though true, is yet better untold." It remained "better untold," for example, that Martha Jane Canary had turned tricks in the end-of-track helldorados of the plains or that she had ridden with General Crook's troops and was banished from camp for swimming nude with the enlisted men. Dime novelist Wheeler turned whoring Canary into kindhearted Calamity. Yet unlike Cooper's swooning ladies, Calamity Jane was a woman who knew how to get things moving. In an age when women's freedom was inhibited by genteel conventions, she captured the public imagination by demanding and receiving equal rights in a man's world. And although readers surely had little trouble recognizing the dime novels as fictions, the intermixture of authentic details encouraged a suspension of their disbelief. All true! Just think of it![10]

The ideal of authenticity also powerfully influenced the art of the frontier. All the major exploring and surveying expeditions mounted by the federal government included artists assigned to record and document the land, animals, and peoples of the West. In 1819 Samuel Seymour and Titian Ramsay Peale became the first westering artists when they signed on as members of Major Stephen Long's expedition. Seymour's instructions were to paint portraits of Indians, to reproduce landscapes noted for their "beauty or grandeur," and to ferret out any and all subjects "appropriate to his art." It was an open invitation to apply his artistic imagination and style to the documentary job at hand. Although he was not a great enough artist to take fullest advantage of the opportunity, Seymour became sufficiently excited about some subjects—his watercolors of Indians, for example—to endow them with a vitality beyond mere record.[11]

The marriage of art and science was a constant for the scores of artists who documented the explorations of the next half-century. "The documentary art of the explorer-artists," writes historian William Goetzmann, "inevitably fused romanticism with realism." The watercolors of the German artist Heinrich B. Möllhausen, who documented the route of one of the Pacific railroad surveys of the 1850s, appear almost surreal. As Goetzmann notes, "Möllhausen never allowed facts, or the demands of literalism, to interfere with his romantic imagination." Riding with the Frémont expeditions of 1845 and 1848 were the brothers Edward and Richard Kern of Philadelphia, scientists who had worked at institutions such as the newly founded Smith-

Portraits of three western Indians. Watercolor by Samuel Seymour, c. 1820. Beinecke.

sonian in the nation's capital. But they were no less artists, exhibiting in such distinguished salons as the Academy of Fine Arts in Philadelphia, and were willing to bend what they saw to fit what they wanted. Making permanent copies of his field sketches, for example, Richard repositioned an Indian pueblo in order to create an illusion of space and order missing from real life, and changed the eye level in an Indian kiva to convey an impression of architectural strength quite different from the fact.[12]

A similar mix of documentary and artistic impulses characterized the work of frontier painter George Catlin. According to Catlin's own account, he experienced a moment of epiphany when, as a young man in Philadelphia, he saw an Indian delegation walk through the city on its way to Washington. He was so impressed with these "lords of the forest" that he resolved that "nothing short of the loss of my life shall prevent me from visiting their country, and of becoming their historian." Enthusiastically he worked his way up the Missouri River to the mouth of the Yellowstone in 1832, sketching practically every Indian he met on the way. It was the first of many trips over the next five years, alternating with periods in the studio transcribing his sketches into finished oils. He asked that the public view his works "as they have been intended, as *true* and *fac-simile* traces of individual life and historical facts." To the backs of his work Catlin attached certificates, signed by Indian agents, army officers, or other government officials, certifying that they had been "painted from the life"; and he included similar testimonials in the account of his travels, *Manners, Customs, and Conditions of the North American Indians* (1841). "The Landscape Views on the Missouri, Buffalo Hunts, and other scenes taken by my friend Mr. Catlin are correct delineations of the scenes they profess to represent," wrote Indian Agent John Sanford, "and further, I know, that they were taken on the spot, from nature, as I was present when Mr. Catlin visited that country."[13]

Yet in truth Catlin aimed at more than mere record. He sought to express a point of view through his art, and he made his views perfectly clear in his writing. "The bane of this *blasting frontier* has regularly crowded upon them," he wrote of the Indians, "and like the fire in a prairie, which destroys everything where it passes, it has blasted and sunk them, where ever it has traveled." Catlin was on a mission of deliverance. "I have flown to their rescue—not of their lives or of their race (for they are '*doomed*' and must perish), but to the rescue of their looks and their modes." The Indians themselves would eventually vanish, "yet, phoenix-like, they may rise from 'the stain of a painter's palette,' and live again upon canvass, and stand forth for centuries yet to come, the living monuments of a noble race." There is much to admire in Catlin's sentiments, especially when they are placed within the Indian-hating context of his times. And clearly they could inspire great art. The men and women of his Indian portraits return the viewer's gaze with a humanity and a dignity that never fail to impress. But because, in the end, he viewed Indian people as victims, helpless against the tide of civilization, he was oblivious to the cultural transformations that in fact would insure their survival. Aside from the necklaces, the feathers, and the paint that adorn his subjects, Catlin's paintings are peculiarly bereft of cultural context.[14]

More successful at capturing images of Indians as people of culture was Karl Bodmer, a Swiss painter who toured the upper Missouri country in 1833 and 1834 with his patron, Prince Maximilian of the small German principality of Wied, providing the visual accompaniment to Maximilian's ethnographic studies. Bodmer, a fine draftsman and colorist, did an extraordinarily good job of placing his subjects in a complicated cultural world. His celebrated study of a Mandan family relaxing around the central hearth of their earth lodge is notable for the abundance of ethnographic detail packed into the image: the shields, lances, and medicine symbols of the warriors, the cooking pots and basketry of the women, the framing timbers and the solidity of the lodge itself. He provided similar images of many Indian cultures. Dennis Hastings, tribal historian of the Omahas, notes the way Bodmer's work helped in the reconstruction of traditional clothing styles, haircuts, and clan rituals, part of a modern revival of ethnic pride among his people. In the face of such testimonials it is difficult to be critical. But like Catlin, Bodmer missed recording much evidence of the history of interaction between Indians and Europeans or Americans.

George Catlin paints a portrait of a Mandan chief. From George Catlin, Letters and Notes on the Manners, Customs, and Condition of the North American Indians, *9th ed. (London, 1857). Beinecke.*

"Interior of the Lodge of a Mandan Chief." Engraving based on a watercolor by Carl Bodmer, from Maximilian, Prinz von Wied, Reise in das innere Nord-America in den Jahren 1832 bis 1834, 2 vols. *(London, 1843–44). Beinecke.*

For both artists, the mission was to capture images of Indians in their "pristine" condition, not to record the contemporary historic moment.

Alfred Jacob Miller, an American artist with European training, was the painter who best captured the cultural mix of the frontier. In 1837 Captain William Drummond Stewart, a Scottish nobleman on leave from the British army, hired Miller to accompany him on the last of his several trips to the Rockies. Miller's watercolors and drawings of this expedition feature Indians and mountain men setting traps, spinning tales around campfires, and resting peacefully together in the midday shade. His remarkable images of the fur trade post of Fort Laramie depict it as a place of intercultural exchange. And more than any other nineteenth-century artist of the West, Miller paid close attention to Indian women—preparing skins and meat, tending children, racing horses, even hunting buffalo. His work provides powerful visual support for the central place of women in fur trade society. Yet all this he delivers in romantic soft focus. Miller's Indian women are nearly always beauties, and frequently unclothed, bringing to mind, as William Goetzmann suggests, the Tahitian works of French artist Paul Gauguin. After all, these paintings were intended for Stewart's pleasure, mementos of days and nights spent in the company of fur trappers and in the arms of Indian maidens. The eroticism of an image like the beautiful *Snake Girl Swinging* (1837) was certainly intended for private male reveries.

Snake Girl Swinging. *Watercolor by Alfred Jacob Miller, c. 1837. Beinecke.*

The documentary concerns that animated these painters of Indians, Missouri artist George Caleb Bingham brought to his images of frontier settlers. Just as Catlin had pledged to preserve a record of the natives, so Bingham declared, at the onset of his artistic career, that art should be history's "most efficient hand-maid," and vowed that the life and politics of his region would "not be lost in the lapse of time for want of an Art record rendering them full justice." Bingham depicted the everyday life he saw around him, settlers at work and at play, at home with their families or in town

Daniel Boone Escorting Settlers Through the Cumberland Gap. *Painting by George Caleb Bingham, 1851–52. Washington University Gallery of Art, Saint Louis. Gift of Nathaniel Phillips, Boston, 1890.*

participating in politics. His most famous series of canvases featured flatboatmen on the Missouri and Mississippi rivers. A Saint Louis critic in 1850 praised the "life-like fidelity" of one of his genre scenes, writing enthusiastically that "it seems an incarnation rather than a painting." If Bodmer's work constitutes a visual ethnography of plains Indians, Bingham's accomplished something similar for midcentury frontier settlers.[15]

That is not to suggest that Bingham's paintings were documentary in any narrow sense. As art historian Barbara Groseclose puts it, Bingham "combined the idea of transcription, a record, with a mood of nostalgia, a memory." River mists evoked the loneliness of trappers; quiet currents provided a backdrop for rough men venting simple emotions by dancing and gambling; slowly moving waters defined the cast of characters—transients loitering and drifting along the backwaters of the frontier. Indeed, so tranquil are Bingham's images that they seem to depict a world in which time stands still. This is especially notable in his masterwork, *Daniel Boone Escorting Settlers Through the Cumberland Gap* (1852). At the head of a column of settlers stretching back through the dark and forbidding pass, Boone leads his family into the clear light of Kentucky. He symbolizes immense courage, unconquerable faith in hard work, and the coming of civilization to a raw West. Executed in the aftermath of the Mexican War, the high tide of American empire, the work is a quintessential celebration of pioneering.[16]

The works of these artists were widely distributed in various printed media. Art historian Martha Sandweiss estimates that between 1843 and 1863 more than seven hundred engravings and lithographs of western scenes appeared in government reports and documents, many with print runs of thousands of copies. The works of Catlin, Bodmer, Miller, and Bingham were issued in authorized prints from private publishers, as well as in unauthorized copies without credit, and often became the basis for drawings in popular books, magazines, and dime novels. Passing through the hands of engravers and hack artists, the images became collaborative products of the imagination. New details might be added, backgrounds filled in, and costumes transformed. The clothing of Richard Kern's Pueblo weavers, for example, emerged in prints looking rather like that of medieval Europeans. Frequently engravers presented Indians as far more fierce and threatening than they appeared in the original sketches or watercolors. "In this way," Sandweiss writes, western artists "influenced popular perceptions of the West through the mediating work of artists who had never ventured west themselves." Though eastern suppositions transformed these pictures, thousands of Americans accepted them as accurate depictions of the West.[17]

In midcentury there was a turn toward grand historical painting. George Caleb Bingham hoped that his *Boone* would catapult him from a painter of simple genre scenes to an artist of national stature, recognized for serious historical works displayed in monumental and patriotic style. In the mid-1850s he lived for a time in Düsseldorf, Germany, a famous center for artistic training, where he joined a group of Americans studying with Emanuel Gottlieb Leutze, the era's most eminent painter of American historical themes, best known for *Washington Crossing the Delaware* (1852), still an icon of American historical commemoration. From Germany, Bingham submitted an entry in a federal competition for a work best illustrating the history of the West. The prize was to be a commission for a mural gracing the walls of the capitol building in Washington.

Leutze, Bingham's mentor, entered the competition himself, and it was he who won the commission (Bingham never forgave him). The resulting work, *Westward the Course of Empire Takes Its Way* (1862), was monumental in scale, filling six hundred square feet in a prominently placed capitol stairwell. It depicts a group of pioneers mounting the summit of a mountain range and celebrating their arrival in the golden West. Leutze had made field studies in the West, and Nathaniel Hawthorne, who observed the work in progress, wrote that the artist was "producing new forms of artistic beauty from the natural features of the Rocky-Mountain region, which

Westward the Course of Empire. *Painting by Emanuel Gottlieb Leutze, 1862. National Museum of American Art.*

Leutze seems to have studied broadly and minutely." Yet the mural depicts a land-scape of Leutze's romantic imagining. The pioneers themselves are a mélange of stereotypes: frontiersmen shouldering their rifles, a young man with a bloody ban-dage on his forehead (a wound, perhaps, from fighting Indians), a stoic pioneer bride, a dead loved one being buried by a grieving family. At the summit is a buck-skinned Boone, joyously indicating the destination to the recumbent mother and child sheltered in his arms. As Hawthorne wrote, the mural is "full of energy, hope, progress, irrepressible movement onward, all represented in a momentary pause of triumph, and it was most cheering to feel its good augury at this dismal time, when our country might seem to have arrived at such a deadly standstill." Completed dur-ing the depth of the Civil War, Leutze's work offered an allegorical visualization of Republican plans for the postwar West.[18]

The artist who best captured the public taste for the monumental was Albert Bier-stadt, an American who studied in Düsseldorf, where he learned to paint castles on the Rhine and snow-capped peaks in the Alps. Returning to the states, he joined a government survey party headed west and found in the Rockies "the best material

The Rocky Mountains, Lander's Peak. *Painting by Albert Bierstadt, 1863. The Metropolitan Museum of Art, Rogers Fund, 1907.*

for the artist in the world." Entranced, he tramped and sketched his way through the Wind River Mountains, then returned to his studio in New York City to paint a number of huge finished works. *The Rocky Mountains, Lander's Peak* (1863) created an immediate sensation when first exhibited. On a canvas measuring six feet by ten, Bierstadt created a panoramic and infinitely receding landscape of valley, lake, and mountains, replete with a busy Indian encampment in the foreground. Dramatic interplays of shadow and sunlight highlight the distant peaks and overwhelm the human subjects. The critics were impressed: "No more genuine and grand American work has been produced of that majestic barrier of the West where the heavens and the earth meet in brilliant and barren proximity." Bierstadt took the canvas on a triumphant tour through the United States and Europe, then sold it for the unprecedented sum of twenty-five thousand dollars (the equivalent of half a million dollars today).[19]

Bierstadt arranged to have the picture engraved and sold subscriptions during the tour, netting him thousands of dollars more. The painting possessed "a geographical and historical value such as few works by modern artists have obtained," he assured potential buyers in an advertising flyer distributed at the exhibitions. Here again was the appeal to authenticity, to the documentary quality of western art. In truth, Bierstadt concocted the landscape in *The Rocky Mountains,* redistributing peaks and valleys and foreshortening distances for dramatic effect. Indeed, in his field studies he had sketched this view of the Wind River range looking east, but in

The Grand Canyon of the Yellowstone. *Painting by Thomas Moran, 1872. National Museum of American Art.*

the finished work he reoriented it 180 degrees in order to take advantage of the dramatic light of an imagined setting sun. Bierstadt suffered considerable criticism for this kind of artistic manipulation. Mark Twain once described one of his Yosemite landscapes as "beautiful—considerably more beautiful than the original," and joked that the painting had "more the atmosphere of Kingdom-Come than of California." But Twain's witty critique missed the point of Bierstadt's art, which aimed not at documenting the western landscape so much as transforming it into something otherworldly, a place of mystery and magic. In the midst of civil war, the country hungered for profound nationalistic images, and the magnificence of the western landscape offered a substitute for a deep American past. This was not lost on everyone. As a perceptive Boston reviewer noted, Bierstadt's work depicted a scene "which does not exist, and in fact hardly could exist. . . . It is the perfect type of the American idea of what our country ought to be, if it is not so in reality." As the stylistic screw turned, however, Bierstadt eventually fell out of favor, and by the time he died in 1902, his huge canvases had been assigned to the nation's attic.[20]

The other great late nineteenth-century painter of monumental western landscapes was Thomas Moran, an artist as well steeped in English romanticism as Bierstadt was in its German form. During a period of study in London in the 1860s he fell in love with the romantic landscapes of J. M. W. Turner, a colorist who seemed to anticipate the Impressionists in his final canvases. Longing for dramatic western vistas appropriate for this kind of art, in 1871 Moran joined the Yellowstone survey

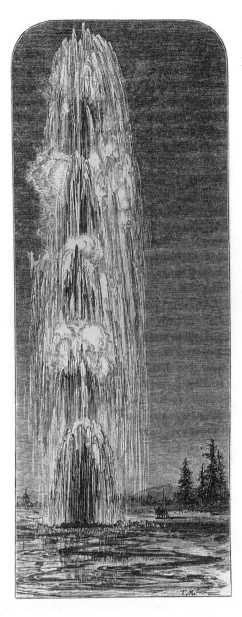

Yellowstone geyser. Engraving based on a watercolor by Thomas Moran, from Scribner's Monthly, *1871. Beinecke.*

party of Ferdinand V. Hayden, financing the trip with a five-hundred-dollar loan from financier Jay Cooke, attempting to generate interest in the region to the benefit of his railroad, the Northern Pacific. Photographer William Henry Jackson, also a member of the Hayden party, later recalled Moran's picturesque appearance—"the jaunty tilt of his sombrero, long yellowish beard, and portfolio under his arm"—and his boundless excitement. "The weird and fantastic towers and pinnacles along the turbulent creek above the falls caught Moran's fancy," Jackson remembered. Upon the completion of the expedition, Moran produced a series of watercolors for Cooke that were engraved for reproduction. Together with Jackson's photographic prints,

Smelting Works at Denver. *Watercolor by Thomas Moran, 1892.* © *The Cleveland Museum of Art. Bequest of Mrs. Henry A. Everett for the Dorothy Burnham Everett Memorial Collection.*

these images were instrumental in persuading Congress to create Yellowstone National Park. For his oils, Moran flung hung canvases over entire walls and, like Bierstadt, gave to western space its image in footage. Congress purchased his *Grand Canyon of the Yellowstone* (1872)—which one critic praised as "the finest historical landscape yet painted in this country"—for the astounding sum of ten thousand dollars. In 1876 Moran arranged for the publication of a set of chromolithographs of his Yellowstone views.[21]

Moran and Bierstadt encouraged the public to think of the western landscape as a spectacular emblem of America. Bierstadt's West was a Gothic cathedral, tuning awe-struck men and women to the infinite beauty of nature. Moran's paintings were stained-glass windows, each small piece of color transmitting an aura of mystical reverence. These paintings were not intended as photographic records. Bierstadt was disingenuous about this, but Moran was more candid. "I place no value upon literal transcripts from Nature," he said to those who questioned his accuracy. "I did not wish to realize the scene literally, but to preserve and to convey its true impression." The National Park Service—which owns the Yellowstone watercolors Moran prepared for Cooke—celebrates him as a pioneer in the conservation movement. Yet making Moran into a Muir with paint misses the point. He was not simply a devotee of spectacular scenery, although that is the effect his most popular work had on the public. One of his most provocative western landscapes is the 1892 watercolor he entitled *Smelting Works at Denver*, in which huge smokestacks belch toxic wastes into the crisp air, the smoke, mountains, and sky dissolving into a haze of yellows, browns, and blacks. Moran's mature painterly interests could find artistic possibilities not only in the towers and pinnacles of Yellowstone but in the cityscapes of the emerging industrial West.[22]

During the long cycle of economic hard times and farmer-worker protest that began with the Panic of 1873 and lasted until the late 1890s, many Americans became concerned about the "close of the frontier"—a catch phrase of the day that included fears of the end of "free land" as well as the exhaustion of the West's natural resources, component parts of the "safety valve," believed to have moderated the country's class tensions. In his influential *Progress and Poverty* (1879), Henry George argued that the nation's economic progress had depended on western expansion. "But our advance has reached the Pacific," he warned. "Further west we cannot go." In 1889 fifty thousand people participated in a frenzied rush to stake claims to two million acres of "unoccupied" land in Indian Territory, almost overnight creating the territory of Oklahoma. That year and the next, six new western states entered the union (North and South Dakota, Montana, Washington, Idaho, and Wyoming), and over the next twenty years the admission of the final four—Utah, Oklahoma, Arizona, and New Mexico—completed the process of statemaking in the nation's contiguous territory that Thomas Jefferson had inaugurated with his Land Ordinance of 1784. Worry over the closing frontier echoed in government reports, scholarly treatises, and ministers' sermons but was not confined to the nation's intellectuals. Humorist and western newspaper editor Bill Nye expressed the fears of ordinary folks: "There ain't no frontier any more."[23]

These apprehensions seemed confirmed by the conclusions of statisticians and cartographers who examined the returns of the federal census of 1890. "Up to and including 1880 the country had a frontier of settlement," they reported. "But at present the unsettled area has been so broken into by isolated bodies of settlement that there can hardly be said to be a frontier line. . . . It can not, therefore, any longer have a place in the census reports." These words fired the imagination of young Wisconsin historian Frederick Jackson Turner. In his essay "The Significance of the Frontier in American History"—delivered in 1893 at a meeting of historians at the World's Columbian Exhibition in Chicago, a celebration of the four-hundredth anniversary of Columbus's first voyage to America—Turner made this famous declaration: "Up to our own day American history has been in large degree the history of the colonization of the Great West. The existence of an area of free land, its continuous recession, and the advance of settlement westward, explain American development." But now, Turner concluded, "four centuries from the discovery of America, at the end of a hundred years of life under the Constitution, the frontier has gone, and with its going has closed the first period of American history."[24]

There were some serious problems with the notion of a closed frontier. Far more land in the trans-Mississippi West, both public and private, was taken up in the years after 1890 than in the years before. And tens of thousands of Americans crossed the northern border to pioneer what the Canadians promoted as the "last best West." Western settlements continued to expand in the years after 1890, yet on the census maps of 1900 and 1910 the "frontier line" made a mysterious reappearance. Geographer Frank Popper reporting on "the strange case of the contemporary American frontier," points out that using Turner's own definition of "unsettled," there are in the late twentieth century 149 "frontier" counties in the West and that many areas of the western Great Plains are steadily losing population. The cartography that so inspired Turner, it turns out, was less a work of science than one of the imagination. A century later, the West has yet to fill up.[25]

The "closing of the frontier" became part of the myth. If expansion was the key to understanding the American past for Turner, for others it seemed also to offer the solution to contemporary problems. After reading Turner's frontier essay Woodrow Wilson wrote that with the continent occupied "and reduced to the uses of civilization," the nation must inevitably turn to "new frontiers in the Indies and in the Far Pacific." Theodore Roosevelt agreed, arguing that American colonies in the Caribbean and the Pacific were the logical and necessary extension of continental westering. He likened Filipinos to Apaches and condemned anti-imperialists as "Indian lovers." If the United States was "morally bound to abandon the Philippines," he blustered during the debate on annexation after the Spanish-American War, "we were also morally bound to abandon Arizona to the Apaches."[26]

Just as expansionists of the 1840s had marshaled public enthusiasm for westering to justify a war against Mexico, so imperialists of the 1890s exploited fears of the end of frontier opportunity in order to build support for the creation of an American overseas empire. As historian William Appleman Williams observed, it offers "a classic illustration of the transformation of an idea into an ideology." But even as Roosevelt was urging his countrymen into battle for imperial possessions, Turner was lamenting the "wreckage of the Spanish War." Rather than overseas expansion, Turner placed his hopes for the American future in the expansion of higher education. "The test tube and the microscope are needed rather than ax and rifle," he wrote. "In place of old frontiers of wilderness, there are new frontiers of unwon fields of science." He made a case for what amounted to a moral equivalent to westering.[27]

Theodore Roosevelt in his hunter's costume. From Theodore Roosevelt, Hunting Trips of a Ranchman *. . . (New York, 1886). Beinecke.*

Simultaneous with Turner's promotion of the frontier thesis, three prominent easterners were doing their part to bring the myth of the frontier to popular attention: politician Theodore Roosevelt, artist Frederic Remington, and writer Owen Wister. Born into prominent families in the era of the Civil War, educated at Harvard or Yale, each of these men went west seeking personal regeneration at a critical point in their early twenties. Historian G. Edward White persuasively argues that these sojourns convinced each man that only by coming to grips with the experience of westering—with the myth of the frontier—could Americans preserve important aspects of their culture being swept away by the rush of industrialization. Most important, they sought to encourage a rugged version of American manhood. Their heroes were all "men with the bark on."

Roosevelt's encounter with the West followed the devastating death of his young wife (in childbirth) and his mother (from disease) on the same dark day in 1884. Leaving his baby daughter in the care of his extended family, the young man abandoned New York and for three years lived on a Dakota cattle ranch, "far off from mankind." For Roosevelt this western sojourn became a critical test of manhood. At first the cowboys ridiculed him as an effete easterner, but things turned around for him once he stood up to a bully and floored him with a lucky punch. Roosevelt learned to hunt, graduating from killing deer to stalking panthers. He joined a posse and participated in the capture of a gang of desperadoes. "We knew toil and hardship and hunger and thirst," he wrote, "but we felt the beat of hearty life in our being, and ours was the glory of work and the joy of living." He returned to New York in 1886, a rough-and-tumble westerner. This experience would inform all his subsequent work—as author of hunting memoirs, including the best-selling *Ranch Life and the Hunting Trail* (1887), his multivolume history *The Winning of the West* (1889–96), and a dozen other popular books with similar themes; as president of the Boone and Crockett Club, conservationist, sports hunter, and advocate of "the strenuous life"; as Rough Rider during the Spanish-American War; and as America's first "cowboy president." What was good for the American male was good for the country. An appreciation of the West and its traditions, Roosevelt believed, would help to cultivate "that vigorous manliness for the lack of which in a nation, as in an individual, the possession of no other qualities can possibly atone."[28]

Frederic Remington went West in 1883 to escape a domineering mother who ridiculed his ambition to be an artist and insisted that he "take a real man's job." Writing that he wished to "cut women out of his life altogether," Remington used a small inheritance to purchase a Kansas ranch. Although he failed to make the operation pay and eventually lost it to creditors, he considered his three years in the West the happiest of his life. Western men "have all the rude virtues," he wrote. They were "untainted by the enfeebling influences of luxury and modern life." His admiration was mixed with a heavy dose of nostalgia. "I saw the living, breathing end of three centuries of smoke and dust and sweat," he later mused. Simultaneously Remington rediscovered his talent and joy for art and, like Catlin and Bingham before him, resolved to capture on paper the last days of the frontier. In 1885 he accompanied troopers through New Mexico during the campaign against Geronimo and placed his sketches in *Harper's Monthly* and *Outing,* one of the new men's sporting magazines. Returning East in the wake of this success, Remington struck his friends as a man transformed. "He had turned himself into a cowboy," wrote a former Yale classmate. Captivated by Remington's work, Roosevelt asked him to illustrate the forthcoming *Ranch Life and the Hunting Trail.* It was the beginning of a lucrative career as fin-de-siècle America's most successful commercial illustrator. Soon oils and bronzes were also pouring from his studio, all commanding top dollar. "It is a fact that admits of no question," wrote an art critic in 1892, "that Eastern people have formed their conceptions of what the Far-Western life is like, more from what they have seen in Mr. Remington's pictures than from any other source."[29]

In his devotion to the cult of masculinity, Remington rivaled his friend Roosevelt. He was always uncomfortable and discontented with women, claiming to have "never drawn a woman—except once, and then had washed her out." This was an exaggeration, but not by much, for amid the thousands of men in his many works women appear only four times. True manliness, he believed, developed in the strug-

A Daring Feat of Horsemanship. *Watercolor by Frederic Remington, from Owen Wister,* The Virginian *(1902; New York, 1911).* Beinecke.

gle with raw nature, the individual pitted against drought and wind. His works include dozens of images of men against a barren landscape. In *Friend or Foe* (1895) a lone rider strains his eyes to identify a barely visible speck on the bleak horizon. The Indians were part of hostile nature, dangerous yet useful as an abrasion against which the white man could prove his mettle. *Downing the Nigh Leader* (1907), one of his most celebrated paintings, features a group of mounted Indians attacking a speeding stagecoach. The lead horse on the left pitches violently to the ground, felled by a spear from a galloping warrior, while the drivers struggle stoically against their impending destruction. In *The Last Stand* (1890), Remington's depiction of the Custer myth, a group of cavalry troopers converge in heroic formation against an unseen enemy. Indians were only one of the enemies threatening the country. In a letter to a friend written at about the same time he painted that image, Remington lumped Indians together with immigrants. "Jews, Injuns, Chinamen, Italians, Huns—the rubbish of the earth I hate—I've got some Winchesters and when the massacring begins, I can get my share of 'em, and what's more, I will." In his art, Remington proclaimed the American male triumphant over nature and the Anglo-Saxon dominant over "the rubbish of the earth."[30]

Owen Wister, the third of this influential trio and a classmate of Roosevelt's at Harvard, went West on a doctor's orders in 1885 when he was twenty-five. According to his daughter, he "freed himself from what to him was a deadly life," a career as a Boston businessman, exchanging it for a position as manager of a large Wyoming cattle ranch. Like Roosevelt and Remington, Wister self-consciously conceived of his western experience as a test of his manhood. He slept outdoors with the cowboys, bathed in an icy creek, drank his steaming coffee from a tin cup, and joined in the roundup. "The slumbering Saxon awoke in him," Wister wrote in a story with auto-biographical implications, and he reinvented himself as "kin with the drifting vagabonds who swore and galloped by his side."[31]

He soon returned east, but over the next fifteen years Wister spent his summers in Wyoming. He began writing about cattle country, publishing short stories, essays, and novels in the 1890s. Ultimate triumph came with *The Virginian* (1902), a run-away best-seller and the most influential and widely read of all western novels. But curiously, although Wister continued writing, he never again wrote about the West. Indeed, after the publication of *The Virginian* he refused to travel West, fearful, per-haps, that the development of the region would destroy the ghost of his past. The mythical country of the open range, the classic setting of the western story, was en-tirely masculine, the playground of young men, Wister called it. But it was far more than play. It restored health, as it had for Wister himself, and it offered to re-create American men as self-reliant individuals. Underscoring self-reliance is the name-lessness of the hero in *The Virginian*. His given name is used but once, in an off-handed manner, and the reader learns precious little of his background, except that he comes from the South. Wister asks that he be judged solely in the present, by what he accomplishes. Moreover, this vagueness contributes to his mystery and power. "It was by design he continued nameless," Wister later wrote, "because I desired to draw a sort of heroic circle about him, almost a legendary circle and thus if possible cre-ate an illusion of remoteness."[32]

He staged *The Virginian* as a series of tests of manhood. The hero rides at the head of a posse that captures and lynches a group of cattle rustlers, including his best friend. They once rode together as wild and woolly comrades, but the Virginian has the foresight to see that the frontier days are passing. He confronts the threatening outlaw Trampas—"When you call me that, smile!"—and in the prototype of the western duel shoots him dead in the dusty main street of Medicine Bow. By dint of intelligence and industry he rises from cowboy to foreman, eventually becoming "an important man, with a strong grip on many various enterprises." But the central test is the Virginian's courtship of Molly Wood, the eastern schoolmarm. In a series of arguments the cowboy convinces the lady to abandon sentimental attachments and accept his moral code, the rule of honor. "Can't you see how it is about a man?" he implores as he rejects her pleas to leave town and avoid the final confrontation with Trampas. She cannot see—but in the end she accepts. After all, Molly had come West because she "wanted a man who was a man." Old South is united with Old East in the New West.[33]

If Turner, Roosevelt, Remington, and Wister brought intellectual respectability to their version of the frontier myth, "Buffalo Bill" Cody was the man who turned that

Sitting Bull and William "Buffalo Bill" Cody. Photograph by W. R. Cross, c. 1885. Kansas State Historical Society, Topeka.

myth into America's most bankable commercial entertainment. Born in Iowa in 1846, William Frederick Cody grew up on the frontier. As a teenage boy he tramped to the Colorado gold rush and rode for the Pony Express. He fought with an irregular force of border Jayhawkers during the Civil War, scouted for the frontier army in

Annie Oakley. Photograph by J. Wood, c. 1885. Beinecke.

campaigns against the Comanches, Sioux, and Kiowas, and earned his nickname hunting buffalo to feed railroad construction gangs. In 1869 dime novelist Ned Buntline (real name Edward Z. C. Judson) met Cody and wrote him up in the fanciful *Buffalo Bill, King of the Bordermen* (1869). Buntline's character was "the greatest scout of the West," skilled in the techniques of wilderness survival, Indian fighting, and vigilante justice. Honor motivated all his actions, whether protecting public virtue by vows of high purpose or rescuing white women from dastardly attacks by Indians or banditti. Before Cody's death in 1917 he had been the subject of no fewer than fifteen hundred dime novels, a score written by Buntline, at least two hundred by Prentiss Ingraham.

Cody was such a showman, such a ham actor, that he tried his best to live the role in which Buntline had cast him. Capitalizing on his moment of dime novel fame, he went on the stage, touring eastern cities in *Scouts of the Plains*, a melodrama written by Buntline. In 1873 he organized the "Buffalo Bill Combination," a troupe of cowboy and Indian actors who dramatized adventures from dime novels and reenacted actual events in western history. This curious alchemy of the spurious and the authentic produced gold for Cody in the spring of 1876, when from the stage he dramatically announced the suspension of his tour so he could join cavalry units fighting the Sioux and Cheyennes. In a minor engagement a few days after Custer's defeat, Cody shot, killed, and scalped a Cheyenne warrior. Within days he was back on stage, reenacting his triumph and displaying the actual dried scalp before droves of sensation seekers. In Cody's hands, dime novel illusions were embodied in flesh and blood, and western history was converted into living melodrama.

In 1882 Cody organized the greatest of his shows, "Buffalo Bill's Wild West," which toured America and the world for the next three decades. The performance began with an overture played by thirty-six "cowboy" musicians wearing flannel shirts and slouch hats. Laced throughout were exhibitions of shooting and riding. Annie Oakley, the sweetheart of the show, entered trippingly throwing kisses. Then her rifle would begin to crack as she dispatched glass balls, clay pigeons, and little three-by-five-inch cards embossed with her picture, thrown high, sliced by her bullets, then thrown to the delighted audience. Buck Taylor, King of the Cowboys, clung to bucking broncs and led a troop in square dances and Virginia reels on horseback.

There was always a large contingent of Indians, mostly Sioux, performing their dances and displaying life as it had been lived on the plains before the coming of men like Buffalo Bill. Sitting Bull joined the tour for the 1885 season, partly because he had met Annie Oakley the year before and had taken a liking to her. He named her "Little Sure Shot," and their relationship appears to have been genuinely warm. But it was difficult for the audience to accept the great Sioux chief into the show. After all, he was Custer's enemy, the embodiment of Buffalo Bill's troubles when he had scouted for the boys in blue. When Sitting Bull came on in his great ceremonial feathers, he was hissed, and in spite of his respect for Annie, he refused to tour for another season. Most of his salary of fifty dollars a week he gave away to bootblacks and street urchins. He was unable to understand why wealthy white men allowed such poverty to exist.

Historian L. G. Moses comments on the ambiguous legacy Cody's Wild West bequeathed to American Indians. On one hand it encouraged Americans to believe that all "real Indians" slept in tepees, wore feathered bonnets, hunted buffalo, and spoke using sign language. The Wild West was the source of many of the negative stereotypes later featured in motion pictures and on television. On the other hand the Indian performances also were critical to the development of the "powwow," an important twentieth-century pan-Indian institution, "a means by which people could retain, restore, or, in certain instances, create through adaptation a modern Indian identity." Reformers complained that Cody exploited his Indian performers, but most of the historical evidence suggests that Indians enjoyed the work and considered themselves well treated. Black Elk, a young Oglala dancer who later became a famous spiritual leader, came down with a bad case of homesickness during a tour of England in the early 1890s. "He would fix that," Black Elk remembered Cody telling him. "He gave me a ticket [home] and ninety dollars. Then he gave me a big dinner. Pahuska [Long Hair] had a strong heart."[34]

Authenticity through historic reenactment was the highlight of the Wild West. "Its distinctive feature lies in its realism," read Cody's promotional copy. "The participants repeat the heroic parts they have played in actual life upon the plains." Hunters chased buffalo, Indians attacked the Deadwood stage, and the Pony Express once again delivered the mail to isolated frontier outposts. The climax was a staging of "Custer's Last Fight," with Buffalo Bill arriving just after Custer's demise, the words "Too Late" projected by lantern slide on a background screen. That was the dark before the dawn. In the grand finale, Cody led a galloping victory lap of all the company's players—"The Congress of Rough Riders of the World"—with the American flag proudly flying in the van. The whole spectacle, in the words of the souvenir program sold during the performance, was designed to illustrate "the inevitable law of the survival of the fittest."[35]

Cody consistently updated these reenactments. In 1899, after the Spanish-American War, he featured Roosevelt's Rough Rider charge up San Juan Hill, then a few years later replaced it with a staging of the American occupation of Beijing during the Boxer Rebellion, the roles of the Chinese played by the company's Sioux contingent. In 1908 he introduced "The Great Train Hold-Up." It was an attempt to compete with *The Great Train Robbery* (1903), the first motion picture to tell a complete story, the first movie western.

George Barnes aims at the audience. Frame from The Great Train Robbery *(1903). The Museum of Modern Art, Film Stills Archive.*

Director Edwin S. Porter based his one-reel film on the holdup in 1901 of the eastbound Union Pacific by an outlaw gang known as the Wild Bunch, led by "Butch" Cassidy and the "Sundance Kid." Porter shot the picture, however, on the tracks of the Delaware and Lackawanna Railroad in New Jersey. The plot built on the Wild West formula pioneered by Cody—a dastardly attack, a dramatic chase, and a violent climactic shoot-out. In the film's final image, one of the outlaws points his gun directly at the audience and fires. People were thrilled. They flocked to nickelodeons to see the picture, and theaters throughout the country installed projectors and screens simply to exhibit it. *The Great Train Robbery* marked the birth of the American motion picture industry, which from its beginnings was preoccupied with western stories. Over the next sixty years at least a third of all the films made in the United States were westerns. "Rather than the cinema inventing the western," suggests film historian Tag Gallagher, exaggerating only a little, "it was the western, already long existent in popular culture, that invented the cinema."[36]

Motion pictures exploited the western with as much gusto as had the dime novel. Film companies churned out short westerns by the hundreds. The first identifiable movie actor to assume the mantle of the western hero was Max Aronson, a traveling salesman from Arkansas whose first screen role was playing one of the outlaws in *The*

Great Train Robbery. When Aronson auditioned, Porter told him the role demanded expert riding. Although he was a complete tenderfoot, Aronson claimed he could "ride as well as a Texas Ranger." When the outlaws make their escape in the film, he is the one attempting to mount his horse from the wrong side! Despite subsequent lessons, Aronson never became comfortable on a horse, but under the stage name of Bronco Billy Anderson he starred in some four hundred astoundingly popular western two-reelers, all with essentially the same plot—Bronco Billy as a "good-badman" redeemed by the love of a virtuous woman or the disarming cuteness of a helpless child. The public eventually tired of Aronson but fell for a new hero of dime novel proportions, Tom Mix, a veteran of wild west shows who was a master of trick riding and fancy shooting. In his snow-white ten-gallon Stetson, hand-tooled boots, and dandified cowboy clothes, Mix cut a fantastic figure, and by the 1920s, in addition to dozens of cheap films, he was being featured in a regular weekly radio program and his own series of comic books.[37]

Bronco Billy and Tom Mix were comic book characters, but other filmmakers went to lengths to emphasize the authenticity of their westerns. In 1912 director Thomas Ince, one of the founders of the southern California film industry, arranged to use the equipment and personnel of the Miller Brothers' 101 Ranch Wild West Show, which kept winter quarters in the Santa Monica mountains near Hollywood. Ince's *Custer's Last Fight* (1912) featured a cast of more than a hundred Sioux that the Miller Brothers had brought to Hollywood from the Pine Ridge Reservation in South Dakota. "The history—the true history—of the Wildest West is being written on film," wrote an enthusiastic critic after seeing an Ince production. Here was "the great West as it really was and is." Ince was soon joined by actor William S. Hart, who made a name for himself playing Trampas in the Broadway adaptation of *The Virginian.* Together they made a series of pictures celebrated for their authentic portrayal of the West. Who cared if the plot of Hart's *Hell's Hinges* (1916) was contrived and maudlin, the acting stilted and melodramatic? The picture's appeal and lasting influence was Hart's good-badman character and the verisimilitude of its mise-en-scène—the wonderfully mangy prairie town populated by authentic-looking western types. Many of the extras in the westerns made during the silent era actually *were* authentic—rodeo cowboys or ranch hands picking up a few extra dollars by wrangling horses on the set, performing stunts, or filling out the ranks of cinematic outlaw gangs and vigilante posses. Until the 1920s there were plenty of places within a few hours of Hollywood that retained the look and feel of the late nineteenth-century West—favorite shooting locations included the old gold rush town of Sonora in the Sierra Nevadas or the arid Owens Valley, frozen in time by the construction of the Los Angeles aqueduct. Viewing these films today, says Kevin Brownlow, "it is possible to stumble across unique glimpses of western history."[38]

The concern for authenticity inspired the production of a number of "epic"

William S. Hart (center). Production still from The Gunfighter *(1917). The Museum of Modern Art, Film Stills Archive.*

westerns during the 1920s. Hart directed and starred in *Tumbleweeds* (1924), an ambitious and gritty depiction of the Oklahoma land rush of 1889. *The Iron Horse* (1924), directed by John Ford, who had been making hard-edged cowboy pictures since 1917, told the story of the construction of the transcontinental railroad. The *New York Times* described it as "an instructive and inspiring film, one which should make every American proud of the manner of men who were responsible for great achievements in the face of danger, sickness, and fatigue." Ford's film was a celebration of the country's epic western adventure, seen as a founding myth that distinguished the United States from all other nations. Perhaps the most impressive of this set of nationalistic westerns from the 1920s was *The Covered Wagon* (1923), a depiction of an overland migration shot on location in Wyoming that included several hundred Indians from nearby reservations as well as dozens of men, women, and children from local ranches, who also supplied the wagons and oxen, lending the film a documentary look that remains startling today. "There is one adjective that one thinks of first" after seeing the picture, wrote the film critic of the *New York Herald*. "That adjective is 'honest.'"[39]

Authenticity thus continued as one of the most powerful attractions of western image-making. There was, however, more artifice than honesty in western films. Most were adaptations of the patterned western stories being published in the "pulps," weekly or monthly magazines printed on cheap paper made of wood pulp, the twentieth-century successors of the dime novels. Growing up on a ranch in Colorado, Carey McWilliams watched as his father's cowboys spent long hours in the bunkhouse "devouring cheap romances," from which they took instruction on how to dress and act in the manner of their western heroes. The most successful writer of western pulp fiction was Zane Grey, a midwestern dentist who wrote serials before hitting the big time with his novel *Riders of the Purple Sage* (1912), in which the lightning-fast gunman Lassiter rescues his lover from Mormon perfidy. Filled with violence, intrigue, cross-dressing, hard-riding women, and plenty of sex, the novel was a blockbuster, eventually selling nearly two million copies. Over the next twenty years Grey published a total of fifty-six westerns, sold at least seventeen million books, and his name was rarely absent from the best-seller list. His were tales of violent action set in spectacular Bierstadtian landscapes of towering peaks and hidden valleys—making them perfect for adaptation to the screen. Between the world wars more than a hundred Hollywood films were based on Grey's novels. Other successful pulp writers of Hollywood westerns included Max Brand (real name Frederick Faust) and Ernest Haycock. An idea of the tone of their work is provided by a character in Haycock's first western, *Free Grass* (1928). "The East is settled, it is orderly, it is governed by women's ideas," he declares, but the West "is still a man's country." He goes on to advise his young friend on the imperatives of western manhood: "No matter how you are hurt, never reveal it to a living creature. . . . This is a rough country. Nobody wants to hear about your feelings." The most notable theme in these stories and films is their obsessive attention to hardshell masculinity.[40]

Indeed, taking the cues provided by Roosevelt, Remington, and Wister, western movies became a primary source for twentieth-century images of American manhood. For sheer masculinity, probably no movie star before World War II was more powerful than Gary Cooper, who appeared in at least a dozen westerns by 1940, including a number of Zane Grey adaptations. In the role that made him a star, Cooper played the greatest western hero of them all in *The Virginian* (1929). The book had already appeared in three screen adaptations by the time Cooper was pitted against Walter Huston's Trampas. But this time their classic confrontation and shoot-out could be heard as well as seen, for the film was the first western to feature sound. In spite of the audio track, however, the picture is most notable for the way Cooper and the other male characters hold their tongues, following Haycock's classic proscription about excessive talking. It was in western films that Cooper developed his screen persona as the laconic all-American male, an object lesson in manhood.

Part of the appeal of westerns undoubtedly lies in the psychological realm. Feminist film critics argue persuasively that Hollywood pictures impose a male-oriented perspective—"the male gaze"—which encourages women as well as men to view women on the screen as the objects of male pleasure. But surely an actor like

Gary Cooper. Production still from I Take This Woman *(1931).*
The Museum of Modern Art, Film Stills Archive.

Cooper—lithe and sexually smoldering—was equally the object of an admiring "female gaze." The strong man with a gun certainly has sexual connotations, and as the roles of women changed and broadened in the twentieth century there may have been women as well as men who looked on images of male dominance with a shiver of nostalgia. But there seems little doubt that the primary audience for westerns was male. The masculine world of the cowboy was especially attractive to boys feeling constrained by the authoritarian controls of childhood.

The myth of the frontier came under serious question during the Depression. No one celebrated the jalopy migration of Okies and Arkies, although they moved for reasons not dissimilar to the covered wagon pioneers of the mid-nineteenth century. Instead their trek was commemorated in Steinbeck's *Grapes of Wrath* (1939), in hard-edged documentary photographs of Dorothea Lange and others working for the Farm Security Administration, and in paintings such as Maynard Dixon's *Destination Nowhere* (1941), which as western historian Howard Lamar notes is the Depression-era version of Leutze's *Westward the Course of Empire.* Tramps move across an arid landscape, but "there is no promised land in the distance." Dixon, by the way, was married to Lange.[41]

At the same time the major Hollywood film studios ceased making "prestige" westerns. Perhaps, as historian Robert Athearn suggested, "viewers were uncomfortable with the idea of watching the triumphal westward march of American civilization on the screen while it was falling apart just outside the door." The genre was abandoned to a group of "poverty row" production companies that turned out cheap "B-westerns"—so-called because theater owners, in an attempt to boost sagging box office receipts, began offering two films for the price of one, with these inexpensive pictures (rented for a flat fee) given second billing to bigger studio offerings (which took a percentage of the box office gross). B-westerns were turned out by the dozens, often as serials or continuing series, using an assembly line of writers, actors, and film crews. Studios sometimes filmed several pictures simultaneously to make economical use of resources.[42]

Of prime importance to the successful B-western was the series star, an actor with a distinctive style whose real identity often merged with the character he played. William Boyd first appeared as the character Hopalong Cassidy in 1935 and continued playing this hero in more than a hundred pictures. He once tried to move on to other parts but found he had become so identified with the role that he was unable to get other work. Singing cowboys Gene Autry, Roy Rogers, and Tex Ritter simply used their own stage names for the characters they played in their films. As historian Richard Slotkin points out, this confusion of the real and the fictive—a phenomenon that harks back to Buffalo Bill—made possible some very odd conjunctions, "a kind of cinematic fourth dimension." In the late 1930s cowboy heroes dressed in Wild West costume battled contemporary gangsters armed with tommy guns. John Wayne, before he became a major star, appeared in a series of B-westerns in which he fought off airplane hijackers, labor racketeers, and evil developers intent on preventing farmers from enjoying the benefits of an irrigation project. With the approach of World War II, the B-western focused on international subversion. In *Cowboy Commandos* (1943) a group of action heroes known as "The Range Busters" prevent Nazi spies from obtaining a secret ore needed for the production of a superweapon.[43]

Slotkin argues that this turn toward politics late in the decade was part of a revival of interest in westerns as a vehicle for examining the tensions in American culture. On the eve of World War II the big Hollywood studios again began to make westerns. *Union Pacific* (1939) and *Western Union* (1941) tell the saga of the transcontinental railroad, while *Dodge City* (1939) and *Frontier Marshall* (1939) chronicle the coming of law and order to the western town. The most successful of this crop of prestige westerns explored the oppositional side of the frontier myth. *Jesse James* (1939) retells the story of the James gang as a populist tale in which Jesse (Tyrone Power) and Frank (Henry Fonda) are driven to lawlessness by evil railroad capitalists who attempt to seize the family farm. The box office popularity of *Jesse James* spawned a series of western "biopics" depicting the life stories of Kit Carson, Brigham Young, George Armstrong Custer, Buffalo Bill, Wyatt Earp, and a score of others.

But director John Ford's *Stagecoach* (1939) was the most impressive and influential western of the late 1930s. A dangerous stagecoach journey through Apache country during Geronimo's uprising throws together a colorful cast of characters drawn directly from dime novels and pulp fiction: a good-badman seeking revenge (John Wayne, in the role that made him a star), a whore with a heart of gold, a traveling salesman, an alcoholic doctor, a respectable army wife, an aristocratic southerner, and a venal banker. The film was mostly shot on a Hollywood sound stage but included location work in spectacular Monument Valley on the Navajo Reservation, with its fantastic buttes towering above the desert—a site fully worthy of Bierstadt's art. There is wonderful B-western action and a stunt sequence in which renegade Apaches (played by local Navajos) chase the stagecoach through the desert until the day is saved by the last-minute arrival of the cavalry, flags flying and bugles blowing. But Ford manipulates and recombines these conventional elements into a film that amounts to considerably more than the sum of its parts. He skillfully reveals the "civilized" members of the party as snobs, hypocrites, or crooks and recruits audience sympathy for the outcasts, who become the heroes of the melodrama. The film celebrates westering while it simultaneously debunks the civilization brought to the West by the East. In the end the good-badman and the whore ride off to spend their

Monument Valley. Production still from John Ford's Stagecoach *(1939). The Museum of Modern Art, Film Stills Archive.*

lives together on a ranch in Mexico, "saved from the blessings of civilization," as one of the characters puts it. *Stagecoach* is able to have it both ways, which is the way the western has always wanted to tell the story of America.

FURTHER READING

Nancy K. Anderson, *Thomas Moran* (1997)
Kevin Brownlow, *The War, the West, and the Wilderness* (1979)

Robert V. Hine, *In the Shadow of Frémont: Edward Kern and the Art of Exploration, 1845–1860*, 2d ed. (1982)

L. G. Moses, *Wild West Shows and the Images of American Indians, 1883–1933* (1996)

Jules David Prown et al., *Discovered Lands, Invented Pasts: Transforming Visions of the American West* (1992)

Michael Edward Shapiro et al., *George Caleb Bingham* (1990)

Richard Slotkin, *The Fatal Environment: The Myth of the Frontier in the Age of Industrialization, 1800–1890* (1985)

———, *Gunfighter Nation: The Myth of the Frontier in Twentieth-Century America* (1992)

William H. Truettner, ed., *The West as America: Reinterpreting Images of the Frontier, 1820–1920* (1991)

Patricia Trenton and Peter H. Hassrick, *The Rocky Mountains: A Vision for Artists in the Nineteenth Century* (1983)

John Tuska, *The Filming of the West* (1976)

G. Edward White, *The Eastern Establishment and the Western Experience: The West of Frederic Remington, Theodore Roosevelt, and Owen Wister* (1968)

16

The Frontier and West in Our Time

When the American novelist James A. Michener died in 1997, he left his papers and a large endowment to the University of Northern Colorado in Greeley. Sixty years before, the young Michener had received an offer to teach there. Anxious for a good job in those depression years, yet equally anxious about leaving his boyhood home in Pennsylvania, Michener had gone to one of his former professors at Swarthmore College for advice. "You'd be making the biggest mistake in your life," the man told him. "The sands of the desert are white with the bones of promising young men who moved West and perished trying to fight their way back East." Without other prospects, however, Michener reluctantly decided he had no choice but to accept the position.[1]

Much to his surprise, Michener fell in love with the West. "Almost all that I saw I liked," he later recalled. He was awed by the landscape—majestic buttes rising abruptly from the plains, mountain valleys crowded with blue spruce and aspen—and astounded by the irrigation systems that turned deserts into thousands of acres of melons and sugar beets. But what struck him most forcefully were the people. "For the first time I caught the fire and fury that characterizes life in the West," he wrote. "A new type of man was being reared in the West. He was taller, ate more salads, had fewer intellectual interests of a speculative nature, had a rough and ready acceptance of new ideas, and was blessed with a vitality that stood out conspicuously to a stranger from the East." Over a long career as the most successful American writer of the twentieth century, Michener traveled to many exotic places, but he always treasured his western sojourn. "One of the good things about my life was that I spent the formative years in Colorado and got away from an insular Eastern-seaboard perspective," he reflected in 1980. "Having had that experience, and having renewed it constantly, I built or acquired an optimism which I've never really lost."[2]

It was his fascination with westerners, Michener believed, that inspired him to be-come a writer. While in Colorado he made several attempts to begin a western novel but gave it up, feeling he did not have the capacity for grandeur that the story re-quired. He did eventually write his big western book—a sprawling epic entitled *Centennial* (1974), one of the best-selling books of all time—but he made his reputation with other topics. Stationed in the Pacific during World War II, Michener penned *Tales of the South Pacific* (1947), a collection of stories about encounters among American servicemen and Pacific islanders that won the Pulitzer Prize. The most noted of the stories—and the one featured prominently in *South Pacific* (1949), the Broadway musical adaptation of Michener's book that also became a major motion picture—features an interracial romance between a Polynesian woman and a GI who is handicapped by racial prejudice. Michener later admitted that while he was working on the book the idea of an American marrying an Asian was "unthinkable" to him, and although the GI of the story overcomes his racism, he dies in combat be-fore he can marry his sweetheart—Michener's way of sidestepping the issue. A few years later Michener published *Sayonara* (1954), another best-selling novel (and suc-cessful movie) that tells of the ill-fated love of an air force officer for a beautiful Japanese woman during the Korean War. It, too, ends tragically, with the death of the lovers.[3]

Not long after *Sayonara* appeared, Michener met an editor who opened her conversation with him by objecting to the book's ending. "An interracial marriage doesn't have to end in tragedy," she announced. The outspoken editor was Mari Yoriko Sabusawa, a daughter of the West, born to Issei parents who grew melons in Los Animas, Colorado. Eventually her family moved to southern California, where during the war they were interned with thousands of other Japanese at the Santa Anita racetrack—confined to a horse stall. It was a humiliation Mari "never got over," according to a friend, and it turned her into a forthright critic of racism and intolerance. Michener had met "a new type" of western woman, and she knocked him off his feet. The couple fell in love, married in 1955, and were constant compan-ions until her death forty years later. Mari Michener deeply influenced her husband, strengthening his hatred of bigotry and racial discrimination. Cross-cultural en-counter was a theme common to nearly all of Michener's novels, but after meeting Mari never again would he feel the need to kill off any of his many interracial cou-ples.[4]

Michener's enthusiasms set up a final, encompassing subject—the shape of the *West* and the *frontier* at the beginning of the twenty-first century. His excitement about the West was typical of post–World War II America. Millions of newcomers poured into the region. Economic development—jumpstarted by the historical projects of the New Deal—reordered the relations between East and West (and much of the South as well). Certainly the postwar West could no longer be consid-

James Michener and Mari Yoriko Sabusawa at their wedding, 1955. Associated Press/Wide World Photos.

ered a colonial periphery, what Bernard De Voto had called the nation's "plundered province." In a historic movement that journalist Neil Morgan described in 1961 as "westward tilt," millions of eastern Americans moved to the booming cities of the Sunbelt. Yet this shift applied not only to migration but to national attitudes. For the first time in American history the West became the economic, cultural, and political pacesetter for the nation. This development had important and somewhat contradictory consequences. So fundamental was the shift that it calls into question the continued relevance of a sectional interpretation of American society. Trans-Mississippi Americans came to think of themselves less as "westerners" than as residents of more discernible cultural provinces. Yet in numerous ways the whole country became a lot more "western" during the second half of the twentieth century. *Western* remained a keyword of the American lexicon, but it signified more about cultural style than regional identity.

Frontier also continued to be a concept of singular importance in the postwar period. The mass migration of Americans into the West from the eastern part of the nation was matched by an equally mass migration of immigrants from Mexico, Central America, and Asia. Millions poured across borders to join in the making of the world's most multicultural society. Indian peoples were very much a part of this diverse world. Against all odds the Indian nations survived, regaining important elements of their sovereignty and reclaiming the proud heritage of their traditions. All this clamor intensified the ongoing struggles over the use and preservation of the environment. Not only did the frontier persist, it began to seem like the wave of the future. "Young and eager, cocky and eternally hopeful," as Neil Morgan put it, "the West seethes with the spirit of *why not*."[5]

World War II was the most significant event in the economic transformation of the modern West. Previous "great and cataclysmic changes," in the words of historian Gerald Nash, took place at half-century intervals—the Louisiana Purchase of 1803, the discovery of California gold in 1848, and the Populist revolt and capitalist reorientation of the 1890s. The war's impact exceeded them all. The New Deal had set out to build an industrial infrastructure in the West, and those efforts laid the foundation for what was to come. But the tidal wave of federal investment during the war "telescoped decades of development into a few years," said Salt Lake City banker Elroy Nelson. Worried about the vulnerability of the Atlantic coast to German attack, military planners sought to disperse vital industries throughout the West. Then, with the Japanese attack on Pearl Harbor, the West became the staging area for the Pacific theater. During the war the government supplied 90 percent of the capital for western industrial growth and directly invested at least seventy billion dollars in industries and military installations. The aircraft industry expanded spectacularly in Texas, Washington, and California; aluminum plants sopped up the hydroelectric power of the Northwest's great rivers; and steel foundries arose in Texas, Utah, Oklahoma, and southern California. "Industry has expanded at a rate never before approached in the history of the area," read the wartime report of Security First National Bank of Los Angeles, "the growth being fully as impressive as that in Detroit when expansion of the automobile industry was underway."[6]

In April 1942 Henry J. Kaiser broke ground for a huge steel mill in the quiet rural town of Fontana, some fifty miles east of Los Angeles. During the 1930s Kaiser had become the West's most prominent industrialist by building the great hydroelectric dams on the Colorado and Columbia Rivers. Now the priority was winning the war, and with federal loans Kaiser built the world's most modern and efficient facility for the production of steel. The Fontana mill turned out mammoth prefabricated plates for the hulls of wartime merchant ships. Many of them went to Kaiser's new ship-building plants at Los Angeles harbor, Richmond on San Francisco Bay, Portland, and Puget Sound near Seattle. By the end of the war Kaiser was launching a new Liberty Ship every ten hours, making him the largest shipbuilder in American history. He drew his workforce—including a large percentage of minorities and women—from all over the country, luring them not only with high wages but with child care facilities and subsidized medical care. The pioneering Kaiser-Permanente Health Plan was one of the first health maintenance organizations in the nation, and it remains one of the strongest.

Kaiser's most important financial partner—aside from the federal government—was San Francisco banker Amadeo Peter Giannini, owner of the Bank of America. Giannini believed in the future of the West, and he invested in many western enterprises. He bankrolled the studios of United Artists and Walt Disney in Hollywood, financed the construction of the Golden Gate Bridge, and (as a strong supporter of the New Deal) came in for more than his fair share of investment opportunities during the 1930s. He was ready for the industrial expansion of the war, providing much of the private financing for western economic growth. By 1945 the Bank of America had become the largest commercial and savings institution in the world. "The West hasn't even started yet," Giannini declared shortly before his death in 1953. Inspired by his example, Bank of America continued as an innovator, the nation's first bank to computerize fully, the first to introduce direct deposit, and in 1958 the first to invent the all-purpose consumer credit card, the BankAmericard (later renamed the Visa card).[7]

Howard Hughes, a tall Texan who inherited a Houston petroleum fortune, was another westerner who touched on many of the most important themes in the economic history of the postwar West. He invested in aircraft and built Hughes Aircraft Corporation into one of the giants of western industry. He won lucrative government contracts during the war and in the subsequent Cold War years developed weapons-guidance systems, satellites, and other sensitive projects for the Central Intelligence Agency. He invested in Trans World Airlines, sold his holdings for half a billion dollars in 1966, and founded Hughes Air West, a carrier specializing in short hauls of passengers and freight that created a new transportation market others would exploit. Hughes also invested in Hollywood's dramatic growth, financing films like *Hell's Angels* (1930), with sex goddess Jean Harlow, and *The Outlaw* (1943), prominently featuring voluptuous Jane Russell. After the war Hughes bought RKO Pictures—one of the major Hollywood studios—and diversified its operations by buying into television stations and broadcasting old movies, a demonstration of how valuable film archives would become to a media hungry for programming. Hughes was also one of the great eccentrics of twentieth-century America, his fear of germs and disease causing him to withdraw almost completely from society, but his investing continued unabated. In 1967 he began buying properties in the gambling city of Las Vegas—whose glowing neon lights were powered by Hoover Dam. By the time Hughes died in 1976 he had become one of the wealthiest men in the world.

The biographies of these men are only the foam on the surface of a phenomenal industrial expansion. The dams and public works of Henry Kaiser had counterparts in the huge construction firms of Stephen Bechtel and John McCone, which moved

Howard Hughes at the controls of the Spruce Goose, *1947. Associated Press/Wide World Photos.*

from building dams in the 1930s to constructing military bases and freeways during and after the war. The Bank of America was only the largest of a number of powerful western banks; in Los Angeles, for example, Security First National financed much of the home construction boom in postwar southern California. Hughes was but a bit player in Hollywood's growth as the capital of the nation's culture industry, and the gamblers he looked down upon from his hermetically sealed Vegas penthouse were part of the growing tourism industry that stretched from the ringing slot machines of desert casinos to the dude ranches of Phoenix and from the ski slopes of the Rockies to the surfing beaches of southern California. Hughes was also just one of a group of western aerospace capitalists that included John Northrop, Allan Lockheed, Donald Douglas, and William Boeing. In the late 1950s both Boeing and Douglas created worldwide markets for their new passenger jets.

The West excelled in high-technology industries. The foundation was laid by the powerful petrochemical industries of Texas and California, but the superstructure was completed during the war. In 1945 a prominent scientist could write that "the center of gravity of scientific talent in the United States had definitely gravitated westwards." An early wartime model was the atomic laboratory at Los Alamos, New Mexico, where the University of California assembled one of the most impressive

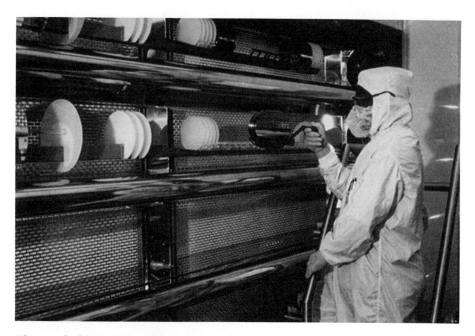

Silicon wafer fabrication facility, Silicon Valley, California, c. 1990.
National Semiconductor Corporation.

groups of scientists in the world to build the atomic bomb. At Hanford, Washington, forty thousand scientists and technicians produced plutonium for those bombs, an assignment that would not have been possible but for the power they drew from the hydroelectric system of the Columbia River. At Pasadena, in southern California, the Jet Propulsion Laboratory of the California Institute of Technology conducted fundamental research in rocketry that later gave it a leading voice in space technology. In the 1950s Stanford University encouraged a consortium of science and industry in the nearby Santa Clara valley, and new electronics companies such as Hewlett-Packard created the critical mass for what became known as Silicon Valley, a place where startups such as Intel, a computer chip maker founded in 1968, could prosper and grow into manufacturing giants.[8]

Defense spending obviously was critical to this growth. In Seattle, where Boeing Aircraft dominated the local economy, military expenditure accounted for 40 percent of job growth in the postwar period. In Denver the military facility at Rocky Flats and the federal Rocky Mountain Arsenal employed more than twenty thousand people. Forty percent of all federal aerospace contracts in the postwar period went to firms operating in California, an annual subsidy to the state's economy that amounted to approximately twenty billion dollars. Writing in 1965, historian James Clayton concluded that "defense spending has been the primary reason for the extraordinarily rapid expansion of industry and population in California since World

War II." Federal military demand, he estimated, had accounted for two-thirds of the state's manufacturing growth since 1945.[9]

The depression that crippled California at the end of the Cold War in the late 1980s confirmed Clayton's point. Yet the West remained "the center of gravity" for high-tech industry. "California had shifted to electronics, the so-called brain factories," James Michener wrote in 1963, and its "horizons seemed unlimited." The most impressive developments were yet to come. In the 1970s Steven Jobs and Stephen Wozniak, two college dropouts tinkering in a Silicon Valley garage, developed an easy-to-use desktop computer they called the Apple. Five years after they financed their startup company with the sale of a Volkswagen bus they were marketing thousands of personal computers and had provoked the eastern computer giant IBM into entering the growing PC market. Microsoft, a company based in Redmond, Washington, organized by westerners Paul Allen and William H. Gates, won the contract to provide the operating software that ran those IBM machines and became one of the great success stories of late twentieth-century capitalism. By the 1990s Bill Gates had become the wealthiest individual in the world, his personal fortune estimated at more than one hundred billion dollars.[10]

The economy of the postwar West, writes historian Gerald Nash, "became a pace setter for the nation." In 1950 only 10 percent of the nation's two hundred largest firms were headquartered west of the Mississippi. By the late 1990s that proportion had climbed to 30 percent. The West was home to some of the nation's largest corporations: in electronics and computers (Hewlett-Packard, Intel, Rockwell, and Apple in California; Compaq, Texas Instruments, and Dell in Texas; Microsoft in Washington), aerospace (Boeing in Washington; McDonnell Douglas in Missouri; Northrop Grumman in California), energy (Exxon in Texas; Chevron and Atlantic Richfield in California), and wood products (Kimberly-Clark in Texas; Weyerhaeuser in Washington). The West's long colonial dependence on the East had finally ended.[11]

Other westerners, however, felt that eastern masters had simply been traded for new ones in the high-rise office towers of Los Angeles and Houston or the corporate "campuses" of Seattle. At the end of the century much of the farming, ranching, and mining West remained tied to a cycle of boom and bust. During the period of national economic stagnation that began in the early 1970s and extended into the 1980s the combined effects of tight money and double-digit inflation created the worst depression in western extractive industries since the 1930s. As the price of commodities fell, mines and lumber mills closed their doors, throwing tens of thousands out of work. Rural westerners by the thousands lost their land. Over the second half of the twentieth century the number of independent western ranchers and farmers fell by half while the size of the remaining operations increased by 125 percent. Farming

and ranching became more concentrated and mechanized, and many small operators were simply priced out. The average cost of a tractor, about a thousand dollars
right after the war, had by the 1970s skyrocketed to as much as one hundred thousand dollars, an increase thirty times the rate of inflation. Corporate "factories in the
fields" became commonplace. Rural depopulation was the result. From 1940 to 1990
the population of the rural West fell from 785,000 to just 172,000, a decline of 78 percent. People abandoned the countryside for the urban centers of Texas, California,
and the Pacific Northwest. The rise of the West as a national economic power was
confined largely to the region's great cities and suburbs.

One of the most powerful forces of western economic expansion was the population boom. Disproportionately large since at least 1900, after World War II it was
staggering. From 1945 to 1970 more than thirty million people moved beyond the
Mississippi, the most significant redistribution of population in the nation's history.
California surpassed New York to become the nation's most populous state in 1964,
and in the early 1990s Texas pushed into the second spot. This growth is predicted to
continue. In the Census Bureau's projections for the first quarter of the twenty-first
century, fifteen states are expected to grow by rates of more than 30 percent—and
all but two are in the West.

Most of this growth is metropolitan. The statistics are stunning. Between 1940 and
1980 the urban proportion of the trans-Mississippi population jumped from 43 to
78 percent. California gained seventeen million new urban residents, Texas nine million, and Washington nearly three million. During the 1980s all but one of the thirty
fastest growing cities were in the West, and eighteen were in California. By the 1990s
eight of the nation's fifteen largest metropolitan areas were western: Los Angeles (2),
Houston (4), San Diego (6), Dallas (8), Phoenix (9), San Antonio (10), San Jose (11),
and San Francisco (14). At the end of the century 86 percent of the population west
of the Mississippi live in cities, making the West the most urban region in America.
Utah has a higher percentage of urban dwellers than New York.

The importance of cities has reordered economic relations. Western cities traditionally acted as funnels for exporting extractive commodities (grain, meat, metals,
lumber) and importing manufactured goods. In the nineteenth century Chicago
and San Francisco served as "gateways" between western resource regions and the
industrial and financial centers in the East. But in the second half of the twentieth
century urban growth became increasingly independent of the countryside. The extractive economy became less significant than urban manufacturing and service industries. As geographer John Borchert argues, the rapid growth of western cities in
the postwar period cannot be explained simply by connections with the hinterland.
Rather, it is the growth of inter-metropolitan links that accounts for development.

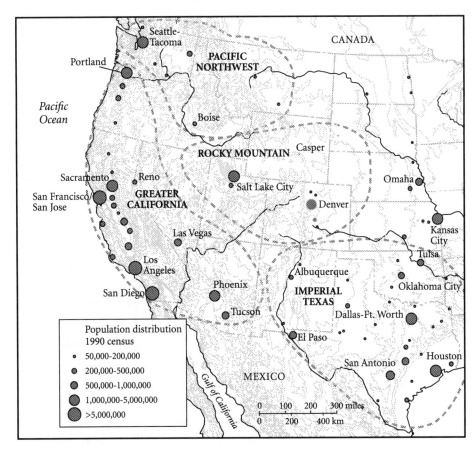

WESTERN CITIES, 1990

"The metropolitan areas have depended for their new growth upon themselves and one another," Borchert concludes. The metropolis now supports the hinterland through its radiating transportation systems, its corporate networks, and its recreational and retirement opportunities.[12]

Rather than thinking of the West as one of the nation's huge sections, it now makes more sense to see it as a series of urban enclaves—"city-states"—with large dependent hinterland districts. "Imperial Texas" centers on the Houston–Dallas–San Antonio triangle and dominates a huge region extending from the Gulf Coast to the oil fields of Oklahoma, from the cattle range of the southern plains to the industrial transborder zone surrounding the twin cities of Brownsville–Matamoros and El Paso–Ciudad Juárez. In the Pacific Northwest an urban empire with its capital at Seattle includes much of Washington, Oregon, Idaho, and Montana, swings north along the coast to pull in Alaska, and encompasses important cross-border ties with Vancouver and international trade with Asia. The granddaddy of western empires is "Greater California," based at Los Angeles, the largest and most diversified urban economy in the nation, with gross revenues totaling more than $342 billion annually. So powerful is the southern California economy that it has swept into its orbit not only the state's other urban centers (including rival San Francisco) but satellite cities and hinterlands, including Phoenix and Tucson, Las Vegas and Reno, Portland and Honolulu.

Each of these economic regions is strengthened by world-class harbors on the Pacific or Gulf Coast. Without such access, the landlocked Rocky Mountain and Great Plains states were forced into subordinate economic relationships. But at the end of the century—in an emerging era of high-tech air transport—the western interior began an economic takeoff. This new empire of the Interior West is centered at Denver, with its state-of-the-art jetport. This region's economic strength has traditionally been in the export of basic commodities (grain, meat, and energy). More recently there has been remarkable growth in the export by jet transport of processed foods (pasta, boxed steaks, frozen chicken) to foreign markets in Russia, Latin America, and the Far East. Meanwhile, high-tech industry is blossoming on the high plains. In Denver the number of highly skilled employees in aerospace, communications, and finance has risen to roughly the same level as Boston. Job growth has stimulated migration into the region. During the 1990s the nation's fastest population growth occurred in the Rocky Mountain states, and the corridor along Colorado's Interstate 25—the spine connecting the Front Range cities of Pueblo, Colorado Springs, Denver, and Greeley (where Michener taught in the late 1930s)—passed through the nation's fastest-growing counties. Symbolic of the Interior West's emergence as a major player in the world economy was the choice of Denver as the gathering place for the meeting of the world's eight leading industrial nations in 1997.

Do these urban empires correspond with the sense of regional identity among residents? "Westerner" continues to have a certain salience—when used as a comparative or oppositional identity to "easterner" or "southerner." But cultural geographers have found that westerners are most likely to describe themselves as natives of more distinct regions, like the Pacific Northwest or the Interior West, divisions that correspond to the nation's other cultural provinces, places like New England or the Lower South. The strongest identification is with local communities and states—for that's where the political action is. Macroregional consciousness is relatively weak by comparison. Ironically, at the moment in the nation's history when sectionalism seemed least relevant, a new group of dedicated western regionalists embarked on a campaign to revivify western regionalism. They would do well to consider what the cultural geographers have to say on the subject. "Regions do not exist," insists Terry Jordan after a scholarly career spent mapping the spatial distribution of cultural traits in the American West. A region is not a living thing but an abstraction—"a classification system, a geographical generalization"—helpful in making sense of a complicated world. But the macroregional West of today is so complex and differentiated, he concludes, that the attempt to define it as a whole is "a fool's errand."[13]

"Give me land, lots of land, under starry skies above—don't fence me in." Cole Porter's tune—recorded by Bing Crosby and the Andrews Sisters—was a monster hit in 1944 and an appropriate anthem for postwar America, expressing widespread desires. Much of the West's urban growth originated in the search for open space, for a freer, cleaner, less encumbered life, especially in an appealing climate. These were the attractions of the Sunbelt, a name that originated among wartime planners who sought to locate the majority of the military's training facilities in what they called the "sunshine belt." The enormous swath of arid country stretching from Texas to southern California became the postwar destination of millions of Americans, and almost overnight there appeared thousands of tracts of detached homes, each framed by ample lawns with clusters of palm, avocado, or banana trees and perhaps a swimming pool in the backyard.

The best known Sunbelt mecca was southern California. "More than anyplace else," writes historian Kenneth T. Jackson, it "became the symbol of postwar suburban culture." But developments there were more than symbol, they were substance. Southern California builders invented the modern home-building industry, moving beyond the innovations of Henry E. Huntington in the early century to consolidate subdivision, home construction, and sales into a single operation. In the late 1930s they invented the techniques of tract construction—in which specialized teams of laborers and craftsmen moved sequentially through the project, grading, pouring foundations, framing and sheathing, roofing, and completing the finishing work. With the boom in wartime industry developers rushed to meet an enormous demand for housing—which was subsidized by federal loans and income tax deductions for home mortgage interest. The combination was explosive, and the resulting development intensified beyond all experience the sprawl of southern California. Builders extended their projects in successive rings outward from central city L.A., bulldozing citrus groves and walnut orchards to make way for housing tracts, factories and offices, shopping centers, and freeways. Homebuilding became a massive engine of economic expansion. It was a good deal for developers and home buyers alike. During the 1950s profits in southern California homebuilding averaged an impressive 21 percent annually, while the steady inflation of real estate prices turned a generation of homeowners into speculators. Buy a bungalow, sit back, and watch its value grow faster than any savings from hard labor. Henry George's "unearned increment" had become everyone's nest egg.[14]

Dozens of "instant cities" appeared, places like Lakewood, where housing for sev-

The intersection of San Vicente and Fairfax Avenues, Los Angeles, 1922 and 1966. The Spence Air Photo Archives, Department of Geography, University of California, Los Angeles.

enty-seven thousand sprouted overnight from former bean fields. Such subdivisions have often been scorned as development gone mad, but places like Lakewood were in fact the result of careful planning. Located near several aerospace plants, and including a huge shopping mall (one of the first in the nation), Lakewood was intended to be a complete community. Rather than establish their own police, fire, and other public services, Lakewood residents contracted with Los Angeles County to provide them, enabling them to keep property taxes low. The "Lakewood Plan" was the model for numerous other developments, essentially forcing the general county taxpayer to subsidize these middle-class enclaves. And like nearly all other southern California subdivisions, Lakewood's developers insisted on "restrictive covenants" that excluded all "non-Caucasians" from ever buying a home there. Racial exclusion was planned, too.

In the words of influential West coast journalist and activist Carey McWilliams, southern California became "the first modern, widely decentralized industrial city

in America." In just twenty years the citrus groves of Orange County, south of Los Angeles, were transformed into one of the world's major metropolitan systems, with an industrial and service economy that by century's end was producing goods and services worth sixty billion dollars annually, equivalent to the economy of Argentina. By the end of the century the vast area from Santa Barbara to the Mexican border, the coast to the mountains, had been converted into a single megalopolis sprawling over seven of the nation's largest counties. By one estimate a full third of the region had been paved over as roads, driveways, and parking lots. Sprawl remained southern California's distinction, and to some its nightmare.[15]

There is no denying that Americans embraced this new kind of urban living with enthusiasm. Despite the cavils of social critics, families delighted in the opportunity to own their own detached house and yard on a cul-de-sac miles from the central city. But with sprawl came a series of bedeviling problems—abandoned inner cities, polluted air, congested freeways. Phoenix, Las Vegas, Seattle, Salt Lake City, and Denver were only a few of the cities that attempted to avoid L.A.'s sprawl (with local groups vowing "Not L.A.") but were unable to come up with an alternate plan. The downside of sprawl was dramatically evident in a national study of "road rage" released in 1999. Sunbelt metro areas led the nation in driving deaths associated with speeding at more than eighty miles per hour, tailgating, failing to yield, or yelling and gesturing lewdly to other drivers. An official of Riverside County in southern California spoke of the frustration of commuters: "Your family is 40 miles away and you're driving one or two hours to get home after putting in 8 to 12 hours on the job, and you're tired and hungry, and you're worried about getting your kids to soccer or keeping the appointment with your child's teacher, or you just want to spend some quality time with your family. But you're stuck in traffic."[16]

The city of Portland, Oregon, was a notable exception to the problems associated with sprawl. In 1973 its farsighted leaders struck at the heart of the problem and drew a line around their city—within that boundary there would be high density settlement, outside it, low density. Jobs, homes, stores were forced into a compact area, catering to pedestrians and served by popular light transit, buses and fewer cars. The downtown freeway was torn up, a park put in its place, and parking restricted to designated areas. Expansionists direly predicted disappearing jobs, decreasing sales, and declining property values, but in fact all have soared. "We have been careful stewards of the land and have fought to protect our natural resources against the urban sprawl that has plagued almost every other metropolitan area in this country," said one of its planners. A number of other western cities are attempting to emulate Portland's success.[17]

Suburban sprawl, congestion, and overdevelopment were not just western problems, of course. In the postwar period subdivisions ate up the countryside on the edges of every major American city. In accounting for this trend, most historical accounts begin with Levittown, the famous Long Island subdivision that opened in 1947, but in fact Levittown was built on the model pioneered by southern California builders (including the racial exclusion). Not only western construction techniques but western home styles went national after the war. Although not everyone moved West, millions looked forward to living in a western house. The classic house of the postwar building boom was the ranch, a domestic style that originated in southern California between the wars, particularly in the work of San Diego architect Cliff May, who was inspired by nineteenth-century haciendas, with their rooms opening onto wide porches and interior courtyards. By the early 1940s the basic design began showing up in architects' plan books. "The style that has captured the attention of the American public is the Ranch-House," wrote the authors of a homebuilder's guide in 1942. The very name evoked myth. "When we think of the West," they mused, "we picture to ourselves ranches and wide open spaces where there is plenty of elbow room." The ranch house sought to capture this feeling with its horizontal orientation: low-slung roof, rooms flowing one into the other, picture windows and sliding glass doors inviting the residents outdoors to the patio (another western loan word) and the barbecue grill. Who needed the Sunbelt when you could live in a ranch

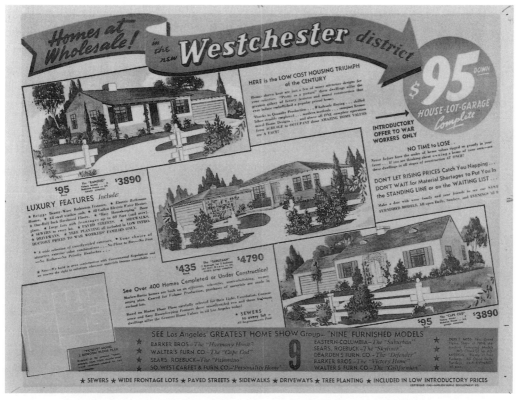

Advertisement for tract homes in Los Angeles, featuring "The Rancho" model, 1942. Westchester/ Playa Del Ray Historical Society.

with elbow room! As cultural historian Thomas Hine suggests, the ranch house "conjured up powerful dreams of informal living, ideal weather, and movie-star glamour." At Levittown ranches commanded a 20 percent premium over Cape Cods, although both were based on the same compact floor plan.[18]

The ranch style in domestic architecture was just one of the many things western that went mainstream in the second half of the twentieth century. Consider the growing popularity of comfortable western clothes. After the war Levi's became the everyday choice of young Americans from coast to coast. By the 1980s not only jeans but western shirts, belts, boots, bandanas, and even Stetson hats were gracing bodies all over the country. Western clothing, writes cultural critic Michael L. Johnson, is "portable Western atmosphere, identity, transWestite statement." And it doesn't cost much—unless you're into custom lizard or snakeskin boots. Meanwhile "country and western" music went urban and national, and by the 1990s "hat acts"—performers such as Garth Brooks and Dwight Yoakam—were selling more CDs and packing more stadiums than rock stars. Then there was the growing popularity of pickup trucks and four-wheel drive "sports utility vehicles"—equipped to brave rough western trails but more frequently used to transport kids from the ranch house to the soccer field. Was it any accident that nearly all of them were named for Indian tribes or western places? Taking a cue from master veteran filmmaker John Ford, television commercials for Durangos and Dakotas, Comanches and Cherokees frequently featured the vehicles driving through the splendors of Monument Valley.[19]

———

Politics ranks high in the list of ways that the country grew more like the West in the postwar period. Consider the ten presidents who served from the end of the war to the end of the century—six were westerners. Harry Truman was born and raised in Independence, Missouri, jumping off place for the Santa Fe Trail, and Dwight Eisenhower grew up in the former cattle town of Abilene, Kansas. Some might object that by the time Truman entered the White House in 1945 Missouri was no longer "western"—but tell that to folks enjoying steaks at the Golden Ox in the Livestock Exchange Building, across from the Kansas City stockyards, the final home of millions of Texas longhorns. Or some might argue that Kansas had little to do with Eisenhower's career—despite his assertion that he had been raised to honor the "code of the West." But the others were clearly western representatives. Texan Lyndon Johnson had been one of the key players in pushing through the New Deal program of western economic development, and George Bush made his reputation as an oil entrepreneur in the postwar boomtown of Houston. Likewise Richard Nixon's political career paralleled the ascent of his native southern California, and Ronald Reagan was California politics incarnate. Add to this list the names of western also-rans: Henry Wallace of Iowa, Barry Goldwater of Arizona, George McGovern of South Dakota, Ross Perot of Texas, and Robert Dole of Kansas. Of the twenty-one major party candidates who stood for election between 1948 and 1996, eleven hailed from the West.[20]

Western and national politics converged in the conservative tendency of American politics late in the century. Conservative "businessmen's governments" had characterized local politics in the West for decades. Their agendas were heavily laden with economic restructuring, big capital projects promoting irrigation, freeway construction, airports, urban renewal, convention centers, and sports and office complexes. The full force of taxpayer financing was put behind the continued growth of urban empires. Private property was sacred, and true to old western traditions, no one had the right to tell developers where or how they could build on their own property. In the mid-1960s this conservative tradition ran headlong into a rising clamor of social protest. African Americans, Mexican Americans, and Native Americans were demanding their civil rights. Students were marching in the streets and demanding an end to the war in Vietnam. Most perplexing was the outcry over the

FROM DODGE CITY TO TOMBSTONE...

HIS GUNS WERE THE ONLY LAW!

UNIVERSAL-INTERNATIONAL
presents

RONALD REAGAN

LAW and ORDER

Color by Technicolor

co-starring DOROTHY MALONE PRESTON FOSTER
ALEX NICOL and introducing RUTH HAMPTON

Ronald Reagan stars as Wyatt Earp, 1954. Beinecke.

"alienated" life of the suburbs—the gross materialism, the excessive competition, the loss of community.

No one exploited these tensions better than Ronald Reagan—a former movie actor who starred in a number of Hollywood westerns and loved nothing better than riding horses and chopping wood on his ranch in the southern California foothills. Emigrating to Hollywood from the Midwest in 1937 at the age of twenty-six, he enjoyed modest success as a leading man but discovered his real talent when he became a leader of the Screen Actors' Guild in the late 1940s. Reagan turned to the right during the era of communist-hunting and blacklisting, and when his movie career began to sour went to work as spokesman for the General Electric Company and added a probusiness, anti–big government perspective to his anticommunism. He burst onto the national political scene in 1964 in a televised speech endorsing Republican right-winger Barry Goldwater's presidential campaign. Two years later he ran for governor in a campaign featuring promises to "cut and squeeze and trim" state government, attacks on ungrateful demonstrators, and endorsements of the California "way of life." Reagan's rhetorical skills and his personal charm combined to win the election. As governor, however, his attacks on state programs were selective. Although he cut funds for mental-health care, higher education, and social welfare ("a

President Ronald Reagan works on his California ranch, c. 1982. Ronald Reagan Library.

cancer eating at our vitals"), he lobbied vigorously for federal defense dollars and supported federal-subsidized water for agribusiness.[21]

Rising property taxes precipitated a tax revolt in California in 1978 that quickly swept the nation. Although Reagan had done little to cut taxes during his two terms as governor, he used that movement successfully to ride into the White House in 1981 after defeating a weary and beleaguered incumbent President Jimmy Carter. He sponsored massive tax cuts while simultaneously pumping up military spending. The deficit spending produced an economic boom but also the biggest deficits in the nation's history. During his two terms better than 50 percent of federal military dollars went to defense contractors in the West, many of them in California.

Reagan's popularity was due in large part to the economic good times that prevailed during most of his tenure. But his advisers were masters of the use of western imagery. An excellent horseman, Reagan had been accustomed to dressing in jodhpurs and riding boots but was told that it wouldn't wash, that he had to act the part of the cowboy. Costumed and frequently photographed in Stetson, Levi's, and Justins, Reagan inherited Teddy Roosevelt's mantle of "cowboy president," a distinction he wore with pride. He not only walked the walk, he talked the talk. In his most soaring rhetoric, he called on the frontier myth. "I have always believed that this land was placed here between the two great oceans by some divine plan," he offered in the first debate of the 1980 presidential campaign. "It was placed here to be found by a special kind of people—people who had a special love for freedom and who had the courage to uproot themselves and leave hearth and homeland and come to what in the beginning was the most undeveloped wilderness possible. We came from 100 different corners of the earth. We spoke a multitude of tongues—landed on this eastern shore and then went out over the mountains and the prairies and the deserts and the far Western mountains of the Pacific building cities and towns and farms and schools and churches." Of course Reagan himself didn't write those lines, but he had the political savvy to know how well they would play with the American people. His oratorical use of the mythic West reached a perfect pinnacle in his second inaugural address: "History is a ribbon, always unfurling; history is a journey. And as we continue on our journey we think of those who traveled before us. . . . The men of the Alamo call out encouragement to each other; a settler pushes west and sings a song, and the song echoes out forever and fills the unknowing air. It is the American sound: it is hopeful, big-hearted, idealistic— daring, decent and fair. That's our heritage, that's our song. We sing it still. For all our problems, our differences, we are together as of old."[22]

Reagan's appeal to the frontier myth was masterful but not unique. In the postwar period the political left as well as the right made use of what historian Warren Susman called "the official American ideology"—the belief that westering defined the nation's unique heritage and that it amounted to the purest expression of American idealism. Accepting the Democratic nomination in Los Angeles in 1960, John F. Kennedy pointed to the "new world here in the West" built by "the pioneers of old" and coined the phrase that would define his administration when he called on Americans "to be pioneers on a New Frontier."[23]

*Western novelist Louis L'Amour, c. 1980.
Western Writers of America.*

Such evocations of the frontier myth were possible because of the continued popularity of westerns. In the postwar period westerns were the most popular fiction genre in America, with paperbacks flying off the racks during the 1950s at the rate of thirty-five million copies a year. In 1958 westerns made up 11 percent of all fiction titles. Western dime novels had never been so popular. The unrivaled master of the postwar western was Louis L'Amour, a North Dakotan who spent years working as a ranch hand, miner, fruit picker, longshoreman, and professional boxer, before enlisting as an officer in the tank corps during the war. He turned to writing after the fighting, scoring his first major success with *Hondo* (1953), made into a hit John Wayne picture the next year. Before his death in 1988 L'Amour had sold two hundred million copies of more than a hundred westerns, at least thirty of which were adapted for motion pictures or television. They are formula fiction, but taut and tough, with the emphasis on the violent endurance of lone gunmen against Indians and bad guys. "When you open a rough, hard country," he once replied to criticism of his stereotyped heroes, "you don't open it with a lot of pantywaists."[24]

Western movies were even more popular than western novels. From 1945 through the mid-1960s Hollywood studios produced an average of seventy-five western features each year, a quarter of all the films released. Most were eminently forgettable, but there were memorable highpoints. John Ford remained the undisputed master of the genre, taking up nearly all the major themes of postwar westerns. His "Cavalry Trilogy"—*Fort Apache* (1948), *She Wore a Yellow Ribbon* (1949), and *Rio Grande* (1950)—masterfully details the life of frontier troopers, encouraging viewers to identify completely with the war against the Indians, who are presented as little more than terrorists. *Wagon Master* (1950) tells the story of the Overland Trail and became the basis for a long-running television series. Perhaps most influential was Ford's lyrical *My Darling Clementine* (1946), in which Wyatt Earp (Henry Fonda) faces down a brutish family of outlaws, a classic confrontation between "savagery and civilization."

The western hero was above all a righteous man with a gun. *Shane* (1952), loosely based on the Johnson County War of the 1890s, features a gunslinger (Alan Ladd) who would like to hang up his holsters but chooses to fight the ruthless cattlemen who are terrorizing homesteaders. Similarly in *High Noon* (1952), the sheriff (Gary Cooper) rejects the pleas of his Quaker bride (a reprise of a very similar scene in *The Virginian*) to stand alone against the outlaws. The proper use of violence was the subject of a remarkable series of films combining the talents of director Budd Boetticher, scriptwriter Burt Kennedy, and veteran western star Randolph Scott—*Seven Men from Now* (1956), *The Tall T* (1956), *Ride Lonesome* (1959), and *Comanche Station* (1959)—that examines self-reliance and individual courage. As Scott asserts in a famous line: "There are some things a man can't ride around." Another series, directed by Anthony Mann and starring James Stewart—*Winchester '73* (1950), *Bend of the River* (1951), *The Naked Spur* (1952), *The Far Country* (1954), and *The Man from Laramie* (1955)—focuses on characters driven by pathological rage but redeemed by their decision to act for the common good.[25]

Westerns also dominated television programming during the 1950s and 1960s. The first cowboy star to make the switch to the small screen was William Boyd, who played good guy Hopalong Cassidy in a long series of B-westerns inaugurated in 1935. In 1948, with the series running out of steam, Boyd quietly acquired the broadcast rights to the films and leased them to local television stations around the country. They proved so popular that NBC quickly signed Boyd to star in a weekly program. Hopalong Cassidy was an immediate hit, with radio, comic book, and merchandising spinoffs adding to Boyd's estimated take of two hundred million dollars. In the wake of this success, westerns quickly became the most popular of children's television programs. Weekly series featured singing cowboys Gene Autry and Roy Rogers, the Lone Ranger and his faithful Indian companion Tonto, and the adventures of mythical frontier characters like Wild Bill Hickok, Kit Carson, and Annie Oakley. In 1954 Disney produced a Davy Crockett series that became a national sensation, and in a few months Americans had spent more than one hundred million dollars on coonskin caps and other Crockettabilia, including four million copies of "The Ballad of Davy Crockett."

The next year westerns appeared on the prime-time network lineup for the first time. *Gunsmoke,* with fictional Dodge City marshal Matt Dillon (James Arness), was the number one show in the country by 1957. Suddenly the rush for western adult programming was on. In 1958 twenty-eight prime-time westerns provided more than seventeen hours of gunplay and Indian fighting each week, and according to the Nielson ratings eight of the nation's top ten programs were westerns. The heroes might be tough sheriffs (*The Life and Legend of Wyatt Earp*) or bounty hunters (*Have Gun Will Travel*), but unlike Hopalong Cassidy or Roy Rogers, these men hung out in saloons, drank whiskey, and cavorted with whores. They wore big guns and used them without hesitation. The violence came in for plenty of criticism. "There must be dead bodies," the costar of *Wagon Train* angrily responded. "In the period of history we're dealing with, it's either kill or be killed. Anybody who studies history knows that." But more significant than the violence was the television writers' casual approach to the law. The administration of justice was always swift and usually delivered by gunplay. Lawyers and judges were rarely seen on camera. The western didn't give a hoot for civil liberties.[26]

Westerns thus had their political side. Most clearly, westerns were a vehicle for promoting America's role in the Cold War. In *Rio Grande* the cavalry pursuit of Apaches provided an oblique commentary on the Korean War, and John Sturges's *The Magnificent Seven* (1960) was clearly a fantasy about Third World counterinsurgency. Metaphors of western violence—showdowns, hired guns, last stands—permeated the language of postwar politics. "Would a Wyatt Earp stop at the 38th Parallel in Korea when the rustlers were escaping with his herd?" a conservative political commentator whined in 1958. "Would a Marshal Dillon refuse to allow his deputies to use shotguns for their own defense because of the terrible nature of the weapon itself? Ha!" The analogy continued into the Vietnam era. President Johnson told a reporter that "he had gone into Vietnam because, as at the Alamo, somebody had to get behind the log with those threatened people." And as a way of explaining the slow progress of political reform in American-controlled territory, ambassador to Vietnam Maxwell Taylor told a congressional committee that "it is very hard to plant corn outside the stockade when the Indians are still around." American troops carried these metaphors into battle. The primary object of the fighting, one veteran later recalled, was "the Indian idea: the only good gook is a dead gook." Taking the ears of enemy dead was "like scalps, you know, like from the Indians. Some people were on an Indian trip over there." Reporter Michael Herr wrote of being invited to join an army company on a Search and Destroy mission. "'Come on,' the captain hailed, 'we'll take you out to play cowboys and Indians.'"[27]

The connection between westerns and political ideology is perhaps best evidenced by the precipitous demise of the genre amid the general cultural crisis of the 1960s and 1970s. Consider the case of filmmaker John Ford. Not since William Cody had an artist better assembled the components of frontier myth as popular entertainment. But in the final westerns of his career, Ford's vision of frontier history turned increasingly sour. *The Searchers* (1956), in which John Wayne plays an incorrigible racist, is an uncompromising study of the devastating effects of Indian hating, and *Sgt. Rutledge* (1960) is a pathbreaking depiction of the black Buffalo Soldiers in the frontier army. In *The Man Who Shot Liberty Valance* (1962) Ford called at-

John Wayne. Production still from John Ford's The Searchers *(1956). Paul A. Hutton Collection.*

tention to the good things lost in the civilizing process, and in his final western, *Cheyenne Autumn* (1964), he finally presented a case for the Indians, exposing the American side of the frontier as murderous and corrupt. Ford's doubts about the meaning of frontier history had become commonplace by the mid-1960s, evident in a flood of films exploiting the widening gap between old images and new ideas. Sergio Leone's *A Fistful of Dollars* (1967)—Clint Eastwood's first star vehicle and the first of dozens of Italian "spaghetti" westerns—and Sam Peckinpah's *The Wild Bunch* (1969) gloried in the amorality of violence, while *Little Big Man* (1970), *Blazing Saddles* (1974), and *Buffalo Bill and the Indians* (1976) lampooned the genre, subjecting the whole ideology of westering to devastating criticism. But this cynical approach quickly wore thin. By the mid-1970s Hollywood studios were producing only a handful of westerns.

In the 1990s there was a modest renaissance. In *Unforgiven* (1992) Clint Eastwood paid tribute to the great westerns of the past while simultaneously calling into question the western myth itself. The film is filled with violence, yet Eastwood does his best to strip it of all honor, romance, and nobility. "It's a hell of a thing, killing a man," his character tells a trembling young gunslinger who has just shot his first man to death—while he sat in an outhouse. "You take away all he's got, and all he's ever gonna have." Never before had the killing come so hard in a western. Another notable feature was Kevin Costner's *Dances with Wolves* (1990), in which the Indians play the good guys and the arrival of the cavalry is treated as a disaster. Costner aptly described his film as "a romantic look at a terrible time in our history." Beautifully shot on location in the Dakotas, it has the production values and the action of a traditional western but a new age sensibility. Although westerns are still not for everyone, it is striking how the genre has been transformed in the hands of directors like Costner and Eastwood. *Dances with Wolves* and *Unforgiven* were both big box-office moneymakers, and both won the Academy Award for Best Picture.[28]

The popularity of *Dances with Wolves* suggested changing American attitudes toward Indians. At the beginning of the twentieth century the assumption had been that Indians and their cultures would vanish, but during the postwar period Native Americans ranked as one of the fastest growing ethnic groups in the country. Their numbers increased from about 350,000 in 1950 to more than 2,000,000 by the beginning of the twenty-first century. How do demographers explain such growth? People self-identify their race on the census questionnaire, and according to demographer Jeff Passel, "there's been a clear trend over the last three censuses for increasing numbers of those people to answer the race question as American Indian." Not only has the number of self-declared Indians grown, but by the 1990s an estimated seven million Americans who identify themselves as "white" also claimed descent from at least one Indian ancestor—as President Bill Clinton did when he remarked, during a televised discussion in 1997, that one of his grandmothers had been a quarter Cherokee. The Cherokee Nation of Oklahoma receives several hundred queries each month concerning enrollment. "We have a lot of people who show up here who may be Indian," the tribal registrar reported, "but they can't prove it." (Neither, it turned out, could President Clinton.) Applicants must demonstrate lineal descent from persons on the 1907 allotment rolls, something few can do. Some may be angling for tribal benefits, but mostly the numbers reflect a cachet now attached to Indians as a people with a proud history. "It's the *Dances with Wolves* syndrome," says Rutgers University demographer Ross Baker. "It has sort of become neat to be an Indian." Such feelings did not emerge spontaneously but were the result of fifty years of concerted Indian activism.[29]

It was not an easy struggle. During the war, 25,000 Indians served in the armed services and another 125,000 worked in war industry. Pointing to this patriotic record, at war's end the National Council of American Indians—a group including leaders from many of the nation's 554 tribes—argued that the time had come for the country to make a fair reckoning with Indians for stolen lands and broken treaties. Congress responded positively, creating the Indian Claims Commission and empowering it to investigate tribal claims and award monetary compensation. By the

Tribal chairman George Gillette weeps as Secretary of Interior J. A. Krug purchases 155,000 acres of the Mandan-Arikara-Hidatsa reservation in North Dakota for use as a Missouri River reservoir. Photograph by William Chaplis, 1948. Associated Press/Wide World Photos.

time the commission finished its work, more than thirty years later, it had heard and considered nearly four hundred cases and awarded more than eight hundred million dollars in damages (much of which remained in the hands of lawyers). There was, however, an important caveat. The settlement of claims, declared Commissioner of Indian Affairs Dillon S. Myer (the federal official who had supervised Japanese internment), would be "the means of removing a major Indian objection" for the termination of official relations with the federal government. That would mean the end of all remaining treaty obligations. The limited sovereignty guaranteed to tribes by the Indian New Deal would be revoked. This program, which became known as Termination, was made official by act of Congress in 1953 and became the primary goal of Indian policy during the Eisenhower administration.[30]

Termination worked in an insidious manner. Consider the example of the Menominee tribe of northern Wisconsin. During the nineteenth century the Menominees ceded millions of acres in exchange for a protected reservation, tribal exemption from state interference and taxation, and the continuing right to hunt and fish. In the early twentieth century the tribe resisted allotment, retaining collective ownership of 230,000 acres of prime timberland, on which they ran a lumbering operation that provided jobs and modest incomes for reservation residents. After the war the tribe filed a suit with the Claims Commission charging federal mismanagement of their trust fund, and in the early 1950s the Menominees won an award of $7.6 million, to be split evenly among tribal members. Then came the kicker: Congress appropriated the funds but made payment conditional on the Menominees' agreement to termination. Tribal leaders opposed the settlement, arguing that maintaining their sovereignty was more valuable, but a majority of members—most of whom lived off the reservation—voted to accept the checks. The results were disastrous. The Menominee nation was abolished, replaced by a tribal corporation. Tribal lands became subject to state taxes, forcing the corporation to sell land to raise revenue. Lumber production fell and workers lost their jobs. Reservation schools and clinics closed. Hunting and fishing rights disappeared. Termination struck at the three most important things to reservation people—sovereignty, land, and culture.

Although termination was completed for only a few tribes, its threat hung over them all. "Fear of termination has poisoned every aspect of Indian affairs," a federal study of the early 1960s concluded. Fear and anger led to a broad movement of pan-Indian activism. In 1961 the National Council of American Indians passed a "Declaration of Indian Purpose," calling on the federal government to end termination and begin a new era of "Indian Self-Determination." The declaration was endorsed by President Kennedy, then in turn by Presidents Johnson and Nixon. By that time western state officials had lost their enthusiasm for termination, concluding that the program would result in higher burdens for state-funded welfare programs. Johnson declared an official end to the policy in 1968, and in 1975 Congress passed the Indian Self-Determination and Educational Assistance Act. This measure strengthened tribal governments by giving them the opportunity and the funds to administer their own programs to promote education, welfare, the administration of natural resources, and the improvement of reservation infrastructure.[31]

Termination, meanwhile, accelerated the migration of young Indians to the cities. Indian reservations in the postwar period were some of the most depressed places in America, with a well-established litany of problems from unemployment to alcoholism, a situation termination did nothing to improve. Like other rural westerners, Indians increasingly looked to western urban enclaves for employment. During the second half of the century the proportion of Indians living in cities rose from 13 to 60 percent. Large Indian communities developed in all the major metropolitan areas of the West, the biggest in southern California, which in the 1990s was home to at least a hundred thousand Indians from more than a hundred tribes. Many Indians maintained their tribal identity by frequent visits to extended family and friends on the reservation, but at least a third claimed no tribal affiliation. A new pan-Indian identity grew increasingly important. As early as the 1920s Indians in Los Angeles were organizing "Powwow Societies" that sponsored informal get-togethers and ceremonial dancing in an eclectic mix of tribal styles. "I knew I lost a lot when I left the reservation," Joe Whitecloud, a leader of L.A.'s "powwow people" told an interviewer. Powwows, he believed, enabled urban Indians "to pass on our traditions to the kids coming up." Many of these traditions, however, had been recently invented.[32]

The best known pan-Indian activist organization of the postwar period, the American Indian Movement (AIM), developed in the urban community of Minneapolis. In the words of Dennis Banks, an intense Chippewa who became the group's most articulate leader, AIM was "a coalition of Indian people willing to fight for Indians." The group quickly became best known for its street patrol designed to check police brutality, which captured the imagination of young urban Indians much as the Black Panthers inspired young urban blacks. In 1969 AIM organizers joined local Indian activists in occupying San Francisco Bay's Alcatraz Island. "We, the native Americans," the occupiers announced, "reclaim the land known as Alcatraz Island in the name of all American Indians by right of discovery." They employed the language of tribal sovereignty, but this was a protest of urban pan-Indians, not tribal people. It was great publicity, and with its slogan of "Red Power," AIM expanded throughout the urban Indian communities of the West.[33]

An important recruit was Russell Means, an Oglala Sioux born on the Pine Ridge Reservation but raised in the San Francisco Bay area. Means quickly proved himself a genius at confrontation politics. In one of his first AIM actions, Means led a group that for three days in 1972 occupied the offices of the Bureau of Indian Affairs in Washington, D.C. The next year he was instrumental in getting AIM involved in the internal politics of the Oglala reservation at Pine Ridge, South Dakota, the most impoverished place in America. Frustrated by a conservative tribal government, AIM activists and a group of reservation supporters armed themselves with rifles and shotguns and occupied a church at the site of the Wounded Knee massacre of 1890, vowing not to leave until the tribal chairman resigned. It was a brilliant bid for national media attention at the site many Americans had recently learned about from historian Dee Brown's best-selling *Bury My Heart at Wounded Knee* (1970). Besieged by FBI agents and federal marshals armed with automatic weapons, tanks, and helicopters, many Americans saw the incident as a replay of the nineteenth-century Indian wars—although this time opinion polls suggested that the majority sympathized with the Indians rather than the cavalry. It was a public relations disaster for the government. After seventy-one days the occupiers finally surrendered with federal promises of negotiations. But afterward the FBI hounded AIM to extinction, and many tribal Indians considered the occupation a disaster.

More effective change came through the struggles of tribal governments to regain

Russell Means and other occupiers of Wounded Knee. Photograph by Richard Erdoes, 1973. Beinecke.

lost lands or treaty rights. One of the most publicized efforts was the struggle of the Taos Indians to regain control of Blue Lake in the Sangre de Cristo Mountains. Seized by the federal government and incorporated within a national forest reserve in 1906, the crystal blue lake not only fed the stream that flowed through Taos Pueblo and gave it life but was one of the people's most sacred places. After nearly a decade of petitions, protests, and bad publicity for the federal government, President Nixon finally returned forty-eight thousand acres, including Blue Lake, to the control of the Taos tribe in 1970. In the Pacific Northwest, meanwhile, Indians staged "fish-ins" to assert their right to fish despite state game laws. In 1974 they won a major victory when a federal judge vindicated their treaty rights to hunt and fish in "the usual and accustomed" place. Using the law, other tribes won an impressive series of Supreme Court cases that reaffirmed limited tribal sovereignty and exemption from state taxes. "What's happening is that tribal governments are becoming a permanent part of the fabric of American federalism," said John Echohawk, executive director of the Native American Rights Fund. "You have a federal government, state governments, and tribal governments—three sovereigns in one country."[34]

Sovereignty was the biggest asset of tribes in their attempt to stimulate economic development on the reservations. At Laguna Pueblo, for example, the tribe created Laguna Industries, which used its tax exemption to advantage in bidding for sub-

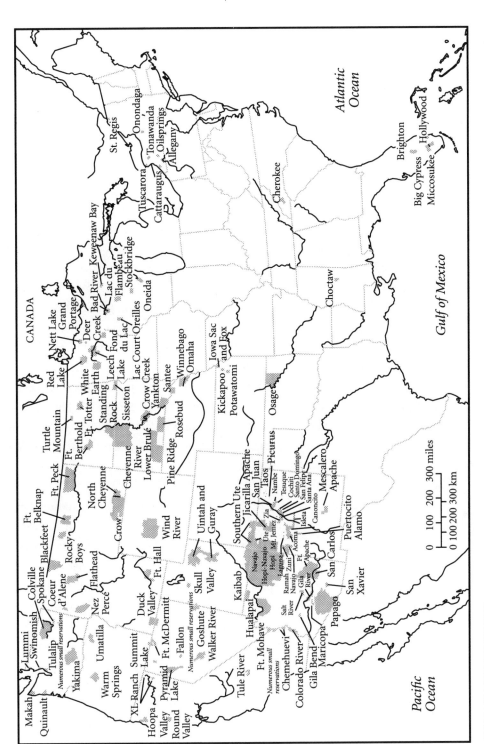

INDIAN RESERVATIONS

CANADA

Atlantic
Ocean

Gulf of Mexico

Pacific
Ocean

St. Regis
Onondaga
Tonawanda
Oilsprings
Tuscarora
Cattaraugus
Allegany

Brighton
Hollywood
Big Cypress
Miccosukee

Cherokee

Choctaw

Red Lake
Nett Lake
Grand Portage
Bad River
Keweenaw Bay
Deer Creek
Lac du Flambeau
Stockbridge
Lac Court Oreilles
Oneida

Turtle Mountain

Ft. Totter
White Earth
Standing Rock
Leech Lake
Lac du Lac
Sisseton
Crow Creek
Yankton
Santee
Winnebago
Omaha

Kickapoo
Potawatomi

Iowa Sac
and Fox

Osage

Makah
Quinault
Lummi
Swinomish
Colville
Spokane
Coeur d'Alene
Tulalip
Yakima

Numerous small reservations

Ft. Belknap
Ft. Peck
Blackfeet
Rocky Boys

Ft. Berthold

Nez Percé
Flathead

Umatilla
Warm Springs

North Cheyenne

Cheyenne River
Lower Brulé
Pine Ridge
Rosebud

Crow

XL Ranch
Hoopa Valley
Round Valley
Summit Lake
Duck Valley
Pyramid Lake
Ft. McDermitt
Fallon

Wind River

Ft. Hall

Uintah and Ouray

Goshute
Skull Valley
Walker River

Southern Ute
Jicarilla Apache
San Juan
Picurus
Taos
Nambe
Tesuque
Cochiti
Santo Domingo
San Felipe
Santa Ana
Canoncito

Mescalero
Apache

Tule River
Ft. Mohave
Hualapai
Kaibab

Numerous small
reservations

Chemehuevi
Colorado River
Gila Bend
Maricopa

Navajo
Hopi
Ute Mt.
Zia
Jemez
Acoma
Laguna
Ramah Navajo
Navajo
Isleta
Zuni
Gila River
Apache

San Carlos

Puertocito
Alamo

San Xavier

Papago

0   100 200 300 miles
0 100 200 300 km

contracting work with the country's major defense industries. During the 1980s and 1990s tribal and Indian-owned businesses grew by a rate nearly five times the national average. Western Indian tribes control a vast resource base: 30 percent of the coal deposits west of the Mississippi, 50 to 60 percent of the country's uranium, 5 percent of the proven oil and gas reserves, fifteen million acres of timber and watershed, and extensive fish and wildlife habitat. The problem is getting the development capital. "We just need to develop more," declared Laguna planner Nathan Tsosie. "People leave the reservation to get jobs. If there were jobs here, they'd stay."[35]

During the 1990s there was great optimism that the source of development capital might come from Indian gaming, perhaps the most significant assertion of Indian self-determination in American history. The boom began when the Seminoles opened a high-stakes bingo parlor near Fort Lauderdale in 1978. Florida sued because gaming was illegal in the state, but a federal appeals court ruled in favor of Seminole sovereignty. Tribes around the country were soon opening gaming operations of their own. In 1988 Congress passed the Indian Gaming Regulatory Act, which required tribes and states to agree on ground rules. Ten years later a third of the nation's 554 tribes were doing a gross annual business of seven billion dollars, about a quarter of which went to tribal governments. But prosperity depended on location. Ten tribes accounted for more than 50 percent of the take—the Mashantucket Pequots and the Mohegans of Connecticut, for example, grew wealthy operating huge casinos and entertainment complexes within easy reach of Boston and New York. But Oglala Pine Ridge, hundreds of miles from a major urban center, remained the poorest community in the country.

Pine Ridge was all too typical. At the end of the century, with the national economy booming, unemployment for adult Indians stood at 15 percent, three times the national average, and a majority of reservation households continued to live far below the poverty line. Moreover, Indian gaming produced a considerable political backlash, with many legislators grousing that wealthy tribes should be paying state taxes and threatening to pass legislation once again eliminating tribal sovereignty.

In spite of such ongoing problems and controversies, the Indian nations had made a remarkable comeback during the postwar period. During the last third of the century tribes founded twenty-seven reservation colleges that annually enrolled more than twenty-five thousand students, and they instituted programs to revive the use of native languages. These developments were part of a cultural renaissance and a resurgence of pride among both reservation and urban Indians. Russell Means remains a controversial figure among Indian people, but he offers a sensible summary of late twentieth-century developments. "We alerted the entire world that the American Indians were still alive and resisting. That fact alone is so stupendous it cannot be measured." The native rights movement inspired Indians and helped to make all

America more aware of their history. "Wounded Knee woke up America," Means insists. "We're still here, and we're still resisting. John Wayne did not kill us all."[36]

If frontiers are what happens when cultures collide and attempt to work out ways of living together, the postwar period deserves prominence in the annals of American frontier history. Not only were Indians resurgent, but Mexican Americans and African Americans mounted an impressive challenge to the ethnic and racial order that had been established during the nineteenth century—the ethnic labor system, the segregation of minorities, and their exclusion from the political process. World War II marked the decisive transition to this new era.

Booming wartime industry in western cities, particularly on the Pacific Coast, encouraged the migration of African Americans from the rural South and Mexican Americans from the rural Southwest. Men and women from both groups found jobs building ships, airplanes, and new housing. They might have lacked experience, but that hardly mattered. At a southern California aircraft plant a black applicant was asked if he had any experience building B-17s. "Man, I didn't know what a P-38 or a B-17 was, but I wanted to learn, I wanted an opportunity," he remembered. "I was honest and told him I didn't know if he were talking about a gun, a battleship, or a plane." The applicant got the job anyway. Jobs drew thousands of migrants. Historians lack good numbers for the growth of the urban Mexican-American population during the war (not until 1970 did the Census Bureau begin the systematic collection of data on Hispanics), but the black population of Seattle, Portland, greater San Francisco, and southern California doubled or tripled.[37]

African Americans were pulled by opportunity and pushed by the daily humiliations of life in the segregated South. "You just don't know what it was like," Theresa Waller told an interviewer about life in her native Houston. "They would try to make you feel like you weren't human." She dreamed of leaving for California, where she could "be somebody." In 1943 she and her husband heard of work in the shipyards and canneries of the Bay Area and he went on ahead to get established. When he called for her to meet him in Oakland, she left Houston "on the Jim Crow car," then changed trains and boarded an integrated car in El Paso. It was filled to overflowing, and a young serviceman rose to offer his seat. "You can relax now," he said when he noticed her shock, "we're at the Mason-Dixon line." Earlier that summer in the Gulf Coast town of Beaumont, just a few miles from Houston, there had been a brutal reminder of why it was difficult for African Americans to relax. Inflamed by false rumors that a white woman had been raped by a black man, a mob of several hundred whites invaded the black side of town looting, burning, and leaving four hundred injured and three dead.[38]

The West might be on the north side of the "Mason-Dixon line," yet racial discrimination and segregation were realities there, too. During the war there was the internment of the Japanese, the so-called Zoot-Suit Riots in Los Angeles, and numerous confrontations between black and white soldiers or workers in western cities. "Things were going to be different out here," remembered Ruth Gracon, a young black woman who migrated to Oakland from Arkansas. "But they weren't like we thought they'd be. They didn't have 'No Colored' signs or anything like that, but they had other ways of telling you they didn't want you." In fact, signs warning "We Cater to White Trade Only" were common in business establishments near western army bases where black units were stationed. African Americans and Mexican Americans were refused service in restaurants and hotels, required to sit in separate sections in theaters, and excluded from using public facilities like parks and swimming pools (except perhaps for a single weekday, usually just before draining and cleaning). A black serviceman stationed in Salina, Kansas, bitterly recalled being turned away with his buddies from a café by the owner—"You boys know we don't serve colored here"—a rejection made all the more painful when he noticed the German prisoners of war eating at the counter.[39]

Jobs were abundant but assurances of equitable treatment few. African Americans in the wartime shipbuilding industry, for example, were subjected to systematic discrimination—not by the companies but by the International Brotherhood of Boilermakers, the American Federation of Labor union that represented workers. The union relegated blacks (though apparently not Hispanics) to subordinate positions and confined them to segregated auxiliary locals without representation at the higher levels of the international. "We pay our dues but what do we get?" complained one black worker. "Nothing but to be discriminated against and segregated." Protests were followed by union-instigated firings of black activists. With the support of the federal Fair Employment Practices Commission, African Americans went to court, and in 1944 the Boilermakers were ordered to end their discriminatory practices.[40]

After the war returning African-American and Mexican-American combat veterans were determined not to sink back into the bad old days. Edward Roybal of Los Angeles told how he had learned to confront racism during his time in the army. "I was assigned to a barracks full of Texans," he recalled, and "one of them woke up every morning and cursed Mexicans in general. Then one day he cursed me. So, I turned around and socked him." To his surprise Roybal found that his commanding officers approved. They wanted no expressions of bigotry—"not because they loved us, but because they wanted things to run smoothly. It dawned on some of us for the first time that the Anglos were divided. And if we united, we could win concessions." In 1947 Roybal made an unsuccessful bid for a seat on the Los Angeles City Council. In the aftermath of that election he was one of the founders of a group called the Community Service Organization that registered fifteen thousand new Mexican-American voters. In a second try two years later, Roybal won the position and became the

Edward Roybal, c. 1950. Roybal Institute for Applied Gerontology, California State University at Los Angeles.

first Hispanic on the council since 1888. He vividly remembered the council president introducing him at his first meeting as the "Mexican-speaking councilman representing the Mexican people of Los Angeles." Calmly Roybal laid aside "the baloney speech" he had prepared and corrected the man: "I'm not a Mexican, I am a Mexican American. And I don't speak a word of Mexican, I speak Spanish."[41]

The mobilization of minority voters was one of the most important of postwar struggles. At first electoral activity focused on the municipal and state levels. Then in 1961 Henry B. Gonzáles of San Antonio became the first Mexican American elected to Congress—like Roybal, he had begun his political career on the city council. In 1962 Gonzáles was joined in the House of Representatives by Roybal, elected to represent East L.A. That same year Los Angeles voters in South Central also sent Augustus Hawkins, an African American born in Louisiana who had emigrated to southern California to escape "the ruthlessness and ugliness of segregation." Most African Americans in Texas could not participate in electoral politics until the Supreme Court declared the poll tax unconstitutional in 1966. That year Barbara Jordan of Houston was elected to the state legislature, and six years later voters elected her to become the first African American to represent Texas in Congress. She later served on the committee deliberating the impeachment of President Nixon.[42]

There were also challenges to segregation. The case of Felix Longoria, a young Mexican-American serviceman killed in action, provided an early symbol. After the war Longoria's family arranged to have his body moved from an overseas cemetery to one near their home in Three Rivers, Texas, but were outraged to discover that the local funeral home would not handle the remains of Mexican Americans. American G.I. Forum, an activist group of Mexican-American veterans, appealed to Senator Lyndon Johnson, who arranged to have the body reburied with full military honors at Arlington National Cemetery. It was one of the first successful challenges to Jim Crow in Texas.

Undoubtedly the most important struggle was the desegregation of public education. The League of United Latin American Citizens (LULAC) had gone to court to end school segregation in Texas during the 1930s, and although they lost, their briefs provided important precedents for later efforts. Immediately following the war LULAC offered legal assistance to a group of frustrated Mexican-American parents in the southern California citrus town of Westminister, whose children were confined to a separate "Mexican school." In a landmark decision, in 1947 the California Supreme Court found for the parents, although the justices declined to make a broad constitutional ruling, preventing the case from setting a national precedent. The decision, editorialized *La Opinión,* the leading Spanish-language newspaper of southern California, was a blow to "those who believe in the anti-Semitic theories of Adolph Hitler." Families who had sent men to fight and die in an antiracist war abroad were not going to tolerate such things at home. The Westminister schools were integrated, and other southern California districts soon followed.[43]

The victory of Mexican-American parents in the Westminister suit inspired others to think that the West was perhaps the place to challenge the national system of segregation. "The die is cast in the South, or in an old city like New York or Chicago," Phoenix activist William Mahoney declared in 1951, "but we here are present for creation. We're making a society where the die isn't cast. It can be for good or ill." Actually, institutional discrimination had been in place in the Southwest for seventy-five years, but Mahoney's views are a good indication of the optimism about civil rights in the immediate postwar period. In 1952 a group of black parents in Phoenix won a state court ruling against the segregation of public schools in Arizona. At the same time black parents in Topeka, Kansas—represented by a group of attorneys that included descendants of Exoduster pioneers—filed a suit in federal court. Although they lost the first round, they quickly appealed. In *Brown v. Board of Education of Topeka* (1954) the Supreme Court unanimously ruled that separate schools were inherently unequal, establishing a precedent that applied directly to the South.[44]

As important as these victories were, however, they were foiled by intractable patterns of residential segregation. Consider the case of postwar southern California, where the increase in the African-American population was double the general growth rate, and Mexican-American expansion was four times greater. Yet restrictive covenants barred "non-Caucasians" from an estimated 95 percent of all the housing constructed in the immediate postwar period. In 1947 James Shifflett, a leader of the African-American community in Los Angeles, moved his family to a bungalow in an all-white district of the city. "I remember a marshal ringing our door-bell and handing my parents a notice to move out," his daughter Lynne recalled. Shifflett's neighbors had filed suit to enforce the white-only covenant. The case went to the Supreme Court, which ruled that such restrictions were "unenforceable as law and contrary to public policy"—yet the practice continued informally for many years. The right of owners to refuse to rent, lease, or sell to anyone they choose was confirmed in 1964 when California voters, by a margin of two to one, approved an initiative known as Proposition 14. The prevailing pattern was that most African-American and Mexican-American newcomers crowded into existing ghettos and barrios, which expanded into fringe neighborhoods as whites fled to outlying sub-urbs. A study of racial segregation in Los Angeles County during the 1960s found that although blacks and Latinos made up 30 percent of the population, fifty-three of eighty-two suburban communities were 99 percent white, which qualified L.A. for the dubious distinction of being the most segregated county in the nation. At about the same time, a California Department of Education survey found that 57 percent of the state's Hispanic students and 85 percent of the African Americans at-tended predominantly "minority schools." Historian Charles Wollenberg concludes that that there was more school segregation by the 1970s than there had been in the 1940s.[45]

Such patterns of discrimination created an ethnic and racial powder keg in the center of the city. As factory jobs moved to new industrial parks in the urban fringe, unemployment rose among minorities. Cars were few in black neighborhoods, and by bus it took almost four hours to get to major industrial plants. Southern Califor-nia was the most industrialized region in the country, yet, as historian Gerald Horne writes, "blacks were left without work, away from higher-wage union jobs." More than 40 percent of African-American families in Los Angeles lived at or below the poverty level. The inevitable explosion was touched off one hot, smoggy August evening in 1965 by a minor traffic accident and a botched arrest in Watts, the most impoverished of L.A.'s black neighborhoods. For four successive days thirty thou-sand angry people fought with police and the National Guard, looting stores and burning hundreds of buildings within a forty-mile radius. Thirty-four people were killed in the Watts Riot. Over the next five years—one of the most tumultuous pe-riods in American history—black urban uprisings affected all the major cities of the West.[46]

The violence was a national phenomenon, of course. Yet the West Coast produced the most influential political movement to come out of the urban violence—the Black Panthers of Oakland, California. Denouncing the strategy of the civil rights movement, they advocated political change by means of armed self-defense and vi-olent revolution. The Panthers jumped from obscurity to infamy in 1967 when lead-ers Huey P. Newton and Bobby Seale, along with a small group of followers, entered

César Chávez at a farmworkers' strike in Tulare County, California, 1965. Archives of Labor and Urban Affairs, Wayne State University.

the chamber of the California state assembly armed with automatic weapons and dressed in their standard-issue uniform of black leather jacket, black turtleneck, black slacks, and black beret. Membership skyrocketed after this successful media event, and soon there were Panther chapters in the ghettos of most western cities— and even offshoots in the East. As with the American Indian Movement, a concerted assault by local police and the FBI eventually brought down the Panthers, but they contributed mightily to their own demise by degenerating into a violent gang of drug runners. Unfortunately the gang mentality was the Panthers' most important legacy to thousands of young blacks and Latinos.

Although many Mexican Americans found employment in the booming industrial economy of the postwar West, thousands continued to labor in the fields as agricultural workers. It was not until the 1960s that they found their champion in César Chávez, an Arizonan whose parents had lost their small farm during the Depression and joined the caravans of pickers following the ripening crops. Once as a boy in the California desert town of Brawley he and his brother were refused service at a diner, the waitress rejecting him with a laugh—"We don't sell to Mexicans." Chávez left in tears. That laugh, he said, "seemed to cut us out of the human race." A few years later he was arrested for refusing to move from the white-only section of a movie theater,

United Farm Workers election poster, c. 1965. Beinecke.

his introduction to political activism. As a young married man in the barrio of San Jose, at the southern end of San Francisco Bay, Chávez went to work as an organizer for the Community Service Organization, then turned his attention to organizing farmworkers.[47]

The Mexican deportations of the 1930s and wartime mobilization had left growers short of farm workers. Pressing the federal government for relief, they secured the passage of legislation permitting the entrance into the country of temporary Mexican farmworkers, or *braceros*. But the Bracero Program outlasted the war. In league with state and federal officials, growers used the program as the means of keeping the lid on wages and preventing strikes. As one grower candidly admitted, he preferred braceros to domestic workers because "they cannot protest [and] work at half the rate." The program also stimulated a huge increase in the number of migrants who came across the border illegally. By the early 1950s border patrols of the Immigration and Naturalization Service (INS) were apprehending more than half a million illegal immigrants each year, and estimates were that perhaps two or three times that many got across successfully. Chávez argued that the presence of a large pool of politically powerless aliens severely hampered the effort to unionize farmworkers who were American citizens. Mobilizing both Mexican Americans and liberals, Chávez's first success came when Congress eliminated the program in 1964.[48]

In his organizing efforts Chávez was joined by an energetic and creative group of young Mexican Americans, including Dolores Huerta, a dynamic young Hispano from an old New Mexican family, and Luis Valdez, an actor and activist, who created a theater troupe called El Teatro Campesino, effectively using entertainment as an organizing tool. Chávez and his colleagues organized the United Farm Workers (UFW), the first independent farmworkers' organization since the 1930s, and in 1966 they launched their first strike ("Huelga!") against grape growers of California's Central Valley. To pressure growers the UFW launched a nationwide grape boycott that had widespread impact. Governor Ronald Reagan of California was reduced to pleading with Americans to eat more grapes, while President Nixon ordered the Defense Department to buy tons more than they needed, sending planeloads to the troops in Vietnam. But Chávez's charismatic and inspirational leadership proved stronger. In 1970 the growers relented and began signing union contracts. In the mid-1970s, with the sympathetic support of Governor Jerry Brown, who succeeded Reagan, the UFW was able to raise the wages and living standards of its members. It was a historic achievement, capping decades of struggle in California's factories in the field. There was considerable slippage during the conservative 1980s, however, and by the time Chávez died in 1993 the UFW was in disarray. It began a revival under new leadership in the late 1990s.

Chávez and the UFW were a critical component in the rise of a broad political and cultural renaissance among Mexican Americans in the Southwest. In New Mexico a volatile leader named Reies Tijerina organized an Alianza of twenty thousand Hispanos demanding an investigation of the wholesale theft of land that had taken place after the Mexican War. Frustrated at the inaction of authorities, he and his followers occupied federal lands at gunpoint in 1966, declaring an independent Hispano nation. "The issue of land is crucial to rural Mexicanos," Chávez said in support, "and reflects the cruel injustices to which they have been subjected." There was a confrontation and an exchange of gunfire in which two officers were wounded, and Tijerina was sent to prison for two years. In south Texas farmworker organizing spilled over into electoral politics and a new political group, El Partido Raza Unita, scored a series of impressive victories in local elections. Among young people throughout the urban Southwest there was a surge of enthusiasm for *mexicanismo*. Amid cries of "Viva la Raza!" activists celebrated the memory of pachucos and zootsuiters. Activists began referring to themselves as *Chicanos*, embracing with pride a slang term Mexican Americans had used for decades to denigrate Mexican newcomers. New slogans were heard on the streets—"Somos uno Porque America Es Una" (We are one because America is one), "Somos un Pueblo Sin Fronteras" (We are one people without borders).[49]

In 1965 Congress reformed the immigration laws, abolishing the system of quotas based on national origins enacted in 1924. Over the next three decades a massive new wave of immigration brought more than seven million Latino and five million Asian newcomers to the country. Most settled near the country's major immigrant gateways—Los Angeles, San Francisco, and Houston in the West, along with New York City and Chicago. LAX—L.A.'s international airport—became the Ellis Island of late twentieth-century America. The Mexican-American population of the Southwest increased by 200 percent from 1970 to 1990, when it stood at nearly fourteen million. Over the same period the Asian population increased more than six times, with more than four million residing in the West by 1990. Demographers project that during the first quarter of the twenty-first century western cities will attract another thirty million Latinos and seven million Asians.

There was also an enormous increase in the number of migrants entering the United States illegally. During the last quarter of the twentieth century about half the illegal migrants during the postwar period crossed into the country from Mexico. In the words of one commentator, they had "an economic gun at their backs"—the turmoil of the Mexican economy. For many other Latinos, the gun was all too real. Armed conflict in Central America created thousands of refugee Guatemalans, Salvadorans, and Nicaraguans (OTMs—"Other Than Mexicans"—in the parlance of the Border Patrol). There were frequent tragedies at the border: corrupt Mexican national police, or *federales,* shaking down refugees; greedy middlemen, known as *coyotes,* extorting high fees for guiding illegals across; violent *banditos* lying in wait to rob vulnerable individuals of their valuables; unknown hundreds, perhaps thousands, dying by drowning or exposure. More than a dozen illegal migrants died in a single early spring snowstorm in 1999. On one California freeway near the Mexican border traffic signs featured the silhouette of a fleeing family as a warning to drivers to watch for illegals darting across traffic lanes. By the early 1990s INS officers along the Mexican border were apprehending and expelling 1.7 million undocumented aliens each year.

Yet by the thousands the people kept coming to take jobs as textile workers, farm laborers, gardeners, nannies, and housekeepers. The rock-bottom wages employers paid for such work depressed the incomes of poor American citizens and made Latino migrants a convenient target for nativist anxiety and anger. In 1994 California voters approved Proposition 187, an initiative that would have denied undocumented aliens or their children access to public services like education and health care, but the measure was eventually thrown out by a federal judge who declared it unconstitutional. Four years later California voters approved another ballot initiative that curtailed bilingual educational programs. Other Americans argued for draconian measures at the border—electrified fences, minefields, the creation of a no-man's-land between the United States and Mexico. A more effective strategy would be to cut off the demand for undocumented migrants by severely fining employers who broke the law by hiring them at subminimum wage, but that would mean challenging powerful business interests.[50]

During the first half of the 1990s a million Latino and three hundred thousand

Asian immigrants settled in southern California, which had become, in the words of historians Leonard and Dale Pitt, "the most ethnically diverse metropolitan area in the world." The city of Los Angeles was home to immigrants from 140 countries, including the largest communities of Mexicans, Salvadorans, Guatemalans, Koreans, and Filipinos outside their homelands, as well as the country's largest concentrations of Japanese, Cambodians, and Iranians. In broad categories, the county was 40 percent Hispanic, 10 percent Asian, 13 percent African American, and only 37 percent "Anglo" (a category including persons from a variety of European backgrounds). The screw turns. "Our modern metropolis is returning to the enduring Pueblo de Los Angeles of years past," declared California State Senator Art Torres, who became chairman of the state Democratic Party in 1998. Essayist Richard Rodriguez, reminding readers that Mexicans were a mestizo people, offered the observation that "Los Angeles has become the largest Indian city in the United States."[51]

By the end of the century the school systems of southern California were attempting to cope with youngsters who spoke eighty-two languages. In San Bernardino County, east of Los Angeles, 40 percent of the students were white, 43 percent Latino. At Victoria School, in the town of Redlands, half of the 680 students were Latino, about a third were white, and the rest came from groups speaking seventeen different languages. According to Loren Sanchez, the San Bernardino County superintendent of schools, Victoria School "reflects what's happening all over southern California. White is no longer the predominant group."[52]

Southern California was one dramatic scene in a larger drama. In a great arc from the Gulf Coast to the Pacific, the Southwest was in the process of turning "majority minority." That was already true for New Mexico, and according to demographic projections California would follow by 2000, Texas and Arizona by 2010. According to Thomas Chan, an international lawyer from Hong Kong who works in Los Angeles, the region was "moving rapidly from being a 'melting pot' of Europeans to a 'world city' with links to virtually every inhabitable part of the globe." In one much noticed phenomena, the diet of the urban West underwent a process of culinary miscegenation, tortillas and guacamole sharing space on the table with egg rolls and fish paste. Urban westerners of the new century would need to learn how to live in a multicultural world. But adjustment was slow. Anglos constituted only 37 percent of L.A.'s population, but they made up 70 percent of the registered voters and 80 percent of the jury pool. They also controlled 90 percent of the fixed wealth. Although the economic gap between whites and minorities was narrowing nationally, it was growing in the Southwest.[53]

The starkest evidence of the problem came with the devastating 1992 Los Angeles riot, the worst urban disorder of the century. For decades the African-American and Mexican-American communities had complained of systematic police brutality. Those charges seemed dramatically confirmed when an amateur videotape of four

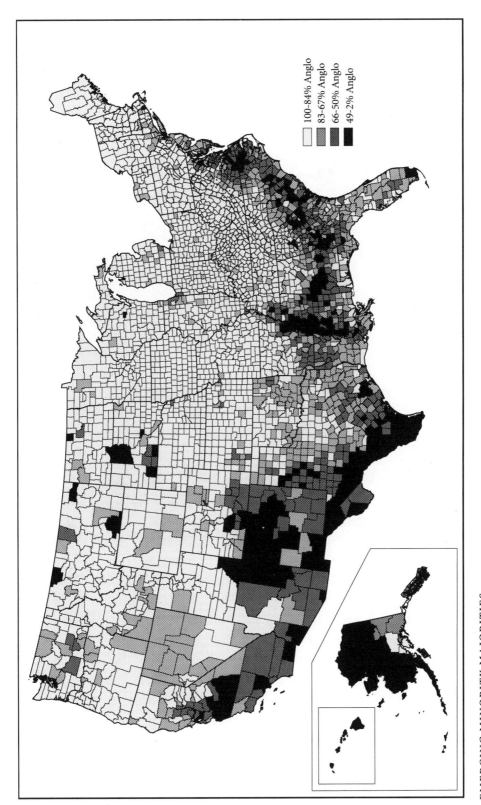

100-84% Anglo
83-67% Anglo
66-50% Anglo
49-2% Anglo

EMERGING MINORITY MAJORITIES

A Korean merchant defends his property during the Los Angeles riots. Photograph by Jean-Marc Giboux, 1992. The Gamma Liaison Network, New York.

white police officers beating a black motorist named Rodney King received wide exposure on television. The officers were indicted, but when a white suburban jury acquitted them of all but one charge, the city exploded in violence. For three days rioters swept through black, Latino, and Asian-American neighborhoods, looting and burning. Fifty-one people died and the equivalent of several square miles was torched before the National Guard restored order. More than twelve thousand people were arrested. There were obvious comparisons with the Watts Riot of 1965, but there were also important differences. Not only was this uprising deadlier and more destructive, it was multicultural. Forty-one percent of those arrested were African American, but 12 percent were Anglo and 45 percent were Hispanic. And much of the violence was directed at the downtown community of Koreans, many of whom owned successful businesses in black ghettos and Mexican-American barrios. The riot exposed the festering ethnic and racial divisions within the "world city."

Doubts about the future of the urban Southwest were also reflected in the considerable outmigration taking place from western cities during the 1990s. About 1.4 million people left southern California from 1990 to 1995, about as many lost by domestic migration as gained by foreign immigration. According to the Census Bureau, most were moving to the Rocky Mountain West, to counties on the outskirts of Denver, Salt Lake City, and Reno. The Boise area of southern Idaho was particularly attractive. "I wanted my children to be able to learn how to light a campfire in the rain and saddle a horse," said a former L.A. resident who relocated there. Often these emigrants brought their suburban values along—the need for two-car garages and swimming pools—and the resentments of locals quickly emerged. Another southern Californian who had relocated to Idaho back in the 1970s warned of the dangers. "I've seen it all happen on the coast," he declared, and "now it's happening here—trout streams dug up for freeways, the smog, the elk herd declining. It's the same old story of unplanned growth." Local sentiments were capsulated in the Boise bumper sticker that screamed, "Don't Californicate Idaho!"[54]

The controversy over the new rush to the Interior West was part of an extended postwar debate over the use of the western landscape. It was a reminder of how special the glorious western vistas were to Americans but also of how fragile they were. The national parks, of course, were to be protected, jewels in the crown of western empire. In the postwar period Congress created twenty-one new parks, increasing the territory for which the National Park Service was responsible to eighty million acres, nine-tenths of it in the trans-Mississippi West and Alaska. But the breathtaking scenery of the parks drew armies of tourists. The number of visits to national parks and forests rose dramatically, from thirty million annually in 1941 to more than six hundred million by the end of the century. The nation's population doubled, but the recreational use of federal lands increased twentyfold. The good news was that support for the federal system of parks and forests had never been stronger. The bad news was that far too many people were trampling fragile meadows, and too many machines were fouling fresh air. The majesty of Yosemite Valley and the Grand Canyon was corroded by traffic jams and gift shops. The danger of Americans' loving the parks to death confronted National Park Service leaders with a fundamental dilemma they are still trying to resolve.

Historian Samuel P. Hays argues that the enormous popularity of outdoor recreation in the postwar period was part of a broad change in values, from an obsession with production to a preoccupation with the "quality of life." New environmental values, he writes, "were an integral part of the continuous search for a better standard of living," which also helps explain the movement of millions to the suburbs. Yet one of the most frequent arguments made for environmental preservation called upon the importance of the frontier in American tradition. "Many of the attributes most distinctive of America and Americans" resulted from "the impress of the wilderness and the life that accompanied it," wrote naturalist Aldo Leopold, whose *Sand County Almanac* (1949) became the bible of the environmentalist movement. Robert Marshall, along with Leopold a co-founder of the Wilderness Society, wrote that only by setting aside wilderness areas could "the emotional values of the frontier be preserved." In the early 1960s the Wilderness Society and the Sierra Club lobbied Congress for legislation that would protect large areas of undeveloped country in the West. The Wilderness Act (1964) set aside as undeveloped wilderness nine million acres of federal land—which Congress had increased to ninety-five million acres by the end of the century. The American, wrote novelist Wallace Stegner in a widely circulated essay supporting the Wilderness Act, "is a civilized man who has renewed himself in the wild," and by preserving wilderness "the hope and excitement can be passed on to newer Americans, Americans who never saw any phase of the frontier."[55]

The problem with this argument was that the frontier could mean different things to different Americans. It was possible to argue, as developers did, that it stood for the process of development that had produced the powerful American economy, providing the standard of living that allowed Americans to live in countrified surroundings and spend their vacations in the national parks. What was "characteristically American" about our civilization, insisted Senator Ernest Gruening of Alaska, was that it had been shaped "in a battle with nature." Echoing Frederick Jackson Turner, he argued that the frontier was "free land, . . . a vast, empty land, waiting for people." Protected parks and wilderness areas made up only a quarter of the nation's federal land. The rest—more than 90 percent of it in the West and Alaska—was intended for wise use. After all, that had been the meaning of conservation as practiced by Gifford Pinchot and Theodore Roosevelt.[56]

The limits of use and exploitation were at the heart of the struggle between utilizers and preservationists in the postwar era. The Bureau of Land Management and the Forest Service administered 258 million acres of western range, issuing grazing permits to thousands of cattle raisers. But by the 1980s overgrazing had destroyed nearly 10 percent of that range and another 68 percent was rated in only fair to poor condition. "Overgrazing, I think, is much too weak a term," wrote novelist Edward Abbey, and he lambasted cattle as those "ugly, clumsy, shambling, stupid, bawling, bellowing, stinking, fly-covered, shit-smeared, disease-spreading brutes" that "crowd and overcrowd our canyons and valleys and meadows and forests." Environmentalists argued that by charging grazing fees only a quarter of the going rate on private range, the federal government actually subsidized the work of destruction. Yet efforts to charge more caused a storm of controversy. In a difficult market, many small ranchers depended on low federal grazing fees and would be put out of business if they were raised. Environmentalists wanted to preserve the range, but might there not be value in preserving the tradition of small ranching as well? The solution would seem to call for better grazing management, but instead the two sides got caught up in mutual recrimination.[57]

There were other controversies. The Forest Service controlled 191 million acres of

Forest Service officials conduct journalists on a tour of clear-cut and terraced hillsides in the Bitterroot Mountains in Montana. Photograph by Dale Burk, 1979. Stoneydale Press.

forest and range land, 92 percent of it in the West. With wartime production needs and the postwar housing boom, timber companies increasingly turned to the public forests to supply their needs. The harvest from federal lands, which averaged a billion board feet annually before the war, rose to eleven billion board feet by the mid-1960s, 25 percent of all domestic production, and that harvest level continued into the 1990s. Vast areas of clear-cut redwood forest in the Pacific Northwest threatened the viability of wildlife and caused serious erosion, choking streams with mud and silt. Stands of old growth forest—a single giant redwood could produce lumber valued at $100,000—were leveled by high-tech equipment. At the harvest rate of the 1980s all the old growth outside the designated wilderness areas would be gone by 2025. In 1991 a coalition of environmental groups sued the Forest Service, citing environmental laws that mandated provision "for diversity of plant and animal communities" and using as their cause threats to the northern spotted owl, designated an "indicator species" for northwestern forests—a kind of "miner's canary" for the entire ecosystem. They won, and for a time the federal timber harvest was halved, although the Forest Service eventually increased the output by salvaging diseased and damaged trees. But those efforts simply put off the day of reckoning, since even those production levels cannot be sustained. The Forest Service itself estimated that in the long run recreational use of the forests would be both sustainable and more profitable. The country needed to learn to get along on the timber harvest from private forest farms, while logging communities needed federal assistance to convert from an extractive to a recreational economy.[58]

The most contentious environmental issue was water, the fundamental resource of the arid West. There was no doubt that the development of the Columbia and the Colorado had been crucial to the spectacular rise of the West, and following the war the Bureau of Reclamation and the Army Corps of Engineers took on the Missouri, the Rio Grande, and dozens of smaller rivers, transforming their raging waters into a series of placid lakes. They became, as historian Donald Worster put it, "a part of nature that had died and been reborn as money." The most powerful western constituency supporting river development was the surging urban population. Los Angeles had drained the Owens Valley, sucked enough northern water into its reservoirs to top off the Rose Bowl every hour and a half, and drew millions of gallons more from the Colorado. In 1963, after a long court battle, Arizona won a Supreme Court decision that cut California's share of water from the Colorado River. "We insist that water must be shipped to the places where people and industry have located," environmentalist Raymond Dasmann commented soon after. "We could equally well insist that people and industry should locate in the areas where water is available." That made good sense. But things were not as dire as they seemed. The fact was, by the 1970s the West had in place a system of dams, aqueducts, and canals that was sufficient to provide for all anticipated urban needs as long as the cities adopted simple and effective conservation measures.[59]

The big water user was agribusiness, which drank up more than 90 percent of western water for crop irrigation. Corporate farms enjoyed a munificent subsidy from the federal government, paying only a fraction of the real costs while cities shouldered most of the fiscal burden. Water was essential if western agriculture was to sustain its amazing ability to feed America and much of the world. But cheap federal water enabled the production of not only the nation's vegetable and fruit crops—but also cotton, rice, and even alfalfa, crops far better suited to other regions. Western agribusiness grew skilled in evading the legislative provision supposedly limiting federal water to 160-acre farms, finally pressuring Congress into dropping the limitation altogether in the 1980s. "The concept of the family farm, long a sham," as Norris Hundley put it, "could now be declared officially dead."[60]

In 1977 President Jimmy Carter caused a furor when he recommended that the

The Trans-Alaska Pipeline, c. 1985. Alyeska Pipeline Service Company.

federal government suspend most of the outstanding water development projects in the West, arguing that they had grown too expensive. He accurately read the signs. The enormous cost of new dams, the narrow interests they served, and the rising clamor of environmentalists all combined to make huge water projects a thing of the past. The tide was running in the opposite direction. The West needed to overcome its lingering dependence on extractive industry and government subsidy. One indication of the new era was in the Owens Valley. After decades of complaints from residents there, the California legislature passed a law requiring the city of Los Angeles to develop a plan to restore the valley to some semblance of its natural condition. The plan announced in 1998 may require L.A.'s Department of Water and Power to cut the water it takes by as much as 15 percent and devote nearly a quarter of its budget to restoring Owens Lake. The screw turned once again.

In another important development, the federal government ordered new protections for the salmon populations of the Pacific Northwest in 1999. To increase the rate of spawning and thus the sustainability of the species, a massive and expensive program would clean up the waterways, limit logging in the watersheds, and even modify some of the great dams blocking freshwater flows on the Columbia and Snake Rivers. Despite the cost and the trouble, however, most residents of the region seemed to welcome the effort, fearing that the natural beauty of the region was being threatened by unchecked development. "As we work to save the salmon," noted Seattle's mayor, "it may turn out that the salmon saves us."[61]

But the struggle between utilizers and preservationists continued. It was at its starkest in the argument over Alaskan development. "Alaska is our last great frontier," President Truman declared in 1948. "It contains known resources of food, timber, and minerals of great value to the national economy, and may have much greater resources as yet undiscovered."[62] Twenty years later, on the far northern shores of the Arctic Ocean, petroleum engineers discovered one of the largest oil fields in North America, and a consortium of oil companies proposed building a 789-mile pipeline across frozen tundra and monumental mountain ranges to the ice-free port of Valdez on Prince William Sound. Here was a project comparable to the construction of the transcontinental railroad or the building of the L.A. aqueduct. Environmentalists threw down the gauntlet, warning that an oil spill in the fragile arctic environment would be "the greatest environmental disaster of our time." But developers were equally determined. Attempting to block the project, one Alaskan asserted, "makes as much sense to us as an attempt to block Daniel Boone from cutting a trail through Cumberland Gap." After a bitter and prolonged debate, Congress approved the pipeline by a single vote—Vice President Spiro Agnew's tie-breaker. Then in 1989, after a decade of operations, the tanker *Exxon Valdez,* which had just loaded up at Valdez, rammed into a reef and spewed eleven million gallons of crude into Prince William Sound. The thick goo spread with the current, blackening fifteen hundred miles of shoreline, killing thousands of aquatic animals, and causing damage of unknown proportions. Development had indeed produced disaster.[63]

———

Thus could the frontier myth be destructive. In our time the frontier myth may have become an anachronism, no more than a refuge for extreme conservatism. But it need not be so. The frontier story must be reformulated and refit to the realities of our history, providing us with a national myth not only to "match our mountains" but to match the needs and aspirations of a new century. The Indians offer heroic examples of resistance, survival, and adaptation. No story in our history is more inspiring than their tale of persistence and resurgence. Although today we may approach the pioneer story with ambivalence, that intellectual experience can be illuminating. The settlers stood alone against authority but also welcomed the assistance of an active government. They went their own way, but they also believed in community. They were not only male but female, not only white and Anglo but German, African, Mexican, and Asian. The frontier is our common past, and it binds us all together, like a continental warming blanket. The frontier is also our common future. The struggle to build a humane and equitable society out of the legacies of colonialism continues, and we must continue struggling to resolve the dilemmas of development. The frontier remains, as Willa Cather expressed it, our "road of destiny." It will not cease to color our next century.[64]

Carl Abbott, *The Metropolitan Frontier: Cities in the Modern American West* (1993)

Edward Buscombe, ed., *The BFI Companion to the Western* (1988)

Peter A. Coates, *The Trans-Alaska Pipeline Controversy: Technology, Conservation, and the Frontier* (1991)

Mike Davis, *City of Quartz: Excavating the Future in Los Angeles* (1990)

Richard Griswold del Castillo and Richard A. Garcia, *César Chávez: A Triumph of Spirit* (1995)

David G. Gutiérrez, *Walls and Mirrors: Mexican Americans, Mexican Immigrants, and the Politics of Ethnicity* (1995)

Samuel P. Hays, *Beauty, Health, and Permanence: Environmental Politics in the United States, 1955–1985* (1987)

Greg Hise, *Magnetic Los Angeles: Planning the Twentieth-Century Metropolis* (1997)

Gerald Horne, *Fire This Time: The Watts Uprising and the 1960s* (1995)

Kenneth T. Jackson, *Crabgrass Frontier: The Suburbanization of the United States* (1985)

Gretchen Lemke-Santangelo, *Abiding Courage: African American Migrant Women and the East Bay Community* (1996)

J. Fred MacDonald, *Who Shot the Sheriff? The Rise and Fall of the Television Western* (1987)

Peter Matthiessen, *In the Spirit of Crazy Horse* (1983)

Gerald D. Nash, *The American West Transformed: The Impact of the Second World War* (1985)

Victor G. and Brett de Bary Nee, *Longtime Californ': A Documentary Study of an American Chinatown* (1973)

Joan Weibel-Orlando, *Indian Country, L.A.: Maintaining Ethnic Community in Complex Society* (1991)

Donald Worster, *Rivers of Empire: Water, Aridity, and the Growth of the American West* (1985)

Notes

Introduction: Dreams and Homelands

1 Woodrow Wilson, "The Proper Perspective of American History," *Forum* 19 (July 1895): 544–59.

2 Loren Baritz, "The Idea of the West," *American Historical Review* 66 (1961): 619.

3 Samuel Eliot Morrison, *Admiral of the Ocean Sea: A Life of Christopher Columbus* (Boston, 1942), 556.

4 Baritz, "Idea of the West," 621.

5 "Emergence Song," *The Portable North American Indian Reader,* edited by Frederick W. Turner III (New York, 1974), 239.

6 James Axtell, *After Columbus: Essays in the Ethnohistory of Colonial North America* (New York, 1988), 142.

7 Carl Ortwin Sauer, *Sixteenth Century North America: The Land and the People as Seen by the Europeans* (Berkeley, Calif., 1971), 203.

8 Axtell, *After Columbus,* 141.

9 Leland C. Wyman, ed., *Blessingway* (Tucson, Ariz., 1970), 32.

10 John Mack Faragher, ed., *Rereading Frederick Jackson Turner: "The Significance of the Frontier in American History" and Other Essays* (New Haven, 1999), 31–60.

11 Sarah Deutsch, *No Separate Refuge: Culture, Class, and Gender on an Anglo-Hispanic Frontier in the American Southwest, 1880–1940* (New York, 1987), 3.

12 Malcolm J. Rohrbough, *The Trans-Appalachian Frontier: People, Societies, and Institutions, 1775–1850* (New York, 1978), 396; Robert G. Athearn, *The Mythic West in Twentieth-Century America* (Lawrence, Kans., 1986), 15; Walter Nugent, "Where Is the American West? Report on a Survey," *Montana The Magazine of Western History* 42 (Summer 1992): 13; Carey McWilliams, *Southern California Country: An Island on the Land* (New York, 1946), 313.

Chapter 1: A New World Begins

1 *The Journal of Christopher Columbus,* translated by Cecil Jane (London, 1950), 57.

2 *Journal of Columbus,* 101–2.

3 *Journal of Columbus,* 194; Crióbal Colón, *Textos y documentos completos,* edited by Consuelo Varela (Madrid, 1982), 302; Francisco López de Gómara, *La conquista de México,* edited by José Luis Rojas (Madrid, 1987), 87.

4 Peter Martyr, *De Orbe Novo,* translated by F. A. MacNutt, 2 vols. (London, 1912), 1:400; Bernal Díaz, *The Conquest of New Spain,* translated by J. M. Cohen (New York, 1963), 33.

5 Hugh Thomas, *Conquest: Montezuma, Cortés, and the Fall of Old Mexico* (New York, 1993), 153; Ronald Sanders, *Lost Tribes and Promised Lands: The Origins of American Racism* (Boston, 1978), 139.

6 Salvador de Madariaga, *Hernán Cortés: Conqueror of Mexico* (Coral Gables, Fla., 1942), 103; Thomas, *Conquest,* 455.

7 Miguel Léon-Portilla, ed., *The Broken Spears: The Aztec Account of the Conquest of Mexico* (Boston, 1962), 17.

8 Miguel Léon-Portilla, *Precolombian Literatures of Mexico* (Norman, Okla., 1969), 87.

9 John Bierhorst, *Four Masterworks of American Indian Literature* (New York, 1974), 37.

10 Thomas, *Conquest,* 193; Léon-Portilla, *Broken Spears,* 23.

11 Léon-Portilla, *Broken Spears,* 51–52.

12 Diaz, *Conquest of New Spain,* 87.

13 Thomas, *Conquest,* 433.

14 Léon-Portilla, *Broken Spears,* 29; Diaz, *Conquest of New Spain,* 214.

15 Thomas, *Conquest,* 301.

16 Diaz, *Conquest of New Spain,* 264.

17 Léon-Portilla, *Broken Spears,* 74–77.

18 Léon-Portilla, *Broken Spears,* 77–79.

19 Léon-Portilla, *Broken Spears,* 84–85.

20 Ronald Wright, *Stolen Continents: The Americas Through Indian Eyes Since 1492* (Boston, 1992), 145; Diaz, *Conquest of New Spain,* 405.

21 Miguel Léon-Portilla, ed., *Coloquios y doctrina cristiana con que los doce frailes de S. Fransisco . . . convertieran a los Indios* (Mexico City, 1986), 96–97.

22 Bartolomé de las Casas, *In Defense of the Indians,* edited by Stafford Poole (DeKalb, Ill., 1974), 201–2.

23 Francisco Guerra, *The Pre-Columbian Mind* (London, 1971), 45–46.

24 Guerra, *Pre-Columbian Mind,* 55.

25 Las Casas, *In Defense of the Indians,* 237.

26 Thomas, *Conquest,* 547.

27 Las Casas, *In Defense of the Indians,* 237.

28 Thomas, *Conquest,* 74.

29 Miguel Rivera, ed., *Chilam Balam de Chumayel* (Madrid, 1986), 72.

30 Nicolás Sánchez-Albornoz, *The Population of Latin America: A History,* translated by W. A. R. Richardson (Berkeley, Calif., 1974), 76.

31 Steven Mintz, ed., *Native American Voices: A History and Anthology* (St. James, N.Y., 1995), 51; David J. Weber, *The Spanish Frontier in North America* (New Haven, 1992), 51.

32 Herbert E. Bolton, *The Spanish Borderlands* (New Haven, 1921), 148–49.

33 Carl Ortwin Sauer, *Sixteenth Century North America: The Land and the People as Seen by Europeans* (Berkeley, Calif., 1971), 131.

34 Ramón Gutiérrez, *When Jesus Came, the Corn Mothers Went Away: Marriage, Sexuality, and Power in New Mexico, 1500–1816* (Stanford, Calif., 1991), 53.

35 Gutiérrez, *When Jesus Came,* 15, 12.

36 Gutiérrez, *When Jesus Came,* 15.

37 Gutiérrez, *When Jesus Came*, 89, 76.

38 Gutiérrez, *When Jesus Came*, 73–74.

39 Gutiérrez, *When Jesus Came*, 114.

40 Tom Lea, *The King Ranch*, 2 vols. (Boston, 1957), 1:112.

41 Quintard Taylor, *In Search of the Racial Frontier: African Americans in the American West, 1528–1990* (New York, 1998), 36.

42 Charles W. Hackett, ed., *Historical Documents Relating to New Mexico . . .*, 3 vols. (Washington, D.C., 1923–37), 1:435.

Chapter 2: Contest of Cultures

1 Colin G. Calloway, ed., *The World Turned Upside Down: Indian Voices from Early America* (Boston, 1994), 34.

2 Carl Ortwin Sauer, *Sixteenth Century North America: The Land and the People as Seen by the Europeans* (Berkeley, Calif., 1971), 59–60.

3 John Bartlett Brebner, *Explorers of North America, 1492–1806* (New York, 1955), 90.

4 Sauer, *Sixteenth Century North America*, 88.

5 Sauer, *Sixteenth Century North America*, 88.

6 Daniel Richter, *The Ordeal of the Longhouse: The Peoples of the Iroquois League in the Era of European Colonization* (Chapel Hill, N.C., 1992), 43; Steven Mintz, ed., *Native American Voices: A History and Anthology* (St. James, N.Y., 1995), 58.

7 Sauer, *Sixteenth Century North America*, 80, 88.

8 Sauer, *Sixteenth Century North America*, 88; Clyde A. Milner II, Carol A. O'Connor, and Martha Sandweiss, eds., *The Oxford History of the American West* (New York, 1994), 80.

9 Walter O'Meara, *Daughters of the Country: The Women of the Fur Traders and Mountain Men* (New York, 1968), 70.

10 O'Meara, *Daughters of the Country*, 140, 28.

11 Olive Dickason, "From 'One Nation' in the Northeast to 'New Nation' in the Northwest: A Look at the Emergence of the Métis," *American Indian Culture and Research Journal* 6 (1982): 7; Jennifer Brown, *Strangers in Blood: Fur Trade Company Families in Indian Country* (Vancouver, B.C., 1980), 65.

12 Reuben Gold Thwaites, ed., *The Jesuit Relations and Allied Documents, 1610–1791*, 73 vols. (Cleveland, Ohio, 1896–1901), 5:113.

13 James Axtell, *The Invasion Within: The Contest of Cultures in Colonial North America* (New York, 1985), 123.

14 Mintz, ed., *Native American Voices*, 52–53.

15 Axtell, *Invasion Within*, 107; W. J. Eccles, *The Canadian Frontier, 1534–1760*, rev. ed. (Albuquerque, N.Mex., 1986), 48.

16 Richard Haklyut, *Discourse on Western Planting*, facsimile ed. (London, 1993), 123.

17 Thomas Hariot, *A Briefe and True Report of the New Found Land of Virginia*, facsimile ed. (New York, 1972), 28.

18 David J. Weber, *The Spanish Frontier in North America* (New Haven, 1992), 72.

19 Samuel G. Drake, *Biography and History of the Indians of North America* (Boston, 1841), 352.

20 Drake, *Biography and History*, 353.

21 Wilcomb E. Washburn, ed., *The Indian and the White Man* (New York, 1964), 22.

22 *Two Broadsides Against Tobacco* (London, 1676), 6.

23 Neal Salisbury, *Manitou and Providence: Indians, Europeans, and the Making of New England, 1500–1643* (New York, 1982), 103; Francis Jennings, *The Invasion of America: Indians, Colonialism, and the Cant of Conquest* (New York, 1975), 24.

24 William Cronon, *Changes in the Land: Indians, Colonists, and the Ecology of New England* (New York, 1983), 88.

25 Salisbury, *Manitou and Providence*, 124; Alfred A. Cave, *The Pequot War* (Amherst, Mass., 1996), 46.

26 Cronon, *Changes in the Land*, 56.

27 Salisbury, *Manitou and Providence*, 191.

28 Jennings, *Invasion of America*, 223; Cave, *Pequot War*, 151.

29 Edmund S. Morgan, *Roger Williams: The Church and the State* (New York, 1967), 122.

30 Richard Drinnan, *Facing West: The Metaphysics of Indian-Hating and Empire-Building* (Minneapolis, Minn., 1980), 50.

31 Jill Lapore, *The Name of War: King Philip's War and the Origins of American Identity* (New York, 1998), 94.

32 Cave, *Pequot War*, 169–70.

33 Richard Slotkin, *Regeneration Through Violence: The Mythology of the American Frontier, 1600–1860* (Middletown, Conn., 1973), 101.

34 Slotkin, *Regeneration Through Violence*, 98, 86, 99.

35 Slotkin, *Regeneration Through Violence*, 173.

36 Richter, *Ordeal of the Longhouse*, 61.

37 Richter, *Ordeal of the Longhouse*, 118.

38 Richter, *Ordeal of the Longhouse*, 153, 155.

39 Richter, *Ordeal of the Longhouse*, 184.

Chapter 3: The Struggle of Empires

1 Terry G. Jordan and Matti Kaups, *The American Backwoods Frontier: An Ethnic and Ecological Interpretation* (Baltimore, 1989), 2.

2 Albert Cook Myers, ed., *Narratives of Early Pennsylvania, West New Jersey, and Delaware, 1630–1701* (New York, 1912), 235.

3 Benjamin Franklin, *Writings* (New York, 1987), 367; Thomas Malthus, *Essay on the Principle of Population*, edited by Michael P. Fogarty, 2 vols. (New York, 1958), 1:305–6.

4 Jacqueline Peterson, "Prelude to Red River: A Social Portrait of the Great Lakes Métis," *Ethnohistory* 25 (1978): 41–67.

5 W. J. Eccles, *The Canadian Frontier, 1534–1760*, rev. ed. (Albuquerque, N.Mex., 1974), 132.

6 Daniel K. Richter, *The Ordeal of the Longhouse: The Peoples of the Iroquois League in the Era of European Colonization* (Chapel Hill, N.C., 1992), 155, 206.

7 Ronald Wright, *Stolen Continents: The New World Through Indian Eyes Since 1492* (Boston, 1992), 130, emphasis added.

8 Richter, *Ordeal of the Longhouse*, 268.

9 Richter, *Ordeal of the Longhouse*, 263, 266.

10 Francis Jennings, *Empire of Fortune: Crowns, Colonies, and Tribes in the Seven Years War in America* (New York, 1988), 402; Richard White, *The Middle Ground: Indians, Empires, and Republics in the Great Lakes Region, 1650–1815* (Cambridge, 1991), 248–49.

11 Jennings, *Empire of Fortune*, 420.

12 White, *Middle Ground*, 269.

13 Gregory Dowd, *A Spirited Resistance: The North American Indian Struggle for Unity, 1745–1815* (Baltimore, 1992), 34–35.

14 Jennings, *Empire of Fortune,* 447.

15 Jennings, *Empire of Fortune,* 463n.

16 Wilbur R. Jacobs, ed., *The Paxton Riots and the Frontier Theory* (Chicago, 1967), 27.

17 Jacobs, ed., *Paxton Riots,* 15–17.

18 Richard Maxwell Brown, *South Carolina Regulators* (Cambridge, Mass., 1963), 135.

19 Hector Chevigny, *Russian America: The Great Alaskan Venture, 1741–1867* (Portland, Oreg., 1965), 50.

20 Philip L. Fradkin, *The Seven States of California: A Natural and Human History* (New York, 1995), 276; George H. Phillips, *The Enduring Struggle: Indians in California* (San Francisco, 1981), 24.

21 Carey McWilliams, *Southern California Country* (New York, 1946), 29; *The First French Expedition to California: Lapérouse in 1786* (Los Angeles, Calif., 1959), 75.

22 Phillips, *Enduring Struggle,* 24–25.

23 Robert Heizer and Mary Anne Whipple, eds., *California Indians, a Source Book* (Berkeley, Calif., 1951), 76.

Chapter 4: The Land and Its Markers

1 John Mack Faragher, *Daniel Boone: The Life and Legend of an American Pioneer* (New York, 1992), 142.

2 Colin G. Calloway, *The World Turned Upside Down: Indian Voices from Early America* (Boston, 1994), 149.

3 Isabel Thompson Kelsay, *Joseph Brant, 1743–1807: Man of Two Worlds* (Syracuse, N.Y., 1984), 172.

4 Ronald Wright, *Stolen Continents: The Americas Through Indian Eyes Since 1492* (Boston, 1992), 139.

5 Richard W. Van Alstyne, *The Rising American Empire* (New York, 1960), 72.

6 Wright, *Stolen Continents,* 227.

7 Henry Steele Commager, *Documents of American History* (New York, 1949), 120.

8 Commager, *Documents of American History,* 123; Clyde A. Milner II, Carol A. O'Connor, and Martha Sandweiss, eds., *The Oxford History of the American West* (New York, 1994), 124.

9 Thomas Jefferson, *Writings* (New York, 1984), 752–53.

10 Henry Nash Smith, *Virgin Land: The American West as Symbol and Myth* (1950; Cambridge, Mass., 1969), 127–28, 206.

11 R. Douglas Hurt, *The Ohio Frontier: Crucible of the Old Northwest, 1720–1830* (Bloomington, Ind., 1996), 147.

12 Faragher, *Daniel Boone,* 70.

13 Faragher, *Daniel Boone,* 5, 60, 326; Harriet Louisa Arnow, *Seed Time on the Cumberland* (New York, 1960), 169.

14 Richard White, *The Middle Ground: Indians, Empires, and Republics in the Great Lakes Region, 1650–1815* (Cambridge, 1991), 441.

15 Donald A. Grinde, Jr., and Bruce E. Johansen, *Exemplar of Liberty: Native America and the Evolution of Democracy* (Los Angeles, 1991), 96–98. Bruce E. Johansen, *Forgotten Founders: Benjamin Franklin, the Iroquois, and the Rationale for the American Revolution* (Ipswich, Mass., 1982), 75–76.

16 White, *Middle Ground,* 441.

17 Francis Paul Prucha, ed., *Documents of United States Indian Policy* (Lincoln, Nebr., 1990), 10.

18 Prucha, ed., *Documents of United States Indian Policy,* 14.

19 Wilcomb E. Washburn, ed., *The American Indian and the United States, A Documentary History,* 4 vols. (Westport, Conn., 1973), 4:2286–90.

20 Prucha, ed., *Documents of United States Indian Policy,* 19; Philip Weeks, ed., *The American Indian Experience* (Arlington Heights, Ill., 1988), 104.

21 Milner, O'Connor, and Sandweiss, eds., *Oxford History of the American West,* 125–26.

22 Faragher, *Daniel Boone,* 250.

23 Anthony F. C. Wallace, *The Death and Rebirth of the Seneca* (New York, 1969), 197.

24 Wallace, *Death and Rebirth of the Seneca,* 203, 206.

25 R. David Edmunds, *The Shawnee Prophet* (Lincoln, Nebr., 1983), 47.

26 Alvin M. Josephy, Jr., *The Patriot Chiefs: A Chronicle of Indian Resistance* (New York, 1969), 159; Robert V. Remini, *Andrew Jackson and the Course of American Empire, 1767–1821* (New York, 1977), 188.

27 R. David Edmunds, *Tecumseh and the Quest for Indian Leadership* (Boston, 1984), 131, 145; John Mack Faragher, *Sugar Creek: Life on the Illinois Prairie* (New Haven, 1986), 31–32.

28 William G. McLoughlin, *Cherokee Renascence in the New Republic* (Princeton, N.J., 1986).

29 Wright, *Stolen Continents,* 210.

30 Wright, *Stolen Continents,* 213.

31 McLoughlin, *Cherokee Renascence,* 353.

32 Wright, *Stolen Continents,* 217.

Chapter 5: The Fur Trade

1 William Appleman Williams, *The Roots of the Modern American Empire: A Study of the Growth and Shaping of Social Consciousness in a Marketplace Society* (New York, 1969), 50; Lloyd C. Gardner, Walter F. LaFeber, and Thomas J. McCormick, *Creation of the American Empire* (Chicago, 1973), 31; Richard W. Van Alstyne, *The Rising American Empire* (New York, 1960), 78, 69.

2 Bernard De Voto, *The Journals of Lewis and Clark* (Boston, 1953), xxiv; James D. Richardson, ed., *A Compilation of the Messages and Papers of the Presidents, 1789–1904,* 10 vols. (New York, 1904), 1:323; Joseph J. Ellis, *American Sphinx: The Character of Thomas Jefferson* (New York, 1997), 212.

3 Francis Wrigley Hirst, *The Life and Letters of Thomas Jefferson* (New York, 1926), 390.

4 E. Wilson Lyon, *Louisiana in French Diplomacy* (Norman, Okla., 1934), 225–26.

5 De Voto, *Journals of Lewis and Clark,* 60, 256–57.

6 De Voto, *Journals of Lewis and Clark,* 70.

7 De Voto, *Journals of Lewis and Clark,* 90.

8 De Voto, *Journals of Lewis and Clark,* lii.

9 Bernard De Voto, *The Course of Empire* (Boston, 1952), 527.

10 Jean Barman, *The West Beyond the West: A History of British Columbia,* rev. ed. (Toronto, Ont., 1996), 36.

11 Van Alstyne, *Rising American Empire,* 93.

12 Michael Allen, *Western Rivermen, 1763–1861: Ohio and Mississippi Boatmen and the Myth of*

the *Alligator Horse* (Baton Rouge, La., 1990), 12–13; Don Berry, *A Majority of Scoundrels* (New York, 1961), 22.

13 Dale Lowell Morgan, *Jedediah Smith and His Maps of the American West* (San Francisco, 1954), 310, 312.

14 William H. Goetzmann, "The Mountain Man as Jacksonian Man," *American Quarterly* 15 (1963): 402–15.

15 David J. Weber, *The Taos Trappers: The Fur Trade in the Far Southwest, 1540–1846* (Norman, Okla., 1971), 23, 35.

16 De Voto, *Course of Empire*, 103.

17 William Clark, "1830 Report on the Fur Trade," *Oregon Historical Quarterly* 48 (March 1947): 31.

18 Weber, *Taos Trappers*, 207.

Chapter 6: From Texas to Oregon

1 Martin Ridge and Ray Allen Billington, *America's Frontier Story: A Documentary History of Westward Expansion* (New York, 1969), 235.

2 Donald Jackson, ed., *The Journals of Zebulon Montgomery Pike*, 2 vols. (Norman, Okla., 1966), 1:390.

3 Jackson, ed., *Journals of Pike*, 1:442.

4 Edwin James, *Account of an Expedition from Pittsburgh to the Rocky Mountains*, 3 vols. (Philadelphia, 1823), 2:361; Walter Prescott Webb, *The Great Plains* (New York, 1931), 152.

5 Jackson, ed., *Journals of Pike*, 2:78–82.

6 Stephen F. Austin, *The Austin Papers*, in *American Historical Association, Annual Report, 1919*, 2 vols. (Washington, D.C., 1924), 2:784.

7 Quintard Taylor, *In Search of the Racial Frontier: African Americans in the American West, 1528–1990* (New York, 1998), 37.

8 William C. Davis, *A Way Through the Wilderness: The Natchez Trace and the Civilization of the Southern Frontier* (New York, 1995), 73–74.

9 Michael Tadman, *Speculators and Slaves: Masters, Traders, and Slaves in the Old South* (Madison, Wis., 1989), 45; Peter Kolchin, *American Slavery, 1619–1877* (New York, 1993), 97–98; U. B. Phillips, *American Negro Slavery* (1918; Baton Rouge, La., 1966), 180–81.

10 Joan E. Cashin, *A Family Venture: Men and Women on the Southern Frontier* (New York, 1991), 103, 114.

11 William C. Davis, *Three Roads to the Alamo: The Lives and Fortunes of David Crockett, James Bowie, and William Barret Travis* (New York, 1998), 166–67.

12 Thomas D. Clark and John D. W. Guice, *The Old Southwest, 1795–1830: Frontiers in Conflict* (1985; Norman, Okla., 1996), 183; Ray Allen Billington, *Westward Expansion*, 3d ed. (New York, 1967), 322–23.

13 David J. Weber, ed., *The Mexican Frontier, 1821–1846: The American Southwest Under Mexico* (Albuquerque, N.Mex., 1982), 125, 128; Susan Calafate Boyle, *Los Capitalistas: Hispano Merchants and the Santa Fe Trade* (Albuquerque, N.Mex., 1997), 66.

14 Donald Day, *Big Country: Texas* (New York, 1947), 10.

15 David J. Weber, ed., *Troubles in Texas, 1832: A Tejano Viewpoint from San Antonio* (Dallas, Tex., 1983), 20, 11.

16 Susan Prendergast Schoelwer, *Alamo Images: Changing Perceptions of a Texas Experience* (Dallas, Tex., 1985), 108.

17 Davis, *Three Roads to the Alamo,* 440.

18 Taylor, *In Search of the Racial Frontier,* 42.

19 Paul D. Lack, *The Texas Revolutionary Experience: A Political and Social History, 1835–1836* (College Station, Tex., 1992), 168, 185.

20 Jesús F. De la Teja, ed., *A Revolution Remembered: The Memoirs and Selected Correspondence of Juan N. Seguín* (Austin, Tex., 1991), 90, 97; Schoelwer, *Alamo Images,* 131–32; David Montejano, *Anglos and Mexicans in the Making of Texas, 1836–1986* (Austin, Tex., 1987), 29.

21 Taylor, *In Search of the Racial Frontier,* 44.

22 David Williams, *The Georgia Gold Rush: Twenty-Niners, Cherokees, and Gold Fever* (Columbia, Ga., 1993), 50.

23 Francis Paul Prucha, *The Great Father: The United States Government and the American Indians,* 2 vols. (Lincoln, Nebr., 1984), 1:189.

24 Ronald Wright, *Stolen Continents: The Americas Through Indian Eyes Since 1492* (Boston, 1992), 219.

25 Francis Paul Prucha, ed., *Documents of United States Indian Policy* (Lincoln, Nebr., 1990), 61.

26 Wright, *Stolen Continents,* 219; Prucha, *Great Father,* 1:212.

27 Wright, *Stolen Continents,* 220.

28 William G. McLoughlin, *Cherokees and Missionaries, 1789–1839* (New Haven, 1984), 135–36.

29 Grant Forman, ed., *A Traveler in Indian Territory: The Journal of Ethan Allen Hitchcock* (Norman, Okla., 1865), 7; Lydia Smith, "Factionalism and the Coming of the Civil War in the Cherokee Nation" (senior essay, Yale University, 1998), 23.

30 Prucha, *Great Father,* 1:232.

31 Donald Jackson, ed., *Black Hawk: An Autobiography* (Urbana, Ill., 1964), 101, 108.

32 Arrell Morgan Gibson, "The Great Plains as a Colonization Zone for Eastern Indians," in Frederick Leubke, ed., *Ethnicity on the Great Plains* (Lincoln, Nebr., 1980), 21.

33 Charles Francis Adams, ed., *Memoirs of John Quincy Adams,* 12 vols. (Philadelphia, 1874–77), 4:438–39.

34 Adams, ed., *Memoirs of John Quincy Adams,* 6:157.

35 Fred W. Powell, ed., *Hall J. Kelley on Oregon* (Princeton, N.J., 1932), 60.

36 Julie Roy Jeffrey, *Converting the West: A Biography of Narcissa Whitman* (Norman, Okla., 1991), 53.

37 Jeffrey, *Converting the West,* 108, 164, 168.

38 Jeffrey, *Converting the West,* 182.

39 Martin Ridge and Ray Allen Billington, eds., *America's Frontier Story: A Documentary History of Westward Expansion* (New York, 1969), 453–54.

40 Ridge and Billington, eds., *America's Frontier Story,* 453; John Mack Faragher, *Women and Men on the Overland Trail* (New Haven, 1979), 163–64.

41 William H. Goetzmann and Glyndwr Williams, *The Atlas of North American Exploration: From the Norse Voyages to the Race to the Pole* (New York, 1992), 159.

42 D. Michael Quinn, ed., *The New Mormon History: Revisionist Essays on the Past* (Salt Lake City, Utah, 1992), 61, 67.

43 George H. Phillips, *The Enduring Struggle: Indians in California* (San Francisco, 1981), 30.

44 Phillips, *Enduring Struggle,* 38.

45 Albert L. Hurtado, *Indian Survival on the California Frontier* (New Haven, 1988), 52.

46 Kenneth N. Owens, ed., *John Sutter and a Wider West* (Lincoln, Nebr., 1994), 33.

47 Thomas Bailey, *A Diplomatic History of the American People*, 8th ed. (New York, 1969), 226, 228.

Chapter 7: War and Destiny

1 Frederick Merk, *Manifest Destiny and Mission in American History: A Reinterpretation* (New York, 1963), 28, 25n.

2 Merk, *Manifest Destiny*, 27–28; *Democratic Review* 17 (July–August 1845): 5–10.

3 Merk, *Manifest Destiny*, 29.

4 Thomas Jefferson, *Writings* (New York, 1984), 1434; William MacDonald, ed., *Select Documents Illustrative of the History of the United States, 1776–1861* (New York, 1905), 224.

5 Sean Wilentz, ed., *Major Problems in the Early Republic, 1787–1848* (Lexington, Mass., 1992), 379; David Donald, *Lincoln* (New York, 1995), 123.

6 Merk, *Manifest Destiny*, 31–32.

7 Richard B. Morris, ed., *Encyclopedia of American History: Bicentennial Edition* (New York, 1976), 225.

8 Richard White, *"It's Your Misfortune and None of My Own": A New History of the American West* (Norman, Okla., 1991), 78.

9 MacDonald, *Select Documents*, 352.

10 Cecil Robinson, ed., *The View from Chapultepec: Mexican Writers on the Mexican-American War* (Tucson, Ariz., 1989), 67; Wilentz, ed., *Major Problems*, 543; William S. McFeely, *Grant: A Biography* (New York, 1981), 30.

11 Wilentz, ed., *Major Problems*, 532–33.

12 Leonard Pitt, *The Decline of the Californios: A Social History of the Spanish-Speaking Californians, 1846–1890* (Berkeley, Calif., 1970), 28–30.

13 Albert L. Hurtado, *Indian Survival on the California Frontier* (New Haven, 1988), 82.

14 Carey McWilliams, *North from Mexico: The Spanish-Speaking People of the United States* (1948; New York, 1968), 102–3.

15 Merk, *Manifest Destiny*, 28.

16 Merk, *Manifest Destiny*, 162.

17 Wilentz, ed., *Major Problems*, 538; John H. Schroeder, *Mr. Polk's War: American Opposition and Dissent, 1846–1848* (Madison, Wis., 1973), 116, 144.

18 David G. Gutiérrez, *Walls and Mirrors: Mexican Americans, Mexican Immigrants, and the Politics of Ethnicity* (Berkeley, Calif., 1995), 17.

19 MacDonald, *Select Documents*, 369.

20 Josiah Royce, *California: A Study of American Character* (Boston, 1886), 472.

21 Howard R. Lamar, ed., *The New Encyclopedia of the American West* (New Haven, 1998), 748; Carlos G. Vélez-Ibáñez, *Border Visions: Mexican Cultures in the Southwest United States* (Tucson, Ariz., 1996), 292; James W. Parins, *John Rollin Ridge: His Life and Works* (Lincoln, Nebr., 1991), 99.

22 W. Eugene Hollon, *Frontier Violence: Another Look* (New York, 1974), 41.

23 Jerry D. Thompson, ed., *Juan Cortina and the Texas-Mexico Frontier, 1859–1877* (El Paso, Tex., 1994), 15, 25, 27; Américo Paredes, *A Texas-Mexican Cancionero: Folksongs of the Lower Border* (Austin, Tex., 1976), 48.

24 Sarah Deutsch, *No Separate Refuge: Culture, Class, and Gender on an Anglo-Hispanic Frontier in the American Southwest, 1880–1940* (New York, 1987), 25.

25 White, *"It's Your Misfortune and None of My Own,"* 58–59.

26 Prucha, *Great Father,* 1:346.

27 Robert A. Trennert, Jr., *Alternative to Extinction: Federal Indian Policy and the Beginnings of the Reservation System, 1846–51* (Philadelphia, 1975), 190.

28 Lloyd C. Gardner, Walter F. LaFeber, and Thomas J. McCormick, *Creation of the American Empire: U.S. Diplomatic History* (Chicago, 1973), 138.

29 James M. McPherson, *Battle Cry of Freedom: The Civil War Era* (New York, 1988), 55.

30 McPherson, *Battle Cry of Freedom,* 145, 147, 149, 152.

31 Michael A. Morrison, *Slavery and the American West: The Eclipse of Manifest Destiny and the Coming of the Civil War* (Chapel Hill, N.C., 1997), 276; Donald S. Frazier, *Blood and Treasure: Confederate Empire in the Southwest* (College Station, Tex., 1995), 5.

32 Alvin M. Josephy, Jr., *The Civil War in the American West* (New York, 1991), 80.

33 McPherson, *Battle Cry of Freedom,* 292, 784, 786.

34 McLoughlin, *After the Trail of Tears,* 210–11.

35 Michael A. Belleîles, "The Origins of Gun Culture in the United States, 1760–1865," *Journal of American History* 83 (September 1996): 455.

36 Frederick W. Turner III., ed., *The Portable North American Indian Reader* (New York, 1974), 517; Prucha, *Great Father,* 1:336.

37 Prucha, *Great Father,* 1:324, 352.

38 Prucha, *Great Father,* 1:439; Gary Clayton Anderson and Alan R. Woolworth, eds., *Through Dakota Eyes: Narrative Accounts of the Minnesota Indian War of 1862* (St. Paul, Minn., 1988), 23.

39 Josephy, *Civil War in the West,* 109; Robert M. Utley, *The Indian Frontier of the American West, 1846–1890* (Albuquerque, N.Mex., 1984), 76.

40 Josephy, *Civil War in the West,* 277.

41 Josephy, *Civil War in the West,* 286.

42 Patrick M. Mendoza, *Song of Sorrow: Massacre at Sand Creek* (Denver, Colo., 1993), 86.

43 Dee Brown, *Bury My Heart at Wounded Knee: An Indian History of the American West* (New York, 1970), 79; Utley, *Indian Frontier,* 91.

44 George E. Hyde, *Life of George Bent: Written from His Letters,* edited by Savoie Lottinville (Norman, Okla., 1968), 147.

45 Josephy, *Civil War in the West,* 307; David Svaldi, *Sand Creek and the Rhetoric of Extermination: A Case Study in Indian-White Relations* (New York, 1989), 291.

46 Hyde, *Life of Bent,* 152.

47 Hyde, *Life of Bent,* 155.

48 Sol Lewis, ed., *The Sand Creek Massacre: A Documentary History* (New York, 1973), 280; Richard Drinnon, *Facing West: The Metaphysics of Indian-Hating and Empire-Building* (Minneapolis, Minn., 1980), 539.

49 Hyde, *Life of Bent,* 181.

Chapter 8: Mining Frontiers

1 Malcolm J. Rohrbough, *Days of Gold: The California Gold Rush and the American Nation* (Berkeley, Calif., 1997), 7; Peter Mode, ed., *Source Book and Bibliographical Guide to American Church History* (Menasha, Wis., 1921), 434.

2 Peter Martyr, *De Orbe Novo,* translated by Francis A. MacNutt, 2 vols. (London, 1912), 2:52.

3 Rodman Wilson Paul, *Mining Frontiers of the Far West, 1848–1880* (New York, 1963), 13.

4 David Williams, *The Georgia Gold Rush: Twenty-Niners, Cherokees, and Gold Fever* (Columbia, Mo., 1993), 97.

5 Kenneth N. Owens, ed., *John Sutter and a Wider West* (Lincoln, Nebr., 1994), 21; Paul, *Mining Frontiers of the Far West*, 13–14; Cheryl Elizabeth Wright, "Life in Topsy-Turvy-Dom: Women and Men in Gold Rush California" (senior thesis, Mount Holyoke College, 1987), 3.

6 Rohrbough, *Days of Gold*, 137–38.

7 Rohrbough, *Days of Gold*, 128; Jean-Nicholas Perlot, *Gold Seeker: Adventures of a Belgian Argonaut During the Gold Rush Years*, edited by Howard R. Lamar (New Haven, 1985), 96–97.

8 Norris Hundley, Jr., *The Great Thirst: Californians and Water, 1770s–1990s* (Berkeley, Calif., 1992), 75; Rohrbough, *Days of Gold*, 197.

9 Richard Hofstadter, *The Progressive Historians: Turner, Beard, and Parrington* (New York, 1968), 160.

10 Eric Hobsbawm, *The Age of Capital, 1848–1875* (New York, 1975), 62.

11 Louisa Amelia Knapp Clappe, *The Shirley Letters from the California Mines, 1851–1852*, edited by Carl I. Wheat (New York, 1949), 121.

12 Bayard Taylor, *Eldorado, or Adventures in the Path of Empire* (New York, 1949), 110, 189.

13 Robert F. Heizer and Alan F. Almquist, *The Other Californians: Prejudice and Discrimination Under Spain, Mexico, and the United States to 1920* (Berkeley, Calif., 1971), 98.

14 Richard H. Peterson, *Manifest Destiny in the Mines: A Cultural Interpretation of Anti-Mexican Nativism in California, 1848–1853* (San Francisco, 1975), 9, 33, 38.

15 Peterson, *Manifest Destiny in the Mines*, 36; Edwin Beilharz and Carlos Lopez, eds., *We Were Forty-Niners!: Chilean Accounts of the California Gold Rush* (Pasadena, Calif., 1976), 119–20.

16 Peterson, *Manifest Destiny in the Mines*, 61–62.

17 Ronald Takaki, *A Different Mirror: A History of Multicultural America* (New York, 1993), 193.

18 Elizabeth Jameson and Susan Armitage, eds., *Writing the Range: Race, Class, and Culture in the Women's West* (Norman, Okla., 1997), 267.

19 Takaki, *Different Mirror*, 195.

20 Heizer and Almquist, *Other Californians*, 230, 233.

21 Liping Zhu, *A Chinaman's Chance: The Chinese on the Rocky Mountain Mining Frontier* (Niwot, Colo., 1997), 150.

22 Zhu, *Chinaman's Chance*, 135, 144; Zhu, "'A Chinaman's Chance' on the Rocky Mountain Mining Frontier," *Montana The Magazine of Western History* 45 (Autumn–Winter 1995): 50.

23 Owens, ed., *John Sutter*, 67; Rohrbough, *Days of Gold*, 13; Albert L. Hurtado, *Indian Survival on the California Frontier* (New Haven, 1988), 104, 112.

24 Heizer and Almquist, *Other Californians*, 86.

25 Heizer and Almquist, *Other Californians*, 28.

26 George Harwood Phillips, *Indians and Indian Agents: The Origins of the Reservation System in California, 1849–1852* (Norman, Okla., 1997), 167; Heizer and Almquist, *Other Californians*, 26.

27 Hurtado, *Indian Survival*, 131; Heizer and Almquist, *Other Californians*, 40, 46, 57.

28 James C. Olson, *Red Cloud and the Sioux Problem* (Lincoln, Nebr., 1965), 32.

29 Wilcomb E. Washburn, ed., *The American Indian and the United States: A Documentary History*, 4 vols. (Westport, Conn., 1973), 4:2519.

30 Robert M. Utley, *The Lance and the Shield: The Life and Times of Sitting Bull* (New York, 1993), 73.

31 Utley, *Lance and Shield,* 116.

32 Louise Barnett, *Touched by Fire: The Life, Death, and Mythic Afterlife of George Armstrong Custer* (New York, 1996), 346.

33 Peter Nabokov, ed., *Native American Testimony: A Chronicle of Indian-White Relations from Prophecy to the Present, 1492–1992* (New York, 1991), 108.

34 Nabokov, ed., *Native American Testimony,* 108.

35 Wayne Moquin, ed., *Great Documents in American Indian History* (New York, 1973), 228; Utley, *Lance and Shield,* 179.

36 Arrell Morgan Gibson, *The American Indian: Prehistory to the Present* (Lexington, Mass., 1980), 392.

37 Peter A. Coates, *The Trans-Alaska Pipeline Controversy: Technology, Conservation, and the Frontier* (Bethlehem, Pa., 1991), 30–31; David Wharton, *The Alaska Gold Rush* (Bloomington, Ind., 1972), 3.

38 Wayne Suttles, ed., *Northwest Coast,* volume 7 of *Handbook of North American Indians* (Washington, D.C., 1990), 124.

39 Suttles, ed., *Northwest Coast,* 149.

40 Harry Ritter, *Alaska's History: The People, Land, and Events of the North Country* (Anchorage, Alaska, 1993), 120–21.

41 Douglas Fetherling, *The Gold Crusades: A Social History of Gold Rushes, 1849–1929* (Toronto, Ont., 1988), 1, 5; Taylor, *Eldorado,* 10.

42 Philip L. Fradkin, *The Seven States of California: A Natural and Human History* (New York, 1995), 88.

43 J. S. Holliday, *The World Rushed In: The California Gold Rush Experience* (New York, 1981), 336, 369–70, 376, 381, 383n.

44 Holliday, *World Rushed In,* 336, 369; JoAnn Levy, *They Saw the Elephant: Women in the California Gold Rush* (Hamden, Conn., 1990), 174.

45 Annette Kolodny, *The Land Before Her: Fantasy and Experience of the American Frontiers, 1630–1860* (Chapel Hill, N.C., 1984), 234–35; Linda Peavy and Ursula Smith, *Women in Waiting in the Westward Movement: Life on the Home Frontier* (Norman, Okla., 1994), 41; Peavy and Smith, *The Gold Rush Widows of Little Falls: A Story Drawn from the Letters of Pamelia and James Fergus* (St. Paul, Minn., 1990), 72, 196.

46 John Mack Faragher, *Women and Men on the Overland Trail* (New Haven, 1979), 165, 167.

47 Faragher, *Women and Men,* 159; Levy, *They Saw the Elephant,* 91, 102.

48 Melanie J. Mayer, *Klondike Women: True Tales of the 1897–98 Gold Rush* (Athens, Ohio, 1989), 6.

49 Rohrbough, *Days of Gold,* 96; Julie Roy Jeffrey, *Frontier Women: The Trans-Mississippi West, 1840–1880* (New York, 1979), 127; Ruth B. Moynihan, Susan Armitage, and Christiane Fischer Dichamp, eds., *So Much to Be Done: Women Settlers on the Mining and Ranching Frontier* (Lincoln, Nebr., 1990), 29.

50 Mary Murphy, *Mining Cultures: Men, Women, and Leisure in Butte, 1914–41* (Urbana, Ill., 1997), 77; Wright, "Life in Topsy-Turvy-Dom," 36; Moynihan, Armitage, and Dichamp, eds., *So Much to Be Done,* 167; Paula Petrik, *No Step Backward: Women and Family on the Rocky Mountain Mining Frontier, Helena, Montana 1865–1900* (Helena, Mont., 1987), 55.

51 Marion Goldman, *Gold Diggers and Silver Miners: Prostitution and Social Life on the Comstock Lode* (Ann Arbor, Mich., 1981), 112.

52 Francis Parkman, *The Oregon Trail* (New York, 1946), 23.

53 Charles Howard Shinn, *Mining Camps: A Study in American Frontier Government* (1885; New York, 1948), 140; Josiah Royce, *California, from the Conquest in 1846 to the Second Vigilance Committee in San Francisco: A Study of American Character* (1886; New York, 1948), 283.

54 Dwight Clarke, *William Tecumseh Sherman: Gold Rush Banker* (San Francisco, 1969), 226.

55 Robert Glass Cleland, *The Cattle on a Thousand Hills: Southern California, 1850–1870* (San Marino, Calif., 1941).

56 Richard White, *"It's Your Misfortune and None of My Own": A History of the American West* (Norman, Okla., 1991), 260.

57 Frederick Hale, ed., *Danes in North America* (Seattle, Wash., 1984), 73–74.

58 Mark Wyman, *Hard Rock Epic: Western Miners and the Industrial Revolution, 1860–1910* (Berkeley, Calif., 1979), 153.

59 William D. Haywood, *Bill Haywood's Book* (New York, 1929), 30–31.

60 Howard R. Lamar, ed., *The New Encyclopedia of the American West* (New Haven, 1998), 546; Carlos Arnaldo Schwantes, *Hard Traveling: A Portrait of Work Life in the New Northwest* (Lincoln, Nebr., 1994), 45.

Chapter 9: The Power of the Road

1 Bret Harte, "What Was It the Engines Said," *Poetical Works* (Boston, 1912), 304; William Cronon, *Nature's Metropolis: Chicago and the Great West* (New York, 1991), 72.

2 Carlos Arnaldo Schwantes, *Hard Traveling: A Portrait of Work Life in the New Northwest* (Lincoln, Nebr., 1994), 6; Richard O'Connor, *Iron Wheels and Broken Men: The Railroad Barons and the Plunder of the West* (New York, 1973), 112.

3 Michael Fellman, *Inside War: The Guerrilla Conflict in Missouri During the American Civil War* (New York, 1989), 75; Oscar Osburn Winther, *The Transportation Frontier: Trans-Mississippi West, 1865–1890* (New York, 1964), 15.

4 Julia D. Harrison, *Métis: People Between Two Worlds* (Vancouver, B.C., 1985), 22; Rhoda R. Gilman, Carolyn Gilman, and Deborah M. Stultz, *The Red River Trails: Oxcart Routes Between St. Paul and the Selkirk Settlement, 1820–1870* (St. Paul, Minn., 1970), 86.

5 Mark Twain, *Roughing It* (1872; New York, 1913), 42.

6 Henry Nash Smith, *Virgin Land: The American West as Symbol and Myth* (1950; Cambridge, Mass., 1973), 27–29; Jan Willem Schulte Nordholt, *The Myth of the West: America as the Last Empire* (Grand Rapids, Mich., 1995), 14.

7 Smith, *Virgin Land*, 42–43.

8 Dee Brown, *Hear That Lonesome Whistle Blow: Railroads in the West* (New York, 1977), 34, 36.

9 James M. McPherson, *Battle Cry of Freedom: The Civil War Era* (New York, 1988), 452; Charles and Mary Beard, *The Rise of American Civilization*, 2 vols. (New York, 1927), 2:53; Robert P. Sharkey in David T. Gilchrist and W. David Lewis, eds., *Economic Change in the Civil War Era* (Greenville, Del., 1965), 27.

10 John Hoyt Williams, *A Great and Shining Road: The Epic Story of the Transcontinental Railroad* (New York, 1988), 78.

11 Stuart Daggett, *Chapters in the History of the Southern Pacific* (New York, 1920), 81.

12 Williams, *Great and Shining Road,* 40.

13 Williams, *Great and Shining Road,* 275.

14 Brown, *Hear That Lonesome Whistle Blow,* 45.

15 Brown, *Hear That Lonesome Whistle Blow,* 17.

16 Lamar, ed., *New Encyclopedia of the American West,* 37; John L. Phillips, "Crédit Mobilier," *American Heritage* 20 (April 1969): 109.

17 Daggett, *Chapters on the History of the Southern Pacific,* 211; David Lavender, *The Great Persuader* (New York, 1970), 128–29.

18 Lamar, ed., *New Encyclopedia of the American West,* 37; Williams, *Great and Shining Road,* 122.

19 Williams, *Great and Shining Road,* 96; Ronald Takaki, *A Different Mirror: A History of Multicultural America* (New York, 1993), 197; William F. Deverell, *Railroad Crossing: Californians and the Railroad, 1850–1910* (Berkeley, Calif., 1994), 184.

20 Williams, *Great and Shining Road,* 99.

21 Brown, *Hear That Lonesome Whistle Blow,* 112.

22 Williams, *Great and Shining Road,* 266; Brown, *Hear That Lonesome Whistle Blow,* 132.

23 Deverell, *Railroad Crossing,* 15.

24 Brown, *Hear That Lonesome Whistle Blow,* 143, 227; O'Connor, *Iron Wheels and Broken Men,* 102.

25 Williams, *Great and Shining Road,* 209.

26 Deverell, *Railroad Crossing,* 19.

27 Robert Utley, *The Lance and the Shield: The Life and Times of Sitting Bull* (New York, 1993), 107; Remi Nadeau, *Fort Laramie and the Sioux Indians* (Englewood Cliffs, N.J., 1967), 250.

28 David Roberts, *Once They Moved Like the Wind: Cochise, Geronimo, and the Apache Wars* (New York, 1993), 111, 113, 260, 263, 300.

29 William Robbins, *Colony and Empire: The Capitalist Transformation of the American West* (Lawrence, Kans., 1994), 88.

30 Schwantes, *Hard Traveling,* 32.

31 Francis Paul Prucha, *The Great Father: The United States Government and the American Indians,* 2 vols. (Lincoln, Nebr., 1984), 1:594.

32 Brown, *Hear That Lonesome Whistle Blow,* 272; Deverell, *Railroad Crossing,* 32.

33 William A. Settle, Jr., *Jesse James Was His Name* (Lincoln, Nebr., 1966), 90, 173; Nat Love, *The Life and Adventures of Nat Love* (New York, 1968), 156.

34 Deverell, *Railroad Crossing,* 39.

35 Deverell, *Railroad Crossing,* 49–50; Lucy E. Salyer, *Laws Harsh as Tigers: Chinese Immigrants and the Shaping of Modern Immigration Law* (Chapel Hill, N.C., 1995), 7.

36 Philip L. Fradkin, *The Seven States of California: A Natural and Human History* (New York, 1995), 369.

37 Deverell, *Railroad Crossing,* 74–75, 80–81.

38 Lavender, *Great Persuader,* 268.

Chapter 10: Open Range

1 E. C. "Teddy Blue" Abbott and Helena Huntington Smith, *We Pointed Them North: Recollections of a Cowpuncher,* edited by Ron Tyler (1939; Chicago, 1991), 105, 334.

2   John A. Lomax and Alan Lomax, eds., *Folk Song U.S.A.* (New York, 1947), 262; Alan Lomax, *The Folk Songs of North America in the English Language* (New York, 1960), 357.

3   Terry G. Jordan, *North American Cattle-Ranching Frontiers: Origins, Diffusion, and Differentiation* (Albuquerque, N.Mex., 1993), 84.

4   Richard W. Slatta, *The Cowboy Encyclopedia* (Santa Barbara, Calif., 1994), 227.

5   Robert R. Dykstra, *Cattle Towns* (New York, 1968), 77.

6   David Dary, *Cowboy Culture: A Saga of Five Centuries* (New York, 1981), 196; James Emmit McCauley, *A Stove-Up Cowboy's Story* (Dallas, Tex., 1943), 72.

7   Dykstra, *Cattle Towns*, 83; Abbott, *We Pointed Them North*, 71–72.

8   Dary, *Cowboy Culture*, 217, 220; William W. Savage, Jr., ed., *Cowboy Life: Reconstructing an American Myth* (Norman, Okla., 1975), 158.

9   Edmond de Mandat-Grancey, *Cowboys and Colonels: Narrative of a Journey Across the Prairie and over the Black Hills of Dakota*, translated by William Conn (Philadelphia, 1963), 279; Roger D. McGrath, *Gunfighters, Highwaymen, and Vigilantes: Violence on the Frontier* (Berkeley, Calif., 1984), 255; Jordan, *North American Cattle-Ranching Frontiers*, 74.

10 Reuben B. Mullins, *Pulling Leather: Being the Early Recollections of a Cowboy on the Wyoming Range, 1884–1889*, edited by Jan Roush and Lawrence Clayton (Glendo, Wyo., 1988), 92.

11 Abbott, *We Pointed Them North*, 63; Américo Paredes, *A Texas-Mexican Cancionero* (Urbana, Ill., 1976), 55; Tomás Rivera, "The Great Plains as Refuge in Chicano Literature," in Virginia Faulkner with Frederick C. Luebke, eds., *Vision and Refuge: Essays on the Literature of the Great Plains* (Lincoln, Nebr., 1982), 133.

12 Samuel D. Herring, "From Shirt-Tailer to Bulldogger: The Experience of the Black Cowboy" (senior essay, Yale College, 1994), 30; Richard W. Slatta, *Cowboys of the Americas* (New Haven, 1990), 26.

13 David Shirk quoted in Will Hale, *Twenty-Four Years a Cowboy and Ranchman in Southern Texas and Old Mexico* (Norman, Okla., 1959), xxiii; Savage, *Cowboy Life*, 94; Jordan, *North American Cattle-Ranching Frontiers*, 108; Richard White, *The Roots of Dependency: Subsistence, Environment, and Social Change Among the Choctaws, Pawnees, and Navajos* (Lincoln, Nebr., 1983), 103.

14 Guy Logsdon, *"The Whorehouse Bells Were Ringing" and Other Songs Cowboys Sing* (Urbana, Ill., 1989), 76, 298, 300; Logsdon, "The Cowboy's Bawdy Music," in *The Cowboy: Six-Shooters, Songs, and Sex,* edited by Charles W. Harris and Buck Rainey (Norman, Okla., 1976), 134; Jordan, *North American Cattle-Ranching Frontiers*, 76; Edgar Breecher Bronson, *Reminiscences of a Ranchman* (Chicago, 1910), 270–71; Kinsey quoted in Jonathan Katz, *Gay American Hsitory: Lesbians and Gay Men in the U.S.A.* (New York, 1992), 512.

15 Abbott, *We Pointed Them North*, 172; Slatta, *Cowboys of the Americas,* 53.

16 Mrs. A. Burks, "A Woman Trail Driver," in J. Marvin Hunter, ed., *The Trail Drivers of Texas,* 2 vols. (San Antonio, Tex., 1920–23), 1:275, 277.

17 Sandra Myers, *Westering Women and the Frontier Experience, 1800–1915* (Albuquerque, N.Mex., 1982), 260; Ruth B. Moynihan, Susan Armitage, and Christiane Fischer Dichamp, eds., *So Much to Be Done: Women Settlers on the Mining and Ranching Frontier* (Lincoln, Nebr., 1990), 270, 271, 281–82.

18 Myers, *Westering Women*, 242, 260; Charles Wallace, *The Cattle Queen of Montana: A Story of the Personal Experience of Mrs. Nat Collins* (St. James, Minn., 1894).

19 Darliss Miller, "The Women of Lincoln County, 1860–1900," in Elizabeth Jameson and

Susan Armitage, eds., *Writing the Range: Race, Class, and Culture in the Women's West* (Norman, Okla., 1997), 154; Teresa Jordan, *Cowgirls: Women of the American West, an Oral History* (New York, 1982), 24.

20 Jordan, *Cowgirls,* 229; Myers, *Westering Women,* 261.

21 David D. Smits, "The Frontier Army and the Destruction of the Buffalo, 1865–1883," *Western Historical Quarterly* 25 (1994): 337.

22 Smits, "Destruction of the Buffalo," 328.

23 Smits, "Destruction of the Buffalo," 330, 337; John G. Neihardt, *Black Elk Speaks* (New York, 1961), 181.

24 Lomax and Lomax, eds., *Folk Song U.S.A.,* 263.

25 Jordan, *North American Cattle-Ranching Frontiers,* 221.

26 Abbott, *We Trailed Them North,* 227–28.

27 Slatta, *Cowboys of the Americas,* 101–2, 124.

28 J. C. Mutchler, "Ranching in the Magdalena, New Mexico Area: The Last Cowboys" (M.A. thesis, University of New Mexico, 1992), 22.

29 Don D. Walker, *Clio's Cowboys: Studies in the Historiography of the Cattle Trade* (Lincoln, Nebr., 1981), 131–32; Slatta, *Cowboy Encyclopedia,* 361–62; Slatta, *Cowboys of the Americas,* 98.

30 Darliss Miller, "The Women of Lincoln County, 1860–1900," in Elizabeth Jameson and Susan Armitage, eds., *Writing the Range: Race, Class, and Culture in the Women's West* (Norman, Okla., 1997), 162; Robert J. Rosenbaum, *Mexicano Resistance in the Southwest: "The Sacred Right of Self-Preservation"* (Austin, Tex., 1981), 96–97.

31 Rosenbaum, *Mexicano Resistance,* 119.

32 Slatta, *Cowboys of the Americas,* 185; Dykstra, *Cattle Towns,* 302; Dary, *Cowboy Culture,* 308.

33 Slatta, *Cowboys of the Americas,* 187; Walter Baron von Richthofen, *Cattle-Raising on the Plains of North America* (1885; Norman, Okla., 1964), 99.

34 Mullins, *Pulling Leather,* 121; Abbott, *We Pointed Them North,* xlviii.

35 Daniel G. Moore, *Log of a Twentieth-Century Cowboy* (Tucson, Ariz., 1965), 169.

36 Mullins, *Pulling Leather,* 80; Mutchler, "Ranching in Magdalena," 24.

37 Sydney B. Spiegel, "Who Were the Cattle Rustlers? A Look at the Johnson County War in Wyoming," *Social Studies* 49 (1958): 225.

38 Abbott, *We Pointed Them North,* 325, 330.

Chapter 11: The Safety Valve

1 Roy M. Robbins, *Our Landed Heritage: The Public Domain, 1776–1936* (Lincoln, Nebr., 1962), 209.

2 Roy M. Robbins, "Preemption—A Frontier Triumph," *Mississippi Valley Historical Review* 18 (1931): 334, 339.

3 Howard R. Lamar, ed., *The New Encyclopedia of the American West* (New Haven, 1998), 998; Robbins, *Our Landed Heritage,* 109, 115.

4 Robbins, *Our Landed Heritage,* 102, 108; Henry Nash Smith, *Virgin Land: The American West as Symbol and Myth* (Cambridge, Mass., 1950), 202.

5 Oscar Micheaux, *The Conquest: The Story of a Negro Pioneer* (Lincoln, Nebr., 1913), 47.

6 Smith, *Virgin Land,* 173; Robbins, *Our Landed Heritage,* 177, 182.

7 Henry Steele Commager, ed., *Documents of American History* (New York, 1949), 410; Gerald D. Nash, *Creating the West: Historical Interpretations, 1890–1990* (Albuquerque, N.Mex., 1991), 41–42.

8 Fred A. Shannon, *The Farmer's Last Frontier: Agriculture, 1860–1897* (New York, 1945), 74–75.

9 Shannon, *Farmer's Last Frontier,* 62.

10 Smith, *Virgin Land,* 192.

11 Shannon, *Farmer's Last Frontier,* 357, 359 (emphasis added).

12 Rudyard Kipling, *The Writings in Prose and Verse of Rudyard Kipling,* 36 vols. (New York, 1899), 28:25–26.

13 Smith, *Virgin Land,* 178.

14 Walter Prescott Webb, *The Great Plains* (New York, 1931), 8–9, 347; Walter Ebeling, *The Fruited Plain: The Story of American Agriculture* (Berkeley, Calif., 1979), 277.

15 Smith, *Virgin Land,* 179, 180, 182.

16 *New York Times,* May 28, 1996.

17 Scott G. McNall, *The Road to Rebellion: Class Formation and Kansas Populism, 1865–1900* (Chicago, 1988), 68–69; Webb, *Great Plains,* 320.

18 Paula Nelson, *After the West Was Won: Homesteaders and Town-Builders in Western South Dakota, 1900–1917* (Iowa City, Iowa, 1986), 124.

19 Webb, *Great Plains,* 374.

20 John A. Lomax and Alan Lomax, eds., *Folk Song U.S.A.* (New York, 1947), 302–3.

21 Mari Sandoz, *Old Jules* (Lincoln, Nebr., 1962), 99.

22 Nelson, *After the West Was Won,* 27–28, 35.

23 Nelson, *After the West Was Won,* 50.

24 Sherry L. Smith, "Single Women Homesteaders: The Perplexing Case of Elinore Pruitt Stewart," *Western Historical Quarterly* 22 (May 1991): 164.

25 Elinore Pruitt Stewart, *Letters of a Woman Homesteader* (1914; Boston, 1982), 215; Dee Garceau, *The Important Things of Life: Women, Work, and Family in Sweetwater County, Wyoming, 1880–1929* (Lincoln, Nebr., 1997), 122.

26 Smith, "Single Women Homesteaders," 167.

27 Smith, "Single Women Homesteaders," 176.

28 Sigmund Diamond, ed., *The Nation Transformed: The Creation of an Industrial Society* (New York, 1963), 363–64.

29 Scott G. McNall, *The Road to Rebellion: Class Formation and Kansas Populism, 1865–1900* (Chicago, 1988), 75; Jeffrey Ostler, *Prairie Populism: The Fate of Agrarian Radicalism in Kansas, Nebraska, and Iowa, 1880–1892* (Topeka, Kans., 1993), 18.

30 Ostler, *Prairie Populism,* 127; Peter H. Argersinger, *The Limits of Agrarian Radicalism: Western Populism and American Politics* (Topeka, Kans., 1995), 71.

31 McNall, *Road to Rebellion,* 214–15; Argersinger, *Limits of Agrarian Radicalism,* 75; Edward T. James, "More Corn, Less Hell? A Knights of Labor Glimpse of Mary Elizabeth Lease," *Labor History* 16 (1975): 408–9.

32 Susan Armitage and Elizabeth Jameson, eds., *The Women's West* (Norman, Okla., 1987), 157.

33 Michael Kazin, *The Populist Persuasion: An American History* (New York, 1995), 44.

34 Smith, *Virgin Land,* 31.

35 William Appleman Williams, *The Roots of the Modern American Empire* (New York, 1969), 301.

36 Williams, *Roots of the Modern American Empire,* 355.

37 Carlos Arnaldo Schwantes, *Hard Traveling: A Portrait of Work Life in the New Northwest* (Lincoln, Nebr., 1994), 47.

38 Cecilia Danysk, *Hired Hands: Labour and the Development of Prairie Agriculture, 1880–1930* (Don Mills, Ont., 1995), 113; Schwantes, *Hard Traveling,* 25.

39 Danysk, *Hired Hands,* 108.

40 Danysk, *Hired Hands,* 108, 166; Schwantes, *Hard Traveling,* 197.

41 Sucheng Chan, *This Bittersweet Soil: The Chinese in California Agriculture, 1860–1910* (Berkeley, Calif., 1986), 104; Ronald Takaki, *A Different Mirror: A History of Multicultural America* (New York, 1993), 199.

42 Don Mitchell, *The Lie of the Land: Migrant Workers and the California Landscape* (Minneapolis, Minn., 1996), 71.

43 Mitchell, *Lie of the Land,* 88.

Chapter 12: A Search for Community

1 John Mack Faragher, *Sugar Creek: Life on the Illinois Prairie* (New Haven, 1986), 50.

2 Faragher, *Sugar Creek,* 51–52.

3 Faragher, *Sugar Creek,* 52.

4 Hamlin Garland, *Son of the Middle Border* (New York, 1920), 402.

5 Sandra Myres, *Westering Women and the Frontier Experience, 1800–1915* (Albuquerque, N.Mex., 1982), 168; Sigmund Diamond, ed., *The Nation Transformed: The Creation of an Industrial Society* (New York, 1963), 333; Everett Dick, *The Sod-House Frontier, 1854–1890* (New York, 1937), 235.

6 Kathleen Underwood, "Schoolmarms on the Upper Missouri," *Great Plains Quarterly* 11 (1991): 228.

7 David L. Kimbrough, *Reverend Joseph Tarkington, Methodist Circuit* (Knoxville, Tenn., 1997), 17; Faragher, *Sugar Creek,* 160–61; T. Scott Miyakawa, *Protestants and Pioneers: Individualism and Conformity on the American Frontier* (Chicago, 1964), 201.

8 Faragher, *Sugar Creek,* 163.

9 Miyakawa, *Protestants and Pioneers,* 44.

10 Dean L. May, *Three Frontiers: Family, Land, and Society in the American West, 1850–1900* (Cambridge, 1994), 197.

11 Sarah Barringer Gordon, "'The Liberty of Self-Degradation': Polygamy, Woman Suffrage, and Consent in Nineteenth-Century America," *Journal of American History* 83 (1996): 823, 828.

12 V. Jacque Voegeli, *Free But Not Equal: The Midwest and the Negro During the Civil War* (Chicago, 1967), 173.

13 Eric Foner, *Reconstruction: America's Unfinished Revolution, 1863–1877* (New York, 1988), 600; Nell Irvin Painter, *Exodusters: Black Migration to Kansas After Reconstruction* (New York, 1977), 158–59, 231.

14 Jane Anne Staw and Mary Swander, *Parsnips in the Snow: Talks with Midwestern Gardeners* (Iowa City, Iowa, 1990), 195, 201.

15 Nupur Chaudhuri, "'We All Seem Like Brothers and Sisters': The African-American Community in Manhattan, Kansas, 1865–1940," *Kansas History* 14 (1991–92): 276, 277, 282, 283.

16 Gordon Parks, *Voices in the Mirror: An Autobiography* (New York, 1990), 1–2, 4.

17 Parks, *Voices in the Mirror,* 331–333; *Gordon Parks: A Poet and His Camera* (London, 1969), n.p.

18 Mark H. Brown, "The Joseph Myth," *Montana The Magazine of Western History* 22 (Winter 1971): 15.

19 Francis Paul Prucha, *The Great Father: The United States Government and the American Indians,* 2 vols. (Lincoln, Nebr., 1984), 1:439.

20 Prucha, *Great Father,* 1:528–29.

21 Philip Weeks, ed., *The American Indian Experience: A Profile, 1524 to the Present* (Arlington Heights, Ill., 1988), 196.

22 Prucha, *Great Father,* 2:647; John H. Bodley, *Victims of Progress* (Palo Alto, Calif., 1982), 107, 117; Fred Hoxie, ed., *Indians in American History: An Introduction* (Arlington Heights, Ill., 1988), 247–48.

23 Prucha, *Great Father,* 2:691.

24 Bodley, *Victims of Progress,* 108.

25 Prucha, *Great Father,* 1:324, 441.

26 Weeks, ed., *American Indian Experience,* 196.

27 Prucha, *Great Father* 2:629, 666.

28 Weeks, ed., *American Indian Experience,* 170.

29 James Mooney, *The Ghost-Dance Religion and the Sioux Outbreak of 1890* (1896; Chicago, 1965), 307; Prucha, *Great Father,* 2:728.

30 Virgil J. Vogel, *This Country Was Ours: A Documentary History of the American Indian* (New York, 1972), 182.

31 John G. Neihardt, *Black Elk Speaks: Being the Life Story of a Holy Man of the Oglala Sioux* (1932; New York, 1972), 217, 220–21.

32 Mari Sandoz, *Old Jules* (Lincoln, Nebr., 1962), 130–31.

33 Frederick C. Luebke, ed., *European Immigrants in the American West: Community Histories* (Albuquerque, N.Mex., 1998), vii; Luebke, ed., *Ethnicity on the Great Plains* (Lincoln, Nebr., 1980), 7; Dorothy Burton Skardahl, *The Divided Heart: Scandinavian Immigrant Experience Through Literary Sources* (Lincoln, Nebr., 1974), 239.

34 Luebke, ed., *European Immigrants in the American West,* 61.

35 Steven Hahn and Jonathan Prude, eds., *The Countryside in the Age of Capitalist Transformation: Essays in the Social History of Rural America* (Chapel Hill, N.C., 1985), 276.

36 Robert C. Ostergren, *A Community Transplanted: The Trans-Atlantic Experience of a Swedish Immigrant Settlement in the Upper Middle West, 1835–1915* (Madison, Wis., 1988), 230.

37 D. Michol Polson, "The Swedes in Grantsville, Utah, 1860–1900," *Utah Historical Quarterly* 56 (Summer 1988): 218.

38 Jon Gjerde, *The Minds of the West: Ethnocultural Evolution in the Rural Middle West, 1830–1917* (Chapel Hill, N.C., 1997), 8.

39 April R. Schultz, *Ethnicity on Parade: Inventing the Norwegian American Through Celebration* (Amherst, Mass., 1994), 29, 37, 58, 117.

40 Sinclair Lewis, *Main Street* (New York, 1920), 26–27.

41 Zona Gale, *Friendship Village* (New York, 1908), 6.

42 Frederick Russel Burnham, *Scouting on Two Continents* (Los Angeles, Calif., 1934), 10.

43 Vachel Linsday, *Collected Poems* (New York, 1927).

44 Sucheng Chan, *This Bittersweet Soil: The Chinese in California Agriculture, 1860–1910* (Berkeley, Calif., 1986), 185–87, 335.

45 Chan, *This Bittersweet Soil,* 332; Lucy E. Salyer, *Laws Harsh as Tigers: Chinese Immigrants and the Shaping of Modern Immigration Law* (Chapel Hill, N.C., 1995), 15; Carey McWilliams, *Southern California Country: An Island on the Land* (New York, 1946), 90.

46 Brian Masaru Hayashi, *"For the Sake of Our Japanese Brethren": Assimilation, Nationalism, and Protestantism Among the Japanese of Los Angeles, 1895–1942* (Stanford, Calif., 1995), 31–32; Carey McWilliams, *Factories in the Field: The Story of Migratory Farm Labor in California* (Boston, 1939).

47 Sayler, *Laws Harsh as Tigers,* 126; Gilbert G. Gonzáles, *Labor and Community: Mexican Citrus Worker Villages in a Southern California County, 1900–1950* (Urbana, Ill., 1994), 49.

48 David Mas Masumoto, *Country Voices: The Oral History of a Japanese American Family Farm Community* (Del Rey, Calif., 1987), 12; Valerie J. Matsumoto, *Farming the Home Place: A Japanese American Community in California, 1919–1982* (Ithaca, N.Y., 1993), 31–32.

49 Masumoto, *Country Voices,* 2.

50 Matsumoto, *Farming the Home Place,* 52–53; Masumoto, *Country Voices,* 65–66, 97, 124.

51 Thomas H. Heuterman, *The Burning Horse: Japanese-American Experience in the Yakima Valley, 1920–1942* (Cheney, Wash., 1995), 26, 49, 98; Philip L. Fradkin, *The Seven States of California: A Natural and Human History* (New York, 1995), 145.

52 Masakazu Iwata, *Planted in Good Soil: The History of the Issei in United States Agriculture,* 2 vols. (New York, 1992), 2:686–87, 690–91.

53 David Montejano, *Anglos and Mexicans in the Making of Texas, 1836–1986* (Austin, Tex., 1987), 112.

54 Montejano, *Anglos and Mexicans,* 127.

55 Mario T. García, *Desert Immigrants: The Mexicans of El Paso, 1880–1920* (New Haven, 1981), 51.

56 Devra Weber, *Dark Sweat, White Gold: California Farm Workers, Cotton, and the New Deal* (Berkeley, Calif., 1994), 61; George Sanchéz, *Becoming Mexican American: Ethnicity, Culture and Identity in Chicano Los Angeles, 1900–1945* (Berkeley, Calif., 1993), 15.

57 David G. Gutiérrez, *Walls and Mirrors: Mexican Americans, Mexican Immigrants, and the Politics of Ethnicity* (Berkeley, Calif., 1995), 49; Don Mitchell, *The Lie of the Land: Migrant Workers and the California Landscape* (Minneapolis, Minn., 1996), 91; Ronald Takaki, *A Different Mirror: A History of Multicultural America* (New York, 1993), 315; Weber, *Dark Sweat, White Gold,* 94.

58 Weber, *Dark Sweat, White Gold,* 74; Mitchell, *Lie of the Land,* 129, 135, 163.

59 Carey McWilliams, *The Education of Carey McWilliams* (New York, 1978), 75.

60 Gonzáles, *Labor and Community,* 189.

Chapter 13: The Urban Frontier

1 John Mack Faragher, ed., *Rereading Frederick Jackson Turner: "The Significance of the Frontier in American History" and Other Essays* (New Haven, 1999), 31, 34; Adna F. Weber, *The Growth of Cities in the Nineteenth Century* (New York, 1899), 20, 27.

2 David Hamer, *New Towns in the New World: Images and Perceptions of the Nineteenth-Century Frontier* (New York, 1990), 97, 118, 185.

3 Richard Wade, *The Urban Frontier: The Rise of Western Cities, 1790–1830* (Cambridge, Mass., 1959), 1; Michael Malone, ed., *Historians and the American West* (Lincoln, Nebr., 1983), 324.

4 Wade, *Urban Frontier,* 322.

5 R. Douglas Hurt, *The Ohio Frontier: Crucible of the Old Northwest, 1720–1830* (Bloomington, Ind., 1996), 239.

6 Carl Abbott, *Boosters and Businessmen: Popular Economic Thought and Urban Growth in the Antebellum Middle West* (Westport, Conn., 1981), 45; Hurt, *Ohio Frontier,* 247–48.

7 Timothy R. Mahoney, *River Towns in the Great West: The Structure of Provincial Urbanization in the American Midwest, 1820–1870* (New York, 1990), 124–25.

8 Hamer, *New Towns in the New World,* 182; Charles N. Glaab, "Visions of Metropolis: William Gilpin and Theories of City Growth in the American West," *Wisconsin Magazine of History* 45 (1961): 26.

9 J. Christopher Schnell and Katherine B. Clinton, "The New West: Themes in Nineteenth-Century Urban Promotion, 1815–1880," *Bulletin of the Missouri Historical Society* 30 (January 1974): 77–78.

10 Jeffrey S. Adler, *Yankee Merchants and the Making of the Urban West: The Rise and Fall of Antebellum Saint Louis* (Cambridge, 1991), 56; Schnell and Clinton, "New West," 80.

11 Schnell and Clinton, "New West," 82; Adler, *Yankee Merchants,* 55, 68.

12 Adler, *Yankee Merchants,* 130, 134.

13 William Cronon, *Nature's Metropolis: Chicago and the Great West* (New York, 1991), 297, 299, 309.

14 Cronon, *Nature's Metropolis,* 283, 308.

15 Weber, *Growth of Cities,* 228; Gilbert Stelter, "The City and Westward Expansion: A Western Case Study," *Western Historical Quarterly* 3 (1973): 189.

16 Richard O'Connor, *Iron Wheels and Broken Men: The Railroad Barons and the Plunder of the West* (New York, 1973), 101.

17 Earl Pomeroy, *The Pacific Slope: A History of California, Oregon, Washington, Idaho, Utah, and Nevada* (Seattle, Wash.,1965), 134.

18 Gunther Barth, *Instant Cities: Urbanization and the Rise of San Francisco and Denver* (1975; Albuquerque, N.Mex., 1988), 210.

19 Bascom N. Timmons, *Jesse H. Jones: The Man and the Statesman* (New York, 1956), 81; David G. McComb, *Houston: the Bayou City* (Austin, Tex., 1969), 112, 116–17.

20 Rodman Paul, *Mining Frontiers of the Far West, 1848–1880* (New York, 1963), 86.

21 Pomeroy, *Pacific Slope,* 125.

22 Carey McWilliams, *Southern California Country: An Island on the Land* (New York, 1946), 98, 100.

23 Pomeroy, *Pacific Slope,* 142; McWilliams, *Southern California Country,* 143; Robert M. Fogelson, *The Fragmented Metropolis: Los Angeles, 1850–1930* (Cambridge, Mass., 1967), 67.

24 Raymond Dasmann, *The Destruction of California* (New York, 1966), 129; Fogleson, *Fragmented Metropolis,* 110.

25 Marc Reisner, *Cadillac Desert: The American West and Its Disappearing Water* (New York, 1986), 77.

26 Fogelson, *Fragmented Metropolis,* 85; Kenneth T. Jackson, *Crabgrass Frontier: The Suburbanization of the United States* (New York, 1985), 122.

27 McWilliams, *Southern California Country,* 235.

28 McWilliams, *Southern California Country,* 212, 237; James M. Cain, *The Postman Always Rings Twice* (New York, 1934), 150.

29 David Rieff, *Los Angeles: Capital of the Third World* (New York, 1991), 41.

30 Joanne J. Meyerowitz, *Women Adrift: Independent Wage Earners in Chicago, 1880–1930* (Chicago, 1988), 9; Bengt Ankarloo, "Agriculture and Women's Work: Directions of Change in the West, 1700–1900," *Journal of Family History* 4 (1979): 118.

31 Hamlin Garland, *Main-Traveled Roads* (New York, 1899), 118–19; *The Needs of Farm Women,* U.S. Department of Agriculture Reports, 103–106 (Washington, D.C., 1915), 103:12–14.

32 David Peterson del Mar, *What Trouble I Have Seen: A History of Violence Against Wives* (Cambridge, Mass., 1996), 1, 24, 25, 31; Susan Armitage and Elizabeth Jameson, eds., *The Women's West* (Norman, Okla., 1987), 113.

33 Meyerowitz, *Women Adrift*, 17–18.

34 Meyerowitz, *Women Adrift*, 18; Mary Murphy, *Mining Cultures: Men, Women, and Leisure in Butte, 1914–41* (Urbana, Ill., 1997), 99.

35 Meyerowitz, *Women Adrift*, 107.

36 Meyerowitz, *Women Adrift*, 118.

37 Bradford Luckingham, "Immigrant Life in Emergent San Francisco," *Journal of the West* 12 (1973): 600.

38 William Issel and Robert Cherny, *San Francisco, 1865–1932: Politics, Power, and Urban Development* (Berkeley, Calif., 1986), 206.

39 Pomeroy, *Pacific Slope*, 127; Ronald Takaki, *A Different Mirror: A History of Multicultural America* (New York, 1993), 215.

40 Charles Wollenberg, "*Mendez* v. *Westminster*: Race, Nationality and Segregation in California Schools," *California Historical Quarterly* 53 (1974): 318; Judy Yung, *Unbound Feet: A Social History of Chinese Women in San Francisco* (Berkeley, Calif., 1995), 207; Victor G. and Brett de Bary Nee, *Longtime Californ': A Documentary Study of an American Chinatown* (New York, 1972), 44.

41 Yung, *Unbound Feet*, 49, 129.

42 McWilliams, *Southern California Country*, 160, 232.

43 McWilliams, *Southern California Country*, 135.

44 Fogelson, *Fragmented Metropolis*, 200; Martha Menchaca, *The Mexican Outsiders: A Community History of Marginalization and Discrimination in California* (Austin, Tex., 1995), 53; Mike Davis, *City of Quartz: Excavating the Future in Los Angeles* (New York, 1990), 163.

45 Gerald Horne, *Fire This Time: The Watts Uprising and the 1960s* (Charlottesville, Va., 1995), 26, 27, 373.

46 Horne, *Fire This Time*, 249, 257; Fogelson, *Fragmented Metropolis*, 204.

47 George Sánchez, *Becoming Mexican American: Ethnicity, Culture and Identity in Chicano Los Angeles, 1900–1945* (New York, 1993), 200.

48 Sánchez, *Becoming Mexican American*, 213; Francisco E. Balderrama and Raymond Rodríguez, *Decade of Betrayal: Mexican Repatriation in the 1930s* (Albuquerque, N.Mex., 1995), 56.

49 Balderrama and Rodríguez, *Decade of Betrayal*, 124; David G. Gutiérrez, *Walls and Mirrors: Mexican Americans, Mexican Immigrants, and the Politics of Ethnicity* (Berkeley, Calif., 1995), 73.

50 Sánchez, *Becoming Mexican American*, 141, 144–45, 225.

51 Horne, *Fire This Time*, 257; Sánchez, *Becoming Mexican American*, 253.

52 Harry H. L. Kitano, *Japanese Americans: The Evolution of a Subculture* (Englewood Cliffs, N.J., 1969), 3; Brian Masaru Hayashi, *"For the Sake of Our Japanese Brethren": Assimilation, Nationalism, and Protestantism Among the Japanese of Los Angeles, 1895–1942* (Stanford, Calif., 1995), 41, 136.

53 Monica Sone, *Nisei Daughter* (Boston, 1953), 42; Hayashi, *"For the Sake of Our Japanese Brethren,"* 85, 93.

54 Valerie J. Matsumoto, *Farming the Home Place: A Japanese American Community in California, 1919–1982* (Ithaca, N.Y., 1993), 94; *New York Times*, June 20, 1998.

55 Richard Drinnon, *Keeper of Concentration Camps: Dillon S. Myer and American Racism* (Berkeley, Calif., 1987), vii, 31, 39.

Chapter 14: Plunder and Preservation

1 James Fenimore Cooper, *The Leatherstocking Tales*, 2 vols. (New York, 1985), 1:246–250.

2 Alan Taylor, *William Cooper's Town: Power and Persuasion on the Frontier of the Early American Republic* (New York, 1995), 86.

3 Donald Worster, *An Unsettled Country: Changing Landscapes of the American West* (Albuquerque, N.Mex., 1994), 71.

4 Cooper, *Leatherstocking Tales*, 1:230, 268, 1103.

5 Roy M. Robbins, *Our Landed Heritage: The Public Domain, 1776–1936* (Lincoln, Nebr., 1962), 246.

6 Michael Williams, *Americans and Their Forests: A Historical Geography* (New York, 1988), 409.

7 William Vogt, *The Road to Survival* (New York, 1948).

8 John F. Reiger, *American Sportsmen and the Origins of Conservation*, rev. ed. (1975; Norman, Okla., 1986), 25.

9 Worster, *Unsettled Country*, 76; Howard R. Lamar, ed., *The New Encyclopedia of the American West* (New York, 1998), 118; David M. Wrobel, *The End of American Exceptionalism: Frontier Anxiety from the Old West to the New Deal* (Lawrence, Kans., 1993), 66.

10 Roderick Nash, ed., *American Environmentalism: Readings in Conservation History*, 3d ed. (New York, 1990), 33–35.

11 Joseph M. Petulla, *American Environmental History: The Exploitation and Conservation of Natural Resources* (San Francisco, 1977), 230; Roderick Nash, *Wilderness and the American Mind*, 3d ed. (1967; New Haven, 1982), 107.

12 Nash, *Wilderness and the American Mind*, 110, 111.

13 Nash, *Wilderness and the American Mind*, 113, 114.

14 Nash, *Wilderness and the American Mind*, 126, 128.

15 Richard West Sellars, *Preserving Nature in the National Parks: A History* (New Haven, 1997), 119; Alston Chase, *Playing God in Yellowstone: The Destruction of America's First National Park* (Boston, 1986).

16 Nash, *Wilderness and the American Mind*, 128, 130.

17 Nash, ed., *American Environmentalism*, 60.

18 Nash, ed., *American Environmentalism*, 44; John Perlin, *A Forest Journey: The Role of Wood in the Development of Civilization* (New York, 1989), 361.

19 William G. Robbins, *Hard Times in Paradise: Coos Bay, Oregon, 1850–1986* (Seattle, Wash., 1988), 18, 20.

20 Nash, *Wilderness and the American Mind*, 137.

21 Wrobel, *End of American Exceptionalism*, 96–97.

22 Charles F. Wilkinson, *Crossing the Next Meridian: Land, Water, and the Future of the West* (Washington, D.C., 1992), 128; Samuel P. Hays, *Conservation and the Gospel of Efficiency: The Progressive Conservation Movement, 1890–1920* (Cambridge, Mass., 1959), 1.

23 Nash, *Wilderness and the American Mind*, 128, 135, 138–39.

24 William Robbins, *Lumberjacks and Legislators: Political Economy of the U.S. Lumber Industry, 1890–1941* (College Station, Tex., 1982), 10; Sandy Marvinney, "Theodore Roosevelt, Conservationist," *New York State Conservationist* 50 (June 1996): 77.

25 Marvinney, "Theodore Roosevelt, Conservationist."

26 Timothy Cochrane, "Early Forest Service Rangers' Fire Stories," *Forest and Conservation History* 35 (1991): 18; G. Edward White, *The Eastern Establishment and the Western Experience: The West of Frederic Remington, Theodore Roosevelt, and Owen Wister* (New Haven, 1968), 197.

27 Polly Welts Kaufman, *National Parks and the Woman's Voice: A History* (Albuquerque, N.Mex., 1996), 65.

28 Kaufman, *National Parks and the Woman's Voice,* 80–82.

29 Kaufman, *National Parks and the Woman's Voice,* 87.

30 Wilkinson, *Crossing the Next Meridian,* 20.

31 Wilkinson, *Crossing the Next Meridian,* 246; Donald Worster, *Rivers of Empire: Water, Aridity, and the Growth of the American West* (New York, 1985), 167.

32 *Oxford English Dictionary,* s.v. "Reclamation" (compact edition, 1987).

33 Norris Hundley, Jr., *The Great Thirst: Californians and Water, 1770s-1990s* (Berkeley, Calif., 1992), 153; Philip L. Fradkin, *The Seven States of California: A Natural and Human History* (New York, 1995), 27.

34 John Muir, *The Yosemite* (New York, 1962), 197; Hundley, *Great Thirst,* 172–73, 175; Nash, *American Environmentalism,* 97; Hays, *Conservation and the Gospel of Efficiency,* 194.

35 Donald Worster, *Dust Bowl: The Southern Plains in the 1930s* (New York, 1979), 58; Marsha L. Weisiger, *Land of Plenty: Oklahomans in the Cotton Fields of Arizona, 1933–1942* (Norman, Okla., 1995), 14.

36 John Steinbeck, *The Grapes of Wrath* (New York, 1939), 126.

37 Worster, *Dust Bowl,* 17.

38 Thomas R. Cox et al., *This Well-Wooded Land: Americans and Their Forests from Colonial Times to the Present* (Lincoln, Nebr., 1985), 217; Wrobel, *End of American Exceptionalism,* 135.

39 Worster, *Unsettled Country,* 103; Richard Hofstader, *The Progressive Historians: Turner, Beard, Parrington* (New York, 1969), 90.

40 Jordan A. Schwarz, *The New Dealers: Power Politics in the Age of Roosevelt* (New York, 1993), 298; Robert G. Athearn, *The Mythic West in Twentieth-Century America* (Lawrence, Kans., 1986), 114.

41 Schwarz, *New Dealers,* 256, 299.

42 Joseph Stevens, *Hoover Dam: An American Adventure* (Norman, Okla., 1988), 20.

43 Schwarz, *New Dealers,* 316–17.

44 Philip Weeks, ed., *The American Indian Experience: A Profile: 1524 to the Present* (Arlington Heights, Ill., 1988), 240.

45 Horace M. Kallen, *Culture and Democracy in the United States* (New York, 1924), 116.

46 Francis Paul Prucha, *The Great Father: The United States Government and the American Indians,* 2 vols. (Lincoln, Nebr., 1984), 2:647.

47 Meghan Fraze, "Legislating Divisions: The Failure of the Indian Reorganization Act on Pine Ridge" (senior essay, Yale College, 1997), 15, 20; Kenneth R. Philip, *Indian Self Rule: First-Hand Accounts of Indian-White Relations from Roosevelt to Reagan* (Salt Lake City, Utah, 1986), 54.

48 Peter Iverson, *When Indians Became Cowboys: Native Peoples and Cattle Ranching in the American West* (Norman, Okla., 1994), 119–20, 181.

49 Weeks, ed., *American Indian Experience,* 254.

50 Fraze, "Legislating Divisions," 38.

51 Richard White, *The Roots of Dependency: Subsistence, Environment, and Social Change Among the Choctaws, Pawnees, and Navajos* (Lincoln, Nebr., 1983), 258, 259.

Chapter 15: The Myth of the Frontier

1 John Mack Faragher, *Daniel Boone: The Life and Legend of an American Pioneer* (New York, 1992), 7, 298.

2 Faragher, *Daniel Boone*, 277, 299–300.

3 Faragher, *Daniel Boone*, 300–301; Faragher, "They May Say What They Please: Daniel Boone and the Evidence," *Register of the Kentucky Historical Society* 88 (Autumn 1990): 391.

4 Richard Slotkin, "Myth and the Production of History," in Sacvan Bercovitch and Myra Jehlen, eds., *Ideology and Classic American Literature* (Cambridge, Mass., 1986), 70, 86; Ralph Samuel, ed., *People's History and Socialist Theory* (London, 1981), 228.

5 Faragher, *Daniel Boone*, 331; James Fenimore Cooper, *The Leatherstocking Tales*, 2 vols. (New York, 1985), 1:888.

6 *Leatherstocking Tales*, 1:250, 324.

7 Carroll Smith-Rosenberg, *Disorderly Conduct: Visions of Gender in Victorian America* (New York, 1985), 97, 103.

8 Henry Nash Smith, *Virgin Land: The American West as Symbol and Myth* (1950; Cambridge, Mass., 1970), 91–92.

9 Rayna Green, "The Pocahontas Perplex," *Massachusetts Review* 16 (Autumn 1976): 704; Smith, *Virgin Land*, 113.

10 Albert Johannsen, *The House of Beadle and Adams and Its Dime and Nickel Novels: The Story of a Vanished Literature*, 3 vols. (Norman, Okla., 1950–62), 1:4.

11 John Ewers, *Artists of the Old West* (New York, 1965), 26.

12 William Goetzmann, *Exploration and Empire: The Explorer and the Scientist in the Winning of the American West* (New York, 1966), 199, 214; Robert V. Hine, *In the Shadow of Frémont: Edward Kern and the Art of American Exploration, 1845–1860* (Norman, Okla., 1982), 158–61.

13 George Catlin, *Letters and Notes on the Manners, Customs and Conditions of the North American Indian*, 2 vols. (1841; New York, 1973), 1:xiv, 3, 13; Jules David Prown et al., *Discovered Lands, Invented Pasts: Transforming Visions of the American West* (New Haven, 1992), 6.

14 Catlin, *Letters and Notes*, 1:16.

15 Michael Edward Shapiro et al., *George Caleb Bingham* (New York, 1990), 54, 126.

16 Shapiro et al., *George Caleb Bingham*, 62.

17 Prown et al., *Discovered Lands, Invented Pasts*, 132; Hine, *Shadow of Frémont*, 160–61.

18 William H. Truettner, ed., *The West as America: Reinterpreting Images of the Frontier, 1820–1920* (Washington, D.C., 1991), 117.

19 Patricia Trenton and Peter H. Hassrick, *The Rocky Mountains: A Vision for Artists in the Nineteenth Century* (Norman, Okla., 1983), 121, 128.

20 Trenton and Hassrick, *Rocky Mountains*, 128; Prown et al., *Discovered Lands, Invented Pasts*, 12–13, 15.

21 Thurmon Wilkins, *Thomas Moran, Artist of the Mountains* (Norman, Okla., 1966), 61; Nancy K. Anderson, *Thomas Moran* (New Haven, 1997), 91.

22 Prown et al., *Discovered Lands, Invented Pasts*, 16.

23 Alan Bogue, *Frederick Jackson Turner: Strange Roads Going Down* (Norman, Okla., 1998), 104, 106.

24 John Mack Faragher, ed., *Rereading Frederick Jackson Turner: "The Significance of the Frontier in American History" and Other Essays* (New Haven, 1999), 31, 60.

25 Paul F. Sharp, "When Our West Moved North," *American Historical Review* 55 (1949): 289; Frank Popper, "The Strange Case of the Contemporary American Frontier," *Yale Review* 76 (Autumn 1986): 101–21.

26 William Appleman Williams, *History as a Way of Learning* (New York, 1973), 148; Fred Hoxie, ed., *Indians in American History: An Introduction* (Arlington Heights, Ill., 1988), 244.

27 Williams, *History as a Way of Learning*, 145; Faragher, ed., *Rereading Frederick Jackson Turner*, 144, 149.

28 G. Edward White, *The Eastern Establishment and the Western Experience: The West of Frederic Remington, Theodore Roosevelt, and Owen Wister* (New Haven, 1968), 80, 85, 91.

29 White, *Eastern Establishment and Western Experience*, 58, 59, 100, 106, 107, 121; Prown et al., *Discovered Lands, Invented Pasts*, 106.

30 White, *Eastern Establishment and Western Experience*, 57, 109.

31 Richard Slotkin, *Gunfighter Nation: The Myth of the Frontier in Twentieth-Century America* (New York, 1992), 171.

32 Lee Clark Mitchell, *Westerns: Making the Man in Fiction and Film* (Chicago, 1996), 287.

33 Owen Wister, *The Virginian: A Horseman of the Plains* (New York, 1903), 29, 474, 503.

34 L. G. Moses, *Wild West Shows and the Images of American Indians, 1883–1933* (Albuquerque, N.Mex., 1996), 272; John G. Neihardt, *Black Elk Speaks: Being the Life Story of a Holy Man of the Oglala Sioux* (1932; New York, 1972), 193.

35 Slotkin, *Gunfighter Nation*, 81–82.

36 Barry Keith Grant, ed., *Film Genre Reader* (Austin, Tex., 1986), 204.

37 John Tuska, *The Filming of the West* (Garden City, New Jersey, 1976), 11.

38 Kevin Brownlow, *The War, the West, and the Wilderness* (New York, 1979), 223.

39 Ralph E. Friar and Natasha A. Friar, *The Only Good Indian . . . The Hollywood Gospel* (New York, 1972), 123–24, 160; Brownlow, *War, West, and Wilderness*, 381.

40 Robert G. Athearn, *The Mythic West in Twentieth-Century America* (Lawrence, Kans., 1986), 267; Ernest Haycock, *Free Grass* (Garden City, N.J., 1928), 9, 14.

41 Prown et al., *Discovered Lands, Invented Pasts*, 138.

42 Athearn, *Mythic West in Twentieth-Century America*, 179.

43 Slotkin, *Gunfighter Nation*, 273.

Chapter 16: Frontier and West in Our Time

1 James A. Michener, *The World Is My Home: A Memoir* (New York, 1992), 448.

2 Neil Morgan, *Westward Tilt: The American West Today* (New York, 1961), vii; *U.S. News and World Report*, Feb. 4, 1980.

3 Michael Sturma, "South Pacific," *History Today* 47 (August 1997): 30.

4 *St. Petersburg Times*, Sept. 27, 1994.

5 Morgan, *Westward Tilt*, 8.

6 Gerald Nash, *The American West Transformed: The Impact of the Second World War* (Bloomington, Ind., 1985), vii; Robert G. Athearn, *The Mythic West in Twentieth Century America* (Lawrence, Kans., 1986), 117; Greg Hise, *Magnetic Los Angeles: Planning the Twentieth-Century Metropolis* (Baltimore, 1997), 130.

7 Paul Rink, *Building the Bank of America: A. P. Giannini* (Chicago, 1963), 182.

8 Nash, *American West Transformed*, 157.

9 James L. Clayton, *The Economic Impact of the Cold War: Sources and Readings* (New York, 1970), 70.

10 Morgan, *Westward Tilt*, viii.

11 Gerald D. Nash, *The American West in the Twentieth Century: A Short History of an Urban Oasis* (Englewood Cliffs, N.J., 1973), 6.

12 John R. Borchert, "America's Changing Metropolitan Regions," *Annals of the Association of American Geographers* 62 (1972): 352–73.

13 Glen E. Lich, ed., *Regional Studies: The Interplay of Land and People* (College Station, Tex., 1992), 11, 18.

14 Kenneth T. Jackson, *Crabgrass Frontier: The Suburbanization of the United States* (New York, 1985), 265.

15 Hise, *Magnetic Los Angeles*, 10.

16 *Los Angeles Times*, Mar. 9, 1999.

17 *New York Times*, Dec. 30, 1996.

18 Gilbert Townsend and J. Ralph Dalzell, *How to Plan a House* (1942; Chicago, 1953), 2–4; Thomas Hine, *Populuxe* (New York, 1987), 49.

19 Michael L. Johnson, *New Westers: The West in Contemporary American Culture* (Lincoln, Nebr., 1996), 45.

20 Erik Barnouw, *A History of Broadcasting in the United States*, 3 vols. (New York, 1966–70), 3:18.

21 *New York Times*, July 17, 1980.

22 *New York Times*, Sept. 22, 1980, and Jan. 22, 1985.

23 Warren Susman, "History and the American Intellectual: Uses of a Usable Past," *American Quarterly* 16 (1964): 254; Maxwell Meyerson, ed., *Memorable Quotations of John F. Kennedy* (New York, 1965), 275–76.

24 Howard R. Lamar, ed., *The New Encyclopedia of the American West* (New Haven, 1998), 608.

25 Edward Buscombe, ed., *The BFI Companion to the Western* (New York, 1988), 321.

26 J. Fred MacDonald, *Who Shot the Sheriff? The Rise and Fall of the Television Western* (New York, 1987), 103

27 MacDonald, *Who Shot the Sheriff*, 108; Richard Slotkin, *The Fatal Environment: The Myth of the Frontier in the Age of Industrialization, 1800–1890* (Middletown, Conn., 1985), 16; Slotkin, *Gunfighter Nation: The Myth of the Frontier in Twentieth-Century America* (New York, 1992), 495–96.

28 *New York Times*, Mar. 21, 1993, and Jan. 13, 1991.

29 Dan Frost, "American Indians in the 1990s," *American Demographics* 13 (December 1991): 28; *Bergen Record*, Mar. 17, 1991.

30 Fred Hoxie, ed., *Indians in American History* (Arlington Heights, Ill., 1988), 260.

31 D'Arcy McNickle, *Native American Tribalism: Indian Survivals and Renewals* (New York, 1973), 107–8.

32 Joan Weibel-Orlando, *Indian Country, L.A.: Maintaining Ethnic Community in Complex Society* (Urbana, Ill., 1991), 104.

33 Peter Matthiessen, *In the Spirit of Crazy Horse* (New York, 1983), 35; Steven Mintz, ed., *Native American Voices: A History and Anthology* (St. James, N.Y., 1995), 175.

34 W. John Moore, "Tribal Imperatives," *National Journal*, June 9, 1990, 1,396.

35 Frost, "American Indians in the 1990s," 26.

36 William Plummer, "Hearing His Own Drum: Activist Russell Means Dances with Hollywood," *People*, Oct. 12, 1992.

37 Quintard Taylor, *In Search of the Racial Frontier: African Americans in the American West, 1528–1990* (New York, 1998), 261.

38 Gretchen Lemke-Santangelo, *Abiding Courage: African American Migrant Women and the East Bay Community* (Chapel Hill, N.C., 1996), 1, 65.

39 Lemke-Santangelo, *Abiding Courage*, 67; Taylor, *In Search of the Racial Frontier*, 257, 265.

40 Taylor, *In Search of the Racial Frontier*, 261.

41 Stan Steiner, *La Raza: The Mexican Americans* (New York, 1969), 180–81; *Los Angeles Times*, July 27 1989, and Jan. 28, 1993.

42 *Los Angeles Times*, July 11, 1989.

43 Charles Wollenberg, "*Mendez* v. *Westminster:* Race, Nationality and Segregation in California Schools," *California Historical Quarterly* 53 (1974): 318.

44 Taylor, *In Search of the Racial Frontier*, 280.

45 *Los Angeles Times*, Jan. 10, 1995.

46 Gerald Horne, *Fire This Time: The Watts Uprising and the 1960s* (Charlottesville, Va., 1995), 249.

47 Richard Griswold del Castillo, *Cesar Chávez: A Triumph of Spirit* (Norman, Okla., 1995), 13

48 Gerald Nash and Richard Etulain, eds., *The Twentieth-Century West: Historical Interpretations* (Albuquerque, N.Mex., 1989), 134.

49 Griswold del Castillo, *Cesar Chávez*, 48–49, 84; David G. Gutiérrez, *Walls and Mirrors: Mexican Americans, Mexican Immigrants, and the Politics of Ethnicity* (Berkeley, Calif., 1995), 191.

50 David Rieff, *Los Angeles: Capital of the Third World* (New York, 1991), 88.

51 Leonard Pitt and Dale Pitt, *Los Angeles A to Z: An Encyclopedia of the City and County* (Berkeley, Calif., 1997), 140; Rieff, *Los Angeles*, 155; *MacNeil/Lehrer Newshour*, transcript, July 3, 1995 (Lexis/Nexis, Mead Data Central).

52 *San Bernardino County Sun*, Oct. 18, 1998.

53 Rieff, *Los Angeles*, 192.

54 *New York Times*, May 30, 1993; *Washington Post*, Apr. 9, 1978.

55 Samuel P. Hays, *Beauty, Health, and Permanence: Environmental Politics in the United States, 1955–1985* (New York, 1987), 34; Roderick Nash, *Wilderness and the American Mind*, 3d ed. (New Haven, 1982), 188, 288; Nash, ed., *American Environmentalism: Readings in Conservation History*, 3d ed. (New York, 1990), 77; Richard West Sellars, *Preserving Nature in the National Parks: A History* (New Haven, 1997), 194.

56 Peter A. Coates, *The Trans-Alaska Pipeline Controversy: Technology, Conservation, and the Frontier* (Bethlehem, Pa., 1991), 89.

57 Charles F. Wilkinson, *Crossing the Next Meridian: Land, Water, and the Future of the American West* (Washington, D.C., 1992), 91.

58 Wilkinson, *Crossing the Next Meridian*, 160.

59 Donald Worster, *Rivers of Empire: Water, Aridity, and the Growth of the American West* (New York, 1985), 276; Raymond Dasmann, *The Destruction of California* (New York, 1965), 169.

60 Norris Hundley, Jr., *The Great Thirst: Californians and Water, 1770s–1990s* (Berkeley, Calif., 1992), 384.

61 *New York Times*, Mar. 18, 1999.

62 Coates, *Trans-Alaska Pipeline Controversy*, 264.

63 *Christian Science Monitor*, Aug. 23, 1993.

64 Willa Cather, *My Antonia* (Boston, 1946), 372.

Index

Page numbers in italics represent illustrations

Bury My Heart at Wounded Knee (Brown), 539
Bush, George, 528
Butte, Montana: copper mining, 269–70; women, 420
Butterfield, John, and Overland Mail, 277–78
Butte Workingmen's Union, 271
B-westerns, 508–10

Cabeza de Vaca, Alvar Núñez, 30, 31
Cahuillas, 195
Cain, James M., *The Postman Always Rings Twice*, 417
Calamity Jane, *479*, *480*
Calhoun, John C. (Sen.), 77, 211
California: admitted to statehood, 220; ceded by Mexico, 212; Chinatowns in, 245–46; citrus belt, 390; cost of winning from Mexico, 205–6; and defense spending, 518–19; Del Rey, 393–94; farm labor strikes, 398–400; gold rush, 234, 235–51; as objective of Mexican War, 204, 205, 207; organizing of migrant workers, 360; petrochemical industry, 517–18; southern (*see* southern California); wheat growing, 342
California Battalion of Volunteers, 208
California Department of Immigration and Housing, 398, 399
California Fruit Growers Exchange, 417
California Institute of Technology, 518
California Redwood Company, land scam by, 335
California Star, on reports of gold strike, 236
California Supreme Court, *People v. Hall,* 246
Californios, 208
Canada: Dominion Land Act (1872), 340; origin of name, 41
Canary, Martha Jane. *See* Calamity Jane
Canasatego (Iroquois chief), 82, 83
Cane Ridge, Kentucky, "Great Revival" at, 366–67
Cannery and Agricultural Workers Industrial Union, 399
captivity narratives, 65–67

Caribbean islands, 29; arrival of Spaniards, 12–14
Caribs, 12, 14; depicted as cannibals, 24
Carleton, James H. (Col.), 227–28
Carlisle Indian School, 378
Carson, Christopher "Kit," 155, 191, 478; campaign against Navajos and Apaches, 227–28
Carter, Jimmy, 558–59
Cartier, Jacques, 41–43
Casement brothers (Jack and Dan), 287; and Union Pacific construction, 285–86
Cassidy, "Butch," 503
Cassidy, Hopalong, 508, 533
Catherine (Tsarina), 93, 95
Catholic missionaries: accommodation with Pueblos, 37–38; assault on Aztec religion, 23; attempts to convert Indians of New France, 49–51; attempts to convert Pueblos, 32, 34–35; and Beaver Wars, 68–69; and conversion among Hurons, 51, 68–69; French vs. Spanish, 50; in Oregon Country, 185; sexual celibacy of, 34–35; in Texas and California, 95–99
Catlin, George, 10, 440; *Manners, Customs, and Conditions of the North American Indians,* 481–82
cattle: branding of, 310; introduced by Spanish, 35, 302–3; Texas longhorn, 303
cattle drives, 304; description of, 305; trails, 307
cattle ranching, 301; and conflict with sheepherding, 322–23; drought and, 325–35; by Indians, 468; investors in, 321; and Johnson County War, 326–28; labor organizing and, 321–22; and Texas economy, 161; and Texas fever, 325; women and, 314–17
cattle rustling, 326–28
Cauauhtémoc, and death of Montezuma II, 21
Cayugas, 44; and Beaver Wars, 67; support of British during Revolution, 102
Cayuse tribe, 185
Central America: refugees from, 551; Spanish invasion of, 14
Central Pacific Railroad, 281; "Big Four," 283;

Chinese labor, 286–87, 298; and Credit and Finance Corporation, 285; and federal subsidies, 282; race to completion, 285–88

Champlain, Samuel de, 44

Chapultepec, capture of, 210

charette, use among métis communities, 276–77

Chávez, César, 548–50

Cherokee Nation v. Georgia (1831), 176

Cherokee Phoenix, 130

Cherokees, 431, 536; cattle herders, 312; cession of land to Britain, 90; declaration of independence, 174, 175; effects of allotment on, 465; and farming tradition, 7; and formation of confederacies, 80; as issue in Georgia, 174–79; literacy among, 130; migration across Mississippi River, 174; as one of "Five Civilized Tribes," 174; opposition to removal, 176; population in mid-18th c., 77; pro-Union faction among, 222; removal from Georgia, 177–79; and support of Tecumseh, 129; Trail of Tears, 373; Treaty of New Echota, 177; Treaty Party, 177

Cheyennes, 251; attacks on Union Pacific workers, 292; and Battle of Little Bighorn, 254–55; Dog Soldiers, 229; at Fort Laramie conference, 218; and Sand Creek Massacre, 228–32; and Treaty of Fort Atkinson, 218; warfare with Crows, 139–40

Chicago: ceded by Ohio confederacy, 123; contest with St. Louis, 406–7; development of metropolis, 406–8; meat-packing industry, 304–5, 408; Union stockyard, 304

Chicago, Rock Island, and Pacific Railroad, 295

Chicago & Rock Island Railroad, 284, 406

Chicago River, pollution, 304–5

Chickasaws: ancestors' attack on de Soto, 31; and Confederate treaty, 222; and formation of confederacies, 80; killed by smallpox, 88; as one of "Five Civilized Tribes," 174; and treaty of removal, 176

Chief Joseph (Nez Percé), 374

chiefs. *See* tribal chiefs

Chihuahua, 160, 168

China Tax (Idaho), 246–47

Chinatowns: in California, 245–46, 390; in San Francisco, 422–24

Chinese Exclusion Act (1882), 298

Chinese immigrants: migrant labor, 359–60; miners, 245–47; railroad workers, 286–87, 298; in San Francisco, 422–24; tenant farmers, 358–59; violence against, 390–91

Chiricahua Apaches, 292–93

Chisholm Trail, cattle drives on, 307

Chivington, John M., 222; and Sand Creek Massacre, 229–31

Choctaws: cattle raising, 312; and Confederate treaty, 222; and formation of confederacies, 80; killed by smallpox, 88; as one of "Five Civilized Tribes," 174; and treaty of removal, 176

Chouteau family, 158; and fur trade, 149

Christianity, 9; influences on Longhouse Religion, 125, 126; and Iroquois society, 69

Church, Benjamin, memoir of, 67

Church of Jesus Christ of Latter-day Saints. *See* Mormons

Cíbola, 30, 32; search for, 234

Cincinnati, Ohio: development of metropolis, 402–3; urban theories on, 405

circuit riders, Methodist, 365–66

Civilian Conservation Corps, 461

Civil Rights Act of 1870, 246

Civil War: controversies leading to, 222–23; Mexican War as precursor to, 219

Clark, George Rogers: in American Revolution, 103–4, *103;* employed by Spanish, 119

Clark, William, 137; on beaver scarcity, 156

Cleveland, Grover: and Forest Reserve Act, 445–47; and Pullman strike, 299

Clinton, Bill, 536

closed frontier, notion of, 493–94

Cody, William "Buffalo Bill," 408–9; and frontier myth, 498–502; with Sitting Bull, *499*

Collier, John, and Indian New Deal, 465–70

Collins, Elizabeth, *The Cattle Queen of Montana,* 316

Colonization Law (Mexico), 168

Colorado, gold rush in, 251, 499

Colt, Samuel, 225

Colter, John, 149

Colt Repeating Firearms Co., 309

Columbia River, 182, 188

Columbus, Christopher, 1, 3, 12–13, 234

Comanches: origin of, 139; and Treaty of Fort
Atkinson, 218

combines, development of, 341

Committee of Vigilance (San Francisco),
267–68

company grants, 112–13, 116

"Company of One Hundred Associates," 45

Compromise Act (1850), 220

Comstock, Henry "Old Pancake," 260

Comstock Lode, 260; and development of
San Francisco, 413–14; discovery of, 240;
Hearst investment in, 269; labor organiz-
ing on, 271

Conestogas, massacred by Paxton Boys, 90–
91

Conestoga wagons, 277

Confederation Congress, 105, 106–9

Congregationalist missionaries, 184, 365

Congress: Agricultural Adjustment Act, 458;
Allotment Act (1888), 379, 464–65; ban on
treaty-making with Indians, 376; Chinese
Exclusion Act (1882), 298; Compromise
Act (1850), 220; creation of Interior De-
partment, 216–17; creation of National
Park Service (1916), 451; Edmunds Act
(1882), 370; Exclusion Act (1881), 360, 395;
Forest Management Act (1897), 447; Forest
Reserve Act (1891), 445–47; Homestead
Act (1862), 109, 221–22, 330, 333–34, 345;
Immigration Act (1917), 360; Immigration
Restriction Act (1924), 298, 393, 430; In-
dian Citizenship Act (1924), 469; Indian
Gaming Regulatory Act (1988), 542; In-
dian Intercourse Act (1790), 120–21, 375;
Indian Removal Act (1830), 175; Indian Re-
organization Act (1934), 466; Indian Self-
Determination and Educational Assis-
tance Act (1975), 538; Interstate Commerce
Act (1887), 350; Land Ordinance of 1784,
461; Land Ordinance of 1785, 107, 109; Log

Cabin Bill (1841), 331; Missouri Compromise, 200; Northwest Ordinance of 1787,
113–16; Pacific Railroad Bill (1862), 281; Pacific Railroad Survey Act (1853), 280–81;
ratification of Articles of Confederation,
105–6; Reclamation Act (1902), 454, 456;
Rural Electrification Act, 462–63; Southern Homestead Act (1866), 370; Taylor
Grazing Act (1934), 461; Timber Cutting
Act (1878), 444; Wilderness Act (1964), 556

conservationism, 453–54; vs. preservation-
ism, 448; in T. Roosevelt administration,
447–50

Cook, James (Capt.), 146

Cooke, Jay, 291, 491; and Northern Pacific
Railroad, 291; proposal for Yellowstone,
442

Coolidge, Calvin, 457–58

Cooper, Gary: 507; in High Noon, 533; The
Virginian, 506

Cooper, James Fenimore: The Last of the Mohicans, 475–76; "The Leatherstocking
Tales," 475; The Pioneers, 434–35, 436, 475,
476; The Prairie, 475; and wildlife destruction, 436

copper mining, 269–70, 294

Cornplanter (Seneca chief), and Quakers, 125

Cornwallis, Charles (Gen.), 104

Coronado, Francisco Vásquez de, 31

Cortés, Hernán: cattle, 302–3; and conquest
of Mexico, 16–23; and gold, 13, 234; invasion of Tenochtitlán, 20–21

Cortez Colony, in Merced County, Calif.,
393–94

Cortina, Juan Nepomuceno, 215–16, 215

Council Bluffs, Iowa, 295

"Covenant Chain," 69

cowboys, 301; African-American, 310, 312; age
of, 307; homosexuality among, 313–14; Indian, 312; Mexican, 310–11; origin of term,
303; as outlaws, 308–10; Spanish, 302;
wages for, 320–21

Crane, Stephen, 339–40

Crazy Horse (Oglala Sioux), 251, 254, 255–56

Crédit Mobilier, and Union Pacific scandal,
284–85

Creeks, 431; cattle herders, 312; and emergence of Seminoles, 81; and formation of confederacies, 80; killed by smallpox, 88; as one of "Five Civilized Tribes," 174; population in mid-18th c., 77; pro-Union faction among, 222; Red Sticks, 129; and treaty of removal, 176

Crees, 139

Creoles, 95

Crèvecoeur, J. Hector St. John de, *Letters from an American Farmer,* 109

Crocker, Charles, 283–84, 289; and Chinese labor, 286–87

Crockett, David ("Davy"), 166, 170, 476–77; at Alamo, 171; television series based on, 533

Crook, George (Gen.), 254; and defeat of Western Apaches, 292

Crows, 139–40; as American allies, 218; at Fort Laramie conference, 218; warfare with Cheyennes, 139–40

Cuba, 14, 22

Cuesta, Felipe Arroyo de la (priest), 97–98

Culpepper's Rebellion (1677), 58

cultural pluralism, 465

Cumberland Gap, 116

Cupeños, 195

Custer, George Armstrong (Col.), 252; and Battle of Little Bighorn, 254–56

Cutler, Manasseh, 112

Daily Alta California, 245, 262

Dallas Weekly Herald, 309–10

Danish settlers, in Delaware valley, 71–74

Dare, Ananias and Elenor White, 52

Dare, Virginia, 54

Davis, Jefferson, and Gadsden Purchase, 222

Davy Crockett Almanac, 476–77

Dawes, Henry (Sen.), 379

Dawson Charley, 259

Debs, Eugene, and founding of ARU, 299

"Declaration of Indian Purpose" (1961), 538

defense spending, western growth and, 518–19

deforestation, 444–47

Deganawida (Iroquois chief), 44

Delaware Prophet. *See* Neolin

Delaware River, origin of name, 71

Delawares, 118; composition of, 71; Iroquois domination of, 82; killed by smallpox, 88; land seized by Pennsylvania colony, 82–83; massacre of, at Gnadenhutten, 104; migration across Mississippi River, 174; and William Penn, 74; support of British during Revolution, 103; and Walking Purchase, 83

Delaware valley, 71–74, 77

Del Rey, California, Japanese community, 393–94

Democratic Party, 199; on expansion, 200–202

Denver, Colorado, 409; development of, 412; and Interior West, 522

Denver Pacific Railroad, 409

Denver Republican, 321–22

Department of Agriculture, survey of farm wives (1913), 418–19

Department of the Interior, creation of, 216–17

desert reclamation, 454–56

Detroit: in American Revolution, 103, 104; ceded by Ohio confederacy, 123; French settlement at, 79; Indian confederacy, 103, 118–19

Devils Tower National Monument, 447

De Voto, Bernard, 514; on Lewis and Clark Expedition, 143; on Louisiana Purchase, 133–34; "A Plundered Province," 461; on trappers, 156

DeWitt, John L. (Gen.), 432

Díaz, Porfirio, 395

Díaz del Castillo, Bernal, 16, 19, 20

dime novels, 477–80, 532; "Buffalo Bill" Cody as subject of, 501

disease: Athabascans decimated by, 260; Beaver Wars and, 68; brought to Oregon, 185; among coastal Indians, 77; death of mission Indians from, 97–98; and decline of Pueblo population, 36; effects on Northeast Indians, 43; as weapon of European invaders, 27

Disney, Walt, and Bank of America, 516

Dixon, Maynard, 508

Dodge, Richard Irving (Col.), 161; on killing buffalo, 317

Dodge City, 307; homicide rate, 308

dogie, origin of term, 302

Dog Soldiers, 229, 232

Dole, Robert, 528

Dominion Land Act (Canada), 340

Donnelly, Ignatius, 351, 354

Douglas, Donald, 517

Douglas, Stephen A., 199, 218, 220

Douglass, Frederick, 211

Drake, Francis, 51

drought: and cattle ranching, 325; during Dust Bowl, 458–59; on plains, 339–40, 354

"dry farming," 340–41

Durango, Colorado, 168

Durant, Thomas C., 284–85; at joining of rails, 289

Dust Bowl, 458–60

Dutch colonists, in New Sweden, 71–72

Dutch traders, 61; in coastal New England, 58

Earp, Wyatt, 308, *309*

Eastwood, Clint, 535

Echohawk, John, 540

Echota, Cherokee capital at, 130

Edmunds Act (1882), effect on Mormons, 370

Eisenhower, Dwight, 528

electric utilities, 462

Eliot, John, 62, 63

Elizabeth I (England), 51–52

Ellis, Edward S., *Seth Jones,* 477–78

Ellis, Joseph, on Jefferson's view of the West, 134

El Partido Raza Unita, 550

El Paso, Texas, Mexican immigration to, 397

El Paso Daily Times, 397

El Teatro Campesino, 549

Emancipation Proclamation, 249, 333

Emerson, Ralph Waldo, 442–43

encomienda, 14, 23, 95–96

English colonization, in New World, 51–64

Erie Canal, construction of, 221

Espuela Cattle Company, 321

Evans, George Henry, 331

Evans, John, 228; and Sand Creek Massacre, 228–29, 231

Exclusion Act (1881), 360, 395, 424

Exodusters, arrival in Kansas, 372

extinction, of North American species, 436

Fairbanks, Alaska, 260

Fargo, William, 277–78

Farmers' Alliance, 350–51, 352, 357

farming: by immigrants, 343–45; tenant, 355, 358; wageworkers, 355–56; as way of life, 6–7

farm mechanization, 341–42

Farm Security Administration, 508

farm women, migration to cities, 418–19

Farnam, Henry, 284

Federal Bureau of Investigation (FBI): and AIM, 539; and Black Panthers, 548

federal subsidies, for railroad construction, 282–83, 335, 409

Fenimore, James "Old Virginny," 260

Ferdinand, King (Spain), 14

fertility, 75, 79

filibusters, 162

film industry: in southern California, 503–10; westerns, 503–10, 532–36

Filson, John, 118; *The Adventures of Col. Daniel Boon,* 472

Fink, Mike, 150–51

Finnish settlers, in Delaware valley, 71–74

firearms, 225; as cause of cattle-town deaths, 308–10

fishing, as way of life, 6

"Five Civilized Tribes": composition of, 174; Confederate alliance of, 222–23; and market culture, 181

Five Nation League of the Iroquois: and Beaver Wars, 67–68; becomes Six Nations, 82; composition of, 44; as intermediaries with English, 67; power of, 80

Fletcher v. Peck (1810), 113

Florida, Spanish invasion of, 29, 30–31

Flynn, Elizabeth Gurley, 355–56

foraging, as way of life, 4–6

Ford, John, 505, 532–33; late career of, 534–35; *Stagecoach,* 509–10

Foreign Miners' Tax (Calif.), 243, 246

Forest and Stream, 439

Forest Management Act (1897), 447

forest rangers, 450–53; women as, 451–53

Forest Reserve Act (1891), 445–47

Forestry Commission, 447

Fort Duquesne, 85, 86

Fort George, 149

Fort Hall, on Oregon Trail, 187

Fort Laramie, 187; 1851 conference at, 218–19; Miller's images of, 484

Fort Lauderdale, Seminole gaming at, 542

Fort Mims, Red Stick attack on, 129

Fort Pitt, 86, 88, 90

Fort Union, 222

Fort Vancouver, 149, 182, 197

Foster, William Z., 294, 294–95, 358

Foxes, war with French, 79

France, and Louisiana Purchase, 133–36

Franciscan missionaries. *See* Catholic missionaries

Franklin, Benjamin: on colonial population growth, 75; on Iroquois model of unity, 119; on Paxton Boys' massacre, 91

Fraser, Alexander and Simon, 144

free trappers, 153, 155, 156

freight rates, for western farmers, 348

Frémont, Jessie Benton, 190, *191*

Frémont, John Charles, *190*, 195; and Bear Flag Republic, 208; in Mexican War, 207–8; as presidential candidate, 221; survey of Oregon Trail, 190–92

French and Indian War, 84–87, 100

French colonial policy, 78–79

French immigrants, in San Francisco, 421–22

French-Indian intermarriage, 47

French Protestants: denied entrance to Canada, 77; establish colony in Florida, 31–32

French settlement, in New World, 43–51, 77–80

Frobisher, Martin, 52

Frontenac, Louis de, 47–48

frontier heroes: Boone, 75, 116–17, 191, 472–75, *473*; Bowie, 169, 171, 478; Bridger, 151, *152*; Carson, 155, 191, 227–28, 478; Crockett, 166, 170, 171, 476–77, 533; Fink, 150–51; for-

est rangers as, 451, 453; Houston, 77, 170, *170*, 171, 172

frontier of exclusion, 57

frontier of inclusion: in Spanish New World empire, 38

frontier preachers, 365–67

frontier squatting. *See* squatting

fur seal, endangered status, 436

fur trade: Chouteau family and, 149; dependence on Indian labor, 143; depression in, 150; Hudson's Bay Company and, 143–44; between Iroquois and Europeans, 42–43; John Jacob Astor and, 146; in New France, 44, 46; North West Company and, 144; in Northwest Territory, 146–49; sea otter, 93, 146, 147; Spanish, 154; and tribal rivalries, 43; wars for dominance of, 80

fur traders: annual summer rendezvous, 153–54, 158; French, 46–47

Gadsden Purchase (1853), 212, 222

Gale, Zona, *Friendship Village,* 388

Gallatin, Albert, 211

Galveston, Texas, rivalry with Houston, 409–10

Galveston Bay, Mexican garrison at, 169, 170

Garakontie (Onondaga leader), 69

Garceau, Dee, 346, 347

Garland, Hamlin, 363; *Main-Traveled Roads,* 349, 389, 418; support for "single tax," 353

Gates, William H., 519

General Land Office, 217; homestead records, 345, 347

Gentleman's Agreement, with Japanese government, 392, 393

George, Henry, 295, 523; *Progress and Poverty,* 353, 493; on San Francisco's "gateway" status, 413; "single tax" idea, 353

Georgia: "Cherokee problem," 174–79; gold rush, 235–36; lands scams, 112–13

German immigrants, 76–77, 384; in San Francisco, 422; in Texas, 343

Geronimo (Apache chief), 292–93, *293*

Ghost Dance: movement, 379–80; as threat to whites, 381; Wounded Knee Massacre and, 381–83

Giannini, Amadeo Peter: and Bank of America, 422; and Hollywood financing, 516; and New Deal financing, 464

Glacier National Park, 444

Glidden, Joseph, invention of barbed wire, 337–38

Glorieta Pass, 167, 222

Gnadenhutten, massacre of Delawares at, 104

Goetzmann, William, 154, 480, 484

gold: Cartier's search for, 41; Columbus and, 13, 234; discovered in Alaska, 257, 258, 259; discovered in Rockies, 222; mining industry in New Spain, 32–33; Spanish greed for, 18; strike on Sioux reservation, 252

Golden Gate Bridge, financed by Bank of America, 516

golden spike, 274, 275, 289

gold rush: in Alaska, 258–60; in California, 234, 235–51; Colorado, 251, 499; effect on Indians, 248–51; in Georgia, 235–36; in Montana, 251; "widows," 262; women and, 262–66

Goldwater, Barry, 528, 529

Gonzáles, Henry B., 545

Goodnight, Charlie, 307; and JA Ranch, 312, 321, 322

Goodnight-Loving Trail, cattle drives on, 307

Gorras Blancas, Las, 323

Gould, Jay, 299

graft, in railroad construction, 285

Grand Canyon National Monument, 447, 555

Grand Coulee Dam, 464

Grange: institution of, 349–50; and Lease, 352; as New Deal influence, 353

Grangers, 282

Grant, Ulysses S., 375; on Mexican War, 205, 210; and railroad summit, 288

grape boycott, by United Farm Workers, 550

Great Depression: and Dust Bowl, 458–60; frontier myth during, 508; and Los Angeles, 427–28

"Great Migration" of 1843, to Oregon, 185, 186

Great Northern Railroad, 291; struck by ARU, 299

Great Plains, 160–61; and Dust Bowl, 458–60; Indians, 138–41; Lewis and Clark on, 137–39

Great Salt Lake, arrival of Mormons at, 193, 367

Great Swamp Fight, 63

Great Train Robbery, The (film), 502–3

Great Treaty Wampum Belt, given to William Penn, 74

Greeley, Horace, 332; on going west, 336; and *Weekly Tribune*, 331, 333

Greenback Party, 349; as New Deal influence, 353; Populists and, 351

greenbacks, 348–49

Green Corn Rebellion, 358

Green Mountains (Vermont), deforestation of, 445

Grey, Zane, *Riders of the Purple Sage*, 506

Grinnell, George Bird, 439

Gronlund, Laurence, *The Cooperative Commonwealth*, 352–53

Gros Ventres, 456

Gruening, Ernest (Sen.), 556

Guess, George. *See* Sequoyah

Guyot, Arnold, 280

Hackensacks, 71

Haidas, 6

Haitian revolt, 135–36

Hakluyt, Richard, "A Discourse of Western Planting," 51–52

Hall, James, 363, 405

Handsome Lake (Iroquois warrior), and Longhouse Religion, 125

Harmar, Josiah (Gen.), 122

Harper's Monthly, 496

Harper's Weekly, 461

Harriot, Thomas, 52–53

Harris, Richard, 258

Harrison, Benjamin: and Forest Reserve Act, 445–47; and Johnson County War, 327

Harrison, William Henry, 200, 331; challenge to Tenskwatawa, 126

Hart, William S., 504–5, *505*

Harte, Bret, *Overland Monthly*, 274

harvesters. *See* wageworkers

Hawaiian Islands, immigrant farmers from, 360

Hawkins, Augustus, 545

Haycock, Ernest, 506

Hayden, Ferdinand V., 338; traveling with Moran, 491; and Yellowstone, 442

Hayes, Rutherford B., and 1887 railroad strike, 297–98

Haywood, Bill, 271–72, 356

Hearst, George, 269

Hearst, William Randolph, 269

herding, 302, 303

Herefords, raised by Apaches, 468

Herrera, Juan José, 323

Hetch Hetchy Valley, 456–57

Hewlett-Packard, 518

Hiawatha (Iroquois), 44

Hickok, James "Wild Bill," 308

High Noon (film), 533

Hill, James J., and Great Northern Railroad, 291

Hispaniola, 14, 25, 27

Hispanos, 216; success in sheepherding, 323

Hoar, George (Sen.), 285

Hochelaga, 41–44

Homestake Mine, 252, 269

Homestead Act (1862), 109, 221, 281, 330; as boon to speculators, 335; provisions of, 333–34; women and, 345–47

homesteading, isolation of, 363–64

homosexuality, among cowboys, 313–14

Hoover, Herbert, 428, 458

Hoover Dam, 464, 469

Hopis, resistance to Christian conversion, 35

Hopkins, Mark, 283, 284

Horne, Gerald, 427, 547

horses, value to Great Plains Indians, 138

Houston, Sam, 77, 170, *170*, 171, 172

Houston, Texas: development of, 412–13; rivalry with Galveston, 409–10

Hudson's Bay Company, 197, 277; chartering of, 80; as competitor in fur trade, 143–44; move to Vancouver Island, 197

Hughes, Howard, 516, *517*

Huguenots. *See* French Protestants

Hunt, Wilson Price, 147–49

Huntington, Collis P., 269, 283, 415; on graft, 285; on quantity vs. quality, 289; on railroad monopoly, 291

Huntington, Henry E., and development of southern California, 415–17

Huntington Beach, California, 425

Hurons: alliance with Champlain, 44; attacked in Beaver Wars, 68–69; Catholic conversion among, 51, 68–69; decimation by smallpox, 50–51; enemies of, 44; near Detroit, 79

hydraulic mining, 239–40, 437

hydroelectric power, 462

Ickes, Harold, 460–61; on Indian policy, 466

Idaho, treatment of Chinese miners in, 246–47

Idaho World, 246

Illinois, admitted to statehood, 159

Illinois Central Railroad, federal subsidy for, 282

immigrant farmers, housing of, 343–44

Immigration Act (1917), 360

Immigration and Naturalization Service (INS), 549, 551

immigration raids, 428

Immigration Restriction Act (1924), 298, 393, 430

Ince, Thomas, 504

Indian, origin of term, 3

Indiana, admitted to statehood, 159

Indian cattle ranchers, 468

Indian Citizenship Act (1924), 469

Indian Claims Commission, 536–37

Indian country, 88, 90; and Indian Intercourse Act (1790), 120

Indian cowboys, 312

Indian Gaming Regulatory Act (1988), 542

Indian Intercourse Act (1790), 120–21, 375

Indian miners, 247–48

Indian New Deal, 464–70, 537; criticism of, 469; and internal sovereignty, 468; reservation day schools, 467

Indian removal, 177–81; of Cherokees from Georgia, 177–79; of Seminoles from Florida, 179–80

Kaiser, Henry J., 464; Fontana mill, 515; and Kaiser-Permanente Health Plan, 516

Kansas: admitted to statehood, 223; African-American migration to, 371–73; cattle inspection regulations, 325; fight over slavery issue, 220–21; public-school segregation, 372–73

Kansas Farmer, 347, 349

Kansas Pacific Railroad, 408; cattle stockyard at, 304

Kearney, Dennis, on Chinese workers, 298

Kearny, Stephen Watts (Gen.), and Mexican War, 206, 207, 208

Kelley, Hall Jackson, 186; "Oregon Colonization Society," 184

Kennedy, Andrew, 199–200

Kennedy, John F., 531; support for "Declaration of Indian Purpose," 537

Kentucky: admitted to statehood, 159; building of Boonesborough, 116; population growth in, 118; survey of, 107

King, Rodney, 554

King George's War, support of Six Nations, 82

King Philip. *See* Metacomet

King Philip's War, 63, 65

King William's War, 80, 82

Kinsey, Alfred C., 313–14

Kiowas, and Treaty of Fort Atkinson, 218

Kipling, Rudyard, 437; on prairie travel, 337

Knights of Labor, 298–99; and Las Gorras Blancas, 323; organizing cowboys, 321; Populists and, 351

"Know Nothings," 208

Knox, Henry, 119–20, 121

Ku Klux Klan, 372; in Los Angeles, 425–26

Kwakiutls, 6

kyowakai, 394

labor organizing: cattle ranches, 321–22; mines, 270–73

labor unions. *See* labor organizing

Lachine massacre, 80

Laguna Industries, 540–41

Lakotas, 139. *See also* Sioux

La Malínche, symbolism of, 19

Lamar, Howard, 195, 508

L'Amour, Louis, 532

Lancaster (Pennsylvania colony), meeting of English and Six Nations, 82

land distribution: following Revolution, 106–9; surveys for, 107–10

land grant colleges, 335

land grants, to railroads, 281–83, 335, 409

Land Ordinance of 1784, 461

Land Ordinance of 1785, 107–9, 282, 330

land scams, 112–13; under Homestead Act, 335–36

Lange, Dorothea, 508

languages, "pidgin," 47

La Opinión, 428, 546

Lapérouse, Jean François de, on Catholic missions, 98–99

la rasa, Malínche as mother of, 19

La Salle, Robert Cavelier de, 48

Las Casas, Bartolomé de, 23–27, 24; *The Destruction of the Indies,* 25

Las Gorras Blancas, 216

Las Manos Negras, 216

Lawrence, Kansas, proslavery attack on, 220

Lea, Tom, 35

lead trade, in St. Louis, 403

League of United Latin American Citizens (LULAC), 546

Lease, Mary Elizabeth, 351–53, *352*

Leatherstocking (character), 434–35, *436*

Lee, Jason (Rev.), 184, 186

Lee, Richard Henry, 113

Lee, Robert E., 216

Leone, Sergio, 535

Leopold, Aldo, *Sand County Almanac,* 555

Leutze, Emanuel Gottlieb, 487–88

Levittown, New York, 526

Lewis, Meriwether, 134, 136–37, *136*

Lewis, Sinclair, *Main Street,* 387, 388–89

Lewis and Clark Expedition, 136–38, 140–43, 182

Lexington, Kentucky, 402

Lincoln, Abraham, 405, 407; elected president, 221; Emancipation Proclamation, 249; on expansion, 200–201

"Lincoln County War," 323

Means, Russell (Sioux leader), *540, 542, 543*; and occupation of BIA, 539

meat-packing industry, in Chicago, 304–5, 408

Melville, Herman, 225

Memphis, Tennessee, 402

Menéndez de Avilés, Don Pedro, 31–32

Mennonite settlers, 77

Menominees, effects of termination on, 538

Meriam Report, 464–65; on stockraising, 467

mestizos, 29, 36; and settling of Los Angeles, 97

Metacomet (Wampanoag chief), 63, 65

Methodist missionaries, 184–85, 365

métis: in French settlements, 79; origin of, 47

Mexican Americans, postwar migration of, 543, 544–52, 554

Mexican cowboys. *See* vaqueros

Mexican immigrants, 395–97; deportation of, 427–29; to Los Angeles, 425, 427–30; as miners, 238, 241–45; to San Francisco, 422

Mexican War, 205–12; Battle of Cerro Gordo, 209; cost to U.S., 205; factors leading to, 202–5; as precursor to Civil War, 219

Mexico: abolition of slavery in, 164, 167; immigrant farmers from, 360; movement for annexation of, 210; passage of Colonization Law, 168; Polk's failed negotiations with, 203; Spanish conquest of, 15–23

Mexico City: heart of New Spain, 29; mission system and, 96

Miamis, 118; support of British during Revolution, 103

Michener, James A., 512–14, *514*, 519; *Tales of the South Pacific*, 513

Michener, Mari Yoriko Sabusawa, 513, *514*

Michigan, admitted to statehood, 159

Micmacs, 6, 39; migratory lives of, 4; response to Catholic missionaries, 49

Microsoft Corporation, 519

migrant labor, and western farms, 358–61

Miller, Alfred Jacob, 484

Miller, Joaquin, 191–92

Miller, John (Sen.), 392

miners: Chinese, 245–47; Indian, 247–48; Mexican, 238, 241–45

Mingos, 118; support of British during Revolution, 103

mining: copper, 294; hydraulic, 239–40; law, 266–68; mercury, 437; placer, 238–39; quartz, 239

Minnesota: development of Minneapolis and St. Paul, 411; Swedish immigrants in, 385

Minnetarees, 137–39

Mission San Juan Bautista, 97, 98

Mission Santa Cruz, 98

mission system, as frontier institution, 95–99

Mississippi, admitted to statehood, 159

Mississippi River, early exploration, 48

Missouri, admitted to statehood, 159

Missouri Compromise, 200

Missouri Fur Company, 149

Missouri Republican, 150

Miwoks, 195; and gold mining, 248

Mix, Tom, 504

Mohawks, 44; attack on Wampanoags, 63; and Beaver Wars, 67–69; support of British during Revolution, 101–3

Mohegans, and gaming profits, 542

Monroe, James, 168; on dominion of U.S., 182

Monroe Doctrine, 183

Montagnais tribe, 43

Montana, gold rush in, 251

Monterey Bay, 95, 97

Montezuma II: and arrival of Spaniards, 16–18; death of, 21; religious dialogue with Cortés, 20–21

Montreal, fur trade and, 44

Moran, Thomas, 490–93; and Yellowstone, 442

Mormons: conflicts with federal government, 367–70; converts, 386; industrial development program, 410–11; plural marriage among, 368–70; policy of isolation, 410; western migration of, 192–94

Morse, Jedediah, *American Geography,* 133

Morse, Samuel F. B., 210

Mount Rainier National Park, 444

"Mudtown." *See* Watts

Muir, John, 442–43, *449;* forest preservation, 447; founding of Sierra Club, 444; and Hetch Hetchy Valley conflict, 456–57; T. Roosevelt and, 448

mules, Mexican, 168

Munn v. Illinois, Supreme Court decision, 349–50

Murrieta, Joaquín, 213–15, *214*

Mustang Hunters, The (Whittaker), 478

Myer, Dillon S., 431, 537

myth, defined, 474–75

Nahuatl language (Aztec), 17

Narragansetts, 59; encounter with Verrazano, 39–40; invaded by English, 63; at war with Pequots, 62; and Roger Williams, 62

Narváez, Pánfilo de, 29

Nashville, Tennessee, 402

Natchez tribe, war with French, 79

National Council of American Indians, "Declaration of Indian Purpose," 536, 538

National Forest Service, 556–58; transfer of forest reserves to, 448

National Grange of the Patrons of Husbandry, 349

"Nationalist Clubs," 353

national parks, creation of, 440–43

National Park Service (NPS), 555; and Albright, 451–53; creation of, 451; and Moran's Yellowstone paintings, 492–93; and women rangers, 451–53

Native American Rights Fund, 540

Native Americans. *See* Indians

Native Sons and Daughters of Kansas, 373

Nature Notes, 452

Nauvoo community (Illinois), 193

Navajos: as actors in *Stagecoach,* 509–10; Blessingway ceremony, 9; Carleton's campaign against, 227–28; and rejection of Indian New Deal, 469; as threat to Pueblos, 37

Nebraska, admitted to statehood, 223

Neolin (Indian prophet), 87–88

Nevada, Comstock Lode discovered in, 240, 260

New Deal, 461; Indian policy of, 464–70; influenced by Populists, 353; public investment program, 462–64; Reconstruction Finance Corp., 464

New Deal Congress, 458

New France, 44, 77–80; Catholic missionaries in, 49–51; and "Company of One Hundred Associates," 45; culture of, 46–49; Iroquois neutrality treaty with, 82; lost to British, 87; population growth in, 77

New Harmony community (Indiana), 192

New Mexico, 33, 34; ceded by Mexico, 212; colonial economy of, 35–36; frontier of inclusion in, 38

New Netherlands, 69

New Orleans, 48–49, 403

New Spain, 29; silver and gold mining in, 32–33; Zebulon Pike and, 160

New Sweden, 71–73

Newton, Huey P., 547–48

New York City, investment in St. Louis, 405–6

New York colony, 69, 76

New York Herald, 505

New York Morning News, 199, 210

New York Post, Bryant editorials in, 406

New York Stock Exchange, crash of 1873, 291

New York Times, 505

Nez Percé Indians, 431; defeat of, 374

Nixon, Richard, 528; and grape boycott, 550; support for "Declaration of Indian Purpose," 538

Nob Hill (San Francisco), 413, 422

Non-Partisan League of North Dakota, 357

Nootka Convention of 1790, 147, 182

North American Review, 285

Northern New Mexico Small Cattlemen and Cowboys' Union, 322

Northern Pacific Railroad, 291, 341, 491; John Muir and, 444; and Yellowstone, 442

Northern Wyoming Farmers and Stockgrowers Association, 327

Northrop, John, 517

North West Company: as competitor in fur trade, 144; sale of, 149

Northwest Ordinance of 1787, 113–16; Indian policy in, 120; slave prohibition in, 115

Proclamation Line, pioneer resistance to, 90

Promontory, Utah, 274; joining of rails at, 288–89

promyshleniki, 93, 95

property qualifications, for voting, 91

prostitution: in cattle towns, 308; at fur trading posts, 46–47; in mining camps, 265–66

public schools: desegregation of, 546; in Land Ordinance, 109; segregation in, 372–73

Pueblos: and Catholic missionaries, 37–38; disease and population decline, 36; and farming tradition, 7; matrilineal descent, 34; Spanish conquest of, 31–34

Puerto Rico, Spanish invasion of, 14

Pullman sleeper cars, and railroad tourism, 441

Pullman Sleeping Car Company, struck by ARU, 299–300

pulp fiction, 506

Puritans, 60–65, 67

Quakers: and Delaware valley, 74; Iroquois ministry, 125; and Paxton community, 90

Quantrill, William, 223, 296

quarantine laws, in Kansas, 325

quartz mining, 239

Quebec, 44, 86

Quebec City, capital of New France, 45–46

Queen Anne's War, 80–81

quitclaims, use by Puritans, 60

racism: against Mexican immigrants, 429–30; in San Francisco's Chinatown, 423–24; "scientific" theories behind, 225; in the West, 543–54

railroad tourism, 441

railroad workers, nationwide strike (1877), 297–98

Raleigh, Sir Walter, 52, 54

rancheros, 161, 194–95

ranch-style houses, 526

Rangers. *See* Regulators

Raritans, 71

Rayburn, Sam, and Rural Electrification Act, 462–64

Reagan, Ronald, 528, 529–31, *530;* and grape boycott, 550

Reclamation Act (1902), 454, 456

Reconstruction Finance Corp., 464

Red Cloud (Sioux chief), 251; on Union Pacific, 292

Red Jacket (Seneca chief), *124;* reaction to Quakers, 125; on treaty provisions, 105

region, defined, 522–23

Regulators, 92–93

religion: Aztec, 20–21, 23; of Europeans vs. Indian cultures, 9; Hurons' loss of faith in, 51; scalping as expression of, 42

Remington, Frederic: and frontier myth, 495, 496–97

Reno, Marcus (Maj.), 254–55

Republican Party, 333, 369

reservation colleges, 542

reservation policy, of Indian Bureau, 226

reservations, removal of Indians to, 374–75

reservation schools, 376–78; day schools, 467

revolver, double-action, 309–10; first modern, 223

Ribault, Jean, 31–32

Richelieu, Cardinal, "Company of One Hundred Associates," 45

Ridge, John: death of, 179; and Treaty of New Echota, 177

right of conquest, 105, 118; failure of, 120

Rio Grande River, 203; rumors of silver, 32

Ritter, Tex, 508

RKO Pictures, 516

Roanoke Island, 52, 54

Robert Bad Wound (Sioux leader), 469–70

Rockefeller Foundation, 465

Rocky Mountain Fur Company, 154, 156

Rocky Mountain Husbandman, 325

Rocky Mountain News, on Sand Creek Massacre, 231

Rodriguez, Richard, 552

Rogers, Roy, 508, 533

Rolfe, John, 55, 57

"Rolling Stone, The" (song), 262–63

Rölvaag, Ole, *Giants in the Earth,* 387

segregation: in Los Angeles County, 547; of Mexican immigrants, 429–30; in public schools, 372–73, 546; in southern California, 427

Seguín, Juan (Capt.), 171, *173*; as mayor of San Antonio, 172

Seminoles, 373; cattle herders, 312; gaming, 542; as one of "Five Civilized Tribes," 4; origins of, 81; pro-Union faction among, 222; removal from Florida, 179–80

Senecas, 44; alcohol abuse among, 84; and Beaver Wars, 67–68; and Quakers, 125; support of British during Revolution, 102

Sequoyah (Cherokee traditionalist), 130, *131*

Serra, Junípero, 97

Seton, Ernest Thompson, 436

Seventh Cavalry, and Wounded Knee Massacre, 381–83

Seward, William Henry, 93, 354

Shackamaxon (Algonquian village), 74

Shakers, 193

Shane (film), 533

Shannon, Fred, 335–37, 348

sharecropping, 355

Shasta Dam, 464

Shawnee Prophet. *See* Tenskwatawa

Shawnees, 118, 431; Daniel Boone hostage of, 116–17; killed by smallpox, 88; migration across Mississippi River, 174; support of British during Revolution, 103

Shays, Daniel, and farmers' rebellion, 110–12

sheep: introduced by Spanish, 35; herding, 322–23

Shelburne, Lord. *See* Petty, William

Shenandoah valley, 77

Sheridan, Philip S. (Gen.), 231; on buffalo hide hunting, 317–18

Sherman, William Tecumseh (Maj. Gen.), 268; on cattle industry, 317

Shinn, Charles Howard, *Mining Camps: A Study in Frontier Government*, 266–67

Shoshones, 5, 431; aid to Lewis and Clark, 141; and origin of Comanches, 139

Siberia, Russian conquest of, 93

Sierra Club, 556; forest preservation, 447; founding of, 444

Silicon Valley, 518

silver, 32, 240, 260

Silver Bow Trades and Labor Assembly, 271

Simpson, Jeremiah "Sockless Jerry," 351; support for "single tax," 353

Sinclair, Upton, *The Jungle*, 305

Sioux: attacks on Union Pacific workers, 292; and Battle of Little Bighorn, 254–55; in "Buffalo Bill's Wild West" show, 501–2; effects of allotment on, 465; at Fort Laramie conference, 218; and Ghost Dance, 380–81; gold strike on reservation, 252; origin of name, 140; removal to Dakota reservation, 227; at Wounded Knee Massacre, 381–83

Sitting Bull (Sioux chief), 251–52, *253*, 254, 256; and Annie Oakley, 501–2; and "Buffalo Bill" Cody, *499*, 501–2; death of, 381; as federal prisoner, 256; and Ghost Dance, 380–81

Six Companies: and building of Hoover Dam, 464; of San Francisco's Chinatown, 423, 424

Six Nation League of the Iroquois: divided during American Revolution, 100–103; emergence of, 82; and French and Indian War, 85; and King George's War, 82; as model of unity, 119; and Treaty of Fort Stanwix, 105

Skookum Jim, 259

slavery: of Chinese women, 245; debate over extending westward, 219–22; as frontier institution, 164–66; legalized in Republic of Texas, 172; prohibition in Northwest Ordinance, 115; as recurring political issue, 200

Sloat, John (Comm.), 208

Slotkin, Richard: on Benjamin Church, 67; on captivity narrative, 65; on film westerns, 508–9; on myth, 474

Smalley, Eugene Victor, 363

smallpox: Aztecs decimated by, 22–23; brought to Hispaniola, 27; effect on Puritan expansion, 61; epidemic at San Juan Bautista, 98; Hurons decimated by, 50–51; used against Ohio Indians, 88

Smith, Henry Nash, 280, 338, 478

Smith, Jedediah Strong, 151–52, 155

Smith, John (Capt.), at Jamestown settlement, 55

Smith, Joseph, 192–94; doctrines of, 368

Smithsonian Institution: founding of, 189; and Pacific railroad survey, 281

Snake River, on Oregon Trail, 188

socialism, 352–53

Society for the Propagation of the Gospel, 62

soddies, 343–44

Soil Conservation Service, 461

Soto, Hernán de, 30–31

South Carolina Regulator movement, 92–93

southern California: aerospace industry in, 517; citrus belt, 390; development of, 413–17; early film industry, 503–8; emigration to, 424–32; farm labor strikes in, 399–400; home-building industry in, 523; restricted covenants in, 426; segregation in, 427; sprawl, 417, 523–26

Southern Homestead Act (1866), 370

Southern Pacific Railroad, 290, 415; and Apache territory, 292; and copper mining, 294; domination in California, 295; and Los Angeles, 414; Muir and, 444; and Yosemite Valley, 441, 442

Southwest Territory, creation of, 115

Spain, formation of, 14

Spanish-American War (1898), 354

Spanish missions, in Texas and California, 95–99

Spindletop, oil gusher, 412

Spotted Eagle (Sioux chief), 292

sprawl: in the East, 526; in Portland, Oregon, 526–27; in southern California, 417, 523–26

Squanto, 59

squatting, 110, 112, 118, 330–31, 335

St. Clair, Arthur, 116; defeat by Little Turtle, 122

St. Louis, Missouri: contest with Chicago, 406–7; development of metropolis, 403–4; financed by eastern capital, 405–6

Stadacona, 43, 44

stag dances, cowboys at, 313–14

Stagecoach (film), 509–10

stagecoach travel, 277–80

Standish, Miles, 59–60

Stanford, Leland, 283, 284; at joining of rails, 289

Stanford University, 518

Stanton, Elizabeth Cady, 370

steamboats, on Mississippi River, 403

Stegner, Wallace: on cowboys, 314; definition of "stickers," 362–63; on preserving wilderness, 556

Steinbeck, John, *The Grapes of Wrath*, 458, 508

Stephens, Ann Sophia, *Malaeska: The Indian Wife of the White Hunter*, 478

Stetson, John B., 307

Stevenson, Robert Louis, 300

Stewart, Elinore Pruitt, *Letters of a Woman Homesteader*, 346–47

Stewart, William Drummond (Capt.), 484

"stickers": in Alpine, Utah, 368; Asian immigrants as, 390; defined, 362–63; German immigrants as, 384

stockmen's associations, 322

Stockton, Robert (Comm.), 208

Stockton Times, 243

Strauss, Levi, 238, 307

strikes: by California farm labor, 399–400; on cattle ranches, 321–22; by IWW, in copper mines, 272; by railroad workers, 297–98

Sturges, John, *The Magnificent Seven*, 534

subsidies. *See* federal subsidies

Sugar Creek, Illinois, 362–63

Sumner, Charles (Sen.): on Alaska, 93, 256; attacked on Senate floor, 220; on Mexican War, 205

Sun Dance, of Great Plains Indians, 138–39

"Sundance Kid," 503

Sun Elk (Taos Pueblo), 378

Sunset Magazine, 453

surveys, for land distribution, 107–10

Susquehannocks, 58

Sutter, John A., 195–96, *196*; on Indian miners, 247–48; and news of gold strike, 236; sawmills, 234, 235

Sutter's Fort, 196